ACKNOWLEDGEMENTS

The publishers and author would like to thank the following for their kind assistance during the compilation of this book:
Steve Baker (Clown Checkers), Carol Crowther and Brian Dewhirst of Clown Cavalcade, David Drummond, Bamber Gascoigne, Jack Gough of Clowns International, William B. Hall III, Pierre Picton, Gary Rae (Clown Patches), Donald M. Stacey, The Master and Fellows of Trinity College, Cambridge (for permission to quote from A. J. Munby's diary of 1869), Harold Whiteley (Clown Rainbow), Mr and Mrs Jack Whiteley.
They would also like to thank the following who took or supplied the photographs: Bibliothèque de l'Arsenal, Paris 6 (left); Bodleian Library, Oxford 6 (above & top); Landes Museum, Braunschweig 15 (above); British Museum, London 9, 16 (right), 49, 50, 51, 52; David Drummond 26; Malcolm Fielding 5, 12, 13, 20, 23, 25, 30, 47, 54-9, 62-8, 71, 72, 75, 76-7, 79, 80, 82-3, 84, 93-101, 103, 106-110, 113 (right), 115, 116, 124-7; Rolph Gobits 28-9 (handcolouring by Amanda Currey), 60, 61, 69, 89, 90; Greater London Council Archive 48 (left); William B. Hall III (photographs by Edward Kennedy) 8, 43, 104, 105, 111, 112, 113 (above); Claus Hansmann, Munich 16 (above); Keystone Press, London 85 (above), 86, 88; Musée du Louvre, Paris 17; Mander & Mitchenson Theatre Archive, London 48 (above); Mansell Collection, London 19, 21 (right), 24 (above), 33 (left), 38 (left), 74 (bottom); Sylvie Mercier, Paris, 31, 78; National Film Archive, London 117 (right & above right); National Museum, Stockholm 10; Popperfoto, London 81, 117 (bottom); Radio Times Hulton Picture Library, London 15 (top), 37, 38 (far left), 44 (below), 73, 117 (far right); G. V. Speaight 21 (above), 27, 32, 74 (below), 87; Homer Sykes 7, 14, 18, 34, 118-123; Theatermuseum, Munich 11; Time-Life Films 85 (right); Victoria & Albert Museum Theatre Collection 33 (below), 35, 36; Wellbeck Gallery, London 39, 41, 42, 45; Harold Whiteley 53.

Copyright © Roxby Press Ltd 1980
All rights reserved. No part of this book may be reproduced or transmitted in any form or by any means, electrical or mechanical, including photocopying, recording or by any information storage and retrieval system, without permission in writing from the Publisher.

Macmillan Publishing Co., Inc., 866 Third Avenue, New York, NY 10022
Collier-Macmillan Canada Ltd.

Made by Roxby Press Productions Ltd
98 Clapham Common Northside, London SW4 9SG

Editors: Louisa McDonnell and Charlotte Parry-Crooke
Design: Ray Gautier
Picture Research: Janet Croall
Typesetting: Pierson LeVesley
Origination: Latent Image
Printed and bound in Spain by Graficromo S.A., Córdoba

Library of Congress Cataloging in Publication Data
Speaight, George.
The book of clowns.
1. Clowns. I. Title.
GV1828.S65 1980 791.3'3 80-16708
ISBN 0-02-612840-3

First American Edition 1980

CONTENTS

EARLY COMEDY AND CLOWNING

The first dramas were performed not as entertainment, but as forms of ritual. Primitive men believed that through dramatic enactments symbolizing the seasonal cycle, the hunt or the harvest, they could perform a kind of sympathetic magic and so gain the benevolence of the forces of nature. Yet an element of foolery and caricature often intruded into the most sacred rites. Man seems to have instinctively recognized a need to exorcize some of the awe of the ritual mystery through comedy.

Clown-like figures appear in many relics of primitive ceremonies. A ritual dance of the Hopi tribe in New Mexico is interrupted by a group of ludicrous interlopers, their faces grotesquely smeared with mud, rabbit fur wigs on their heads, who mock the serious dance and end by collapsing in a heap on the ground. In English village festivals today, fools appear with blackened faces, fox tails on their heads, paper ribbons hiding their clothes and brooms in their hands to sweep a space clear for the performance.

The earliest forms of folk theatre in Greece included comic characters, absurd figures in grinning masks. As these dramatic games began to settle into a formal pattern, certain types of performance can be distinguished. We are not concerned here with the great Greek tragedies or even the comedies of Aristophanes, but with mimes and farces whose texts were never written down and of which our only evidence is the odd literary allusion, or a few statuettes and vase paintings.

Some of the first comic dramas seem to have been the Mimes enacted by the Dorians, one of the earliest Greek peoples, some time in the sixth century BC. A little later, Greek colonists in southern Italy and Sicily developed the Phylax Comedy. Thanks to the survival of a number of vases painted with dramatic scenes, we have excellent pictorial records of this theatre, which bears distinct points of resemblance to what we know of the Dorian Mimes. The Phylax Comedy disappeared with the decline of Greek influence, but its place was taken in the Roman civilization, at about the time of the birth of Christ, by a roughly similar form of native drama.

Clowning has hardly changed over the centuries. Dimitri plays with the Circus Knie in Switzerland. The bells and asses' ears on his hat and his array of musical instruments are reminiscent of early minstrels and travelling players.

NE MERGANTUR

Top: Fools have often been introduced into traditional folk plays. A modern jester wears the traditional motley and carries an inflated bladder at the Abbots Bromley Horn Dance, held in Staffordshire each year on 'Wakes Monday'.
Above: Claus Narr, the famous German jester, strangles his goslings to save them from drowning during a flood in this illustration from the Douce Portfolio.

This was the Atellan Farce which originated from the Oscan district in Italy, now called Campania.

Certain characteristics recur in all these forms of drama, throughout a period of over 500 years. Performers wore grotesque masks; often a player wore a long formalized phallus hanging between his legs, or a costume which was absurdly padded on stomach or buttocks, or he might be disguised as an animal. They were acrobats as much as actors. They turned somersaults, enacted fights when they beat each other with sticks, and sometimes danced. Although often described as mimes, these dramas were not necessarily without speech. The plots, in so far as they were standard, appear to have consisted of burlesques of the legends of the gods, intermixed with farces of domestic life.

Stock characters, whose names may change but whose function is clear, also crop up in every play. There is the bald-headed fool, the old fool, the fat fool, the fool with warts on his face. In the Atellan Farce there is Bucco, the comic slave; Maccus, the country bumpkin; Pappus, the old dotard; Dosennus, the sharp-tongued hunchback; Manducus, grinding his teeth and frightening the children. Although the plays have vanished these personalities are with us still. They are the universal clowns.

Any organized theatre in Europe disappeared with the collapse of the Roman Empire, and few written records survive from the Dark Ages. Yet the instinct for dramatic foolery could not be suppressed and we see clowning reappear throughout Europe in the entertainments of wandering medieval minstrels. The minstrels often travelled round in bands, led usually by a *trouvère* or poet. Although they might entertain the local nobility, they more often put on a show for the ordinary people at a street corner, or in the market-place, gathering a crowd with drum and trumpet. The troupe included acrobats, animal trainers, jugglers, conjurers or puppet showmen. Many minstrels combined all these skills, and all could make a little music or tell jokes.

Performers often painted their faces or wore masks, which

might be of animal heads. Sometimes they played the drunkard or danced grotesquely in a circle with wild gestures, sporting bright costumes ornamented with bells which jangled as they moved.

From the fourteenth century and possibly before, the custom had grown up of keeping a tame fool, or jester, at court. Some of these people were simply idiots; it was a pleasant feature of medieval society that the lunatic was regarded with some awe as one 'possessed by God'. Similarly, dwarfs, who had been kept in the homes of the rich in Roman times, were often given a place at medieval courts and treated somewhat as pets. In the ducal palace of the Gonzaga family at Mantua in Italy, there is a complete set of small-size apartments created as living quarters for the court dwarfs. This custom survived in Russia up to the eighteenth century, when the Tsar kept seventy-two dwarfs as a guard of honour.

From these simple-minded fools there developed the profession of court jester, who was probably recruited from the ranks of the minstrels. The jesters represented a safety-valve in feudal society, the innocent who could answer back to bishop and king, the fool with licence to poke fun at anyone. Some jesters adopted a kind of uniform of motley-coloured coat and hose, with a hood like a monk's cowl, often decorated with asses' ears and a peak like a cock's comb. Bells tinkled from their skirts and elbows, and they carried a mock sceptre, decorated with a fool's head or attached to an inflated bladder with which they could deal out mock blows.

Behind their foolery, the jesters could conceal some sharp comments on contemporary society. A jester called Claus Narr, for example, was employed by the Elector of Saxony. At this time his master could not manage to beget an heir. 'You should study the methods of the monks,' said Claus; 'they have no wives, but they manage to have plenty of children, so no doubt they grow them in their gardens.'

The medieval delight in fooling was well exemplified in the custom of the Lord of Misrule. On one day in the year, usually the octave of Epiphany, the minor clerics in French cathedrals would take over the ceremonies themselves, dressing up as bishops, burlesquing the Mass, braying at the responses, and pouring water

Top: In this seventeenth-century allegorical engraving, a jester is revealed beneath the robes of a figure, symbolizing Royalty and Government, while Morris dancers circle him to the sound of rough music. La Danse du Monde *was engraved by Joan Baptista Vrints and is in the Douce Portfolio.*

Above: The Abbots Bromley Horn Dance. In addition to the jester, the dancers include six men carrying reindeer antlers, a boy with a bow and a fixed arrow, a hobby-horse man and a man-woman figure, the Maid Marion of the Morris dance, accompanied by two musicians.

Left: In the Middle Ages fools found a place in the courts of kings. In this miniature from a fifteenth-century manuscript, a court jester wears traditional dress and carries a mock sceptre.

over the precentor instead of sprinkling him with holy water.

When the Church succeeded in banning these profanities the lay people took over. Confréries Joyeuses sprang up all over France consisting of young men who adopted jesters' costumes and elected one of their number as Prince des Sots or as Mère Folle, a man dressed up as a woman, to preside over their revels. By the sixteenth century these displays of animal spirits had developed into little plays, called *sotties*, which often used clowning to underline their satire in those days of fierce religious controversy. In one of these Mère Eglise, the Catholic Church, appears in splendid ecclesiastical robes, but at a dramatic moment in the play her dress is pulled up to reveal the fool's motley underneath.

The stage fool or clown of the *sottie* acquired the name of Badin. There is an interesting description of a Badin of the early sixteenth century, 'with his shirt all dirty, his face covered with flour, and with a baby's bonnet on his head, decorated with cock's feathers'. This is one of the earliest references to a white-faced clown, a figure that will reappear many times in our story. In Spain the role of Badin was taken by a character called Bobo, from which the English term booby comes. In Germany the fool or *Narr* played a leading part in the Fastnachtspiele, or Carnival plays, that were acted at Shrovetide by groups of young artisans.

While these secular forms of drama were struggling to find expression, another type of drama had been developing in the churches in the form of mystery plays based on biblical themes. But even here the instinct for broad comedy expressed itself. In the

Nativity plays the shepherds who visit the Christ Child are often shown as foolish and clownish, as when in one famous example they steal a sheep and hide it in a baby's cradle; in the story of the Murder of the Innocents, Herod rants and raves in such an exaggerated way that the tragedy turns to farce; Joseph, the husband of Mary, was sometimes depicted as a simpleton.

In England the biblical stories came to be replaced by morality plays and interludes, which were dramas of personified sins and virtues. The clowning in these pieces was provided by the Vice, a kind of abstraction of wrongdoing, who turned himself into a comical buffoon. He would indulge in backchat with the audience, speak in a nonsensical gabble or wail, and he delighted in verbal perversions and pretended misunderstandings. When Lucifer himself appeared and commanded him to repeat a salutation: 'All hail, O noble prince of hell,' the Vice replied, 'All my dame's cows fell down in the well,' and so on. At the end of the play the Vice was often carried off to hell on the devil's back, but we may be sure that he clowned as he made his exit.

It was above all the devils in these mystery and morality plays, strutting and scampering with such glee in their black, horned masks, that provided the element of farce. Today at the Munich Christmas Market in the city square this tradition continues when St Nicholas – a mitred old gentleman similar to Father Christmas – pays his annual visit; he is accompanied by a couple of black-visaged devil imps. As they charge into the crowd from time to time to snatch an onlooker people run from them screaming; but as soon as the foray is over they press after them laughing.

Opposite: Dwarfs were traditionally kept in both the homes of rich Romans and medieval lords. This tradition is preserved in the Circus. This is Jimmy Armstrong, an American circus dwarf who worked for both Ringling and Clyde Beatty and Cole Brothers in the 1950s.

Left: A medieval buffoon called Marculf leads a dance of grotesque characters with bare feet. This scene, reminiscent of the sotties was etched by Daniel Hopfer. Above: A ship of devils and fools pulled through the streets of Nuremberg in a pageant of about 1500.

Scenes from Commedia dell' Arte performances as recorded in the sixteenth century in the Recueil Fossard. Top left: Horacio and Arlecchino on a donkey. Top right: Arlecchino, Zany Cornetto *and Pantaleone making music. Above left: Zany Cornetto with Arlecchino as an acrobat. Above right: Pantaleone and Zany fight a duel over Francheschina.*

Devils and physical deformities were terribly real to the men of the middle ages, but they allayed their fear with laughter. The devils of the medieval plays and the dwarfs of the medieval courts were treated as figures of fun. A strand of horror and the grotesque runs very close to laughter in the story of clowning through the ages.

A new form of drama grew up in Italy in the middle of the sixteenth century which was to have a lasting influence on the development of the clown. Small companies of professional actors began touring Italy playing in secular comedies. They called their theatre *dell' Arte*, that is 'skilled', a professional type of theatre as opposed to the amateur troupes who played at court or at universities. This type of theatre was marked by three distinctive elements that still make it unique in the entire history of the stage.

Firstly it was played by stock characters, and an actor having settled into one role might continue playing it throughout his entire career. Every play had, in effect, the same cast: a lecherous old merchant, usually called Pantaleone; a pompous Doctor of Law, who might be called Balanzone or Tartaglia; a boastful army Captain, probably called Spavento or Scaramuccia; young lovers, with names like Flavio or Leandro and Isabella or Silvia; and a clutch of servants, tradesmen and other humble supernumeraries, called Arlecchino, Pedrolino, Brighella, Scapino, Mezzetino, or Pulcinella among the men and Francheschina, Colombina, or Lisetta among the women. Many of these characters were firmly associated with certain regions of Italy, and spoke in strong local dialects: Pantaleone, for instance, came from Venice; the Doctor from Bologna; the Captain was a Spanish invader; Arlecchino came from Bergamo; Pulcinella from Naples.

The second distinctive feature of the Commedia dell' Arte was that many of the characters wore masks. The Greek drama had been acted in masks many centuries earlier, but the Italian Comedy was unique in that it mixed masked and unmasked actors in the same plays. Certain characters, like the lovers and the female

Above: In this watercolour of about 1750 Pantaleone, Arlecchino and Colombina appear in a scene from the Commedia dell' Arte. The other character is played by a German clown similar to Hans Wurst.

servants, were never masked. Other characters were immediately recognizable from their masks and their costumes: Pantaleone by a hooked nose, jutting beard and moustaches, and tight red breeches; the Doctor assumed a bulbous nose, huge red wart, and loose black costume; Arlecchino had a devil-like black face, a jacket and trousers covered with irregular coloured patches, and a flat wooden bat stuck in his belt; Pulcinella was given a hook nose and a loose white costume, belted at the waist.

The masks worn by these characters did not cover the entire face, as had those of the Greek and Roman theatre. They were half masks over the upper part of the face, but leaving the mouth and jaw free. This enabled the actors to speak more clearly, and to act more naturalistically, than if their faces had been completely covered. At the same time they could mingle less inappropriately with the unmasked characters.

The third feature of this type of theatre was that the plays had no written scripts. The author, so far as there was one, sketched out a plot, and the actors made up speeches to fit it. Presumably, after a number of performances, the dialogue tended to become fairly standardized, but at its inception it was a true improvised drama. At any performance an actor might add a new speech or a fresh bit of business and his companions on the stage had to be ready to respond. Actors performing in this way have been compared to a group of musicians playing jazz. It was a form of theatre that demanded agile and creative acting, and if contemporary reports are to be believed the players in these troupes were some of the most skilful in the history of the theatre.

The plots of the plays varied enormously in detail, but tended to fall into a fairly standard pattern in which the old merchant and the Doctor are avaricious or lecherous, the lovers have every obstacle thrown in their way but are eventually united, and the servants, or *zanni* as they were called, contribute broad humour and tricks to complete the mixture.

Clowning played a large part in these performances and, despite the lack of any written texts, pictorial records and eye-witness

Knockabout acts at the traditional Cirque à l'Ancienne in Paris are reminiscent of the humour in the Commedia dell' Arte.

Above: Dédé tries to douse his companion with water from his mouth, but bursts out laughing and sprays water everywhere.

accounts make it possible to recapture some of the ways it was performed. There was verbal humour. Pulcinella is left by his master to guard the house; on his master's return he is asked if any one has called. He replies, 'Not a fly.' The master, however, finds three thieves inside. On being upbraided, Pulcinella replies, 'You didn't find any flies – only men.'

There was much miming. A popular effect was the night scene, which went something like this. Two men enter, in of course the bright light of the open stage, carrying candles as if at night. Each one is looking for an intruder he thinks he has heard. A gust of wind blows the candles out. They grope about as if in pitch darkness, hearing the other's movements, feeling their way towards one another, just missing, embracing the furniture, finally grappling furiously together only to find that they are friends living in the same house. There was situation comedy. Pantaleone recommends Arlecchino to marry a widow for her money. He does so, only to find that she has eight children, all of whom look like little Pantaleones. The old man has been fathering off his bastards.

There was the joke of repetition. Pantaleone is just returning home when he meets one of the characters coming out of his (Pantaleone's) house, who bows to him, without a word, and enters the house next door. Then another character leaves, bows, and enters next door. And another and another and another. Finally Pantaleone, quite bemused, bows to the audience and enters the house next door.

There was much parody and burlesque. Music was made on a bellows or a gridiron; singers warbled in extravagant imitation of madrigalists; old fools cast themselves on the ground in ridiculous wooing of pretty young girls; duels were fought with quillpens; tattered knights rode forth to battle mounted on a donkey.

Trickery and thieving were found funny. Eating and drinking were a great source of humour. Two thieves spot a countryman with a basket of fruit, and sit down on either side of him; one tells a story, to which the countryman listens open-mouthed, while the other eats up half the basket; then this thief tells another story while the first finishes the basket. They leave the countryman

amazed at the tales he has heard, till he looks down at his basket, finds it empty, and bursts into tears.

Knockabout humour was introduced all the time. Water was thrown about, and characters spat fountains of water out of their mouths to drench their companions. Some character fell down dead, and every one else tumbled over him as they ran on to the stage. Here is an example of some typical funny business.

Trivelino stretches on the ground and tricks Arlecchino into helping him up. As Arlecchino does so he loses his wooden bat which Trivelino promptly grabs to whack the other's bottom. Then Arlecchino turns round and Trivelino bumps him in the stomach so that he falls over. Arlecchino tries to help Trivelino again and carries him across the stage, and props him up against the wings at stage right. While Arlecchino is wiping his brow and looking at the audience, Trivelino crosses over behind him to lean against the wings at stage left. Arlecchino cannot find Trivelino and is very puzzled, but after much searching finds him. While he expresses his relief to the audience, Trivelino crosses back to stage right. And so on, *ad infinitum*, adapting their actions to the audience's responses. By this time the audience will be shouting advice which Arlecchino misunderstands every time. One can see just this sort of interplay between performers and audience in almost any pantomime or Punch and Judy show today.

Top left and right: Alexis Gruss, the white-face, and Dédé, the auguste, are shown in a typical double act.

Above: Dédé recovers from a retaliatory knock on the head during his act at the Cirque à l'Ancienne.

The actors were often good acrobats. One Arlecchino, in a moment of surprise, could throw a back somersault without spilling a drop of wine from the glass in his hand; another could walk on stilts, and so kiss pretty girls in the first floor windows of their houses. Sometimes the humour was coarse and vulgar. Arlecchino's hand found its way up women's skirts; his bat was employed as a phallus; the chamber pot was emptied over serenaders in the street below; enemas were administered by a monster syringe. This was particularly funny if someone was hiding in the commode that the victim now had to sit on!

The acting troupes of the Commedia dell' Arte had found their way all over Europe by the year 1600. Shakespeare and Molière were influenced by them. The characters they had originated were adopted and transformed in the lands they visited; so that in France, for example, the patchwork Arlecchino became an elegantly patterned Arlequin, the peasant Pulcinella a dandified Polichinelle, and the dreamy Pedrolino a love-sick white-faced Pierrot. In England they became Harlequin and Punch. The style of improvised comedy that these actors originated did not survive, but the clowning in which they delighted was copied everywhere and is with us still.

A secular form of theatre evolved in England towards the end of the sixteenth century, with companies of professional players appearing at the new theatres in London and travelling round manors and inns throughout the country. Clowns played a prominent part in the entertainment. They burst in upon all kinds of plays with comic business that had very little relation to the plot. A contemporary comment gives some idea of a typical act: 'Why, if thou canst but draw thy mouth awry, lay thy leg over thy staff, saw a piece of cheese asunder with thy dagger, lap up drink on the earth, I warrant thee they'll laugh mightily.' This could well describe a clown act today.

In his character the Elizabethen stage clown was a guzzler of food and drink, and a hater of hard work; he was fond of practical jokes, but was often duped himself; he was boastful but cowardly; he spoke either in a peasant's dialect or in an absurd parody of high-flown speech; if he was married his wife was a shrew. A popular effect was to let his voice be heard off stage, and then suddenly poke his head between the curtains, which was enough, we are told, to set the audience laughing. These are the age-old tricks of clowns everywhere.

The dramatic writers complained bitterly at the way the clowns intruded into their plays with impromptu jokes. Hamlet is certainly speaking for Shakespeare when he advised the players, 'And let those that play your clowns speak no more than is set down for them.' In the end the clowns were either absorbed into the dramatic structure of the play, or allowed to have their own way in short

At the Festival of Fools, held in the West of England, the colour and excitement of the fairs of the seventeenth and eighteenth centuries are revived. Below: Fools perform on a booth stage. Bottom: The procession makes its way up a hill.

Opposite: A modern juggler keeps alive a traditional fairground entertainment at the Festival of Fools in the West of England.

Above: The Italian Commedia dell' Arte actors were expelled from France in 1697. This engraving shows their departure.

apparently stupid partner always ends up best. An example from France at the end of the seventeenth century went something like this. Two Arlequins – Arlequin and Arlequin Clumsy – appear on the stage. Arlequin is a brilliant acrobat, and Arlequin Clumsy tries to imitate him. Arlequin shows off by turning a somersault with a glass of wine in his hand without spilling any, and then sips it with relish; Arlequin Clumsy won't be caught – he puts his glass down, throws an awkward somersault, picks the glass up again, and drinks it down at one gulp. Arlequin hits Clumsy on the back; Clumsy hits Arlequin in the stomach; Arlequin says, 'If you do that again I'll hit you'; Clumsy says, 'As you've done that again I'll hit you', and does so. Arlequin knocks on his girl friend's door, eager to make love to her; Clumsy runs through the door as soon as she opens it, and Arlequin is left outside. This is a classic comic situation that recurs constantly in the story of clowning.

Similar to this is the joke of the pompous person deflated. In another French sketch of the same period Arlequin is having a bath in a tub of water; there is much funny business involving getting out of the bath, having his hair curled, and dressing himself up in a fine costume. The clock strikes, he thinks he will be late for his appointment with his mistress and rushes towards the door, only to fall fully clothed into the tub.

When the Italian comedians were banished from France in 1697 because of the indecency of their performances, the spirit of the Commedia dell' Arte went on to flourish in the theatres of the French fairs. But here they had to face opposition from the established theatres, who claimed a monopoly for the performance of plays. A similar situation arose in England, where the patent theatres had been granted a sole right to perform drama. The fair booth proprietors were, therefore, forced to adapt their performances into a form that did not conflict with the licensed theatres, and their shows tended to fall into a succession of disjointed scenes rather than a developed plot.

This, however, was not enough; and to protect themselves from the legal injunctions of the licensed theatres, the fair booth proprietors fell back upon two courses of action. They either acted their plays in dumb show, without any dialogue; or they dismissed their human actors and performed their plays with puppets. Puppet shows have a long history, closely linked with the popular theatre in every civilization in which they have flourished, and in late seventeenth and eighteenth-century Europe they came into their own.

Wherever the puppet theatre has existed there has been a tendency for *one* character to become the ubiquitous comic hero of all its plays. In the Italian puppet theatres of the seventeenth century this was Pulcinella, the Neapolitan zany. As Italian puppet players travelled across Europe, Pulcinella acquired new characteristics; in France there was an old tradition of hunchbacked clowns, and here

Opposite: Clowns and puppets have many characteristics in common. This young white-face clown is from the Elleboog children's circus in Amsterdam.
Above: Punch kills his wife Judy in this illustration from a nineteenth-century children's book.
Right: In this scene from a German Kasperl play, Kasperl asks for contributions to his collecting box so that he can go to the inn for a glass of beer, having beaten death and the devil.

Pulcinella seems to have become grotesquely hunchbacked, often with a counterbalancing protruding breast as well. These physical deformities, added to the hooked nose of his black mask, provided a wonderful opportunity from which the puppet carvers could create a figure of extravagant fantasy, and in France Pulcinella became Polichinelle, discarding his white Neapolitan clothes for a bright costume of red and yellow.

So when the theatre booths of the early eighteenth-century French fairs were driven to make use of puppet actors, they adopted Polichinelle as the comic hero of their pieces. He delighted the public with his witticisms, which were sometimes somewhat saucy. A poem of 1708 describes a performance at a local village festival as follows:

And there the famed Polichinelle,
The hero of these little plays,
Although a bit free in his ways
In no way made the ladies blush;
They smiled and laughed at him so much.

In England, an Italian puppet showman had arrived, taking advantage of the removal of restrictions on theatre after the restoration of Charles II. In 1662 a Pulcinella show was presented in Covent Garden, and the English quickly took him to their hearts, changing his name to Punchenello and then to plain Punch. As Punch he absorbed much of the character of the Vice of the morality plays and of the Elizabethan stage clowns; he appeared in a large repertory of plays, mostly folk stories and biblical themes, intruding with jokes and vulgarities into any kind of plot, and was carried off by the Devil at the play's end in the medieval tradition.

During all this time Punch had been a marionette – that is, a puppet moved by wires or strings from above; but at the end of the eighteenth century he began to appear as a hand puppet in a simple booth in the streets. It was here that there developed the basic form of the Punch and Judy show, which consists of little more than a series of short dialogues between Punch and various members of the cast, each of which ends with Punch bashing the other on the

head with his stick. Finally Punch is taken off to be hanged, but in an immortal bit of business he tricks the hangman into putting his own head into the noose; and the piece traditionally concludes with Punch triumphing even over the Devil. This is the show that can still be seen in England today.

By the eighteenth century Pulcinella had taken root in almost every country of Europe, and in North America, but in the social fervour of the French Revolution and the nationalistic upsurge of the Napoleonic Wars a very curious thing happened. All over Europe new regional comic heroes sprang up to displace the progeny of Pulcinella from the puppet stage. In France, a character called Guignol was created in Lyons by a puppeteer, Laurent Mourguet; Guignol was a typical workman of the district, lively, good-humoured, and fond of a bottle of wine. In Vienna a character called Kasperl was created by an actor, Johann Laroche. Kasperl was in the tradition of Hanswurst, a peasant of the Austrian mountains, but in time he acquired an appearance rather closer to that of Punch. In other cities the same thing was happening – Hänneschen in Cologne, Tchantchès in Liège, Jan Klaasen in Holland, Lafleur in Picardy, and many another, most of whom can still be seen performing in their local puppet theatres today. Of the older figures, only Punch in England and Petroushka in Russia survived; but Petroushka vanished with the Russian Revolution.

Puppets do, of course, possess a certain distinct character and puppet clowns cannot be exactly equated with human clowns. But there is one respect in which the puppet and the human clown blend. A great feature of many puppet clowns is the way the puppets hit each other on the head without getting hurt. If a real person were hit a crushing blow on the head, the audience would be concerned; but with puppets the spectators know it is not for real and they laugh. But exactly the same thing applies when a clown is hit on the head. However realistic the blow, the spectators know that no harm is done and they find the idea enormously funny. The clown with his painted face and stylized appearance is a step removed from the ordinary man. He is almost a puppet.

CLOWNS ON THE STAGE

Many troupes from the French fairground theatres came to play in London in the early years of the eighteenth century. They gained great popularity, and their acts inspired the development of English pantomime. Their style derived from the Italian tradition; in 1702 a French troupe performed *A Night Scene by a Harlequin and Scaramouche after the Italian Manner* at Drury Lane, and acts similarly described were presented in several theatres during the next twelve years.

From contemporary accounts it is clear that not all these 'Night Scenes' actually depicted events happening in the dark, and it would seem that the description 'Night Scene' was used for any kind of performance, largely in mime, by characters from the Commedia dell' Arte. We have already seen how a night scene was a popular act in the performances of the Italian comedians, giving full scope for their genius in comic mime, and the term became adopted for any kind of act presented by these French players, who had inherited the tradition of the original Commedia dell' Arte.

Their appearance on the London stage sparked off attempts to imitate them. In 1702 John Weaver claimed to have produced what he called a pantomime at Drury Lane; and in 1716 John Rich, the manager of Lincoln's Inn Fields, produced a pantomime called *Harlequin Executed*. Within a few years this new form of entertainment had attracted a wide following. A few statistics illustrate just how popular it had become: at Rich's theatre the number of programmes introducing pantomimes grew from four in 1720-1 to 57 in 1723-4 and 91 in 1729-30. In 1722-3 the average receipts for a programme without a pantomime were £36, while for a programme with a pantomime they were £114.

These early eighteenth-century English pantomimes were short afterpieces, performed after the main play of the evening. The pantomimes comprised two unconnected sections; one told some mythological story and the other displayed characters from the Commedia dell' Arte. The performance was largely in mime, but with some songs and dances; and elaborate scenery, tricks and

Nola Rae, the versatile clown and mime, perpares to go on stage in London to perform her one-woman show.

stage effects were made an important feature. It was influenced by the Commedia dell' Arte tradition, but became a form of entertainment in its own right. Pantomimes were bitterly attacked by serious dramatists as 'monstrous Medlies' of nonsense but they exactly caught the spirit of the age.

As pantomime developed, the Commedia dell' Arte element tended to settle into a pattern built round the love adventures and misadventures of Harlequin and Columbine, danced and mimed in dumb show and interrupted by comic and grotesque incidents. Harlequin's bat was often used as a kind of magic wand to effect mysterious or amusing transformations. The so-called serious part of the pantomime consisted of a mythological story expressed in song, recitative and dance, with a little dialogue. And the whole thing often carried a parody of contemporary entertainment, in which the new craze for Italian opera provided an easy butt.

Much of the success of pantomime must be attributed to the genius of John Rich. As a young man he was a flashy figure, keeping race horses and mistresses. In old age he became an eccentric theatre manager surrounded by innumerable cats, but throughout his career he was a wonderful silent actor, always billed as Lun, in the role of Harlequin. He is often said to have acted in dumb show because he was practically illiterate and could not speak the part. But this is based on a misunderstanding. He was not illiterate; he was a brilliant mime, and so set his stamp upon the development of English pantomime, because he acted through his body rather than through his mouth.

The tradition that English eighteenth-century pantomime was presented largely in dumb show proceeds, therefore, from two sources: from the tradition of dumb show acting imposed upon the actors in the French fairs, and from the natural genius for mime of John Rich. And in this tradition of dumb show acting clowning, too, played a part. Some of Lun's mimes became famous. There was a scene in which he was hatched from an egg; he cracked the shell, peered out, moved cautiously, put one foot to the ground, tested it, took a step, a little leap, and then a dance of wild delight. It was a masterpiece of dumb show. In another act he mimed catching a butterfly, an act that was to be repeated in many circus rings in years to come. Another act that can be seen in circuses today was introduced in the pantomime *Merlin in Love*. Harlequin lolls back comfortably in an armchair. Suddenly the chair sneezes which gives him a fright. Then one arm of the chair taps Harlequin on the shoulder. He tries to get up, but the other arm seizes his hand. When he struggles to escape both arms encircle him in a grip of iron and he collapses, a helpless prisoner.

The following description of a pantomime called *Harlequin Sorcerer* of 1741 gives an idea of this type of entertainment. The scene opens showing Columbine looking out from a balcony. Harlequin enters, Columbine calls to him, they strike attitudes of love, but Pantaloon and his servant surprise them, and they run off hotly pursued by Pantaloon. The lovers come to a half-built house and Columbine hides behind a pile of bricks while Harlequin clambers up a ladder. Pantaloon chases Harlequin who slides down the ladder, and the scaffolding collapses bringing Pantaloon down with it. Next, Pantaloon imprisons Columbine in his house; an ostrich is delivered to the door, and brought in by the servant; it dances before Columbine, and then it is revealed to be Harlequin in disguise; they run off together. Harlequin now appears disguised as a washerwoman, with a big washing tub. When Pantaloon and his servant rush in looking for Columbine, Harlequin trips them up so that they fall headlong into the tub and emerge covered with soap suds. Finally we see the statue of a horseman about to be unveiled. The man on the horse is actually Harlequin and the servant thinks he recognizes him. He climbs up to peer under the cover, the horse bites him and kicks him down.

Pantaloon's servant in this pantomime was probably not one of the Commedia dell' Arte characters, but the traditional English clown, who came to enter more and more into these pieces. He might be called Clodpoll, Clodpate, Blunder, Dulman, or Simon and he was normally dressed as a simple country yokel. He played a subordinate role in the piece as the stooge or feed to the clowns of

Above: John Rich, the brilliant mime and manager of Lincoln's Inn Fields, in the character of Harlequin. An impression by a later artist.

Opposite: Clowns at the Circus Knie today perform a variation of a traditional entrée. Their act is set in a haunted castle where a chair suddenly comes to life.

MONS. LOUIS AS CLOWN. 44.

London Published by J. REDINGTON, 73 Hoxton Street, Formerly called 208 Hoxton Old Town.

Italian origin. In *Queen Mab*, for instance, of 1771, it is Harlequin who disguises himself as a dog, hides in a dog kennel, and jumps out to bite Clown as he passes by. But in a few years the structure of pantomime was to be transformed, when the Clown emerged as the dominant character.

I n the last two decades of the eighteenth century a young boy called Joey Grimaldi could have been seen playing small parts in the melodramas and pantomimes at Sadler's Wells and Drury Lane. This boy had a theatrical background. His grandfather had been a noted performer in the theatrical booths of the French fairs; his father had been a ballet master and Pantaloon on the London stage and his mother was a Cockney dancer in the chorus at Drury Lane. The manager at Sadler's Wells, Charles Dibdin the younger, had noted the liveliness of young Grimaldi, the faces he pulled and the antics he played, and in 1800 he decided to give him his chance in the new pantomime, where he would play a second Clown.

In a few years he shot to the top, clinching his position as London's funniest clown in the famous pantomime *Mother Goose* at Covent Garden in 1806. From that time he played, on average, in three or four new pantomimes each year and became the darling of English audiences, but it was a brief triumph. By 1820 his health was giving way, his body was wracked with pain, his limbs were stiff, his muscles knotted, and in 1823 he played his part on the stage for the last time. He died fourteen years later, leaving behind him a legend and bestowing the name of Joey upon all clowns thereafter. Descriptions and pictures of Grimaldi's performances have survived in such richness that we can gain some idea of the nature of his artistry. In the first place, it must be remembered that he grew up in the theatre and that he was a good actor. He could have made his mark as a comedian in straight plays if the hierarchical structure of the patent theatres had let him; as it was, he played the second gravedigger in *Hamlet* with success and stamped his way through a whole catalogue of melodramatic villains.

More important than this, he was a brilliant mime. Again and again we come back to the art of mime as the secret of clowning, and here he was supreme. In one of the melodramas in which he played he took the part of Orson, a Wild Man of the Woods, and gave a wonderful impersonation of the impression made by music upon a savage mind. In one scene he was about to tear a child to pieces, when the father, desperate to find some means of communication, began to play upon a flageolet. Grimaldi gave a start, his hands hung as if arrested, his body seemed to soften; as the plaintive music continued his frame shook convulsively, he clasped his hands to his eyes in an agony of tears. Finally, as he restored the child to its father and the music played a more lively air, he danced in wild abandon in the ecstasy of a liberated spirit.

Another observer has recalled how he acted the dagger scene from *Macbeth*. No word of Shakespeare was uttered, only a few elocutionary sounds, but the effect was such that – despite his clown's dress – the whole audience was transfixed, and young and old seemed to tremble with awe as if they were watching a great tragedian. Such effects were not just the result of careful rehearsal. He was, above all, a marvellous impromptu performer. One night at Covent Garden there was a hitch in the pantomime, and the prompter begged Grimaldi to go on and hold the audience for five minutes while the accident was put right. Grimaldi looked round backstage, saw a bottle of beer, and told a boy to come in after him, carrying the bottle on a tray. Grimaldi walked on stage, followed by the boy. Grimaldi eyed the beer, winked at the audience, drew the boy's attention to somebody in one of the boxes, and neatly stole the bottle while the boy was looking the other way. The boy went off in bewilderment.

Grimaldi produces the bottle from behind his back and raises it to his mouth. Suddenly he is interrupted by Conscience – that is to say by himself as Conscience. Conscience lectures Grimaldi with a stern face and a wagging finger. Grimaldi answers Conscience with a cheeky face and a rude gesture. Conscience forbids Grimaldi to drink. Grimaldi insists on drinking. All this without a word being

Opposite: Grimaldi established a tradition of clown costume and business which is still alive today. A Victorian clown of about 1850, pictured after a raid on the butcher's and fishmonger's stalls.
Top and Above: These two drawings by W. Heath *show Grimaldi in various acts from the pantomime of* The Golden Fish *of 1812. Grimaldi riding in his 'Tandem', a joke of construction in which a laundry basket is transformed into a coach, and Grimaldi playing leap-frog.*

spoken. As Grimaldi puts the bottle to his lips Conscience strikes it away. They fight. At the end of the first round they retire to their corners, and Grimaldi takes a pull at the beer. In the second round Conscience boxes with powerful straight lefts and Grimaldi is left in poor shape, but as he reels back to his corner he takes another long swig from the bottle. At the end of the third round Grimaldi is knocked down and Conscience is declared the winner. But by this time Grimaldi has finished the bottle! This little act indicates two of the characteristics that have marked clowns in every age. Grimaldi was a guzzler and a thief. But he stole in such an artless, droll way, and stuffed his mouth with tarts or his pockets with sausages with such good humour that nobody could take offence.

Grimaldi's acts were not entirely in mime. He did speak from time to time, in a thick, chuckling voice, but usually only after a long silence, perhaps happily munching gingerbread, to pronounce the word 'Nice'; or when he was suffering the most apalling torture he would eventually utter the one word 'Don't'. He sang, too, in a light baritone, and many of his songs gained enormous popularity. The words were not remarkable, it was the way in which they were sung that created the effect. Some were complete nonsense, like *A*

Typitywitchet, in which successive verses ended with a chorus of hiccups, sneezes, yawns, cries, and laughs. Some were clever parodies, like *An Oyster Crossed in Love*, which guyed the style of grand opera. The most famous of all his songs was *Hot Codlins*, about an old woman selling toffee apples in the street, who trotted off to the pub for a drink to keep herself warm, with dire consequences. The last word of each verse was left for the audience to sing, which they certainly did, bellowing the key responses of 'gin', 'drunk', and – according to verbal tradition – 'pissed'. The music for these songs looks back rather to the eighteenth century than to the rollicking style of Victorian music-hall, and I imagine that Grimaldi took the songs pretty slowly, with many a nod and a wink, making each word tell.

As well as actor, Grimaldi was an acrobat. He was noted as a swordsman in stage fights before he ever became a clown, and his training at his father's hands stood him in good stead in the business of clowning on the Regency stage. The essence of pantomime at this period consisted of chases and escapes, and the performers had to be ready to leap through traps in the stage floor, to slip on butter slides, to be bashed on the head and beaten on the bottom, and to

Opposite: Clowns from all over Britain attend the memorial service which is held annually at Holy Trinity, Dalston, London, in honour of Grimaldi.

Above: After the service they all congregate for a lively entertainment in the church hall, which houses a unique collection of clowning memorabilia.

dive through trick pictures or clock faces in the scenery, where flaps opened to let them through. If they hit the wrong part of the scenery they struck a wooden beam, and if they didn't tip the stage hands sufficiently there might be no one waiting to catch them as they landed on the other side. It was the effect of over twenty years of this kind of activity that crippled Joey Grimaldi before he was forty-five.

Beyond all this, Grimaldi had a genius for satirical observation. He ridiculed fashionable clothes, by dressing himself up as a fine lady with a coal scuttle for a bonnet, an iron stove pipe for its crown, and a bunch of flowers picked off a street barrow for its decoration. He ridiculed the uniform of hussar officers by parading with coal scuttles on his feet for boots, candlesticks for spurs, and a lady's muff for a helmet. He burlesqued the craze for coaching by harnessing two little dogs to an upturned cradle, fitting an iron fender inside it, and perching himself on the top as the coachman.

He was marvellously inventive in devising jokes of construction like these, in the most famous of which he assembled the contents of a greengrocer's shop to form a vegetable man, who then fought a boxing match with him; the vegetable man was presumably some

kind of loosely articulated marionette. In another trick Grimaldi would suddenly shove a mop stick through a big round cheese, thrust it into Pantaloon's hands, seize his legs, and turn him into a wheelbarrow.

And what did this demon of anarchy look like? He transformed the appearance of Clown by formalizing and exaggerating it. Clowns before Grimaldi had been dressed as country yokels or gentlemen's servants, with red wigs and bright, jolly faces. Grimaldi, partly guided by Charles Dibdin, transformed the servants' liveries into what Dibdin called 'a whimsical mixture of colours and compositions'. He puffed the breeches out to allow room to stow away the objects he pilfered; the red hair became a cock's comb or three tufts on a bald wig; and the ruddy cheeks became neat red triangles on a whitened face. It was not a uniform, but rather a series of experiments that quickly became standardized into the traditional clown costume and make-up that we recognize today.

But beneath it all, there was the face of Joey Grimaldi. That big, good-humoured, round phiz with the twinkling eyes and the 'oven mouth', 'a living jest book' as it was called by his contemporaries. And behind the face was the personality of Joey Grimaldi, the half-Italian, half-Cockney acrobatic mime, who exuded good humour as soon as he stepped on the stage, who could project himself to the gallery of great theatres like Covent Garden and who could drop a delicate wink to the front row of the pit at Sadler's Wells. He has come to be recognized by generations who never saw him as *the* clown of all time.

Sometime in the 1930s a public relations man with the Bertram Mills Circus had the idea of getting some clowns from the Olympia Christmas Circus to lay a wreath on Joey Grimaldi's grave outside the church of St James in Islington. Grimaldi had nothing whatever to do with circuses and never played in one, but it made a picture for the evening papers and a bit of publicity for Bertram Mills, and it became an annual event. When the Olympia circus was discontinued a Clowns' Club took up the idea, and a service was held in the church till a new vicar threw the clowns out. But the clowns found another church in the east end of London, Holy Trinity at Dalston, which could claim a doubtful association in being built the year after Grimaldi had died. Here they still meet, once a year, in their make-up and motley, for an annual service and an entertainment in the church hall. They arrive in every rig of fantasy and fun to take part in a ceremony to honour the craft they practise and the man who did so much to create it.

At about the same time as Grimaldi transformed the character of Clown in English pantomime, a brilliant clown in France developed another character from the Commedia dell' Arte which gave rise to a contrasting tradition of clowning.

From the 1760s there had grown up along the Boulevard du Temple in Paris a row of theatrical booths, marionette shows, rope-dancing exhibitions, and similar attractions. So many murders were enacted upon the boards of these little theatres that the street was christened 'le boulevard du crime'. One of the smallest and dirtiest of these shows was the Théâtre des Funambules, and it was at this theatre that a troupe of tumblers and rope dancers, directed by Philippe Deburau, was engaged in 1816. In, but scarcely of, this troupe was Philippe's son, an awkward boy called Jean-Gaspard, whose gangling legs made

him too clumsy to dance the rope but who worked as a stage hand.

Jean-Gaspard may have been clumsy as an acrobat, but as he brought his long, loose arms and legs under control he began to show some ability as a theatrical mime. Nine years later he made his first appearance in one of the pantomimes that made up the repertory of this theatre. He played the part of Pierrot, a character derived from the Pedrolino of the Commedia dell' Arte and the Gilles of the eighteenth-century French fairs. He wore an all-white costume with a white-face make-up, just relieved by eyebrows and eye sockets picked out in black and rouged lips, with a black skull cap. He left off the big ruff that traditionally flopped over Pierrot's shoulders, thus leaving his neck and chin free and visible for expressive movement, and he adopted long wide sleeves that accentuated his arm gestures. The romantic image of Pierrot that was to haunt poets and writers throughout the nineteenth century was born.

But Deburau was not just a love-sick spirit striking romantic attitudes in the pale moonlight. That is a later and decadent interpretation of the character. He was a true clown, capable of all the leaps and tricks of the French form of pantomime, but performing with a style that soon astonished Paris and drew artists and writers to sit with the rabble at the Funambules to watch this extraordinary new actor. In the words of one of his literary admirers, Pierrot became 'a character whose infinite nuances are difficult to render. Ingenuous like a child, cowardly, crafty, lazy, mischievous by instinct, obliging, jeering, gluttonous, thieving, blustering, greedy, clumsy . . he is a naïve and clownish Satan.'

This might almost serve as a description of Grimaldi's clown across the Channel, but there was a fundamental difference. Whereas Grimaldi was coarse and jolly, Deburau was subtle and sinister. Baudelaire described him as 'pale as the moon, mysterious as silence, supple and mute as the serpent, thin and long as a gibbet'. And he was totally silent, a true mime, expressing every emotion through the fluid movements of his long limbs.

Deburau was recreated by Jean-Louis Barrault in Marcel Carné's fine film, *Les Enfants du Paradis*. But while Barrault and Baudelaire have conveyed the poetic and sinister quality of Deburau's miming, they have failed to give weight to the elements of traditional clowning that he inherited with the role of Pierrot. These were demanded by the rough and boisterous audiences at the Funambules, and must have been touched with the magic of his art.

The sinister element that many spectators sensed in Deburau's

Rough and tumble acts (such as those on the right) were an important part of the pantomimes given at the Funambules Theatre in Deburau's day, but his interpretation of the Pierrot character added a new element to the tradition. The modern Pierrot (opposite) is much more of a romantic than Deburau's innocent yet mischievous figure.

Go to
W. WEBB'S
Juvenile
Theatrical Print
Warehouse
140
Old Str. St Lukes
for the Best Plays
ever Published

Pompey   Fairy   Harlequin   Fairy   Squire's Servant

Desperate Fight for Scene 12
Printed & Pub. W. WEBB 140 Old Str. St Lukes, London

Above: Characters and a scene from a toy theatre play of 1854. The 'Desperate Fight for Scene 12' features a clown, a policeman and tradesmen who are brandishing fishes, legs of mutton and other similar weapons.
Right: Harlequin from a page of illustrations of pantomimes shown in five London theatres in the mid-nineteenth century.

performance was, indeed, an element in his personality. One day in 1836, by which time he was famous and recognized all over Paris, a youth called out insults at him as he was walking in the street with his wife. Cooly and cold-bloodedly Deburau stepped up to him and struck him on the head with his stick. The boy died that evening. Deburau was Pierrot that evening at the Funambules. As with all great clowning, laughter is just round the corner from horror, and Deburau emphasized the dark side of the clown character. Deburau is remembered as a mime rather than as a clown, but it was not easy to separate the two skills at the Funambules. Nor is it easy now. A good clown must be a good mime. A great clown must be a great mime. True clowning means acting with the body.

Before the advent of Grimaldi, the clown had been a minor character in English pantomime and Harlequin had been the star. Grimaldi had changed all that. By the time he had retired, Harlequin was a gorgeous figure in a skin-tight costume of red, yellow and green lozenges, effecting magical transformations with a touch of his bat, but basically little more than a striker of elegant attitudes. Clown was the creative star of the pantomime.

The pattern into which early Victorian pantomime developed was that of an Opening, in which some nursery or legendary story was enacted in rhyming couplets. At a certain point in the proceedings the Fairy Queen or other benevolent agent appeared and transformed the young hero and heroine into Harlequin and Columbine, and a couple of the villains in the plot into Pantaloon and Clown. A Dandy Lover was often added to this foursome. The transformation was sometimes effected by the removal of large papier mâché heads and loosely-tied costumes that were worn in the first part of the show; but later there were sometimes two casts, so that Harlequin, for example, was acted by a different actor to that of the young nursery rhyme hero. In either case, after the transformation came the harlequinade, which had no connection with the previous story but which, for most spectators, was the best part of the entertainment.

There was no plot, strictly speaking, in the harlequinade. It consisted of a long chase in which Harlequin and Columbine were pursued by Pantaloon and Clown. It was played out before a rapid succession of backcloths depicting typical London scenes of the time, and on a stage peopled by the characters of the London streets: one-legged beggars, old clothes men, hawkers, nurses with babies, soldiers of the Queen, tradesmen, mobs of urchins, watchmen and later policemen. In this setting, Clown played his tricks, stole sausages from the butcher, spread a butter slide on the pavement for unwary pedestrians, brandished his red hot poker, laughed and sang. It was not at all the kind of pretty-pretty ballet that some recent revivals have suggested, but a full-blooded acrobatic tumble, calling into play every resource of stage carpenters and mechanics. It was anarchy allowed to run wild in the familiar streets of London, with Clown leading a satirical rampage in which the newest fashions and the latest inventions were the object of his mordant but usually genial wit.

The clowns who followed Grimaldi were legion, though none of them matched his genius. There was his contemporary, James Kirby, who wore a razzle-dazzle costume with zigzag lines running vertically up and down it and who originated the burlesquing of military uniforms; there was Paulo Redigé, the son of a rope dancer from the French fairs, who replaced Grimaldi for one season at Sadler's Wells; there was Tom Matthews, generally regarded as Grimaldi's pupil. There are descriptions of Matthews that mark him as a true successor to his master, recalling how he would waddle in bow-legged, pilfer in the most innocent manner possible, or knock at shop doors and then lie down in the doorway so that the incautious tradesman fell over him as he rushed out. He once sang a duet with a mouse (whose voice was provided by a boy off stage), and he gave such a clever burlesque of a famous ballerina, Mlle Duvernay, in a Spanish dance that she came night after night to sit in a stage box and watch him.

The harlequinades of the Matthews era are almost impossible to

Left: Columbine from a page of illustrations of pantomimes shown in five London theatres in the mid-nineteenth century.
Below: Three clowns of the 1820s, Paulo, Kirby and Bradbury, appearing together in The Three Fishermen *at the Surrey Theatre, London.*

Above: A modern variation of the wash-tub harlequinade performed at the Circus Hoffman in London. Frankie Bailey takes the boy clown's overalls and puts them into the Atomic Washing Machine, but they come out stretched beyond belief.

He then attempts to put them back in the machine to shrink them, but falls into it and apparently reappears shrunk himself.
Opposite: Tom Matthews was Grimaldi's most famous successor.

describe in print and little indication of their nature can be gleaned from the playbooks. But here is one whose business has been preserved in manuscript, which may serve as an example.

The scene represents a public bath and wash house with a crowd of women at the wash-tub. Enter Clown and Pantaloon dressed as old women, each carrying a bundle of dirty linen; they stand at either end of the wash-tub, pull very long pieces of soap out of their pockets, and start scrubbing. Enter a crowd of sweeps, dustmen, coal-heavers, etc., each carrying a dirty child or two; they hand them to their wives, who plunge the children into the wash-tub and start scrubbing them. Meanwhile the Clown and Pantaloon start to iron their washing, smoothing the linen upon their neighbours' backs and, of course, scorching them in the process and producing a satisfactory pandemonium. When this has quietened down the Clown puts his washing through a mangle, and it comes out torn into rags; Pantaloon interferes and is pushed through the mangle himself; he comes out as thin as cardboard; so he is pushed into the hot wash-tub and jumps out his normal self. More hot water is needed in the baths, so Clown and Pantaloon go to the hot water cistern and start pumping it into the baths. Steam comes pouring out of the cubicles, and the bathers – as scarlet as lobsters – come screaming out, wrapped in towels, and chase Clown and Pantaloon round the stage, catch them, and pitch them into the wash-tub.

It will be noted that this harlequinade repeats much of the comic business of Rich's pantomime of a hundred years earlier and pantomime actors and circus clowns are tumbling into water in much the same way today. The beauty of clowning is that nothing has ever changed! Descriptions like this make it all sound pretty fast and furious, but totally lacking in subtlety. Yet delicate effects could be achieved too as was shown in a letter written by the great tragic actor, William Macready, to Tom Matthews.

I was never so diverted in my life as at your admirable entertainment last evening. There is, however, one little suggestion which I would wish to offer you. I have been thinking of it all night. You may remember that a gentleman is coming out of a shop with a brown paper parcel in his hand. As he advances across the stage, the parcel is abstracted from his possession by the pantaloon, who is, in his turn, deprived of it by a policeman, apparently in the discharge of his legitimate duties. The policeman upon that makes a vulgar sign at pantaloon, whom he has robbed. You, then, Mr Matthews, with admirable dexterity, pilfer the same parcel from the policeman, at which the pantaloon makes the same sign to you. Now, it occurred to me, that inasmuch as the pantaloon, when he has robbed the gentleman, makes that sign to the policeman, and the policeman, when he has robbed the pantaloon, repeats it, you, when *your* turn comes for larcenous dexterity, should accompany the same act by the same gesture. This was my idea as it occurred to me after witnessing the performance, and I merely put it before you, Mr Matthews, as the suggestion of a person wholly without experience in such matters.

This charming letter, with its careful observation of the minutiae of comic business, certainly shows the eminent tragedian in a new light. Every actor discovers that the precise timing of tiny and subtle gestures can make all the difference between a bit of business going for nothing and bringing the house down.

Later clowns tended to be specialists rather than all-round actors. Wieland was so flexible an acrobat that it was said he was 'apparently a creature of whalebone and rubber'. Jefferini's long legs made acrobatic leaps dangerous, and indeed he injured himself severely, but he made his mark in telling jokes and reciting monologues. Harry Boleno and Richard Flexmore were famous as comic dancers; Flexmore, in particular, gave clever imitations of the noted ballet stars of the day; he adapted his clown's costume in order to leave his legs free for dancing, replacing the traditional voluminous breeches by a knee-length frilled skirt.

Many pantomime clowns introduced circus tricks into their acts. Huline, a dexterous clown of the 1850s balanced on two chairs that were themselves balanced on four bottles; and he danced on stilts in a ludicrous *pas de deux* with a giant effigy of a Negress.

Other clowns walked on barrels or played the fiddle with their knees. It was all clever stuff, but not the essence of clowning.

Although pantomime in the English sense failed to take root in other countries, it had enjoyed a brief vogue in America in the 1860s, when all New York came to the Old Bowery Theatre to watch a clown of genius called George L. Fox. Pantomime in the French style, that is true mime, had been successfully played in America in the 1830s by the Ravels with much additional use of acrobatics and scenic transformations. Fox saw this company as a young boy and it is possible that it influenced him. In due course Fox became an actor, specializing in the roles of comic Yankees or burlesque heroes, but he could turn his hand to almost any kind of comedy.

In 1850 he appeared as Harlequin in a Ravel-style pantomime at the National Theatre, New York, and when the clown walked out Fox took over his part. Six years later he produced and acted in an English-style pantomime which proved enormously popular, and from then on he specialized in pieces of this type, transferring to the Bowery in 1858. He continued to amaze and delight American audiences with his pantomimes for nearly twenty years.

His skill lay in combining within the structure of English pantomime the light acrobatic tricks of the French pantomime clown with the broad humour of the English clown. The result was something that was uniquely American. The scenes of the harlequinades were set in familiar New York settings, like a German billiard saloon, with actors guzzling beer and pretzels, or City Hall in construction. The action consisted of violent slapstick, with policemen being thrown into ovens, babies being kidnapped, red hot pokers being thrust at tight bottoms, and stomach pumps disgorging disgusting messes on to the stage floor. When the actors sat down to a Thanksgiving dinner the turkey got up off the table and chased the diners round the room, flourishing a carving knife. When a customer ventured into Clown's barber's shop he found his face being lathered with a whitewash brush and a butcher's cleaver being stropped in preparation for shaving him. When Clown and Pantaloon went to bed, rats came out and pulled the bedclothes off them. An actor was captured and put down the barrel of a gun, there was a big bang, and there he was, flat against the wall of the scenery, to be peeled off like a sheet of paper.

Fox wore the costume of an English harlequinade clown, but his make-up was bald-head and white-face. He played mostly in silence, and performed the most extravagant absurdities in complete seriousness. His whitened Pierrot-like face was a screen across which passed a succession of changing expressions. At moments of consternation his eyebrows went up and his jaws dropped as if pulled by opposing magnets. This was a very different clown to that of Grimaldi. If Grimaldi's coarse geniality reflected something of the character of the Regency Londoner, Fox's wild, almost mad violence reflected that of the mid-nineteenth century New Yorker.

The madness in Fox's performance was, indeed, a trait in his own character. As he grew older his actions became more and more unpredictable. His grimaces grew increasingly hideous. He would suddenly break out into obscenities during a performance, and his dresser had to be kept in the wings, ready to dash on to the stage and bring him to his senses whenever this happened. One night in 1875 he was taken away after the first act of *Humpty Dumpty in Every Clime* and committed to an asylum. He never acted again.

Perhaps the last clown in the tradition of Grimaldi and Matthews was Harry Payne. He came from a theatrical and pantomimic family, and his first appearance on the stage was as Moth in *A Midsummer Night's Dream*. He was appearing as Harlequin at Covent Garden in 1859 when the Clown, Flexmore, was taken ill. Payne hurriedly filled the gap, and played so well that he became a regular Clown in pantomimes year after year until he died in 1895.

Payne was not just the chief actor in the harlequinade but the deviser and producer too. He used to lie in bed thinking out new bits of comic business, and then wrote it out with every action and movement carefully plotted. Like all good actors he was nervous every night before going on the stage, but, he told an interviewer, 'once on the stage, my nervousness goes and I am myself again'. This somewhat portly, genial gentleman, who grew a moustache

Above: In the pantomime The King of the Castle *of 1858, James Huline appears as Clown with his son as a little sprite. Opposite: Richard Flexmore, billed as the* 'Celebrated Dancer Comique', in the pantomime of King Jamie *at the Princess Theatre, London in 1850, combined the arts of ballet and clowning.*

Dan Leno was one of the most popular music hall comics. Here he is seen as a railway guard with an oversize whistle and a lamp (far left) and in an auguste-like costume (left). The song for which he was best known was The Beefeater *and he is featured in an appropriate costume on the cover of the music sheet (opposite).*

between Christmas engagements, seems to embody the genteel clowning of the late Victorian age.

By the time of Harry Payne's death the great days of the harlequinade were over. The harlequinade itself had become shorter and shorter, and was filled up with dioramas and scenic effects. The opening section of the pantomime was now much more important, and the roles were filled by music-hall performers, with strapping girls as Principal Boys and wise-cracking comics as Dames.

The harlequinade was soon to disappear completely from the pantomime, however the music-halls themselves provided the last great setting for stage clowning. Many strands of popular entertainment began to come together as the music-halls grew up in the London of the 1860s. There was the tradition of the Song and Supper Rooms, where Regency men had gathered for drinks and light refreshments and bellowed out the choruses of popular, sometimes bawdy songs. In the eighteenth-century Pleasure Gardens, wafer-thin ham and indifferent wine had been consumed to the accompaniment of *al fresco* concerts. There were also the music rooms which enterprising proprietors had started to build adjoining their taverns in the 1840s, culminating in the opening of the Canterbury Hall in 1851.

The chief performers in the music-hall programmes were always the singers, but there was much variety in the show. Many ideas were gleaned from the circus, and many circus artistes – jugglers, acrobats, trapezists, animal-trainers and clowns appeared on the stage. A largely new style of clowning developed in this framework and a school of legendary comedians grew up as its exponents.

One of the best-known music-hall comedians was Dan Leno. He was a cockney child, brought up in poverty, who first made a name for himself in the 1870s as a clog-dancer – that speciality of working-class entertainment originating from the north of England. In the next decade he began to build a reputation as a comic singer, and he became the most popular Dame – the transvestite comic role in the later nineteenth-century pantomime – at Drury Lane. Like

George Fox and other brilliant clowns, his reason failed him at his life's end. At his funeral in 1904 crowds lined the streets, three deep.

Dan Leno was only five foot high, with a marvellously expressive face, heavy eyebrows, and tragic eyes. He would rush on to the stage like a whirlwind and deliver his songs in a small, husky voice with comic patter between each verse. He was no real singer, but he gave brilliant female impersonations. Max Beerbohm wrote that 'he had, in a higher degree than any other actor I have ever seen, the indefinable quality of being sympathetic ... The moment he capered on, with that air of wild determination, all hearts were his.'

His material grew out of the working-class life in which he had been reared and which his audiences shared. He was the archetypal cockney comic. There was a famous song about a beefeater at the Tower of London, which he described in one of his unexpected throw-away phrases as 'supplying a long-felt want'. There was a sketch about two plumbers, a song about a shop-walker, those dignified overseers of Victorian emporia, and so on. His humour was not merely verbal: his tiny figure, auguste-like costume, mobile face and darting movements must certainly rank him among the authentic clowns.

The music-hall artiste who became known as Little Tich had the unlikely advantage of an extraordinary physical appearance. He was born with an extra finger on each hand, and never grew taller than four foot six. His nickname was acquired from a supposed facial resemblance to the bloated Tichborne claimant – the protagonist in a celebrated Victorian legal *cause célèbre*. Tich's first appearance on the music-halls was as a black-face minstrel, but he suddenly shot to fame in the 1890s as a zany comic, combining song, mime and dance.

He made some appearances in pantomime, but he really established his reputation with burlesque interpretations of characters like the gas inspector, the sergeant-major, and the Spanish señora. Despite the ludicrous contrast between his appearance and the characters he impersonated, his acute observation brought them vividly to life.

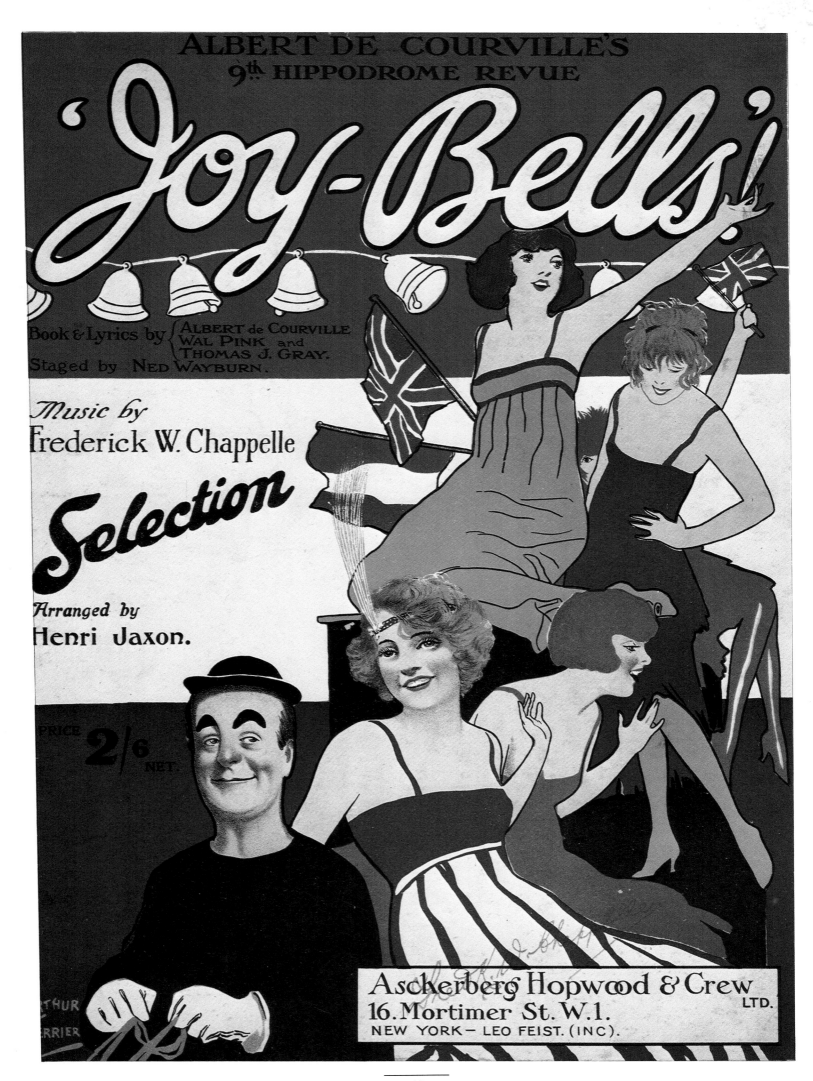

Opposite: George Robey is shown on this music sheet from the revue Joy-Bells, *which was first performed at the Hippodrome, London in 1919.*
Right: Little Tich, one of music-hall's most versatile performers, is depicted on this music sheet wearing his big boots for his most famous act.
Far right: George Robey's sober stage costume contrasted with the expressive humour of his face.
Below right: Little Tich in private life.

TO LITTLE TICH

Big Boot Dance

AS PERFORMED WITH IMMENSE SUCCESS

BY LITTLE TICH.

Composed by

JOSEPH FREDERICKS

LONDON
L. WILSON & Co
5. OXFORD CIRCUS AVENUE. 231 OXFORD St W.

Little Tich was not only a gifted actor and mime but a brilliant dancer and acrobat. His most famous act was the Big Boot dance. For this he wore enormously long boots, half his own height. He would start softly, as in a soft shoe routine, and then work up to a crescendo, slapping the floor noisily with one sole after the other, and finally rising up and balancing on the tips of his huge shoes. He could lean with them, too, at a forward angle of nearly 45 degrees, picking his hat up from the floor without bending his knees. Then he would juggle with his top hat, balancing it on his chin and on the toe of his boot.

But Tich was not just an acrobatic dancer. He was, or could have been with a normal physique, a really great dancer. There are no lack of tributes to his skill. Osbert Sitwell wrote that Tich was 'surely a dancer of genius'. Nijinsky always asked to be taken to see Little, as he called him, when he came to London with the Russian Ballet. Something of Tich's secret seems to have been the breathtaking speed with which he would suddenly break into movement and then out of it, together with the fluidity and grace of his seemingly awkward limbs.

He had a gift for matching a phrase to his visual comedy. When he did the old clown's trick of kicking just out of reach the hat that he was stooping to pick up, he would quietly announce 'Comic business with *chapeau*'. He had a juggling act in which he failed the trick the first time and muttered 'very difficult'; when he failed at the second attempt he threw the balls away, saying 'too difficult'.

Like other eccentric English clowns before him he practised a type of humour that greatly appealed to French intellectuals. Sacha Guitry spoke of his 'great comic acting'. French intellectuals have, in general, been readier to appreciate clowning than their English or American counterparts, but J. B. Priestley was always ready to recognize quality in popular entertainment, and he summed up Little Tich's appeal after his death in 1928 in a memorable appreciation: 'In the antics of this gargoyle there was all the time the suggestion of a companion spirit winking and nodding and shrugging at you over the crazy jumble and tangle of things.'

George Robey is the third character in our gallery of music-hall clowns. He first appeared professionally in 1891 and soon established a reputation as an off-beat comedian. Where other comics dressed smartly or eccentrically, he walked soberly on to the stage in a black semi-clerical suit with a hard flat black hat; only the swishy cane in his hand hinted at the joke behind this exterior. But he had the kind of round, humorous face that people warm to instinctively, and laughter swept the theatre as he gazed about him. Then, lifting a minatory finger and raising his bushy black eyebrows, in a voice that rang through the largest auditorium, he intoned, 'No mirth. Desist.' And, of course, the audience laughed more than before.

Robey was a good all-round actor, working in pantomime, musical comedy and operetta. He played Sancho Panza to the Don Quixote of Chaliapin in a film; and acted the part of Falstaff in Shakespeare's *Henry IV*. Less physical in performance than Dan Leno or Little Tich, he had the true clown's ability in burlesquing a character to keep it funny but true. He created dozens of comedy characters like Clarence, the last of the Dandies, the Mayor of Mudcumdyke, the German professor of music, and Daisy Dillwater, District Nurse. Despite the honest vulgarity to which some objected, he was knighted just before his death in 1954.

Many music-hall comedians made their mark in the role of a pantomime dame. Male actors had been appearing in comic female roles for centuries – Grimaldi had played the Baroness in *Cinderella* in 1820 – and with the late Victorian pantomime this character became an essential member of the cast. The tradition is still very much alive in England today with grand old-time actors like Arthur Askey and George Lacy. It did not matter much what the story of the pantomime was: whether the show was entitled *Aladdin* or *Mother Goose* or *Jack and the Beanstalk*, a place was found for a female of uncertain age and a heart of gold, but addicted to broad comedy and ancient jokes. You can hear them today, every January, at almost every English provincial theatre: 'My boy is teacher's pet, you know; she keeps him in a cage at the back of the class'; 'I've got the turkey all ready, stuffed and plucked; all we've got to do now is kill it.' Sometimes, as pantomime is essentially popular theatre, the jokes are vulgar too: 'My boy's learning his three Rs, 'reading, 'righting and 'rithmetic; so he'll always have his Rs to fall back on', 'I call this my religious jersey, because it's "Lo and behold",' cries the Dame as he pulls his dress down almost to reveal his ballooning imitation breasts.

And then there is the visual business, with the Dame going to bed and discarding one improbable article of underclothing after another, culminating with whalebone corsets and scarlet knickers; and he is sure to dislodge one of his breasts in the process, and hunt all round for it till he finds it sticking out of his bottom.

Although the pantomimes of the latter part of the nineteenth century and of today have diverged increasingly from the pantomimes of Rich and Grimaldi, some of the features remain unchanged. There is the 'slosh scene', with custard pies or wallpaper paste being splashed into the faces of characters, who then sit on their hats, or tread in the glue pot, or fall in the bath. And there is the chase, with a set containing two doors. The guards chase the Dame who runs out of one door and in at the next with such rapidity that soon he is chasing them, and when he pops up through a trap door to trip up the guards, you realize that the Dame has a 'double'. The invasion of pantomime by music-hall performers may have killed its dramatic consistency, but it introduced a rich vein of clowning into this uniquely British form of entertainment.

Another facet of music-hall clowning was provided by the blackface minstrels, or Ethiopian Serenaders as they were sometimes called. This form of entertainment originated in the United States in the 1830s with white performers blacking their faces and singing songs that were supposed to reflect the life of the American Negroes. The entertainment soon acquired a formal structure, with a row of musicians and singers, a chairman or 'interlocutor' in the middle, and the two comics, Mr Bones and Mr Tambo, at each end.

Minstrel troupes enjoyed enormous popularity for some forty or fifty years, often appearing as an after-show or concert in American circuses, and they became a great vogue in Britain. The humour consisted largely of puns and riddles delivered with excruciating slowness and ponderous repetitions in fake Southern accents:

Now, Mr Bones, can you tell me why did de chicken cross de road?
You want me to tell you why did de chicken cross de road?
Yes, Mr Bones, dat is so. Why did de chicken cross de road?

And so on, so that the most dim-witted member of the audience can see the point of the joke a good two minutes before it finally explodes.

The black face of the minstrels was like the masks of the Commedia dell' Arte or the painted face of a clown behind which individuality disappeared and gave way to the delineation of a type. In the particular circumstances of nineteenth-century America, with a civil war to abolish slavery combined with strong social pressures to keep the Negroes a race apart, the minstrel show flattered the social conscience of its audience by portraying the American black as a happy, carefree innocent, singing his ballads in the cotton fields or 'Way down upon the Swanee ribber'.

American popular entertainment did in due course produce genuine Negro comedians, often dancers and singers, although sometimes in acts of true clowning. But other forms of ethnic comedy, Jewish Vaudeville and innumerable German, Italian and Irish sketches alongside the traditions of medicine shows and carnival midways, came to flourish in the burlesque show. This was totally different to burlesques in Victorian England. It was a mixture of comic backchat, honest vulgarity and striptease which brightened up many a shabby downtown street during the early years of the twentieth century.

Visual clowning did sometimes play a part in the burlesque show as in the popular *The Hammer Scene*. In this an opera singer is trying to sing an aria, a workman is hammering on the stage, and the theatre manager does his best to resolve the discord. Every time he comes in he complains how hot it is, and each time the lady piano accompanist removes an article of clothing. A high note of

Below: This song sheet cover shows Walter Howard of the Mohawk Minstrels who sang a parody of the sentimental ballad I Dreamt that I Dwelt in Marble Halls.

Opposite: Carrying on the traditions of the pantomime Dame, clowns often appear in drag. Ernie 'Blinko' Burch is dressed as a parody of Carmen Miranda.

NEW BANJO SONG.

I DREAMT THAT I DWELT ON THE TOP OF St PAUL'S

HUMOROUS PARODY
ON
BALFE'S POPULAR SONG.
WRITTEN BY
HARRY HUNTER.
SUNG BY
WALTER HOWARD.
OF THE MOHAWK MINSTRELS, AGRICULTURAL HALL, LONDON.

the aria, a crescendo of hammering, the final strip, and the collapse of the manager bring the curtain down.

Clowning was, of course, developing in countries other than Britain and the United States. In France, Italy and Spain the best clowning was to be found in the circuses, but in Germany, though the circuses were excellent, the most gifted clowns were to be found in cabarets and beer halls. One such was Karl Valentin, who was born in Munich in 1882 and who was always most at home in the tobacco-laden, beer-swilling atmosphere of the singing halls of the Bavarian capital. In appearance he was a gaunt, lanky individual, his legs encased in skin-tight trousers, his boots too large, his nose elongated, and with a dead-pan expression on his deeply-lined face. He sang songs, told jokes, invented absurd machines (like a nose-picking machine for children), and played in little sketches, usually opposite the homely figure of Liesl Karlstadt.

In one of his sketches, *The Christmas Tree*, Valentin, the father of a family, returns home with a miserable shrub of fir that he has bought for a Christmas decoration. First he has to assemble a platform to put it on, and his work is constantly being interrupted by barking dogs and howling children. An enormously tall chimney sweep sets up a tiny ladder to clean the stove pipe, and then sits on the Christmas cake; Valentin's struggles with the planks end with him knocking down the chandelier; and amidst the resultant chaos Valentin discovers that he has forgotten to tear the dates off the calendar hanging on the wall and Christmas day is long past.

Bertolt Brecht worked for a time in Valentin's company and always preserved a high opinion of him as an artist. He described *The Christmas Tree* as 'a dramatic production of quality' and Valentin himself as 'one of the most impressive spiritual figures of the age'. Ten years after his death in 1948 a museum in his memory was opened in the old city gateway in Munich and he is still remembered and much loved in Bavaria.

Music-hall and vaudeville comedy at the end of the nineteenth century was basically verbal in style and a little removed from true clowning, which is essentially visual in nature. Genuine slapstick, however, did exist and the most famous exponents of this were the troupes directed by Fred Karno. As a boy, Karno had appeared in a small circus busking on the sands of Skegness in the north of England. He performed on the trapeze, and after each trick he would lower a bucket for the spectators to put a halfpenny in before continuing his act. Later he developed a horizontal bar and trapeze act on the music-halls, either alone or with partners, and it was while he was appearing as a straight acrobat at the Metropolitan, London, that he was asked to fill a gap in the programme with a knockabout acrobatic act. This proved so successful that he developed this line during the 1890s and in a few years had five companies on the road.

The acts they presented were, at first, in pure mime, with titles like *Hilarity*, *Jail Birds*, *Early Birds* and *The New Woman's Club*, skeleton plots with a mixture of eccentric acrobatics and slapstick comedy. After 1901 some spoken dialogue was added, but the emphasis was always upon broad visual clowning. Their most famous sketch, *Mumming Birds*, is set in a variety theatre, with an Inebriated Swell in one stage box and a schoolboy munching buns in the other. These two characters play havoc with the unfortunate but totally incompetent artistes who are trying to perform on the miniscule stage.

Karno had a wonderful feeling for comic movement. He took the basic language of somersaults and tumbles and moulded it into a series of hilarious wordless plays. And then he added something else: 'Do it *wistful*,' he used to instruct his actors. He blended pathos into farce – the secret that lifts knockabout into great clowning. He continued producing until 1932, but his greatest contribution to the development of clowning had come in 1907 when he took on a seventeen-year-old boy called Charles Chaplin to join his company. Eventually the music-hall and vaudeville craze waned in the face of the cinema and the arts of stage clowning were to be transferred to the screen.

Below: The Ethiopian Serenaders in a typical line-up. The two end characters are Mr Tambo and Mr Bones, named after the instruments they play. The 'chairman' in the centre initiated the comic dialogue and was known as the Interlocutor. Opposite: This song sheet cover shows one of the Manhattan Minstrels.

If You See Lucy, Let Me Know,

OR

SEND ME WORD BY THE FIRST BALLOON.

CHORUS. "If you see Lucy tell that girl I'm coming by & bye,
I'm going to mount the mountains & I'm going to sky the sky,
So when you see me in the moon, playing the old banjo,
Just send me word by the first balloon, if you see Lucy Crow."

WRITTEN & SUNG BY

HARRY HUNTER,

IN THE

MANHATTAN MINSTRELS' POPULAR ENTERTAINMENTS,

THE CIRCUS CLOWN

Clowns have played against many backgrounds but perhaps their true home is the circus ring. Circus began in London in the mid-eighteenth century when showmen devised a new type of popular entertainment which relied on a display of physical skill. Riding masters began to give exhibitions of trick horse riding in open spaces adjoining an inn or tea garden. They would ride in a circle within a roped-off enclosure, standing on the saddle of one horse, with feet astride on two horses, then on three horses; they would leap over a galloping horse, pick up a whip from the ground while hanging from the stirrups, or ride with a child standing on their heads.

The earliest of these display horsemen was an Irishman, Thomas Johnson, who rode in a field adjoining the Three Hats Inn in Islington in 1758. He was followed by half a dozen or more competitors during the next ten years. These displays proved a great attraction, but after a time it became apparent that some variety was needed in the entertainment. The first example of this was in September 1768, when Mr and Mrs Wolton, who gave exhibitions of trick riding at St George's Spaw in Lambeth, added a performance of rope dancing and tumbling to their display. At Christmas time that year Philip Astley, who gave similar exhibitions at Halfpenny Hatch also added a display of tumbling as well as a monkey riding on horseback. From these beginnings there sprang the idea of a varied entertainment of trick horse riding, acrobatics and animal training, presented in a circular ride, or ring. The Circus was born.

The name of Philip Astley is closely associated with the development of the Circus. He did not invent it, as is often incorrectly stated, but he was largely responsible for popularizing it. He built a permanent circus theatre by Westminster Bridge, the famous Astley's Amphitheatre, which survived – in various rebuildings – until 1893, and he erected others in many English towns as well as in Paris. But he was not the only man to spread the idea of the Circus.

English riders were taking their little companies all over the

Clown Dusty outside the performance tent
at the Clyde Beatty and Cole Brothers
Circus in Savannah, Georgia.

Left: William Capon's drawing of Astley's Amphitheatre in 1777 when it only consisted of an open air arena. The white 'clown to the horsemanship' is the earliest known illustration of a circus clown. Above: One of the first clowns to perform in the circus was Carlo Delpini, here shown 'shooting at the Spaniard' with his leg. Opposite: 'The Valorous Jump', an equestrian act in which the clown plays a humorous part, is depicted in The Children's Circus and Menagerie Picture Book *of 1882 by J. L. Blamire.*

world. There was Charles Hughes, a partner in the Royal Circus in Lambeth, which was the first to use the name 'Circus', who took the idea to Russia; there was Bates in Holland, Hyam in France, Prices in Austria and Scandinavia, Southby in Spain, and John Bill Ricketts in America. By the beginning of the nineteenth century the Circus was a well-established performing art. One further ingredient, however, was necessary to create a fully rounded form of entertainment – comedy.

In his very first year of performing Astley had sensed this, and in July 1768 he introduced a comic act of pretended bad riding which he called *The Taylor Riding to Brentford*. The origin of this act is a curious one, and has only recently been revealed. In 1768 a radical politician and scourge of the government, called John Wilkes, had been prosecuted for publishing seditious and obscene libels, and had been expelled from the House of Commons. He determined to challenge the government by standing as a candidate for parliament for the county of Middlesex. The election was held at Brentford, then a village a few miles to the west of London. It attracted enormous public interest; Wilkes was the hero of the mob, and his supporters streamed from London by every possible means of transport in order to vote for him. Among them was a tailor who was determined to register his vote and hired a horse to take him to the poll. But the poor fellow had no idea how to ride it, and his perilous journey to Brentford became a joke of the town for a few weeks.

Astley took advantage of this to introduce an act in which Billy Button, the tailor, first cannot mount his horse. When he eventually succeeds it will not move; then it gallops so fast that he is thrown off and finally it chases him round the ring. It was the first clowning act in the history of the Circus, and it was performed all over Europe and America until at least the end of the nineteenth century.

Another comic riding act, which was popular in the early circuses and for many years afterwards, was known as *The Peasant's Frolic* or *The Flying Wardrobe*. It was often performed in America where it was known as *The Canadian Peasant* and there is a good

account of it in *Huckleberry Finn* by Mark Twain. The performance of a display of classic equestrianism is interrupted by what appears to be a drunken countryman who clambers from the audience into the ring and insists upon mounting the horse. Despite the ringmaster's remonstrations he finally manages to seat himself the right way round. The finale of the act is vividly described by Twain:

and the next minute he sprung up and dropped the bridle and stood! and the horse agoing like a house afire too. He just stood up there, a-sailing around as easy and comfortable as if he warn't ever drunk in his life – and then he begun to pull off his clothes and sling them. He shed them so thick they kind of clogged up the air, and altogether he shed seventeen suits. And then, there he was, slim and handome, and dressed the gaudiest and prettiest you ever saw, and he lit into that horse with his whip and made him fairly hum – and finally skipped off, and made his bow and danced off to the dressing-room, and everybody just a-howling with pleasure and astonishment.

I can well remember seeing this trick performed at the first circus I ever attended, in about 1920, in a Hertfordshire village. Like Huckleberry Finn, I thought it was all for real.

The Taylor Riding to Brentford and *The Peasant's Frolic* were necessarily performed by skilled horse riders rather than by specialist comedians, but the demand for comedy in the Circus soon led to the introduction of specific clowns. Two of the earliest and most important of these were Carlo Delpini and Baptiste Dubois.

Delpini had been a Pierrot and a deviser of pantomimes at Drury Lane, where he had worked under Garrick. By all accounts he was an excellent mime; there are prints of him wiping his eyes in exaggerated mourning, and pointing his leg, as if it were a gun, to 'shoot Spaniards'. He went to the Royal Circus as manager and clown in about 1785, and he became noted for his catch phrase 'What you please'. Meaningless catch phrases of this kind have always been the trademark of comedians. It is not what they mean, it is how they are said that matters. Later Delpini devised entertain-

ments at Astley's. His name indicates his Italian origin and he may well have inherited some of the skills of the Commedia dell' Arte; he certainly had experience in mounting English pantomimes. Two strands of clowning were being brought together in the circus ring.

Dubois had played as clown at many theatres, especially at Sadler's Wells, a small playhouse on the northern outskirts of London, which was famous for its light entertainments. Here he used to appear as the clown to give variety to the rope dancing; one of his tricks was to set up to thirteen conical hats spinning on the stage floor, to dance a reel with them, and then to kick them up and catch them, one on top of the other, on his head.

He went on to play at several circuses, including the Royal Circus and Astley's Amphitheatre. He was billed as clown at Astley's in 1780, and is probably the first named clown in the whole history of the Circus. Like almost all true circus clowns, he was an expert acrobat as well as comedian. One of his most popular acts was *Frolics of my Granny*. He seems to have originated this as a tightrope act at Sadler's Wells in 1792, and later it was transferred to horseback in the circus. An old woman in bonnet and black bombasine skirt came riding in, while perched on her back was a young fellow waving his arms about and generally making things very uncomfortable for the elderly grandmother. After various near tumbles it is revealed (or guessed by the audience) that there is actually one rider, a young man who is standing on the horse. The lower part of his body is hidden in a wicker frame covered in an old woman's skirt; the old woman's head and body, and the young man's legs, are dummies. In a similar deception called *Jim Crow's Ride to the Devil*, it looks as if an old witch is carrying Jim Crow off in a basket while she dances on horseback. Jim Crow was the name given to the performer of a highly popular song and dance routine, based on that of an American Negro, which had been introduced into England in 1836.

At some time in the early nineteenth century this act became combined with the introduction of a miller and a chimney sweep. The miller dressed in a white smock, entered with a sack of flour, and the black-coated chimney sweep carried a sack of soot. They started to argue and the chimney sweep laid a hand on the miller, leaving a black smudge on the white smock. The miller retaliated, leaving a white mark on the black coat. They eventually came to blows and the white smock and the black coat were soon covered in soot and flour respectively. The climax of the fight was when the combatants emptied their sacks over each other so that the miller ended up all black, and the chimney sweep all white!

The other comic horse act introduced by Dubois was usually called the *Metamorphosis of a Sack*. The clown, wearing some loose all-over costume, was persuaded by some means or other to be put in a sack. Perhaps he was hiding from an enemy. The sack was put on a horse's back, and the horse cantered off round the ring, with the sack bobbing and twisting about on its back. And then, suddenly, there sprang out of the sack not the original clown, but what appeared to be a smartly dressed lady. Dubois is an important figure in the development of the circus clown. He used to dress as a comical yokel, with a red wig and ruddy face, and represents a very English influence in clowning.

By the end of the eighteenth century many different traditions of clowning had been united in the Circus. There was the tradition of the Commedia dell' Arte, of French mime, and of English pantomime from Delpini; there was the tradition of the folk fool and of the English stage clown from Dubois. But it was the influence of Grimaldi's Clown in pantomime a few years later that was to give the final touch to the character of the circus clown.

As the Circus developed during the early decades of the nineteenth century, clowning became a more and more essential part of the entertainment. The clowns were not usually actors from the theatres but circus performers who combined comedy with their feats of skill. There was, for instance, Mr Porter, the clown at the Royal Circus in 1801, who was a great leaper. He jumped from a springboard over a ribbon 12 ft high, and then through a hoop surrounded

Above and Opposite: More scenes from The Children's Circus and Menagerie Picture Book. In 'Our Whimsical Favourite' a clown pours water over the ringmaster. In 'Hands Full Once More' he executes a skilful balancing act.

by blazing fireworks, firing off two pistols as he did so. Mr Bristow, the clown at Astley's Amphitheatre in 1815, did a strong man act. He allowed a blacksmith's anvil to be laid on his chest while he stretched himself across two chairs, and two blacksmiths then hammered steel bars on the anvil until they made the sparks fly.

Other clowns were retired acrobats who still had the instinct of the ring in their blood. One such was Jack Clarke, who was a celebrated equestrian and once billed as 'the Northern Wonder'. He ran his own circus at the fairs round London during the 1820s; although he was warm-hearted he had a hot temper, and the boys in the audience delighted in baiting him. They would shout rude remarks and blow peas from pea-shooters at him when his back was turned, and he would brandish his stick and threaten to deal with them, but he never managed to catch anyone. In his old age he lost the ownership of his circus and was reduced to playing the role of clown, but his children and grandchildren became some of the greatest circus performers in the world.

Circus performances in this period largely consisted of displays of trick riding and of rope dancing. Clowns were used mainly to introduce comic relief into these displays. They did not, at this period, perform complete comic acts on their own.

Horse-riding acts often featured a beautiful and graceful girl posing and leaping on the back of a horse, and the clown would pretend that he was smitten with love for her, falling into absurd attitudes of adoration every time she passed him. Her act would last for much longer than is usual in circus programmes today, and to give her and the horse time to rest the clown would have to fill in with spots of comic business. There is a nice description of such a performance in *Sketches by Boz* by Charles Dickens. He is describing a performance at Astley's Amphitheatre in about 1835.

When Miss Woolford, and the horse, and the orchestra, all stop together to take breath, the riding-master urbanely takes part in some such dialogue as the following (commenced by the clown): 'I say, sir!' – 'Well, sir?' (it's always conducted in the politest manner.) 'Did you ever happen to hear I was in the army, sir? – 'No, sir.' – 'Oh, yes, sir – I can go through my exercises, sir.' – 'Indeed, sir!' – 'Shall I do it now, sir?' – 'If you please, sir; come, sir – make haste' (a cut with the long whip, and 'Ha' done now – I don't like it,' from the clown). Here the clown throws himself on the ground and goes through a variety of gymnastic convulsions, doubling himself up, and untying himself again, and making himself look very like a man in the most hopeless extreme of human agony, to the vociferous delight of the gallery, until he is interrupted by a second cut from the long whip, and a request to see 'what Miss Woolford's stopping for?' On which, to the inexpressible mirth of the gallery, he exclaims, 'Now, Miss Woolford, what can I come for to go, for to fetch, for to bring, for to carry, for to do, for you ma'am?' On the lady's announcing with a sweet smile that she wants the two flags, they are, with sundry grimaces, procured and handed up; the clown facetiously observing after the performance of the latter ceremony – 'He, he, oh! I say, sir, Miss Woolford knows me; she smiled at me.'

The clown was expected to help the grooms by holding one end of the ribbons or lengths of cloth over which the equestrians would jump, and he would often make this comic. He might make a great business of adjusting the ribbon to the correct height, climbing on a stool to get high enough, and then falling off it; finally he'd get it right. 'That's right, now', the groom would call out. 'Good, I'm glad I've done that properly', says the clown, dropping the ribbon and sauntering off just as the horse is ready to start.

In a rope-dancing act one of the clown's jobs was to rub the rope and the performer's shoes with powdered chalk to prevent slipping. When he had done this he would carefully chalk his own nose. He had to hand the balance pole to the rope dancer, and he would sometimes make absurd attempts to balance the pole in the saw-dust, pretending to misunderstand the use of the 'balance' pole. He might try to walk the rope himself, and would fall off in a ridiculous way, catching it with one hand, waggling his feet, and screaming like a baby. At this period the ropes were only some 8 or 10 ft off the

Opposite: Clowns and acrobats perform together in the circus in this illustration of 1882 by J.L. Blamire.
Above: Circus performers, including clowns, started at a very early age. This photograph from the family albums of Harold Whiteley (Clown Rainbow) shows a young clown and acrobats, who are thought to be members of the Whiteley and Mellors families.

Opposite: Comic interplay between ringmaster and clown is often featured in circus acts. At the Circus Knie, Dimitri carries on playing his lute despite the presence of the elegant ringmaster right behind him.
Right: Clowns often combine many circus skills in their acts. Oleg Popov's performance at the Moscow State Circus includes juggling, tight-rope walking and animal training.
Overleaf: Oleg Popov in his snake charming act at the Moscow State Circus.

ground, so that a fall need not be dangerous. But if the clown were a funambulist himself he would, of course, only pretend to fall. It is much more difficult to nearly fall, and then recover oneself, than to present a perfectly straight act. Some of the greatest clowns in the history of the Circus – like Auriol, Poodles Hanneford and Charlie Rivel – have been exceptionally brilliant acrobats.

Quite early in the development of the Circus we begin to find a distinction developing between acrobatic clowns and talking clowns. Circuses were at first presented in buildings specially designed for the purpose. Tents did not come into use until the 1840s in England, when they were introduced from America, where they had been used since 1825. At first these tents were very small. So, whether in a circus building or tent, the performance was an intimate one and dialogue in the ring could be clearly heard by all the spectators. There was no possibility of using – and fortunately no need to use – that bane of the modern circus, the microphone.

A popular feature of all early circuses was comic dialogue and funny business between the ringmaster and the clown. Certain phrases became standardized to be repeated decade after decade till the end of the century. On first bounding into the ring the clown would cry 'Here we are again', a phrase also always used on his first appearance in the stage harlequinade. When the horses were led out the clown would tell the groom 'to rub them well down with cabbage puddings', and he might announce that 'the horses are as clever as the barber who shaved bald magpies at twopence a dozen'. A piece of paper might be tied to the end of the ringmaster's whip, and the clown mistakes it for a butterfly; as the ringmaster flicks his whip about the ring the clown dashes after it, trying to 'catch the butterfly' in his hat. A variant of this, still to be seen today, is for the clown to have an imitation butterfly at the end of a long curved wire that is fastened to his hat. Every time he advances to seize the butterfly it flutters exactly the same distance away from him.

Sometimes the clown was able to turn the tables on the ring-master. The ringmaster might say he is thirsty; the clown brings him a pint of beer in a pewter mug; the ringmaster asks for it to be served, more elegantly, in a tumbler; the clown promptly drinks the beer, throws a somersault, and announces, 'Here it is, in a *tumbler!*' On leaving the ring the ringmaster holds the clown back, saying 'I never follow the fool, sir', at which the clown lets him go first and follows after with the parting shot, 'Then I do!'

The ringmaster in these circuses was traditionally an imposing individual, dressed in military-style uniform or, later, in evening dress. The contrast between this somewhat pompous personage and the grotesque clown provided humour that is difficult to recapture from a mere reprinting of their dialogue. However, for the record this is an authentic bit of dialogue between a ringmaster and a clown in about 1840.

CLOWN Oh dear! oh dear!
RINGMASTER Why, what's the matter, you great fool?
CLOWN Oh! my precious legs! oh dear!
RINGMASTER Legs! why what on earth is wrong with them? They are there all right, ain't they?
CLOWN No, sir; oh dear no, they ain't all right at all, sir. Don't you see they are gone to a shadow – two drumsticks, sir; and yet they're not strong enough to be played with, I can tell you.
RINGMASTER Come, come, sir; jump about, sir, and no capers, sir!
CLOWN But my legs won't jump at all now, for they have no strength.
RINGMASTER How does that come about, sir? Let us hear how they lost their strength, will you?
CLOWN Why, you see, sir, it's a melancholy story, but won't take long to tell. My father, being a very economical man, had our shoes always made for our growth, and to keep them on our feet we stuffed them with hay; and oh! sir, my calves came down one day to have a feed upon the hay, and they forgot to go up again, sir!

Sometimes the talking clown would deliver long monologues. A

Opposite: Noe Noe (Ernie Stevenson) has
played with many of the best known
circuses in England.
Right: Many clowns are proficient
musicians and perform musical entrées.
Noe Noe rehearses while his son, Gary,
who joins him in the act, watches from the
window of their caravan.

success in the 1860s, had a trick in which he used to dive through what looked like a paper-covered hoop, and when he emerged through the torn paper on the other side he was seen to be wearing a long nightdress. This actually had been concealed between the two sheets of paper stretched on either side of the hoop. An amusing variant of the long dress idea was seen in a circus recently, when a clown and partner, dressed as bride and bridegroom, marched across the ring; the bride had a very long train to 'her' wedding-dress which had to be supported by quite a procession of 'brides-maids'. It went on and on, even after the bridal pair had left the tent on the opposite side and was still being manhandled by the brides-maids when the wedded pair appeared at the entrance to the ring carrying the end of the bride's train themselves!

A very effective clowning act, which was first introduced as early as 1912 by Pimpo, one of John Sanger's clowns, is the comic motor car. The clown drives into the ring in an old crock of a car that produces a series of bangs and explosions and finally shudders to a halt. He opens up the bonnet and a gigantic explosion sends the steering-wheel soaring into the air; he takes off the radiator cap and is met with a fountain of water; he jumps on it to keep it down, and it seems to shoot out of the top of his head; he cranks the starting-handle, and the car starts on its own and chases him out of the ring. There is, of course, a very small man or dwarf hidden inside the vehicle, who controls the mechanism and directs its progress.

Many clowns nowadays are equipped with secret ducts of water that will squirt fountains of tears from their eyes. Some have big boots, weighted with lead, permitting them to incline their bodies at an alarming angle without falling over. Good clowning, however, does not need elaborate equipment. A traditional trick was balanc-ing a peacock's feather, the clown blowing it up into the air and catching it on his hand, his foot, his nose or his chin as it floated slowly down. Jimmy Chipperfield has recalled how his father would set the audience 'crying with laughter, just at this feather. . . . He made the tent sound like a football match.'

Sometimes the spectators were brought in to add to the fun. The clown would invite two members of the audience to play blindman's buff with him while he carried a live duck under his arm. The two players were given pillows with which they were to try to hit the clown. The first man to do so would win the duck. When all was set, the clown took up his position between the two blindfolded competitors and gave the duck a pinch; the duck quacked; the competitors advanced towards the noise, swinging their stuffed pillows; the clown stepped out of the way; and they hit each other! This could go on for quite a long time.

Various other ways of persuading the spectators to provide their own comedy have been exploited in circuses, and it must be admitted that the results are sometimes funnier than the efforts of the official clowns. One is the unrideable mule, which members of the audience are invited to ride round the ring. I have never seen anyone succeed. True clowning is involved when a 'plant' in the audience clambers into the ring; his wife tries to restrain him; in the struggle his spectacles are knocked off and his wife gets kicked by the mule over the ring fence. Finally his trousers fall down and the mule chases him out of the ring.

Another similar piece of audience participation is the riding mechanic, which was introduced in America as a genuine help to circus equestrians when practising. The rider has a belt round his waist which is fastened to a rope which in turn is taken over a pulley over the centre of the ring. If a groom holds the free end of the rope he can support the rider in mid-air should he fall off the horse. Spectators rarely negotiate a circuit of the ring successfully on horseback, although it is probable that the circus grooms tend to pull the riders off if they look too good. It is certainly very funny to see them flying spreadeagled in the air at the end of the rope. One girl who volunteered to try the riding mechanic in the Bertram Mills Circus was so athletically funny in the way she tried and failed that the circus engaged her as a permanent member of the company. Simple clowning of this kind is the very stuff of circus. It has hardly changed in two hundred years. However, within this framework, there have been many distinct styles and trends in clowning.

The costume of the circus clown was influenced by the costume of the harlequinade clown, as standardized by Grimaldi, but it never settled into any strict pattern. The baggy breeches, for instance, that were so useful in the harlequinade for hiding joints of beef stolen from butchers' shops, were often replaced in the Circus by Dutch-style loose trousers, fastened at the ankles, which might be of one piece with the shirt. There was often a frill round the neck, and the three-tufted wig that Grimaldi had made familiar was sometimes replaced by a single cock's comb – a style that can be found as far back as the jesters of the middle ages. One of the most distinctive features of the circus clown's costume was the round pointed hat, with a rim strengthened so as to keep its shape. Dubois used hats like this as spinning tops, and a common act between two clowns was for one to send one after another of these hats skimming across the ring for the clown on the other side to catch on his head.

Wallett was very proud of the costume that he based on a miniature of a medieval jester; and Auriol, the acrobatic French clown, wore a somewhat similar type of costume. In fact, although one can always recognize a circus clown by his costume there was great diversity of detail in how it was carried out. Acrobatic clowns, in particular, could not use the loose garments worn by talking clowns, and they usually adopted a style of close-fitting shirts and skin-tight breeches or tights.

Whatever the cut of the costume, it was recognized as clownish by its colour and decoration. Some costumes were marked with bright stripes, and almost all were decorated with circles, triangles, and other geometric shapes. The costumes of the Price brothers, the acrobatic musical clowns, were particularly striking and beautiful, with a pattern of butterflies over a violet background.

As the century went on the clown's costume became more and more elaborate, and early in the twentieth century the French clown, Antonet, who was Grock's partner, introduced the loose spangled dress, with calf-length trousers, that is the hallmark of European white-face clowns today.

Behind the scenes, the clowns of the American Clyde Beatty and Cole Brothers Circus prepare their costumes and make-up. Kaye (opposite), whose costume seems to be influenced by the European white-face and Pierrot tradition, puts the finishing touches to his face. In the wardrobe (below left and right) Oscar and Dusty dress for their acts. Bottom: Oscar in full make-up.

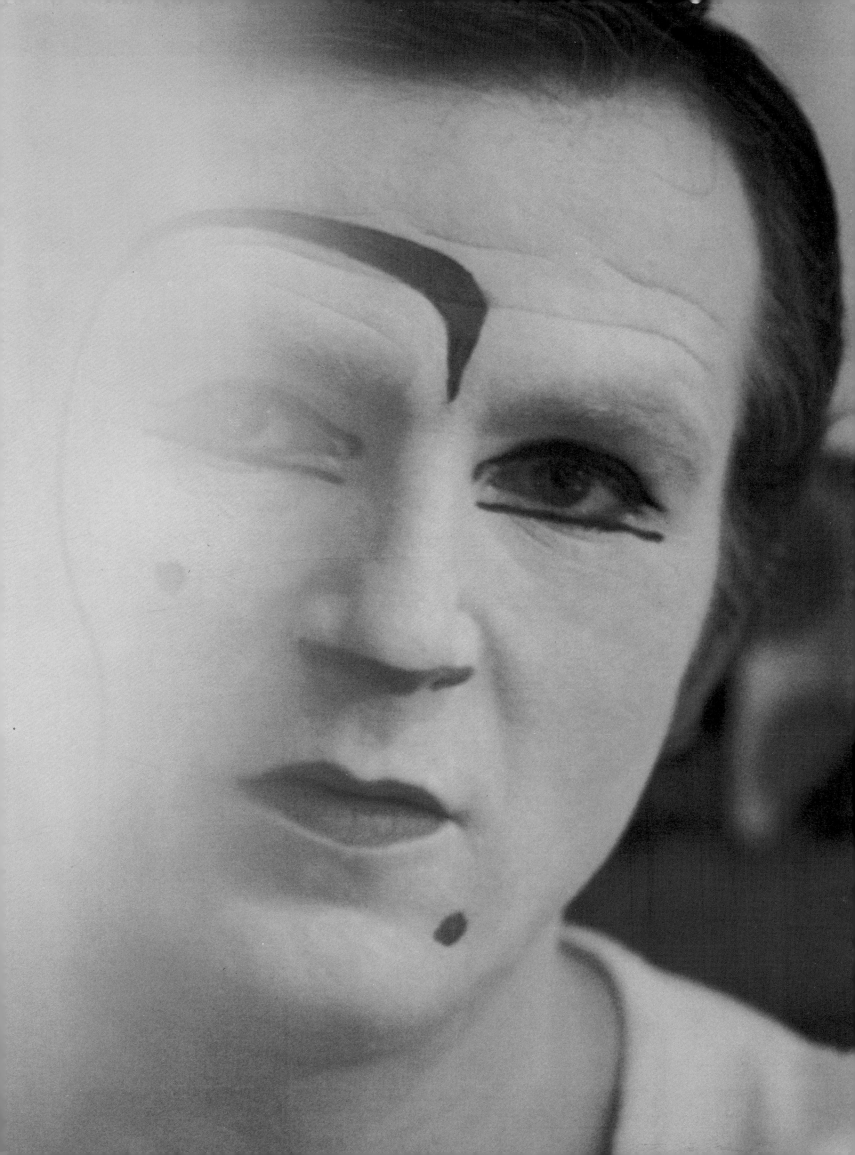

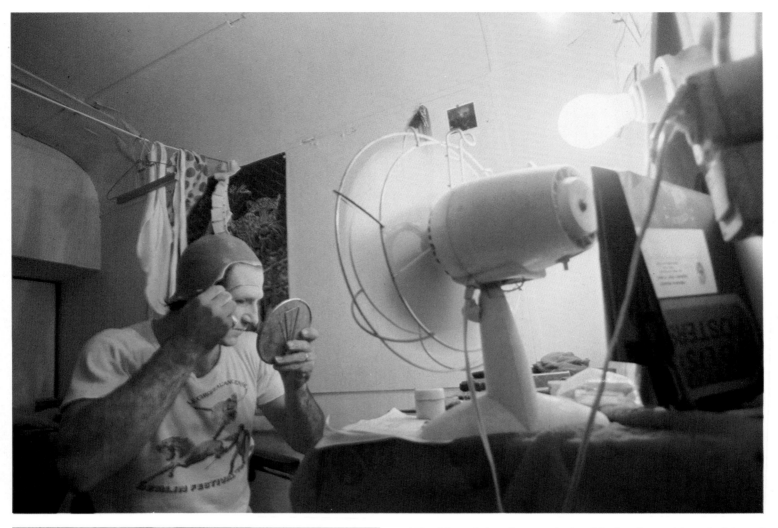

Previous page, top and above: Alexis Gruss, the white-face at the Cirque à l'Ancienne in Paris. The traditional distinction between white-face clown and auguste is today best preserved in France. Opposite: In the ring, Alexis Gruss epitomizes the tradition of the elegant sequinned white-face clown.

The idea of the clown painting his face is as old as the idea of clowning. But there were two quite different traditions. The tradition of Gilles and Pierrot, which had been brought to the Circus by Delpini and was later reinforced by the influence of Deburau and the French pantomimists, was for the chief comic character to have a white face. This was originally achieved with the application of flour, and later, before the invention of greasepaints, with a mixture of oxide of zinc, lard and tincture of benzoin, which was not without danger to the skin. The other tradition was that of the ruddy cheeks of the English stage yokel which had been formalized by Grimaldi into neat painted red triangles.

Both of these traditions have continued in the Circus ever since. The elegant European clown still retains his white face, though with red lips and perhaps one eyebrow drawn down into an enormous curve. English and American clowns have tended to exaggerate their make-up with huge red mouths, thick eyebrows, and other grotesque features. However as the clown's costume became more colourful and elegant, the clown himself became less suited to the rough slapstick humour. It was not surprising that a new kind of clown appeared in the ring. This was the auguste.

One story goes that an American acrobat called Tom Belling, who was employed in the great Circus Renz in Berlin, had offended the mighty proprietor in some way and was taken off the bill for a few nights. With nothing else to do, he was sitting idly in the dressing-room and decked himself up for fun in some of the shabbiest and most ridiculous clothes he could lay his hands on. Stepping out into the corridor to entertain his friends with his unusual attire he saw the stern-faced proprietor of the circus advancing towards him. In great alarm, he turned and ran in the opposite direction and suddenly found himself in the ring. Tripping over the tails of his overlength coat he fell flat on his face. Staggering to his feet and crimson with shame he blundered back behind the scenes to the accompaniment of roars of laughter and cries of *August*, a slang term in Berlin dialect for a stupid booby. Renz met him, clapped him on the back, and told him to repeat the act at

Small hats, oversize boots, baggy checked clothing, shock-headed wigs and red noses are the trademarks of auguste clowns. Top, above left and right: Auguste clowns at the

American Clyde Beatty and Cole Brothers Circus. Opposite: Jacko Fossett is one of the best-known augustes in England today.

every performance. The kind of clown to be henceforth known as an auguste was born!

Like most such stories, this has almost certainly been much embroidered over the years. Claims have been made for several other performers as having invented the auguste character at other times and at other places. But there may be a grain of truth in the Belling story. The character did almost certainly receive its name at Renz's Circus in Berlin in the 1870s, but he was probably so called because a performer called Agoust, one of a well-known circus family, caught the audience's fancy.

Whatever the origin of the name, no one person invented the character. The idea of a clown wearing ridiculous clothes, coats too long, trousers too short, boots too big, hats too small, and so on, is as old as the hills. Elizabethan clowns wore that kind of outfit and it was not so different from the old-fashioned livery worn by Dubois. But however old the idea might be, the concept had fallen out of use in the circuses of the nineteenth century, and it was not until the 1870s that it was revived.

So there were now two kinds of clown in the Circus. The white-face clown, wearing an elegant costume in bright colours, and the auguste, wearing any kind of old ridiculous clothes, with a shock-headed wig, a false nose, a grotesque make-up, and a generally zany appearance. The auguste kind of clowning spread rapidly through the circuses of Europe and America, and clowning tended to develop into double acts with a white-face clown and an auguste working together. The white-face clown began to take over the role hitherto played by the ringmaster, that of the haughty, pompous individual who gives orders; while the auguste became the incarnation of lawlessness and disorder, always misunderstanding what he is told to do, stupid but artful, beaten, drenched with water, but finally triumphant. With the auguste the art of clowning was given a fresh dimension. Today the traditional clown and the auguste have largely become merged. The white-face clown survives, mainly in Europe, as little more than a picturesque feed to the auguste, who is the life and soul of the act.

EUROPEAN CLOWNS

Many of the contributors to the tradition of clowning have been unknown, like the jesters and actors of the Commedia dell' Arte troupes. But some of the most important developments have been inspired by the genius of a few individuals. In this chapter we concentrate on some of the famous European clowns whose personalities, original gags or interpretations of old entrées have influenced clowning everywhere.

From the 1830s to the 1860s there was a curious craze in the Circus for what were known as Shakespearean clowns. It is not at all clear how Shakespearean these clowns really were. Some clowns certainly used to parody familiar speeches from the plays of Shakespeare. One such speech began like this:

Now is the winter of our discontent
We have not enough money to pay the rent.
And by all the clouds that tip our house
We've not enough food to feed a

At this point the clown paused, the audience waited in expectation for 'louse' (or perhaps 'mouse') to complete the rhyme, and the clown said 'barley sugar'. Dan Rice, the famous American clown, was Shakespearean in style; he would work genuine Shakespearean quotations into his speeches, but he also often parodied them. This was a period when burlesques and parodies of Shakespeare were enormously popular in the theatre, and the Circus was joining in a general trend.

Some clowns, however, seem to have called themselves Shakespearean clowns without necessarily uttering a word of Shakespeare. They apparently adopted the title if they specialized in a wisecracking type of act, full of the word play that is a feature of many of Shakespeare's comic characters. They were really more sophisticated successors to the Mister Merrymans, whose rather feeble jokes had enlivened the circuses of the first decades of the century.

The most famous Shakespearean clown was W. F. Wallett. On the strength of a royal command appearance at Windsor Castle he used to describe himself as 'the Queen's Jester'. Contemporary

The great tradition of European clowning is today being carried on by Annie Fratellini at the Ecole Nationale du Cirque.

playbills described him as 'the King of the Clowns'. At various times in his career he was scene-painter, property-maker, marionette-carver, designer of circus parade wagons, posturer (or contortionist), man-monkey, poser in the Grecian Statues act, actor in pantomime and of course, circus clown. He even ran his own circus for a time. His autobiography gives some interesting descriptions of circus life in England and America, but it tells us very little of how his own act was performed. However, an extract from a speech made by Wallett at a grand fête in Bristol in 1857 gives some idea of his style. It was a wet afternoon which explains the relevance of his opening patter.

> The weather tonight is like Queen Victoria – 'long to reign over us'. Talking of fools, the generality of mankind do not like to be called fools. Three or four hundred years ago was the time to be a fool, when kings and queens used them in their palaces. In those days fools were great men, but now great men are fools. In those past days fools were well fed and paid, but now so many people make fools of themselves for nothing that fools have become too numerous. . . .

A critic wrote of Wallett that, 'he has a tongue with all the velocity of a railway, streaming out a fund of wit, censure, and satire that appears unbounded and interminable – there is no pause, no hesitation – not a jot – all flows like a stream of a mighty river – sometimes smooth and graceful, sometimes powerful and overwhelming.'

Wallett was very much a clown of his age. This was the period when Charles Kean was attracting large audiences to his productions of Shakespeare in which all the details of costume and scenery were reproduced with historical accuracy. Wallett, too, prided himself on having adopted a costume 'copied from an illuminated drawing in the British Museum'.

Surprisingly English Shakespearean clowns were a great rage in Paris, where they delivered their French quips in an atrocious English accent. It was in Paris, moreover, that Shakespearean clowning stepped right out of conventional comedy into almost surrealistic tragedy.

There is an extraordinary description of James Boswell, a Shakespearean clown at Astley's in the 1850s, who became an intellectual cult figure in the Parisian circuses. We are told that he would sometimes pause in the middle of his foolery and run round the ring, declaiming the most frightening lines of Shakespeare with a kind of nervous frenzy, at once grotesque and ferocious. Trailing a length of white material streaked with red over his costume, his white face with a great crimson mouth, he resembled some spectral caricature wrapped in the bloody winding sheet of a corpse. Boswell fell dead in the ring at the age of 39 while balancing on his head on the remaining upright spar of a come-apart ladder. It seems a fitting finale to this strange black comedy.

There are many tributes to the success and popularity of these Shakespearean clowns, but they seem quite distinct from true clowning and should be seen, rather, as the origin of the wisecracking comedians of the music-halls. As the music-halls became popular towards the end of the nineteenth century the lure of higher wages drew many performers away from the Circus, and clowns in the Circus reverted to what has always been their true role – visual comedy.

There have been acrobatic clowns since the days of the early fools, and in the Circus this seems a natural combination. A particularly notable one was the French clown, Auriol, who played between 1835 and 1873. He was a superb acrobat, achieving remarkable feats of leaping and balancing, but he added to this, in the words of Théophile Gautier, 'a jolly, seemingly Chinese face, on which a grimace was enough to set the audience in a roar'. He wore a bright, medieval-style costume, with bells tinkling from his fool's cap.

However, the combination of clowning and acrobatics reached its apogee with the Hanlon-Lees, who developed this into an extraordinary dramatized form which took Europe and America by storm in the 1870s. The story began with the six Irish Hanlon brothers, who created a very good straight acrobatic act under the tuition of an old acrobat, 'Professor' John Lees. They first appeared

Opposite: The skills of Shakespearean clowns survive today in the small circuses; Pipo at the Cirque à l'Ancienne impersonates a ringmaster talking to a flea.

Above: Wallett, shown here at the Alhambra Palace, Leicester Square, London, was the best known Shakespearean talking clown.

in London in 1846, and even after the death of Lees they kept his name in the title of their act.

The Hanlons were playing in Chicago in 1865 when they met a juggler, Henri Agoust, who was a member of a well-known French circus family. Agoust persuaded them to extend their acrobatics and juggling into dramatized comic scenes, and under his guidance they invented some of the weirdest, surrealist plots that have ever been conceived. Some of their effects came to them in dreams, and indeed their playlets sound like nightmares transferred to reality.

There was, for instance, a bull fight in which the bull appears actually to devour one of the clowns; a butcher's shop in which the carcases of meat come alive and human limbs are exposed for sale; a drawing-room in which a crazy pianist dives head first into the piano; and an orchestra in which the anarchic musicians ignore and then attack the conductor. Their most famous piece was *A Trip to Switzerland*, in which a coach is upset and a train is derailed and when the travellers finally arrive at their Swiss hotel they are met by juggling waiters and have to endure a mad chase in and out of boxes and cupboards before a final explosion sends bodies hurtling in every direction. This mixture of farce and violence was rather strong meat for the British, but it was hailed fervently in France, especially by intellectuals. Edmond de Goncourt wrote:

> Great Britain has developed an entirely new form of satirical comedy, largely created by unknown performers. . . . It was as if the Italian comedies had been rediscovered. . . . In recent years the art of the English clown has developed a sinister quality . . . the clown's art is now rather terrifying and full of anxiety and apprehension, their suicidal feats, their monstrous gesticulations and frenzied mimicry reminding one of the courtyard of a lunatic asylum.

The performances of the Hanlon-Lees were based on highly skilled trick work and acrobatics, but the dramatic form in which they were presented demonstrates again how close laughter lies to horror and violence. It was Punch and Judy brought to life, and there has never been anything quite like it since.

Many English clowns found greater appreciation in France than in their own country during the nineteenth century. One of the first was Billy Hayden, who had started his career as a black-faced minstrel. As a clown he wore huge boots and did a popular act with a trained pig. Sadly he fell from favour and died in poverty.

The most successful of all the English clowns in France was George Footit, who was not only a remarkable clown but created the most famous double act in the history of the Circus. Footit was the son of an English clown and was working as a horse rider in a French circus when he decided to try his luck as a clown. He did not seem to be a natural comedian. He had an ugly face, a big nose, a bull neck, small eyes, and a haughty expression. But he was a mime of

Many clowns have been expert acrobats. Among these were the Hanlon Brothers, who incorporated acrobatics into extraordinary dramatized scenarios (below), and Auriol, who is shown here in two poses, including his famous bottle dance (bottom). This tradition is carried on today by Dimitri (opposite).

At the Circus Knie, Dimitri's act combines acrobatic expertise with a dramatic element reminiscent of the Hanlon-Lees. Here he juggles on a slack rope (below) and walks blindfold on it (right).

genius; he could throw his body into an attitude that just seemed to sum up the character of whoever he was impersonating. At one moment he might be an English tourist, stomping round the Paris Exhibition; at another one of Napoleon's old guard dragging his steps through the snows of Russia, the very picture of a proud but failing warrior; or he gave a delicious caricature of a female oriental dancer, all wrists and elbows at awkward angles. He was a particularly brilliant female impersonator, and once gave a parody of Sarah Bernhardt as Cleopatra, with a fuzzy red wig and a rubber snake instead of an asp at his throat. Bernhardt herself came to see it, and laughed with the rest to see him leap up after the suicide and run round the ring with wig awry and train gathered up under his arm.

In 1889 Footit teamed up with a dark-skinned Cuban whose professional name was Chocolat. Chocolat was not quite the typical auguste; he dressed nattily rather than disreputably but he fulfilled exactly the role of 'he who is slapped'. The essence of the Footit and Chocolat act was the contrast betwen the haughty, commanding, white-faced Footit and the dim-witted, humiliated, black-skinned Chocolat. In the act Footit would storm at Chocolat. 'Fool, idiot', he screamed, again and again, louder and louder; until at the end Chocolat turned to him, beaming innocently, and lazily replied, 'I heard you the first time.' Chocolat could play the simple idiot to perfection, as in this piece of dialogue:

FOOTIT Now, Chocolat, listen to this and try to give the answer. Do you know who is the child of my mother and father and yet isn't my brother or sister?
(Chocolat scratches his head a long time and finally gives up.)
FOOTIT It's me!
(Chocolat, delighted, now runs up to the ringmaster.)
CHOCOLAT Can you tell me who is the child of my mother and father and yet isn't my brother or sister?
RINGMASTER I can't think.
CHOCOLAT It's Footit!

Footit and Chocolat revived the already popular entrée of *The Railway Station*. Footit is the guard, ringing his bell as a warning for the start of the, imaginary, train. A rich passenger arrives, travelling first class; Footit bows and scrapes, spreads an imaginary red carpet on the platform, and pockets the tip. A bourgeois family arrives, travelling second; Footit is all smiles, gallant with the mother, deferential to the father, roguish with the maid, and joking with the children. Chocolat arrives, travelling third; 'Where's your ticket?' screams Footit. 'Where are you going? Hurry up there, don't take all day, you stupid fool. Not in that carriage, you idiot!' And finally Footit bundles him down the platform and throws him into his compartment with a kick up his backside.

The Railway Station touches us today on a sensitive nerve. It seems to us socially and racially degrading. But are we looking at it with the benefit of hindsight? The Parisian audiences of 1900 found it marvellously funny. They were not sadistic or racialists, just blind to the deeper issues that lay beneath the comedy.

It does seem that a real situation sometimes lay behind the pretended confrontations in the ring. When Chocolat showed any disposition to argue Footit would say, 'Chocolat, I shall be obliged to box your ears'. These were not just pretence slaps. When Footit first engaged Chocolat it is said that he gave him an extra forty sous a night on the understanding that he must accept without flinching all the real slaps that he gave. The clown was, at first, the master out of the ring as well as in it. The auguste was a secondary, badly paid, assistant. The clown despised the auguste, and the auguste felt inferior to the clown.

But gradually the situation changed as the augustes became more and more popular with the audiences. Sometimes they answered back, in the ring as well as outside it. There was a famous, but quickly hushed up, incident between the clown C.W. Ilès, and the auguste, Little Walter, at Amiens. The strain grew too great and partnerships split up.

Footit and Chocolat went their separate ways, but alone they made little impact. Together they had complemented each other's qualities. But when they were reunited for a brief season the old magic had been lost. The age that had found something funny in

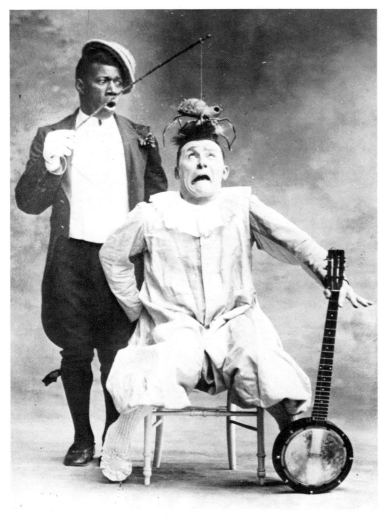

The essence of the Footit and Chocolat partnership lay in their use of the contrast between the traditional haughty white-face, such as Alexis Gruss (opposite), and his partner. However in this scene (above) Chocolat gets his revenge.

the scorn of Footit and the subservience of Chocolat was soon to vanish. Humour is a strange phenomenon. A clown can make us laugh at the most painful subjects – aggression, failure, disaster, adultery and – in the immortal partnership of Footit and Chocolat – contempt and humiliation.

I f Footit and Chocolat were the classic double act in the art of clowning, the Fratellini brothers were the classic triple act. Like almost all clowns they were born in the atmosphere of the sawdust; their father was a rider, acrobat, clown and proprietor of a small circus. The sons were horse-riders, jugglers and acrobats.

In 1902 François and Albert were engaged to present a juggling act at the London Hippodrome. It was entitled *The Original American Bar*, and was performed in evening dress. While at the Hippodrome the theatre manager asked them to fill a gap in the programme by appearing as clowns. Rather unwillingly they thought up an act, and it was at this time that Albert had the idea for the costume and make-up that was later to become famous. Wandering round the poor streets in the East End of London he went into a pub and saw a man dressed in an ancient frock-coat, green with mildew, the tails dragging the ground. The man's trousers fell in concertina folds to his feet. Albert persuaded the man to sell the clothes he stood in and they formed the costume of an outrageous auguste. Then Albert painted his face with a huge red mouth and enormously extended eyebrows with a potato-shaped nose upon a white base.

The act began to take shape when they moved to Europe, and were joined by their brother, Paul. The reason why it became a threesome is interesting. It was nothing to do with artistic or dramatic effect. Paul had been playing in an act with a fourth brother, Louis. Louis had died, leaving a widow and five children. It was the brothers' mother who decided what must be done.

'You can't leave Paul on his own. It will be difficult for him to find a new partner,' she said. 'Take him into your act; what you are doing with two you can do with three. And each of you will put a little aside from your salaries for Louis' widow and children.' In this way, on the basis of family loyalty and brotherhood, the trio of the Fratellini was formed.

Paul adopted a role and costume midway between the elegant white-face François and the grotesque auguste Albert. He was called the notary, black-coated, with top hat and little make-up. In a sense he was the auguste to François, and the clown to Albert.

During the years between 1910 and 1914 they travelled from circus to circus across Europe: in Germany, Hungary, Russia and Spain. At last they came to France and were engaged at the Cirque Medrano, the intimate circus building in Montmartre in which Toulouse-Lautrec had painted and which is now unfortunately destroyed. And here they triumphed.

Historians debate as to what it was that made them unique. Other clowns have played the same acts in the same way, without achieving the same success. Perhaps they just happened to be in the right place at the right time. But perhaps they had that touch of genius that cannot be described in words. Whatever it was, during the years between the wars they enjoyed not only a great popular following but became the darlings of the intellectuals. Writers and critics sang their praises, Jacques Copeau took his theatre students to watch and study them, artists painted them, the President of France honoured them.

Some indication of their style is given by a description of one of their most famous entrées, *Firemen*. Paul and François – the black-coated notary and the sequinned clown – enter the ring, humming an operatic aria. They place their hats – a top hat and a clown's pointed hat – on the chairs behind them. Albert – the auguste – enters playing an enormous trombone which emits such discordant noises that he crams the hats into the mouth of the instrument to quieten it.

'What are you doing here?', asks François; 'you're interrupting our singing. Get out'. And, helped on his way with a kick, Albert retreats. But naturally he creeps back again. After some argument as to who shall sing first, François puts on his hat (which he has

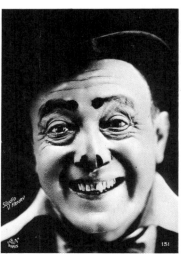

The famous Fratellini Brothers triumphed all over Europe with their triple act, in which Albert (right) payed an outrageous auguste, François (top right) a white-face, and Paul (bottom right) a character called the notary.
Opposite: Paul's granddaughter, Annie, uses François's classic trick from the Fratellini's Firemen entrée.

retrieved from the trombone) and begins to hum. Meanwhile, Albert, standing a bit behind the others, lights an enormous pipe. It catches fire. Albert tries to put it out, but finally empties the burning tobacco onto François' hat (which is provided with an iron cavity for the purpose). As François breaks into song flames are seen rising from the top of his hat. François is quite unaware of what is going on and continues to chant his ballad while behind him Albert and Paul rush up, with firemen's helmets on their heads and axes in their hands, pulling a miniature pump. Albert erects a little ladder against François' back and squirts water from the hose over him. François, still singing blithely, puts up his umbrella to keep the rain off. At the end of their act the trio break into a flurry of somersaults and tumbles, in the course of which Albert's trousers fly off and are whisked up to the gallery.

Acts like this were decked out with an assortment of comic props. There was the huge watch that Albert produced from his pocket and which then flew out of the ring. There were the guitars that were smashed on Albert's head, or exploded scattering hams and sausages over the ring. And the child's bicycle that collapsed into numerous pieces when Albert sat on it, and which looked like something quite different when he tried to put it together again.

Other clowns have used, and still use props like these. But for the Fratellini they were incidentals to their personalities. During the decades of their triumphs they raised the art of clowning to a degree of critical appreciation that it had never achieved before, and that it has today, alas, totally lost. One of the most telling of all the tributes they received was from a French poet, who said simply: 'The Fratellini are poets'.

The family tradition is kept alive today by Annie Fratellini, the granddaughter of Paul, who plays as an auguste. Her performance, worthy of her name, is one of charm and zany humour. She runs a circus school in Paris with her husband, a white-face clown. Many circus skills are studied there, but not clowning, for she believes that although clowns can be taught acrobatics and other tricks of the trade, they are born not made.

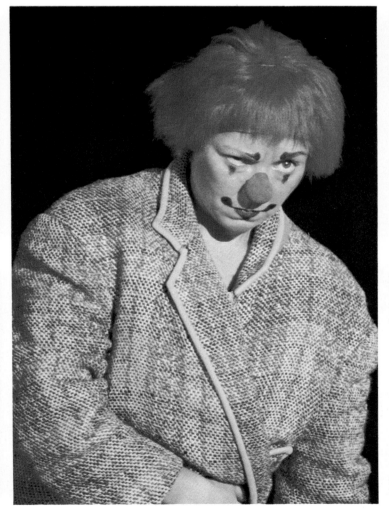

Annie centres her clowning act around her impish personality. Her mobile face expresses a range of emotions that recalls the magic of her Fratellini forebears.

Grock is exceptional among clowns as he was not brought up in the Circus. He was born Adrian Wettach, the son of a Swiss watchmaker who had some ambitions to become a circus acrobat but settled down as an innkeeper. Young Wettach grew up with a passion for acrobatics and longed to become a circus performer. He was sent to Hungary, like several Swiss children at that period, to speak French with the children of an aristocratic family, and here he eventually found a regular job in a small circus. He eked out a hard livelihood, tumbling in circuses and playing music in restaurants.

In 1903 Wettach was working as cashier in a small German circus when a comic double act called Brick and Brock broke up. Brick needed to find a new partner; Wettach volunteered for the job, and took the name of Grock.

Brick and Grock's act was a musical burlesque, and by all accounts nothing very brilliant. Grock's face was festooned with a huge red beard and he wore tartan trousers over a padded stomach. He must have looked like a hundred other indifferent augustes at the time and there was no hint of the fame to come.

After four years the Brick and Grock partnership broke up, and Grock teamed up with the French clown, Antonet. Antonet was the very model of the classic white-face clown, with exquisite sequinned costumes and an almost feminine grace. Before meeting Grock, Antonet had worked with an auguste called Little Walter, and it is clear that Grock modelled his new style and costume upon that of Little Walter. His costume was basically that of the first European augustes, a shabby waiter's black tail-coat and trousers, badly fitting but worn with a certain dash, rather than the extravagantly absurd rig of later augustes.

Antonet and Grock played in circuses until 1911 and were very successful. In that year they were given a booking at the Winter Garden in Berlin. But this was a variety theatre not a circus, and they soon discovered that what went down well in the ring fell absolutely flat on the stage. Very few circus clowns have succeeded in transferring their acts to the stage. The reverse holds equally true, indeed it is difficult to think of a single stage clown who has subsequently made a success in the Circus.

However, Antonet and Grock were among the few who eventually succeeded in both mediums. But they had to change the whole character of their act. In the Circus it was played with broad effects and big props. The piano could not be played and they found a woman's corset wrapped round the strings; Grock fell through the big drum; and so on. In the theatre they had to evolve a new style, more subtle and delicate but no less funny.

Two years later Grock broke up the partnership. Antonet was a good clown, but in a traditional circus double-act the clown was the master, the auguste his assistant. Grock wanted to be the chief. He engaged other actors as partners but they were always subsidiary to him. Henceforth it became Grock with an assistant, who was a straight character, not a clown.

Grock achieved great fame and wealth. He played mostly in variety houses, though he did return to the Circus from time to time. He finally retired in 1954. Many people say he was the greatest clown of his age. He was always a perfectionist. Through the greater part of his career he played only one entrée, the musical burlesque, but he was continually polishing and improving it. Eventually it lasted over an hour. It is impossible to recapture the effect of his tricks on paper, still, here is some kind of a description.

His partner enters and begins to play on the violin. Grock follows him, lugging an enormous double-bass case on to the stage. From it he produces a tiny violin. Having adjusted it under his chin he throws the bow up in the air in delight, but fails to catch it. Mortified, he retires behind a screen, and the audience can see the bow thrown up several times as he practises the trick. Apparently satisfied, he returns to the audience, throws the bow up, and drops it again. Finally he gives up; settles down to study the score, absent-mindedly throws the bow up, catches it, starts to play – and suddenly realises what he has done. He stops playing and a delighted grin spreads over his half-moon face. He had a quiet, sing-song voice that could suddenly explode into a deep foghorn for his

Above: Grock at the age of 74 makes his last appearance in Hamburg in 1954.
Right: In the film Au Revoir Mr Grock, *Grock played the great musical entrée for which he was so well known.*
Opposite: Popov also plays a violin entrée in the Russian circus today.

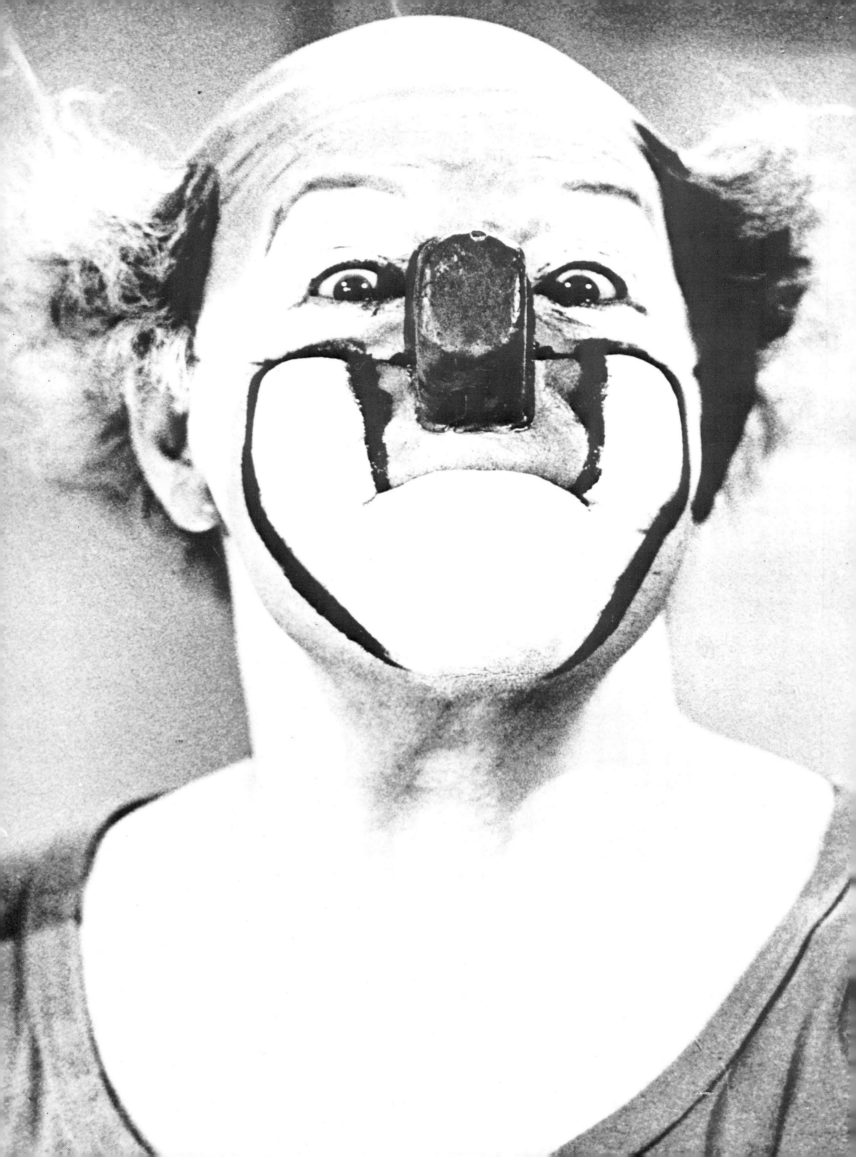

famous catch phrases, like 'sans blague' – 'no kidding'. Here is a scrap of dialogue with his partner, Max:

MAX What instrument can you play?

GROCK I play the wztdhp.

MAX What on earth's that?

Grock launches into an elaborate description, with much pantomime, of the instrument. There are banks of strings arranged so, tubes and pipes curling and twisting so, a mouth-piece here, a keyboard there, and so on.

MAX That sounds more like an entire orchestra. But at the end of the strings, at the end of the pipes, at the end of the keyboard, what is there?

GROCK There is some cheese.

MAX Some cheese! What on earth for?

GROCK To eat.

The act usually ended with piano playing. Grock seats himself before the piano, but the stool is too far away. With great effort he pushes the heavy grand piano nearer the stool. He prepares to play, stands up, bows, tinkles the keys, pulls up his cuffs, prepares to play. Then he feels something itching his back; he tries to scratch it, but can't reach it; he rubs the back of his chair against it; no good; he takes Max's violin bow and sticks it inside his coat; Max snatches it away.

Grock prepares to play. He strikes a chord, and the piano lid falls down on his fingers. He blows on them and tries again. Again it falls. The third time he waits for it, snatches his hands away just in time, and leaps to his feet in triumph.

He takes off his gloves and places his hat and gloves on the piano. His bald head glistens. He begins to play, and as he plays the vibration sets his hat and gloves sliding across the piano. He reaches out to hold them with one hand while still playing with the other. But they escape from him. Grock leaps after them on to the piano. They slide away down the sloping piano top. Grock slides after them – whoosh – on to the floor.

Grock sits again at the piano. His fingers run up and down the keyboard. He rounds off a vibrant arpeggio with a crashing chord, and leaps in triumph to stand on his chair. The seat falls in and he is left standing inside the four chair legs. Baffled, he jerks himself into the air and lands neatly to sit on the chair back. Another jerk to sit in the chair, and his bottom falls through the open seat and he is stuck in it, feet and arms waving helplessly in the air. Those who remember it all agree that Grock's piano playing was a masterpiece.

Few great clowns have grown up without a circus background. The story of Charlie Rivel's birth is therefore not that unusual. In 1896 a small cart was pulled by a man into a village near Barcelona. The man was an acrobat, beside him walked his old mother, and in the cart was his young wife who was heavily pregnant. They set up a tight wire, the old mother beat a drum, the man performed some acrobatic feats, and the young wife danced on the wire. But she had to stop in mid-act and the baby was born that night. He was called José Andreu and was destined to become the most famous clown of our time.

The little family continued plodding from village to village across the plains and hills of Spain and France. A horse and caravan was acquired. Other children followed. And from a very early age they learnt to balance and walk the wire and present a simple act. They were booked for circuses here and there, and began to be noticed for the skill, grace and subtle charm of their performance. It was not all acrobatics. At that date many circuses included a mimed dramatic spectacle in their programmes, and at the age of seven José found himself playing roles in them. These scenes sharpened the boy's sense for mime that was to blossom in later years. Whenever an opportunity presented itself he would take part in a bit of clowning in the ring.

In 1916, at Madrid, when he was twenty years old, José saw a Charlie Chaplin film and was inspired to attempt a parody of Charlie Chaplin on the trapeze. He hit upon the name Charlie Rivel for this act. The act was successful from the first and was played in small circuses up and down Europe, but it was not until 1929,

CIRKUS SCHUMANN
CHARLIE RIVEL

Opposite: Charlie Rivel's bold make-up makes him a distinctive auguste.

Above: Rivel appears on a poster for the Cirkus Schumann.

Opposite: Sacha Coco revives his father's costume and make-up and plays today with the Circus Hassani in England.

Above: Coco, hair on end, makes his well-remembered entrance into the ring at Bertram Mills Circus.

when it was presented as a quite minor item in the bill at the Cirque d'Hiver in Paris, that it hit the headlines. Suddenly he was catapulted into fame. United Artists, as Chaplin's agents, at first tried to stop imitators appearing. But the Charlie Rivel trapeze act was not an imitation; it was a new creation, a brilliant parody of Chaplin as he might appear if he were a trapeze artiste. Subtle observation was added to considerable acrobatic skill to create an act that was hailed all over Europe and America for the next 28 years, until, at the age of 61, Charlie felt he was getting too old for the physical exertion involved.

Meanwhile, however, he had been developing other clowning acts. He teamed up with his brothers in a threesome, with René as the white-face clown, Polo as the 'straight auguste', and Charlie as the 'outrageous auguste' in outsize black trousers, a red jersey, large black shoes, a false square-shaped red nose and a bald wig with red hair sprouting from the temples. One day his red jersey needed washing. When it came out of the wash it had stretched to twice its length and came down to his knees. There was no time to change it and he had to put it on as it was. It looked funnier than ever. The costume of Charlie Rivel the clown, as distinct from Charlie Rivel as Charlie Chaplin, was complete.

The act of the three Rivels was a good one. It was balanced in much the same way as that of the three Fratellini. Each of the brothers made his own contribution. René was a white-face clown in the restrained, elegant style of Antonet. Polo, in exaggerated bourgeois costume, was considered by some good judges to be the cleverest and most original of the three. But it was Charlie, with his grotesque appearance and broad style of playing, who caught public attention and whose picture went up on the hoardings.

This led to jealousy and friction within the family troupe. We only have Charlie's account of what happened so we cannot be sure as to what lay behind the trouble, but the result was that in 1935, at the height of their success, the act broke up. Polo and René went their own way, to make a significant contribution to the art of clowning. Charlie had to find new partners. Some people think his act has never been the same since.

In 1979, at the age of 83, Charlie was still occasionally performing. His act is now polished and refined to a subtlety of gesture and interpretation that belongs more to the cabaret than the circus ring. It is difficult to describe the act, for the effect is achieved by a thousand little touches, each insignificant in itself. He enters as a violin maestro in shabby evening dress, but nothing will go right: the bow of the violin gets caught in his braces; the violin gets mixed up with the microphone; confusion mounts upon confusion to a well-orchestrated climax and the act ends in total anarchy.

Then he returns in the familiar long red jersey but with an enormous head-dress as an operatic soprano in an act originally conceived as a parody of Maria Callas. The throat is cleared, the large breasts settled into place, the music score studied, but co-ordination with the accompanist at the piano eludes him. The music falls on the floor, is picked up, and the first notes are sung in a deep bass. Astonishment from the accompanist! A hurried consultation. The music is being held upside down! It is turned the other way up, and the voice utters a piercing squawk. Further confusion. Collapse of the accompanist. Chaos on all sides as the prima donna assoluta soars into an unquenchable aria.

Coco is a famous clown whose children have followed him into the ring. His daughter has performed as a clown, calling herself Cocotina, and his son can be seen working today in an English circus, wearing an identical costume to his father. Coco was born as Nikolai Poliakoff in 1900 in Russia. As a little boy he used to amuse army officers by dancing and singing in their club near Leningrad, and when he was only eight years old he ran away with an organ grinder and got himself a job as an assistant to a well-known circus clown called Lazarenko. He was sent back home, but his father saw that his heart was in the Circus and he was apprenticed to the Circus Truzzi, one of the best in Russia at the beginning of the twentieth century.

He wanted to be a clown from the first, but he was told, 'My boy, if you want to be a successful clown, first you must be an acrobat, then a trapeze artiste and a tumbler; in fact you must be able to do everything, and *then* you can think about being a clown.' That is the golden rule for circus clowning. While he was with the Circus Truzzi he adopted the name of Coco. It was the idea of Truzzi, who was an Italian, and he just liked the sound of it. He probably did not know that three clowns had already used it.

Coco moved on in due course, travelling all over Russia, usually by hiding under the seats of railway carriages, and was eventually arrested as a vagrant. When the First War broke out he joined the army, but he was wounded and then caught up in the Revolution, playing in entertainment troupes for the soldiers of both sides as the fortunes of the civil war swept to and fro. When the War was over Coco found work as an acrobatic clown in a circus in Latvia, but he slipped while rehearsing some acrobatic feat and injured his leg, so that he could hardly walk. For some time afterwards he had to perform sitting in a chair, accompanied by his little four-year-old daughter. When at last his injured leg was cured he discovered that the audience laughed much less now that he could walk about in an ordinary way during the act.

At last Coco started his own small circus, touring in Lithuania, but here disaster struck. In one of his acts he used to fill a samovar with boiling water, place it on a table, balance the table on his forehead, strike the table away, and catch the samovar as it fell. One day all went as it should until, in catching the samovar, the handle broke, the samovar tilted sideways and drenched him with boiling water. He was terribly scalded and for a long time lay in hospital. When he came out his money had all gone and his circus had been disbanded. The Russian circuses were at a low ebb and although they were to recover their standards, it was not the moment for an independent artiste to look for work with them.

So Coco turned his steps towards Berlin and found work with the Circus Busch, one of the best in Germany. Here he was spotted by Bertram Mills and offered a job as a run-in clown in the famous English circus. That was in 1929. He continued to work with Mills for the next 37 years.

It is doubtful if Coco could be described as a great clown, but he became one of the best-loved clowns in English history and almost a living symbol of the Bertram Mills Circus. Although he appeared in fairly standard water entrées and similar acts in the ring, usually with Percy Huxter as the white-face clown, he is really remembered more for the way in which he would walk round the ring, shaking hands with children in the ringside seats. He would walk halfway across the ring, step out of his big shoes, and the shoes would go on walking by themselves. (This seems to be originally a Russian gag – it was repeated in the fine new Moscow Circus recently.) Then the tufts of wild hair on his red wig would jerk up into the air. And so on. It was enough to create an impression that audiences remembered and welcomed year after year.

Above all, Coco was a magnificent, if unofficial, advertisement for the Bertram Mills Circus. One day, it is said, a small boy came up to him after a performance to ask for his autograph. Coco signed his name and the boy ran quickly across the road to rejoin his parents, looking neither to right nor left; a car, unable to stop, knocked him down and killed him. This incident made a profound impression upon Coco, and he dedicated his life to teaching children the elementary rules of road safety. Wherever the circus went, Coco offered to give a talk on road safety in local schools and the children's wards of hospitals. It was a magnificent work, for which he was awarded the OBE. It was an honour richly deserved. But it must also be said that his appearance served as a very useful reminder of the fact that the Bertram Mills Circus was in town.

When the Bertram Mills Circus was suspended during the Second World War, Coco organized a highly successful concert party to entertain the troops. And after Bertram Mills had closed down in 1960, due to economic conditions, Coco found he could not keep away from the ring, and he went on clowning till he was

Charlie Cairoli in his customary simple make-up and bowler hat.

quite an old man with a much smaller and more modest family circus. Coco died in 1974 and was accorded the unique honour of a memorial service in St Paul's Cathedral. A large congregation attended to pay tribute to this much-loved clown.

If Footit, like others before him, was an English clown who made his reputation in France, Charlie Cairoli was a French clown who gained his reputation in England; the Circus is, indeed, an international art. Cairoli's father, Jean, was a juggler who was persuaded to turn clown in the Cirque Pinder. After a few years with other partners he formed a successful trio with his younger son, Carletto (Charlie) and the auguste, Porto. In this company Jean was the white-face clown, very elegant, graceful in his movements, and a gifted musician who made the bow of his violin or the keys of his saxophone seem to dance in his hands. Porto was the eccentric, a brilliant but unpredictable comedian, who tended to put his partners in the shade with the exaggeration of his miming. Carletto, at that time, was very much the junior auguste. One of the entrées that they presented at the Cirque Medrano in Paris, went as follows. Jean Cairoli appears as a magician who can create anything in his magic cauldron. Porto asks for a beautiful princess.

'Do you want her blond or brunette?'

'Red', replies Porto.

'Eyes, blue, green or black?'

'Yellow'.

Cairoli mixes the ingredients in the bowl. Then he asks:

'Do you want large . . .?'

'Yes, large, like this', as Porto pantomimes big breasts.

'Do you want her to be musical?'

'Large . . . large,' Porto continues.

'Clever?'

'Large, I tell you, large . . .'

Carletto, as the magician's assistant, pours bucket after bucket of fat into the magic bowl, from which emerges the shape of a gross, barely human figure who towers over Porto and rains a shower of blows on his head for having created her so fat.

After some years Porto left the group to continue his successful career with other partners whom he could more easily dominate, and Jean took his eldest son, Filip, into the trio. During their years at the Medrano, from 1927 to 1937, the Cairolis devised over seventy different entrées, including a number of short unrelated episodes, called 'blacks' because the lights were momentarily extinguished between each. This was an attempt, not entirely successful at the time, to introduce some new ideas into circus clowning and it indicates the creative thought that the Cairolis gave to their performances. Clowning is a very traditional art, but it does require infusions of fresh ideas from time to time.

In 1939 the Cairolis came to England to play at the beautiful Tower Circus at Blackpool. They were an immediate success, and Charlie stayed on, eventually taking British nationality. He appeared there for 40 successive seasons and retired not long before his death in 1980. Charlie appeared in what one might call a modified auguste style, with a red nose and big black eyebrows, but not otherwise grotesquely made up; he wore a bowler hat and a kind of shabby businessman's suit reminiscent of the image of the 'little man' created by the cartoonist, Strube. As soon as he walked into the ring he was greeted with acclamation from the audience, with whom he established a wonderful relationship. The children, especially, loved him and he never did anything to frighten them.

He usually produced two new entrées each season. One might be a skit on a conjuring show, with the tricks all going wrong; or a musical entrée, with Charlie producing music from a weird and wonderful array of instruments, including a vacuum cleaner. He was, in fact, a fine musician himself and could play up to top G after top C on the trumpet. The other entrée always involved water and slosh (the ring at Blackpool can be filled with water), and everyone got drenched by the time it was over. But this was not just crude slapstick. Every gag had been carefully thought out, and was polished and refined during the season.

CLOWNING IN RUSSIA

Many brands of humour and characters from national folklore have become interwoven in the travels of circus clowns; yet distinct traditions and variations on the clown character have developed in countries outside the mainstream of European clowning.

Circus came from England to Russia at the end of the eighteenth century. Many of the great European troupes found warm appreciation at the court of St Petersburg. But a native Russian tradition did not appear until the 1870s, when the Nikitin brothers founded their own show. Within the indigenous Russian circuses the role of clown was taken by a red-headed comic, drawn from Russian folk tradition, known as the *r'izhii*. A typical act of the *r'izhii* is described by a Russian writer as follows:

> The clown tumbled down from the banks of benches into the ring, accompanied by the crashing and banging of a huge watering-can. He collapsed, sprawled across the ring fence; then, seating himself on it, he brought out a handkerchief and blew his nose. The sound was atrociously magnified by the drums and trumpets of the band. When he removed his handkerchief, his false nose was seen to be lit up by an electric lamp inside it. It went out, but suddenly his red hair stood up straight on his head . . . He got in the way of the ring boys as they rolled up the carpet, until they put him with it in a wheelbarrow and wheeled him off, crying like a baby.

Early in the twentieth century the crude clowning of the *r'izhii* could have been contrasted with the more subtle wit of the Durov brothers, Anatoli and Vladimir. Both of these artistes were wonderful animal trainers, and their comedy was in a quiet, witty style. Vladimir, in particular, had a gift for persuading usually incompatible animals to perform together. He taught a cat and rats to play in the same act; he had a school with eight different species of animals all sitting on benches before him; he had a special love for rats, and used to show a model railway with rats as engine driver, guard and passengers as the train chugged round the ring.

Anatoli was particularly noted for the humour he introduced

Russian clowns, like Yevgeny Kudrjashov who is shown here during the Moscow State Circus tour in Holland, have adopted a more naturalistic and less grotesque style of performing.

into his act, which sometimes included political satire. When his trained pig went over to a box in which some unpopular government officials were sitting, Durov exclaimed, 'You wretched animal, you're deserting me to rejoin your own family.' When he was forbidden to make political jokes, he appeared in the ring with a big padlock fastened over his mouth.

Just as Auriol was a gifted acrobat who performed in a fancy costume with a touch of humour, so the Durovs were gifted animal trainers who performed in fancy costumes with comedy and satire. They were not, perhaps, primarily clowns, but they laid the foundations of a new style of Russian clowning that is such a marked characteristic of Russian circus entertainment today.

It was a clown called Karandash, however, who led the development of Russian clowning from the coarse buffoonery of the past towards a simpler, more naturalistic form of humour. A former student at the Moscow Circus School, he began his career by performing in a Charlie Chaplin guise. But by 1936 he felt the sad tramp role was out of place in the society in which his audiences lived, and he adopted a new style. He put on a shapeless coat, baggy trousers, bootlace tie, and soft round hat, all black, relieved only by a crumpled white shirt. He played without make-up what he described as 'a normal, healthy, happy man, with the innocence of a child'.

He was often accompanied by a donkey and two Scotch terriers. In one act he led his donkey on with bicycle handlebars on its collar, a bicycle seat on its saddle, and a registration number on its rump. He produced a bicycle pump, and with an air of great seriousness pumped up the donkey's hind leg. Then he rode it round the ring. During the war he raised the spirits of the Russian people in innumerable sketches, such as when he placed his dog before a microphone, let it bark for a good minute, and then announced, 'The speech of propaganda minister Goebbels has now finished.'

A famous act he played was *A Scene in the Park*. He is walking in a park and sits down on a bench; when he gets up he finds that it had been freshly painted, and his trouser seat is coloured green. How to get it off? He tries rubbing himself against a passer-by which is not very well received! Then he tries rubbing himself against a nude statue of Venus but he only knocks the statue over, and it breaks into pieces. In alarm he tries to piece it together again, but he cannot get the pieces to fit. What does a woman's body look like? Breasts in hand he studies the ladies who pass, trying to figure out where that piece goes. Before he can get it right a park keeper comes along. Karandash leaps on to the plinth, posing as the statue himself. 'This looks odd', thinks the park keeper, scratching his head. You can imagine the rest. The idea of the living statue is at least as old as the Commedia dell' Arte.

Although Karandash belonged to the new school of naturalistic Russian clowns he did not entirely abandon traditional circus gags. One that he played was *The Funnel Trick*. In this he demonstrates how to place a funnel in the waistband of his trousers, then balances a coin on his forehead, and with a flick of the head tips the coin into the funnel. He then offers the coin as a reward to a second clown if he can do the trick. The clown places the funnel in position, casts his head back to balance the coin, and Karandash pours a jug of water down the funnel. Clown number 2, having learnt the trick, then plays it on clown number 3. At this point Karandash wanders innocently in and clown number 3 offers to show the trick to him. Karandash apparently allows himself to be fooled, but he has concealed a hot water bottle inside his trousers, into which he fits the funnel. Triumph of Karandash!

This is a gag that has been played by hundreds of clowns, but the secret of Karandash's success lay in his personality. He would transform his soft black hat into a woman's bonnet and hitch up his floppy trousers with an elegant air. He would drive into the ring in a little cart, radiating such a spirit of happiness and fun that audiences warmed to him immediately. He had that instinctive rapport with the public, without which a clown cannot succeed.

Russian clowns have been seen in Western Europe and in America during the many tours of the Moscow State Circus. These musical clowns and augustes appeared at the historic Circus Carré in Amsterdam.

In 1950 Karandash was provided with an assistant at the Moscow Circus. He was Oleg Popov, a recent student at the Moscow Circus School. At the school he had showed an aptitude for the low wire, and his teachers had observed that he balanced with a certain sense of humour that was worth developing. He was encouraged to work up a comic act on the wire.

Popov learnt a great deal from working with Karandash, above all his mastery in playing upon the emotions of the audience; he could make them laugh just whenever he wanted. After this apprenticeship, Popov resumed his role as a comic wire performer. It was while he was playing at Saratov that the main clown of the company was taken ill; there was no time to send a replacement, and young Popov was asked to take his place. In the first half of the programme he did his best to repeat the standard buffooneries of the old-style clown, but the laughs did not come and he sensed that he was a failure. During the interval he tore off the clown's motley and washed the make-up off his face; he just couldn't face going on. In a mood of despair he wandered into the circus kitchen, and suddenly had an idea. He borrowed the chef's white hat and jacket and a pile of pots and saucepans and hurried back to the ring.

He had absolutely nothing prepared, but his circus training had included some practice in juggling and inspiration came to his aid. He greatly pleased the audience in the role of a simple, happy cook, tossing his pots and pans up and down and catching his potatoes on the points of a fork. A new clown was born.

As he developed this type of clowning in the years to come, Popov strengthened and deepened his characterization. He was essentially what he describes as 'a simple, happy lad, a little tender and lyrical'; he tried to create a character that would be naïve but also poetical; he was always smiling, and became known as 'the sunshine clown'. He completely abandoned the gross burlesque and buffoonery of the old school of clowning. He wore only slight make-up and for his costume he adopted, like Karandash his master, a simple black coat and striped trousers with a white shirt. But he wore – as a kind of trademark – a cap patterned in big black and white chequers like a chess board.

By 1957 he had already built up a repertoire of over 80 entrées, many of which were parodies of the previous circus act. Some were simple mimes. He appeared as an orator, nervously sipping water before his speech, rising anxiously to his feet, losing his place in his notes, gesticulating, ringing his bell to call the audience to order, all without uttering a word.

In another sketch he used sounds but not words. It was the traditional entrée of *You Can't Play that Here*, in which the clown comes in with half an orchestra of instruments, but each is confiscated by the ringmaster except for a whistle, which – in a moment of panic – he swallows. From that moment the clown is unable to speak, he can only whistle. But in the tone of his whistling he conveys all the sentiments of apology, indignation, impertinence and delight in his dialogue with the ringmaster. The same idea had been used by Chaplin in one of his films, but Popov was sufficiently original to stamp it with his own interpretation.

Many of Popov's sketches are gently satirical. The pre-Revolutionary Russian clowns had been adept at poking fun at the Tsarist government; attacks on the present-day communist government would not be permitted, but Russian clowns do have considerable freedom in satirizing the bureaucracy and inefficiencies of the economic system. In one sketch Popov is a doctor who has been called to the aid of a nearly drowned man who has been rescued from the river; after examining him in a very off-hand manner he gives him an injection from an enormous syringe which shocks him back to consciousness. The doctor promptly demands his name and address, and on hearing them he orders the man to be thrown back into the river; 'He lives in a district for which a different doctor is responsible.'

Some satires are directed against fashions of which the authorities disapprove. In one of these Popov comes on carrying a plaster statue of a naked lady. It is, he says, a portrait of his grandmother in 1859 and he is taking it to the Academy. But at this moment he stumbles, falls on the ground, and the statue breaks

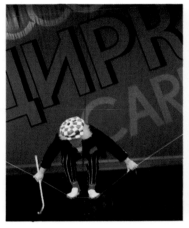

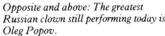
Opposite and above: The greatest Russian clown still performing today is Oleg Popov.

Overleaf: Popov takes a rest after the exertions of his act, and fans himself with the hat that has become his trademark.

Above: Popov lends his fun to an exciting display of acrobatic tricks.
Right and opposite: Popov is still performing today the chef's juggling act

which began his career as an all-round clown. He improvised it at the last minute when called upon to stand in for the regular clown who had been taken ill.

into pieces. With great care he pieces them together again, but the order has been muddled and the result is an angular monstrosity. Popov, however, is perfectly happy, 'It is a portrait of my grandmother in 1959', he announces 'and I'm taking it to the Exhibition of Abstract Art.'

Popov has written seriously and well about his role as a truthful clown of the people, but his acts do not entirely ignore the basic elements of traditional clowning. Here is a description of one of his entrées called *The Fishermen*. Popov and Tchijik are two fishermen sitting, rod in hand, side by side. Because Popov has taken some of Tchijik's bait, Tchijik swings his rod so that a fish that he has just caught hits Popov in the face. Popov then makes the hook of his line catch Tchijik's cap. Tchijik disentangles his cap and hits Popov on the face with it. This hurts Popov, so he takes the upturned bucket on which Tchijik has been sitting, fills it with water, and bathes his face in it. Then he puts it back behind Tchijik, who – thinking it is still upside down – sits down in it. Screams! A lobster in the pail has fastened its claws on his bottom. Popov produces a revolver and shoots the lobster.

Friends again, they decide to celebrate by drinking a bottle of wine. But they have not got a corkscrew. So they try to shoot the cork out of the bottle by punching the base of the bottle; but it flies out of Tchijik's hands into the river. Popov jumps in to rescue it and fishes for it with a net, but he brings up a big sturgeon. The fishermen land it with delight, and proceed to cut it open to extract the caviare, but they find the bottle of wine in its stomach.

At last they can celebrate, but just as they clink glasses the big fish comes alive and stands up on its tail. Popov in a panic fires his pistol at it. He misses, the bullet goes into the ground and a jet of water spurts up. Tchijik puts up his umbrella. Popov produces a huge pair of scissors and cuts off the jet of water 'at its roots'. They run out pursued by green frogs which scramble out of the water.

Popov's poetic spirit is brought out in an entrée called *The Spotlight*. A spotlight lights up a circle in a darkened ring. Popov enters, tired out as if at the end of an exhausting day. He warms his hands in the spotlight, smiles, and settles down to rest in its beam. Suddenly the spotlight is switched to a different spot in the ring. Popov chases after it, finds it, heaves a sigh of relief, and snuggles down in it again. Again the spotlight is switched. Popov chases after it, and then with gentle gestures of his hands, almost carressing the light, he – as it were – wafts it back to its original spot. He settles down again, smiling, contented, brings a bottle of milk out of his sack and raises it to his mouth.

At this moment a discordant sound is heard. The beam of the spotlight narrows. Popov is dismayed. The sound is repeated. The beam narrows to a pencil point. In desperation Popov seizes his sack and seems to put the beam into it. The spotlight goes out, but inside the sack a tiny point of light still gleams. Clutching the sack on his back, Popov leaves the ring. The pathos with which Popov plays this entrée gives his clown figure a universal quality. The ray of light he catches seems to become a symbol of happiness and the traditional entrée transmits a new message.

AMERICAN CLOWNS

The most famous American clown entered the Circus almost accidentally in the course of a frantically varied career. Dan Rice was born in 1823 and as a young boy he was a jockey, riding horses in Kentucky and Ohio. Then, when he became too heavy to be a jockey, he found that life could be amusing and profitable living on the river steamers, which passed up and down the Mississippi, card-sharping for a living.

He had an all-round talent. He could sing after a fashion and dance a jig, and wrote his own words and music. He played for a time in a black-face minstrel troupe. Somewhere in his travels he met circus people and began to study their skills. He learnt to lift heavy weights and to toss a cannon ball. And he had a genuine gift for training animals.

In 1844 he appeared as a circus clown. He was a talking clown in the small, one-ring circuses of those days, and worked in the tradition of Shakespearean clowns. He used to recite a doggerel version of *Hamlet*, beginning,

Hamlet, the Dane, of him just deign to hear,
And for the object lend, at least, an ear.
I will a tale unfold, whose lightest word
Will freeze your soul, and turn your blood to curd.

It was for the wit of his impromptu repartee, however, that he is best remembered, and for his skill with animals. He trained a giraffe, a buffalo, a rhinoceros and a pair of mules. His pig, Sybil, was famous. He would ask it to pick out the biggest rascal present. It went off, sniffing round the audience, and then came back and rubbed its snout against Rice himself.

At one time Rice was earning the, then, enormous salary of $1000 a week, but he never settled with any company for long. After playing for some time with Spalding in New Orleans, he set up in opposition and engaged the English clown, Wallett, to play alternately as clown and ringmaster with him. At this time he was engaged in a bitter war of insults and abuse with Spalding, his ex-employer. Spalding retaliated, but the local people tended to

*Checkers pauses in his patriotic parade
around the ring at the Bill Gray Circus
at the Texas State Fair in Dallas.*

side with Rice. According to Wallett, 'Dan was a sort of martyr in the eyes of the New Orleans people; they believed that the proprietors [of Spalding], who were rich and powerful, had come on purpose to crush his company. In fact, the feeling rose to such a height that it was dangerous for the Spalding managers, or any of their company to be recognized by the populace after dark.'

Rice might engage the sympathy of the people for an underdog, but his attacks on Spalding grew so virulent that Spalding called in the law and Rice was sent to prison for slander. He came out, with no money, and started up a very modest little circus that had only one horse. It is said that Spalding taunted him with running a one-horse show; Rice countered by proudly billing his circus as 'Dan Rice and his One-Horse Show'. That seems to have been the origin of the saying.

In the ring Rice devised his own striped costume. He wore no make-up, but his Uncle Sam beard made him instantly recognizable, and he is believed to have inspired the traditional image of Uncle Sam that was spread over the world by cartoonists. Rice was never content to be merely a circus clown. He lectured up and down the country, supported President Zachary Taylor, for which he was made an honorary colonel, and stood for Congress and for Republican presidential nomination, though unsuccessfully in both cases. In his later years he drank heavily and circus proprietors despaired of engaging him, for he could never be relied on to honour a contract. He made his last tour in 1885. We have to take the quality of Rice's wit largely on trust, but he must have had a remarkable personality. Wallett writes of him warmly, describing him as 'the great American clown'. He was a complete individualist, gifted, difficult to deal with, and egoistical, but something of a folk hero to the American people.

The American tradition gave birth to a new clown character, taken from folklore. The European idea of the disreputable auguste was taken a stage further at the end of the nineteenth century with the development of the hobo or tramp clown. This character originated in the vaudeville theatres. The hobo, bumming free meals up and down the length of the United States, had become a kind of folk hero, and in the theatres he was sometimes portrayed as a homespun philosopher, sometimes as a juggler, which was the role in which W. C. Fields first made his reputation on the stage. It was an easy step from a hobo juggler, performing with skill and comedy, to a hobo circus clown.

One of the greatest hobo clowns was Emmett Kelly. He started life as a farm boy in the mid-West with a talent for drawing and an ambition to be an artist. When he left for Kansas City in 1917 he drifted through a series of jobs, always fascinated by circuses and fairs but not part of them.

To show off his skill with chalk and paper he worked up a kind of lightning cartoon act, and he had a proper easel made with a curtain to pull in front of it. He needed to present this act in some kind of character, and he tried it out with himself as a 'silly kid' type, with white wig, white shirt and baggy short pants held up by comic suspenders.

This was, in fact, very close to a traditional American comic character, the Toby, who appeared as a red-headed, freckle-faced, country boy in a host of simple rustic farces from the late nineteenth century almost up to the present day. The stock Toby, as he evolved in tent shows and touring companies, developed into a more zany character, with grotesque make-up and exaggerated behaviour, who tended to take over the whole show as a vehicle for his clowning.

When he was not sketching and clowning in the streets, Kelly got jobs – if he could – as an artist with advertising agencies or similar firms. And it was while he was working with a company that made cartoon films that he had an idea. He created the character of 'a forlorn, melancholy little hobo who always got the short end of the stick and never had any good luck at all, but who never lost hope and just kept on trying'.

It was just an idea. He made a few sketches, but his heart was

Opposite: Dressed in his customary tatters and clutching an old paper bag, Emmett Kelly, one of America's most famous hobo clowns, is shown here during his time with the great Ringling Brothers and Barnum & Bailey Circus.
Above: The most noticeable characteristic of the tramp clown was his forlorn and dejected appearance and his refusal to smile, yet audiences identified with him and roared with laughter in sympathy with the hobo's disastrous exploits. Of all the tramp clowns, Otto Griebling had perhaps the most sensitive and expressive face.

now set on something else. He had been bitten by the circus bug. He had worked up a single trapeze act, and with this and the lightning cartoon act he had something to offer. He had played in a dog and pony show and he was then offered a modest contract with Howes Great London Circus, one of the titles that have passed through the hands of dozens of American circus proprietors since Howes and Cushing came back from a tour of England in 1864.

In this circus he clowned with a white face, applied with zinc oxide and lard, doubling with his trapeze act. In the lightning cartoon act he would pretend to be sketching another clown, who kept on asking 'Is it like me?', at which he nodded vigorously and when he turned the paper round it was a drawing of a jackass. He married a girl trapeze artiste, and they travelled around playing a double act, and he also clowned in white-face. It was while he was with the John Robinson Circus that he had the idea of clowning in the hobo role that he had drawn some years earlier. But the boss clown did not like the concept as he thought the costume looked dirty, so the idea was shelved for some time.

While Kelly was with the Cole Brothers and Clyde Beatty Combined Circus his marriage broke up, which left him feeling very unhappy. It was then that he began to present the hobo character, which reflected something of his feelings at that time. The act was admirably suited to the conditions of the American three-ring circus, in which it was often difficult for the average clown to make much impact. Kelly worked in close to the audience, not just playing to the expensive seats at the ringside, but moving right up the aisles to the 'bleachers' at the back.

Kelly's brilliant idea was to appear the complete opposite of everyone's preconception of a clown. He would wander round the track, dirty, ragged and unshaven, as if looking for something. He might pause before a woman spectator and fix her with a long mournful stare, while he nibbled on wisps of leaves from a big cabbage. He would take a board, prop it across a seat, and slowly saw it in half, studying a blueprint as he did so. He would pick up a peanut, try to crack it with his teeth, and find it too hard; then he would place it on the floor, fetch a great sledge-hammer, and smash

Many other American clowns have added their individual adaptations of costume and make-up to the original hobo clown figure. Rex 'Boxcar' Young's rough make-up (opposite) contrasts with that of Checker's partner, Patches (below). The neat make-up of Patches (Gary Rae) is a superbly stylized version of the tramp face.

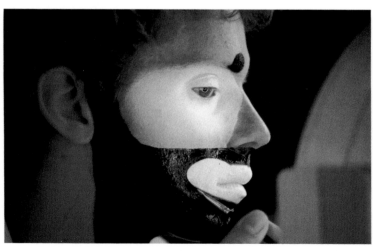

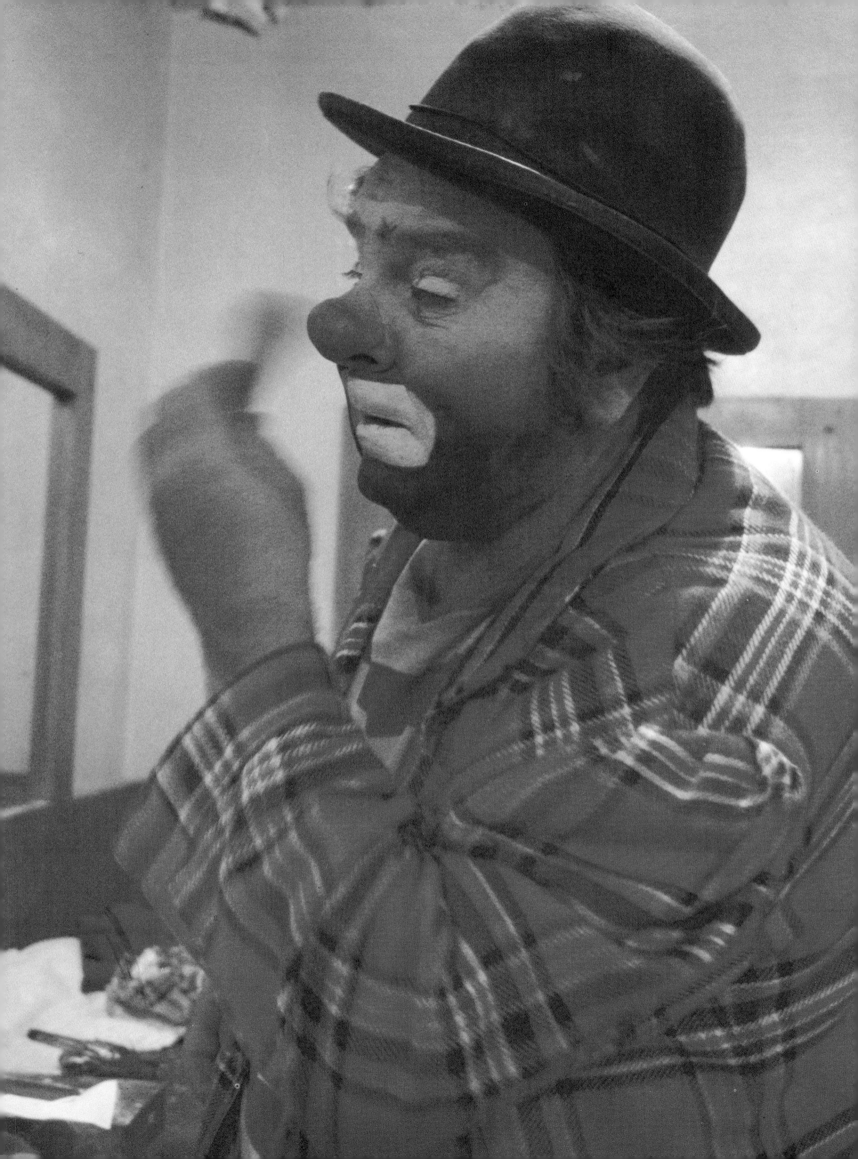

Top: The grand opening parade at the Texas Shriner's Circus in San Antonio. To achieve a good rapport with the audiences in such vast three ring circuses, clowns either produce eye-catching acts in the outside track or mingle closely with the spectators. A clown from the Clyde Beatty and Cole Brothers Circus (above left) performs a walk-round, while another autographs programmes (above right).

it down on the peanut; the result, of course would be just a tiny pile of fragments. Sadder than ever, he would mournfully drift away. He never smiled, but his melancholy figure made his audience howl with laughter. People who were not too successful themselves saw a caricature of their failures in this sad, incompetent little tramp. They could laugh at his incompetence, and feel better for it.

In 1937 he was spotted by Bernard Mills and offered a job at the Bertram Mills Olympia Christmas Circus in London. He found the English audiences a little slower to respond than the American ones, but once they warmed to him, they were happy that he kept repeating the same routine and generous with their applause. Bertram Mills liked him and engaged him for the summer tenting tour as well. When he was with Bertram Mills he used to warm up the audience before the show started by introducing a gag that had been originated by 'Shorty' Flemm in America some years before. He came on, in his usual tramp outfit, carrying a broom and started to sweep the ring. A spotlight was turned on, casting a bright spot of light around his feet. He swept at it with his broom, but could not get rid of it; he tried sweeping in the opposite direction, but it was still there; he leant on his broom and gazed at it mournfully. Then he produced a toy balloon, blew it up steadily and slowly until it burst. With a resigned expression he dug a little grave for it in the sawdust, and buried it. He had established his character right from the start.

It was while he was with Bertram Mills that he was seen by John Ringling North and booked for the great Ringling Brothers and Barnum & Bailey Circus. Here, as a special concession, he was allowed to work just his solo hobo act all through the show and was excused taking part in the general clown numbers. He had now achieved special appearances in the two best English and American circuses.

Emmett Kelly made one appearance on the stage in a Broadway spectacular, in which he stole the show by taking the worn stub of a toothbrush out of his pocket and cleaning his teeth with it after munching a sandwich on a park bench. As he says, 'I don't know what made it funny.'

The same comment could be made about his whole clowning style. Anything less funny than the idea of his act it would be difficult to imagine. His success, of course, lay not just in his off-beat ideas but in his personality. He was a truly original clown who exploited the difficulties of playing in an American three-ring circus. In such a show the attention of the audience is not concentrated, as it is in a European one-ring circus, upon the action in the ring. The spectator's attention is somewhat diffused, and he is not likely to be irritated by a bit of clowning competing for attention with what is going on elsewhere. When he played with Ringling, however, Kelly was careful not to clown during the star acts, and when he was with Bertram Mills he kept his appearances to before the show and between the acts. Wherever he was, it was Emmett Kelly's genius to develop a quiet, subdued kind of clowning in a style that had never been seen before.

In due course Kelly tried to run his own circus, but it did not meet with much success. He died in 1979, and his son has carried on his act, safeguarding the copyright of his father's costume and make-up. It sounds an easy act to copy, but it is unlikely that anyone else will ever repeat Emmett Kelly's original success. There have been innumerable other tramp clowns, most notably, men like Otto Griebling. Following in the same tradition, of course, come Charlie Chaplin and his imitators in the circus ring. But the tramp clown remains an American speciality.

Circuses in the United States had grown very large by the 1880s, but the size of a circus ring cannot constantly be altered, because the horses become accustomed to working in a standard size ring; ever since Astley's first covered Amphitheatre this has been approximately 13 metres in diameter. The only way to expand the size of the show was to put several rings side by side in a huge tent, with a track running round them that was used for spectacular processions and for clown 'walk-rounds', gags which are designed to be walked or

Below: At the Clyde Beatty and Cole Brothers Circus in Savannah, Georgia, a clown troupe performs a walk-round.

A mock horse-race takes place and in the last stretch one 'horse' takes the lead by elongating his neck to win by a 'head'.

pushed round the track encircling the three rings.

Here is a clown walk-round which was devised by Jerry Bangs for use in the Ringling Brothers and Barnum & Bailey Circus in the 1930s: a blackened raffia-skirted 'cannibal' is seated before a table on which stands a big plate covered with a lid. The whole contraption rolls on wheels. At intervals it stops, the cannibal brandishes his knife, removes the lid, steam billows out beneath it, and there on the plate looking anxiously at him is the head of a live man. The cannibal makes as if to carve a slice of human meat, but the victim shoots a stream of water out of his mouth into the cannibal's face. End of act. The show wheels on to the next stop round the track. The cannibal is actually a walking clown with fake legs and the victim is a dwarf, with a plate fitting like a collar round his neck.

The three-ring circuses presented new problems for the clowns: they needed not just individual clown acts but producers able to fill the massive arena with action and comedy. This has given rise to the producing clown, who is not only a star clown himself but who will devise acts for a whole troupe of fifteen or twenty other clowns and will direct their appearance.

One of the first of these was Felix Adler, who was born in 1895 and ran away from home to join a circus when he was a boy. He eventually came to star with Ringling Barnum. His appearance was distinctive, with grossly padded hips and buttocks and long, long yellow shoes; he wore a tiny hat and carried a tiny umbrella opened above it – the old joke of sartorial opposites. He was particularly good at training pigs, and during his career is said to have persuaded more than five hundred piglets to take part in his acts. He would walk in, carrying the piglet in his arms like a baby, feed it out of a bottle, and it would then climb a step-ladder and slide down a plank on the other side. In another act, when Walt Disney's film was playing at every cinema, he disguised himself as the Big Bad Wolf, and then let three little piglets chase him round the arena.

Adler had a good understanding of the philosophy of clowning. He explained this as follows: 'The clown's humor is based on two things. The first is doing something that looks serious, but turns out to be funny. Cutting the man in half, for instance. There is a

Below: This disappearing act in the single ring at the Circus Hall of Fame in Sarasota, Florida, includes some of the ingredients of Adler's comedy, though it bears more resemblance to European single ring entrées. One of the clowns climbs into a box; the lid is shut and the others stick swords through it to prove the original clown has disappeared. However when they try to conjure him back again he surprises them by jumping out of the box, his head transformed into that of a grotesque monster!
Opposite: Felix 'King of the Clowns' Adler, one of the first great producing clowns, during his Ringling career.

Opposite: Paul Jung was a noted producing clown who played with Ringling and Barnum & Bailey. Above: The familiar face of Lou Jacobs. Right: Mechanical inventions are often used by producing clowns in American circuses. Here Rex 'Boxcar' Young examines the radiator of his 'cannon car'. Later in his act he attempts to launch himself from the cannon but fails and is shot out of the back, minus his overalls!

very narrow dividing line between comedy and tragedy, and the clown finds it. The second essential for him is surprise; the unexpected makes people laugh.... My gags are not elaborate. The simpler the trick the better, so long as it contains an element of surprise.' Adler appeared before three American presidents at the White House. He died in 1960, but by that time other producing clowns had succeeded him under the big top.

The face of Lou Jacobs has appeared on millions of circus posters and achieved the supreme accolade of being chosen as the design for a five cent United States postage stamp in 1966. It is the quintessential image of clown. Jacobs was originally a German contortionist but he has been a clown with the Ringling Barnum Circus for many years. His superb make-up is based on that of Albert Fratellini, but he has made it even more effective and suited to the vast size of American circuses by extending the height of the head. He is a tall man, and this extra height gives him a commanding ring presence.

In his act he sometimes drives into the ring in a minute motor car. The way he extricates himself from this car brings the house down. A foot appears, which looks enormous, and then a long, long leg stretches out. And then another foot and leg. And finally he towers over the car as if it were a toy shop model. No one can understand how he got himself inside it. But he was not a contortionist for nothing. He milks this business for all it is worth; in its way it stands comparison with John Rich getting out of his egg shell.

In another act he is hunting rabbits. He sees one and aims his gun, but it is really his pet dog with fake rabbit ears on, sitting up and waiting to be shot. Bang, the dog falls over, is picked up and put in his bag. But the bag has a false bottom, the dog falls out, scampers away, and poses to be shot again. Finally Lou recognizes him and pulls the false ears off. The dog has made a fool of him.

The best-known producing clown of all is Paul Jung. Some of Paul's mechanical inventions are brilliantly clever. There is the Reducing Machine. A fat man gets into this contraption. Some one turns a handle and steam comes pouring out at the cracks. Then the door is opened and out comes a dwarf, dressed just like the fat man who went in.

Dwarfs and midgets are much used for comedy in the Circus. Another of Jung's inventions was the Atom Smasher. A clown gets into the atom-smashing box. An implement like a pile driver descends on him. The doors open and out run four midgets, each the dead spit of the original clown.

Another good act with dwarf clowns is the rocket gun. A dwarf gets into the barrel of the gun. There is a loud explosion and the clown is seen flying up towards the roof of the building. And then a spotlight picks him out prancing on the seats at the back of the gallery as if he has just landed there. Actually the clown in the gallery is a double; what came out of the gun is a dummy that is caught in a net in the roof. (The Ringling Brothers and Barnum & Bailey Circus does not play in tents any more; since 1956 it has abandoned tenting as impracticable in modern conditions, and now plays entirely in covered arenas.)

Paul Jung also devised a steam-roller that rolled over a clown street cleaner, who was swallowed up into the innards of the machine, leaving a squashed flat image of himself on the ground behind. This, of course, is a variant of an old trick in the pantomime harlequinade.

Much of American circus clowning today is necessarily devoted to thinking up visual gags of this kind. Some of them are very ingenious, but they need not be complicated. Fred Stone used to stroll round the track puffing a cigar. Of course, this was not allowed. So whenever the boss was looking at him he hid the cigar behind his back and surreptitiously puffed the smoke in his mouth down inside his overcoat. But the smoke came billowing out from under the back of his overcoat. A simple rubber tube did the trick.

One of the most amusing walk-round gags was one that Emmett Kelly used to work with Otto Griebling. They entered in the guise of ice men – those figures of pre-refrigerator American folklore. They walked round the track after the first act pulling a trolly with a huge lump of ice on it, calling out for Missus Jones to whom they seemingly had to deliver it. After the second act they came in again, with a smaller lump, still calling for Missus Jones. And so on after every act, the lump of ice becoming smaller every time. After the last act there is no lump and no calling, they just walk round licking an ice-cream cornet.

MODERN TIMES FOR CLOWNS

Clowning is essentially popular entertainment and clowns have had to assimilate current trends quickly in order to keep in touch with audiences. They moved from pantomimes and the fairgrounds to the newly-founded circus and then many returned to the stage when the music-hall craze was at its height. The circus has always had to battle against the competition of the day whether it be music halls or, as in the early years of this century, cinema. With the coming of the silent movies some of the greatest twentieth-century clowns had enormous success in this new medium. The early film comedies grew directly out of the traditions of the theatre, and in their use of acrobatics and other skills they certainly drew much inspiration from the circus.

The first great comic director was Mack Sennett. He learnt the elements of his trade in New York burlesque, with its simple situation comedies, ethnic jokes and fat dancing girls, and he became familiar with the earthy humour that made American audiences laugh. In 1912 he was made manager of the Keystone Film Company, formed specially to make comedies. He ran Keystone for the next five years, producing about 500 short comedies, which represent the first important vehicles for clowning in the cinema. Later comedians were to develop film clowning with greater skill and subtlety, but Mack Sennett led the way by harnessing the age-old traditions of clowning to the requirements of a new technology.

Charlie Chaplin himself had his roots in the music-hall in England, in which his parents had been small time performers. The influence of the music-hall was to mark everything he did in the future. By the time he joined the Fred Karno troupe he was an able performer. In 1910 he was seen on an American tour by Mack Sennett, who booked him for the Keystone studios. The famous tramp character was born in 1914. Asked to put on a comedy make-up, Chaplin tells how he wandered into the wardrobe and chose a tight jacket and baggy pants, large shoes and a small hat – the eternal rule of juxtaposing opposites. It all came about in a

A child clowns at the Elleboog Circus
in Amsterdam, where performances are
given for and by children.

matter of minutes, without any planning. The character of the little tramp evolved over the next year or so. By 1916 he was famous, and the rest is history.

Little can be added to what has already been written about Chaplin's art. He is the supreme and greatest clown, whose genius has been preserved for the joy of future generations. But it is worth making the point that this personal genius was built upon traditions of clowning that had evolved over centuries.

His talent for acrobatic clowning is shown in *The Gold Rush* when the cabin teeters on the edge of a precipice; this is the clowning of the Hanlon-Lees. His genius for choreographic clowning appears in the boxing match in *City Lights*, in which he agilely keeps the referee between himself and his ferocious opponent; this is the clowning of the harlequinade, and of John Rich. In *Modern Times* he swoops and glides on roller skates to the edge of a broken balcony railing, showing his fluidity of movement; this is the clowning of Little Tich, of Flexmore and the burlesque ballets. His ability to give life to inanimate objects is shown by every twirl of his cane, and above all, in the glorious dance of the bread rolls in *The Gold Rush*; this is the clowning of the puppets.

The influence of circus clowning is illustrated both in *The Circus* and earlier in *The Floorwalker*. The way in which he turns a clowning routine upside down may be seen when he treats that old stand-by of the Elizabethans and the Commedia dell'Arte – food guzzling. And there is slapstick in everything, but he elevates the knockabout humour of generations of clowns to a more subtle level. Added to all this, there is the gift of pathos, indulged in film after film as we see the little fellow sadly but bravely walk away into the sunset.

Chaplin's early films were all shorts. Preceding him in the production of full-length feature films was Harold Lloyd. In 1919 Lloyd saw a film of a bespectacled parson and this gave him the idea of creating an apparently weak and soppy character who battled through to success. He donned a pair of horn-rimmed lensless glasses and a straw boater and became the typical American boy,

eager and honest, but shy and innocent. The character is funny not for what he is, but for what happens around him. In *Safety Last* (1923) Lloyd introduced one of those stunt comedies with thrills for which he is today chiefly remembered. They are classic examples of clowning that succeeds by appearing dangerous. Lloyd can be compared to the Russian circus clowns, who, at much the same period, were succeeding by looking very ordinary rather than grotesque. He was loved by his audiences, and his athletic and inventive (rather than subtle or zany) clowning provided them with a fantasy of success.

Buster Keaton had a very different personality. Sad, poetic in spirit and blessed with a superbly athletic body, his face was impassive, but the finely modelled features and expressive eyes seemed made for the camera. There was nothing grotesque about his appearance, the only distinctive feature of his costume was a flat hat of some kind, but behind the apparent immobility of the frozen expression there lay a sharp intelligence and the gifts of a very great clown. This genius was expressed in the delicacy with which he built up what in other hands might have been no more than a succession of slapstick gags. Keaton's acrobatic stunts were all real, and it is this lack of faking which makes his clowning close to the traditional clowning of the ring. After his virtual retirement from filming, he did, in fact, appear in circuses in Europe.

The golden age of clowning in films was during the era of the silent movies. In one exceptional case, however, movie clowns did succeed in surviving the transition from silence to sound. Stan Laurel had worked in the same Karno troupe as Chaplin but in 1927 he teamed up with Oliver Hardy, and they created the finest double-act ever seen in the movies. It was not exactly a clown-auguste double, as they were both augustes, but they were complementary. Laurel was fat, Hardy was thin; Laurel was timorous, Hardy was commanding, and so on. They both had characteristic voices and made good use of them after the advent of sound, but their comedy was always basically visual.

A rare clowning partnership that flourished entirely during the

Right: Among the greatest clowns in the silent movies were Charlie Chaplin, Buster Keaton and Harold Lloyd, who is shown here in Safety Last *as he desperately clutches the hand of a clock at the top of a soaring skyscraper. Laurel and Hardy are seen in a typical pose from* The Music Box. *The influence of these movie clowns worked its way back into the circus and many look-alikes appeared on the scene. Opposite: Dédé, from the Cirque à l'Ancienne, is a similar type of auguste to Oliver Hardy.*

The Fossetts are a well-known English circus family. Several members of the family perform as clowns in circuses *around England today. Sonny Fossett is pictured here while clowning with Gerry Cottle's Circus.*

era of the talkies was that of the Marx Brothers. Their approach was so eccentric and original that it could, indeed, have triumphed in any conditions – on the stage, in the ring, in silent movies or talkies. They gained their early experience on the stage in vaudeville and their first film, *The Coconuts* (1929), sprang from their musical stage act. Madly individual though they were, their clowning, like Chaplin's, had deep traditional roots. There was more than a touch of manic incongruity about their work which recalls Boswell declaiming Shakespeare's tragedies in the ring, and in several ways the contrasts and complementary talents of Groucho, Chico and Harpo recalled those of the Fratellini.

The stress on verbal humour in film today has generally made it suitable for other breeds of comic. Television too has developed its own style of humour for the broad style of traditional clowning can seem incongruous on the small screen. So there is still a place for the circus clown. He still plays a similar role, although he has not remained oblivious to the developments of clowning in other media. Indeed Chaplin's influence was widespread as many circus parodies like those of Charlie Rivel bear out.

But it is useless to pretend that all is well with circus clowning today. In England, and Europe generally, there are a handful of good clowns, but in many large circuses they rely too much on mechanical tricks, and in some small circuses the clowns simply keep the audience occupied while the props are set up for the next act. In difficult conditions many do their best, but, frankly, some do no more than run round the ring calling 'Hi ya, kids'. Children can be a wonderful audience to play to, but circus clowning can and should be something more than just keeping the kids amused. Clowns are often the worst paid members of circus companies, and it is a vicious circle with poor clowns earning low pay which discourages ambitious artistes from becoming circus clowns.

An attempt to improve this state of affairs was initiated some

forty years ago in England by the formation of the International Circus Clowns' Club, which still exists. Among the measures it took was the registration of a clown's make-up by having it painted on an egg-shell, which was kept at the club's headquarters. It is a matter of professional etiquette not to copy another clown's make-up. But not all clowns wanted to join the club, and it lacked the teeth to have much effect on working conditions or professional standards. Still, every circus must have clowns, and all honour is due to those clowns who keep the tradition of circus clowning alive. And if you look for it you can still be surprised and delighted, perhaps in a leaking tent on a wet English meadow, perhaps behind a canvas surround beneath a Mediterranean sky, perhaps in some little show on a dusty downtown parking lot, to find a clown giving new life to his traditional art.

In America, the three-ring circus has both killed the old style of intimate clowning and has encouraged much ingenuity in the devising of visual comic effects. Many of these visual gags are extremely clever and entertaining, but they cannot replace the personal contact of a performer who holds the attention of his audience in the palm of his hand. Yet, there are signs that there may be a return to the intimacy of one-ring circuses, and even in the large circuses artistes like Emmett Kelly have devised ways of working without mechanical tricks in close rapport with the audience. There is still some truth in the words of Phineas Barnum that 'clowns and elephants are the two pegs you hang the circus on.'

In Russia, circus clowning seems to be at a higher level than elsewhere in the world. It may be that the more natural, less grotesque, style of playing adopted by Russian clowns in recent years, will spread to circuses elsewhere. It does not make them any less funny. The cause of clowning in the Soviet Union is not helped by Party officials who declare that clowns must play their part in the national struggle, ridicule western fashions, and generally advance the Marxist-Leninist education of the people. But there is a germ of truth in the idea that clowning, if it is to be a living force,

In small travelling circuses today clowns have to help out with the day to day running of the circus. Sonny Fossett's work

at Gerry Cottle's Circus includes selling programmes, and helping put up and take down the big top as well as clowning.

The revival of interest in clowning has resulted not just in the establishment of official circus schools but also in some more informal training schemes. This circus workshop (above and opposite) took place in Cardiff, Wales, and was followed by a parade in which the children demonstrated their new skills.

should spring from contemporary life. There is a real danger that clowning in the West may become fossilized in a highly stylized and no longer funny tradition of character and costume. Clowning does need some fresh ideas from time to time. Artistes like Oleg Popov and Anatoli Martchevski have given an indication of these ideas when they have appeared on tours of the Moscow Circus in Western Europe and America; there are others playing in the same style in the circuses of the USSR – look out for Mai (Yevgeny Maikhrovsky) if he ever comes West! But where are the new clowns with a fresh approach to come from?

In the past, clowns almost always sprang from the circus families. They were brought up in the tradition and were masters of all the circus skills. Often they were acrobats or trapeze performers who turned to clowning after an accident, or when their limbs grew stiff. They had the instinct of the ring in their blood. There are clowns playing in European and American circuses today who can count three or four generations of performers who preceded them.

For instance, there is Harold Whiteley, an English clown who played under the name of Clown Rainbow. On both sides of his family he can trace three generations of circus performers. His father was one of twelve children, who were born in nine different cities – London, Cologne, Florence, Modena, Palermo, Genoa, Paris, Lisbon and Laibach – wherever their parents' circus engagements took them. His mother was a noted equestrienne, and her mother was one of twenty-one children brought up in a horse-drawn caravan.

But clowning as a hereditary profession is dying out. The conditions of life are hard and easier money can be made elsewhere. The future of the Circus, however, may be preserved through the growth of circus schools. The most famous and the first of these was founded in Moscow in 1927, and at present houses some 400 students. Children may enter at the age of 11-12 for a seven-year course, or at the age of

15-16 for four years. As well as a general education, training is given in all the basic circus skills. Students who show any aptitude for clowning are encouraged to develop their own ideas.

This is one of the entrées which was performed by three students at the Moscow Circus School at a passing-out performance last year. Two young people wander in – a boy and a girl – and begin to play with a doll on the sand. A big boy enters with a noisy transistor radio. They ask him to turn it down. He pays no attention. They ask again, indicating that their doll does not like the noise. His only reply is to seize the doll and break it in pieces. The little boy squares up for a fight; the big bully towers over him with contempt. But the little boy, like a David against Goliath, flies at the big boy and a hilarious comic fight ensues, introducing all the tricks of acrobatics. In the end, of course, the little boy wins, the radio is turned off, the big bully slinks away, and the boy and girl gather up their disjointed doll and wander off quietly, hand in hand.

This sort of thing may seem a long way from conventional circus clowning. There may be something in the argument that clowning is essentially anarchic and disruptive of society, and to turn it into a didactic medium (even in the admirable cause of turning off noisy radios) is to emasculate it and rob it of its true character. Clowns cannot become mouthpieces of Big Brother and remain true to their calling. Traditional clowning has always found objects for ridicule in the agents of authority. But, equally, traditional clowning has always reflected the instincts of its audience, the common people. I personally am delighted that the students at the Moscow Circus School can make me laugh with a theme that satisfies the official line that clowning should contribute to the education of the people, while at the same time reflecting the instincts of all decent people at the discomfiture of a noisy bully.

There are now circus schools in several other countries of Eastern Europe and there are two in Paris. In the United States several universities teach circus skills as well as the rapidly growing academic subject of circus history. There is a School for Circus Arts in

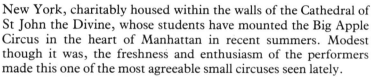

New York, charitably housed within the walls of the Cathedral of St John the Divine, whose students have mounted the Big Apple Circus in the heart of Manhattan in recent summers. Modest though it was, the freshness and enthusiasm of the performers made this one of the most agreeable small circuses seen lately.

Nowadays many clowns play in street theatre and more impromptu settings than the circus ring, ranging from amateur occasions such as this street parade in Cardiff, Wales, (above and top left) to the professional acts of Clown Cavalcade, a travelling clown troupe based in London, (left and top right). Unusually for a modern troupe, Clown Cavalcade includes a white-face, Brian Dewhirst (opposite).

None of these schools specifically teach clowning. Effective clowning is something one either can or cannot do; it cannot be taught. But one *can* teach the basic elements of the art, and this has been the aim of the Clown College established by the Ringling Barnum Circus. In 1967, conscious of the declining standards of clowning in American circuses, this great organization started an eight-week course for potential clowns. The original idea was really no more than a publicity gimmick, but it has developed into a regular institution, attracting thousands of applications every year. Some of the students are offered contracts with the show, but this does not guarantee an easy life. In 1974 the Ringling management was so disgusted with the lack-lustre performances and off-the-ring behaviour of their clowns that they fired fifteen of them in mid-season. Their sleeping cars, it was said, 'were being turned into whorehouses'. Circus clowns must adopt the same standards of dedication and hard work shown by other artistes in the Circus if they are to be worthy of their heritage.

The Moscow Circus School receives about 3,000 applications for entry each year, of whom only a few can be accepted. The Ringling Clown College accepts only fifty students from the thousands who apply. There is a hunger among young men and women today to express themselves through the medium of clowning. Perhaps they seek some escape into a world of fantasy from a too rigid and materialist civilization; or perhaps they sense an abysmal catastrophe hanging over our society and can find no other response but to laugh at it. Whatever the reason, more people are trying to be clowns today than ever before in history.

The Circus cannot absorb them all, and increasingly clowning is being practised by fringe theatre and mime groups in street theatre, in children's playgrounds, on the sidewalk, on the beach, wherever

an audience can be found. If no patron offers himself, the hat is passed round. These groups may range from performers of modest ability who are perhaps merely amusing themselves to some very talented artists.

Among the artists who are clowning today but who do not belong essentially to the world of the Circus one might mention the Swiss mime, Dimitri. He studied with Marcel Marceau and Etienne Decroux and has adopted a style of white-face make-up, with red lips outlined in black, thickened black eyebrows, and black surrounds to the eyes running down to points on either side of his nose. He can juggle and balance with skill; he is a good musician, able to play no less than four saxophones simultaneously; and he performs almost entirely without speech, only punctuating his act with piercing squeals of delight which he has made recognizably his own. His whole approach is that of an innocent at large in a wonderful world.

He comes in strumming a guitar and humming a tune. The ringmaster orders him to be silent. He continues strumming and humming. The ringmaster stuffs a ping-pong ball into his mouth, without effect. He stuffs in a second ping-pong ball. Dimitri pops them out of his mouth onto the strings of the guitar, dancing them there and producing the same tune. Then he pops them back into his mouth before the ringmaster can snatch them away, and proceeds to juggle them, shooting them in and out of his mouth high into the air. The ringmaster strikes him on the back, and Dimitri pretends to swallow a ping-pong ball. But he produces a rolling-pin, hits himself on the stomach, and the ping-pong ball pops out of his mouth again. Finally he balances, juggling, on the rolling-pin.

He comes in carrying a little chair, seating himself on one side of the ring; the ringmaster orders him away; he shifts the chair to the other side; again he is ordered to move. He takes the chair up to the little platform to which his tightrope is attched; the ringmaster orders him off it. He edges the chair along the wire, balances it on two legs, and seats himself on it with delicate ease. Then he discards the chair, stretches out at full length and falls asleep on the wire. The next act is ready, but Dimitri sleeps on. Ring boys are summoned, and lower the wire towards the ground, while Dimitri sleeps on, rocking gently as if in a hammock. In all this he adds the grace and artistry of mime to traditional circus skills. In everything his timing is measured and subtle and his movements are beautifully choreographed. Dimitri normally gives full-length solo performances, lasting up to two hours, but he has worked in the Circus with the famous French white-face clown, Louis Maïsse, and has been engaged for several tours with the great Swiss Circus Knie.

Another contemporary artiste is Victoria Chaplin (Charlie's daughter) who with her husband, Jean-Baptiste Thierrée, presents a programme called *Le Cirque Imaginaire*. Victoria plays in silence with an expressionless, mask-like face, but with immensely expressive movements, on the tight-wire, in a fan dance, or as a one-man band. Thierrée talks all the time as he performs conjuring tricks that sometimes go wrong and sometimes have their secrets revealed. The two performers admirably complement each other in a programme that has enormous charm.

When *Le Cirque Imaginaire* began in 1971 it was on a much bigger scale, but over the years the show has been pared down to the bare essentials in which mime and clowning meet. The atmosphere is half circus and half a kind of family joke, for the Thierrées' small children immensely enliven the proceedings.

In Paris today George Carl is to be seen at the Crazy Horse Saloon. He shared the coveted Golden Clown award at the Monte Carlo Circus Festival in 1979, that splendid array of circus talent that Prince Rainier brings together for a week each December in his Principality. Carl's act, like that of other clown mimes, is played without speech, but with the music of his harmonica. His comedy is created from the simplest materials, like a flamboyant walk reminiscent of Max Wall's, or his struggles with the microphone, but the response of the audience leaves no doubt that here is another performer who gives new life to clowning.

Bob Berky was originally trained as a classical musician, but is

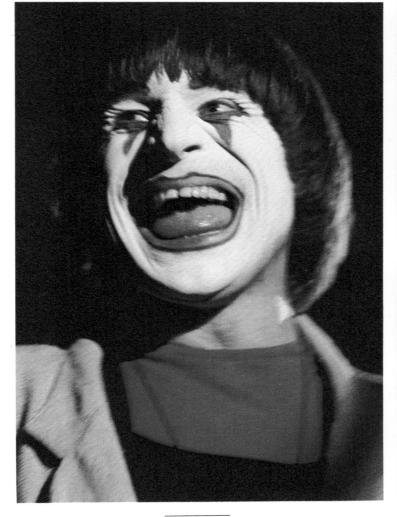

The elegant mime and clown, Dimitri, is shown here at the Circus Knie playing, among others, his famous ping-pong ball entrée. Of all his different props, Dimitri makes particularly imaginative use of strange 'musical instruments', as when he 'plays' a saw with a feather duster (opposite) and accompanies his mime by making appropriate musical noises.

Annie Fratellini not only preserves the traditions of European clowning at the Ecole Nationale du Cirque but makes her own unique contribution by performing as a female clown. She plays an equivocal auguste with a quality of pathos reminiscent of Chaplin and the other great historical clowns.

now widely regarded as America's leading mime and theatre clown. He wears brightly striped trousers with a black and white striped tee-shirt and a battered old top hat; his white-face make-up is broken by a tie-on squashed red nose. He 'talks' without words, but with complete understanding through a squeaker in a gibberish that has some affinity with the squeaking voice of Punch and other folk puppets. He has some circus skills, for he is a clever juggler and rides a unicycle, and he plays the concertina with a plaintive beauty to open and close his act. But his most original contribution is inviting members of the audience to join him in miming the actions of motor-bike riders or ballet dancers. The results are highly entertaining.

It is natural that traditional circus clowns are somewhat scornful of newcomers who have learnt none of the circus skills but merely plaster some clown-white over their faces, prance into the street (and often into the newspapers and the television), and call themselves clowns. Their scorn is sometimes merited. But clowning today is not confined to the circus ring, and among the new, young breed of actor- and mime-clowns there is an enthusiasm and an inventiveness that is keeping the art of clowning alive.

In the past, clowning has been largely a male preserve, but female clowns were beginning to appear in the 1860s. In 1869 Arthur Munby, who made a study of working women, recorded in his diary seeing a female clown at the Metropolitan, Edgware Road, 'drest exactly like any male clown in a pantomime, her face daubed with chalk and red ochre, grinning and jabbering, making ugly faces and thrusting her tongue in her cheek, her legs knock-kneed, her elbows thrust out, her shoulders up to her ears'. In the 1880s an English girl, Josephine Matthews (the great-aunt of Clown Rainbow), appeared with Barnum & Bailey as Josey the Lady Clown; in the 1890s the Nouveau Cirque in Paris boasted a bevy of half a dozen clownesses. Today Annie Fratellini has taken a leading place in the clown world in France, where she is director of the Ecole Nationale du Cirque. She charms audiences with her individual brand of humour. One of her entrées begins as follows:

Her husband, Pierre Etaix, a noted film director and actor, opens the act as a resplendent white-face clown. He performs a few simple conjuring tricks, but just as he is reaching the climax Annie appears behind him in the auguste role. She slides in with an equivocal smile, eccentrically costumed in a long, ill-fitting overcoat and grey bowler-hat, red haired, red-nosed and cheeky, male in costume, feminine in her movements, half sexless mime, half the kind of street urchin that the French call *gamin*. She captures the audience's attention by picking up a bottle of milk that the clown has brought in, pouring it into an invisible tumbler (it is a trick bottle from which the contents appear to disappear when tilted), and then drinking the invisible milk.

The clown resumes his conjuring, this time with a rope that knots and unties itself. But again Annie slides in behind him, holding a dog lead – with no dog at the end of it. The invisible dog sniffs round the ring, pauses at the ringmaster's elegant top hat which has been placed upside down on the ground, cocks up an invisible leg, and deposits an invisible offering inside it.

So it goes on, with a kind of mad poetic logic. Some invisible liquid has disappeared; some invisible liquid has been produced. This is not the usual slapstick but a type of feminine comedy that extends the boundaries of circus clowning. More and more clownesses are appearing in clown troupes today; female clowning calls for a somewhat different style to that of the male, but it has its own special qualities.

In private life, clowns are not funny men; they are often reserved, often sad and lonely. Perhaps the ultimate appeal of the clown lies in this double image. When they don the motley they become agents of a great reversal of everything that is taken for granted in ordinary life. They may be tricked, beaten and humiliated, but in their hands these things become matters for laughter, and the sadness of life is transformed. To see a great clown is a wonderful thing; but to see any clown is, for a child or a philosopher, wonderful too. The world is turned upside down. In the words of Henry Miller, 'Clowns and angels meet together.'

THE WHITE HOUSE

ITS HISTORIC FURNISHINGS AND FIRST FAMILIES

BY BETTY C. MONKMAN
CATALOG BY WILLIAM G. ALLMAN
PRINCIPAL PHOTOGRAPHY BY BRUCE WHITE

Second Edition

THE WHITE HOUSE HISTORICAL ASSOCIATION
WITH THE SUPPORT OF THE WALTER H. ANNENBERG WHITE HOUSE PUBLICATIONS FUND
Washington, D.C.

ABBEVILLE PRESS PUBLISHERS
New York   London

Jacket Illustrations:

Front Cover: *The Red Room, Barack Obama administration.*

Back Cover: *The Lincoln Bedroom, George W. Bush administration.*

Endpapers: *A patchwork quilt made of silk fabrics used between 1897 and 1901 for upholstery in the East Room, Green Room, and Red Room. (Detail)*

Page 1: *One of a pair of gilded silver soup tureens made in London by James Young after a design by Robert Adam, 1779.*

Page 2: *The North Portico of the White House.*

Page 3: *Carved and gilded crest of an overmantel mirror frame, 1853. (Detail)*

Page 5: *The Green Room, Barack Obama administration.*

Page 6: *National emblem taken from a Tiffany presentation cup, 1899. (Detail)*

Abbeville Press

First Edition
Project Manager: Susan Costello
Editor: Walton Rawls
Art Director: Patricia Fabricant
Designer: Joel Avirom
Design Assistants: Meghan Day Healey and Jason Snyder
Copy Editor: Marian K. Gordin
Production Manager: Louise Kurtz

Second Edition
Editor: Joan Strasbaugh
Production Manager: Louise Kurtz

The White House Office of the Curator

Curator: William G. Allman
Assistant Curators: Lydia S. Tederick, Melissa Naulin
Collections Manager: Donna Hayashi Smith

White House Historical Association

The White House Historical Association is a nonprofit organization, chartered on November 3, 1961, to enhance understanding, appreciation, and enjoyment of the Executive Mansion. Address inquiries to 740 Jackson Place, N.W., Washington, D.C. 20503; whitehousehistory.org.

President: Neil W. Horstman
Vice President of Publications: Marcia Mallet Anderson
Production Manager for Books & Special Projects: Abby Clouse-Radigan
Editorial Consultant: Lauren A. Zook

Board of Directors

Chairman: Frederick J. Ryan Jr.; *Vice Chairman:* John F. W. Rogers; *Secretary:* James I. McDaniel; *Treasurer:* John T. Behrendt; *President:* Neil W. Horstman; Michael R. Beschloss, John H. Dalton, Henry A. Dudley Jr., Alice C. Foultz, Cathy Gorn, Janet A. Howard, Knight Kiplinger, Martha Joynt Kumar, Anita McBride, Mike McCurry, Robert M. McGee, Roger B. Porter, Harry G. Robinson III, Gary J. Walters, Gail Berry West; *Ex Officio:* James H. Billington, G. Wayne Clough, David S. Ferriero, Earl A. Powell III, Estevan Rael-Gálvez; *Directors Emeriti:* Nash Castro, Jeannine S. Clark, George M. Elsey, Nancy M. Folger, Clayton W. Frye Jr., David I. Granger, Elise K. Kirk, Floretta D. McKenzie, Leonard L. Silverstein, Alfred R. Stern; *Liaison Member:* Jonathan Jarvis; *Honorary Member:* Bernard R. Meyer

All photographs contained in this book unless otherwise noted are copyrighted by the White House Historical Association and may not be reproduced without permission. Requests for reprint permissions should be addressed to Photo Archivist, White House Historical Association, 740 Jackson Place, N.W., Washington, D.C. 20503.

Text and photographs copyright © 2014 White House Historical Association. Compilation—including selection of text and images—copyright © 2014 Abbeville Press and White House Historical Association. All rights reserved under international copyright conventions. No part of this book may be reproduced or utilized in any form or by any means, electronic or mechanical, including photocopying, recording, or by any information storage and retrieval system, without permission in writing from the publisher. Inquiries should be addressed to Abbeville Press, 137 Varick Street, New York, N.Y. 10013. The text of this book was set in Requiem.

Printed in Italy

Second Edition
10 9 8 7 6 5 4 3 1

The Library of Congress has cataloged the first edition as follows:

Monkman, Betty C.
 The White House : its historic furnishings & first families / by Betty Monkman ; photos by Bruce White.
 P. Cm.
 "With the support of the Hon. Walter H. Annenberg White House Publications Fund."
 ISBN 0-7892-0624-2 (alk. paper)
 1. Furniture—United States—Washington, D.C.—History. 2. White House (Washington. D.C.)—History. I. Title

NK2438.W37 M66 2000
917.5304'41—de21   00-027085

Second edition: ISBN 978-0-7892-1179-8

CONTENTS

THE PRESIDENT'S HOUSE IN THE EARLY YEARS, 1789–1814

THE WHITE HOUSE

FRENCH TASTE AT ITS WHITE HOUSE ZENITH, 1817–29

THE BLUE ROOM 77

THE PEOPLE'S PRESIDENT AND THE JACKSONIAN ERA, 1830s–40s

THE GREEN ROOM 107

FOREWORD:
THE FIRST LADIES

It's so important, the setting in which the presidency is presented to the world, to foreign visitors. All the things we did so well, pictures, furniture—I think that this house should be the place where you can see them best.

Jacqueline Kennedy

When I walked through the rooms of the White House, I had a constant sense of a host of companions. I knew that I walked with history—the long line of presidents and their wives and their children who had occupied this house. Each family has left something of itself there, through some material change, more especially through some touch of the individual human spirit. I was delighted to accept for the White House a historic silver coffee urn, a possession of John and Abigail Adams, the first occupants of the President's House. It was the most historic acquisition during my residence there.

Lady Bird Johnson

We love this house because it lives and grows—as does the Nation. There is much to savor in the White House—the beautiful paintings, the fine old furniture and china, its aura of simple elegance and great dignity.

Patricia Nixon

I took great interest in the presidential porcelain services when the president and I entertained at the White House. We frequently chose porcelain that would not only complement the occasion, but also give our guests an opportunity to see the historic collection of which we were so proud. At small dinners with family and friends, our favorite was the colorful Hayes service with the assorted wildlife animal and plant designs. We used settings from the Abraham Lincoln, Benjamin Harrison, and Franklin D. Roosevelt services, as well as the various dinner plates chosen by Frances Cleveland at the end of the nineteenth century. It is a rare privilege to live in the White House and be surrounded by great history and beauty.

Betty Ford

Soon after we moved into the White House, we discovered a nearby repository of furnishings used by former presidents and their families. It was fascinating to browse in this "museum" of White House history, which held everything from a rocking chair that had belonged to President McKinley to a room full of andirons. We chose for Amy's room an adorable little sofa and chair set, which had been a gift to Caroline Kennedy, and Chip brought back a Truman chiffonier. Jeff and Annette chose the greatest treasure of all: a chair that Mary Todd Lincoln had purchased. We found three large oriental carpets to replace the long red runner in the hall on the third floor. This made the hall, with its crystal chandeliers and groupings of furniture, into a livable and elegant area—which is how our family viewed the entire White House.

Rosalynn Carter

I always felt that the White House should represent this country at its best. It is an important symbol in our country, and every morning when thousands of tourists line up for a brief look at some of the public rooms, I think they should be impressed. From White House storage we selected dozens of White House treasures—chairs, desks, tables, and mirrors—had them restored, and moved them into the White House. Hopefully, everyone took away the wonderful memories that I have.

Nancy Reagan

I wanted to have that great big house feel more like home, so one of the first things I did was unpack some of our personal photographs to put around on tables. In one of our sitting rooms, I placed a needlework rug I had made while we lived in China. George and I took great pleasure in sharing the President's House with our children and grandchildren, with foreign heads of state, and especially with the American people. It made us very happy to show off our lovely house, Lincoln Bedroom and all. We saw reflections of its history in every room and corridor.

Barbara Bush

When our family walked into the White House on Inauguration Day, 1993, we knew we were stepping into a place of history. Wherever we looked there was something that held magic from the past, some link to the presidents who shaped our nation. As history buffs, Bill, Chelsea, and I never tire of learning new stories about objects in these rooms. For me, it's been a tremendous honor to help refurbish several White House rooms, and I'm particularly proud of our efforts in the Blue Room, whose furnishings had become faded after years of wear and tear. We wanted to make sure there was no mistaking the color for which the room was named, and we reupholstered the gilded furniture from President Monroe's time in a new and rich shade of sapphire blue. The White House is indeed a living museum. Not only is it a repository of America's storied past, but history is being made within these walls every day. It has been a great privilege for my family to be tenants of this extraordinary home—and stewards of all these treasures.

Hillary Rodham Clinton

My first priority was the White House itself. I knew what a remarkable collection of art and furniture the White House had, exceptional pieces by many of America's best furniture makers, pieces that had been owned by other presidents. I was eager to start making the White House residence our home. There is a unique community to knowing your predecessors have walked these halls, have written on these tables, have sat in these chairs. And a comfort as well. We both felt that comfort in the rooms of the White House.

Laura Bush

Living at the White House is an honor for our family, and every day we feel the history that surrounds us. The White House is one of our nation's most iconic landmarks, and while it is an impressive, inspiring place, it is a home too. It is this duality that makes the White House not just the president's residence, but truly the People's House.

Michelle Obama

INTRODUCTION

WENDELL GARRETT (1929-2012)

A French gilded bronze clock made by Thomire & Co., with works by Moinet, depicts Minerva, the Roman goddess of wisdom, and has graced the White House since 1817.

The American capital in the early nineteenth century was an anomaly. Other towns and cities of the United States grew up on a commercial foundation; even the frontier settlements laid out in advance of the arrival of permanent householders usually had some assured prospects of trade by river or rail. But the well-informed founders of this nation—statesmen familiar either through travel or study with the great cities of Europe—envisaged even more for the national capital than a meeting place for Congress and a seat of the executive branch of government. Their carefully prepared plan for the city of Washington in itself proclaimed their dream of embodying in the stones of her buildings, in her parks and fountains, and in the broad sweep of her avenues a dignity and beauty that would symbolize the ideals of the new republic. With the federal city a reality, architectural competitions were held in 1792 for the new nation's two most important buildings, the Capitol and the President's House.

President George Washington, Secretary of State Thomas Jefferson, and the commissioners of the Federal City gave William Thornton the prize for the Capitol and James Hoban the commission for the residence of the president. Hoban apparently drew inspiration for his somewhat conservative design from Leinster House, Dublin, and from other English and Irish country houses shown in James Gibb's *Book of Architecture* (1728). His original plans called for a structure three stories high, but as funds were meager, two stories would suffice. Construction had begun in the fall of 1792, but when, in November 1800, President and Mrs. John Adams took up residence, the building set within Virginia sandstone walls was still unfinished. Abigail Adams wrote her daughter, complaining: "There is not a single apartment finished. . . . We had not the least fence, yard, or other convenience, without, and the great unfinished audience-room [the East Room] I make a drying room of, to hang up the clothes in." Though conditions were drafty and unpleasant, John Adams nonetheless bestowed a lasting benediction on the house, following his first night there: "May none but honest and wise men ever rule under this roof."

Thomas Jefferson, the mansion's first long-term resident, from 1801 to 1809, was not overly enamored of the building either, grousing that it was "big enough for two emperors, one Pope, and the grand Lama." A diligent amateur architect, he designed low terrace-pavilions for either side of the main building, thinking they would soften the structure's grandiloquent impression. Jefferson appointed architect Benjamin Henry Latrobe to finish the structure, and he had completed numerous projects before it was burned by the British in August 1814 during the War of 1812. To rebuild the gutted mansion, President James Madison (1809-1817) rehired James Hoban.

By 1817 President James Monroe (1817-1825) was able to move into the reconstructed house, and he ordered the elaborate French Empire furnishings that remain at the core of the historic White House collection. Hoban was still on the scene in 1824 when Monroe hired him to add the semicircular South Portico, a Latrobe-Jefferson pastiche. Five years later, Andrew Jackson (1829-1837) engaged Hoban to build the North Portico, again following Latrobe's Jefferson-sanctioned plans. Throughout the nineteenth century, creature comforts brought about by advancing technology were added, including water closets, running water, central heating, gas lights, and electricity by 1891.

The symbol of continuity and stability, the White House in reality has been continually in revision over the past two centuries—as Betty Monkman's engaging narrative so ably demonstrates. Ever since the Adamses moved into the house, first families have furnished and redecorated the White House in the prevailing styles of their times or the exigencies of the moment. Because the house was not only the president's home but his office as well, the structure endured the stress and strain of daily use by numerous visitors.

Chester A. Arthur (1881-1885) undertook a major refurbishing of the mansion in 1882, having wagon-loads of old furniture carted away to public auction, and then calling on the celebrated New York designer Louis C. Tiffany to redecorate the interior. When Theodore Roosevelt (1901-1909) became president, the house underwent another revamping when the prominent architectural firm of McKim, Mead & White was selected to survey the building and make recommendations. Extensive greenhouses that had flanked the building for decades were demolished, and interior facilities were modernized. The Roosevelt renovation began the process of reshaping the White House into what was envisioned as its original appearance—a process extending through succeeding presidencies. By the early 1960s, Mrs. John F. Kennedy, recalling the period when the White House was first occupied, redecorated the state floor rooms in the Federal style. Earlier, during the administration of Harry S. Truman (1945-1953), the White House had been gutted to create more space and to provide structural stability within the original walls. This involved disassembling the rooms, removing the internal fittings of the building, then piecing the interior back together over a steel structural frame.

It is difficult to know whether to be more astonished at the boldness and courage or at the originality and genius of that generation of incomparable leaders who launched this nation. The founding fathers formulated the paradox of democracy and limited government, and they and their successors institutionalized it with such practical devices as written constitutions, bills of rights, a system of checks and balances, and judicial review—all sanctioned by the primacy of law.

That the American cause had opened a new chapter in the history of mankind was reaffirmed by foreign liberal intellectuals throughout the nineteenth century. The French social philosopher Alexis de Tocqueville wrote: "In that land the great experi-

ment of the attempt to construct society upon a new basis was to be made by civilized man; and it was there, for the first time, that theories hitherto unknown, or deemed impracticable, were to exhibit a spectacle for which the world has not been prepared by the history of the past." America was not just one more empire but a transforming presence whose emergence at the center of history had been made possible not only by the providential wealth of a virgin continent, but by the first successful application of a new principle in human affairs. "The present year," Martin Van Buren said in 1838, "closes the first half century of our Federal institutions. . . . It is reserved for the American Union to test the advantages of a government entirely dependent on the continual exercise of popular will." Andrew Jackson's prophecy that America was "manifestly called by the Almighty to a destiny which Greece and Rome, in the days of their pride, might have envied" was coming true.

Between the time of Washington and Lincoln, America was searching for its identity to give meaning to its past, present, and future. One reason Americans tried so compulsively to explain America was that the country kept changing beyond the conception and even the recognition of its people. The belief that America was different, that America was exceptional, evolved into a national mythology of sorts. All expected us to become the most splendid empire since Rome, indeed the first true empire of liberty in the history of mankind. The principal instrument of collective progress was an exceptionally functional elite, a swarm of achievers, largely self-taught, who had earned rather than inherited their places. They were rigorously continental in scope and vigorously capitalist in thrust, this multitude of uncommon men and women whom Lincoln hailed as "the fairest portion of the earth."

The diverse, changing, and in many ways unique White House collection of decorative arts featured here vividly reflects the disparate strands of this emerging American culture. "Democratic nations," De Tocqueville observed, "will therefore cultivate the arts that serve to render life easy in preference to those whose object is to adorn it. They will habitually prefer the useful to the beautiful, and they will require that the beautiful should be useful." Romantic beliefs led artists to seek truth and beauty in the commonplace of daily life, and there is a functional beauty in these peculiarly American household objects of utility and adornment. Ralph Waldo Emerson urged young American writers to find their inspiration and materials in the "meal in the firkin; the milk in the pan; the ballad in the streets; the news of the boat"; and, as for himself: "I embrace the common, I explore and sit at the feet of the familiar, the low." This kind of art would be democratic and practical, moral and optimistic. And in that spirit, over the next several decades, literature was written and arts, both ornamental and useful, were created all across this broad continent. Herman Melville called Americans the advance guard of mankind, "sent on through the wilderness of untried things, to break a path in the New World that is ours." — Wendell Garrett, 1998

PREFACE

BETTY C. MONKMAN

I t is timely that a book on the historic furnishings of the White House should appear on the two-hundredth anniversary of the building's first occupancy by a president and first lady, John and Abigail Adams. Built to be the residence of America's presidents and their families, the White House has been a symbol of the nation since 1800. Within its stone walls, presidents have led both public and private lives, and the house has also served as the president's office and as a stage for ceremonies of state.

Today, the White House is also a museum of American history and art. Open to the public since 1801, it now receives many thousands of visitors each year. No other house in America has been so accessible. Americans always have been interested in the home of the president and first family, the historic events that have taken place at the center of American life, and in the objects and original documents connected to the presidency. After President James Monroe had furnished a few rooms, a Virginia senator visited the house in 1823 and noted that the quality of the elegant French furnishings was worthy of a private gentleman and that one room was "splendidly" done and would impress upon foreign ministers proper respect for the government of the United States.

In meeting the residential needs of first families, the office functions of the president, and the continuous demands of ceremony and entertaining, the White House, over the years, has accumulated a very special collection of decorative objects. Many have rich historical associations with occupants of the house, and several bear emblems of national sovereignty—the American eagle and the shield from the Great Seal of the United States, as well as the president's own seal; others were especially acquired as examples of the highest quality in American and European decorative arts. These historic furnishings (furniture, ceramics, glass, metals, lighting fixtures, clocks, and textiles) duly reflect and document the tastes and daily life of White House residents, who, from diverse backgrounds and various regions of the country, helped shape the collections. From Abigail Adams who was faced with fitting eighteenth-century furnishings from the former President's House in Philadelphia into a much larger setting, to recent first ladies who have been actively involved in refurbishing several of the state rooms, the residents have left a legacy. The objects in the house resonate with meaning, imparting inspiration and a glimpse into past presidential lives and significant White House events for each new first family. They are also evidence of changes in the nation's taste and technology, its styles of decoration, and an increasing interest in the country's history and its cultural heritage.

A rare American porcelain vase, one of a pair made in Philadelphia in the 1830s, bears patriotic motifs and, on the reverse, an image of the Marquis de Lafayette.

As residents moved in and out every four or eight years, the furnishings and decorations of the nineteenth-century President's House were in constant flux, and heavy demands on a house used for large-scale entertaining necessitated regular refurbishing of the state rooms. As early as 1797, when George Washington left office, Congress authorized the disposition of "decayed" presidential furnishings through local auctions, and these were staged sporadically until the last sale in 1903. In authorizing these sales, Congress conveyed the idea that most White House furnishings were to be viewed as expendable utilitarian items of little historic value to the nation. The final auction in 1903 resulted in the wholesale dispersal of most of what remained of the nineteenth-century furnishings, except for Monroe's gilded-bronze treasures from France and the elegant silver from Jackson's era, as well as objects that had come to be identified with Abraham Lincoln, and a few other pieces such as furniture from the Grant-era Cabinet Room still in use. In recent decades, many of the items bought at those sales have been returned to the White House as donations from generous American citizens, including examples of the gilded French furniture purchased by James Monroe for the Oval Room in 1817 and sold at auction in 1860.

On occasion, a president's political opponents focused upon the rich furnishings of the President's House and the amounts allocated or spent for them as a way of discomfiting the incumbent; such issues played a role in the defeat of President Martin Van Buren for reelection in 1840. In the 1860s, even a president's wife, Mary Todd Lincoln, was widely criticized for prodigal spending of government funds for White House furnishings during the Civil War.

Until the 1876 Centennial Exposition in Philadelphia increased public awareness of America's history and led to a serious interest in objects connected to the country's past, there had been little sense of the historic value of decorative objects associated with the White House. As this awareness grew, efforts were begun to identify and preserve articles that had to do with the lives of past presidents. First lady Caroline Harrison, in the 1890s, began to assemble examples of surviving porcelain from the state table services ordered and used by earlier presidents. This first attempt to document a group of White House objects eventually resulted in the setting aside of the China Room in 1917 as a place to display historic china, glassware, and silver. However, much of what was known about the history of these pieces came from word of mouth stories handed down by the Executive Mansion staff, many of whom had employment stretching back several administrations. The recollections of a White House doorkeeper recorded in 1898 were the main source of information for several decades on the origin and history of objects in the state rooms.

Increasing historical consciousness toward the end of the nineteenth century would lead to an attempt in 1902 to return White House interiors to an imagined colonial past, through architectural and design changes in the rooms and through objects made for those spaces. In the 1920s, Grace Coolidge sought to create in the state floor rooms a sense of the nation's early history. She was guided by the first advisory committee formed for

"Substantially good and majestically plain; made to endure."

ONE

THE PRESIDENT'S HOUSE IN THE EARLY YEARS, 1789–1814

George Washington, John Adams,
Thomas Jefferson, James Madison

The precedent for providing and furnishing an official residence for the President of the United States was set in April 1789 when the government rented for President-elect George Washington the home of Postmaster General Samuel Osgood on Cherry Street in New York City. From the beginning, as the first elected head of state in the Western world, Washington was concerned about setting precedents for the office he was about to assume. Before he left his Virginia home at Mount Vernon for his inauguration in New York City, the initial seat of government, he expressed concerns to James Madison about the arrangements for his official lodgings: ". . . as it is my wish and intention to conform to the public desire and expectation, with respect to the style proper for the Chief Magistrate to live in, it might be well to know . . . what these are before he enters upon it."[1]

Congress authorized funds to prepare the house for Washington and appropriately furnish it. A visitor to the house the day before Washington moved in observed, "the best of furniture in every room, and the greatest quantity of plate and china I ever saw. The whole of the first and second story is papered & the floors covered with the richest king of Turkey . . . carpet. . . . they spared no pains nor expense on it."[2] An extensive list of objects purchased for the house from New York merchants in 1789 included furniture, plate, looking glasses, linens, carpets, glassware, and china.[3] In the White House collection is a pair of mahogany side chairs with a history of use in Washington's official New York residence. Made in Philadelphia, circa 1760–85, they may be from a group of "plain" mahogany chairs purchased by the United States government from Thomas Burling in 1789.[4] Burling, a cabinetmaker and merchant, supplied not only chairs but also a wide selection of

OPPOSITE:
TEA OR COFFEE URN
Sheffield, England, c. 1785-88

Abigail and John Adams may have purchased this graceful neoclassical urn when they lived in London while Adams served as American minister in the 1780s. Abigail Adams viewed England as the source of everything elegant.

BELOW:
The United States government rented a house on Cherry Street in New York for George Washington in 1789 and purchased a substantial amount of furnishings for it.

mahogany bedroom, dining room, and parlor furniture for the first "President's House." Washington also bought objects for the house through his personal accounts, including furniture from Burling. (A desk chair survives at Mount Vernon.) He declined a salary for his office and, instead, was granted $25,000 annually for his expenses, so he retained many of the items used in his official residences. Gouverneur Morris, an American busi-

nessman and diplomat in Paris, was asked to secure porcelain and silver for Washington's table from France, and Morris responded that it was of "very great importance to fix the taste of our Country properly, and I think your Example will go so very far in that respect. It is therefore my Wish that every Thing about you should be substantially good and majestically plain; made to endure."[5] Washington wished to avoid the trappings of luxury and ostentation, but was, nevertheless, accused by his political opponents of extravagance and living in an aristocratic manner. European ministers to the new republic saw things differently. The French minister described the Osgood residence as "squalid," and a member of the Dutch legation observed that Washington had a "simple and frugal mode of living."[6] President and Mrs. Washington did live a simple life when compared with European monarchs, but few Americans lived on the same scale as the Washingtons.

In February 1790, Washington moved from Cherry Street to a larger residence on Broadway near Federal Hall (where Congress was meeting), which had been occupied by the French legation and the French minister, the Comte de Moustier (1751–1817), who had been recalled to Paris in 1789. With a bigger house to furnish and in which to entertain, Washington chose to purchase many items from Moustier, including French furniture (twelve armchairs, six small chairs, one sofa, mirrors, and sideboards), porcelain, and a glass chandelier.[7] An eighteenth-century carved and painted French armchair in the Louis XVI style, donated to the White House with a

OPPOSITE:

SIDE CHAIR
Philadelphia, c. 1760-85

This chair may be from a group of "plain" mahogany chairs purchased in 1789 for George Washington from New York cabinetmaker and merchant Thomas Burling who supplied household furniture for the first presidential residence.

LEFT:

SAUCE BOAT
Royal Porcelain Manufactory of Sèvres, France, c. 1778

President and Mrs. Washington used a white and gilded French porcelain service made by various manufacturers as their state service during his presidency. He bought this sauce boat from the former French minister, Comte de Moustier, when the Washingtons moved into his New York house in 1790.

BELOW:

During the ten years (1790-1800) that Philadelphia was the capital of the nation, George Washington and John Adams lived and entertained in a house rented from Robert Morris on High Street.

family history of use in the President's House in Philadelphia, may be one of the twelve armchairs bought from Moustier. French chairs, with similar histories, exist in other collections, including Mount Vernon. Another object in the White House from the Moustier purchases is a *saucière* (sauce boat), one of four, made by the Royal Porcelain Manufactory of Sèvres, circa 1778. It is part of a large group of white and gilded French porcelain by various manufacturers used as a state service by President and Mrs. Washington. The purchases from Moustier were the largest group of personal furnishings acquired by Washington while he lived in New York, and they supplemented the government purchases of 1789.

In the summer of 1790, Congress agreed upon a permanent site for the national capital, somewhere within a ten-mile-square federal district established along the Potomac River rather than in Philadelphia, which, nevertheless, was named the temporary capital until 1800, when the new district was expected to be habitable.

When the United States government left New York, the furnishings of the President's House were moved to Philadelphia under the supervision of Washington's secretary, Tobias Lear. The government had secured for Washington and his family the home of Robert Morris at 190 High Street, where Washington had been a guest during the Constitutional Convention. He observed that it was "the best *single house* in the City," but indicated that additions would be required to accommodate his family.[8] On the first floor were the family dining room and what would be designated the State Dining Room; on the second

floor were two drawing rooms where guests were received and entertained, Washington's study and dressing room, and space for Mrs. Washington and the grandchildren. A third story held Washington's public office, accommodations for Lear and his wife, and two additional family rooms.

Washington was intimately involved in many decisions about the furnishings of the Philadelphia house. He specified the placement of objects on the sideboards in the dining room and in the drawing room and rejected the use of tapestries or rich and costly papers, as they would not suit his furniture.[9] He expressed his desire that the additions and alterations to the house be done in a "*plain* and *neat* manner, not by any means in an extravagant style," because he wanted nothing to detract from his use of and comfort in the house and thought that the furniture and everything else should relate in style to the interior work.[10] When the Pennsylvania legislature considered building a permanent house for the president in Philadelphia, Washington expressed his adamant reservation about such a project, saying that he was perfectly satisfied with the Morris house and that he had, at considerable expense, "accommodated his furniture" to that residence and did not think it could be made to "suit another house so well." Getting new furniture for a new house was "out of the question."[11] The state of Pennsylvania proceeded to build the house, but it was never occupied by Washington or his successor John Adams.[12]

A pair of mahogany armchairs, circa 1793–97, attributed to the Philadelphia cabinetmaker Adam Hains (1768–after 1820) and acquired by the White House in 1975, may have been in the Philadelphia house. In the French taste popular in Philadelphia, Boston, and New York, these chairs exemplify the French influence on American cabinetmakers in the late eighteenth century.

Examples of the porcelain services used by the Washingtons in Philadelphia are in the White House. They include a Chinese export porcelain plate, circa 1784–85, from the Society of the Cincinnati service, commissioned for officers who served in the American Revolution and purchased for Washington by General Henry Lee in 1786, and a Chinese export porcelain sugar bowl and plate from the "States" tea service given to Martha Washington in 1796 by Andreas Everardus van Braam Houckgeest, a Dutch-American who had directed the Dutch East India Company's operations in Canton from 1790 to 1795. A border of chain links represents the fifteen states of the time, and in the center of each piece are Mrs. Washington's initials, "MW."

President and Mrs. Washington lived in the Morris house until his two terms in office ended in March 1797. There they held weekly state dinners, levees, and "drawing

OPPOSITE:
ARMCHAIR
*Attributed to Adam Hains,
Philadelphia, c. 1793-97*

American-made chairs modeled after French styles were popular in urban centers at the end of the 18th century. This mahogany chair, possibly from the Philadelphia house of President Washington, exemplifies the French influence on American cabinetmakers.

ABOVE:
SUGAR BOWL AND
TEAPOT COVER
China, 1795

Martha Washington was presented with a Chinese export porcelain service in 1796 by a director of the Dutch East India Company. Decorated with a border of chain links representing the fifteen states of the Union, the service was used in their Philadelphia residence.

LEFT:
DINNER PLATE
China, 1784-85

The Society of the Cincinnati service, with a figure of Fame holding the Society's badge, was commissioned for officers in the American Revolution. This plate is from the service purchased for Washington by General Henry Lee in 1786.

ARMCHAIR
France, c. 1780-85

Among Washington's 1790 purchases
from the Comte de Moustier were
twelve armchairs. This Louis XVI style
chair may be from that sale.

rooms" and received the public on New Year's Day and the Fourth of July. In anticipation of his return to Mount Vernon, Washington prepared two lists of the contents of the Morris house, separating those items that were "furnished by the U. States" from the furnishings and works of art "Purchased by GW." On both lists were plated ware, furniture, clocks, lighting fixtures, looking glasses, counterpanes and blankets, rugs, flatware, and fireplace equipment. He added a note regarding the condition of the items supplied by the government. "Nothing here has been said relatively to the Table Linens, Sheeting, China and Glassware which was furnished at the expense of the United States, because they have been worn out, broken, stolen and replaced (at private expense) over & over again."[13] Most of the kitchen furniture suffered the same fate, and the carpets were entirely worn out. Still, the list of furnishings left for the new president was substantial. The "public cabinet-work" included dozens of mahogany chairs, ten chairs covered with yellow damask, three yellow silk sofas, two mahogany dining tables, cabinets, bookcases, bureaus, sideboards, and bedsteads; most had been purchased in 1789 for the first New York residence.

Washington offered his successor John Adams the French furniture from the Green Drawing Room, which he had purchased from the Comte de Moustier in 1790, believing that Adams would surely want to purchase the set, but after much consideration Adams declined to do so, and the furnishings were offered for sale at public auction. The green silk window curtains, a sofa, twenty-four armchairs, two stools, a chandelier, and carpet from the room were sold in Philadelphia in March 1797, when Washington decided not to ship these articles to Mount Vernon.[14] Nothing was sold of the public furniture, according to Lear.[15]

Adams did not have the personal wealth of Washington, and the costs of furnishing and maintaining a presidential residence were worrisome to him. When the official announcement of his election to the presidency was made in February 1797, Adams expressed to his wife Abigail, who was at their home in Quincy, Massachusetts, the necessity for funds from Congress to enable them to furnish a proper house; otherwise, he explained, they would have to wait until fall to acquire "a very moderate one, with very moderate furniture."[16]

Abigail Adams had not lived in Philadelphia during Adams's second term as vice president and told her hus-

PRESENTATION SABER
Klingenthal Armory, Alsace, France, c. 1799-1800

French volunteers in the American Revolution commissioned this gilded brass saber for presentation to George Washington, but it was not finished before his death in 1799. The French government donated it to President Franklin D. Roosevelt in 1933.

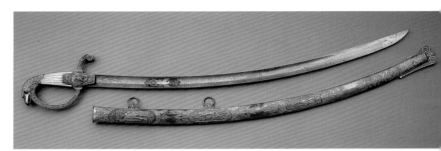

Abigail Adams sat for her portrait by Gilbert Stuart in 1800, the same year she moved into the White House. She was concerned about moving to the new city of Washington and her responsibility for furnishing such a large house. (Detail)

band that she would not be available to assist in finding a house in Philadelphia or in furnishing it and that Congress should appoint a committee to do so. "I desire to have nothing to do with it. There are persons who know what is necessary and proper," she replied.[17] She did agree to manage the household, hire the female servants, and assume the social responsibilities of first lady.

Two days before Adams's inauguration on March 4, Congress appropriated $14,000 for furnishing a presidential house, and Adams finally decided to move into the one Washington had occupied since 1790. The bill also authorized the sale of furnishings "as may be decayed, out of repair, or unfit for use," but none of the public furnishings was sold in 1797.[18] This authorization for the sale of presidential furnishings was the first of many similar provisions that continued to be included in appropriations bills for the White House throughout the nineteenth century. The sales were intended to provide extra funds to supplement the government appropriations. Succeeding presidents often sold White House furnishings that were no longer in style or were damaged or beyond repair. The last such sales took place in 1903 and 1905 after Theodore Roosevelt's renovation of the White House.

When Abigail Adams arrived in Philadelphia in May 1797, after the death of John Adams's mother, she complained about the poor condition of the public furniture left in the house. "There is not a chair to sit in. The beds and bedding are in a woeful pickle."[19] Nonetheless, she received guests each day, hosting an endless succession of dinners, teas, and receptions. She received as many as sixty callers a day and arranged dinners for forty guests. By the end of June, all of Congress had dined with the Adamses. However, she declined to receive at formal "drawing rooms" because, she explained, her health was precarious, summer was approaching, and "I am not prepared with furniture for a Regular drawing Room."[20]

Little is known about the furnishings purchased for the Philadelphia house by the Adamses since the accounts have not survived. However, in 1797, $8,300 was spent; in 1798, $1,000; and in 1799, $3,595. By 1800, only $1,102 remained of the $14,000 appropriation; much of the fund was probably utilized in purchasing such expendable items as table and bed linens and tableware, and in the constant maintenance of the house. The furnishings that remained from the Washington era and those acquired from 1797 to 1800 by Adams were moved by wagon and ship to the new capital city of Washington in the District of Columbia during the summer and fall of 1800.

The new federal city of Washington had been established by Congress in the Residence Act of 1790, which authorized the commissioners of the District of Columbia to "provide suitable buildings for the accommodation of Congress, and of the President." President Washington himself, who had been authorized to select its precise location, was a strong advocate for the new capital city on the Potomac and chose the French engineer Pierre Charles L'Enfant to provide a grand plan for it. Together they selected a site for the President's House, and in 1792 Secretary of State Thomas Jefferson suggested a

*Royal Porcelain Manufactory of Sèvres,
France, 1782*

*John and Abigail Adams lived in France
while he was American minister in 1784-
85. They may have acquired this family
service when they purchased china, glass,
and plate for official entertaining in 1785.*

house.) Secretary of State and Mrs. James Madison arrived in May 1801 and stayed for three weeks while they prepared to move into their own house. It was almost two years before Jefferson's married daughters, Martha Randolph and Maria Eppes, arrived for a visit that lasted from November 1802 to January 1803. Martha returned in late 1805 and stayed for several months in 1806, giving birth to the first child related to a president born in the White House, James Madison Randolph, in January 1806. Their husbands, Thomas Mann Randolph and John Wayles Eppes, both members of Congress, stayed with Jefferson when Congress was in session.

In March 1801, congressional debates over appropriations for the new administration centered on the incomplete state of the President's House. The furniture was "by no means sufficient to furnish it in that style it demanded," commented one congressman; another mentioned that "the largest and most elegant rooms were not yet furnished"; another voiced reservations on the amount of the suggested appropriations, stating that if the style of furniture was raised too high he would not be surprised if there were proposals to raise the salary of the president to match the style of the furniture.[36] Washingtonians also commented on the state of the furnishings. Margaret Bayard Smith, wife of the editor of *The National Intelligencer* and a friend and admirer of Jefferson, recalled that Jefferson found the house "scantily furnished with articles brought from Philadelphia and which had been used by Genl. Washington," but, she continued, Jefferson retained the worn and faded pieces out of respect for Washington.[37] The furniture added by the government was "plain and simple to excess," she observed.

A little over $10,000 remained from the $15,000 that had been appropriated in 1800 for furnishings. Jefferson also had available funds from the sale of the seven horses and two carriages that Adams had bought with appropriated funds intended for furnishings. Congress was critical of this use of the funds and ordered the sale, with the proceeds ($1,575) added to the furniture account.[38] Jefferson's first priority was to improve the house by making it structurally habitable and comfortable, and in the first few months the grounds were cleaned up and a post-and-rail fence was erected. In 1803, after two years in residence, he appointed the English-born architect Benjamin Henry Latrobe to the new position of surveyor of public buildings. Latrobe completed the main staircase, and in 1804 replaced the leaking roof. Water had entered every part of the building and "injured the furniture, exceedingly," he reported to Jefferson.[39] The majority of the $11,928.29 spent in 1804 was expended on the roof, but a small amount was also spent on finishing one of the chambers on the second floor, work that was overseen by Latrobe, who also purchased furnishings for Jefferson.

From 1801 through 1804, Jefferson spent $12,242 from the furnishing fund. Claxton continued to be responsible for Jefferson's expenditures for furnishings, as he had been for John Adams. Few government accounts of specific purchases survive, but existing records indicate that in 1801 and 1802 funds were spent on carpeting, cabinet and upholstery work, a clock, china and crockery ware, grates, and kitchen furniture. Purchases continued to be made for items of a utilitarian nature and those that needed replacement in a house where there was continuous entertaining. In 1805 at the start of Jefferson's second term, Congress made available an additional $14,000, and upholstery and cabinetwork, flatware, silverware, gilt waiters, china and glassware, as well as copperware, tinware, table and bed linens were purchased. A local Georgetown silversmith and retailer, Charles A. Burnett (1769–1848), was paid $113 for silver, and John Letelier (dates unknown), also of Washington, supplied silver tureens for $479.35.[40] Accounts from 1807 and 1808 record expenditures for painted floor-cloths and for window blinds. Most of these items were probably secured in Baltimore and Philadelphia, where there was a wider selection of craftsmen and goods. Jefferson lived simply in the President's House, among the furnishings that had been used

OPPOSITE:

Architect Benjamin Henry Latrobe, appointed surveyor of public buildings by Thomas Jefferson, drew this plan of Jefferson's White House rooms in 1803. Jefferson's office was in the "Library or Cabinet" (lower left).

THE WHITE HOUSE

32

The surrounding Ground was chiefly used for Brick yards,
it was inclosed in a rough post and rail fence.—(1803)

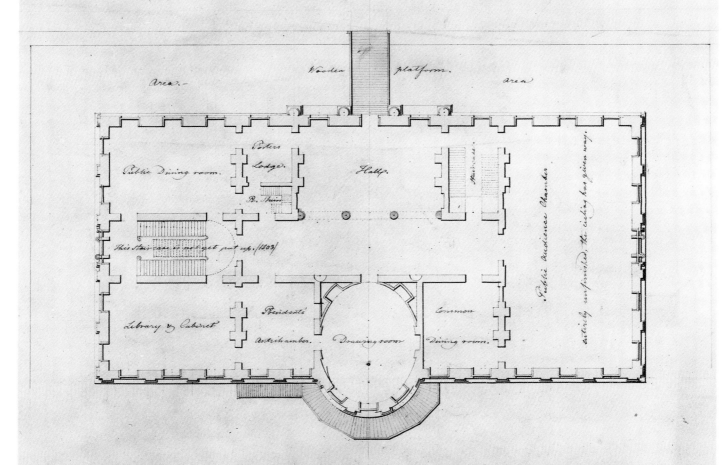

Area.—   Wooden   platform.   area

Public Dining room.   Porters   Hall.
                       Lodge.

                       P. Stair

This Stair case is not yet put up. (1803)

Library & Cabinet   Presidents   Common
                       Antichamber. Drawing room. Dining room.

Public Audience Chamber

entirely unfinished, the ceiling has given way.

During the short residence of President Adams at Washington, the wooden stairs & platform were the usual
entrance to the house, and the present drawing room, was a mere Vestibule.

Plan of the Principal Story in 1803.

B Henry Latrobe
1807

by Washington and Adams. And yet, at the end of his administration, there were many pieces described as "elegant" or "fashionable" in the official inventory. Perhaps these objects were acquired in Philadelphia or Baltimore from cabinetmakers copying the designs of the English cabinetmaker Thomas Sheraton, whose pattern books were available in the urban centers along the eastern seaboard in the 1790s. Many of the black and gold chairs listed in various rooms were probably black-painted chairs with gilded ornamentation, some in the English style popular in America in the early nineteenth century. They had been in the house since Adams's residency.

Jefferson's taste for French objects is well documented, but there is no indication that French furniture was purchased by Jefferson for the President's House.[41] In 1790, at the end of his stay in Paris as American minister to France, he shipped eighty-six cases of furniture and other goods to his Virginia home, Monticello. As his daughters lived there and he spent several months there each year while president, it is unlikely that any of these furnishings accompanied him to Washington. A French Louis XVI style painted *fauteuil* (armchair), circa 1784–89, acquired for the White House in 1972 with a history of ownership by Dolley Madison, may be from a suite of furniture that left Monticello after Jefferson's death in 1826.[42] Also in the White House is an English silver tablespoon, circa 1768–69, made in London by Elizabeth Tookey (working 1767–74), which came to Jefferson upon his marriage to Martha Skelton and descended in the family of their daughter, Martha Jefferson Randolph. It bears the monogram of Martha and her first husband, Bathhurst Skelton, to whom she was married from 1766 to 1768.

The southwest corner of the state floor, a levee room in Adams's time, became Jefferson's office and cabinet room, and he took great interest in it, arranging things according to his own taste and convenience. A spacious room, it had a long table in the center with draw-

OPPOSITE:
ARMCHAIR
France, c. 1784-89

This chair, with a history of ownership by Dolley Madison, may be from a group of furnishings Jefferson purchased in France in the 1780s, which left Monticello after his death in 1826. It is unlikely that much of Jefferson's personal furniture was moved to the White House in 1801 or that French furnishings were purchased for the White House during his presidency.

BELOW:
TABLESPOON (DETAILS)
Elizabeth Tookey, London, 1768-69

Jefferson came into possession of this spoon through his marriage to Martha Wayles Skelton, widow of Bathurst Skelton. She died in 1782, almost twenty years before he became president.

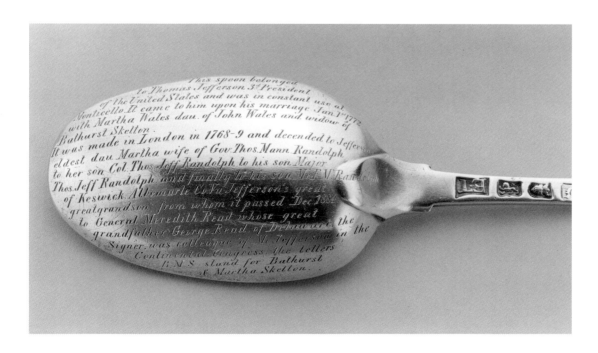

The first work of art purchased for the White House in 1800 was the portrait of George Washington by Gilbert Stuart completed in 1797. Dolley Madison assured its survival when she arranged for the painting to be removed from the President's House before the British set fire to it in 1814.

ers containing a set of carpenter's tools and garden implements. Maps, globes, charts, and books stood along the sides of the room, and in the windows were flowers and plants. By 1809 the room had three long mahogany tables covered with green cloth, two mahogany windsor stools covered with haircloth, one letterpress, a desk and bookcase, a set of mahogany steps for the library, six small mahogany paper cases, twelve black and gold chairs that had been in the Adamses' dining room, one sofa, and two mahogany armchairs.[43]

According to the 1809 inventory, to the east of his office was the President's Sitting Room (the present Red Room), with "elegant" girandoles, mantel ornaments, an "elegant" timepiece, an inkstand, three sofas covered with black haircloth, an "elegant" mahogany drink table with a marble top, a mahogany card table, sixteen "fashionable" black and gold chairs, and an "elegant" Brussels carpet.

The full-length Gilbert Stuart portrait of Washington was placed in the President's Drawing Room (the present Blue Room), where the president received guests on New Year's Day and the Fourth of July, the two occasions on which Jefferson held large receptions for the public. In contrast to the sparseness of this room in the Adams administration, it was now well furnished with four large mahogany sofas covered in haircloth, two large mahogany card tables, and twenty-four "fashionable" chairs upholstered in blue and gold. Four girandoles with glass lustres provided light, as did a large chandelier. At the windows hung chintz curtains. Although the room was furnished, the decorations may not have been harmonious, since the room received immediate attention when James and Dolley Madison moved into the house in 1809.

The East Room remained unfinished, but the south end was partitioned for an office and bedroom for Jefferson's secretary, Meriwether Lewis, and after 1804, Lewis Harvie. The adjacent room to the west (the present Green Room) served as the dining room where Jefferson hosted dinners daily at 3:30 in the afternoon, often having only four guests and seldom more than twelve.[44] Wives of the cabinet secretaries would serve as his hostess, the most favored of whom was Dolley Madison. Here were an "extra large" mahogany dining table, a small dining table, an oval breakfast table, fifteen black and gold chairs, a large mahogany dumbwaiter, an elegant sideboard with urn knife cases, two looking glasses, three large Japanned waiters, and a canvas floor-cloth painted green. The dining room table was oval or round so that the guests could see one another and conversation would flow freely. As at Monticello, Jefferson installed through the door a set of circular shelves that rotated so dishes with food could be introduced into and removed empty from the room without having servants enter. At intimate dinners, a small dumbwaiter was placed by each individual with everything that was needed, so that guests would not be interrupted by servants.[45] There was also a glass case containing silver and plated ware, such as two large punch urns and ladles, bread baskets, casters, and ten salt stands, which remained from Adams's residency; much of this silver appeared on George Washington's 1797 list of items that had been furnished by the United States government in 1789 for the first President's House in New York.

In the second-floor private apartments, six rooms were fitted as bed chambers. Jefferson occupied the large southwest corner room, furnished with a corniced bed, a mahogany washstand, a "machine" to hang clothes on, "fashionable" chairs upholstered in crimson and gold, and prints of Washington, Adams, and Jefferson.

In the Ladies Drawing Room, the second-floor oval room that continued to be used as a family sitting room, Jefferson kept the mahogany furniture with crimson damask bottoms (twenty-two chairs and two sofas) that had been moved from Philadelphia in 1800; the suite was still there when he left office in 1809, along with the "elegant" glass chandelier mentioned in the Adams inventory that had been removed from its crate and hung.

Mrs. Margaret Bayard Smith, often a guest of Jefferson, reflected that during his eight years in office, "republican simplicity was united to Epicurean delicacy; while the absence of splendour ornament and profusion was more than compensated by the neatness, order and elegant sufficiency that pervaded the whole establishment."[46]

In March 1809, James and Dolley Madison became the third set of principal residents of the President's House, but their occupancy would be unexpectedly interrupted toward the end of the War of 1812 when British forces invaded the city in 1814. The Madisons were very familiar with the official demands of the presidency. They had lived in Philadelphia in the 1790s and moved to Washington in 1801 when Madison was appointed secretary of state by Jefferson. Dolley Madison entertained official Washington in their home and often served as Jefferson's hostess in the President's House. They moved into a house that Jefferson had completed structurally and to which he had added domestic conveniences such as a water closet, and there was a substantial quantity of furnishings already in the house. The Madisons directed their attention to decorating in an elegant manner the state rooms used for the ceremony and entertaining that would be an important emphasis of the new residents, especially for Dolley Madison who enjoyed company and social life. Catharine Mitchell, wife of Senator Samuel L. Mitchell of New York, attended a Madison levee in 1811 and observed Mrs. Madison: ". . . I never

Dolley Madison, seen here in an 1804 portrait by Gilbert Stuart, and James Madison, painted by John Vanderlyn in 1816, oversaw extensive work in the state rooms so that the spaces would be elegant venues for ceremony and entertaining.

saw a Lady who enjoyed society more than she does. The more she has round her, the happier she appears to be."[47]

The Madisons expanded entertaining from the small, intimate dinners given by Jefferson to larger dinners for thirty, and Dolley Madison held weekly "drawing rooms" to which anyone with an invitation or introduction to the Madisons could come.[48]

A month before his inauguration, James Madison delegated to Benjamin Henry Latrobe, who remained surveyor of public buildings until 1811, the responsibility for interior design of the house and named him his agent for the furniture fund. Latrobe's wife, Mary, was a childhood friend of Dolley Madison, and the Madisons knew the Latrobes well. He worked closely with Dolley Madison on the decoration of the Oval Room (the present Blue Room), her sitting room (the Red Room), and the State Dining Room, which Jefferson had used as his office and cabinet room.[49]

In 1809 Congress appropriated $14,000 for the furniture fund; an additional $14,000 was provided at the beginning of Madison's second term in 1813. From 1809 to 1811, $12,669.31 was spent by Latrobe, who bought looking glasses, silver, china and crockery, furniture and upholstery work, books for the president's library, carpeting, linens, and kitchen wares in Philadelphia, New York, Baltimore, and Washington. Included in these costs was the furniture Latrobe specially designed and had made for the Oval Room.[50]

The first room to be completed was Mrs. Madison's sitting room—"Mrs. Madison's Parlor" (the present Red Room)—which was finished in May 1809. The furniture left from Jefferson's time, described by a visitor in 1813 as "elegant and delicate," was reupholstered in bright yellow satin, although another observer noted that the high-back sofas and stiff chairs had "no pretense of comfort."[51] The sunflower-yellow damask curtains had valances of swags over the two windows, and the valance continued around the room. There was also a new carpet, pier tables and card tables, and a pianoforte and a guitar. Throughout the nineteenth century, pianos were placed here, and the room was often used as a music room in which musicians and entertainers visiting Washington would perform for the president and first lady and their guests.

The Oval Room had a substantial amount of furniture in it at the end of Jefferson's term, but the room now received attention to create an ensemble effect. Latrobe and Dolley Madison expended their energies and talents to create an elegant interior in which the president and first lady could receive guests. Latrobe knew the vocabulary of Greek and Roman architecture and turned for inspiration to the fashionable designs in the Grecian style advocated by the English designer Thomas Hope, who had published his book, *Household Furniture and Interior Decoration,* in 1807. Latrobe interpreted and adapted the Greek klismos form for the Oval Room chairs, with saber-cut legs but stretchers added between the legs, probably for strength. Just four months after the room had opened, Latrobe reported that three of the chairs were broken by men leaning back in them, an occurrence that would be a constant refrain in a house in which the furnishings were in constant use.

OPPOSITE:

Benjamin Henry Latrobe was commissioned by President and Mrs. Madison to design furnishings for the Oval Drawing Room in 1809. Inspired by Grecian forms made fashionable in London, he adapted the Greek klismos form for the chairs and incorporated the shield from the Great Seal on the sofas. The painted suite, made by the Baltimore firm of Hugh and John Finlay, was destroyed in the 1814 fire.

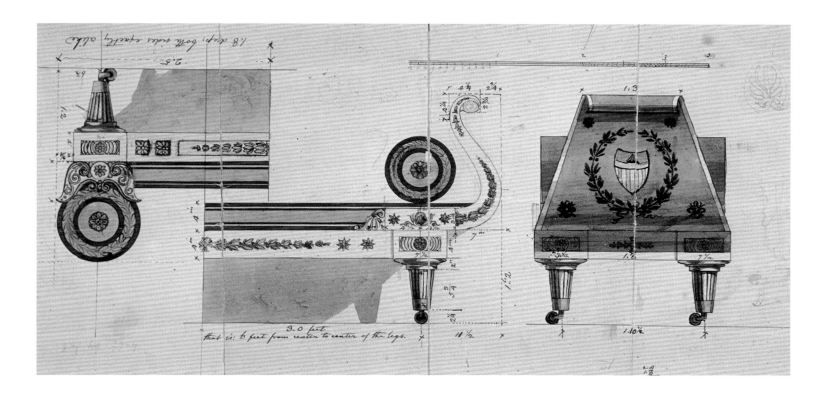

18 deep, both sides exactly alike

2.5

3.0 feet
that is: 6 feet from center to center of the legs.

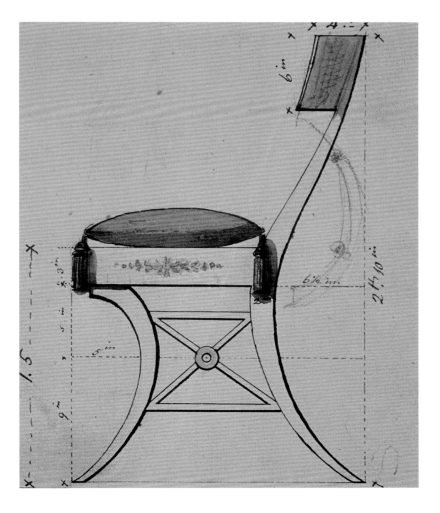

Six days after Madison's inauguration, Samuel Smith, a United States senator from Baltimore and friend of the Madisons, wrote to Dolley Madison introducing a Mr. Finlay, "our man of taste" who "wishes to have the honor of presenting to you specimens of his work, his object to obtain your friendly interference with Mr. Latrobe, that he may participate in furnishing the Presidential house."[52] The Finlay firm furnished thirty-six cane-seat chairs "made to a Grecian model, painted, gilded & varnished, with the United States arms painted on each" at a cost of $20 a chair. Two matching sofas at $80 each and four settees at $40 each completed the order for a total cost of $1,111, including freight.[53] It has been suggested that the frames for the furniture were made in Philadelphia by John Rae, but the only invoice for the work is that of the Baltimore firm of John and Hugh Finlay. Latrobe mentioned Rae's role to Dolley Madison: "The furniture of the drawing room, as far as depended on Mr. Rae has been finished since the beginning of July. But Mr. Finlay of Baltimore who has the Chairs & Sofas in hand, appears not to have been equally attentive. . . . I have written to Rae, and desired him to come immediately with his part of the furniture and to stop at Baltimore for Finlay's."[54] When it arrived, the furniture was arranged along the sides of the room with the settees in the windows. The seat cushions were in the same red velvet as the draperies that Dolley Madison would rescue in 1814. Latrobe also designed an overmantel looking glass with anthemions, but the glass was broken in transit, and two smaller glasses were installed in its place. A Brussels carpet covered the floor. The room was ready for the New Year's Day reception on January 1, 1810, and met with much acclaim, but a Scottish barrister, Lord Francis Jeffrey, who visited the room in 1813, saw a room "plainly but handsomely furnished but rather insufficiently lighted."[55]

To the east of the Oval Room was Madison's "handsomely furnished" sitting room (the present Green Room), and to the east was the large, unfinished room (the East Room) with its rough stone walls, a portion of which Madison used as a cabinet room.[56]

The third room on which Latrobe and Dolley Madison collaborated was the State Dining Room, the southwest room Jefferson used as his office and cabinet room. Latrobe closed off two windows on the west side of the room, and President Madison requested that the Gilbert Stuart portrait of George Washington be placed there. Anna Cutts, Dolley Madison's sister, showed the room to the son of Vice President Elbridge Gerry in the summer of 1813; he thought it was "furnished in the most elegant manner, and the furniture is so large, that Mrs. Cutts says, the sideboard would cover the whole side of a large parlour."[57] Lord Jeffery attended a dinner the same year and saw a "large lofty handsome room . . . with five or six tall narrow windows without any drapery or curtains. The walls are papered, the floor covered with an ordinary Scotch carpet—the chairs petty little rushbottomed articles, and a long table with a tarnished flat plateau in the center."[58]

In 1810 Madison instructed Latrobe to arrange for the first auction of furnishings from the President's House. Handled by the Washington firm of Andrews & Jones Auctioneers, the sale netted $435.42.[59] Sold were several brass lamps, fireplace and kitchen equipment, a set of china, a variety of plates, and numerous pieces of furniture including twenty-seven chairs, six of which Latrobe purchased for himself.

Latrobe and Dolley Madison's efforts were short-lived. In August 1814, British forces invaded the city, and on the evening of August 24 some of them entered the President's House, which had been vacated by the Madisons. After dining on a meal prepared for Madison, they gathered the furniture into the center of each room and then threw flaming torches through the windows, setting fires that destroyed everything in the house.[60] Only the portrait of George Washington and a few other items were saved. Dolley Madison recounted the dramatic event: "Two hours before the enemy entered the city, I left the house where Mr. Latrobe's elegant taste had been so justly admired. . . . and on that very day I sent out the silver (nearly all) and velvet curtains and Gen. Washington's picture, the cabinet papers, a few books and the small clock—left everything else belonging to the publick, our own valuable stores of every description. . . ."[61]

A silver tea service (teapot, creamer, and sugar bowl) was donated to the White House in 1986 with a family history of being given in gratitude by President and Mrs. Madison to Jacob Barker, one of the men to whom Dolley Madison entrusted the George Washington portrait for safekeeping and a major financier of the War of 1812. Engraved

TEA SERVICE (TEAPOT, CREAM PITCHER, SUGAR BOWL)
[John] Sayre and [Thomas] Richards, New York, c. 1803-13

This silver tea service with the monogram "JM" descended in the family of Jacob Barker, a major financier of the War of 1812 and one of the men Dolley Madison entrusted with the Stuart portrait of Washington during the British invasion in 1814. President and Mrs. Madison may have presented the service to Barker in gratitude for his assistance.

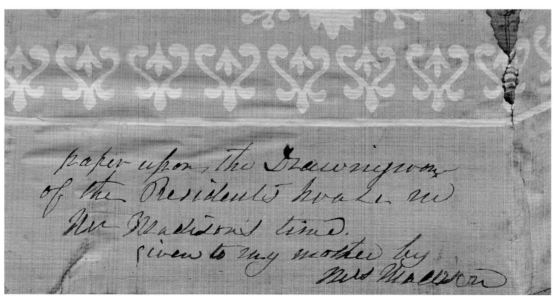

paper upon the Drawingroom
of the President's house in
Mr Madison's time.
   given to my mother by
            Mrs Madison

with the monogram "JM," it was made by John Sayre and Thomas Richards in New York, circa 1803–13. The Madisons may have purchased the service shortly after arriving in Washington when they began to entertain extensively. One can only speculate as to whether this particular service was part of the silver saved by Dolley Madison in 1814.

The Madisons took up temporary residence at the Octagon, the nearby home of John Tayloe, but in 1815 they moved to a larger house at 19th Street and Pennsylvania Avenue where they lived until the end of Madison's term in 1817. That house was furnished with secondhand objects secured at auctions, from private individuals, and from the diplomatic corps, including the French minister. The Madisons purchased new furniture, including several bedsteads, settees, and chairs, from William Worthington, a local Georgetown cabinetmaker, in 1815 and fireplace equipment, glassware, and silver from Charles Burnett, another Georgetown merchant.[62] They also bought twelve chairs from John Finlay of Baltimore who had made the Latrobe-designed suite for the Oval Room.[63] These purchases were moved to the White House when it was reoccupied in 1817 by the new president, James Monroe.

The fire of 1814 consumed all of the furnishings that Washington and Adams had purchased for the presidential residences in New York and Philadelphia from 1789 to 1800 and those Adams, Jefferson, and Madison had selected for the White House from 1800 to 1814. Many objects believed by their owners to have been in the pre-fire White House have been brought to the attention of White House curators, but it is very unlikely that they would have survived the fire. "It is feared that very little property had been saved out of the President's House," Mrs. William Thornton recorded the day after the fire.[64]

The Madisons' friendship with Benjamin Henry Latrobe and his wife, Mary, resulted in the preservation of one of the few surviving artifacts from the pre-1814 President's House. It is a section of a French wallpaper border that lines the inside of a Chinese lacquer tea box of 1811. The wallpaper pattern, with green leaves and white floral decorations on a pink ground, was printed from woodblocks used by the Parisian firm of Jacquemart et Bénard, active between 1791 and 1825.[65] Inscribed on the paper in the hand of Julia Latrobe, the Latrobes' daughter, is the following: "Paper upon the Drawing Room of the President's House in Mr. Madison's time. Given to my mother by Mrs. Madison." Descriptions of the Madison period do not reveal the room in which the paper was hung; it may have been installed in the second-floor oval room in the private apartments where the Madisons received personal friends.

Several Madison-associated objects now in the White House collection were owned by them personally and were in their Virginia home, Montpelier, in 1814. Their taste for French objects is reflected in a pair of neoclassical silver candlesticks and a pair of silver cruet stands, all made in Paris for James Monroe in 1789 by Roch-Louis Dany (working 1789–1820) and sold to the Madisons in 1803. A white and gilt cup and saucer from a French porcelain tea service was acquired at the same time from Monroe, and Dolley Madison later added a gilded "M" to the cups. Dinner plates, a soup tureen, and a

OPPOSITE:
TEA BOX
China, c. 1811 (box); Jacquemart et Bénard, Paris, France, c. 1809-11 (wallpaper)

One of the few surviving artifacts from the pre-1814 President's House is the French wood-block wallpaper preserved inside this tea box. Given by Dolley Madison to her friend, Mary Latrobe, wife of architect Benjamin Henry Latrobe, the wallpaper is the only evidence of such papers in the White House before 1814.

CRUET STAND AND CANDLESTICKS
Roch-Louis Dany, Paris, 1789

These beautiful pieces of French neoclassical silver reflect the taste of early presidents for French objects. They were purchased by James and Dolley Madison from James Monroe in 1803 and were used at the Madisons' Virginia home, Montpelier.

pair of dessert coolers from a French porcelain dinner and dessert service ordered by the Madisons when he served as secretary of state in 1806 are also in the White House. Made in Paris by the Nast factory, the orange and black pinwheel-bordered service may have been used as a state service by the Madisons in the post-fire presidential residences.[66]

A rare early example of the American glass industry is a diamond-cut glass decanter (one of a pair) made in Pittsburgh by the firm of Bakewell, Page & Bakewell and presented to President Madison in 1816. Engraved with the arms of the United States and the monogram "M" in the shield, these decanters were still owned by Dolley Madison's son from her first marriage, Payne Todd, in the 1840s.[67] One was acquired by the White House in 1986.

The responsibility for furnishing the rebuilt President's House fell to the incoming president, James Monroe, who succeeded Madison in March 1817.

DESSERT COOLER AND
SOUP TUREEN
Nast manufactory (Jean-Népomucène-Herman Nast), Paris, c. 1806

James and Dolley Madison purchased this service in 1806 when he was secretary of state and used it when entertaining official Washington and later, at their Virginia home.

DECANTER
*Bakewell, Page & Bakewell, Pittsburgh,
1816*

*One of the finest examples of early 19th-
century American glass, this cut and
engraved decanter, one of a pair presented to President Madison by its Pittsburgh manufacturer in 1816, bears his
"M" monogram.*

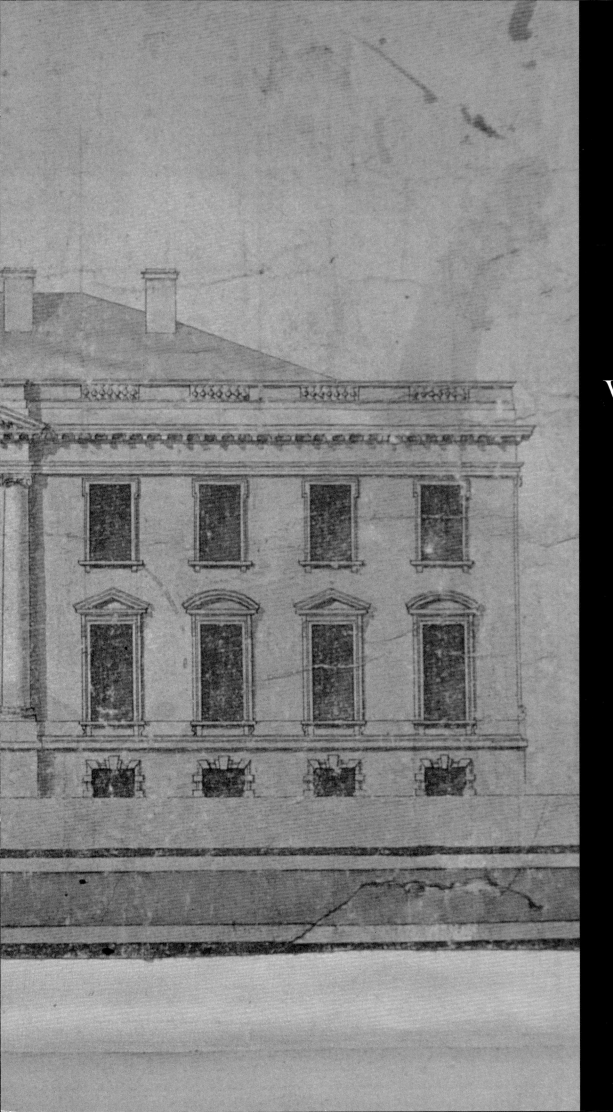

THE WHITE HOUSE: FROM DESIGN TO DESTRUCTION 1793–1814

LEFT:
Architect James Hoban's final design, 1793

By Mr Blodgett   Sketch of the North front   196 feet

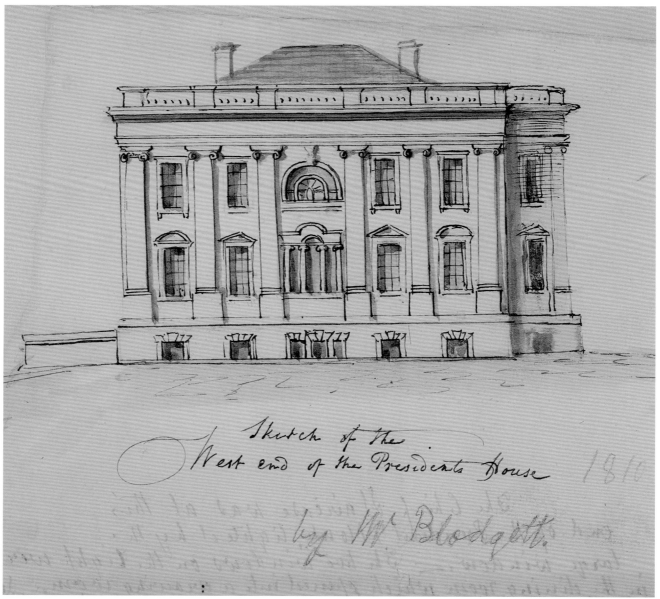

Sketch of the
West end of the Presidents House   1816

by Mr Blodgett

OPPOSITE, ABOVE:
North elevation by Samuel Blodget, Jr.,
c. 1800

OPPOSITE, BELOW:
West elevation by Samuel Blodget, Jr.,
c. 1800

LEFT, AT TOP:
North Front of the President's
House, *by Benjamin Henry Latrobe,*
c. 1811

LEFT, CENTER:
North Front of the President's
House following the fire of 1814,
watercolor by George Munger, c.1814-
1815

LEFT, AT BOTTOM:
St. John's Church in the City
of Washington . . . ,
by Benjamin Henry Latrobe, 1816

"Something of splendor is certainly proper."

TWO

FRENCH TASTE AT ITS WHITE HOUSE ZENITH, 1817–29

JAMES MONROE, JOHN QUINCY ADAMS

A few months after the British invader's devastating arson, which destroyed the White House, parts of the Capitol, and other public buildings, Congress, at the urging of President Madison, made the decision to go forward with rebuilding everything. There had been discussion of moving the nation's capital again, this time beyond the Eastern seaboard, but once Congress decided to rebuild the public buildings and appropriated funds for the restoration of the President's House and the unfinished Capitol, the city of Washington was destined to remain the capital of the federal government. In the spring of 1815, James Hoban, the original architect of the White House, was recalled to supervise its reconstruction. By the fall of 1817, it was deemed ready for occupancy by the new president, James Monroe, who had served as secretary of state and secretary of war under James Madison, but reconstruction work was to continue until 1820. Since his inauguration in March 1817, Monroe and his family had lived in his own home a few blocks from the White House at 2017 I Street (now the Arts Club of Washington). After a sixteen-week official tour of New England and the West as far as Detroit, which launched what was called "the era of good feelings," Monroe moved into the not-yet-finished President's House and held his first public reception on January 1, 1818. The rebuilt White House came to symbolize the resiliency of a strong, united country that had successfully survived a war with one of the world's most powerful nations. It was Monroe's aim to provide within the President's House settings that would convey the dignity and grandeur befitting such a state.

To furnish the house, Congress appropriated $20,000, but that would not even cover the French and American purchases already being selected by Monroe—an additional $30,000 was required for all the costs of refurnishing. The extant furnishings,

OPPOSITE:

BASKET
Attributed to Denière et Matelin, Paris, c. 1817 (Jean-François Denière; François Matelin)

Three gilded bronze baskets, each with figures of the "Three Graces," the Greek goddesses who dispensed beauty and charm, accompanied a rich centerpiece acquired for the State Dining Room in 1817. The baskets held fruit or flowers.

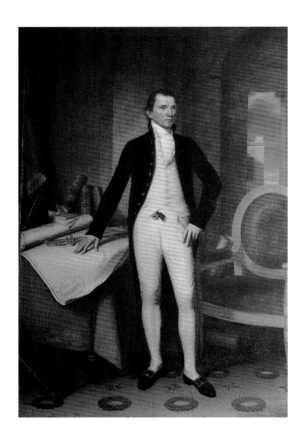

ABOVE:

James Monroe lived in France during the Napoleonic era and was impressed with the aura of the French state. He turned to France to furnish the Oval Room, the major reception room, and the State Dining Room when the President's House was rebuilt in 1817. He stands by one of the thirty-eight chairs made for the Oval Room.

OPPOSITE:

WINE COOLER

Jean-Baptiste-Claude Odiot, Paris, 1798-1809

Monroe sold many of his personal furnishings to the government for use in the White House. Four silver wine coolers by Odiot, a highly skilled silversmith who was one of the first to incorporate sculptural elements in silver, remain in the White House.

many secondhand, which had been secured for the temporary residences of President and Mrs. Madison, were worn out and unusable except for some chairs, a sideboard, and two pier tables for the dining room and a set of French chairs and two looking glasses to be used in the private apartments. What remained of the old silver was exchanged for new plate. None of the china, glassware, or linens was deemed fit for service.

Until new objects could be secured, Monroe offered to sell the government his personal furnishings for use in the President's House, much of which he had acquired while living in Europe as American minister to France from 1794 to 1796 and from 1803 to 1807 when he had been sent to Paris to help negotiate the Louisiana Purchase treaty. (During that period he also served as minister to England and on a diplomatic mission to Spain.) These possessions he described as "a small service of excellent plate, made for my own use, by the best artists in France and England" and "dining room, drawing [room] and bed room furniture, French china and kitchen furniture, all of good quality, and in good state."[1] Of these items, four silver wine coolers with an engraved border of grapevines, lion's mask handles, and sphinx-shaped feet are still in the White House. Made between 1789 and 1809, they are the work of the French silversmith Jean-Baptiste-Claude Odiot (1763–1850), who worked from 1785 to 1827. Odiot, one of the most highly esteemed metalworkers in Paris, created numerous works for Napoleon, his family, and nobility throughout Europe. Technically accomplished, he was one of the earliest French silversmiths to incorporate such sculptural elements in silver as the cast handles and feet on the coolers. Engraved on the coolers is the early-nineteenth-century epigraph "President's House," which continues to be engraved on most White House silver.

The furnishings Monroe sold to the government and the arrangements relating to their sale became the source of a long, complicated financial dispute that was only settled near the time of Monroe's death in 1831.[2] Many of the items remained in the White House after he left office, but several pieces of the Louis XVI–style furniture he had purchased in France, including the desk on which he drafted the Monroe Doctrine, stayed in his family and are in the James Monroe Museum in Fredericksburg, Virginia.

Monroe also turned to local Washington craftsmen to supply furniture for the President's House, especially for the family quarters. An 1817 newspaper article reported that "all the furniture of the small saloon, sitting room, dining room, and bed rooms, are made or making in the city of Washington."[3] To Samuel Lane, the superintendent of public buildings who was charged with disbursing funds for the orders, Monroe stated: "The chairs, for the East room, and tables, and any other articles, for that room, and the mahogany benches, small tables, and chairs for the hall, will be made by Mr. Worthington and Mr. King."[4]

In 1818 William Worthington (dates unknown), a Georgetown, D.C., cabinet-maker and upholsterer, delivered a mahogany sideboard, a French bedstead with fluted

posts, and five large dressing tables and washstands.[5] Of the objects made in Washington, only a suite of seat furniture made for the East Room by William King, Jr. (1771–1854) of Georgetown has survived and can be identified.[6] King, who had apprenticed with the Annapolis cabinetmaker John Shaw (represented in the White House by a desk-and-bookcase and a pair of armchairs), worked in Georgetown from 1795 until his death in 1854. The twenty-four mahogany armchairs and four sofas, made in 1818 at a cost of $28 per chair and $184 per sofa, sat unupholstered along the walls of the unfinished and unused East Room until they were finally covered in blue damask satin when the room was completed in 1829. They had stood in the East Room for fifty-five years when they were removed by President Ulysses S. Grant in 1873 and later sold at auction. Three of the chairs have been returned to the White House, the Smithsonian Institution has one of the sofas, and other chairs are in public and private collections. These solid, well-made pieces with square backs and scrolled arms, in the latest style of the day, are examples of the quality of cabinetmaking in early Washington. King's design may have been inspired by the gilded French chairs by Pierre-Antoine Bellangé that had arrived in the President's House in 1817.

A Georgetown silversmith and retailer, Charles Burnett (1769–1848), who had supplied silver to the President's House of both Thomas Jefferson and James Madison, received orders for silver and plated ware as well as fireplace equipment. Three small spoons by him survive in the White House and may be from the Monroe order for a half-dozen spoons.[7]

Table linens, Brussels carpets for the dining room and other rooms, floor cloths for the Entrance Hall, glassware, flatware, candlesticks, and fabrics were secured in Philadelphia from James Yard and George Bridgport. Monroe also ordered a large glassware service that included decanters engraved with the United States coat of arms from the Pittsburgh firm of Bakewell, Page & Bakewell after visiting the factory on his western trip in 1817.[8] None of these items has survived.

The most impressive furnishings of the Monroe era were the rich and elegant French pieces he selected for the President's House in 1817, which continue to be the most treasured objects in the White House. Their grandeur has impressed visitors since 1818. James Monroe was one of only a handful of national leaders of the late eighteenth and early nineteenth centuries to have lived abroad. He had admired the French Revolution and while minister to France in the 1790s was accused of being too pro-French. The time he spent in France, from 1794 to 1797 and from 1803 to 1807, influenced his taste for French culture and resulted in the extensive collection in the White House of objects in the style of the French Empire.

The gilded bronze *surtout de table* (centerpiece), clocks, candelabra and vases, silver tureens and plates, porcelain dessert service and

MUSTARD SPOON
AND SALT SPOONS
Charles A. Burnett, Georgetown, D.C.,
c. 1817-30
Jacob Leonard, Washington, D.C.,
c. 1817-27 (left)

Washington, D.C., silversmiths were patronized by Monroe and later presidents as they had been by Jefferson and Madison. Burnett supplied silver, plated ware, and fireplace equipment in 1817.

ARMCHAIR
William King, Jr., Georgetown, D.C., 1818

*Washington cabinetmakers made furniture
for the Monroe family quarters, the dining
room, and the East Room. The design of this
mahogany chair, from a suite of twenty-four
chairs and four sofas for the East Room, may
have been inspired by French furniture that had
been placed in the Oval Room in 1817. The suite
remained in the East Room for fifty-five years
until removed by President Grant in 1873.*

vases, and the carved and gilded furniture secured in Paris represent works of the highest quality by some of the finest French craftsmen of the Empire period: Pierre-Philippe Thomire, Jacques-Henri Fauconnier, Deniére et Matelin, Pierre-Louis Dagoty, and Pierre-Antoine Bellangé.[9] Napoleon, as consul and as emperor from 1804 to 1815, promoted and patronized French industry by commissioning artisans to furnish the residences of the imperial court, and many of them worked with his official architects, Charles Percier and Pierre Fontaine. The attention to detail and finish, excellent workmanship, and use of the finest materials by these craftsmen resulted in interiors that lent prestige to the French court and set the tone for the rest of Europe.[10] There was also an aura of solidness, dignity, and richness about the well-proportioned objects acquired for the President's House; many of them reflect the new interest in symbols of ancient Rome and Egypt, which were predominant in the decorative arts of France during Napoleon's reign. Designs were influenced by engravings of ancient world discoveries made during Napoleon's 1798 Egyptian campaign and archeological artifacts of the Roman world uncovered at Pompeii and Herculaneum in the eighteenth century. Designers incorporated such Egyptian motifs as sphinxes, obelisks, figures of gods, and lotus flowers and from the Romans drew upon a vocabulary of displayed armaments, laurel wreaths, and olive branches, all of which appear on White House objects.

When the Monroes lived in Paris in the 1790s, they lived very well—beyond the purchasing power of funds supplied by the government. In 1795 Monroe bought an elegant house and furnished it with his own purchases. Mrs. Charles Cotesworth Pinckney, wife of the new American minister to France, visited the house in 1796 before the Monroes' departure and noted, "Mr. Monroe's furniture is handsome, but as he ordered it with a view to take it to America, the chairs are not gilt, and do not suit the rooms."[11] Many examples of this furniture are in the Monroe Museum in Fredericksburg, Virginia.

To assist American minister Robert Livingston in the Louisiana Purchase negotiations, Monroe began his second mission to France in 1803. His exposure to the tastes of the French Empire on this mission would later result in the 1817 purchases for the White House. In 1803 the French court was under the Consulate, but in December 1804, Monroe would attend the coronation of Emperor Napoleon, who rejected the furniture of the Louis XVI period, determined to "create the new, not buy the old."[12] He mobilized the energies of an enormous class of artisans, and his requirements of simplicity and solidity were characteristic of the Empire style. Paris was the center of luxury and taste, and Napoleon's example influenced others in developing a style admired from St.

Petersburg to Washington, D.C.; among the style's admirers was President Monroe who sought to create a setting of dignity and stability for the presidency and for a government that under attack and invasion by the all-powerful British had persevered. Monroe was personally involved in the selection of the furnishings for the President's House, as indicated in a message he addressed to Congress in 1818: "The furniture in its kind and extent is thought to be an object, not less deserving attention than the building for which it is intended. Both being national objects, each seems to have an equal claim to legislative sanction. . . . Many of the articles being of durable nature, may be handed down through a long series of service."[13]

A month after his inauguration, Monroe delegated to William Lee, a former American consul in Bordeaux now appointed to a position in the Treasury Department, the task of ordering the furnishings. Mrs. Monroe had lived in France, admired the elegance of French interiors, and wore the stylish French fashions of the day, but she does not appear to have been involved in the French orders. Monroe did defer to her in the matter of drapery fabrics for the East Room and in the decision as to whether they should be made in France or the United States, but that seems to have been the extent of her involvement. Two French-born citizens of Washington, draper René de Perdreauville and upholsterer Charles Alexandre, were hired to execute the decorative work inside the house.

The American firm of Russell and La Farge in Le Havre was engaged to acquire the furnishings in Paris and was given three months in which to secure the needed items since Monroe hoped to move into the house in time for the fall social season. They found that everything had to be made to order except for an available gilded bronze chandelier (which they described as being of superior workmanship) originally ordered for the French government. Orders were placed in June, shipped in September, arrived in November, and were in place in time for the New Year's Day open house in 1818. No record of the original order has been located, but agent Joseph Russell presumably reiterated certain requirements spelled out in that order. He wanted to make sure, he explained to Monroe, to obtain articles that "united strength with elegance of form, and combining at the same time simplicity of ornament with the richness suitable to the decoration of a house occupied by the first Magistrate of a free Nation."[14]

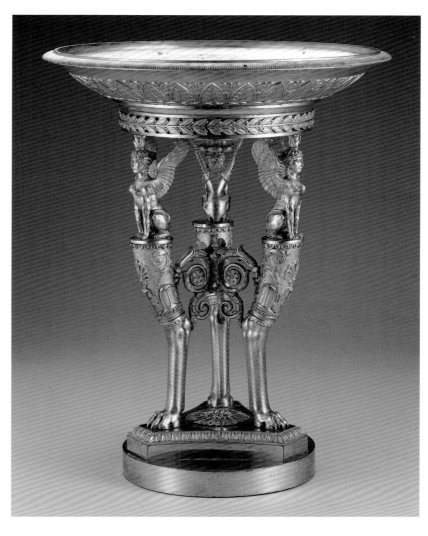

OPPOSITE:

CANDLESTICK
France, c. 1817

A pair of gilded bronze candlesticks with lotus-decorated columns in the Egyptian style stood for decades on the mantel in the Blue Room, the room for which they were purchased.

ABOVE:

STAND
Possibly by Denière et Matelin, Paris, c. 1817

Two gilded bronze tripieds (stands) copied from l'antique were part of the State Dining Room ensemble. They, like other pieces made in France during the French Empire, feature motifs derived from ancient Egypt, Greece, and Rome.

The majority of the French pieces were ordered for two rooms where formal entertaining in the President's House took place, the Oval Room (the present Blue Room), which was the main drawing room where the president and first lady received guests and where foreign ministers presented their credentials in a formal ceremony, and the State Dining Room where frequent dinners were held during sessions of Congress with members of Congress, the Cabinet, justices of the Supreme Court, foreign ministers, visitors to the city, and local citizens as guests.

The carved and gilded suite of furniture for the Oval Room was made by Pierre-Antoine Bellangé (1758–1827), referred to by the Russell and La Farge firm as the "first *Eben-este* in Paris."[15] Other cabinetmakers such as François-Honoré-Georges Jacob-Desmalter, the official cabinetmaker to the emperor, had larger shops and supplied more furnishings to the French palaces, but Bellangé had worked for the monarchy before the Revolution and had survived to work for the *Garde-Meuble Impérial,* the successor to the *Garde-Meuble Royal,* which had been created in the seventeenth century to commission furniture for the French royal palaces. Bellangé furnished suites for Napoleon and Josephine at the Palais des Tuileries and at Chantilly for the duc de Bourbon. Furniture by him survives today in Paris at the Salon of the Four Seasons in the Hotel de Beauharnais (one of Napoleon and Josephine's residences) and the Musée Marmottan, at Versailles, and in England and Germany. He continued to be active under the *Restauration* and would later be granted the title "Cabinetmaker to the King."

Monroe had wanted mahogany furniture, but the pieces were made of gilded beechwood because, Joseph Russell noted, "mahogany is not generally admitted in the furniture of a Saloon, even at private gentlemen's houses."[16] This was not entirely true, since mahogany was widely used in furniture made in the Empire period, but it had become scarce by 1814 after Napoleon prohibited its importation into France, and cabinetmakers turned to local woods. This suite, arranged around the walls of the Oval Room, consisted of fifty-three pieces of excellent craftsmanship, solid, heavy, and carved with olive branches: a pier table, two sofas (each nine feet long), two *bergéres* (enclosed armchairs) made for use by the president and first lady, eighteen *fauteuils* (armchairs), eighteen *chaises* (side chairs), four X-shaped *tabourets* (stools), six footstools, and two fire screens.[17] Cartier et fils of Paris made the costly upholstery fabric of crimson silk with laurel leaves and an eagle in shades of gold, and the furniture was uphol-

SOFA, ARM CHAIRS,
AND SIDE CHAIR
Pierre-Antoine Bellangé, Paris, c. 1817

A large suite (fifty-three pieces) of carved and gilded furniture was ordered for the Oval Room from Bellangé, who had created furniture for the French royal palaces. All pieces of the suite, including eighteen chaises *(side chairs), were arranged along the walls, and two* bergères *(enclosed armchairs), larger than the other chairs, were made for the president and first lady. Ten of the original pieces are in the White House collection.*

ABOVE:
CANDELABRUM
Paris, c. 1817

*In the Monroe Oval Room were placed
a pair of candelabra with bases having
military trophies in relief. Although not
marked, the candelabra resemble examples
by Pierre-Phillipe Thomire.*

OPPOSITE:
PIER TABLE
Pierre-Antoine Bellangé, Paris, c. 1817
MANTEL CLOCK
*Case by Thomire & Co. (Pierre-Philippe
Thomire), works by Louis Moinet, Sr.,
Paris, c. 1817*

*On the gilded beechwood pier table from the
Oval Room suite is a gilded bronze clock
with the figure of Minerva, the Roman
goddess of wisdom. Thomire, one of the
finest bronze makers of the French Empire,
often depicted mythological subjects. The
table, with carved and gilded olive branches,
is the only piece of the Bellangé suite that
always remained in the White House.*

stered by the *tapissier* Laveissier. (The pieces were first upholstered in blue fabrics in 1837.) Most of the suite remained in the Oval or Blue Room until 1860 when President James Buchanan sold the furniture, considered by then outdated in style, at public auction, except for the pier table, which has always remained in the house.[18] Since 1961 seven of the original chairs (two side chairs bear Bellangé's stamped mark) and a sofa have been returned to the room.

In addition to the furniture, other objects that would always remain in the White House added to the richness of the Oval Room. A gilded bronze clock marked "Thomire et Cie" depicts a seated figure of Minerva, the Roman goddess of wisdom. Pierre-Phillipe Thomire (1751–1843) was one of the finest bronze makers of the reign of Louis XVI and the Empire and worked for all the major European courts, employing nearly eight hundred craftsmen at one time in his shop. A pupil of Pierre-Joseph Gouthière (1732–1813/14), he was an innovator in the technology of bronze-casting. Many of Thomire's works depict mythological subjects, of which this clock is an excellent example. Russell and La Farge had trouble acquiring the kind of clock specified by Monroe, as they found "great difficulty in getting *Pendules* [clocks] without *Nudities*, and were . . . *forced* to take the two models we have bought on that account."[19] To accompany the Minerva clock on the mantel was a pair of gilded bronze candelabra, not marked, but resembling examples of Thomire's work. Each has a central shaft of a classically draped woman and bases with military trophies in relief, a familiar motif of the Empire period and a reminder of the military might of the emperor. A second clock acquired for the sitting room (the present Red Room) depicts the Carthaginian general Hannibal, after the battle of Cannae; on its base are reliefs of his other victories at Trebia and Trasimene during the Second Punic War (218–201 B.C.). This clock, made by Denière et Matelin, a large shop of highly skilled bronze makers in Paris, was accompanied by another pair of gilded bronze candelabra with standing classical female figures, each holding six lights above her head, much like those for the Oval Room attributed to Thomire.

Few Americans had seen objects of such grandeur, and visitors to the White House remarked on their elegance and splendor. "We entered a Saloon which is elyptical—crimson papering, with rich gilt bordering. The windows are corniced with large, gilded, spread eagles. . . . This is a most splendid room," commented a guest in 1819 in describing the Oval Room.[20] Another guest, in 1823, observed, "There is only one room, splendidly furnished . . . designed to impress upon foreign ministers a respect for the government, which may have a valuable influence upon our foreign relations."[21] With its crimson flock paper, crimson draperies and upholsteries, and gilded furniture and ornaments, the Oval Room was furnished to impress the visitor, whether it be an American citizen or a foreign minister. President and Mrs. Monroe received guests there before dinners and receptions and on public days such as New Year's and the Fourth of July. Mrs. Monroe also received visitors there once a week; her aloofness and the regal setting led some to make references to "Mrs. Monroe's court." The artist Samuel F. B. Morse, a house guest while painting a portrait of James Monroe in 1819, observed that the draw-

ing room and other rooms were furnished and decorated in "the most splendid manner; some think too much so, but I do not. Something of splendor is certainly proper about the Chief Magistrate for the credit of the nation."[22]

No large suites of furniture came from France for other rooms, but one piece survives from the Monroe sitting room. Described on the original bill as *"une table ronde en bois d'acajou,"* this round mahogany table with a marble top and three columnar legs with gilded bronze capitals has been on display in the center of the Blue Room in recent years. In the Monroe sitting room were placed a pair of French porcelain vases with painted scenes of the Greek poet Homer and the Byzantine general Belisarius, attributed to the Paris firm of

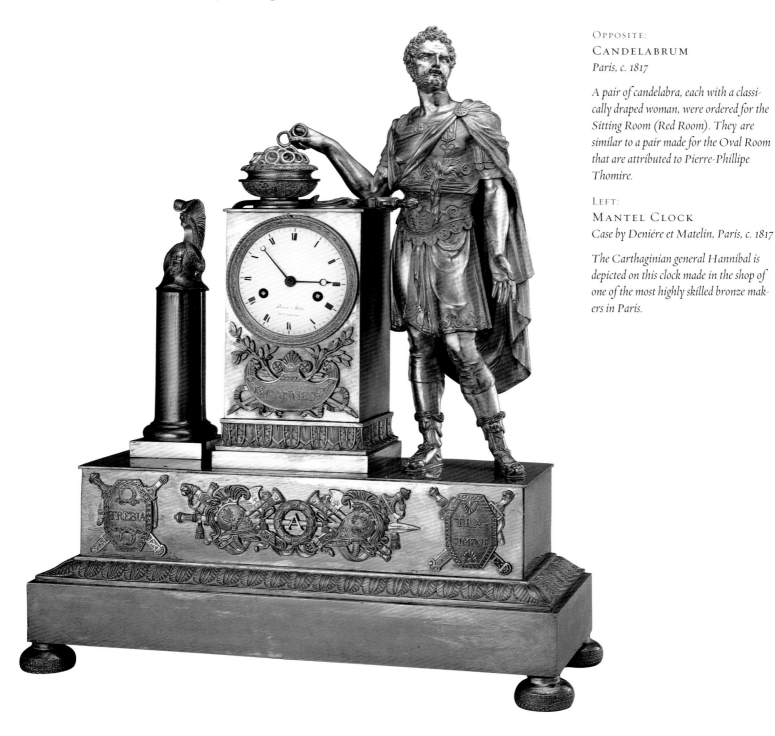

OPPOSITE:
CANDELABRUM
Paris, c. 1817

A pair of candelabra, each with a classically draped woman, were ordered for the Sitting Room (Red Room). They are similar to a pair made for the Oval Room that are attributed to Pierre-Phillipe Thomire.

LEFT:
MANTEL CLOCK
Case by Deniére et Matelin, Paris, c. 1817

The Carthaginian general Hannibal is depicted on this clock made in the shop of one of the most highly skilled bronze makers in Paris.

P. L. Dagoty that also supplied the porcelain dinner and dessert services. The figures on one vase appear to be after a painting of Belisarius by François Gerard (1770–1837), a French artist working during the Empire period. A pair of gilded bronze candlesticks with lotus-decorated columns by an unknown maker accompanied the vases.

A second pair of porcelain vases, unmarked but probably by Dagoty, were acquired for the Card Room (the present Green Room). The painted landscape scenes on these cobalt blue and gilt vases depict the house of Benjamin Franklin at Passy, where he lived while American minister to France, and another view of Passy.

The richest objects were supplied for the State Dining Room where official entertaining of government officials, foreign ministers, and other guests took place at weekly dinners for thirty to forty people. The most elaborate piece was a gilded bronze *surtout de table* centerpiece, or plateau, for the dining room table made by Denière et Matelin. These long, rectangular pieces were in vogue at official residences in France at that time, and two rare American-made silver plateaus (one in the White House) were made by the New York silversmith John W. Forbes in the 1820s. Reflected in the mirrored base of the French plateau are sixteen classical female figures holding crowns for candles and standing on globes mounted on pedestals within a gallery of fruit and vine leaves with figures of Bacchus and Bacchantes. When extended to its full length, the plateau measures more than fourteen feet. The plateau bears the mark of Denière et Matelin, and an existing drawing of a design for a centerpiece attributed to the firm

CENTER TABLE
France, c. 1817

French tables in this form were copied in America. This table, one of only two mahogany pieces ordered from France in 1817, clearly matches a table described as being in the Sitting Room (Red Room).

LEFT:

VASES
Paris, c. 1817

The landscape scenes on these cobalt blue vases show the house of Benjamin Franklin at Passy where he lived while American minister to France, and a view from Passy. They were ordered for the Card Room (Green Room).

BOTTOM:

VASES
Paris, c. 1817

The Greek poet Homer (left) and the Byzantine general Belisarius (right) appear on these vases that may have been made by the Paris firm of P. L. Dagoty, which produced a dinner and dessert service for the President's House in 1817. Swans (on the handles) were used often on French Empire objects.

FAR LEFT:

PLATEAU

Denière et Matelin, Paris, c. 1817

The gilded bronze surtout de table centerpiece or plateau, over 14 feet in length, impressed White House dinner guests; few Americans had seen such an elegant piece, although they were in vogue in France (detail, above). Charles Percier, Napoleon's architect, may have designed the plateau with its gallery of fruit and vines and figures of Bacchus and Bacchantes.

LEFT:

PLATEAU

JOHN W. FORBES, NEW YORK, 1820–25

American-made plateaus were rare. This is one of two silver plateaus (detail) with neoclassical motifs by Forbes.

has many similarities to the White House piece.[23] Three gilded bronze baskets to hold fruit or flowers, each with figures of the Three Graces, a pair of "Etruscan" shaped vases ornamented with garlands of flowers, and a pair of *trepieds* (stands) with sphinx-shaped legs, described as copied from "l'antique," were part of the plateau ensemble and continue to be displayed together. A congressman who attended a dinner in 1818 exclaimed that the plateau was "the most elegant thing that I ever saw. . . . The whole had a most pleasing and brilliant effect and as you looked across the table you saw in the mirror the ladies and gentlemen who were sitting opposite you with their faces inverted."[24] Another dinner guest in 1823 noted that the plateau was covered with vases containing artificial flowers and that the large size of the plateau "left room only for a string of insignificant side dishes."[25]

Little of the Monroe silver, which included six dozen fluted place settings, remains in the White House, except for two elegant soup tureens with eagle finials on the lids and borders with scenes of classical musicians in relief made by Jacques-Henri Fauconnier (1776–1839), who was described by Joseph Russell as an excellent artist and honest man who had worked under Odiot. A service of *vermeil* (silver gilt) flatware for thirty-six was ordered, but only a few pearl-handled fruit knives with gilded coats of arms, made by J. B. Boitin, have survived. They have been reproduced over the years for use at state luncheons and dinners.

The Monroes' gilt porcelain dinner service for thirty people is no longer in the White House and cannot be identified elsewhere, but pieces from the dessert service made by P. L. Dagoty and Edouard Honoré are in the White House and other collections. The Monroe agents in France commented that all the manufacturers in Paris competed for this order. The variety of forms in the service indicate the elaborateness of dessert services produced in the early nineteenth century. The pieces are decorated with an amaranth border, a color admired by the Bonapartes as symbolic of immortality, and vignettes representing agriculture, commerce, art, science, and strength; a spread-wing eagle with a shield from the arms of the United States graces the center of each plate. Many other objects from Monroe's French purchases have long since disappeared from the White House. They included chandeliers, wall sconces, lamps, looking glasses, fireplace sets, and a piano made by Sebastian Erard (1752–1831). Five cartons of French wallpapers were received, and a green carpet with the arms of the United States in the center was specially made by Roger & Sallandrouze of Paris for the Oval Room. Among the lasting architectural elements that remain from the Monroe era are two Italian Carrara marble neoclassical mantels with female column supports, originally installed in the State Dining Room in 1819 but moved to the Red and Green Rooms in 1902.

William Lee, the government agent who aided President Monroe in securing these items, defended the costs incurred, noting that the articles from France were of the

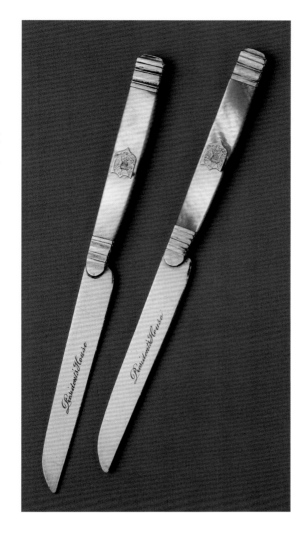

OPPOSITE:

SOUP TUREEN
Jacques-Henri Fauconnier, Paris,
c. 1817

Fauconnier, one of the silversmiths favored by Napoleon, produced two elegant tureens for Monroe. Classical musicians appear in relief in the border; an American eagle finial perches atop the cover.

ABOVE:

FRUIT KNIVES
J. B. Boitin, Paris, c. 1817

A gilded flatware service for thirty-six was ordered in 1817. These knives with small shields engraved with an American eagle have been reproduced for continuous use.

DESSERT PLATE, DESSERT
COOLER, BASKET
*Pierre-Louis Dagoty and Edouard
Honoré, Paris, c. 1817*

*A dessert service with a variety of forms,
made for thirty people, was decorated
with an amaranth border, a color
admired by the Bonapartes as symbolic of
immortality, and vignettes representing
agriculture, commerce, art, science, and
strength.*

"very first quality, and so substantial that some of them will last and be handsome for 20 years or more." He continued: "... in furnishing a government house, care should be taken to purchase substantial heavy furniture, which should always remain in its place and form as it were a part of the house, such as could be handed down through a succession of Presidents, suited to the dignity and character of the nation ... the convenience, solidity, and usefulness of the public furniture has a decided preference."[26] The objects that survived have indeed retained their fine quality and continue to be among the historic treasures of the home of the President of the United States.

Monroe recognized the necessity of committing the care of the furnishings to a public agent and urged Congress to assign that duty to the office of the superintendent of public buildings. That officer and his successors became responsible for the care and accountability of the public property in the White House. Congress passed a resolution requiring an inventory to be taken at the end of the Monroe administration, and it was completed in March 1825 before President John Quincy Adams and Mrs. Adams moved in. This inventory indicates that the house was fully furnished, although it was noted that there were card tables, bureaus, chairs, stools, fire screens, lamps, fabrics, china, and silver broken, injured, or damaged, and that the carpets were "much worn."[27]

The Adamses were shocked by the condition of the house and its contents and delayed moving into the house for more than a month after the inauguration. Congress appropriated $14,000 for the new administration to furnish the house (a year later, an additional $6,000 was made available), and Adams turned to some of the same local craftsmen who had received commissions from Monroe, such as the Georgetown cabinetmaker William Worthington, for a small writing desk, a bureau, a mahogany washstand and knife box, and two bedsteads; his apprentice Benjamin Belt, for two high-post bedsteads; and silversmith Charles Burnett, for plated ware and a looking glass. From Philadelphia came lamps from Fletcher & Gardiner and Gardiner & Veron and twenty mahogany chairs and a "conversation" table from M.[Michael] Bouvier (1792–1874), the French-born cabinetmaker who was the great-grandfather of future first lady Jacqueline Bouvier Kennedy. Washington cabinetmaker Henry V. Hill supplied a pair of French bureaus, wardrobes, and fourteen cherry chairs, and from Baltimore cabinetmaker John Needles (1786–1878) came a mahogany secretary and bookcase. One dozen green "fancy" chairs were ordered from A.[Aloysius] Clements, a Washington cabinetmaker who advertised "Cane and Rush Seat Fancy Chairs" for sale at his Pennsylvania Avenue shop three blocks from the White House.[28] Other items were purchased at auctions and private sales in the city. New curtains, upholsteries, and carpeting were installed throughout the house.[29] Yet in 1827, a visitor to Adams's southeast corner office on the second floor remarked that that part of the house was not very splendid and that the furniture was "mostly old and plain."[30]

Adams was very aware of the problems caused by Monroe's financial difficulties with his personal and government accounts, and he delegated control of his accounts to

LEFT:
William J. Clinton administration, 1999

BELOW:
*Earliest image of the Blue Room,
United States Magazine, September 1856*

RIGHT, ABOVE:
Ulysses S. Grant administration, 1870

RIGHT, BELOW:
The Colonial Revival style,
William McKinley administration, 1900

OPPOSITE, ABOVE:
Blue Room, The White House,
by Charles Bittinger,
Theodore Roosevelt administration, 1903

OPPOSITE, BELOW:
William J. Clinton administration, 1995

"Everything announces the august simplicity of our government."

THREE

THE PEOPLE'S PRESIDENT AND THE JACKSONIAN ERA, 1830S–40S

Andrew Jackson, Martin Van Buren, William Henry Harrison, John Tyler, James K. Polk

Duing the eight years of Andrew Jackson's presidency, objects of the highest quality were purchased for the President's House, and many are still there. Furniture made in Philadelphia by the French émigré Antoine-Gabriel Quervelle for the East Room, glassware from the Pittsburgh firm of Bakewell, Page & Bakewell, and silver by noted French silversmiths Martin-Guillaume Biennais and Jacques-Henri Fauconnier are among the treasures of the White House collection. There is some irony in their auspices and their survival. The inaugural reception at the President's House for the new president on March 4, 1829, did not augur well for the preservation of valued furnishings. As the candidate of the common man and first president from the West, Andrew Jackson attracted throngs of supporters to Washington for his inauguration. After the ceremony at the Capitol, everyone descended on the President's House, creating such a crowd that there was total chaos; Jackson had to be rescued through a window from the crush of people wanting to greet him personally. Washingtonians, accustomed to more controlled receptions, were aghast. Margaret Bayard Smith, a keen observer of the Washington social scene who had lived in the city for almost thirty years and was no Jacksonian democrat, commented that "the whole house had been inundated by the rabble mob. . . Ladies and gentlemen, only had been expected at this Levee, not the people en masse. But it was the People's day, and the People's President and the People would rule."¹ A more sympathetic view was reported in a local newspaper, the *National Intelligencer* of March 6, 1829: "At the mansion of the President, the Sovereign People were a little uproarious, indeed, but it was any thing but a malicious spirit." Glass and china were broken in the struggle to get refreshments, and men with "boots heavy with

OPPOSITE:
WINE GLASS, CELERY GLASS, AND WATER BOTTLE, *Bakewell, Page & Bakewell, Pittsburgh, Pennsylvania, 1829-30, and/or unidentified American glass houses, c. 1833-46*

In 1829, Andrew Jackson ordered a 425-piece state service of "richest cut" glassware from the Pittsburgh firm that had made a service for James Monroe in 1818.

mud" stood on the "damask satin-covered chairs" to see Jackson.[2] Finally, the floor-length windows were opened to allow people to exit onto the lawn where punch and liquor were placed to relieve the congestion inside the house.

A week later Jackson took up residence in the house. His beloved wife, Rachel, had died in December 1828, several weeks after his election, but other family members and friends accompanied him to Washington and to the President's House. His nephew, Andrew Donelson, served as his private secretary and brought his twenty-year-old wife, Emily, and their three-year-old son. Three of the Donelson children would be born in the White House. Emily assumed the role of White House hostess, to be assisted later by Sarah Yorke Jackson who married Andrew Jackson, Jr., Jackson's adopted son, in 1831. He succeeded Andrew Donelson as Jackson's secretary in 1836, the year Emily died, and Sarah Jackson assumed her responsibilities of running the household and preparing for Jackson's eventual return to his Tennessee home, The Hermitage.

In 1829 there were other Tennesseans and friends living in the President's House. Nineteen-year-old Mary Eastin, a friend of Emily Donelson and a ward of Jackson's, stayed until her marriage in 1832. The artist Ralph Earl, married to Rachel Jackson's niece, moved in, as did Major William B. Lewis, an old friend and political advisor appointed by Jackson to a position at the Treasury, and to whom Jackson delegated responsibility for overseeing the furnishing of the house. African-American servants from The Hermitage completed the household.

The day before the inauguration, Congress appropriated $14,000 for furnishings, and the money was immediately put to use to refurbish the interior and replace broken glass and china after the tumultuous inaugural reception. Major Lewis, in March, bought four-and-a-half dozen punch tumblers, two dozen wine glasses, and other glassware from Michael Shanks, who operated a wholesale and retail china store on Pennsylvania Avenue, and, in April, nine dozen wine glasses, two dozen cordial glasses, and eight dozen tumblers were ordered from the same merchant.[3] Several pieces of furniture were repaired, and common tableware was purchased.

The White House into which Jackson moved was not yet fully finished. Construction of the North Portico, under the direction of White House architect James Hoban, was under way and completed in the first year of Jackson's term. The prime interior space that remained unfinished was the East Room, the largest room in the house, which Hoban had designed as the major audience or reception room. In 1818 after the house had been rebuilt following the 1814 fire, Hoban had had the walls plastered and installed a plaster frieze of gilded anthemia, and James Monroe commissioned a suite of mahogany furniture for the room from William King of Georgetown. These twenty-four chairs and four sofas still stood unupholstered against the walls of the room in 1829, for the space was not in any condition to be used for entertaining, although from time to time overflow crowds were admitted and it was used for dancing. For over ten years it had served as a storage or catch-all room, and the doors remained closed most of the time. A

Scottish visitor in 1828 saw the room "entirely unfurnished and bare. Even the walls were left in their unpainted plaster. Here was a degree of republican simplicity beyond what I should have expected, as it seemed out of character with what I saw elsewhere. . . . Congress asked 'what was the use of spending so much public money, when people could dance as well, or even better, in the empty room, than in one crowded with furniture.'"[4]

In 1826 Congress had approved spending $6,000 to "finish the large room," but the money was not made available until 1827 and appears to have been spent by John Quincy Adams on other repairs. With sufficient funds for the work to begin in 1829, Major Lewis, as Jackson's agent, took charge and turned to Philadelphia to the French-born Louis Veron who had a "Fancy hardware etc. store" on Chestnut Street. Veron's shop was one of a new type of furniture supplier where customers could choose from among a variety of goods on display rather than have to order objects directly from a cabinetmaker or manufacturer. How Veron came to be recommended to the White House is unknown, but he handled the entire East Room project, supplying lemon-colored wallpaper with a cloth border, seven sets of light blue moreen curtains with yellow draperies surmounted by gilt eagle cornices, 498 yards of fawn, blue-and-yellow Brussels carpet with a red border, mahogany furniture by Quervelle, overmantel mirrors in "rich" gilt frames, and fireplace equipment. A variety of fashionable lighting fixtures included astral and mantel lamps, gilt bronze wall brackets, and three eighteen-light cut-glass chandeliers. The chandeliers received much comment when the room opened in December 1829. Their style "is entirely new; the color of the glass and cutting perhaps *exceed any thing of the kind ever seen*."[5] The splendid chandeliers "give the appearance of a rich and consistent style of decoration and finish," recounted one astute observer.[6] There is no record of the manufacturer of the East Room's first set of chandeliers. They were replaced by Veron with another more costly set in 1834, which graced the room until 1873. (The original chandeliers were placed in the two dining rooms.)

The only objects from the East Room that have survived from this period in the White House are the three monumental mahogany center tables, with black-and-gold marble slabs inset into the tops, and one of the four pier tables, all made by Anthony Quervelle and bearing his Philadelphia label. French-born Antoine-Gabriel Quervelle (1789–1856) settled in Philadelphia in 1817 and by the late 1820s had become one of the foremost cabinetmakers in the city, where he received several awards in competitive exhibitions of the mechanical arts at the Franklin Institute and was patronized by Philadelphia's leading citizens. By 1827 he had supplied work in Washington to Secretary of the Navy Samuel Southard.[7] The East Room tables, with mahogany and rosewood veneers, are robust exam-

Jackson purchased elegant furnishings for the President's House during his term (1829-1837). The East Room was furnished for the first time in 1829 with fashionable Philadelphia furniture and elegant lighting fixtures that included chandeliers "magnificent in every respect." Jackson is portrayed here in one of Monroe's French chairs from the Oval Room (Blue Room) still in its original crimson fabric from 1817.

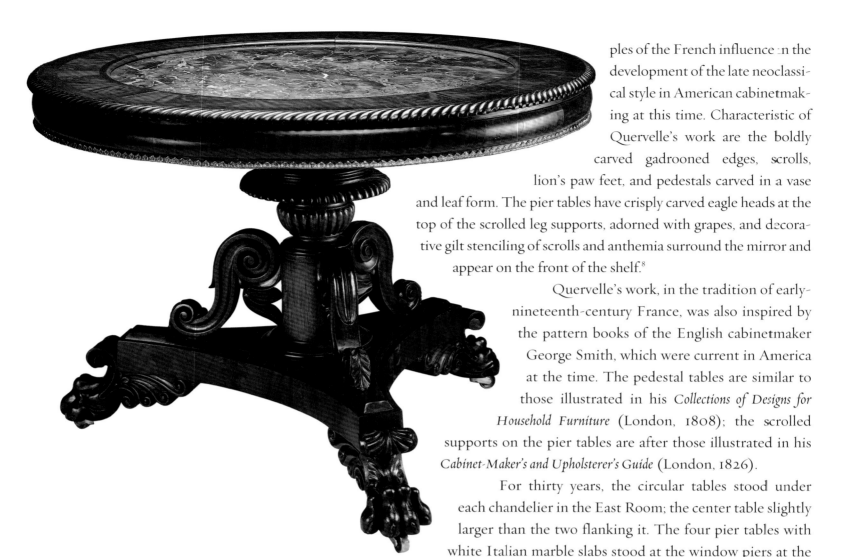

ples of the French influence in the development of the late neoclassical style in American cabinetmaking at this time. Characteristic of Quervelle's work are the boldly carved gadrooned edges, scrolls, lion's paw feet, and pedestals carved in a vase and leaf form. The pier tables have crisply carved eagle heads at the top of the scrolled leg supports, adorned with grapes, and decorative gilt stenciling of scrolls and anthemia surround the mirror and appear on the front of the shelf.[8]

Quervelle's work, in the tradition of early-nineteenth-century France, was also inspired by the pattern books of the English cabinetmaker George Smith, which were current in America at the time. The pedestal tables are similar to those illustrated in his *Collections of Designs for Household Furniture* (London, 1808); the scrolled supports on the pier tables are after those illustrated in his *Cabinet-Maker's and Upholsterer's Guide* (London, 1826).

For thirty years, the circular tables stood under each chandelier in the East Room; the center table slightly larger than the two flanking it. The four pier tables with white Italian marble slabs stood at the window piers at the north and south ends of the room. After the Civil War, the center tables were moved to the second-floor private quarters, and two of the pier tables were placed in the Family Dining Room.

The room "has lately been fitted up in a very neat manner," relayed a Washington guidebook in 1830.[9] "All the furniture corresponds in color and style," reported *The People's Magazine* in 1833. The suite of furniture made by William King in 1818 was finally upholstered in blue damask satin to match the blue draperies.

Veron was paid $9,358.27 for the refurbishing of the East Room, which also included the creation of ornamental rays with a dozen gilt stars over the large west door through which Jackson would enter the room.[10] The elegant existed with the practical. The last item on the bill was twenty spittoons costing $12.50. Many visitors to the Jackson White House, as well as the press, commented on the completed East Room, where "Here congregate . . . all the fashion that flocks to Washington during the sessions of Congress."[11] An anti-Jacksonian visitor who had heard much about the elegance of the

CENTER TABLE
*Anthony Gabriel Quervelle,
Philadelphia, c. 1829*

*Three monumental mahogany tables
with black-and-gold marble slabs inset
into their tops stood under the East
Room chandeliers. Made by the French-
born Quervelle, they are robust examples
of French and English influences on
American cabinetmakers working in the
1820s in the late neoclassical styles.*

furniture and beauty of the finish of the interior found that it fell short of the reality, except for the East Room, which "by far excels any one in this country."[12] When a Kentucky friend of Jackson's, Major Thomas H. Shelby, Jr., dined with him in 1831, he requested a look at the East Room, "of which so much has been said." Jackson walked with him through the room and pointed out the different articles of furniture and their cost. Shelby found it "magnificent in every respect."[13]

The other public rooms did not require or receive such extensive decorative changes, although Veron supplied a variety of lighting fixtures, wallpapers, and carpets for them. When the French aristocrat Gustave de Beaumont, traveling with the statesman and author Alexis de Tocqueville, met Jackson, he observed that the president of the United States occupied a palace that in Paris would be called a fine private residence. "Its interior is decorated with taste but simply, the *salon* [the Blue Room] in which he receives is infinitely less brilliant than those of our ministers."[14] The Oval Room still retained the crimson paper, crimson silk draperies, and gilded furniture upholstered in crimson silk, all imported from France in 1817 by James Monroe.[15] Major Shelby was told by Jackson that the chairs of this room cost almost as much as all the furniture in the East Room.[16]

PIER TABLE
*Anthony Gabriel Quervelle,
Philadelphia, c. 1829*

Four pier tables were placed between the windows on the north and south ends of the East Room in 1829. This table, the only one that survives, has crisply carved eagle heads on scrolled leg supports and its original gilt stenciling.

The English traveler and author Frances Trollope recounted that "the reception rooms are handsome, particularly the grand saloon, which is elegantly, nay, splendidly furnished,"[17] and *The People's Magazine* in 1833 reported that the Oval Room furnishings "give the appearance of a rich and consistent style of decoration and finish."[18]

Handsome, but less richly furnished than the Oval Room, the other state rooms had their walls covered with new green, yellow, white, and blue French papers sprinkled with gold stars and with gilt borders, all supplied by Louis Veron. One commentator in 1830 observed that the "ornaments are sparse and not of high order."[19]

The demands of official entertaining required a large service of glassware, and one was ordered in 1829 from the same Pittsburgh firm, Bakewell, Page & Bakewell, that had made a pair of decanters for Madison in 1816 and a state service for Monroe in 1818. This glassware was engraved with the coat of arms of the United States, grapevines, and grapes.[20] Veron supplemented this service with additional glass from Bakewell in 1833 and supplied a blue-bordered French dinner and dessert service for fifty decorated with the American eagle at a cost of $2,500 in 1833.[21]

By 1831 the $14,000 allocated to Jackson had been spent, and a supplemental appropriation was made to pay for a table service from Robinson Tynsdale in Philadelphia. After Jackson's reelection in 1832, $20,000 was provided by Congress, and in 1834 an additional $6,000 was appropriated to make up for a deficiency in buying, among other things, new chandeliers for the East Room. When the request for additional funds was made to Congress in 1834, Jackson's representative argued that "many new articles were absolutely necessary for the domestic comfort of the establishment which had not been renewed since Mr. Monroe's administration."[22] The elegant furniture was "much abused from the crowds of careless visitors."[23] During his eight years in office, Jackson spent a total of $45,000, an enormous sum in the 1830s.

In December of 1833, old furniture, glassware, and china from the White House were sold by P. Mauro, an auctioneer on Pennsylvania Avenue, and old silver was sold in Philadelphia. The two sales resulted in proceeds of $4,300, which Jackson used to purchase 464 pieces of elegant French silver costing $4,308.82 of which 130 remain.[24] The newly acquired dinner and dessert silver services had been owned by the Russian minister to the United States, Major General Baron Feodor Vasil'evich Teil'-fan-Serooskerken, known as Baron de Tuyll. He died in 1826 enroute to Europe, and in 1833 this silver was sold from his estate at the direction of his successor as Russian minister, Baron Krudener.[25] The plates and a coffee pot made by Fauconnier are engraved with a shielded "S," probably the Cyrillic cypher of the Baron de Tuyll; the larger pieces are engraved "President's House."

This fine quality French silver was the work of the most talented French silversmiths of the Napoleonic period: Martin-Guillaume Biennais (1764–1843), Jacques-Henri Fauconnier (1776–1839), François-Dominique Naudin (working 1806–34?), and Pierre-Joseph Dehanne (working 1800–1820?). Pieces included finely executed soup

tureens, vegetable dishes, sauce boats, large and small round plates, cruet stands, salt and mustard stands, bottle stands, a coffee service, and a variety of flatware that included dessert flatware of gilded silver. They arrived in two massive trunks with compartments for each piece, each trunk bearing an engraved silver plaque with the baron's name. The silver was stored in these trunks until a silver pantry was built in the White House in the early twentieth century.

Most of the pieces were made in Biennais's Paris shop between 1809 and 1819. Biennais had been appointed silversmith to Napoleon and Josephine by 1805. He received major commissions from the French court for its palaces and was also a favorite of the Russian aristocracy. The decorative elements include supports topped by winged female torsos in the Egyptian style and other neoclassical motifs such as anthemions, palmettes, and dolphins reflecting the widespread interest in the classical world of Greece and Rome in the early nineteenth century. Much of the plate from Biennais's studio was based on the designs of the French architects Percier and Fontaine. The coffee pots, in the shape of ancient amphora, stand on three splayed legs with paw feet.

Biennais also made a set of thirty-six gilded-silver fruit knives (twenty survive), but most of the flatware (ladles and a variety of spoons) were by Naudin, one of 600 craftsmen employed by Biennais; Dehanne made the gilded-silver dessert spoons. All

OPPOSITE AND LEFT:
PART OF DINNER SERVICE
(SAUCE BOAT, MUSTARD
STAND, CRUET STAND,
VEGETABLE DISH)
Martin-Guillaume Biennais, Paris, 1809-19

In 1833 Jackson purchased an elegant French silver service of 464 pieces from the estate of the Russian minister to the United States, Baron de Tuyll. Most of it was made by Biennais, who had been appointed silversmith to Napoleon in 1805. He oversaw a workshop of several hundred artisans that received commissions from the French and Russian courts. Decorative details on the silver—winged female torsos, palmettes, and dolphins—reflect the widespread interest in the ancient world in the early 1800s.

The French silver acquired in 1833 was stored in its original trunks in the White House until a pantry was constructed in the early 20th century.

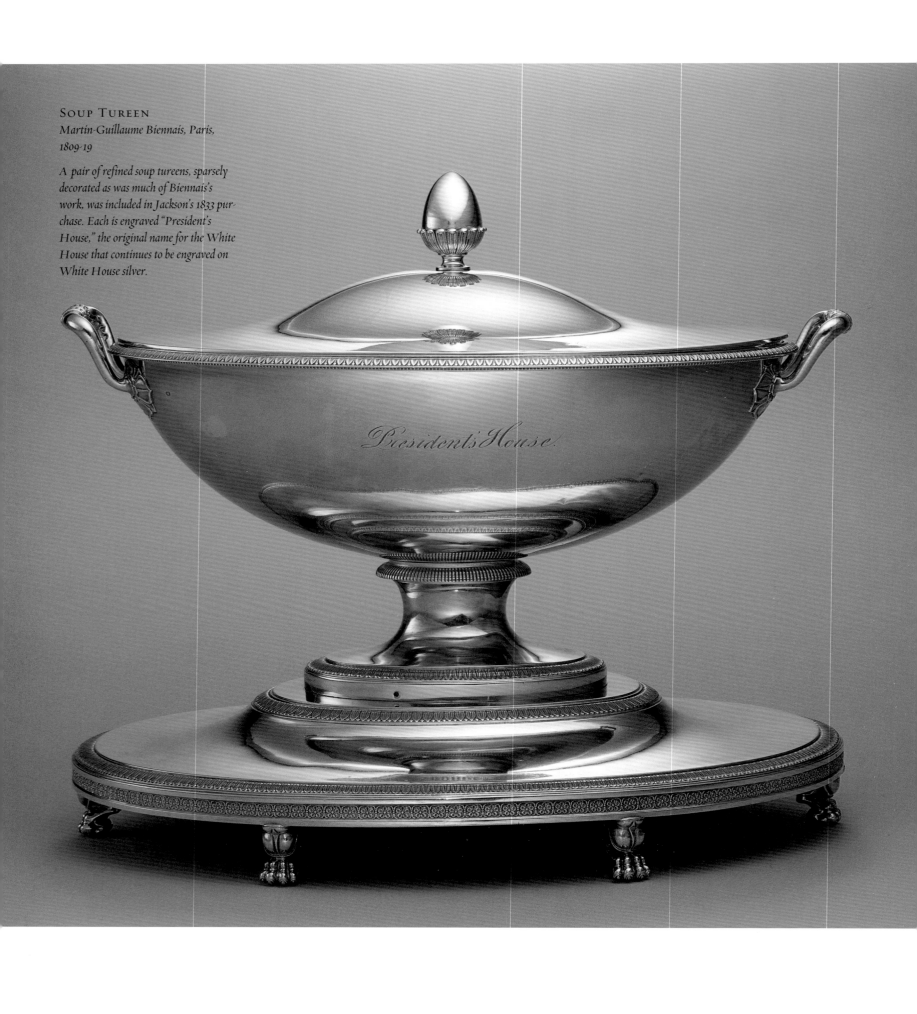

SOUP TUREEN
Martin-Guillaume Biennais, Paris, 1809-19

A pair of refined soup tureens, sparsely decorated as was much of Biennais's work, was included in Jackson's 1833 purchase. Each is engraved "President's House," the original name for the White House that continues to be engraved on White House silver.

bear Paris hallmarks of 1809–19. Fauconnier, who received the commission for silver for the White House in 1817, which included a pair of soup tureens still in the White House, is represented in the de Tuyll service by platters, plates, and a coffee pot in the same style as the Biennais pots.

That much of this extraordinary group of French silver has survived in the White House is a testament to its quality, since it was heavily used throughout the nineteenth century. Jackson's critics in Congress decried the expenditure at the time, but his purchase in 1833 was money well spent.

In Jackson's second term, the house received more attention, primarily in the refurbishing of the public and family spaces. In 1833 and 1834, Charles Alexandre, a Washington upholsterer with a shop on Pennsylvania Avenue who had first worked for the President's House in 1817, cleaned and replaced carpets and draperies throughout the

COFFEE SERVICE (COFFEE POTS AND CREAM JUG)
Martin-Guillaume Biennais, Paris, 1809-19

Much of the silver produced in Biennais's shop was inspired by the designs of French architect Charles Percier. These coffee pots, in the shape of ancient amphorae, stand on splayed legs with paw feet. The handles are ivory.

ABOVE:
TORCHÈRE
France, c. 1830-37

A pair of gilded bronze torchères stood near the Blue Room mantel in the mid-19th century. According to a longtime White House employee, they had been a gift to President Jackson from a political supporter.

OPPOSITE:
MANTEL CLOCK
France, c. 1833

Typical of French clocks made for the American market between 1820 and 1840, this clock stands on the Lincoln Bedroom mantel where it stood, under a glass dome, when the room was Lincoln's office. A four column black marble clock was purchased for the "audience room" in 1833.

house. Louis Veron was again called upon to provide mirrors for the Green Room and State Dining Room, new chandeliers for the East Room, an oil cloth for the corridor, and other goods such as table linens, Brussels and Wilton carpeting, flatware, glassware, a French dinner and dessert service, and French silk curtain fabric and trim made in Lyons.[26] A French mantel clock with four black marble columns, an elaborate metal dial, a rosette and lyre pendulum, and gilded bronze wreath-shaped mounts on the base was purchased for the "audience room" at a cost of $75. Typical of French clocks made for the American market between 1820 and 1840, it is now back in the Lincoln Bedroom where it was during the Lincoln era, covered then by a glass dome.

Local cabinetmakers such as James Green of Alexandria, Virginia, who had a furniture warehouse on Pennsylvania Avenue, made beds for the servants and mahogany chairs and sofas for the dining room and audience room. Charles Burnett of Georgetown, who had produced silver for the President's House since Jefferson's time, sold flatware, a common dinner service, ewers, basins, and chamber pots.[27]

When Jackson occupied the President's House there were thirty-one rooms in the house: seven on the state floor, thirteen in the second-floor private quarters, which included offices for the president and his staff, and eleven on the ground-floor basement level where the kitchen and pantry were located. Jackson's office in the large southeast room on the second floor was a room "where everything announces the august simplicity of our government."[28] The center table in his office, used for Cabinet meetings, was covered with books and papers, as was the smaller table near the fireplace used by Jackson.

The only outright gift to the President's House in Jackson's administration that remains in the White House is a pair of French gilded bronze torchères, each with leaf-scrolled candle arms and a scrolled tripod base. A longtime White House doorkeeper related that they were presented to Jackson by Robert Patterson of Philadelphia, an early supporter of him for the presidency.[29] According to Patterson family history, the candelabra were bought from Point Breeze, the Bordentown, New Jersey, home of Joseph Bonaparte, the eldest brother of Napoleon, who served as king of Naples and king of Spain before moving to New Jersey, where he lived from 1815 to 1839.

Jackson's popularity is reflected in the decoration of American and French porcelain vases made in the 1830s and acquired by the White House in the twentieth century. A rare near-pair of American-made vases imitating French forms was produced by the most significant early-nineteenth-century American porcelain factory, Tucker and Hemphill of Philadelphia, circa

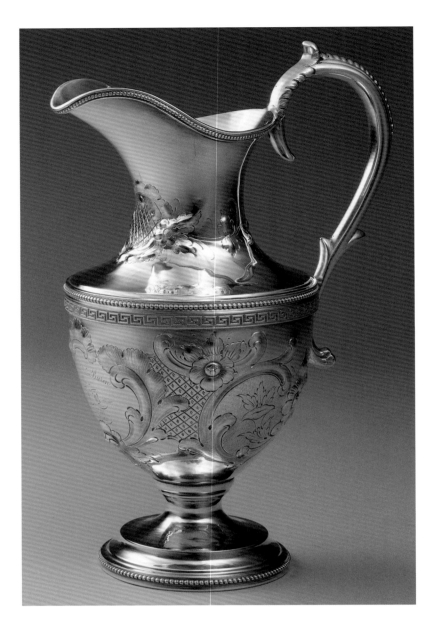

WATER PITCHER
G. C. Allen, New York, 1858

*President Van Buren's former law partner
and U. S. attorney general, Benjamin F.
Butler, bequeathed funds for the purchase
of three pieces of silver for Van Buren
after he left office. Two pitchers and an ice
bowl were presented to him.*

sonal relief, or to the private advantage of the President. He is . . . the host of the nation. His guests are the guests of the People. Here ambassadors and ministers. . . are received and entertained in the name of the hospitality of the nation! . . . The house . . . open to all, and is daily visited by many. Is it too much, then that the place and its appendages are beyond the requirements of private station?" He refuted Ogle's relentless criticism of the style and fashion of the objects that had been purchased: Congress had appropriated funds "without restriction or qualification." As to the purchase of dozens of cups and saucers, they were used for the hospitable entertaining of visitors and friends and were "a means, among others, of offering the courtesies of place to those who called upon the President as the Representative of the People."[39]

Ogle's speech was widely disseminated by the Whig party and published in Whig newspapers such as the Baltimore *Log Cabin Advocate,* which supported Harrison's candidacy. The speech clearly had an effect on Van Buren's electoral defeat in 1840, and the controversy had not ended by the time he left office in 1841. The commissioner of public buildings, William Noland, was called to respond to congressional inquiries relating to the use of gold knives, forks, and spoons in the White House. A local silversmith had to provide a certificate stating that the pieces were not gold but silver gilt.[40] Van Buren was also accused of stripping the house of its furnishings and carrying them away with him when he left office. The boxes sent to New York, Noland reported, contained only those items that belonged to Van Buren. (Mrs. Lincoln would be faced with the same accusations and rumors in 1865.) An inventory of the plate and furniture in the President's House was taken a few days before the inauguration and a copy was provided to an aide of the new president.[41]

An object associated with Van Buren, a gift to the White House in 1913, is a silver water pitcher with repoussé flowers and scrolls made in New York by G. C. Allen (working 1844–58). Benjamin F. Butler, Van Buren's old friend, former law partner, and United States attorney-general during his administration, bequeathed funds to purchase three pieces of silver for Van Buren after he left office. The pitcher, inscribed "Martin Van Buren from BFB December 3, 1811 [the year Butler became Van Buren's law clerk] November 8, 1858 [Butler's death date]," is part of a service that also included another pitcher and an ice bowl.[42]

Despite the bitter campaign of 1840, Van Buren met with William Henry Harrison and offered to vacate the White House prior to the inauguration; Harrison declined his generosity. A Richmond newspaper, *The Jeffersonian*, rebuked the new administration in March 1841 for requesting an additional $6,000 for furnishings when the Whigs had so roundly condemned Van Buren's furnishings. Harrison supporters claimed that the house was denuded of any article of comfort, that there were only three beds in the house, and that it was destitute of furniture for the comfort of the family. One congressman suggested selling the gold spoons; another promptly had to deny that they were gold. On and on the argument went, but the funds were finally approved by Congress for the new president, as they had been for each of his predecessors.[43]

The day after the inauguration, Harrison received guests in the Blue Room, assisted by his daughter-in-law, Jane Findlay Harrison, as Mrs. Harrison had not yet made the journey to Washington. A few days later a visitor commented on the Harrison White House, "I was delighted; of the contrast between the log cabin with its wings, and this republican palace. Yet the old General walked round these rooms as if he had been always accustomed to such grandeur." She described the "chairs all gilded with blue satin medallion cushions, the Green Room with white spotted paper with gilt stars and the East Room which was more 'antique' and had eight immense mirrors with 'broad carved frames which rise nearly to the ceiling.'"[44] During Harrison's one month in the White House, he received the diplomatic corps and held only one formal dinner. He died on April 4 of pneumonia aggravated by his two-hour-long inaugural speech, the first president to die in office.

CAMPAIGN TEXTILE
American, c. 1840

William Henry Harrison adopted the log cabin as a symbol of his rustic background in the 1840 presidential campaign. He defeated President Van Buren but died after a month in office.

Little was purchased for the house during Harrison's short residence except miscellaneous French and English tableware. Queen's ware and glassware were purchased in Alexandria, Virginia, from Hugh C. Smith, in Baltimore from the firm China Hall, and in Washington from Thomas Pursell, who would continue to be patronized by the Virginian John Tyler, who had been Harrison's vice president.[45]

Ten days after Harrison's death, Tyler moved into the President's House with his invalid wife, Letitia, and their seven children. Mrs. Tyler, who died in the White House in 1842, was too ill to attend public functions. Priscilla Tyler, wife of the Tylers' son Robert, served as Tyler's hostess for three years, assisted by the Tylers' daughter Letitia Semple. In

1844 Tyler married the much younger Julia Gardiner, who with great enthusiasm assumed the role of first lady during the last eight months of his term.

With Tyler's Whig opponents in control of Congress and a period of depression in the country in 1841, no additional funds were appropriated for furnishings or the maintenance of the house, so Tyler had to make do with the $6,000 appropriated for Harrison and spent his own funds for fuel and lights. Not surprisingly, when Julia Gardiner arrived in 1844 she found the house a "dirty establishment," and it was rumored that she used Gardiner family funds to refurbish the house.[46]

The schedule of public entertaining was heavy. Each week, two evening receptions and two formal dinners were held during the social season when Congress was in session. Once a month, the house was opened for a public levee. There was a constant need to supplement items required for entertaining, and dozens of "rich gilt" plates and coffee cups and saucers were purchased.

The office areas on the second floor received utilitarian items such as a mahogany case with pigeonholes made by William McLean Cripps (working 1827–40s), a cabinet-maker with a shop on Pennsylvania Avenue, and tables for maps and newspapers. The purchase of a crib and a child's chair reflected the needs of Tyler's large extended family. Maple bedsteads and two dozen cane-seat chairs came from Edwin Green, a Washington cabinetmaker. In 1843 John Tyler, Jr., who served as his father's secretary, bought an ornamental table for $100 from Joseph Camera, and two rosewood concert pianos were acquired for the grand sum of $1,050 from E. N. Scherr of Washington in exchange for two secondhand pianos to lessen the cost.[47]

Charles Dickens compared the Tyler mansion to an English clubhouse. When he visited one morning in 1842 he observed people in the public rooms with "no particular business there, with some lounging on the chairs and sofas. . . . A few were closely eyeing the movables, as if to make quite sure that the president (who was far from popular) had not made away with any of the furniture, or sold the fixtures for his private benefit." He characterized the president's reception room next to his office, its tables covered with newspapers, as being as "unpromising and tiresome as any waiting-room" in a public establishment and observed the "energetic" spitting of several men who "bestowed their favours so abundantly upon the carpet."[48] He and his wife returned for an evening levee where the rooms were, he wrote, "crowded to excess."

A handsome French porcelain centerpiece, circa 1820–30, with an oval, pierced gilded basket upheld by two bisque winged angels kneeling on a cobalt blue-and-gilt oval base is one of the few objects in the White House associated with President Tyler. Purchased at the sale of his effects with a history of White House use, it was donated to the White House in 1957. It is unmarked but similar in style and form to another basket marked by Parisian porcelain manufacturers and merchants Marc and Victor Schoelcher.

The Washington silversmith Robert Keyworth (1795–1856) established a shop in the city in 1817 and supplied silver to the President's House from the 1820s to the

OPPOSITE:
FRUIT BASKET
France, c. 1820-30

When John Tyler succeeded to the presidency on the death of William Henry Harrison in 1841, the country was in a period of depression and Congress did not provide funds for furnishings or maintenance of the house. This French porcelain centerpiece, a Tyler family possession, was sold after his death.

*Robert Keyworth, Washington, D.C.,
c. 1835-51*

*Keyworth had a shop on Pennsylvania
Avenue and supplied silver to the White
House from the 1820s to the 1850s.*

1850s. In 1840 he had been called upon to verify that Van Buren's "gold" spoons were not gold but silver gilt. Examples of a tea service marked "R. KEYWORTH"—a footed waste bowl and creamer with grapevine and leaf motifs and a pair of sugar tongs—remain in the White House, but no accounts have been found for the purchase of these specific objects made between 1835 and 1850.

One of the few newspaper accounts of the state of the house during the transition from one nineteenth-century administration to another was recorded before Tyler left office in March 1845. The reporter's observations reflected a suspension of time during changes of administration. He found the East Room "in real Mayday [the traditional moving day] order. The carpets had been rolled up and lay in bundles about the halls; the chairs . . . with their sky-blue satin seats and trimmings hanging in rags over the sides. . . . [T]hose notorious mirrors seemed to give back a misty reflection; and everything about strongly indicated that Tyler glory was in its winter hues."[49]

Tyler's successor James K. Polk—the last of the political heirs of Jackson to become president—arrived with his wife, Sarah, to a house that required attention. They had lived in Washington when he served in the House of Representatives and had many friends in the city. Entertaining these friends and others was demanding, and although Mrs. Polk, a strict Presbyterian, did not allow dancing in the White House, the couple received guests at weekly receptions and dinners. Congress provided $14,000 in 1845 for repairs, maintenance, and furnishings. In the first year of Polk's term, both the exterior and interior of the building were repaired and painted, and in 1848 gas was introduced into the house. Cornelius & Company of Philadelphia fitted the great East Room chandeliers installed by Jackson for gas, with President Polk witnessing the initial lighting; Cornelius manufactured several additional new chandeliers.

Polk delegated William W. Corcoran, a Washington banker who helped finance the Mexican-American War, as his agent for the furniture fund. Corcoran, a man of wealth, an art collector, and founder of the Corcoran Gallery of Art, turned to fashionable New York merchants for goods for the President's House. James Knox Walker, Polk's nephew and private secretary who lived with the Polks, also authorized purchases. Glassware came from Ebenezer Collamore (hocks, wines, and claret glasses) and Baldwin Gardiner (goblets, champagnes, wines, liquors, and decanters, wine coolers, and green finger bowls).[50] Although many reports indicated that Mrs. Polk banned alcoholic beverages from the house, these orders and accounts by guests at White House dinners indicate otherwise. (She did ban hard liquors.)

In the summer months of 1845, cleaning and refurbishing of the public and private rooms went forward, as happened during most summer months when presidents and their families traditionally vacated the house. Joseph Boyd, a local upholsterer, supervised carpet cleaning; taking down, cleaning, and replacing draperies; and gilding, upholstering, finishing, and polishing furniture, and recovering the gilt chairs in the Red Room. When Elizabeth Dixon, wife of Connecticut congressman, James Dixon, attended a reception in December of 1845 she was received by Mrs. Polk in the "Receiving or Red Room" with new crimson velvet curtains and chairs. (This was the first use of the name "Red Room"; it also continued to be called the Washington parlor, as the large Gilbert Stuart portrait of the first president hung there.) The room looked "warm and comfortable," according to Mrs. Dixon.[51] Rosewood armchairs, two couches and ten chairs in the fashionable Louis XV style, upholstered in crimson plush, were purchased in 1845 from the New York cabinetmakers John (1801-75) and Joseph W. Meeks (1806–78).[52] The earliest illustration of the room, published in 1856, shows the high-backed upholstered chairs in the popular "French antique" style.

In 1846 and 1847, Meeks also supplied twenty-four black walnut "Gothic" chairs at $8 each.[53] These Gothic Revival chairs were probably made for the second-floor Cabinet Room where they were located in the 1850s. They later became identified with their use in President Lincoln's Cabinet Room when they appeared in widely distributed prints of Frances Carpenter's painting of *The First Reading of the Emancipation Proclamation*. The chairs continued to be used by the Cabinet until 1869. Four of the chairs, with four Gothic lancet arches in the cyma-curved back and three trefoil piercings in the crest rail, remain in the White House. Furniture in the Gothic style was adapted from the forms and ornaments of Gothic architecture that were popularized in America by the architect Alexander Jackson Davis, who

RIGHT:

SIDE CHAIR

J. & J. W. Meeks [John Meeks and Joseph W. Meeks], New York, c. 1846-47

The Meeks shop made a set of twenty-four black walnut chairs in the Gothic Revival style for the Cabinet Room in 1846 and 1847; they were used there until 1869. The chairs appeared in prints of Lincoln's Cabinet Room in the 1860s and came to be identified with him.

OPPOSITE:

SIDE CHAIR

Charles A. Baudouine, New York, c. 1845

The French-born Baudouine made forty-two rosewood chairs covered with purple velvet for the newly redecorated State Dining Room in 1845. Mrs. James Polk installed matching purple-and-gold draperies to create what a dinner guest described as a "very splendid" room.

designed furniture in this style, often for libraries. Many chairs similar to the style and form of the White House chairs were made by other cabinetmakers in other woods and are in private and public collections. Without a White House history, it is not possible to verify that they were from the set purchased by the White House in 1846 and 1847. The Meeks firm had retail and wholesale outlets in many cities, but the White House pieces came directly from its New York shop. When Meeks died in 1868, his obituary noted that he produced the "most expensive, elegant and durable cabinet work made in America."[54]

Mrs. Dixon attended a dinner for forty people in the State Dining Room in 1845 where the windows were hung with purple-and-gold figured curtains and the guests sat on purple velvet chairs with carved rosewood frames. "As the furniture is all new and fresh and all the decorations newly gilded, it was very splendid."[55] The forty-two rosewood chairs "in plush" were made by the French-born New York cabinetmaker Charles A. Baudouine (1808–95) for $13.50 each.[56] Sixteen of these balloon-backed chairs with cabriole legs and heart-shaped crests carved with two large rosettes and a central fan remain in the White House. In the earliest photograph taken of a president inside the White House, President Polk and his Cabinet can be seen seated in these chairs in the State Dining Room, where the chairs continued to be used until 1882; some remained in the adjacent Family Dining Room until 1902. Balloon-backed chairs became popular in America about 1840 after first being introduced in England in the 1830s, and they continued to be made for thirty years.

The dinner courses were served in silver dishes, tureens, and wine coolers from the Monroe and Jackson purchases, with "the famous gold forks, knives and spoons for dessert."[57] The china service was the blue-and-white and gilt French dinner service Jackson ordered in 1833 along with blue and gilt dessert plates decorated with painted fruit and flowers in the center. A new service, ordered by the Polks, arrived in 1846. Made in France by E. D. Honoré, the dinner and dessert service, with its rococo-shaped gilded edges, is decorated with the shield from the Great Seal of the

United States in the border. The plates, fruit baskets, and compotes in the dessert service have apple green borders and elegant hand-painted flowers in the center.

Seven rooms on the second floor were used as bedrooms by the Polks and their relatives; many had French bedsteads. Rooms for the housekeeper and household staff were located in the basement and the west terrace wash house.[58] Joanna Ruckner, a niece of Mrs. Polk and White House guest during 1845 and 1846, left a vivid account of life in the Polk White House. Once she was disturbed by a stranger in the private quarters who, she wrote, pretended to have lost his way to the president's office. "There is but little privacy here, as the house belongs to the Government and everyone feels at home and they sometimes stalk into our bedrooms and say they are looking at the house."[59]

She described a constant factor of life for residents of the White House with its lack of privacy; other visitors noted the problems incurred with the house open constantly to the public and its heavy use for public entertaining. "Some of the furniture of the house is elegant, but in general it looks much abused from the crowds of careless visitors," wrote a visitor in the last year of Polk's administration.[60]

VEGETABLE DISH, SOUP PLATE, FRUIT BASKET, DESSERT PLATE
Edouard Honoré, Champroux, 1846

President and Mrs. James Polk ordered a handsome rococo French dinner and dessert service decorated with the shield from the Great Seal of the United States in 1846. The apple green dessert plates, with hand-painted flowers, are among the most attractive pieces of any state service.

THE STATE FLOOR:
THE
GREEN ROOM

LEFT:
George W. Bush administration, 2007

BELOW:
Engraving, United States Magazine,
September 1856

LEFT, TOP:
Rutherford B. Hayes administration, c. 1880

BELOW, TOP:
Calvin Coolidge administration, c. 1927-28

LEFT, BOTTOM:
Harry S. Truman administration, 1952

BELOW, BOTTOM:
John F. Kennedy administration, 1963

OPPOSITE:
George W. Bush administration, 2007

"The appearance of comfort and comparative beauty."

FOUR

REVIVALS OF THE "ANTIQUE" AT MID-CENTURY, 1850s–60s

ZACHARY TAYLOR, MILLARD FILLMORE, FRANKLIN PIERCE, JAMES BUCHANAN, ABRAHAM LINCOLN, ANDREW JOHNSON

In the 1840s, the taste and style of furnishings in America changed. A mix of styles influenced by English and French revivals of historic sources became popular, and objects were designed heavier in form and decoration. Whole room ensembles were now created, often in the "French antique" or Rococo Revival styles, which were rich interpretations of eighteenth-century French styles. Furnishings increased in dimension (much exaggerated in comparison to the eighteenth century), and chairs and sofas with curved frames were made more comfortable. There was also a change from individual handcrafted objects to those mass-produced and factory-made as a result of new technologies. Beginning in the 1850s, German and French immigrant craftsmen dominated cabinetmaking in several eastern cities, especially New York and Philadelphia, and they increasingly set the styles. Many supplied furnishings for the White House, either directly or through retailers, in the last half of the nineteenth century.

In the years prior to and after the Civil War, motifs symbolic of the Union, such as the shield from the Great Seal of the United States, were often incorporated into gilded mirrors, sideboards, and tableware made for the White House. Naturalistic carving of fruit, flowers, and vines symbolized the bounty of this country and appeared on White House mirror frames and furniture.

Two rosewood chairs in the "French antique" style, circa 1850, bear witness to this period. On the crest rail of each of the chairs is a carved likeness, Martin Van Buren of New York on one and Zachary Taylor of Virginia on the other, presidents with no apparent connection. Furniture carved with images of the presidents is rare, but perhaps these chairs were part of a set that included likenesses of other presidents.

The presidency of Polk's successor, Zachary Taylor, was destined to be short-lived. He died on July 9, 1850, after a brief illness, a year and four months after his inau-

OPPOSITE:
CENTER TABLE
Attributed to John Henry Belter, New York, c. 1861

Mary Todd Lincoln selected this "quite costly and exceedingly beautiful" rosewood table for a White House guest room in 1861. Belter was highly skilled in working with laminated wood, and he carved vines, grape clusters, and roses for the apron and exotic birds for the legs.

111

guration. His wife, Margaret Taylor, in poor health, had remained in the family quarters during their occupancy of the White House, and his youngest daughter, Betty Taylor Bliss, had assumed the responsibilities of hostess. Another daughter, Ann Taylor Wood, with her husband and their children were in residence also. Official dinners were held once a week when Congress was in session, and Taylor met guests on Wednesday and Friday afternoons and at Friday evening receptions.

Concerns were increasingly raised about the healthfulness of living in the President's House, located so near the "miasma" of Tiber Creek and the swampy area to the south of the house. The ground-floor kitchen areas were damp with moisture, the roof leaked, the furnace and plumbing were faulty, the house needed painting, but the second-floor family quarters were made livable.[1] Many improvements were made in 1849, but little was done about conditions outside the building.

William W. S. Bliss, the president's son-in-law and secretary, was authorized by Taylor to be the purchasing agent for the house. Congress provided $14,000, and in the spring of 1849 several pieces of bedroom furniture for the family—dressing bureaus, mahogany washstands and wardrobes, and a bed—were shipped from Baltimore along with a dozen fancy chairs. In the summer and fall, several articles of furniture were repaired and regilded, probably including the French furniture in the Blue Room. New York cabinetmaker Joseph Meeks, who had made furniture for the Red Room in 1845 and chairs for the Cabinet Room in 1846 and 1847, supplied a rosewood canterbury.[2] Two months before his death in 1850 Taylor accepted a gift of a "rustic" settee from its Baltimore manufacturer, Cotten Bride, which he placed on the porch of the South Portico.

Several Taylor-associated objects have been donated to the White House by family descendents. A pair of brass, urn-shaped andirons resting on rococo supports with a Chinese influence and a brass fender with a grilled panel came from relatives of Betty Bliss with a family history of use in the Taylor White House. In 1915 and 1916, the White House received a pair of Sheffield silver candlesticks from the daughter of Taylor's son Richard, and glassware owned by Taylor came from descendants of his daughter, Ann Taylor Wood.

Taylor, a career Army officer and hero of the Mexican-American War, won major victories at Monterrey and Buena Vista. A commemorative sword commissioned by his native state of Virginia and presented to him at the White House in 1849 attests to his popularity. Made by the Ames Manufacturing Company of Chicopee, Massachusetts, in 1848–49, its gilded silver scabbard has chased and engraved vignettes of those battles, and it is an excellent example of the skill of its craftsmen.

OPPOSITE:
GOBLET
Bohemia, c. 1840-60

Glass with American views, made for the American market, was popular at mid-century. This White House view was taken from an English print of 1831 that was widely distributed.

ABOVE:
SIDE CHAIR
American, c. 1850-60

Furniture with carved likenesses of presidents is rare. This rosewood chair in the "French antique" style depicts Zachary Taylor and is a near pair to a chair that shows Martin Van Buren. They may have been part of a set that included images of other presidents.

REVIVALS OF THE "ANTIQUE"
AT MID-CENTURY

Taylor's vice president Millard Fillmore and Abigail Fillmore, along with their daughter, Mary Abigail, and son, Millard, moved into the house in July 1850 after Taylor's death. The cultured and well-read Mrs. Fillmore convinced her husband to request a special appropriation from Congress to establish a permanent collection of books for a library in the second-floor oval room, the family's sitting room, and the White House library for most of the late nineteenth century. Washington cabinetmaker William Mc. L. Cripps, who had been in business since the 1820s, made two ten-foot-high mahogany bookcases for the Fillmores during the summer of 1850 and a year later supplied two circular bookcases. He also made mahogany and rosewood desks, a large sideboard, a black walnut fire screen, a mahogany map stand, and a rosewood music stool for the music-loving Fillmores (their daughter played the harp) who bought a rosewood pianoforte for $475.[3] It is probably the large piano that is mentioned in the Red Room in 1856.

Household items for family rooms, purchased from C. S. Fowler, included several banded cups and saucers and plates and three rich "mitre cut" water bottles.[4] Vendors such as Thomas Pursell, who had supplied goods to presidents for decades, continued to be patronized and provided eighteen cut glass decanters in 1850. Washington upholsterer David A. Baird made new draperies for the library and the president's office and upholstered several pieces of furniture in horsehair. Fillmore used the funds appropriated for Taylor in 1849 to make these purchases.

A visitor to the Fillmore White House in August 1850 saw the gilded French furniture of Monroe's time still in the Blue Room and the Jackson-era tables in the East Room,

GARDEN SETTEE
*Attributed to Janes, Beebe & Co.,
New York, c. 1852*

Millard Fillmore loved gardening and supported plans for landscaping the area south of the White House. This Rococo Revival cast-iron settee is one of several purchased for the White House grounds while he was president.

which remained draped in black crepe out of respect for Taylor, who had died a month earlier. He noted the up-to-date gasoliers and the "splendid" Turkey carpets and furniture upholstered in velvet, probably referring to the State Dining Room.[5] Fillmore invited an old friend to the White House later that year. "We have one spare room in this temple of inconveniences, neatly fitted up," he wrote, "and just the thing for you and Mrs. H."[6]

In the early 1850s, there was great interest among Washingtonians in plans for landscaping the grounds of the Mall and the area south of the President's House. Andrew Jackson Downing, the leading landscape designer in the country, was commissioned by Fillmore, who loved gardening, to make recommendations, but Downing met an untimely death in a steamboat explosion in 1852. A group of Rococo Revival style cast-iron garden settees, painted bronze green, with elements of Gothic style in the arches in their backs, were purchased for the White House grounds in 1852. They are attributed to Janes, Beebe & Co. of New York whose estimate for sixty benches for the grounds of the Capitol and White House at a cost of $14 each was accepted.[7] Several remain on the White House grounds 150 years later. Cast-iron benches in this style were first patented in England in 1846, and by the 1850s several American companies were producing them.[8]

A two-handled silver hot-water urn, inscribed "Millard Fillmore No. 2" and a sugar bowl inscribed "Mrs. Millard Fillmore, No. 7" are from a twelve-piece service made to order for President and Mrs. Fillmore after his presidency. In 1858 Fillmore sold a carriage and horses that had been presented to Mrs. Fillmore in 1850, and the proceeds from the sale were used to purchase the silver service by Wood & Hughes, a major New York firm. Resting on a stand of four scrolled legs with anthemion-shaped feet, the paneled urn has a spout fashioned in the form of a bird's head. The dome-shaped lid has a fruit and leaf finial.

Fillmore's successor Franklin Pierce and his wife, Jane, were still burdened with grief at the recent death of their young son when they arrived at the President's House in March 1853. Mrs. Pierce led a life of retirement from society during the four years she lived in the White House although she did attend official dinners on occasion following the end of a year of mourning. Work and entertaining proceeded nonetheless with Abby Means, an aunt and childhood friend of Jane Pierce, as hostess. A larger than normal appropriation of $25,000 was granted for the furniture fund, and Pierce delegated his secretary, Sidney Webster, as his personal representative to approve expenditures from the fund.

Thomas U. Walter, architect of the Capitol, was called on to plan and supervise the installation of a new heating system, new bathrooms, and decorative work throughout the state rooms. Several new marble mantels were installed, decorative fresco painting was executed on the ceilings of several rooms, and many rooms received new wallpaper. At the direction of the president, L. R. Menger of New York sent gilded frames for mantel and pier mirrors for the East Room and gilt window cornices and gilt frames for mirrors for the Green Room, Blue Room, Red Room, the two dining rooms, and the new Library. He also furnished two overscaled gilt pier tables with white marble slabs for the Green and Red Rooms at a total cost of $3,141.[9] Proceeds from the sale of old furniture netted $350.64 in 1854.

The pair of gilded mirror frames purchased for the Green Room survived there until 1902 and remain in the White House collection. Of wood and gesso, they are carved with elaborate scrollwork and leaves, and in the center of the crest is a large carved shield derived from the Great Seal of the United States. Other overmantel mirrors were carved with fruit and corn, symbols of the bounty of the nation.

The Pierces ordered a handsome white porcelain French dinner and dessert service with blue and gilt decoration, by an unknown manufacturer, and a large service of cut glassware from Haughwout & Dailey in New York, both for sixty people. Examples in the White House include a large centerpiece and baskets from the porcelain dessert service, which was decorated in New York.[10] The design of the porcelain service was selected from a sample shown at the Crystal Palace Exhibition in New York in 1853. Bailey & Co. in Philadelphia was called upon to regild the Monroe plateau, and repair and replate silver tea services and flatware.[11] Several pieces of walnut and mahogany furniture, including beds, wardrobes, walnut side tables, and sideboards were purchased from Baltimore cabinetmakers Anthony and Henry Jenkins (1837–57) who also recovered chairs and settees.[12] The four carved console tables that appear in photographs of the State Dining Room late in the nineteenth century may be the four walnut side tables from the Jenkins firm.

Official entertaining centered on dinners for congressmen and their wives. At a dinner for thirty people in the State Dining Room in 1855, the newly regilt Monroe plateau occupied the length of the table along with seven vases of flowers and a setting of five glasses at each place. The guests were served from silver trays.[13]

OPPOSITE:
HOT WATER URN
AND SUGAR BOWL
Wood & Hughes, New York, c. 1858

The names of Mr. and Mrs. Fillmore are engraved on these objects, part of a twelve-piece silver service made after his presidency by a leading New York firm. Proceeds from the sale of a carriage and horses presented to Mrs. Fillmore in 1850 were used to purchase the service.

BELOW:
COMPOTE
France, decorated by Haughwout & Dailey, New York, 1853

WATER BOTTLE
AND WINE GLASS
Possibly Haughwout & Dailey, New York, 1853, or later reorder

President and Mrs. Franklin Pierce placed orders for a French dinner and dessert service and cut-and-engraved glassware, both for sixty people, in 1853. At a White House dinner in 1855, five glasses were set for each guest.

A large pair of French porcelain vases was a gift from the French government during the Pierce administration, according to late-nineteenth-century White House staff accounts. The vases, with a magenta ground and rococo gilded-metal mounts, have hand-painted scenes from the French Revolution of Marie Antoinette appearing before Robespierre and the sentencing of Charlotte Corday.

The earliest published images of White House interiors were presented in 1856 in *United States Magazine*. The wood engravings illustrate Thomas U. Walter's work along with the accumulation of objects from previous administrations. Monroe's French candelabra and clocks rested on mantels; chairs from 1817–18 still stood in the East Room and the Blue Room; part of the gilded suite from the Blue Room appears in the Green Room, probably placed there in Polk's time if not earlier. At the end of the Pierce administration, John B. Blake, commissioner of public buildings, reported to Congress that the house, throughout, "was never in a better condition on the close of an administration than at present."[14]

The pre–Civil War White House of James Buchanan would reflect the tensions in Washington as volatile national issues were discussed and argued before the rupture of the Union in 1860 by South Carolina's secession. Buchanan was the only president never to marry, and he chose his niece, Harriet Lane, as his White House hostess. Southerners had been very involved in Washington social life and continued to welcome the glittering receptions and dinners that Lane arranged throughout her uncle's term.

With $20,000 available from Congress, Lane began to make changes in the house. Most of her purchases came from Philadelphia: a marble clock and serving ware from Bailey & Co., walnut furniture from Gottlieb Vollmer, a black walnut office table from Klauder, Deginther & Co, a Sèvres flower stand and china for bedrooms from Tyndale and Mitchell, new lighting fixtures, including chandeliers, from Cornelius and Baker, Brussels carpets from James H. Orne, and an oval, gilt-framed mantel mirror from A. S. Robinson.[15]

A major change was made in the Blue Room in 1860 when the Monroe French suite, in the room since 1817 and long out of style by mid-nineteenth century, was sent to auction. Most of the furniture in the suite, except for the pier table, which remained in the White House, was sold at the Washington auction house of James C. McGuire & Co.[16] In its place, Harriet Lane selected a suite of gilded furniture in the Rococo Revival style that became popular in America in the mid-nineteenth century after being favored by Empress Eugénie, who had married Napoleon III in 1853. With high backs and cabriole legs, the suite of four sofas, four armchairs, four window chairs, four "reception" chairs, two ottomans, and a center divan, all upholstered in blue brocatelle, were pro-

OPPOSITE:

OVERMANTEL MIRROR
L. R. Menger, New York, 1853

This elaborately carved and gilded mirror frame is one of two made for the Green Room in 1853.

ABOVE:

CENTERPIECE
France, decorated by Haughwout & Dailey, New York, 1853

In the Pierce dinner service, the most prominent piece was a porcelain centerpiece with three figures representing love, peace, and abundance.

CENTER DIVAN,
ARMCHAIR, AND OTTOMAN
Gottlieb Vollmer, Philadelphia, 1859

*Harriet Lane, niece of James Buchanan
and his White House hostess, chose a
Rococo Revival suite for the Blue Room
that remained there from 1860 until
1902. Nineteen gilded pieces, all covered
in blue brocatelle, were made by
Vollmer, who had received an earlier
commission in 1858 for decorative and
upholstery work and also produced an
ebony suite for the Green Room in 1859.*

*The most prominent piece in the
suite was a circular divan that stood in
the middle of the Blue Room. In the center of its top sat a rich, gilt, vase-shaped
ornament that was later replaced with
potted plants.*

duced by Gottlieb Vollmer, who been commissioned to do extensive decorative and upholstery work for the White House in 1858. In 1859 he received the order for the Blue Room and also for a suite of ebony and gilt furniture to be placed in the Green Room; only the Blue Room furniture remains in the White House collection. Born in Germany, Vollmer came to the United States in 1832, settling in Philadelphia where he worked as an upholsterer and cabinetmaker. He developed a growing furniture business in the 1860s and owned it until his death in 1883. His bill of sale states that G. Vollmer was a "manufactory of fashionable furniture for parlor, chamber, dining or drawing room."[17]

The most prominent piece in the new suite, a circular divan, referred to in France as a *causeuse*, a place for small talk, stood in the middle of the Blue Room. In the center of the divan's top sat a rich, gilt vase-shaped ornament that was replaced later in the nineteenth century with potted plants. The divan and other pieces in the suite, covered several times over the years in various shades of blue fabric, continued to be used in the Blue Room for more than forty years, until removed in 1902.

In May 1860, the first diplomatic delegation from the Empire of Japan arrived in Washington, and its members were received at the White House. Some examples of Japanese lacquerware—a *chigai-dana* (cabinet), a low rectangular table, and a small box— are known to have been in the White House since the mid-nineteenth century and may have been among the gifts presented to Buchanan by the delegation. Issues of *Frank Leslie's Illustrated Newspaper* with engravings featuring the diplomats' visit show an elaborate shipping box, "containing the lacquered cabinet," and a sketchily drawn cabinet, in a view of gifts being unpacked by the Japanese at the Willard Hotel. However, Buchanan directed that those presents be deposited in the Patent Office, and neither he nor the aide who dealt with the gifts remembered that anything was kept at the White House. It is therefore possible that these lacquered objects were among the items brought back from Japan by Commodore Matthew C. Perry in 1855 and presented to President Franklin Pierce, who exhibited them to the public in the White House. Benjamin Brown French, who would become commissioner of public buildings, was shown the Perry gifts by Pierce in 1855 and mentioned that objects "proper to be kept at the President's House as ornaments & furniture are to remain. . . . Some of the things are magnificent."[18] In the same year, a visitor saw cabinets from Perry's trip in one of the parlors when he met with Pierce in his office. Pierce recommended that the visitors see the "interesting specimens from Japan."[19] Whatever their provenance, the objects are excellent examples of Japanese craftsmanship of this period and would be the earliest Japanese artifacts seen in America. If not the finest work made for Tokugawa palaces, they are of a quality appropriate for state gifts. Decorated in the *maki-e* (to sprinkle) style, they depict landscapes with plum trees, blossoms, and cranes in relief, highlighted in gold leaf and with gold powders.[20]

The crisis in the nation stemming from secession and the election and inauguration of the Republican Abraham Lincoln focused attention on the President's House in March 1861 when Lincoln and his wife, Mary Todd Lincoln, along with their three sons,

Robert, Willie, and Thomas (Tad), took up residence. Lincoln's secretaries, John Nicolay and John Hay, also lived in the house, in a second-floor bedroom across the hall from Lincoln's office and the Cabinet Room. Just a few days after the inauguration, Nicolay commented on the "very pleasant offices and a nice large bedroom, though all of them sadly in need of new furniture and carpets. That, too we expect to have remedied after a while."[21] Another secretary, William Stoddard, wrote, "The East Room had a faded, worn, untidy look in spite of its frescoing and its glittering chandeliers. Its paint and furniture require renewal; but so does everything else about the house, within and without."[22]

These views of the house were ones that Mrs. Lincoln would readily have agreed with. Very quickly she began to plan changes for the house. The day after the inauguration she and her cousin, Elizabeth Todd Grimsley, explored the house from attic to basement and noted that the only elegance to be found was in the East Room and the Blue and Red Rooms. The shabby condition of the private quarters, cluttered with furniture, broken and in disrepair, prompted Cousin Lizzie to note that some pieces looked as though they had been "brought in by the first President."[23] Other visitors commented on the condition of the "miserably furnished" rooms.[24]

With the approach of outright war, threats to the president and the White House increased, and volunteer soldiers were quartered in the East Room. "The White House is turned into a barrack," wrote John Nicolay.[25] In July 1861, a visitor came upon two soldiers fast asleep on a sofa in the room.

Congress provided $20,000 for refurbishing, but by the fall of 1861 the funds already had been expended, and two additional appropriations were necessary to pay the outstanding bills incurred by Mrs. Lincoln. She frequently signed the bills, attesting to their correctness—the first wife of a president to do so. As problems arose with deficits in the government accounts, President Lincoln was forced to become involved and to authorize that the expenditures be paid. When Benjamin Brown French was appointed commissioner of public buildings in the fall of 1861, Mrs. Lincoln requested that he meet with the president to seek his approval for paying the overruns in the appropriations. She wanted French to tell Lincoln that it was common to overrun appropriations. French recounted the meeting with Lincoln: "He said it would stink in the land to have it said that an appropriation of $20,000 for furnishing the house had been overrun by the Pres. when the poor soldiers could not have blankets and he swore he would never approve the bills for *flub dubs for that darned old house*. It was, he said, furnished well enough when they

OPPOSITE:
CHIGAI-DANA
Japan, circa 1854

One of the earliest Japanese works seen in America, this lacquer cabinet has been in the White House since the mid-19th century. Once thought to possibly have been presented by the first Japanese delegation in 1860, it is more likely to have been one of the gifts brought back from Japan in 1855 by Commodore Matthew C. Perry. He presented several gifts to President Pierce that were displayed to the public in the State Rooms.

ABOVE:
The Chigai-Dana *appeared in the Green Room during the Theodore Roosevelt administration.*

Dessert Wine Glass and Compote
Christian Dorflinger's Greenpoint Glass Works, Brooklyn, New York, 1861

Dinner Plate
Haviland & Co., Limoges, France, decorated by E. V. Haughwout, New York, 1861

On Mary Todd Lincoln's first shopping trip to New York in the spring of 1861, she selected a French porcelain dinner and dessert service and a breakfast and tea service, all decorated in her favorite "solferino" purple color. She also ordered "one set of Glass ware rich cut and Engraved with the U.S. Coat of Arms." Both services were reordered several times by succeeding administrations.

came, better than any house they had ever lived in and rather than put his name to such a bill he would pay it out of his own pocket."[26]

Lincoln did not personally have to come up with the money since Congress provided additional funds to cover outstanding bills of $6,858 in early 1862, and French arranged a sale of "some old furniture." Perhaps a portion of the receipts were applied to the debit.

No first lady since Dolley Madison had taken such personal interest in the furnishings and decoration of the house. Mrs. Lincoln's interest was less in its historical associations than it was to provide a comfortable home for her family, to furnish a showcase for entertaining, and to reflect the high status of the presidency. Since 1800 the president or someone to whom he delegated the task had assumed responsibility for ordering furnishings and overseeing the interior decorations; in the Lincoln era, this was the commissioner of public buildings. However, it was Mrs. Lincoln who made the decisions on purchases. She had the assistance of her cousin Elizabeth, who traveled with her on her first major shopping trip to New York in May 1861, shortly after the shelling of Fort Sumter and the secession of the final four of eleven states, and she took "great delight" in purchasing new carpets and bedroom furnishings.[27] Mrs. Lincoln bought $1,006 worth of carpets from Alexander T. Stewart & Co., reputedly the largest retail store in the world, including a crimson Wilton for the Red Room, chintz Wilton for the "Prince of Wales" room (the major guest room), and "G & O" Wilton for the president's office. Sheepskin mats for beds and velvet and Brussels hassocks were purchased from G. S. Humphrey & Co.[28] She also selected a French porcelain dinner and dessert service and a breakfast and tea service decorated to match from E. V. Haughwout & Co. in New York, which later supplied a toilet set decorated in the same manner in her favorite color "solferino" (purple), with a gilt border and the arms of the United States, and three dozen gilded silver forks, ten dozen silver-plated and iron-handled dinner knives, and six dozen dessert knives, and also replated and repaired other flatware.[29] Additions to the porcelain dinner service and "one set of Glass ware rich cut and Engraved with the U.S. Coat of Arms," made in Brooklyn by Christian Dorflinger in 1861, were reordered several times in the late nineteenth century.[30]

Mrs. Lincoln continued her shopping in Philadelphia where she went to William H. Carryl & Bro., "importers and dealers of curtain materials and trimmings of every description." Carryl's fashionable designs for drapery treatments were illustrated in Godey's Lady's Book and Magazine in the 1850s and set the standard for design. "Here the skill and the art of every part of the civilized world are exhibited to an extent unsurpassed in any single establishment in our country."[31] She spent $7,500 for satin damask curtain cornices, lace curtains (14 pairs in an extra-large size), rich French brocades and gimps, purple French satin, and large, carved gilt-wood cornices. Among the furniture on the bill were "1 Rosewood Bedstead, 2 Arm Chairs, 4 Wall Chairs with 1 Wash Stand, 1 Bureau & 1 Sofa" costing $800 and "1 Rich Rosewood Centre Table" for $350. President Lincoln approved the expenditures in June.[32] It is the bedstead in this order that has come to be known as the "Lincoln" bed, although it was not selected for his room but for the state guest room in the northwest corner, the "Prince of Wales" room, where the prince had stayed on a visit in 1860. Mrs. Lincoln completely refurnished the room with a Wilton carpet and a light-tinted purple paper with a golden figure of a moss rose tree in bloom. The bed, made of rosewood veneers and wood grained to resemble rosewood, is almost six feet wide and eight feet long. The pierced headboard has richly carved exotic birds, grapevines, and clusters of grapes, and the footboard has similar but simpler carvings. Attached to the wall high above the headboard was a large gilded canopy carved in the form of a crown with an ornamental center shield. From it were draped bed hangings of purple figured satin and gold lace. In the early twentieth century the canopy was removed and sent to storage and eventually disappeared.

Also purchased for the guest room was a rosewood center table, "quite costly, and exceedingly beautiful."[33] This round table with a white marble top is made of layers of laminated rosewood. (Rosewood was inherently brittle, so lamination of several sheets of veneer glued together in curved shapes made furniture lighter but stronger and fanciful shapes possible.) Its cabriole-shaped legs, carved with prominent, elongated, exotic birds' heads and grapes on the knees, terminate in unusual ball and claw feet. The solid-wood stretcher, an extension of the birds' backs, supports a bird's nest with eggs in the center. The pierced apron, made of eight laminated sheets, each 1/20th-inch thick, and carved with naturalistic vines, leaves, grape clusters, and roses, is very similar to that of a labeled table

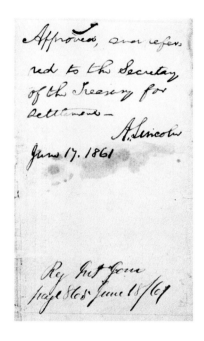

INVOICE
President Lincoln officially approved the bills for Mrs. Lincoln's expenditures in 1861.

FOLLOWING SPREAD:
THE LINCOLN BEDROOM

The room that President Abraham Lincoln used as his office and Cabinet room was furnished with objects from the Lincoln era at the request of President Harry S. Truman in 1945.

in the Museum of the City of New York by the German-born John Henry Belter (1804–63) who had operated a shop in New York since the 1840s and distributed furniture to retail outlets outside of New York City. The firm continued in business four years beyond Belter's death in 1863.[34]

Two armchairs (one of which was possibly sold at the last major White House sale in 1903) and four side chairs purchased from William Carryl, which were placed in the "Prince of Wales" bedroom, may also be by Belter, the best-known nineteenth-century cabinetmaker working with laminated woods; other New York cabinetmakers, such as Charles A. Baudouine, Joseph Meeks, and Alexander Roux who worked in the Rococo Revival style, also produced laminated furniture. The White House chairs with balloon-shaped backs made of seven layers of laminated rosewood, are of high quality and superb construction and execution. The plain, molded, and curved frames have upholstered backs and seats; the short cabriole front legs have simple, elegant carving, and the rear legs are splayed.

The Carryl purchases also included a bureau; in the White House is a dressing bureau of the 1860s with a marble top and carved mirror *étagère* in three sections that may be the one purchased by Mrs. Lincoln, or it could be another rosewood and glass bureau purchased by her in 1864. Like the other bedroom furniture, it is made of rosewood with rosewood veneers. The crest of the mirror has a central carved cartouche flanked by cherubs.

Fine French wallpapers also came from Carryl for the president's room, Mrs. Lincoln's room, guest rooms, and the nursery and were installed in the summer of 1861. In October, Mrs. Lincoln bought French papers for the East Room, the Red, Blue, and Green Rooms, along with 1,600 feet of gilt molding. In approving this bill, Mrs. Lincoln wrote, "Mr. Carryl has bought the papering according to order, he particularly desired to select it for the rooms, of the richest style."[35] Carryl's bill for $3,549 stated that the papers were "as selected by Mrs. Lincoln," and Carryl wrote to the commissioner of public buildings stating

OPPOSITE:

BED
American, c. 1861

This bed, often called the "Lincoln Bed," was purchased by Mrs. Lincoln in 1861 for the principal guest room. President Lincoln did not sleep in the bed although other presidents did. Made of rosewood veneers and wood grained to resemble rosewood, the bed, eight feet long, has a headboard richly carved with exotic birds, grapevines, and clusters of grapes.

BELOW, LEFT:
The original gilded canopy and bed hangings of purple satin and gold lace appear in this photograph from the 1870s but were removed in the early twentieth century. They were replicated for the bed in 2005.

BELOW, RIGHT:
In the early 1890s, the Lincoln era bed, center table, and chairs were still in the guest room.

ARMCHAIR AND SIDE CHAIR
American, c. 1861

Two armchairs and four side chairs were among the items purchased in 1861 for the guest room. The excellent construction and execution of these balloon-shaped chairs, made of seven layers of laminated rosewood, suggest the work of New York cabinetmaker John Henry Belter.

that they had purchased the paper in Paris at Mrs. Lincoln's order. The earliest photograph of the East Room shows the patterned paper ordered for it "in Parisian style of heavy velvet cloth paper, of crimson, garnet and gold. It gives a massive appearance to the room, and is quite rich. In the daytime it seems rather dark; but when the soft light of the great chandeliers fills the room, it develops its full richness and harmonizes to a shade."[36]

During the summer of 1861, the upholsterer and paperhanger John Alexander was engaged to put the house in order. He cleaned and replaced curtains and carpets, reupholstered furniture, and repaired and regilded furniture and frames. Each summer when there was no entertaining and the family lived three miles away at the Anderson Cottage on the grounds of the Soldier's Home, he continued much the same kind of work throughout the Lincoln administration.

Northern newspapers reported on Mrs. Lincoln's shopping trips and her expenditures, and critics viewed them as excessive and extravagant. By the end of 1861, the refurbishing had been completed, and in the spring of 1862 a positive review of

responsibilities to her daughter, Martha Patterson, who lived at the White House with her husband, a senator from Tennessee, and their two children. Two of the Johnsons' sons, Robert and Andrew, and their widowed daughter, Mary Stover, with her three children, were also in residence.

The commissioner ordered a dozen "comfortable" parlor chairs and instructed G. M. Wright, a local cabinetmaker and furniture dealer, to call on Mrs. Patterson to see what wardrobes and bureaus were needed to match the furniture already in use.[50] Wright supplied a large amount of oak and walnut furniture for family rooms, including rocking chairs.[51]

President Johnson instructed Commissioner French to order silver and additional pieces of the "solferino" china selected by Mary Todd Lincoln. E. V. Haughwout & Co. in New York was requested to examine the old silver and china and "replace such of the silver as has been lost and such of the china as has been broken."[52] At the end of 1865, Congress appropriated $30,000 to refurnish the house, and in 1866 another $40,000 was requested since the Johnsons had to buy basic housekeeping items such as beds, bedding, table linens, and furniture for the family quarters and silver and china. Also, during the summer of 1865, a flood in the house from overflowing gutters resulted in ruined carpeting and furniture that had to be repaired and replaced. When the new silver arrived in 1866, French oversaw its unpacking and ordered a new inventory, which he sent to Mrs. Patterson. He also appointed a steward to oversee and be accountable for the silver, china, and glassware.

Although Congress had authorized $76,000 for the President's House since 1865, it still was not enough, and French went to President Johnson to ask him to request more funds from Congress. Johnson told him that if he could not "fit up the public portion of the house in a manner creditable to the Nation" that he should not do it at all. Johnson wanted the public part of the house to be handsomely furnished, but he told French that he cared nothing about the private quarters. "It was good enough for him."[53] Johnson did move the Cabinet Room one room to the west, where the Cabinet met until 1902.

In May 1866, the interior of the house was dismantled to repair and refurnish it. French met with Mrs. Patterson and arranged for the work to be done in the public rooms. When money ran short, French brought members of the appropriations committee to show them what was needed, and they agreed to provide another $20,000; in January 1867, another $35,000 was appropriated. More than $135,000 was spent on White House interiors from 1865 to 1869. Mrs. Johnson left decisions to Martha Patterson, only once expressing her wishes, that the painting of the East Room ceiling be of the best quality. The importance of pleasing the family was expressed by the commissioner: "All repairs at the President's should be made in the very best manner and with all possible economy but with the ulterior object, always, of giving satisfaction to the family. Whatsoever Mrs. Patterson desires should be done."[54] It was Mrs. Patterson's desire and determination that whatever was done was done properly and thoroughly and that there should be "no mingling of the old and the new."[55]

OPPOSITE:

DECANTER AND FRUIT BASKET
E. V. Haughwout, New York, 1866, and Haviland & Co., Limoges, France, decorated by E. V. Haughwout, New York, 1866.

President Andrew Johnson requested that additional pieces of the Lincoln dinner service be reordered in 1865 and the glassware in 1866 and 1869. Much breakage had occurred since 1861.

The State Dining Room, shown here in 1893, reflected Louis C. Tiffany's decoration of a decade earlier and the alterations made in 1891 when electricity was installed. The four walnut side tables, which had been placed along the walls by 1867 (visible beneath the sconce at the right of the photograph), would remain in the room for nearly fifty years.

Hubert Shutter was engaged to paint, fresco ceilings, and gild centerpieces and cornices in several rooms in the summer and fall of 1866, the first such work since 1853. The East Room and parlors were repapered with panels surrounded by black-and-gold borders, lace curtains made in Europe were hung, carpets cleaned, and furniture regilded, repaired, and upholstered. Except for the East Room, the state rooms were ready for the New Year's Day reception on January 1, 1867. In the family and office quarters much of the old carpeting, curtains, and furniture was repaired and reused.

In the last year of the administration, a large order for diamond-cut and engraved glassware with the arms of the United States was placed with the Washington firm of J. W. Boteler. This service was probably a duplicate of the Lincoln service.[56]

Four large walnut console tables with carved shields in the center were placed in the State Dining Room. The 1867 inventory listed "4 side tables to fit the piers" as in the room, and they appear in early photographs.[57] These rectangular tables, with spiral-turned rear legs and molded and carved front legs, have shields derived from the Great Seal and could be the four walnut side tables purchased in 1853 when gilded mirrors with similar shields were acquired.

Few administrations received such largess in furnishings' funds from Congress as were granted in the Johnson era, despite the acrimony of an impeachment trial. In 1868 nearly all parts of the White House were accessible to visitors, and "something of interest may be found in all apartments," recounted a Washington guidebook.[58] With the costly expenditures and extensive changes to the interior, it would have seemed that the house was in good order for Ulysses S. Grant and his family. However, it did not take long before work began again.

SIDE TABLE
Attributed to A. & H. Jenkins, Baltimore c. 1853

Four walnut side tables, each with the shield from the Great Seal of the United States, were in the State Dining Room by 1867. They may be the four side tables purchased in 1853 when gilded mirrors with similar shields were placed in other state rooms.

THE STATE FLOOR:
THE
RED ROOM

LEFT:
William J. Clinton administration, 2000

BELOW:
Engraving, United States Magazine,
September 1856

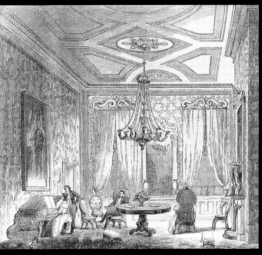

LEFT:
Rutherford B. Hayes administration, c. 1877

BELOW:
Louis C. Tiffany decor of 1882

RIGHT:
Theodore Roosevelt administration, 1902

OPPOSITE, TOP LEFT:
Franklin D. Roosevelt administration, 1940

OPPOSITE, TOP RIGHT:
Harry S. Truman administration, c. 1948

OPPOSITE, BELOW:
John F. Kennedy administration, 1962

"On the whole, isn't the people's parlor a pleasant place?"

FIVE

RENAISSANCE REVIVALS AND THE AESTHETIC MOVEMENT, 1870S–1890S

ULYSSES S. GRANT, RUTHERFORD B. HAYES,
JAMES A. GARFIELD, CHESTER A. ARTHUR, GROVER CLEVELAND,
BENJAMIN HARRISON, WILLIAM MCKINLEY

U lysses S. Grant, elected to unify the country after the tumult over Reconstruction policies that led to Andrew Johnson's impeachment trial, was the only nineteenth-century Republican president to serve two full terms. He and his wife, Julia Dent Grant, with their children, Frederick (Fred), Ulysses Jr. (Buck), Ellen (Nellie), and Jesse, as well as Mrs. Grant's parents, Col. and Mrs. Frederick Dent (he died in 1873), entered the White House in 1869 and remained until 1877. Fred, who was at West Point until 1871, and Nellie were each married in Grant's second term, with Nellie having a large East Room wedding in 1874. After the initial confusion of moving from their I Street home and of selecting household staff, Julia Grant settled in and grew to love the house. ". . . If I could have my way, would never have it changed. Eight happy years I spent there—so happy! It still seems as much like home to me as the old farm in Missouri. . . ."[1] Fond of society, she relished her role as hostess and "enjoyed to the fullest extent the opportunity afforded me at the White House."[2]

During the spring and summer of 1869, Mrs. Grant began to set the house in order for her family. She replaced hall carpets that, she said, were "much worn and so ugly I could not bear to look at them" and rearranged furniture that she found scattered about the family quarters, placing the pieces in suites since she wanted each room to have its own set. The Grants' youngest son, Jesse, recalled the state of the President's House: ". . . I remember that I was very unfavorably impressed by the dingy, shabby carpets and furniture in this new home. I was often at the White House during the incumbency of President Lincoln, but I do not recall that these things impressed me then. Perhaps it was my mother's disap-

OPPOSITE:

PLATTER
Haviland & Co., Limoges, France, 1880

President and Mrs. Rutherford B. Hayes's French porcelain dinner service of 1880 included a dinner platter, "Wild Turkey." Etchings of each design (below), based on watercolors by American artist Theodore R. Davis, were made in France for transfer to individual pieces.

proval of the furnishings, rather than my own, that I now recall. But I do know that the interior of the house was not attractive when we first arrived there but as new furnishings were installed and the old rearranged under mother's skillful direction, the White House became a real home."[3]

With a $25,000 Congressional appropriation, Julia Grant first concentrated on the family quarters and the suite of offices for the president and his staff at the east end of the family floor. In the first month of the Grants' residency, the Washington firm of W. B. Moses supplied several pieces of walnut and rosewood furniture (wardrobes, marble-top tables, rocking chairs, book stands) and one "fine parlor suite covered in blue satin,"[4] and it continued to supply additional furniture for family and office areas in 1870 and 1871.

While the Grant family summered at their cottage in Long Branch, New Jersey, the work proceeded. By the fall of 1869, workmen had begun to arrange furniture in the domestic areas of the house, but the offices of the president and his secretaries were uninhabitable while the repairs were still ongoing. Boxes of furniture were shipped by rail from New York, and the White House was billed $6,409.75 for furniture and decorating by the Pottier & Stymus Manufacturing Company of New York, which had been in business since 1859. The French-born Auguste Pottier (1823–96), a cabinetmaker, had arrived in New York in 1847, worked with Gustave Herter in the 1850s, and subsequently established with William Pierre Stymus, an upholsterer, one of the leading decorating firms in New York. (By 1871 it had grown to include a factory that occupied a full block on Lexington Avenue; by the 1890s Pottier & Stymus had wealthy clients such as Henry M. Flagler, William Rockefeller, Fred T. Steinway, Mark Hopkins, and Leland Stanford.)[5]

Pottier & Stymus had received commissions for work in the Treasury Department offices of Salmon P. Chase in 1863 and in the Navy Department under Gideon Welles in the early 1860s. Perhaps one of these former Cabinet officials had recommended the firm to President and Mrs. Grant, who may also have earlier admired the offices themselves. The firm had "a world wide reputation for the superior grades of furniture and wood-work which they manufacture as well as for their artistic conceptions of interior decoration. . . The articles they manufacture are from special designs of their own, or from designs of architects. . . . There are no stock patterns . . . but individual creations, unhackneyed, special, unique and worthy to endure for centuries as noble heirlooms. The foremost point of interior decoration is to have a firm like Pottier & Stymus and Co. attend to all parts of the work, so that the whole may be harmonious."[6] Although this glowing review was

OPPOSITE:

The Lincoln Sitting Room served as an office for the president's staff until 1902. It contains several White House objects from the Victorian era, including the marquetry center table shown below.

BELOW:

CENTER TABLE
American, c. 1875-85

This table with an intricate marquetry center panel originally was in the Green Room in the 1880s and 1890s.

SOFA AND ARMCHAIR
Pottier & Stymus Manufacturing Co.,
New York, 1869

A suite of Renaissance Revival style wal-
nut furniture of monumental propor-
tions was made for President Ulysses S.
Grant's Cabinet Room in 1869 by one of
the leading New York decorating firms.
The United States shield is carved on the
crest of the sofa.

written over two decades after completion of the White House project, the Grants probably turned to this prestigious firm for similar reasons.

Mr. Stymus came to Washington to personally supervise the work. Among the
items on the bill for the Cabinet Room were a suite of French walnut furniture, including
a sofa, 10 stuffed back chairs, 4 arm chairs—all covered in tapestry. In addition the bill
listed "1 Revolving chair, 1 Rack, 1 Patent Revolving Secretary, 1 Table for 8 persons, 1 Gilt
Mantelframe/Best French plate, 2 Window Cornices, 2 Sets Draw'g Curtains with
draperies." Among other purchases were a fire screen, a walnut side table, a seven-foot
chandelier, wall brackets with globes, and a Rose du Var marble mantel.[7] Pottier & Stymus
had the Cabinet Room painted in yellow tints and hung tapestry and lace curtains looped
back at the windows. The firm also supplied items for the secretary's room used by General Horace Potter, Grant's longtime aide, in Lincoln's former office and Cabinet Room.

The Pottier & Stymus furniture incorporated many elements of the Neo-Renais-
sance or Renaissance Revival style that became popular in France during the reign of
Emperor Napoleon III and Empress Eugénie. This massive style appeared at the Crystal
Palace Exhibition in London in 1851 and in New York by 1853, where it was interpreted by
several American firms. The White House black walnut furniture is of monumental proportions and bears motifs typical of the style—massive crests or rounded pediments enclos-
ing a crest (the secretary and the sofa both have a carved shield from the arms of the United
States); vase-turned legs with rings above the feet; decorations with incised lines (arrows
and stars), angular scrolls and pilasters, and machine-carved ornaments and panels.

During the Grant administration, the Cabinet met on Thursdays and Fridays,
with each member seated around the Pottier & Stymus "Table for 8 persons" in order of
the establishment of his department. The eight drawers, with locks, were made so that each

official could safely leave state papers between meetings. The furniture remained in the Cabinet Room—it was often an office for the president as well—from 1869 until an office building (the West Wing) was built with expanded spaces for the president, his staff, and Cabinet in 1902. The chairs were then offered as souvenirs to the Cabinet, and the "Patent Revolving Secretary" was bought for $10 by President Hayes's son, Webb, who had used the desk while serving as his father's personal secretary in the White House.[8] In 1961 Jacqueline Kennedy reinstalled the six surviving pieces from the Pottier & Stymus suite of furniture in their old location and renamed the room the Treaty Room.

The table from the suite, selected by Presidents William J. Clinton, George W. Bush, and Barack Obama as their desk in the Treaty Room office, has been witness to important events in the nation's history. Several international treaties and agreements have been signed on the table: the peace protocol ending the Spanish-American war (1898), the Kellogg-Briand Peace Pact (1929), the Arms Limitation Treaty with the Soviet Union [SALT] (1972), the Egyptian-Israeli Peace Treaty (1979), the Israeli-Palestinian Declaration of Principles (1993) and other Middle Eastern agreements and accords in 1994, 1995, and 1998.

An unusual black marble and malachite clock was selected from the New York importer Browne & Spaulding Co. in 1869 for the Cabinet Room. The case contains three dials—a clock, a perpetual calendar, and a barometer—and a thermometer. Made in France, the clock does not bear maker's marks, but is similar to other works by S. Marti et Cie. Several French marble mantel clocks were selected by the Grants for the state rooms and remain in the White House.

At the beginning of Grant's second term in 1873, $100,000 in additional funds from Congress were used for major furnishing projects. On the state floor, the East Room was extensively renovated and decorated in the taste of the "Gilded Age" under Alfred B. Mullet,

CONFERENCE TABLE
Pottier & Stymus Manufacturing Co., New York, 1869

The Cabinet table has eight locked drawers, one for each Cabinet member in 1869. Several international treaties and agreements have been signed on the table.

RIGHT:

MANTEL CLOCK

France, c. 1869

This black marble and malachite clock with three dials—a clock, perpetual calendar, and barometer—and a thermometer sat on the Cabinet Room mantel.

BELOW:

President Hayes shown at a Cabinet meeting in 1879 in what is now the Treaty Room, with the Grant era furnishings in use.

OPPOSITE:

The Treaty Room was the Cabinet Room from 1866 until 1902 when the West Wing was built. Since then, several presidents have used it as their private office on the second floor. The Grant Cabinet table has been chosen by recent presidents as their desk.

the supervisory architect of the Treasury. The William King furniture that had been in the room since 1818 was later sold at auction, and the handsome chandeliers that had hung there since Andrew Jackson's time were removed. The ceiling, divided into three panels, was newly frescoed, the walls were papered a delicate pearl gray and gilt, and the room was further embellished with a double row of white-and-gold columns, three immense cut-glass chandeliers that "blazed like mimic suns," and four large white-painted mantels. The room was "pure Greek" according to a Washington guidebook; another visitor commented approvingly, "On the whole, isn't the people's parlor a pleasant place?" But a later critic remarked that it "resembled the main salon of that time, seen on the Long Island Sound steamers."[9]

The walls of the adjacent Green Room were papered a vivid emerald touched with gold and the rosewood furniture cushioned with green-and-gold brocatelle used also in the draperies. In 1875 Mrs. Grant undertook the refurbishing of the Red Room and called upon Herter Brothers in New York, which had supplied bedroom furniture in 1872 when it was paid $5,016.30 for a "rich" walnut bedstead, bureau with glass, and a washstand, two rosewood wardrobes, two dressing mirrors, a sofa covered in satin, and six chairs.[10] For the Red Room, Herter Brothers acted as the interior decorator, one of the earliest cabinetmaking firms to do such work, making and installing draperies of golden bronze Japanese satin damask. The Red

CENTER TABLE
Herter Brothers, New York, c. 1875

Julia Grant called on Herter Brothers, a renowned New York firm that supplied sophisticated interiors and furniture, to decorate the Red Room in 1875. This rosewood center table, with carved lion's heads, has intricate marquetry inlays of satinwood, holly, and boxwood. It stood in the center of the room.

Room order included two rosewood and gilt sofas and six chairs, all covered in bronze satin damask, two "all gilt" reception chairs, covered in black and gold Japanese velvet, and two lady's chairs, one covered in blue lampas, another with red and gold Japanese brocade, one "rich rose-wood inlaid & gilt centre table," and a black-and-gilt screen with "real" Aubusson tapestry.[11] Only two pieces remain in the White House—one of the lady's chairs (a gilded armchair) and the rosewood center table.

The armchair, of gilded ash, has armrests that terminate in carved lion heads with open jaws and a stylized mane surmounted with an acanthus leaf. Its turned and tapered fluted leg forms also appear on other Herter pieces. The rectangular center table, also with carved lion heads, bears the remains of the only known surviving Herter Brothers paper label. Made of solid and veneered rosewood on walnut, the table has intricate marquetry inlays of satinwood, holly, and boxwood; traces of gilding remain on the stretcher. The shaped rectangular top has unusual inlays—in the rounded corners are lion heads and around the edge of the top and on the apron are stylized floral motifs. The elaborately carved stretcher originally supported a classical urn; it was removed at some time, perhaps after it was damaged, and a replica made.

The renowned Herter Brothers firm, founded in 1865 by two German cabinet-makers, Gustave and Christian Herter, was among the most important New York firms in the 1880s supplying sophisticated furniture and interiors influenced by the English Aesthetic Movement. It was one of the first American firms to incorporate Japanesque elements in their furnishings, such as the ebony suite made for the Red Room.[12] The firm continued to work for the White House until 1902 when it received a commission for interior work in Theodore Roosevelt's State Dining Room, Red Room, and Green Room.

In 1876 President and Mrs. Grant attended the Philadelphia Centennial Exposition, organized to celebrate the one hundredth anniversary of the Declaration of Independence by focusing on the most advanced manufacturers in the United States and Europe. Interest in the country's history increased, and the White House began to be recognized as historic. While vacationing at their New Jersey beach home, Mrs. Grant visited the exposition several times. "I took much pleasure in selecting a piece of silver for the Executive Mansion and was happy in securing a piece entirely American in history,

ARMCHAIR
Herter Brothers, New York, c. 1875

Herter Brothers made thirteen pieces for the Red Room, including two lady's chairs, one of which survives. The arm rests terminate in carved lion's heads, a motif that appears in other Herter pieces.

ABOVE:

FIRE SCREEN
Edward A, Richter, Vienna, Austria,
c. 1876

After this gilded screen was exhibited at
the Centennial Exposition in 1876, it
was donated to President Grant and
placed in the Red Room.

RIGHT:

TOBACCO BOX
George B. Sharp, Philadelphia, c. 1869

President Grant's secretary of the navy
presented him with this box containing a
wheel to cut cigars in 1869.

ideal, skill, and material," she wrote concerning a large center-piece exhibited by the Gorham Manufacturing Company.[13]

Made in 1871, the centerpiece depicts the story of Hiawatha from Henry Wadsworth Longfellow's poem. On each side of the base is an inscription, "All Alone Went Hiawatha Through the Clear Transparent Water" and "Swift or Slow at Will He Glided Veered to Right or Left at Pleasure." The mirrored base representing a lake, is supported by crouching bears and surrounded by a border of grasses, bulrushes, and water lilies, a turtle and lizards. On the mirror is a high-masted canoe modeled after Longfellow's description of Hiawatha's birch-bark canoe. Hiawatha is seated on robes of fur in the stern, and atop the mast is a squirrel, perhaps the one named "Adjidaumo" in Longfellow's poem. "You can imagine the effect," exclaimed Julia Grant.

The centerpiece was placed on the Herter table in the Red Room and later moved to a sideboard in the State Dining Room; as the century progressed, the White House domestic staff began calling it the "ship of state." It remained on prominent view for decades in the Family Dining Room. Often filled with flowers such as violets, primroses, and lilies of the valley, it also served as a centerpiece for state dinners and, in the twentieth century, for teas.

A small silver piece associated with President Grant is a more personal item—a tobacco box engraved with flower heads and the inscription "President U. S. Grant from A. E. Borie." A Philadelphia businessman, Adolph E. Borie, served briefly as secretary of the Navy in 1869. Made by George B. Sharp of Philadelphia, the box has two hinged compartments with gilt interiors, one fitted with a revolving wheel to cut cigars.

A gift presented through the Austrian government to President Grant in 1877 has remained in the White House collection. Carved and gilded, this fire screen surmounted by a large eagle has an embroidered panel of a European domestic scene by Edward Richter of Vienna. After the screen had been exhibited at the Philadelphia Centennial in 1876, Richter requested that it be given to President Grant, who accepted it on

CENTERPIECE
Gorham Mfg. Co., Providence, R.I., 1871

On a visit to the Centennial Exposition in 1876, Julia Grant selected this "Hiawatha Boat" centerpiece, based on Henry Wadsworth Longfellow's poem.

"ALL ALONE WENT HIAWATHA THROUGH THE CLEAR TRANSPARENT WATER"

COMPOTE, CAKE STAND,
AND DINNER PLATE
*Haviland & Co., Limoges, France,
1869-70 and 1874*

*A beautifully decorated French dinner and
dessert service with hand-painted flowers
was ordered by President and Mrs. Grant
in 1869 and reordered by them in 1873 in
preparation for the White House wedding
of their daughter, Nellie, in 1874.*

the condition that it become part of the furnishings of the Executive Mansion, as the White House was then called. The screen was placed next to the Red Room mantel where it stood during the last quarter of the century.

The Grants entertained often during their eight years in the White House. From the Washington retailer J. W. Boteler & Brother they purchased a beautifully decorated French buff-bordered dinner and dessert service with hand-painted American flowers, made by Haviland in 1870. Additional pieces were purchased in 1873 when the Grants began preparing for the 1874 wedding of their daughter, Nellie. In 1870 Boteler also supplied a rose-banded dinner service, again made by Haviland. A less formal service, it was not commissioned exclusively for the White House, but was an open stock pattern. Examples of both sets are in the White House.[14]

In the Grant White House, the elegant existed with the practical. Spittoons (forty were in the house in 1869) and water coolers were placed in spaces frequented by the public and in the office areas; a blue china card receiver in the main hall was provided for visitors who left their calling cards with the expectation of an invitation to a tea or reception.

The presidency of Rutherford B. Hayes began in a cloud of controversy over the results of the election of 1876. Hayes had not received a majority of the popular vote, and several of the Electoral College votes were contested. The election was finally decided in Hayes's favor by a congressional commission. The official inauguration day, March 4, fell on a Sunday when no public ceremony would take place, so President Grant invited Hayes and his family to the White House for dinner on Saturday evening, March 3, 1877. Before dinner Hayes took the oath of office in the Red Room—the only nineteenth-century president inaugurated in the White House. The Grants' personal effects were removed from the White House that afternoon, but the Grants stayed in the house for another day and a half as Mrs. Grant had arranged a luncheon for the Hayeses when they returned to the White House after the public inaugural ceremony at the Capitol on March 5.

Lucy Webb Hayes, the first first lady with a college degree, brought to the White House a "home-iness not often found in official residences."[15] Like the Grants, the Hayeses also had young children—Fanny and Scott. Another son, in his early twenties, Webb, served as secretary to his father, and his two brothers, Rutherford (Rud) and Birchard, were away at college. Many of the Hayeses' Ohio relatives and friends visited and stayed with them during their four years in the White House, including a cousin, Emma Foote, and a niece, Emily Platt, who assisted Mrs. Hayes as her secretary and was married in the Blue Room in 1878. Living accommodations for a large family and guests were inadequate, although there were eight rooms, a library, and one bathroom for family use. "Never during the time my father was President, did I have a bedroom or even a bed to myself," recalled their son Rutherford. He slept on cots in halls, couches in reception rooms, on the billiard table, and even in bathtubs.[16]

Two pairs of maple side chairs, in imitation bamboo, probably made in New York, were in President and Mrs. Hayes's bedroom in the late 1870s. No order for the suite has been found, and it may have been purchased in the prior administration by Julia Grant. In 1878 a reporter, permitted a rare tour of the family quarters, described their bedroom. "The furniture is Eastlake, and the woodwork light in color; the upholstering and hangings are blue cretonne."[17] A guest bedroom had another set of furniture in the same light wood, style, and finish. Imitation bamboo furniture became popular in Europe and America after Commodore Perry's expedition to Japan in 1854, and interest further increased as

ABOVE:
SIDE CHAIR
Probably New York, c. 1873-77

Maple furniture made in imitation bamboo became popular in America following Commodore Perry's return from Japan in 1855 and the later influence of the British Aesthetic movement. Two sets were in White House bedrooms in the 1870s.

LEFT:
President and Mrs. Hayes's bedroom shown in the late 1870s, with a suite of imitation bamboo furniture.

RENAISSANCE REVIVALS AND
THE AESTHETIC MOVEMENT

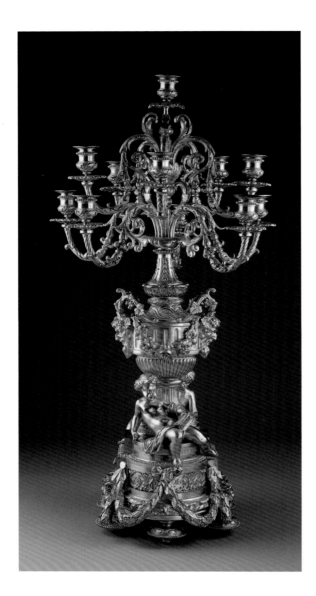

ABOVE:

CANDELABRUM
Probably European, c. 1880

Lucy Hayes selected two pairs of gilded brass candelabra from Tiffany and Company for the State Dining Room in 1880. They have been there ever since.

OPPOSITE:

DINNER SERVICE
Haviland & Co., Limoges, France, 1880

The unusual shapes and designs of the Hayes state service were created by Theodore R. Davis who suggested that each of the five courses—soup, fish, game, dinner, and dessert/fruit—feature American plants and animals.

Americans followed the British Aesthetic Movement from the mid-1870s to 1890. Like other Americans, White House occupants selected it for their rooms.

Mrs. Hayes immediately assumed the duties of the nation's hostess, arranging receptions for the diplomatic corps and the Army, Navy, and Marines, as well as the first of her Saturday public receptions, all within her first few days in residence. As was true of earlier administrations, the receptions were crowded affairs. After the public receptions, a member of the White House staff went around with a basket of glass pendants, replacing those taken from chandeliers by souvenir seekers who also cut sections from the bottoms of draperies.[18]

President and Mrs. Hayes were antiquarians, interested in history and art, and loved old houses. They took a special interest in assembling a collection of presidential portraits for the house and were the first family to begin to look at the historic nature of the White House and its collections. "I love this house for the associations that no other could have," said Lucy Hayes.[19] Because of the less than cordial relations between Hayes and Congress, that body was not as generous with appropriations for the house as it had been in previous administrations. Two years passed before any funds were forthcoming. In the meantime, Lucy Hayes purchased furnishings at auctions, and the Hayeses personally assumed many of the costs of keeping the house presentable and "in harmony with what is expected of the Chief Executive's mansion."[20] William Crook, a longtime White House employee and the disbursing agent for funds for the Executive Mansion, observed Mrs. Hayes looking in the attic and basement for old furniture to be restored and wrote that "many really good things owed their preservation to this energetic lady."[21] Writing desks and reading lamps in each room and books placed everywhere were indicative of the Hayeses' intellectual interests.

When funds became available, Mrs. Hayes spent much of the money converting the billiard room between the State Dining Room and the conservatory into a room for plants. In 1880 the dining room received new carpets and lace curtains, and Mrs. Hayes selected two pairs of gilded brass candelabra for the table, which have been in continuous use ever since in the State Dining Room.[22] Purchased from Tiffany & Company for $125 each, the three-tiered fixtures are heavily worked in classical motifs of floral swags, satyr heads, and figures of reclining children on the bases. The candelabra may have been made in Europe; there are no maker's marks evident on them. These heavy, solid Victorian candelabra stand in contrast to the elegant early-nineteenth-century French gilded bronze table ornaments from Monroe's time, with which they are often displayed.

The major expenditure of the Hayes administration was for a state dinner and dessert service ordered in 1879 and received in 1880 at a cost of $3,120. Made by the Havi-

land company in Limoges, France, its original designs were by the American artist Theodore Russell Davis (1840–94), an illustrator of the American West, who created unusual shapes and designs with subjects such as American plants (okra and corn), animals (turkeys, antelope, and buffalo), seafood and fish, snowshoes on an ice cream plate, and "Ohio Goldenrod" and "Maple Sugar" on dessert plates. Mrs. Hayes had wanted an American-made service, but since no American company could execute the fine porcelain required for the White House, she agreed to Davis's suggestions to have American plants and animals depicted on it. After the service arrived, Lucy Hayes wrote to Davis, "It is a delight to study the beautiful forms and paintings. One almost feels as if such Ceramic Art should be used for no other purpose except to gratify the eye."[23] The new service was first used at a dinner in the fall of 1880 to honor President-elect James Garfield. Presidents Chester A. Arthur and Grover Cleveland reordered pieces in 1884 and 1886, and more than five hundred pieces from the five-course service remain in the White House. It elicits comments from all who view this extraordinary service. Many pieces with the same design as the White House service, but with different marks on the reverse, were made by Haviland for commercial sale in 1880 and often appear at auctions and sales.

The Hayeses also commissioned a large, robust mahogany table and sideboard from Henry L. Fry (1808–95) of Cincinnati for the adjacent Family Dining Room, and the Hayes china was displayed on the sideboard. Two massive legs of the table, in the form of winged eagles, are based on the side supports of the pier tables made for Andrew Jackson's East Room in 1829 by Anthony Quervelle, two of which had been moved to the Family Dining Room. Carved with the eagles are shields from the arms of the United States. Two years later, in 1882, President Arthur had the table altered to become a side table; it remains in the White House collection.[24] Fry, born in England, taught wood carving beginning in the 1870s, and his classes began the art furniture movement in Cincinnati.[25]

One of the best-known objects in the White House is a large oak desk, the *Resolute* desk, presented to President Hayes by Queen Victoria in 1880 as a "memorial of the courtesy and loving kindness which dictated the offer" of the earlier American gift of the refitted HMS *Resolute*. When the desk arrived on November 23, 1880, Hayes sat at it and wrote to the historian George Bancroft that this was the first note he had composed at the desk.[26]

The American whaler *George Henry* discovered and extricated the abandoned British ship *Resolute* in the Arctic in 1855, and Congress appropriated $40,000 to refit and send it to England as a gift to Queen Victoria from the president and people of the United States, as a token of goodwill and friendship. The *Resolute* had been part of an expedition sent in 1852 in search of Sir John Franklin, who had left England in 1845 on a voyage to discover the Northwest Passage and was lost. The ship was trapped in ice and abandoned in 1854.

The double-pedestal desk has been used by nearly every president since 1880. Until 1961 when President John F. Kennedy selected it for the Oval Office, it was used in the

presidents' offices in the family quarters or in the ground-floor Broadcast Room. Several recent presidents—Carter, Reagan, Clinton, Bush and Obama—have also used it in the Oval Office.

When HMS *Resolute* was decommissioned in 1879 and dismantled, its best timbers were selected to make a desk for the pres-ident of the United States and a design was submitted to Queen Victoria for approval. A drawing, published in the December 11, 1880, issue of *Frank Leslie's Illustrated Newspaper,* featured front pan-els with carved medallion portraits of President Hayes and Queen Victoria, side panels with arc-tic subjects in relief and other motifs such as English and American flags and drawer handles formed of two hands illustrating the good will between the two countries. None of these motifs was included in the completed desk made by William Evenden, a skilled wood carver and joiner at the Chatham Dockyard where the ship was taken. Instead, the desk features simpler, carved moldings and floral swags. A center panel, with the carved seal of the President of the United States, was added to the front of the desk at the request of President Franklin D. Roosevelt who wished to hide his iron leg braces from view and to conceal a safe to be placed behind the panel. White House architect

PARTNER'S DESK
William Evenden, Royal Naval Dockyard at Chatham, England, probably from a design by Morant, Boyd & Blanford, London, 1880; kneehole panel by Rudolph Bauss, Washington, D.C., 1945

Queen Victoria presented President Hayes with an oak desk made from the timbers of British ship HMS Res-olute. A panel carved with the presiden-tial seal was added in 1945 for President Franklin D. Roosevelt. The desk has been used by almost every president since 1880.

A drawing of the desk featured portraits of Queen Victoria and President Hayes and side panels with arctic subjects and the English and American flags.

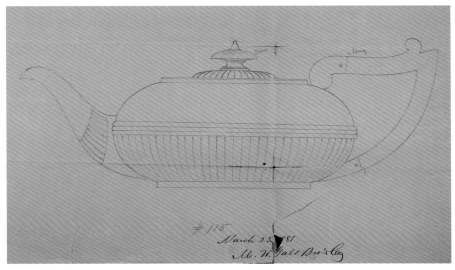

TEAPOT
Dominick & Haff, New York, 1881

Lucretia Garfield requested a silver tea pot through the established Washington firm of M. W. Galt Bro. & Co. in 1881. She selected a large pot after seeing the above drawing submitted by a New York firm with a reputation for excellent work.

Lorenzo Winslow designed the panel, and it was constructed of hard oak in the White House carpenter shop by Rudolph Bauss, who altered the original design of the eagle.[27] President Roosevelt did not live to see the panel completed before his death in 1945.

President and Mrs. Hayes left the White House in 1881, and their successors, fellow Ohioan James Garfield and his wife, Lucretia (Crete), would live in the White House less than seven months, for President Garfield died on September 19, 1881, after a disgruntled office seeker shot him at a Washington railroad station in July. Mrs. Garfield, a reticent, retiring woman, had become ill shortly after entering the White House and was on the New Jersey shore recuperating when her husband was shot. James Garfield and his interests were her chief concern, and she had had no ambition to lead Washington social life, although the Garfields did give several large receptions shortly after the inauguration. Like the Lincoln, Grant, and Hayes families, the Garfields had young children, Mary (Mollie), Irvin, and Abram, as well as two teenage sons, Harry and James. President Garfield's mother attended the inauguration, the first mother of a president to do so, and stayed in Washington to live in the White House. Garfield ordered an elevator installed for her use but it was not finished before his death.

Lucretia Garfield was interested in the house and thought that refurbishing was called for, as it had not received much attention since the Johnson and Grant administrations. President and Mrs. Garfield went personally to the Library of Congress and requested that librarian A. R. Spofford research the history of the White House and its contents, "of which very little seems to be known," wrote Garfield.[28]

Five days after the inauguration, a four-foot-square black walnut desk was commissioned from George A. Mills of Baltimore, and a few months later an "extra fine" black walnut cabinet desk with a carved top was purchased for the Cabinet Room from H. O. Towles of Indianapolis, who advertised the latest styles of cabinetware. The long-established Washington firm of M. W. Galt Brother & Co. was requested to furnish a silver tea pot for Mrs. Garfield. They sent a small pot for her to examine, along with the drawing for a larger pot, which she ordered. The silver pot, with a gadrooned body and an ebony handle, is engraved "President's House/1881" and bears Galt's mark, but it was made by Dominick & Haff of New York, which had a reputation for quality design and excellent execution.[29]

With $30,000 from Congress, Lucretia Garfield approved plans to refurbish the Green Room in the summer of 1881, and a set of ebony furniture was ordered for it, but it had not arrived before she departed in the fall. After Garfield was shot, he was taken to his southwest corner bedroom where an artist for an illustrated newspaper was permitted to make sketches of his room, furnished with the bamboo set used by President and Mrs. Hayes. The images were widely published before Garfield was moved to New Jersey to recuperate, but where he died.

Garfield's vice president, Chester A. Arthur, did not move into the White House until December 1881; he lived in the Washington home of Nevada senator John P. Jones near the Capitol for three months. Arthur was a widower; his wife, Ellen Herndon Arthur, had died a year before his presidency. Their two children, Ellen (Nell), ten years old when Arthur assumed office, and Chester (Alan), a college student, spent most of their time away at school, but joined their father at the White House for holidays and vacations. Arthur's sister, Mary McElroy, served as his White House hostess during the four-month social season each year, and she often brought her daughter with her as a companion for Nell. Another of Arthur's sisters, Malvine Haynesworth, also came from time to time to take care of Nell and assist with social functions.

Arthur was a cosmopolitan New Yorker with sophisticated, refined tastes and adamant about not moving into the White House following an inspection shortly after assuming office. Because of the mourning period following Garfield's death, no public entertaining took place until the New Year's Day open house in 1882. During the fall of 1881, Arthur went from his temporary quarters to the White House each evening after dinner, going from room to room and giving orders on what was to be changed. "He wanted the best of everything, and wanted it served in the best manner," observed William Crook, a White House clerk since Lincoln's time.[30]

Arthur instructed the officer in charge of public buildings to clean out the house and sell furnishings in disrepair and those that were no longer fashionable. Thirty barrels of old china were packed for sale, and in April 1882, twenty-four wagonloads of furniture and "junk"

President Chester Arthur sent unfashionable furniture and objects in disrepair to auction in 1882. Thirty barrels of china and twenty-four wagonloads of furniture and "junk" made this one of the largest White House sales.

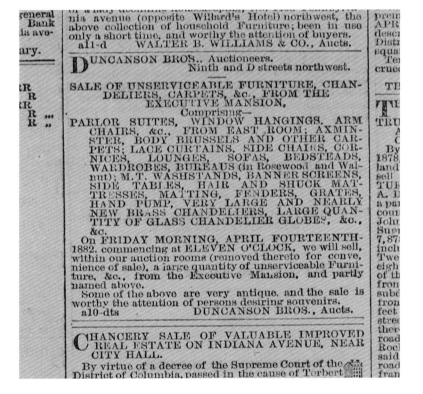

were sent to the Washington auction house of Duncanson Brothers for the first large sale of White House furnishings since 1860. Duncanson advertised several items as "very antique" and worthy of the attention of persons seeking souvenirs. Five thousand people attended the sale on April 14. The articles were "well worn" and of little value, but the bidding was "spirited" and yielded about $3,000. There was no official listing of everything in the sale, but among the known items were carpets and parlor sets, including those of the Green Room, "well worn and moth eaten," and some from the Red Room, "in better condition," furniture from the East Room, chandeliers, lambrequins, and lace curtains, four marble mantels, bureaus and bedsteads, leather-covered sofas, dining room chairs, and many utilitarian objects—water coolers, stoves, and cuspidors.[31]

Arthur relished society, took great pleasure in entertaining well, appreciated excellent dinners, and was a fastidious dresser. Mrs. James Blaine, wife of Garfield's secretary of state, attended a dinner in 1882 and observed "hardly a trace of the old White House taint being perceptible anywhere." The flowers, silver, damask, "all showing the latest style and an abandon in expense and taste."[32] The same was true for the interiors and the furnishings. Arthur had the two dining room centerpieces—the silver Hiawatha boat and the gilded Monroe plateau—and several other pieces, repaired, polished, or regilded before he began to entertain.

Washington retailer W. B. Moses & Son, on Seventh Street and Pennsylvania Avenue, which had worked on the White House since Lincoln's time, received the commission to refurnish the second-floor library and Arthur's bedroom with new wallpapers and several new chairs upholstered in satin damask, red embroidered plush, pomegranate silk plush, and olive embossed plush. Moses also supplied a four-foot-long walnut library table, revolving bookcases and walnut book racks, a cabinet, a Chinese carved table, and an ebony table and four ebony chairs and many other utilitarian furnishings for office spaces.

For the Family Dining Room where Arthur entertained personal friends, Moses provided a large extension table and a mahogany buffet table; a large oak sideboard with marble top was made by John C. Knipp & Brothers of Baltimore. Eighteen mahogany side chairs, upholstered in leather, came from Hertz Brothers of New York in the spring of 1882 for use as dining chairs, and twelve more were requested in 1883. Twenty-two copies of the chairs were made by Daniel G. Hatch & Company, whose Washington letterhead referred to its business as "Artistic Furniture and Interior Decorations."[33] In 1901 these forty chairs were in use in the State Dining Room, but all were sold at the last big White House sale in 1903. A chair purchased at that sale was donated to the White House in 1972.

Mrs. Garfield had begun planning the refurbishing of the Green Room in 1881 and Arthur permitted the work to continue. W. B. Moses repapered the walls, refrescoed the ceiling, and installed new comfortably upholstered furniture. By December 1881, the Moses firm had finished their work in the East Room, Red Room, Blue Room, and Green Room and in the two dining rooms. The official in charge of the work, Colonel A. F. Rock-

OPPOSITE:

White House families took their private meals in the Family Dining Room adjacent to the State Dining Room. The room's decor changed frequently, and it was photographed for the first time in 1889 (above, left) and in 1892, after electricity was installed (above, right). The Colonial Revival decor appeared about 1900 (below).

An ebony sofa carved with fan-shaped elements in the Japanese manner was part of an East Room suite purchased from a Washington firm in 1882.

RIGHT:
The Family Dining Room features Federal period furnishings and nineteenth-century silver services.

well of the Army Corps of Engineers, reported that the East Room had received new furniture and window hangings. An ebony sofa from the East Room, returned to the White House in the Kennedy administration, is from a suite of furniture that included sofas, arm and side chairs, and corner chairs supplied by W. B. Moses in 1882. The recessed back of the sofa has an elaborately carved crest rail with a classical mask, and its ornamental seat rail is carved with fan-shaped motifs in the Japanese manner. The arms terminate in lion's head masks.[34]

Arthur supported the proposal for a new White House to be built on the south grounds, but opposition arose to the idea of America's president no longer living in the historic house, and the plan died. He was intent on improving the appearance of the house, and less than a year after its 1881 refurbishing Arthur turned to Louis C. Tiffany & Co./Associated Artists to execute major decorative work in the East Room, Blue Room, Red Room, State Dining Room, and the Entrance Hall and Cross Hall in 1882–83. Arthur was a close friend of Tiffany's father, the jeweler Charles Louis Tiffany, who was often Arthur's houseguest. Associated Artists, whose partners were Louis Comfort Tiffany, Samuel Colman, Lockwood de Forest, and Candace Thurber Wheeler, had been created only three years earlier, in 1879, and was dissolved in 1883. The firm saw itself as an arbiter of good taste and sought to elevate aesthetic standards. The Aesthetic Movement, which emphasized art in the production of furniture, ceramics, glass, textiles, wallpaper, and metalwork, was at its height in America in the early 1880s and received its highest expression in interiors created by firms such as Associated Artists. The total environment of the White House rooms, with an emphasis on the effect of light, was in the forefront of a new way of thinking about interiors.[35] Although each member of the firm had his or her speciality (Colman—color and pattern; de Forest—carving and wood decoration; Tiffany—stained glass; and Wheeler—textiles), it is not clear how involved each of them was in the White House since all correspondence and billing was handled by Tiffany. Most of the White House work was decorative painting using gold and silver leaf and bronze pow-

ders, and it is likely that Colman was involved, as de Forest would have been in the design of new mirrors and the striking Red Room mantel. Furniture from previous administrations was retained, but stained glass, lighting fixtures, mantels, and overmantel mirrors were specially designed or made by Associated Artists. No furniture was commissioned, and the only surviving piece of furniture bought from Tiffany is a small, carved ebony stand with unusual bird supports terminating in paw feet and a base with oriental fretwork that may be either the pedestal or carved cherry wood stand bought for the Red Room in 1883. Tiffany's bill for the decorative painting, mantels, mosaics, carpeting, upholstery, mirror frames, and the regilding of several mirror frames was $12,120.[36]

The pale colors selected for the oval Blue Room reflected the enthusiasm for the arts of Japan that had grown since the London International Exposition in 1862, when Japanese objects were shown publicly in the West for the first time. (In the White House, Japanese objects had been displayed earlier, in 1855 from the Perry expedition and again in 1860 from Japan's first diplomatic mission.) The walls of the oval room were tinted a light blue-green called "robin's egg blue," which became lighter toward the ceiling and culminated in a seven-foot ivory and silver frieze of hand-pressed paper that complemented the ceiling with its oval patterns of light bluish-gray and silver. The suite of Rococo Revival furniture made by Gottlieb Vollmer in 1860 was kept, and Associated Artists regilded, repaired, and reupholstered it in blue silk canvas, a new upholstery fabric, with gold threads woven in to change its appearance. The white marble mantel was altered and inlaid with blue opalescent glass framed in silver, and Tiffany supplied a handsome brass fender and andirons that have survived. Four new sconces, three feet in diameter, had diamond-shaped mosaics of glass jewels and small mirrors, and the seven brass gas jets in each sconce added to the light effects in the room. *Artistic Homes* commented that they produced a "scintillating effect of great variety and brilliancy."[37]

In the Red Room, the Herter Brothers furniture of 1875 was reupholstered and a few new pieces added, including a large cabinet from Joseph Cabus, a New York cabinetmaker who was doing work for Tiffany in the early 1880s. This cabinet is probably the large, heavily carved ebony piece that appears in photographs of the room. The walls were painted Pompeiian red with a richly decorated tawny red frieze of abstract stars and stripes. The cornice and ceiling medallion had a golden tint with stenciled decoration in gold leaf, and the star pattern in the ceiling was executed in gold and copper tones. Fireplaces became very prominent in Aesthetic interiors, and a new cherry mantel, stained a deep amaranthine red, had brown, amber, and brown-red glass tiles that changed in tone with the light; it was surmounted by a large mirror with glass mosaics in the latest fashion.

Tiffany's *pièce de résistance*, and the first thing visitors saw as they entered the house through the front door, was the large stained-glass screen he made to link the spaces between the Ionic columns that separated the Entrance Hall from the Cross Hall. The screen was composed of sheets of opalescent glass encrusted with vitreous jewels of topaz,

OPPOSITE:

President Arthur commissioned Louis Comfort Tiffany and the firm Associated Artists to execute decorative work in the Blue Room in 1882-83. The walls were tinted a light blue-green called "robin's egg blue," which became lighter toward the ceiling and culminated in an ivory and silver frieze of hand-pressed paper. This photograph shows the room in the Cleveland administration, after the furniture had been upholstered in velvet.

Louis Comfort Tiffany's stained-glass screen with its sheets of opalescent glass encrusted with glass jewels could be seen in the Entrance Hall from 1882 until it was removed and sent to auction in 1902. The large oval in the center had patriotic motifs of eagles surrounding a shield and the monogram "US" in red, white, and blue.

ruby, and amethyst arranged in abstract panels on the sides. The doors in the central space comprised a large oval composition of patriotic motifs that included four eagles surrounding a shield and the monogram "US" in vivid red, white, and blue colors. The screen was best viewed in natural daylight rather than in the artificial light of evening. Guests commented on the "harmonious and sparkling arrangement of rich color," which was set off by the pale olive walls and gilded niches of the corridor.[38] In January 1883, Louis C. Tiffany & Company billed the White House $10 a square foot for 338 square feet of glass mosaic for the screen, for a total cost of $3,380. Later that year Tiffany also furnished "artistic" glass for the transom over the north door and the semi-circular window at the west end of the second floor for an additional cost of $1,042.94.[39] All of the glass was removed in 1902 when Theodore Roosevelt commissioned McKim, Mead & White to strip the house of its late-nineteenth-century interiors. An admirer of Charles F. McKim commented that the screen was totally out of place in the hall and "not suitable for the residence of a cultured gentleman."[40] The glass was broken up and sold at an auction of discarded White House property in 1903, where a local real estate agent for a resort development on the Chesapeake Bay purchased the glass for $275.[41] The glass may have ended up in a hotel at Chesapeake Beach, Maryland, which burned to the ground in 1923. No example of the glass has ever been brought to the attention of the White House. Of all the work done by Tiffany in 1882–83, it is his glass screen that is of most interest to White House visitors as Tiffany's work continues to be highly admired and valued.

Tiffany also selected miscellaneous porcelain and silver for President Arthur. He placed a large pair of "Satsuma" vases, made in China, on either side of the Red Room mantel; they remain in the White House as does a porcelain oval plaque painted with a Renaissance domestic scene that found a home on the mantel. A group of English and French decorative porcelain plates of various designs (used as decoration rather than as tableware), made by the Worcester Royal Porcelain Company, William Brownfield & Son, and other English manufacturers, and Haviland & Co., reflect the Aesthetic taste. Arthur admired the Hayes dinnerware, used it often, and displayed pieces prominently on the sideboards in the Family Dining Room. The table silver, all made or supplied by the firm of Louis Tiffany's father, Tiffany & Company, consisted of oyster forks, salt spoons, pepper shakers, salad bowls, serving tongs, serving stands, and candy stands.

Louis Comfort Tiffany's work for President Arthur was one of the most important White House decorative projects in the nineteenth century; however, it did not remain intact for long as presidential families in the 1890s made changes of their own to the rooms; his interiors disappeared completely in 1902. They endure only in the photographic record and in descriptions from the 1880s.

When Arthur left office in 1885, he was succeeded by Grover Cleveland, who, in 1886, married his young ward, Frances Folsom, in Tiffany's Blue Room— the only wedding of a president in the White House. Almost twenty-two, Frances Cleveland was the youngest woman to be first lady and was mentored in the role by Harriet Lane, who had served as hostess for her uncle, James Buchanan. President Cleveland's sister, Rose Cleveland, assisted as his hostess prior to the marriage.

To protect their privacy Cleveland bought a private home in the city, and they spent most of their time there, staying at the White House only during the official social season. Cleveland went to the White House each day, selecting the second-floor oval room—the traditional family sitting room and library—as his office, where he worked at the *Resolute* desk. The rooms in the private quarters

VASE (top)
China, c. 1883

VASE (bottom)
American, c. 1884

Tiffany placed a large pair of "Satsuma" vases on either side of the Red Room mantel, but he replaced them with another pair of earthenware vases from his shop that were modeled after a form made at Sèvres in the early 19th century. One of the vases has a hand-painted scene of Cupid being locked away for his mischief.

TOP RIGHT:

PLATE
*Worcester Royal Porcelain Co.,
England, 1881, painted by Charles
H. C. Baldwyn*

PLATE
Probably England, c. 1881

*A selection of decorative porcelain plates
by English and French manufacturers,
supplied by Tiffany, reflect the Aesthetic
taste of the 1880s.*

RIGHT:

PEPPER SHAKER
*Adams & Shaw Co., New York,
for Tiffany & Co., c. 1882*

COMPOTE, OLIVE DISH,
OYSTER FORK, AND SALT
SPOON
Tiffany & Co., New York, c. 1882

*President Arthur was a good friend
of the jeweler Charles Louis Tiffany
(Louis C. Tiffany's father), and a
variety of silver came from that firm.*

took on a lighter appearance, reflecting the changing decor in American homes in the late 1880s. Shortly after the president's marriage, the Washington firm of W. H. Houghton & Co. was asked to repaper and provide furniture for the northwest corner room overlooking Pennsylvania Avenue, which the Clevelands selected for their room: chairs, a cheval glass, a chiffonier, a mirror wardrobe, a ladies writing desk, a washstand, and a bureau, all in cherry as had been requested.[42] From the same firm, the officer in charge of public buildings, Colonel J. M. Wilson, requested a large, strong desk for Mrs. Cleveland, as she "writes a good deal." A desk was sent, and Mrs. Cleveland was "charmed" with it, but the chair's armrests tired her writing arm and needed to be adapted. She required wardrobes for her dresses, and two of them—"plain, strong and substantial"—were ordered from Houghton, which also supplied a special plush sofa for the space under the Palladian west window in the second-floor corridor where Frances Cleveland spent much time.

Little was done to the state rooms before Cleveland was defeated in 1888, but Houghton provided a gold plush divan for placement under the center chandelier in the East Room. Several types of decorated porcelain plates were purchased from J. W. Boteler & Son of Washington, who had supplied tableware to the President's House since the Grant administration. These plates were open-stock patterns, and the small number ordered indicated use by the family rather than for official functions.[43]

Before she departed the White House, Frances Cleveland reflected on the three years she had been first lady and on her attachment to the White House: ". . . I am not saddened by the thought of leaving the White House. One thing, though, would make me very sad—if any change should be made to this beautiful house. It is to me the most beau-

During his first term, President Grover Cleveland worked at the Resolute desk in his office in the oval room on the second floor—a room often used over the years as a family sitting room and library.

tiful house in the world. . . . It is not only the beauty of the old house that I love, but I have a feel of reverence for its past. . . . Oh, I could not bear to think of it as changed and different after I leave it."[44]

The large extended family of Benjamin and Caroline Harrison stretched the available space in the presidential living quarters to the limit. The families of their married son, Russell, and daughter, Mary McKee, joined the Harrisons, as did Mrs. Harrison's aged father, John Scott, and her niece, Mary Dimmock. The needs of this extended family led to the purchase, one day after Harrison's inauguration in 1889, of a cherry wardrobe bed, two brass beds, and one mantle bed, all acquired on the open market by W. H. Houghton & Co. of Washington.[45] More beds were ordered, including two iron bedsteads, in 1890. Popular with the Harrisons, five rocking chairs and six wicker sofas were purchased in 1890–91.

To ease the increased space demands on the second-floor family quarters and presidential and staff offices, Caroline Harrison strongly supported a proposal to construct large, winged extensions east and west of the historic house (one wing for offices; the other for social functions and an art gallery), but Congress was not forthcoming with an appropriation and the plan died.

Mrs. Harrison was a lifelong art student who had a studio in her Indianapolis home, and she set up another one in the White House. She brought her own kiln and organized china-painting classes for Cabinet wives and others in the city. At the suggestion of Mrs. Harrison, a new White House china service (including a breakfast and tea service) with a deep blue border decorated with gilded goldenrod and corn was made in Limoges, France, by Tressemannes & Vogt, and reflected her interests and love of her native state of Indiana.[46] Her interest in china painting led to her searching White House storage areas for old services that she had repaired and preserved, and she had a china closet constructed in the butler's pantry to store them. Through her concern and interest in preserving these and other historic pieces from past administrations, she can be credited with beginning the collection of White House china now in the China Room. She also chose a handsome glassware service in the "Russian" pattern in the "brilliant" style, popular in the 1880s, produced by C. Dorflinger & Sons of White Mills, Pennsylvania, with the United States coat of arms on each piece.[47]

Her interests in the house were broad. She took pride in her household management and ordered a thorough cleaning of the house from attic to basement, and she set aside furnishings she felt worthy of preservation. With $35,000 from Congress she engaged W. H. Post & Co. of Hartford, Connecticut, to refurbish several rooms after the house was wired for electricity in 1891. The Post company and its chief decorator, Edgar S. Yergason, received the White House work in 1891 through the Treasury secretary, William Windom.[48] The Green Room, the Blue Room, the Entrance Hall, the State Dining Room, the East Room, and several rooms in the family quarters—all received decorative wall and ceiling painting, new draperies, curtains, and carpets. Just nine years after the Louis C. Tiffany/Associated Artists work for President Arthur, new draperies and

OPPOSITE TOP:

BREAKFAST PLATE AND
DINNER PLATE
*Tressemannes & Vogt, Limoges,
France, 1891*

WATER GOBLET
*C. Dorflinger & Sons, White Mills,
Pennsylvania, 1891*

*Caroline Harrison suggested that a new
White House state service be decorated
with the goldenrod and corn of her native
state of Indiana. She also chose new
glassware in the "brilliant" style popular
in the 1880s and 1890s.*

OPPOSITE BOTTOM:

SCONCE
American?, c. 1891

*Electric wall brackets were installed
in the Family Dining Room when
the White House was wired for
electricity in 1891.*

fabrics in a different shade of blue, repainted ceiling and woodwork, and grillwork at the windows completely changed the appearance of the Tiffany-era Blue Room, which no longer had the ensemble effect Tiffany had achieved in 1882. The same was true for the State Dining Room, with its brownish-yellow walls and its five-foot stenciled frieze in several shades of yellow with the "lustrous" effect created by the new electric lighting. The furniture in the East Room was recovered in gold brocatelle, and new silk damask draperies and 515 yards of Axminster carpet were installed.

During the summer of 1891 while the Harrisons were away on a trip West, the changes were made. When President Harrison returned in the fall, he wrote to Mrs. Harrison (Carrie), telling her that the house looked very clean and "much improved," and he hoped that she would "find the relief from housekeeping cares a comfort." He noted the "very tasteful" rooms but was most impressed with one of the new bathrooms, with its white tile and marble and porcelain-lined tubs that he said would "tempt a duck to wash himself every day."[49]

When electricity was first installed in 1891, the gas lighting fixtures were refitted or removed to be replaced by fifteen electric chandeliers. Gone from the Blue Room were the Tiffany sconces of mosaic glass, replaced by small gilded electric brackets. Four electric wall sconces with cherubs, of brass and cut glass, were installed in the Family Dining Room by the Edison General Electric Company of New York and remain in the collection.[50]

White House rooms were extensively photographed for the first time in the late 1880s and 1890s by Frances Benjamin Johnston. Her views captured the array of objects accumulated since 1817, as seen in this detail of the State Dining Room in 1893.

Public attendance at White House receptions increased in the last decades of the nineteenth century and wreaked much havoc on the house. The large formal receptions held in the social season of January and February became restricted to those with invitations and the parlors were closed to the public, but President Harrison received all public callers "without regard to color or previous or present condition" in the East Room each afternoon.[51]

Granted rare access to the White House and the Harrisons' living quarters in 1892, the Washington photographer Frances Benjamin Johnston provided the most

extensive photographic documentation of nineteenth-century White House rooms. Johnston's beautifully composed prints reveal a house filled with an array of objects in various styles acquired for the house since 1817.[52]

In ill health during much of the time she lived in the White House, Caroline Harrison died of tuberculosis two weeks before the 1892 election in which her husband was defeated by Grover Cleveland, and her funeral was held in the East Room. She left the White House in "better order, with more modern conveniences and handsomer decorations and furnishings than ever before in its history," observed Johnston.[53]

President and Mrs. Cleveland ("the most popular woman in America") returned to the White House in 1893 with their two-year-old daughter Ruth. Two more daughters, Esther and Marian, were born in Cleveland's second term; Esther was the only child of a president to be born in the White House. As in his first term, the Clevelands purchased a private home in the city where they lived much of the time, seeking privacy, which became more difficult with the press and public's interest in the attractive first lady and their children. Press coverage of the White House and its residents increased, and by 1893 the Clevelands were written about extensively. Before the inauguration, one newspaper speculated on the Clevelands' life in the house and wrote that all Mrs. Cleveland needed to do to have an article of furniture renewed or any alterations made to the mansion was to communicate a request to the officer in charge of public buildings and "the matter would be attended to at once."[54]

In 1894 W. H. Houghton Mfg. Co., in business six blocks from the White House, papered the large northwest bedroom and the small northwest room used by the Clevelands and supplied white iron bedsteads, a Louis XIII sofa, a "gents" chair and lady's chair, and two Turkish chairs. Since several rooms had been refurbished at the direction of Caroline Harrison, few changes were made to the state rooms except for the Red Room. A Washington firm, Johnston & Kennedy, decorated it with brighter red walls and a neoclassical frieze and a ceiling in lighter tones, doing away with Tiffany's terra cotta and gilt colors of 1882. The old pine wood trim surrounding the doors was replaced with carved mahogany moldings that matched details in the mantel installed by Associated Artists in 1882.

A set of dark oak furniture (four sofas and two easy chairs) was specially made for the state floor Cross Hall by A. H. Davenport of Boston in 1895. The same firm would be commissioned in 1902 to produce a substantial amount of furniture for Theodore Roosevelt.

By the mid-1890s, the White House required additional flatware for official dinners, and Mrs. Cleveland selected a pattern ordered from Harris & Shafer and later from Galt & Brother of Washington. Old, miscellaneous White House flatware was melted down by the Treasury and the metal supplied to the firm commissioned to make new flatware. Gilded silver dinner and breakfast forks in a beaded-edge pattern were made by William B. Durgin (1833–98) whose Concord, New Hampshire, firm was one of the country's largest manufacturers of high quality flatware. The pieces were engraved by Galt's with the arms of the United States and the name "President's House," which continues to be engraved on

DINNER FORK AND
BREAKFAST FORK
*Wm. B. Durgin Co., Concord, N.H.,
1894*

New gilded silver in a beaded-edge pattern was selected by Frances Cleveland in 1894. Old, miscellaneous White House flatware was melted down by the Treasury and supplied to Durgin, one of the country's largest manufacturers of high quality flatware. This pattern is still used for state occasions.

some new pieces of White House silver. Copies of this flatware, still in use, were made in 1950 and 1993 by the Kirk firm of Baltimore. Galt's also supplied silver salad and vegetable bowls.

Another proposal to enlarge the house and create an office wing and larger rooms for public receptions was floated in the mid-1890s, but year after year Congress failed to provide the funds. Receptions continued to be extremely crowded—"great crushes"—and the masses of guests were often immovable because of lack of space.

With increased interest from the press and its focus on the lives of White House families, reporters began to write about the objects in the White House for the first time. During the presidency of William McKinley, from 1897 to 1901, articles such as "Art in the White House" and "The Bric-a-Brac of the White House" appeared in popular journals.[55] With the permission of Mrs. McKinley in 1901, the commissioner of public buildings, Theodore A. Bingham, engaged Abby Gunn Baker, a Washington journalist, to research White House china and write about it because there was so little known about the history of the services, and he thought it important to preserve the existing pieces. Baker began searching in government records and contacted former occupants of the White House and their families for accounts of their china services. She continued her work for two decades and later sought examples of the china and other memorabilia connected to its use in the White House. Baker's article on the china—the first on the subject—appeared in 1903.[56]

Commissioner Bingham's interest in the historic White House also led to the first attempt to record the history of objects other than presidential china. At Bingham's direction the doorkeeper, Thomas Pendel, who had been on the staff since Lincoln's time, went room by room recalling stories relating to the objects and when and how they had come into the White House. The accuracy of some of his stories has not held up under archival research, but the efforts to document this history began to instill a consciousness about the historical origin and importance of objects in the President's House.

President and Mrs. McKinley made few changes to the White House in their five years of occupancy except in their private quarters. Their two children had died years before, and Ida McKinley was in frail health with various chronic illnesses. She participated in White House social functions when feeling well, but she had little strength for an active social life. Most of her time was spent reading and making embroidered or crocheted work for charities. The McKinleys had lived well during their private years in Ohio, and while he was governor of Ohio, and they appreciated luxuries and refined living. In the White House, Ida McKinley's health limited her involvement to the selection of paint colors and fabrics, but in 1899 she agreed to a major refurbishing of the Blue Room, which had last received attention in 1891. Bingham, who supervised the work, commissioned W. B. Moses & Sons of Washington to change the character of its decoration planned by E. S. Yergason, who had overseen earlier work in the room for Caroline Harrison. The Vollmer furniture, in the room since 1860, was regilded and reupholstered in new light-blue fabrics chosen by Mrs. McKinley. When the room was reopened in the fall of 1899 its style was referred to as "Colonial"; an effort had been made to create a harmonious rather than a "composite" decoration, as would be seen in most rooms in the White House by the end of the century. (This approach had been reflected earlier in the 1882–83 work of Louis C. Tiffany.)

The 1899 Blue Room was the first major example of the Colonial Revival style on the state floor. Selecting what was termed the "English Colonial" influence of the late-eighteenth-century English designer Robert Adam, with its use of floral motifs derived from classical sources, the walls were covered with dark blue paper and lighter blue patterned silk framed in ivory and gold frames over which were gilded brackets with branches containing electric bulbs. Below the egg-and-dart cornice was an embossed frieze of garlands and wreaths in low relief that resembled lace embroidery. Two large gilded and ivory mirrors "of English colonial type" were placed over the mantel and over the gilded French console table that had been in the room since 1817. With broken pediments, urn finials, and Corinthian columns, the mirrors reflected the growing incorporation of late-eighteenth- and early-nineteenth-century architectural details into American homes.

Placed along the south wall of the Blue Room was a large pair of cobalt blue French porcelain vases made by Sèvres, presented to President McKinley in 1898 by Félix Faure, president of France. Donated to commemorate the inauguration of the new Franco-American cable under the Atlantic on August 17, 1898, the vases reflected the growing involvement of the United States in international affairs.

CANDELABRUM
Gorham Mfg. Co., Providence, R.I., c. 1898

At the 1899 dinner honoring Admiral George Dewey, the hero of the Spanish-American War, several pair of four-arm candelabra made of heavily chased silver plate stood in splendor on the dining table.

An 1899 dinner for Admiral George Dewey, the hero of the Spanish-American War who had defeated the Spanish navy in the Philippines, was the social highlight of the McKinley administration. The State Dining Room was not large enough to hold all of the guests, so the dinner was arranged in the long transverse corridor. Residing in splendor on the table were several pair of four-arm candelabra made of heavily chased silverplate by the Gorham Manufacturing Company in 1898. Large quantities of silver were ordered in the late 1890s and early 1900s through Galt & Brother of Washington, which contracted with companies such as Gorham to manufacture six large meat dishes, a dozen gilt bon-bon dishes, and flatware such as table, dessert, and coffee spoons and oyster forks. All remain in the White House. Reorders of the Harrison dinner and breakfast service and the "Russian" cut glass were placed with Dulin and Martin, a Washington firm with which the White House continued to place orders for tableware in the twentieth century.

A handsome three-handled silver cup commissioned from Tiffany & Company in 1898 as a gift from President McKinley to Jules Cambon, the French ambassador to the United States, is associated with the signing of the peace protocol with Spain that ended the Spanish-American War. Cambon represented Spain in the negotiations and was among those who signed the protocol in the Cabinet Room on August 12, 1898. Under the cup's openwork handles of leaves and berries are elaborate medallions with the coats-of-arms of the United States, Spain, and France. Three eagles connected by a garland of leaves support the bowl.

The last White House sale of the century occurred on December 20, 1899, when "unserviceable" furniture, china, tapestries, draperies, lace curtains, carpets, etc., were sold at the Washington sale rooms of James W. Radcliffe. Another attempt to enlarge the house was made by Commissioner Bingham in 1900 on the one hundredth anniversary of John Adams's occupancy of the house, but it, like the proposals of the 1880s and 1890s, was not successful. President McKinley's assassination in September 1901 and the assumption of Vice President Theodore Roosevelt to the presidency led to massive changes that continued to shape the White House in the twentieth century.

VASE
National Porcelain Manufactory of Sèvres, France, 1898

America's increasing involvement in international affairs is reflected in a large pair of cobalt blue porcelain vases presented by the president of France to President McKinley in 1898 to commemorate the inauguration of the Franco-American cable under the Atlantic.

PRESENTATION CUP
Tiffany & Co., New York, 1899

This silver cup was commissioned for presentation by President McKinley to the French ambassador who aided negotiations that ended the Spanish-American War.

THE STATE FLOOR:
THE
EAST ROOM

LEFT:
William J. Clinton administration, 2000

BELOW:
Engraving, Gleason's Pictorial, *May 6, 1865*

BELOW, LEFT:
Earliest photograph of Lincoln's East Room, c. 1862-67

AT BOTTOM:
Lithograph, pre-Civil War, c. 1861

BELOW, RIGHT:
Ulysses S. Grant administration, c. 1869

OPPOSITE:
William McKinley administration, 1898

WASHINGTON

EAST ROOM IN THE PRESIDENT'S MANSION.

"A house always on exhibition should look its best at all times."

SIX

NATIONAL IDENTITY AND THE COLONIAL REVIVAL, 1900–1950S

Theodore Roosevelt, William Howard Taft,
Woodrow Wilson, Warren G. Harding,
Calvin Coolidge, Herbert Hoover, Franklin D. Roosevelt,
Harry S. Truman, Dwight D. Eisenhower

D
ramatic change came to the President's House with Theodore and Edith Roosevelt and their six active children (four sons—Theodore Jr. [Ted], Kermit, Archibald [Archie], and Quentin—and two daughters, Alice and Ethel). Alice's debut in 1902 and marriage in 1906 and Ethel's debut in 1908 were major White House social events. When the family moved into the house in the fall of 1901, the need for additional living space in the private apartments became critical. The president, his staff, and the family all faced crowding and inadequacies since the staff had expanded when the Spanish-American War increased the role of the United States in world affairs.

Roosevelt succeeded where other administrations had failed when Congress passed an appropriation bill in 1902 for a temporary office building to be constructed west of the house, which resulted in the removal of government offices from the east end of the second floor and allocated the space for family bedrooms, sitting rooms, and additional bathrooms. The legislation provided $475,445 for repairs and refurnishing of the house and grounds, with $131,500 of these funds for new furnishings. The proposal came as urban designers on the McMillan Commission focused on a major plan for the city of Washington at the turn of the century. The White House was to be made structurally strong, the public spaces rearranged for more dignified and comfortable entertaining, and the State Dining Room enlarged. Extraneous additions that detracted from the architecture of the house, such as the greenhouses on the west, were to be removed. Seeking the

OPPOSITE:
CHANDELIER
William Parker, London, c. 1774

One of a pair of cut-glass chandeliers created by the preeminent London maker of fine lighting fixtures. It is among several English chandeliers donated to the White House in the 1940s.

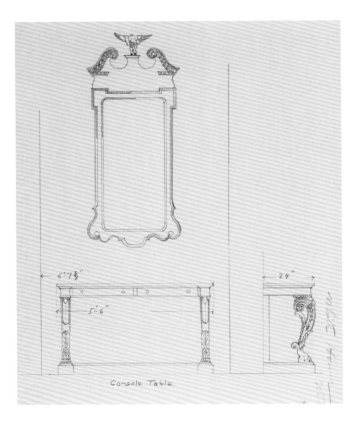

Console Table.

ABOVE:

Colonial Revival furnishings were designed for the Family Dining Room by McKim, Mead & White in 1902. The scrolled legs of the console table were inspired by an East Room table from 1829.

OPPOSITE:

SIDE CHAIR AND ARMCHAIR
A. H. Davenport, Boston, 1902

Stanford White designed chairs in the Queen Anne and William and Mary styles for the State Dining Room. The side chairs remain there today. Davenport, one of the leading manufacturers of Colonial Revival furniture, made all of the furniture for the two dining rooms.

highest quality work in America, President and Mrs. Roosevelt selected the renowned New York architectural firm of McKim, Mead & White for the extensive project, which was completed in the fall of 1902.[1]

The goal was to make changes so that the house would not have to be altered again—no longer would it be subject to changing fashion—and to modernize living conditions for its occupants, a major principle of the Colonial Revival movement in America at the turn of the century. Interior decoration in the White House continued to change in the new century, but the architectural spaces of today's house remain essentially those created in 1902. While it was the architects' intention to recreate the original early-nineteenth-century interiors, their work in major rooms such as the East Room and State Dining Room drew inspiration from French and English interiors rather than the 1790s rooms of White House architect James Hoban.

Criticism of the existing nineteenth-century interiors had come from many quarters. Architect Glenn Brown—secretary of the American Institute of Architects, Washington representative of McKim, Mead & White, and superintendent of the White House project—referred to the East Room as an "over-ornamented salon, loaded down with crude decorations." Of Tiffany's glass screen in the Entrance Hall, he noted that it was possibly beautiful in itself, "but totally out of place in this hall." The Red Room was "totally out of sympathy with the refined Georgian Mansion."[2] Another critic wrote that Tiffany's screen was "ill advised" and that the removal of it and other "anachronisms and offences to the purity and taste of the building" restored a simple dignity to the house.[3] Brown commented, too, on the furnishings, which he thought were "crude in the extreme, with poorly designed frames and no taste in the color or materials of the covers."[4]

The McKim, Mead & White interiors reflected widespread interest in the creation of a national identity that had been developing since the 1876 Philadelphia Centennial Exposition. Americans looked back to the origins of the country and an idealized past and sought antiques or reproductions of furnishings of the earliest periods of the country's history to represent that past.[5] There was a growing reaction away from pattern in wallpaper, fabrics, and carpets and away from the typical busyness in number and arrangement of objects that was very evident in the White House. This emphasis on lighter spaces was reflected in the new interiors and furnishings designed in 1902 by McKim, Mead & White for the White House and made by American manufacturers that produced work of the highest quality—A. H. Davenport of Boston, Leon Marcotte and Edward F. Caldwell of New York. (Colonial Revival designs with neoclassical motifs of floral swags, ribbons, etc., had appeared in the Red Room, Blue Room, Entrance Hall, and Cross Hall in the 1890s and on White House china services in the 1880s and 1890s.)

During the summer of 1902, while the Roosevelts were at their home in Oyster Bay, New York, Edith Roosevelt reviewed Charles McKim's proposals for paint colors, furniture, wallcoverings, and fabrics. She and the president, avid students of history, selected the "Lincoln" bed and the carved rosewood Belter table purchased by Mary Todd Lincoln for their southwest corner room. When Mrs. Roosevelt requested a desk for her use, she asked McKim to supply one that matched the rosewood table. After they had been approached by a Michigan congressman, she and the president brought up to McKim the possibility of having Grand Rapids furniture in one of the drawing rooms. McKim recommended against Grand Rapids pieces in the state rooms and suggested that all of the furniture be made by one firm, "in order to be consistent throughout."[6] Instead the new furnishings came from several firms that McKim had worked with on other projects. However, in 1903 a few pieces of Grand Rapids furniture (a bookcase and three mahogany tables) were added to the Red Room, a gift from the Grand Rapids Furniture Manufacturers Association, and made by Retting and Sweet in the Federal style after McKim's designs.[7] He turned down offers from Washington firms that had worked in the house for decades.

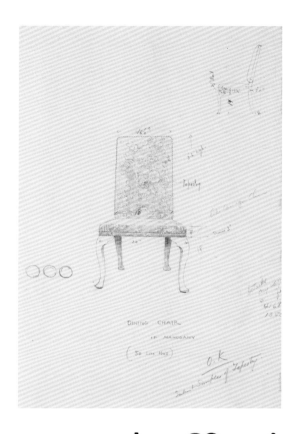

For the State Dining Room (enlarged through incorporating the space of a removed staircase) with its carved oak walls made by Herter Brothers, a New York firm that had done decorative work and supplied furnishings for the White House since 1872, Stanford White designed mahogany Queen Anne style side chairs, William and Mary style oak armchairs with caned backs, and three mahogany serving or console tables with carved eagle pedestals and marble tops modeled after Italian console tables in White's own New York house, all made by A. H. Davenport.

For the adjacent Family Dining Room, Davenport produced mahogany chairs and a mirror in the late-eighteenth-century Chippendale style and tables, a Sheraton style mahogany sideboard, and a china cabinet, all from special designs and larger in scale than those made in the early nineteenth century. A new mahogany con-

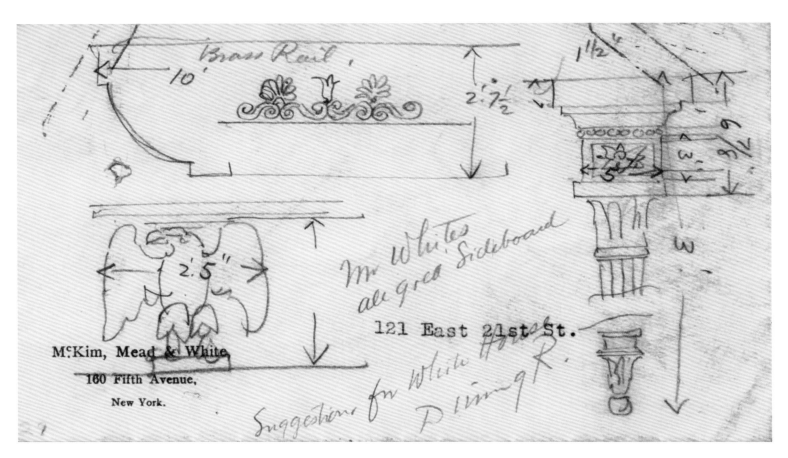

Brass Rail.

Mr White's
all green Sideboard

121 East 21st St.

Suggestions for White House
Dining R.

McKim, Mead & White
160 Fifth Avenue,
New York.

OPPOSITE:

CONSOLE TABLE
A. H. Davenport, Boston, 1902

Three mahogany console tables with carved eagle pedestals were made for the State Dining Room. The design (detail, above) was based on an Italian console table in Stanford White's New York home. Above the double pedestal table is a carved and gilded English pier mirror, c. 1790, donated in 1946.

sole table with eagle supports was inspired by the pier tables made by Anthony Quervelle for Andrew Jackson's East Room in 1829 that had resided in the Family Dining Room since the late 1860s. Davenport also received the commission for the Green Room and made a large caned-back sofa and chairs, some with rolled backs, others with shield backs, derived from early-nineteenth-century French and English designs, all painted white. The company also made Colonial Revival mahogany bedroom furniture imitating early-nineteenth-century American pieces for the four rooms in the family quarters that were converted from office spaces, and an oak bookcase for the president's study.[8]

A. H. Davenport was one of the leading manufacturers of furniture in Colonial Revival styles, and the quality of the firm's work had recommended it to McKim, Mead & White who had commissioned work from Davenport for other projects. Designs came from the firm's extensive library and also from Charles McKim and Stanford White.[9]

For the major reception room on the state floor, the Blue Room, McKim turned to Leon Marcotte of New York to produce a suite of furniture in the French Empire style. McKim was aware that a French carved and gilded suite had been made for the room in the Monroe era, but the pieces designed and created for the room in 1902 were not reproductions of the 1817 suite, which had been removed and sold in 1860. Rather, Marcotte's copies of French furniture of the Napoleonic period were very likely derived from a painted and gilded suite by François-Honoré-Georges Jacob-Desmalter (1770–1814) at the Château de Compiègne outside Paris. (McKim incorporated several

architectural details from Compiègne in the East Room paneling.) All of the furniture, including small shield-back chairs derived from English Hepplewhite designs, was painted white with gilt trim to imitate bronze mounts. The eclecticism of the furniture in the rooms was typical of Beaux Arts architects such as McKim who copied historic objects in an evolution of styles. The suite (one sofa, four armchairs, ten side chairs, and four footstools) remained in the Blue Room until 1961 when some of the original Monroe pieces were returned to the room. Marcotte also executed the interior decoration in the Blue Room, covering the walls and upholstery in a dark blue silk rep with a gold Greek key border, selected by McKim.

More than the other rooms, the Red Room retained a vestige of Victorian decor with its red velour–covered walls and large red silk overstuffed sofas and chairs, made by Marcotte, who also made small carved and caned white-and-gold painted chairs like those in the Blue and Green Rooms. In the next decade, President Wilson's daughter, Eleanor, thought the room with its velour walls, heavy velvet draperies, "hideous" rug, and overstuffed furniture "gloomy beyond words."[10]

Herter Brothers created the East Room wood paneling, but Marcotte did all the decorative work in the room—the carved and gilded window cornices, four richly carved and gilded marble-top console tables, and thirteen carved and gilded banquettes, all in the Louis XVI Revival style. Marcotte also supplied andirons and fire tools for several rooms, probably from Marcotte's Paris branch. For the Blue and Red Rooms came two identical pairs of brass andirons, in the Egyptian Revival style with reclining sphinxes on rectangular bases, copied from early-nineteenth-century French *chenets*. The Egyptian Revival style had become popular again after new archeological discoveries in Egypt.

The fashionable New York decorating firm of L. Marcotte & Co. had been in business since 1861, although the French-born architect Leon Marcotte had worked in New York with his father-in-law, Rinquet LePrince, since the early 1850s. Along with

BELOW:
ANDIRON
France, 1903

Two identical pairs of brass andirons, copied from early-nineteenth-century French chenets, *were supplied by Marcotte for the Blue and Red Rooms.*

BOTTOM:
BENCH
L. Marcotte & Company, New York, 1902

Marcotte produced carved and gilded banquettes in the Louis XVI Revival style as well as window cornices and console tables in the same style for the East Room.

Herter Brothers and Pottier & Stymus, Marcotte dominated the new field of interior decoration in the 1870s and 1880s. These firms were furniture manufacturers as well as suppliers of fabrics for draperies and upholstery and did decorative painting and interior woodwork to create unified effects in rooms such as Pottier & Stymus had done in President Grant's Cabinet Room in 1869.[11] Marcotte not only supplied furniture, but his craftsmen gilded mirror frames, painted walls, varnished doors, made draperies, and installed wall coverings. Herter Brothers' contribution was limited to interior woodwork and ornamental plasterwork in the State Dining Room, East Room, and Red and Green Rooms, and wall coverings and draperies for the Red Room and Green Room. No furniture came from the firm, which went out of business in 1905.

The nineteenth-century furniture that was not reused on the state floors was moved to the newly renovated ground-floor rooms or used in the family quarters, which were sparsely furnished with old or historic objects used by past occupants. One official

ARMCHAIR AND
SIDE CHAIR
L. Marcotte & Co., New York, 1902

Furniture copied from a painted and gilded French Empire suite in the Château de Compiègne outside Paris was commissioned from Marcotte for the Blue Room along with shield-back chairs based on English designs. L. Marcotte & Co., a fashionable New York decorating firm, executed all of the interior decoration of the Blue Room.

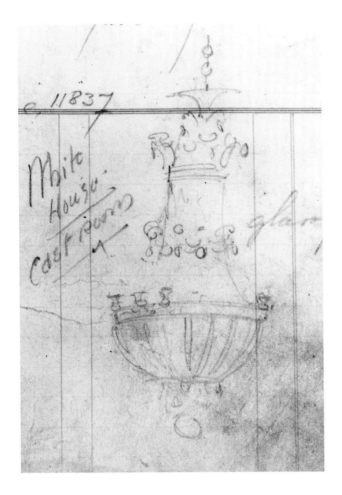

OPPOSITE:

CHANDELIER

Christoph Palme & Co., Parchen,
Bohemia (Austria-Hungary), 1902, for
Edward F. Caldwell & Co., New York

Edward F. Caldwell & Co., a firm
prominent in lighting design, supplied
new electric lighting fixtures for the
White House in 1902, including three
large Bohemian glass chandeliers (sketch,
above) for the East Room. They were
modified and shortened in 1952.

recalled that there were not a half-dozen pieces of furniture in the house worth keeping.[12] At Roosevelt's direction, condemned furnishings were sold at a major public auction in 1903 and a smaller one in 1905—the last sales of White House objects. The larger sale was held January 21, 1903, at Sloan's in Washington. Much of what was sold was office or bedroom furniture, but among the items were Tiffany's glass screen from the Entrance Hall, the large sideboard made in Cincinnati for the Hayes Family Dining Room, large gilded mirrors, mantels, furniture from the East Room, and numerous lighting fixtures. The three elaborate East Room chandeliers installed by President Grant in 1873 and chandeliers from the Blue and Green Rooms and Library were sent to the United States Capitol.[13]

Eleven years after the White House was first wired for electricity, the contract for new electrical lighting fixtures was awarded to Edward F. Caldwell & Co. of New York at the suggestion of McKim, Mead & White who approved all the designs and supervised the work. In business since 1895, Caldwell was a prominent designer of lighting fixtures. He had worked on earlier McKim, Mead & White projects and gave personal attention to the manufacturing and installation of the White House fixtures.[14] Architect Glenn Brown observed that the White House fixtures were probably the "most artistic that have been designed in the country."[15] Caldwell was paid $23,588.50 for three large Bohemian glass chandeliers for the East Room; a silver chandelier and eight six-branch silver wall sconces for the State Dining Room; a gilded metal chandelier and sconces for the Red Room; cut-glass chandeliers and sconces for the Blue Room, Green Room, and Family Dining Room; lanterns for the Entrance Hall and North Portico; eight gilded light standards/torchères for the Cross Hall and Entrance Hall; four light standards and four pairs of candelabra for the East Room; and ceiling lights throughout the house, lamps for the private quarters, and repairs and new parts to old gas fixtures that were reused. Caldwell also supplied electrical fixtures for the new office wing. Of the highest quality craftsmanship, these elaborate custom-made lighting fixtures are still in the White House. They were designed in a variety of styles derived from European precedents—the East Room light standards, modeled after a French candelabrum of the Empire period, have Egyptian motifs such as winged lions in the bases; the cut-glass chandeliers were copied from eighteenth-century English and French chandeliers.[16]

With the dramatic changes in the architecture and interior furnishings also came changes in protocol. Edith Roosevelt hired the first social secretary to assist a first lady, and the Roosevelts' formal entertaining became more structured and organized than in previous administrations. The only state service with enough pieces for larger dinners in the newly expanded State Dining Room was the Hayes service from 1880. The Roosevelts ordered

LIGHT STANDARD

Edward F. Caldwell & Co., New York,
1902

Four gilded metal and glass light stan-
dards, modeled after a French Empire
candelabrum with Egyptian motifs of
winged lions on the bases (sketch, above),
were made for the East Room and
remain in place.

another, more restrained dinner service for 120 through the Van Heusen Charles Company in Albany, New York, known to them from Roosevelt's tenure as governor of New York. Made in England by Wedgwood, the cream-white service with gold lines in the border was an adaptation of a Wedgwood pattern, "Ulunda," with the addition of the Great Seal of the United States hand-painted in color on the borders of each piece.[17] Edith Roosevelt also ordered additional pieces of Caroline Harrison's French service. Glassware supplements of Lincoln's service and of the "Russian" pattern, first made for the White House by C. Dorflinger & Sons in 1891, were also purchased.[18]

Edith Roosevelt's interest in American history and her view of the White House as a national treasure led to her support of journalist Abby Gunn Baker's research on White House china services and the donation of several pieces by presidential descendants to begin what is now the extensive White House china collection. (Mrs. Roosevelt made contributions, too.) In 1904, two tall oak cabinets with glazed doors and sides were purchased to display examples of the historic services along the walls of the Ground Floor Corridor. The cabinets, in the Arts and Crafts style, have the red decal mark of Gustav Stickley (1857–1942), an innovator in furniture design at the turn of the century. After

TEA CUP AND SAUCER
AND OYSTER PLATE
*Josiah Wedgwood & Sons, Ltd.,
Etruria, England, 1903*

In keeping with the architectural changes made in 1902, President and Mrs. Theodore Roosevelt selected a restrained pattern for their state service adapted from the Wedgwood pattern "Ulunda."

ABOVE:

CABINET

Gustav Stickley, Eastwood, New York, c. 1904

Edith Roosevelt first exhibited former state dinner services in the Ground Floor Corridor (top right). They were housed in Arts and Crafts style oak cabinets by Gustav Stickley, an innovator in furniture design at the turn of the century.

RIGHT:

The Family Dining Room shown with the Colonial Revival furnishings made for the room in 1902.

seeing White House china displayed in these cabinets, Theodore Roosevelt proposed that examples from every administration be represented in the collection, and four additional cabinets to house even more pieces were made by a Washington company.[19]

An extraordinary rug, reflecting the quality of gifts to presidents by foreign officials, was presented to Theodore Roosevelt in 1909 by the Persian consul general in New York. This rare silk prayer rug, inset with jewels, was made in Tabriz, circa 1850. Its field is inset with emeralds, tourmalines, aquamarine, turquoise, and pearls; the fringe is seed pearls. On two panels, in Arabic script, are lines of poetry from the noted thirteenth-century Persian poet Saadi (Sheikh Muslih-ud-Din).[20]

The newly renovated and refurbished house was opened to wide and positive acclaim on New Year's Day, 1903, and photographs and drawings appeared in major publications such as *The Century Magazine* and *The Architectural Record*. Visitors noticed the dignified, tasteful, yet simpler and starker interiors that gave the rooms a more spacious look and reflected the nation's larger role in international affairs. Charles Moore, who later became chairman of the Commission of Fine Arts, stated that forms and materials, "belonging to all times," had been used to express ideas of permanence and dignity.[21] Others noted that it was an "an intelligent as well as a sensitive restoration. But it is none the less a restoration," adding, "the Colonial note is struck at once" when one enters the Entrance Hall.[22] The replacement of dark wood molding with enameled ivory paint was indicative of the changes throughout the house. The philosophy that had governed the redecorating—to furnish the interior of the building in harmony with its exterior architecture—continues to influence the furnishings of White House State Rooms.

When President and Mrs. William H. Taft arrived in 1909, the house was in good order, and they made no changes in the furnishings of the state rooms, which they often used as family rooms, gathering in the Red Room each evening after dinner. Helen Taft

PRAYER RUG
Tabríz, Persia, c. 1850

Silk rugs inset with jewels are very rare in the West. This carpet, with emeralds and tourmalines and colored stones framed with seed pearls, was presented to Theodore Roosevelt by the Persian consul general in New York in 1909.

was very complimentary about McKim, Mead & White's work, and when President Taft sat for his official portrait by Anders Zorn in 1911 he chose to be portrayed seated in one of the new Blue Room armchairs. The most noticeable architectural change was President Taft's addition of an oval office to the south elevation of the 1902 office wing. The Caldwell firm supplied lighting fixtures for it as it had done for the 1902 offices.

"I was always conscious of the character which a century of history had impressed upon the White House," Mrs. Taft wrote, but "it came . . . to feel as much like home as any house I have ever occupied."[23] Her experience as a house guest of President and Mrs. Hayes in 1877 instilled in her a dream to live in the White House. Once she was first lady she took an interest in the old furnishings of the house but quickly removed the "Lincoln" bed from their bedroom, stating that "whatever its historic interest" she did not like it as a bed to sleep in.[24] She appreciated the Colonial Revival furniture made in 1902 but was less enthusiastic about the remaining Victorian bureaus and wardrobes that were scattered in various rooms. From A. H. Davenport she ordered a suite of Colonial mahogany bedroom furniture to replace the Lincoln-era pieces. In the second-floor oval room where the Tafts received personal guests she placed several of their own treasured pieces, including oriental tapestries and teakwood furniture from their earlier life in the Philippines where Taft had served as governor.

Their daughter, Helen, eighteen, who often assisted her mother as hostess, occupied the large northwest corner room, and their two sons, Robert, twenty, who was often away at school, and Charles, twelve, shared a room under the North Portico. Mrs. Taft hired a housekeeper, Elizabeth Jaffrey, who lived across the hall from the boys, and introduced several changes in the management of the household; her transfer of the steward's responsibilities to the housekeeper was one of them. Under Mrs. Taft's direction, White House silver, long stored in its original silver chests and boxes, was given its own special closet with locked vault doors across from the ground-floor kitchen. Special compartments and velvet-lined trays for flatware replaced the old trunks in which the silver purchased by James Monroe and Andrew Jackson had always been kept. Mrs. Taft did not select a new state porcelain service as she was satisfied with the Wedgwood china chosen by Edith Roosevelt, but she reordered pieces to supplement the service. As she enjoyed using the older services at small luncheons and dinners, she continued to support the efforts of Abby Gunn Baker to acquire examples of china from past administrations for display, and several additional pieces from the Jackson, Polk, Fillmore, Pierce, and Buchanan administrations were donated by presidential descendants.

The major social event of the Taft years was the celebration of their twenty-fifth wedding anniversary on June 19, 1911, when they gave a large evening garden party on the south lawn for several thousand people, an event "not to be forgotten" by all who had witnessed it. Among the gifts of silver showered on them was a three-piece cobalt blue ceramic coffee and tea service with silver overlay in a floral design made by Lenox in Trenton, New Jersey. This is an early example of Lenox since it had been in business only

from 1906. In the center of each piece is an engraved "T" above a shield with the dates "1886–1911." The Tafts also received a stemmed silver creamer and sugar bowl in a latticework design with cobalt glass liners by an unknown American manufacturer. All of these pieces were donated to the White House in 1966 by their son, Charles P. Taft, as a lasting reminder of this highlight of his parents' life in the President's House. In 1959 their daughter, Helen Taft Manning, also donated several examples of family porcelain and ironstone dinner and dessert services made in Bohemia and in England by Wedgwood and Minton.

With Theodore Roosevelt, the Progressive party candidate, drawing away Republican voters in the presidential campaign of 1912, the Democrat Woodrow Wilson defeated Taft and entered the White House in March 1913 with his wife, Ellen, and their three daughters, Margaret, Jesse, and Eleanor. Two had White House weddings—Jesse to Francis Sayre (1913) and Eleanor to Secretary of the Treasury William McAdoo (1914). President Wilson's cousin, Helen Bones, also lived with them and assisted with the supervision of the household. Considering that only ten years had elapsed since

TEA AND COFFEE SET (COFFEEPOT, SUGAR BOWL, AND TEAPOT)
Lenox, Inc., Trenton, New Jersey, 1911

President and Mrs. William H. Taft celebrated their 25th wedding anniversary at a large garden party on the White House lawn. This service with silver overlay engraved "T" and "1886-1911" was among the many gifts they received on the occasion.

McKim, Mead & White's restoration, few changes were made in the state rooms, but the Wilsons adapted the family quarters as their home and furnished the rooms with books and the first lady's paintings. Ellen Wilson, an accomplished artist of landscapes, set aside a small studio for herself in the third-floor attic and furnished her own room with flowered chintz to resemble an indoor garden. New suites of bedroom furniture, painted white enamel, were installed in several newly created bedrooms for guests and household staff in the attic, and W. B. Moses furnished brass beds and a white enameled desk and chiffonier for a second-floor bedroom. During the summer of 1913, several family rooms were stripped of old wallpapers and the rooms painted light yellow or blue or covered with grass cloth. An imported blue-and-white figured paper was hung on the walls of President Wilson's room where the "Lincoln" bed resided.

A strong supporter of projects to aid education in Appalachia and provide assistance to its mountain craftswomen, Ellen Wilson selected blue-and-white handwoven textiles by Elmeda McHargue Walker (1837–?) of Tennessee to cover furniture and for draperies, and fabrics and rugs woven in strips by Allie Josephine Mast (1861–1936) of North Carolina, as well as baskets and a cream-colored coverlet for the "Lincoln" bed, which she purchased with government funds at the Southern Industrial Educational Association craft show in Washington held to assist mountain women in marketing their work.[25] Mrs. Wilson served as honorary president of that association until her death. The room she decorated, known as the "Blue Mountain Room," and her support of the mountain craftswomen received wide attention.[26]

Ellen Wilson loved gardens, and in 1913–14, she converted Edith Roosevelt's Colonial garden, east of the West Wing, into a rose-filled flower garden—the Rose Garden. She

Textiles made by Appalachian weavers were selected for President Woodrow Wilson's bedroom by Ellen Wilson, a strong supporter of projects to assist mountain craftswomen.

invited the noted landscape designer Beatrix Jones Farrand in 1913 to redesign the east garden—later to become the Jacqueline Kennedy Garden—and she lived to see it completed before her death in 1914. Garden benches introduced then are still there. The benches—of painted limestone with naturalistic carvings of grapevines, corn stalks, and animals such as weasels, dogs, and birds, and bases carved to simulate intertwined rustic tree branches—are probably of northern European origin. Four limestone chairs and four seats with similar motifs were also placed in the garden.

Ellen Wilson's death in 1914 brought to a halt any changes in the house. When Woodrow Wilson married Edith Bolling Galt in 1915, she moved many of her own furnishings into her room and brought her piano and books, as she "felt more at home with some of my own things around me."[27] After Wilson's 1916 reelection, she oversaw several changes in the state floor and living areas. She did not like the two square dining tables in the State Dining Room and discovered in the White House kitchen a large round table that could seat fourteen to sixteen people and had it moved to the dining room. The chairs in the room were reupholstered and the draperies replaced, as were those in the East Room, and wall coverings, upholsteries, and draperies were replaced with duplicate fabrics in the Blue Room and Green Room. One of her lasting contributions to the White House was the creation of a room in which to display the historic china and glass services from previous administrations. In 1917 a room on the south side of the Ground Floor Corridor was arranged with built-in glass-front cabinets

GARDEN SETTEE
Northern Europe, c. 1900

Ellen Wilson invited landscape architect Beatrix Jones Farrand to redesign the East Garden in 1913, and limestone garden furniture with naturalistic carvings of animals, rustic tree branches, and corn stalks was installed there.

along the walls. The China Room continues to be the one room in the White House in which the tastes of presidents and first ladies are represented. From 1913 to 1917, several more examples of presidential china, glass, and silver from the Washington, Jackson, Van Buren, William H. Harrison, Taylor, Tyler, Buchanan, Lincoln, and Grant eras entered the collection through donations from presidential families. Edith Wilson also ordered the first American-made state service for the White House in 1918 from a Washington firm, Dulin & Martin Co. The 1,700-piece service was made in Trenton, New Jersey, by Lenox China, one of the first companies in the country to produce high-quality dinnerware. The service, with its ivory borders and gilt decoration, reflects the twentieth-century taste for elegance combined with simplicity, and continues to be used for state dinners. Additional pieces were ordered during the Harding, Coolidge, and Hoover administrations, and in 1994 Hillary Rodham Clinton ordered replacements of the handsome cobalt blue and gilt service plates. President Wilson was the first chief executive to have a presidential seal and flag, and, at his suggestion, the Wilson state service was the first to incorporate the presidential seal rather than the Great Seal of the United States.[28]

With the entry of the United States into the war in Europe, Mrs. Wilson sought ways for President Wilson to relax and, in 1918, she created a new billiard room in the west end of the Ground Floor Corridor, in the present-day Map Room, close to the China Room. After the Wilsons' trip to and from France in 1918–19 for the Versailles Peace

SERVICE PLATE,
ENTREE/FISH PLATE, AND
RAMEKIN AND PLATE
Lenox, Inc., Trenton, New Jersey, 1918

*The Wilson state service was the first
White House service made in the
United States and the first to bear the
arms of the presidential seal rather than
the Great Seal of the United States.*

Conference, several pieces from their suite on board the USS *George Washington* were transferred to the White House for use in a guest bedroom and the Ladies Diplomatic Room. They were removed to the presidential yacht, USS *Mayflower,* in 1921 by the Hardings, except for a few chairs that remained in the White House.

Government accounts of White House furniture reflect the poignant as well as the utilitarian. After President Wilson's stroke in 1919, a spring cushion for an "invalid" chair was ordered, and a single rolling chair with 18-inch wheels and tires was purchased for him in the spring of 1920.[29] A wheelchair in White House storage is almost certainly Wilson's chair.

The house and grounds were closed to the public during the war and Wilson's illness. When Republican Warren G. Harding succeeded to the presidency in 1921 with his strong-willed wife, Florence, they opened the house immediately to the public on a scale not seen previously. As the wife of a former United States senator, Mrs. Harding knew many people in official Washington, but she never felt accepted by them, and the Hardings chose to entertain a broader range of people, such as World War I veterans who were guests at large garden parties. The Hardings granted the press much more access than had previous administrations. A visitor to a private dinner was invited to their quarters in 1921 and described their "living room"—the West Sitting Hall—as furnished with a grandfather clock, a grand piano, a huge French vase filled with pussy willows, soft-toned rugs, Mrs. Harding's pet canary, and a large bowl of goldfish. "Just like home," wrote the reporter.[30] When Mrs. Harding requested decorative changes to this area in 1923, she requested that the piano, clock, fish bowls, and canary cages remain, as they "have sentimental value."[31]

The Hardings occupied the same southwest suite as had their predecessors, with the oval Library as a place to entertain guests, one of the few rooms to receive any attention in 1921. Florence Harding sought to economize and not spend government funds allocated for their private quarters, and moved much personal furniture from their Washington home into the house. The Lincoln-era furniture was moved across the hall to the large northwest guest room, its location in 1861. Mrs. Jaffrey, the housekeeper since 1909, still resided in a room on the north side, and during Mrs. Harding's illness in 1922 two doctors lived in. There were no significant acquisitions for the house in the Harding administration, but the Harding Memorial Association later donated examples of gilded glassware that the Central Glass Works of Wheeling, West Virginia, gave to Mrs. Harding in 1921 and examples of the Lenox dessert service personally owned by the Hardings.[32] After Harding's sudden death on a western trip in August 1923, Mrs. Harding remained in the house long enough to pack their belongings and Harding's papers and then moved to the Willard Hotel.

President and Mrs. Calvin Coolidge had lived at the Willard Hotel during the two and a half years he served as vice president, and they stayed there until Florence Harding left the White House. The Coolidges and their two sons, John and Calvin Jr., who were away at school most of the year, had a brief time together in the White House before Calvin Jr., sixteen, died of blood poisoning in July 1924. His funeral was held in the East Room, and his death left a pall over the Coolidge White House years.

When they first moved into the White House, Grace Coolidge saw the house as a home "rich in tradition, mellow with years, hallowed with memories," and she enjoyed sharing it with guests.[33] They brought no furniture of their own and made few other changes in the short time before the election of 1924 when Coolidge was reelected. Family and guests gathered before meals in the West Sitting Hall, surrounded by family photographs and comfortable, overstuffed chairs and sofas "full of honorable years."[34] Grace Coolidge was interested in the history of the house and requested to see the old photographs of White House rooms taken by Frances Benjamin Johnston in the late 1880s. She searched the attic and storehouse for original White House furnishings but was disappointed to find little left.[35] She did locate a few pieces and had them repaired and refinished—a brass inlaid table, a chair bearing the tag "Andrew Jackson's chair," and an old

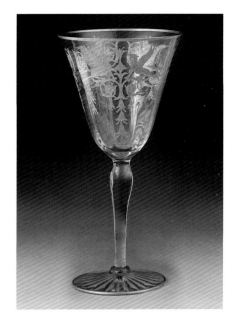

TOP:
WATER GOBLET
Central Glass Works, Wheeling,
West Virginia, 1921

ABOVE:
DESSERT PLATE
Lenox, Inc., Trenton, New Jersey,
c. 1920

American services, given to or personally owned by President and Mrs. Warren G. Harding, reflect the tastes of the 1920s.

mahogany dining table with brass claw feet—and she moved the "Lincoln" bed into its former location in the southwest suite that she used as a personal sitting room. She enjoyed sewing, knitting, and crocheting, and in 1925—with the hope that she would begin a first lady tradition of leaving a memento of family life in the White House, a visible link between past and present—she began to crochet a coverlet for the "Lincoln" bed, finishing it in 1927. Incorporating patriotic symbols such as the Liberty Bell, eagle and shields from the Great Seal of the United States, and the motto E Pluribus Unum, she also included her name and the dates of Coolidge's term of office, "August 3, 1923–March 4, 1929," before Coolidge announced that he did not choose to run again. Public interest in the coverlet prompted Mrs. Coolidge to agree to publish instructions for making the coverlet in Washington, New York, and Boston newspapers in 1928.[36] The coverlet was left on the bed for the new White House occupants in 1929.[37]

Grace Coolidge's strong interest in history expressed itself in her desire to refurnish some of the rooms with furniture of the period in which the house was built. Drawing on the precedent of the new American Wing of the Metropolitan Museum of Art in New York, she hoped that treasures from private collections would be donated to the White House instead of requiring government funds to purchase them. With the advice of Mrs. Harold I. Pratt, a wealthy New York collector of Americana, she convinced President Coolidge to request Congress to authorize the acceptance of gifts for the White House by the officer in charge of public buildings and grounds. A joint resolution provided for the presidential appointment of a temporary committee to advise the White House on furnishings and the acceptance of gifts.[38] This was the first effort to bring antique objects into the house through donations and was the beginning of a museum role for the White House. (A few donations had been made in earlier administrations, but they were new pieces or gifts to presidents that were left in the White House. In 1903 the Steinway Company donated a specially designed piano, now at the Smithsonian Institution, and Grand Rapids furniture was donated for Theodore Roosevelt's Red Room.) Congress also increased the appropriation of funds available for furnishings at the beginning of each administration to $50,000.

In 1925 an advisory committee of experts was appointed to evaluate and make recommendations on the decor of the state rooms and review offers of gifts, the first such committee formed to advise presidents and first ladies on White House interiors. One of the appointees, New York businessman R. T. Haines Halsey, was a collector and scholar who in 1924 had assisted in the creation of the Metropolitan Museum's American Wing, which featured decorative arts collections and historic rooms. His view was that the White House rooms should reflect the late-eighteenth- and early-nine-

BELOW:
RUG DESIGN
Bollentin and Thompson for Tiffany Studios, New York, 1926

Two Aubusson-style rugs were specially designed and made for the Red and Green Rooms in 1926-27. This drawing was for the Green Room, the first White House room where an advisory committee was involved in its decoration and assisted with donations of antiques for it.

OPPOSITE:
COVERLET
Grace Goodhue Coolidge, Washington, D.C., 1925-27

Grace Coolidge hoped to begin a tradition of first ladies' leaving a memento of family life in the White House. She crocheted for the "Lincoln Bed" a coverlet with patriotic symbols and the dates of President Coolidge's term of office.

GRACE COOLIDGE
E PLURIBUS UNUM
AUGUST 3 1923 - MARCH 4 1929
THE PRESIDENT'S HOUSE

teenth-century style derived from designs of English architect Robert Adam, rather than the early Colonial period.[39]

When other committee members began to express their ideas publicly as to what should be done to the rooms, there was tremendous press interest. A magazine poll of artists, architects, and decorators discovered that the majority favored the "Colonial" style for White House furnishings, but there were those who thought the house should be left alone or decorated with modern furniture; some favored retaining the French Empire style furniture found in the Blue Room.[40] "Colonial furniture will always possess a strong grip on the affections of the American people. . . . It seems to embody, in its lines and shapings, many of the characteristics of rugged worth and stern necessity that were identified with the early struggles of our ancestors," commented one expert.[41] Just what people meant by "Colonial" was not always clear, but it did seem to reflect furnishings of the Federal period (1790–1815) rather than the earlier Queen Anne and Chippendale styles often referred to as Colonial. The increasing popularity of the American Colonial style after World War I was reflected in the strong preferences of the committee members.

The advisors disparaged the variety of styles of furnishings already in the house and recommended their replacement with those of the Colonial style. Controversy arose when the American Institute of Architects, which saw itself as custodian of the White House, became concerned that changes would be made to McKim, Mead & White's state floor rooms with their French style furnishings. The AIA wanted to retain and preserve the 1902 work and expressed its views to President Coolidge who was not pleased with the public controversy.[42] Consequently, no changes were made on the state floor until 1928.

The advisory committee also recommended that Colonial style furnishings replace the odds and ends of old White House furnishings that had accumulated in the family quarters over the years. Mrs. Coolidge gave instructions for the family quarters to be painted during the summer of 1925, and Halsey coordinated portions of the project, securing a reproduction French scenic wallpaper for Mrs. Coolidge's room. Architectural and decorative changes were made in several other rooms by W. & J. Sloane of New York under Halsey's direction.

Two years later, during the summer of 1927, the White House roof was rebuilt and the third-floor attic spaces converted into larger guest and servant rooms and storage rooms for linens and family personal effects. Colonial style maple bedroom suites were purchased for the new guest rooms, and a glass-paneled bookcase and a table were made from the old roof timbers. A sky parlor surrounded by glass, the current Solarium, was added on the south to provide a sun-filled space overlooking the south grounds. It was furnished simply with a cot bed, a writing table, porch furniture, a phonograph, and a radio. With the roof project completed and unused funds available, U. S. Grant III, the officer in charge of public buildings, asked Mrs. Coolidge about the state rooms, and she selected the Green Room to be refurbished as the 1902 furniture was in bad condition and the fabrics shabby. The advisory committee, dormant since 1925, did not approve of

the painted furniture designed by McKim, Mead & White and was delighted to participate in acquiring new furnishings. The intent was to create a room with a homogeneous
character of the Federal period. Two specially designed Aubusson-style rugs with the
arms of the United States in the center had been commissioned for the Green Room and
Red Room from Tiffany Studios in 1926, and a change in the damask wall covering from
a garish green to a "proper" color was recommended but was not completed before the
Coolidges left the White House in 1929. There had been little response from the public
for donations since the 1925 legislation, but advisory committee member Harriet Pratt
donated one of a pair of English cut-glass girandoles and some small tables; and an eight-
foot-long Sheraton-style sofa, copied from an "old example" believed to have been owned
by George Washington, was made by the New York firm of Ginsberg & Levy, Inc., in
1928. Oval-back mahogany chairs in the Hepplewhite style, covered in yellow brocade,

SOUP SPOON, DINNER
KNIFE, AND DINNER FORK
*International Silver Co., Wallingford,
Connecticut, c. 1926-60*

*A silver flatware service in the "Minuet"
pattern was selected by Mrs. Coolidge
in 1926; supplements were reordered for
nearly fifty years.*

and a pair of mahogany console tables, all reproductions, were purchased from New York dealers and gradually added, either through donation or with donated or appropriated funds.[43] With this mix of sparse delicate furnishings, the Green Room did not achieve the committee's goal of creating the type of harmonious interior they imagined there in the days of Jefferson and Madison. Nevertheless, it was the first attempt by a committee to advise a first lady on interior decoration and set a precedent for continuing review and donation of objects offered to the White House.

After the 1928 election, Mrs. Pratt continued to press for a new advisory committee chosen for its knowledge of the needs of the White House and appointed by the Smithsonian. She was willing to contribute and raise funds for acquisitions only if such a committee was appointed. She thought that furnishings should not be restricted to American-made objects, but should also include English and other pieces.[44] A smaller group continued to function through the 1930s as a Committee on Furnishings and was incorporated later under the Commission of Fine Arts that reviewed and approved acquisitions through the 1950s.[45]

With her warm personality and interest in people, Mrs. Coolidge was a very popular first lady. As wife of the vice president, she had been involved with wives of senators who had organized during World War I to assist the Red Cross. Mrs. Coolidge had served as president of the Ladies of the Senate, and when she left the White House in 1929, as a token of their friendship and in recognition of her White House refurbishing efforts, the Ladies presented her with a silver inkstand made in London by J. Wakelin and Robert Garrard, circa 1800–1801, an eighteenth-century slant-front mahogany desk of Pennsylvania origin, and an early-nineteenth-century maple side chair. They were donated to the White House in 1982 by John Coolidge who had presented examples of the Coolidge family English Spode and Copenhagen porcelain services for the China Room exhibits in the late 1950s.

Interest in the White House grew after President and Mrs. Herbert Hoover took up residence in 1929. Well educated, well traveled, and with broad interests, the Hoovers sought to provide a feeling of history to the public areas as well as to the family quarters. President Hoover wrote that he felt the invisible presence of the former presidents within the White House rooms and enjoyed studying the objects for their history.[46] Mrs. Hoover introduced paintings of historical events, presidential portraits, and objects with historical associations in a foyer on the ground floor where tourists congregated before tours. President Hoover selected the former Lincoln Cabinet Room as his study, and the Hoovers hung their personal prints there. In the well-known print of Lincoln and his Cabinet, they recognized the Lincoln Cabinet chairs still in the house, and returned them to the room. Objects from the Anderson Cottage at the U. S. Soldiers' Home where nineteenth-century presidents such as Lincoln had lived during the summer months were identified and transferred in 1929 at Mrs. Hoover's request. A small French clock, circa 1830, and a Victorian desk, believed to have been the desk on which Lincoln drafted the

Emancipation Proclamation, were placed in Hoover's study, the room Lincoln had used as his office. When the presidential yacht, the USS *Mayflower,* was decommissioned in 1929, Lou Hoover saw that many of the furnishings were transferred to the White House and placed in office and family areas. Among them were twenty-four small oriental rugs and several pieces of silver. In 1931 descendants of the Washington auctioneer James McGuire, who had sold White House objects at nineteenth-century auctions, donated handsome late-eighteenth-century French silver candlesticks and cruet stands once owned by James and Dolley Madison, which McGuire had received from her son, Payne Todd. As the 1932 bicentennial of George Washington approached, Mrs. Hoover accepted the gift of a sideboard made of paneling from Sulgrave Manor, the English ancestral home of the Washington family.

She desired to emphasize the historic nature of White House furnishings, but also sought to create a comfortable home for family and guests, placing cozy chairs in every room for visiting and reading. Mrs. Hoover had a great appreciation for the outdoors and transformed the West Sitting Hall into a garden sitting room with wicker furniture, palms, ferns, flowering plants, and birds. Their family possessions resided in the oval drawing room.

As her interest in the house grew, Lou Hoover proposed a study of all objects in the White House to determine their history and past associations with former occupants.

INKSTAND
John Wakelin & Robert Garrard,
London, 1800-1801

In recognition of Mrs. Coolidge's efforts to have American antiques donated to the White House, the Ladies of the Senate presented her with an English inkstand when she left Washington in 1929.

OPPOSITE:
DESK
Morris W. Dove, Washington, D.C., 1932

Lou Hoover sought to provide a sense of history in White House rooms. She created the "Monroe Room" (above) in the family quarters and had reproductions made of furniture James Monroe had purchased in France in the 1790s, including a secrétaire-a-abattant *(fall-front desk) on which he drafted the Monroe Doctrine.*

Intending to do the work herself, she soon realized that time constraints and her other responsibilities as first lady made it impossible to devote the time the project needed, and she assigned the work to Dare Stark McMullin, the daughter of friends, who lived in the White House where she assisted Mrs. Hoover with a variety of matters. She researched every object in the White House and interviewed White House staff to elicit the oral history of each item. Mrs. Hoover personally subsidized the project and granted permission for documentary photographs to be taken in rooms in the private quarters, something that had rarely been done in the past. Lou Hoover wanted the research to be published, and a draft document was prepared, but it was not published before the election of 1932 and left the White House with the Hoovers in 1933.[47] This was the first extensive attempt, other than Abby Gunn Baker's research on White House china, to document White House furnishings, and McMullin's work of the early 1930s, now in the Hoover Library, provided the only information on these objects until the National Park Service began research in National Archives records in 1946 to prepare a history of White House furnishings.

On one of Lou Hoover's drives to the family's weekend getaway at Camp Rapidan in the Virginia Blue Ridge mountains, she stopped to visit the James Monroe Law Office in Fredericksburg, Virginia, and was inspired to create a room in the White House, "The Monroe Room," with reproductions of several pieces of Monroe's Louis XVI furniture from the 1790s, including the *secrétaire-a-abattant* (desk) on which he drafted the Monroe Doctrine. In the 1866–1902 Cabinet Room, which had been used by twentieth-century presidents as an office, she placed a French mahogany table from 1817, other Monroe-associated objects from the White House collection, and copies of seven pieces from the Monroe Office, which she commissioned in 1932 from Washington cabinetmaker Morris W. Dove (1878–1968) who had made chairs for the Cabinet Room since 1913.

A fire in the West Wing in 1929 ruined many of the furnishings in the Oval Office. The Grand Rapids Furniture Association saw an opportunity and offered to donate furniture for the room to give "the appearance of a well preserved suite of Colonial furniture.[48] Mrs. Hoover approved a design scheme for the room that included sev-

it to Roosevelt to reaffirm the "tribute of a free people to the noblest figure in the struggle for freedom."[57] Regrettably, after the war, the demand for office space continued, and Roosevelt's idea of a museum wing did not come to fruition.

The Roosevelts entertained a great deal, and it became necessary to consider whether to reorder pieces of the Wilson state dinner service or have a new service designed. Mrs. Roosevelt decided to have a new service made by Lenox China in 1934 as she said it was less costly than ordering replacements. The new service with a narrow blue border with gilt stars of the forty-eight states included a narrow gilt band that incorporated roses and plumes from the Roosevelt family coat of arms.[58] After the 1939 New York World's Fair closed in 1940, a service from the Federal Building was transferred to the White House, with pieces made by Lenox and by the Shenango Pottery Company. Mrs. Roosevelt also ordered a new glassware service in 1937 made by the T. G. Hawkes Company of Corning, New York. Its "Venetian" pattern was renamed "White House," and the United States coat of arms was added to the White House pieces. This was the first new glassware service ordered for the White House since the Harrison administration in 1891, and pieces continued to be reordered until 1955.[59]

In 1938, the Steinway Company offered to donate to the White House a new piano (Steinway's Number 300,000) to replace a piano it had made in 1903 for the East Room.[60] The offer was accepted, and Eric Gugler was selected by the Commission of Fine

WATER GOBLET AND
FINGER BOWL
T. G. Hawkes & Company, Corning, N.Y., 1938, on blanks by Tiffin Glass Co., Tiffin, Ohio

SALAD PLATE
Lenox, Inc., Trenton, New Jersey, 1934

The first new glassware service since 1891 was ordered in 1937, and Hawkes's "Venetian" pattern was renamed "White House." A state china service for 120 people, decorated with an inner band of gilt roses and plumes from the Roosevelt family coat of arms, was chosen by Mrs. Roosevelt in 1934.

PIANO AND BENCH
Steinway and Sons, Long Island City, New York, 1938; design by Eric Gugler; legs by Albert Stewart; decoration by Dunbar Beck

A concert grand piano was especially designed for the White House when Steinway offered to replace an earlier instrument in 1938. Gilded scenes of American dance forms appear on the Honduran mahogany case, which is supported by three gilded, eagle-shaped legs in the Art Deco style.

Arts to design a full-size concert grand piano with President Roosevelt's approval of the final design. It was to be a special "state" piano that would be unique to the White House. The Honduran mahogany case stands on three large gilded legs carved in the shape of eagles in the Art Deco style by the sculptor Albert Stewart (1900–1965), and gilded scenes of American dance forms were painted along the sides by Dunbar Beck (1902–86), including the Virginia reel, a barn dance, an Indian ceremonial dance, African Americans dancing, and a cowboy with a guitar.[61] Accepting it in 1938, President Roosevelt dedicated it to "the advancement of music in every city, town, and hamlet in the country."[62] Eleanor Roosevelt encouraged a variety of musical performances in the White House and thought that the donation of the piano was symbolic of an increased interest in music in the country.[63] Josef Hofmann performed the first concert on the piano, which has been a major presence at White House musical events, receptions, and dinners.

ABOVE:
President Harry S. Truman's study in the second floor oval room, as it appeared in 1952. The New York department store B. Altman and Company executed all of the interior design work in the house during the Truman Renovation.

OPPOSITE:
French objects from the late eighteenth and early nineteenth centuries and an American painted armchair, c. 1815, frame the south view from the Yellow Oval Room at the end of the twentieth century.

After the death of President Roosevelt in 1945, Mrs. Roosevelt sorted through and packed the accumulations of twelve years. It took twenty big army trucks to transport their possessions to Hyde Park. Only one truck was required to move the belongings of President and Mrs. Harry S. Truman from their Connecticut Avenue apartment. They brought only their clothes and the piano of their daughter, Margaret. With the faded walls of the family rooms showing outlines of the Roosevelts' many photographs and prints and the shabby furniture, the house gave the appearance of an abandoned hotel, according to usher J. B. West.[64]

Mrs. Truman worked with a decorator from Kansas City to select new paint colors and fabrics for the family rooms, and arranged the furniture to suit their family. They moved in on May 7, the day before the German surrender ended the war in Europe. Wanting to have Margaret with them at the west end of the second floor, President Truman had the Lincoln-era furnishings moved from the large northwest bedroom to the southeast room that had been Lincoln's office, creating the room that has since been called the Lincoln Bedroom. Mrs. Truman selected for herself the rooms Eleanor Roosevelt had used, and President Truman chose Roosevelt's oval study as his private office.

Serious structural problems and safety issues with the White House led the Trumans to move to Blair House late in 1948 where they stayed during the massive renovation and reconstruction of the house from 1949 to 1952. White House furnishings from the Green Room, Red Room, and Family Dining Room were sent to Blair House for the Tru-

mans to use.[65] They returned to a freshly renovated house with many new amenities such as central air conditioning, modern bathrooms, and built-in closets. Visitors familiar with the state rooms would not have noticed dramatic changes. Many of the furnishings had been returned to their previous locations, and the same bright emerald green silk damasks from the mid-1940s were reinstalled in the Green Room that, like the Red Room, contained a mix of English and American pieces from 1902 and more recent additions, many of them reproductions, suggesting neoclassical styles of the late eighteenth and early nineteenth centuries. The most dramatic change was in the State Dining Room where the oak-paneled walls of 1902 were painted celadon green. This decision, like all others dealing with changes in the rooms, was approved by President and Mrs. Truman. Howell Crim, the White House chief usher, had assured Mrs. Truman that she and the president would have the "last word" on the interior decorating on the second and third floors, and he made sure that they saw and approved all samples and sketches for the state rooms.[66] Truman, keenly interested in White House history, wrote: "I am very much interested in the proper replacement of the furniture in the White House in the manner in which it should be placed, and since I am the only President in fifty years who has had any interest whatever in the rehabilitation of the White House, I am going to see that it is done properly and correctly."[67]

In the fall of 1950, a little more than a year before the Trumans hoped to move back into the White House, the Commission on the Renovation of the Executive Mansion met to consider what to do about the interiors and furnishings. The New York firm of B. Altman and Company had removed and stored the contents of the house that were

SERVICE PLATE, SOUP PLATE, AND BOUILLON CUP AND SAUCER
Lenox, Inc., Trenton, New Jersey, 1951

The state service designed for President and Mrs. Truman has a green border to correspond with the newly painted celadon green walls of the State Dining Room.

not transferred to Blair House, at the direction of Chief Usher Crim, who had a good working relationship with Altman's, which had done work for the White House since 1945. The director of Altman's design department, Charles T. Haight, had consulted on numerous projects from repairs to carpets, new fabrics for the Green Room and State Dining Room, and the redecoration of Truman's Oval Office and Cabinet Room. At Crim's suggestion, Altman submitted the sole proposal to supply and install the new furnishings, and Haight oversaw the complete refurbishing.[68] He also designed a new green-bordered state dinner service for the Trumans made by Lenox.[69]

The commission intended to preserve the original character of the building in its interior decoration. To the members, that meant the Georgian style of the late eighteenth century—the period of the building's construction. By the late 1940s, the Colonial Revival interiors of 1902 contained a varied mix of furnishings selected by White House occupants, architects, and furnishing committees. Altman's submitted plans for furniture placement and proposals for new furniture. The company also oversaw repairs to old furniture and the design, manufacture, and installation of furniture, wallcoverings, and draperies. The budget of $200,000 for the interiors limited the purchase of antique objects to supplement historic and utilitarian objects, some of which had been in the house since the mid-nineteenth century. William Adams Delano, who had served on the advisory furnishing committees from the 1920s to the 1940s, wanted to be involved in decisions on the furnishings, and he was given supervision over the interior decoration and worked closely with Haight. The Advisory Committee on Interior Decoration of the Executive Mansion was appointed to give overall approval to Altman's proposals. The Commission of Fine Arts, involved for decades in decisions relating to White House interiors and acquisitions, was represented by its chairman, David Finley, who brought in Mrs. Dwight Davis, a former member of the White House furnishings committee, as a consultant. Throughout 1951 the advisory committee met with Haight on a weekly basis, and Chief Usher Crim represented the Trumans' interests by showing all drawings and samples to them for approval and consulting with them on numerous details.

Increasing construction costs ruled out diverting additional funds to the purchase of early-nineteenth-century furniture in the Federal style comparable to what would have been in the house in the early years. Purchases were restricted to neoclassical reproductions of English and New England furniture made in Massachusetts by the Kaplan Furniture Company and by Drexel and the Kittinger Company. (Most of the 225 new

CHIFFONIER
Kaplan Furniture Co., Cambridge, Massachusetts, 1951

A lack of funds with which to purchase antiques during the Truman Renovation led to the purchase of reproductions of English and New England neoclassical furniture for family rooms.

NATIONAL IDENTITY AND
THE COLONIAL REVIVAL

221

ABOVE:

OVERMANTEL GLASS
WITH PAINTING
England, c. 1695

OPPOSITE:

MANTEL CLOCK
*Case possibly by Pierre-Joseph Gouthière,
movement by Michel-François Piolaine,
Paris, c. 1780-90*

*Gifts for the newly restored White House
were presented to President Truman by
King George VI of Great Britain and
President Vincent Auriol of France.
An English carved and gilded overmantel
glass was installed in the State Dining
Room, and a French musical clock with a
case made by one of the most accomplished
bronze casters and sculptors of late eighteenth-century France was placed on the
Red Room mantel.*

pieces purchased were for the private quarters.)[70] Donations were offered, but the commission responded that it was not attempting to collect items to add to the historic "relics" already in the White House.[71] It did accept several elegant late-eigh-teenth-century English cut-glass chandeliers—as the advisory committee recommended the addition of such chandeliers—a mahogany table in the Hepple-white style for the State Dining Room, and a nine-teenth-century tall-case clock. While the renovation continued, President Truman researched what for-mer presidents had done to the house. He found in the attic of the Treasury Department four of the Lincoln-era Cabinet Room chairs with mouse-eaten upholstery and broken legs, which he had restored and placed in the Lincoln Bedroom.[72] His television tour of the house in 1952 elicited several leads to old White House objects, but led to few donations.[73]

In addition President Truman received gifts for the newly renovated house from foreign heads of state. On behalf of her father, King George VI of Great Britain, Princess Elizabeth brought to Wash-ington a late-seventeenth-century English overmantel glass with a still life painting and a pair of elegant gilded bronze and bluejohn candelabra by the renowned Birmingham metalsmith Matthew Boulton, circa 1770. They were displayed prominently in the State Dining Room. The president of France, Vincent Auriol, personally selected a late-eighteenth-century French musical clock with a gilded bronze and marble case possibly made by Pierre-Joseph Gouthière (1732–1813/14), one of the most accomplished bronze casters and sculptors in late-eighteenth-century France, with works by Michel-François Piolaine (working from 1787 to circa 1810). President Truman had the clock and a pair of French gilded bronze candelabra, also a gift from Auriol, placed on the mantel in the Red Room.

The renovated rooms had a fresh, clean, rather spare appearance that was well received by the American public and press. Reporters commented on the "smartness" of interiors that had been "purified" in authentic fashion.[74] The Trumans were delighted with the success of the project. If it no longer seemed like the old house filled with 150 years of national life, it was prepared for the vast expansion of the presidency that had come with World War II.

A month after the election of General Dwight D. Eisenhower in 1952, Bess Tru-man welcomed Mamie Eisenhower for a tour of her new home. In his memoirs, President Eisenhower recalled that his family "liked the place and all it stood for . . . it conveyed to us

much of the dignity, the simple greatness of America."[75] As the house had just been completely refurbished, Congress did not provide the $50,000 given to each new administration for redecoration and new furnishings. The feminine Mrs. Eisenhower furnished her personal rooms with objects she found in other spaces and made the home comfortable for her family. Her mother lived with them until 1956, and the Eisenhowers' son, John, and his family were frequent guests.

Mamie Eisenhower did inquire about purchasing historic furniture for the house but was told that such items could be obtained only through donation. After her selection in 1955 of 120 service plates by Castleton China with gilded borders to complement the gilded flatware, she developed a strong interest in the White House china collection and arranged for a Smithsonian Institution curator to study and research the White House china and identify and rearrange the displays in the China Room.[76] Several gifts of personal services from past presidential families were received, and she accepted a reproduction set of plates from the Washington "Society of the Cincinnati" service and a set of porcelain plates with painted portraits of first ladies from Martha Washington to Edith Wilson made by the Royal Berlin Factory in 1923, which she displayed in the Diplomatic Reception Room.

In 1955 a collection of furnishings, including thirty-eight pieces of English furniture (many were reproductions), was donated by William A. M. and Shirley C. Burden, who were associated with the Metropolitan Museum of Art in New York. A Victorian rosewood sofa and three chairs were donated for the Lincoln bedroom, and a sofa believed to be from the Monroe era was placed in the Monroe Room. Handsome late-eighteenth-century Chinese porcelain jars decorated with exotic birds and peonies were also received.

Mamie Eisenhower's friendship with Margaret Thompson Biddle, who had entertained the Eisenhowers in Europe while he was with NATO and was a White House guest on several occasions, led to one of the most extensive collections in the White House. Upon her death in 1956, Mrs. Biddle bequeathed to the White House a collection of 1,575 pieces of vermeil (gilded silver). When it arrived in 1958, special cabinets were constructed for it in a ground-floor room that has since been renamed the Vermeil or Gold Room. Biddle, born in Montana and heir to a mining fortune, spent much of her life in Paris where she entertained on a grand scale and collected silver gilt for her homes. Primarily European in origin, the tureens, baskets, plates, wine coolers, candelabra, trays, flatware, boxes, and vases represent works by the finest English and French silversmiths of the eighteenth and nineteenth centuries. English craftsmen such as Thomas Farren (apprenticed 1695, died circa 1743), James Young (apprenticed 1749), George Wickes (1698–1761), and the renowned English Regency silversmiths Paul Storr (1771–1844) and Philip Rundell (1743–1827) and Parisian silversmiths Jean-Baptiste-Claude Odiot (1763–1850) and Denys Frankson (working 1765–91) are represented.

BELOW & OPPOSITE:
WINE COOLER
Paul Storr, London, 1809-10, for Rundell, Bridge & Rundell

Over 1,000 silver gilt objects from a private collection were donated in 1956 (selection, opposite). Some of the finest French and English silversmiths of the eighteenth and nineteenth centuries are represented as well as contemporary American work. Four urn-shaped wine coolers with classical Roman scenes are by the renowned English Regency silversmith Paul Storr.

Some pieces were made for English and French royal families such as that of King George II of England and King Louis XV of France, and others bear family crests of former owners such as the duke of Northumberland. There are contemporary American pieces in the collection, too. Margaret Thompson Biddle's monogram appears on dinner plates made by Gorham in 1916 and goblets by Tiffany, 1907–47.[77]

In 1960, the last year of the Eisenhower administration, President and Mrs. Eisenhower accepted a substantial gift of furnishings for the Diplomatic Reception Room. The donation of early-nineteenth-century American furnishings of superb quality was suggested by the National Society of Interior Designers, which selected and assembled donations from private individuals and the country's foremost dealers in Americana. It was the beginning of the growth of a museum-quality collection of furnishings for the White House that has continued to be supported by succeeding first ladies. Among the Federal-style pieces made in New York, New England, and Maryland were a mahogany sofa of unusual bowed form, easy chairs, lolling chairs, side and armchairs, card tables, and three other tables. A gilded bronze French mantel clock with a figure of George Washington, handsome fireplace equipment, and four pair of Georgian sconces with hurricane shades were added as was an oval carpet with seals of the fifty states specially designed for the room.

This gift of furnishings from the period of the building of the White House and its earliest occupancy was the first successful attempt to furnish a room in the White House with American antiques of the highest quality, and it set a precedent for Jacqueline Kennedy's efforts in the early 1960s to bring a historic character to the house.

TALL CASE CLOCK,
Effingham Embree, New York, c. 1800

Mamie Eisenhower accepted a donation of American federal furniture for the Diplomatic Reception Room in 1960 (right), to begin a collection of American furniture of the highest quality from the period when the White House was constructed. Those objects have been supplemented over the years by additional pieces such as a tall case clock with musical works and a French wallpaper, "Views of North America," in the room today (opposite).

THE STATE DINING ROOM

LEFT:
William J. Clinton administration, 2000

BELOW:
Engraving, A State Dinner at the White House,
Harper's Weekly, *March 12, 1870*

RIGHT, ABOVE:
Ulysses S. Grant administration, 1870s

RIGHT, BELOW:
Theodore Roosevelt administration, 1903

OPPOSITE, ABOVE:
*Harry S. Truman administration,
pre-renovation, 1948*

OPPOSITE, BELOW LEFT:
*Harry S. Truman administration,
post-renovation, 1952*

OPPOSITE, BELOW RIGHT:
Harry S. Truman administration, 1952

E PLURIBUS UNUM

Dubuc
Rue Michel-le-Comte N°33
A PARIS

WASHINGTON
First in WAR, First in PEACE,
First in the HEARTS of his COUNTRYMEN

"Enhancing the historic and artistic values of the White House."

A MUSEUM EVOLVES
FROM A COLLECTION

JOHN F. KENNEDY, LYNDON B. JOHNSON, RICHARD M. NIXON,
GERALD R. FORD, JIMMY CARTER, RONALD W. REAGAN,
GEORGE H. W. BUSH, WILLIAM J. CLINTON, GEORGE W. BUSH, BARACK OBAMA

T he arrival of President and Mrs. John F. Kennedy in January 1961 set in motion a completely new approach to enhancing the character of the White House and its collections. Less than ten years after the Truman renovation, the house contained historic furnishings from the last half of the nineteenth century, furniture designed by McKim, Mead & White in 1902, a variety of objects donated to the house since the 1920s, and, in the family quarters, reproduction furniture supplied by B. Altman & Company in 1952, which Mrs. Kennedy referred to as "early Statler." Dismayed to find so little evidence of the past, she embarked on an extensive program of bringing America's history to life in the President's House. Her interest in history, aesthetic sense, organizational ability, and attention to detail led to a new way of thinking about the historic character of the house and the institutionalization of its museum role that influences attitudes about the site in the twenty-first century. President Kennedy supported her efforts, stating that presidents "receive stimulus from the knowledge of living in close proximity to the people who seem legendary but who actually were alive and who were in these rooms. . . . Anything which dramatizes the great story of the United States—as I think the White House does—is worthy of the closest attention and respect by Americans who live here and who visit here and who are part of our citizenry. That's why I am glad that Jackie is making the effort she's making."[1]

Jacqueline Kennedy was given an album of photographs and floor plans of the rooms in the family quarters following her postelection visit with Mrs. Eisenhower and, in the weeks before the inauguration, she studied them and made decisions on decorative changes to the living quarters. Her initial priority, as for all first ladies, was to create a comfortable, "cozy" living area in the house for her husband and two young children. Making use of the $50,000 congressional appropriation provided each new administration, she worked

OPPOSITE:

MANTEL CLOCK
Dubuc (possibly Jean-Baptiste), Paris, France, c. 1815

Gilded bronze clocks with figures of George Washington were made by Dubuc, a skilled French clockmaker, for the American market after Washington's death in 1799. The scene in relief on the base depicts Washington's resigning his commission as commander in chief of the Continental Army in 1783.

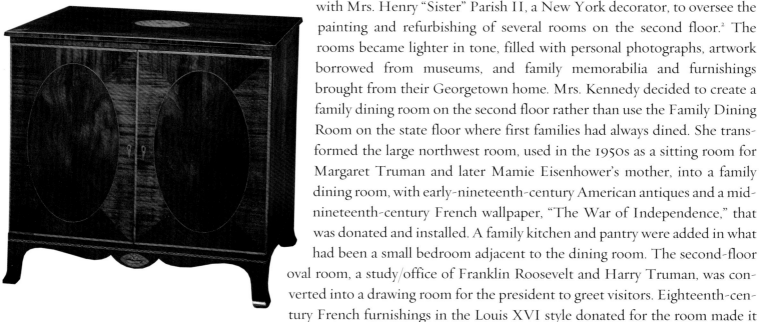

ABOVE:

LINEN PRESS
Annapolis, Maryland, c. 1790-1800

Pictorial inlays—patera, lily of the valley, a floral urn—and the veneer ovals on the doors contribute to this handsome storage piece for clothes that once belonged to the family of William Paca, a signer of the Declaration of Independence and governor of Maryland.

OPPOSITE:

LIGHTHOUSE CLOCK
Simon Willard & Son, Roxbury, Massachusetts, c. 1825

Clocks in the unusual shape of a lighthouse were advertised for sale by Willard in 1822. This clock is the only one with a portrait of the Marquis de Lafayette, who was received at the White House in 1824 and 1825 when he returned to America on a farewell visit.

with Mrs. Henry "Sister" Parish II, a New York decorator, to oversee the painting and refurbishing of several rooms on the second floor.[2] The rooms became lighter in tone, filled with personal photographs, artwork borrowed from museums, and family memorabilia and furnishings brought from their Georgetown home. Mrs. Kennedy decided to create a family dining room on the second floor rather than use the Family Dining Room on the state floor where first families had always dined. She transformed the large northwest room, used in the 1950s as a sitting room for Margaret Truman and later Mamie Eisenhower's mother, into a family dining room, with early-nineteenth-century American antiques and a mid-nineteenth-century French wallpaper, "The War of Independence," that was donated and installed. A family kitchen and pantry were added in what had been a small bedroom adjacent to the dining room. The second-floor oval room, a study/office of Franklin Roosevelt and Harry Truman, was converted into a drawing room for the president to greet visitors. Eighteenth-century French furnishings in the Louis XVI style donated for the room made it one of the most elegant in the house. It was to become Mrs. Kennedy's favorite room.[3] She left the Lincoln Bedroom as it had been since Truman moved the Lincoln-era bed and other objects there in 1945. It was, she said, "the one room in the house with a link to the past."[4]

Young and energetic, with a sense of style that captured the attention of the nation, Jacqueline Kennedy took a hands-on approach to changes in the house. She read old magazine articles and books describing its history, examined old photographs of White House rooms, searched its storerooms and closets for historic objects, and wrote detailed memoranda to Chief Usher J. B. West with her ideas. "I want to make this a grand house," she told him.[5] She also wanted to transform it into a place where visitors would learn about the history of the country, and she began to formulate ideas on how to achieve her goals. Shortly after the inauguration she consulted with David Finley, chairman of the Commission of Fine Arts, on how to form a committee to solicit and receive donations of objects. On February 23, 1961, she announced the appointment of a committee of advisors to work with the Commission of Fine Arts, which had been created in 1910 and involved in reviewing White House donations for decades. The mission of the new Fine Arts Committee for the White House was to locate authentic furniture of the early years of the White House and to raise funds to purchase such furniture for a permanent collection. Two months later, she added notable museum directors, curators, and presidential historians to advise her Fine Arts Committee in order to focus national attention and stimulate regional interest in the work of the committee.[6] Mrs. Kennedy selected as chairman of the Fine Arts Committee Henry Francis du Pont, director of the Winterthur Corporation that operated the Wilmington, Delaware, museum of decorative arts he founded in 1951—the Henry Francis du Pont Winterthur Museum. Du Pont's reputation as a collector of eighteenth- and early-nineteenth-century Americana of the highest quality lent credibility to the project.[7] Jacqueline Kennedy served as honorary chairman and was very involved in myriad details and decisions. The committee included David Finley and John Walker, director of the National Gallery of Art, as well as several wealthy and socially prominent private collectors and patrons of the arts. Although the committee did not convene formally after an initial meeting, its members participated actively in seeking furnishings and funds; several made substantial donations or contributed funds to purchase objects and/or pay for refurbishing rooms. Du Pont reviewed the numerous letters from the public and from dealers and collectors offering objects for the White House and consulted with Mrs. Kennedy and White House staff on plans for the public rooms. In the fall of 1961, a Special Committee for White House Paintings was formed with art historian James W. Fosburgh as chairman. Its goal was to expand the existing presidential and first lady portrait collection and replace copies of presidential portraits with those painted from life. The inclusion of representative landscape and still-life paintings by America's finest artists was also a priority, and many important works by major nineteenth-century artists were added.

Du Pont requested that historians and curators on the advisory committee draft a statement of philosophy to govern the committee's work. The Smithsonian Institution, with its First Ladies Hall containing many nineteenth-century presidential and White House furnishings, submitted an initial report that was expanded by advisory committee members Lyman H. Butterfield and Julian P. Boyd, editors of the papers of John Adams and Thomas Jefferson. They commented that "no other residence reflects so meaningfully the struggles and aspirations of the American people" and suggested that the White House continue to represent the living, evolving character of the presidency and the variety of backgrounds of presidents and their families rather than be furnished in a uniform style or period. While certain periods such as the early nineteenth century could be favored, they advocated representation from the late nineteenth and early twentieth centuries. They recommended that the project be grounded in thorough research into the history of the White House and its contents and the lives of its occupants and that a special White House archives or research file be established. They also suggested a variety of interpretative publications and supported the Smithsonian Institution's suggestion of installing visual materials in historical exhibits along the public tour route.[8] These principles guided the committee as it began to formulate its policies.

Mrs. Kennedy sought a professional museum curator for the White House to oversee the museum functions of research, acquisition, interpretation, and the care and preservation of a

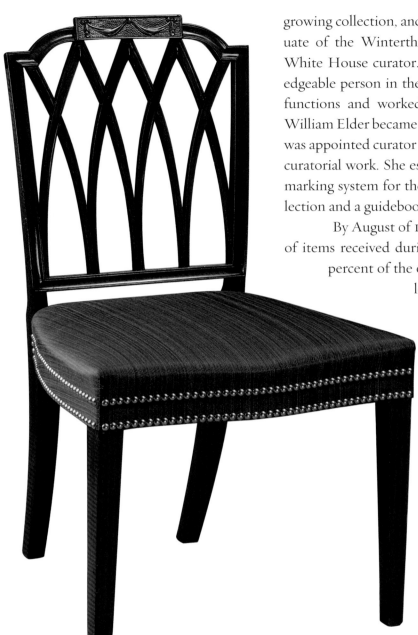

SIDE CHAIR
Salem, Massachusetts, c. 1800, carving possibly by the shop of Samuel McIntire

One of eight White House chairs of the same design, this chair bears a rectangular tablet with a carved drapery and a star-punched ground, a detail often associated with McIntire, one of the foremost Salem carvers working in the Federal style.

growing collection, and in the spring of 1961, Lorraine Waxman Pearce, a graduate of the Winterthur program in early American culture, was appointed White House curator. For the first time, a professionally trained and knowledgeable person in the White House assumed responsibilities for its museum functions and worked with the advisory committee.[9] A few months later, William Elder became registrar and began to catalog the incoming donations; he was appointed curator in 1962. Mrs. Kennedy took an interest in every aspect of curatorial work. She established goals for the office, proposed a cataloging and marking system for the collection, and planned to publish a catalog of the collection and a guidebook.[10]

By August of 1963, Elder reported to Mrs. Kennedy that the cataloging of items received during the Kennedy administration was completed and 50 percent of the objects in the White House prior to 1961 had been cataloged. Earlier, Lorraine Pearce had been assigned to write the text for the White House's first guidebook, *The White House: An Historic Guide*, to be published by the White House Historical Association. Mrs. Kennedy oversaw every detail of its publication, from the selection of photographs to approving the copy. She had suggested the creation of this non-profit association, since she wanted informative materials published on the history of the White House so that visitors would leave with a memorable experience; the sale of such publications would also provide a source of funding for restoration projects and the acquisition of objects.[11] For more than fifty years, the association has continued to financially support the collections and the public rooms. The guidebook has been in print continuously since 1962, with nearly five million copies sold.

Initially, there had been consideration given to declaring the White House a national monument to protect the building and its historic objects, but President Kennedy was not supportive of such a designation as he did not want to live in a national monument. Instead, the Kennedy administration worked with Congress to establish legislation that provided for the preservation and interpretation of the museum character of the public rooms and the protection of articles of furniture and decorative objects in the White House and those acquired in the future. The 1961 Act of Congress stated that White House objects, "when declared by the President to be of historic and artistic interest . . . shall be considered to be inalienable and the property of the White House."[12] For the first time, there was legal protection for historic White House objects, which could no longer be sold at auction, disposed of, or given away. The legislation was important in assuring potential donors that their gifts would remain permanently in the White House through changes of administration. A provision was included to transfer any historic object not on display in the White House to the Smithsonian Institution for study, exhibition, and storage.[13] The primacy of the house as a home and office was noted in the legislation; nothing was to conflict with the use and occupancy of the house as a home for the president and his family or the administration of the executive offices of the president. This congressional bill recognized the national importance of the White House collections and their preservation as part of the nation's heritage.

Mrs. Kennedy searched throughout the house and its storerooms for items of historic interest. In the ground-floor Broadcast Room she found the *Resolute* desk, and President Kennedy selected it as his desk in the Oval Office where it joined marine paintings and ship models he had chosen for the room. One of her important discoveries was the gilded pier table purchased in France for the Oval Room (Blue Room) in 1817 during the Monroe administration and used there until 1902. The only remaining piece of the suite was found at Fort Washington, Maryland, where White House furnishings had been sent for storage since the late 1940s. The table was repaired and regilded, and when photographs of it were published, a citizen recognized that a chair she owned was from the same Monroe suite and offered it to the White House, thus beginning the return of important documented pieces to their original home. Jacqueline Kennedy also uncovered the nineteenth-century porcelain state services from the Lincoln, Grant, Hayes, and Harrison, administrations, which she began to use on special occasions when entertaining privately. (There were not enough pieces in the services to use for official dinners.)

By the summer of 1961, the response to Mrs. Kennedy's call for donations to the White House began to bear fruit, and on the Fourth of July the White House announced the first gifts that would make it possible for the White House to become a museum of the country's heritage and a "testimonial to American fine arts and cabinetmaking."[14] The announcement stressed the efforts to obtain objects associated with past presidents and American historical figures. Several objects associated with Washington, Madison, Monroe, and Lincoln were among the donations, including the important gift of an original chair from the Monroe suite, major examples of New York furniture in the American Empire style for the Red Room, handsome early-nineteenth-century Maryland pieces for the two small dining rooms, as well as major paintings, sculpture, and historic prints. At the end of 1961, the committee's account of the large number of donations coming into the White House from all

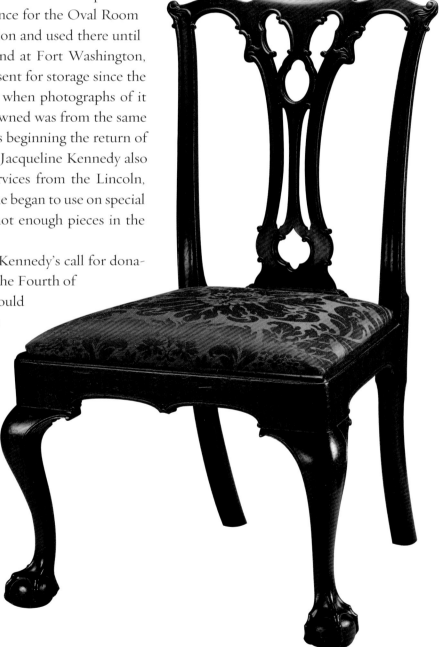

SIDE CHAIR
James Gillingham, Philadelphia, c. 1768-73

Based on designs of the English cabinetmaker Thomas Chippendale, with its pierced back splat, this chair bears a rare label of its maker who was among the highly skilled cabinetmakers in Philadelphia before the Revolution.

SETTEE
Philadelphia, c. 1800-1810

This richly carved mahogany chairback settee, with four matching armchairs all featuring plumes and double curved arms, epitomizes the highest level of work produced in Philadelphia in the Federal period.

over the country reflected the wide response to her efforts. The committee had found it more practical to identify appropriate objects and then locate donors who would pay for them, but thousands of people offered their family heirlooms. Among the objects accepted were rare examples of American porcelain pitchers made in Philadelphia in the 1830s and fine Federal furniture made by Maryland cabinetmakers in Baltimore (a bookcase-desk by Joseph Burgess, circa 1805) and Annapolis (a serving table attributed to John Shaw, circa 1790). In a handwritten letter to contributors of several pieces of early-nineteenth-century American furniture, Mrs. Kennedy wrote, "I hope you can realize what this means to us. We worked so hard to find some lovely things—and when they were all there it still seemed as if hardly a dent had been made—Every room was still mainly B. Altman 1948 and I wondered if we would ever be able to have all period rooms. . . . I do hope you will come this fall to the White House—then together we will see what a difference your things have made—and how much they have done towards making the White House the beautiful place that it should be—and can and will be."[15]

With extensive media interest in her project, Mrs. Kennedy granted a rare interview to *Life* magazine in an extensively illustrated article in which she made it clear that her project was to be a restoration based on scholarship, not simply a redecoration. Her goal was to bring to the interior of the house the beauty and strong feel of national tradition implicit in the building's exterior.[16] A few months later she was approached by CBS with plans to feature her in a special television program about her White House project. Broadcast as "A Tour of the White House with Mrs. John F. Kennedy" in February 1962, the program was viewed by almost a third of the nation and caused the White House to be inundated with correspondence. Typical of the responses was a telegram from Florida: "Your endeavor to restore the historical dignity to the White House is an inspiration to all the nation."[17] Her knowledgeable and gracious account of the history of the White House and her plans for it led to thousands of offers of objects and to a major increase in the number of visitors to the White House.

During the time the search for objects and placement of donated pieces throughout the house was proceeding, Jacqueline Kennedy also consulted with French designer Stéphane Boudin about the interior design of the rooms. Boudin, president and the leading designer of the Parisian firm of Jansen, had an international clientele and had done extensive work at Malmaison, the home of Josephine Bonaparte outside of Paris. Introduced to Mrs. Kennedy by Jayne Wrightsman, a wealthy New York collector of eighteenth-century French decorative arts and a member of the Fine Arts Commission, Boudin worked through Jansen's New York office to plan the dramatic window and wall treatments in the state rooms, where his aesthetic sense resulted in a strong visual impact. His background of working in grand European houses appealed to Mrs. Kennedy who thought that he provided a sense of state and grandeur to the White House. He also assisted her with redoing several rooms in the private quarters.[18] He advised Jacqueline Kennedy on paint colors, fabrics, and drapery treatments and arrangements of furniture, lighting fixtures, and paintings. The American furnishings being offered were reviewed by du Pont and other members of the Fine Arts Committee along with Mrs. Kennedy and the curatorial staff, but it was Boudin who provided the settings for them in the state floor rooms. The collaborative efforts resulted in a combination of historically authentic objects and a separate design aesthetic governing the totality of a room. As the rooms had continually changed over the years, there was no attempt to recreate rooms of a specific time in White House history, although the ambiance of the early nineteenth century was favored in the parlors.

Shortly after the election, the National Society of Interior Designers (NSID) wrote to Mrs. Kennedy about the donations it had made for the Diplomatic Reception Room in 1960, and she responded with additional suggestions to complete the furnishing of the room. When a historic French wallpaper, "Views of North America," printed from woodblocks by Zuber et Cie in 1834, was removed from a Maryland house and brought to her attention, she approached the NSID to donate the paper for the room, which it did, along with an unusual pair of mahogany window seats made in New York, circa 1825–30, Louis XVI bouillotte lamps, and several pieces of Chinese export porcelain. The historic paper with scenes of Boston harbor, West Point, Niagara Falls, the Natural Bridge of Virginia, and New York was based on engravings by French artists published in the 1820s. It

BOOKCASE
Philadelphia, c. 1800-1810

Made for a Philadelphia banking family, this bookcase is from the only known pair of Federal period bookcases extant. In the center of the pediment are delicate inlays of urns and scrolls; the drawers and doors have inlaid bands with fans in each corner.

continues to provide a romantic view of America and its landscape to foreign ambassadors and other guests received in the Diplomatic Reception Room.

Another group of designers, the American Institute of Interior Designers (AID), offered to contribute their efforts to the refurbishment of the ground-floor White House Library in 1961. Mrs. Kennedy accepted their offer and worked with the group's members and du Pont to create an attractive setting for a collection of books relating to American life that was assembled under the direction of James T. Babb, librarian of the Beinecke Library at Yale University.[19] The initial proposal to assemble an important collection of books by American authors, suggested by Lyman Butterfield and Julian Boyd, "was a most fascinating suggestion . . . and one that interests my husband and myself very much," wrote Jacqueline Kennedy.[20] She strongly supported their proposal. Among the furnishings for the Library, acquired with funds raised by AID, was a rare suite of caned furniture (two sofas and eight chairs) attributed to the New York workshop of Duncan Phyfe, 1800–1810, a library desk, work and card tables, a tole and glass chandelier from the home of American author James Fenimore Cooper, a pair of Argand lamps that had been a gift from the Marquis de Lafayette to the Revolutionary War general Henry Knox, and a handsome Aubusson carpet.

In the Red Room, the first state room to be refurnished, the neoclassical marble mantel that had been in the house since 1819 and Jacqueline Kennedy's longtime interest in French furnishings led to its decoration in the "Grecian" style of the period 1810–30, often referred to as American Empire. Influenced by the early-nineteenth-century French and English taste for revivals of Greco-Roman forms and motifs, American cabinetmakers interpreted English pattern books to produce objects with richly figured woods such as mahogany and rosewood, lyres, gilded supports such as winged females or eagles, animal paw feet, brass inlays and moldings, and gilded mounts. Curator Lorraine Pearce's scholarship on the French-born New York cabinetmaker Charles-Honoré Lannuier (1779–1819) resulted in the acquisition of handsome examples of Lannuier's work. Presidents had not purchased New York furniture for the President's House in its early years, but the ideas of Greece and Rome incorporated into the cabinetmakers' work had been expressed in the political philosophy of the early Republic and been manifested earlier in Benjamin Henry Latrobe's klismos chairs commissioned by President and Mrs. James Madison in 1809. Mrs. Kennedy's committee also recognized the French taste of early presidents such as Washington, Jefferson, Madison, and Monroe, all of whom had turned to Paris as a source of taste and for the quality of craftsmanship. A *gueridon*, a circular table, of superb design and construction with a geometric

ABOVE:

PITCHER
Tucker & Hulme, Philadelphia, 1828

With its delicate hand-painted floral design, this rare American-made porcelain pitcher was produced by a short-lived Philadelphia factory patronized by Andrew Jackson.

LEFT:

WALLPAPER
Jean Zuber et Cie, Rixheim, France, c. 1834-36

A set of French wallpaper "Views of North America" was installed in the Diplomatic Reception Room in 1961. This woodblock-printed paper with scenes of Boston (seen here), Niagara Falls, West Point, the Natural Bridge of Virginia, and New York Harbor was based on French engravings published in the 1820s and continues to be printed by the original maker.

ABOVE:

ARGAND LAMP

Matthew Boulton, Soho, England, 1784

One of several pairs of Argand lamps in the White House, this is from a pair presented to the Revolutionary War general Henry Knox by the Marquis de Lafayette in 1784. Argand lamps produced a stronger light than earlier lighting devices and were used by Washington, Jefferson, and Madison.

RIGHT:

SETTEE AND SIDE CHAIRS

Duncan Phyfe, New York, c. 1810

LOOKING GLASS

Probably New York, c. 1810

The White House Library, refurbished in 2007 with a new color scheme, textiles, and drapery design, holds a suite of Federal caned and reeded furniture (two settees and eight chairs) with scrolled backs carved with panels of drapery and ribbon-tied reeds, all characteristic of Phyfe's most complex creations. The table in the center of the room is also attributed to Phyfe. Above the settee is an unusual looking glass with a gilded architectural frame and a glass panel with an American eagle painted on the reverse.

patterned marble top supported by gilded bronze caryatids atop beautifully carved legs adorned by lion head masks was the highlight of the Red Room. Bearing Lannuier's label, this unique table was one of the earliest pieces acquired, to be followed by a pier table, architectural in form, also bearing Lannuier's label. Pearce noted that Lannuier's work was "ideally suited" to the White House, not only in period but in quality and construction.[21] An early-nineteenth-century sofa with boldly carved dolphin-shaped arms and feet, a rare form in America, was placed prominently in the room, along with a mix of early-nineteenth-century neoclassical French and American chairs and tables. The cerise red silk wall covering and upholstery fabrics with gold medallions and basket designs were copied by an American firm from a French textile document, circa 1810–15, supplied by Boudin. The finished room with its dramatic fabrics and furnishings influenced by designs from the classical world of Rome, Greece, and Egypt focused attention on an underappreciated period of American furnishings and led to an increased interest in the period among scholars and collectors of Americana. The influence of the room became evident in attempts by other historic houses to recreate the look of the Red Room.

The existence of an original pier table and the donation of original chairs (one armchair and two side chairs, both with the stamp of the French cabinetmaker Pierre-Antoine Bellangé) from Monroe's Oval Room led to the continuance of the French Empire style in the Blue Room, which had been reintroduced by McKim, Mead & White in 1902 when reproductions were made. The original 1817 furnishings were supplemented with copies of the Monroe chairs placed around the perimeter of the room, as during the Monroe era. More than any other room, it was here that Boudin's decor

DESK AND BOOKCASE
John Shaw, Annapolis, Maryland, 1797

*Bearing the label of its maker and the
date "1797," this desk with its delicately
carved and pierced pediment is one of the
finest works of the Scottish-born Shaw,
the most prominent cabinetmaker in
Annapolis. A large inlaid conch shell
appears on the fall board.*

would find its most theatrical expression. He drew inspiration from nineteenth-century European documents to hang a blue silk valance that encircled the room below the cornice with the same fabric carried over to the draperies. The walls were covered in a two-toned cream striped silk, a departure from blue papers or fabrics that had covered the walls for more than one hundred years. To the French gilded bronze clock and candlesticks from Monroe's 1817 purchases were added a pair of French Empire bronze torchères, wall sconces, and a gilded bronze and glass chandelier to create a ceremonial room in the French style. In this formal room, Mrs. Kennedy wanted a sense of state, ceremony, and grandeur, and she thought the finished room was very successful in meeting her criteria. She called it Boudin's "masterpiece" and said that she was "so proud" of his work in the room.[22]

Henry du Pont 's aesthetic was most clearly seen in the Green Room, with its handsome examples of American furnishings of the Federal period—the time when John Adams and Thomas Jefferson lived in the house. A pair of New England card tables, circa 1790–1810, typical of the style of furnishings in the early-nineteenth-century White House, acquired for the room in the 1946 (a donation from Mrs. Francis B. Crowninshield, Henry du Pont's sister), governed the acquisition of the delicate early-nineteenth-century chairs, tables, and sofas/settees modeled after the designs of the English cabinetmakers George Hepplewhite and Thomas Sheraton and made in Baltimore, New England, and Philadelphia. Boudin executed the decorative work, covering the walls with a moss green watered silk also used in the draperies that hung in panels.

In the East Room and State Dining Room, the McKim, Mead & White furnishings of 1902 were retained, but alterations were made to finishes. The red marble mantels in the East Room were painted to resemble white marble, and the celadon green walls of the State Dining Room were painted ivory. The Monroe gilded bronze centerpiece was brought out of storage and placed prominently on the dining room table, the 1902 silver chandelier and

SOFA
New York, c. 1810-25

"Grecian" style sofas with painted and gilded scrolled arms and feet fashioned as dolphins were made by New York cabinetmakers influenced by English Regency and French Empire forms.

ABOVE:

CARD TABLE

Probably New York, c. 1825

Carved lyres were fashionable motifs used on tables and chairs in the 1820s. This table, with its beautiful veneered oak top, has unusual glass mounts on the columns.

RIGHT:

SOFA TABLE

New York, in the manner of Charles-Honoré Lannuier, c. 1815-20

Made for placement before sofas and used for drawing or writing, sofa tables were seldom made in America. This mahogany table with its gilded winged caryatids and verde antique *feet displays elements from the ancient world adapted by Americans, especially in New York.*

OPPOSITE:

The Blue Room was created as a ceremonial room in the style of the French Empire when, in 1962, Jacqueline Kennedy assembled many original White House furnishings of the James Monroe era.

wall sconces were gilded to match, and at Boudin's direction, the mahogany console tables were gilded and painted. Although Mrs. Kennedy gave much thought to a new state dinner service and considered various samples, no decisions had been made by the time of the assassination of President Kennedy in November 1963. Mrs. Kennedy did, however, order a new set of glassware. Encouraged to order fine French glass, she turned, instead, to the state of West Virginia where her husband had gained support in his 1960 primary campaign. The restrained glassware, with no cutting or engraving, named "President's House," was produced by the Morgantown Glass Guild.[23] When the Guild went out of business, replacements were produced by Fostoria Glass Company, Moundsville, West Virginia (1974), and by Lenox Crystal, Mount Pleasant, Pennsylvania (1994).

The reach of Jacqueline Kennedy's project extended to the private quarters. For the room that had been the nineteenth-century Cabinet Room, she brought from storage the remaining pieces from Ulysses Grant's Cabinet suite made by Pottier & Stymus in 1869, and Boudin created a Victorian ambiance with green flocked walls on which were displayed facsimiles of foreign treaties. With the assistance of Vice President Lyndon B. Johnson, she secured on loan from the United States Capitol one of the elaborate cut-glass chandeliers from the 1873 East Room that had been sent to auction in 1903. (It was returned to the Capitol in 1978.) Throughout rooms such as the Lincoln Sitting Room, Queens' Bedroom, and several third-floor guest rooms, American furniture, ceramics, textiles, and other decorative arts invoked a sense of America's past.

In the two years and eight months since Jacqueline Kennedy announced a Fine Arts Committee to advise her, almost all the public rooms and most of the family rooms had been furnished with early-nineteenth-century American and French decorative arts in furniture, looking glasses, clocks, lighting fixtures, ceramics, glass, and silver. Among the major acquisitions were three of the original French chairs from Monroe's Oval Room, a chair made for

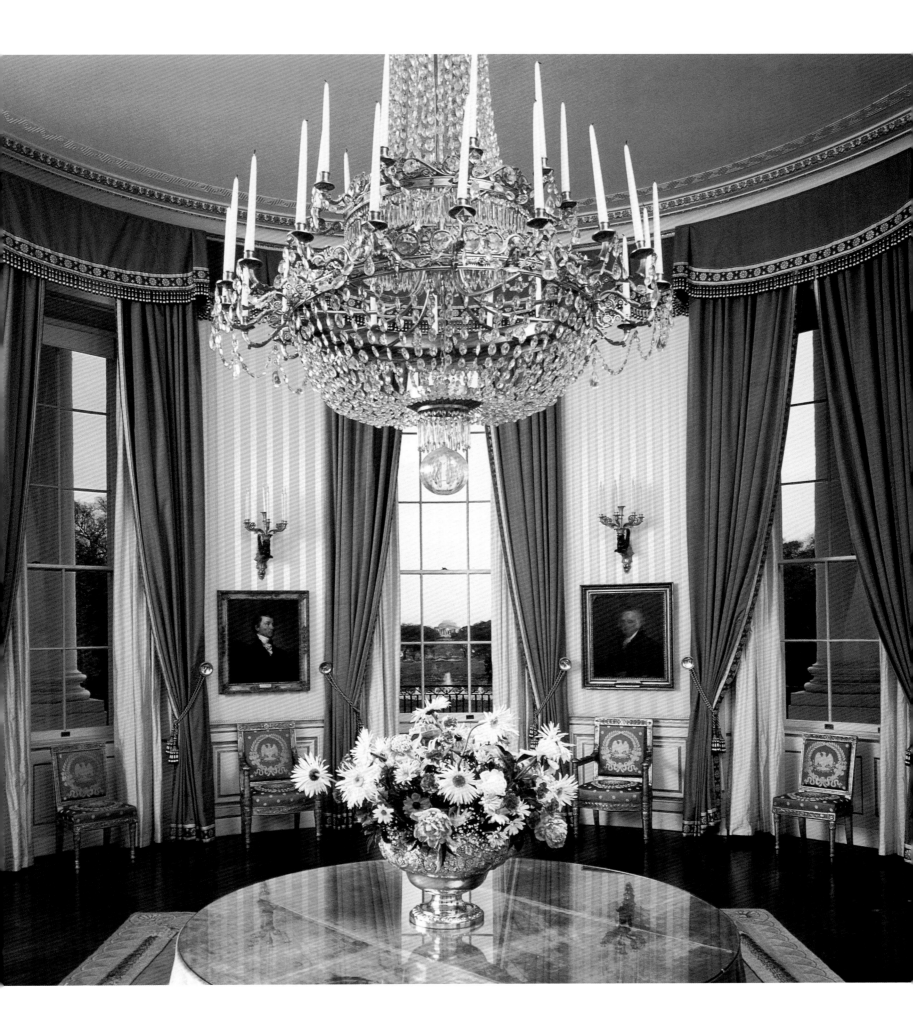

RIGHT:

*The Queens' Bedroom, where seven
queens have been guests, contains several
fine examples of New England and
Maryland Federal-period furniture.*

BELOW:

CANDELABRUM
Paul Storr, London, 1810-11

*A set of heavily chased silver candelabra
with three beautiful scrolled branches
decorated with anthemia and flower-
heads was made by this highly esteemed
English Regency silversmith. Storr made
many candelabra of this form that can be
used as single candlesticks when the
branches are removed.*

the East Room in 1818, examples of American cabinetmakers John Shaw (Annapolis), Joseph Burgess (Baltimore), Duncan Phyfe and Charles-Honoré Lannuier (New York), as well as many unattributed pieces from Baltimore, Philadelphia, Boston, and New York. American, French, English, and Chinese export porcelains and earthenware graced the rooms. A superb silver plateau, a rare form in America, made by John W. Forbes of New York, circa 1825, was placed in the Family Dining Room, as was an important group of English Regency table silver, made 1806–7, by the London silversmith Paul Storr. Rare French (Aubusson and Savonnerie) and English (Axminster) carpets were placed on the floors, and important historic documents relating to the house were added.

Mrs. Kennedy's efforts in recapturing a sense of the nation's history in the context of the White House influenced historic houses and state governors' mansions and led to the revival of interest and new appreciation in American neoclassical furnishings of the period 1810–30. She set a standard for future refurbishing projects in the White House. Her legacy endures in the policies and standards established by the Fine Arts Committee, her appointment of a curator with responsibility for the museum functions of the White House, and her commitment to the interpretation of the house through the establishment and the publications of the White House Historical Association. So strong was the perception of her project that many Americans believe that White House interiors have not changed since 1963.

President and Mrs. Lyndon B. Johnson recognized the precedent-setting efforts of Mrs. Kennedy and her advisory committees and thought it vitally important that they be continued and preserved. After discussions with attorney and advisor Clark Clifford and Jacqueline Kennedy, Lady Bird Johnson expressed her thoughts. "If we can do anything to perpetuate what has been done and move forward in acquisitions that is my great ambition."[24]

In 1964 President Johnson issued an Executive Order establishing a permanent advisory committee, the Committee for the Preservation of the White House, to report to the president on its responsibilities for the "preservation and the interpretation of the museum character of the principal corridor of the ground floor and the principal public rooms on the first floor of the White House."[25] The committee was charged with making recommendations on the articles used or displayed in the White House and the "decoration and arrangement best suited to enhancing the historic and artistic values of the White House." With the director of the National Park Service as its chair and other government officials such as the director of the National Gallery of Art, secretary of the Smithsonian Institution, chairman of the Commission of Fine Arts, White House chief usher, and White House curator as ad hoc members, the order also provided for the appointment of private individuals by the president. Henry du Pont and James Fosburgh, chairs of Mrs. Kennedy's committees, were appointed to the new committee to provide continuity. The aim of that committee was to continue "the high standards of beauty, history and maintenance of the White House," said Mrs. Johnson.[26] Recognizing the need for the preservation and protection of the growing collections, the Executive Order provided for the permanent position of a White House curator charged with making recommendations on historic and artistic objects in the White House and their care and preservation. Mrs. Johnson wanted the position to be a permanent one, "so the house will not be at the whim of any First Lady."[27]

Building on the philosophy that had governed the Kennedy Fine Arts Committee, the new committee developed further guidelines and goals for White House collecting, emphasizing the acquisition of objects associated with the White House or its occupants and those that reflected the highest tradition of American craftsmanship. Donations such as an eighteenth-century Sheffield silver coffee urn once owned by John and Abigail Adams, nineteenth-century presidential china, important examples of American silver, two neoclassical marble mantels from the Washington, D.C., home of the city's first mayor, Robert Brent, and the beginning of a collection of letters written by presidential families while they lived in the White House were testament to the desire to continue the dedicated efforts of Mrs. Kennedy and her committee. Mrs. Johnson felt that the committee's work was one of the most important things she was associated with in the house.[28] Under the direction of curator James R. Ketchum, who had been appointed in 1963, a catalog of the donations to the

RUG
France, c. 1815

French carpets, including this Savonnerie, were placed in the state parlors in the early 1960s. It has been copied and reproduced for current use in the Red Room.

LEFT:
DESSERT COOLER
France, c. 1815-25

Dessert coolers, made to hold ice to cool ice cream or other chilled desserts, were a particularly French innovation. This is one of a pair of porcelain coolers with the monogram "WCE" that was given to Massachusetts governor William Eustis by his friend, Marquis de Lafayette.

RIGHT:
URN
Barr, Flight & Barr, Worcester, England, c. 1807

With its seashell and dolphin-shaped handles and other decorations relating to the sea, this commemorative urn was made to honor a British naval captain whose ship captured a French frigate during the Napoleonic Wars. The captured frigate, used by the British Royal Navy in the War of 1812, was sunk by the USS Constitution.

OPPOSITE:
The Queens' Sitting Room has its Kennedy-era decoration still intact. Mrs. Kennedy engaged French designer Stéphane Boudin to execute interior work in the state rooms and in the family quarters.

White House from 1961 through 1964 was prepared.[29]

In 1967 Lady Bird Johnson accepted the gift of a late-eighteenth-century Italian crèche, made in Naples, with more than thirty carved wood and terra cotta figures, many with original fabrics. It was placed on view in the East Room during the December holiday season and has remained a focus of the holidays ever since. She also chose a new state dinner service for 216 people, consisting of 2208 pieces, the first service made for the White House since the Truman administration. Designed by Tiffany and made by Castleton China, it was decorated with borders of American wild flowers and, on the dessert plates, painted flowers of the fifty states and the District of Columbia, all representing Mrs. Johnson's deep interest in the natural world.[30]

The White House has never been a static house frozen in time; its rooms and collections change as do its occupants. By the time that President and Mrs. Richard Nixon took up residence in 1969, thousands of visitors and guests and the normal wear and tear on the silk fabrics in a heavily used house had taken their toll and necessitated changes. After the 1970 appointment of Clement E. Conger as curator, Mrs. Nixon and the Committee for the Preservation of the White House embarked on changes to several rooms and an ambitious acquisition program to secure examples of the highest quality American decorative arts from 1800–1825. Mrs. Nixon took a personal interest in the work, approved designs, wall coverings, and fabrics and strongly supported the efforts of Conger, who brought in Edward Vason Jones as a consulting architect and interior design expert. Jones, with his clear sense of Federal period design, had assisted the American Wing at the Metropolitan Museum of Art with its reinstallation of nineteenth-century interiors in 1970 and championed the neoclassical furniture of New York cabinetmakers Duncan Phyfe and Charles-Honoré Lannuier with its excellent proportions and skillfully executed carving and ornamentation.[31] With Conger appealing to donors and raising private funds, major examples by Phyfe and Lannuier were acquired for the Green Room and Red Room, where substantial decorative changes were made in the replacement of plaster architectural ornaments from the 1950s and in the design of the draperies copied from early-nineteenth-century French and English

documents.[32] Superb examples of early-nineteenth-century New York cabinetmaking replaced the delicate furnishings in the Green Room. Among the pieces were two extraordinary work tables in a "sarcophagus" form with interior compartments of sliding trays, a bookcase-desk with a cylinder front, a pair of window seats signed by Duncan Phyfe's upholsterer, a sofa, sofa table, pole screen, easy chairs, and a pair of lyre-back armchairs, all handsomely carved with motifs characteristic of highly skilled New York cabinetmakers. An exceptional pair of pedestal tables with marble tops, long separated, were located and joined the other New York pieces. In the Red Room, an unusual table or stand labeled by Lannuier, diminutive in scale and with balusters with water-leaf carving, canted corners, and green and black marble inset into the top, joined the Kennedy-era pieces. A pair of card tables with brass moldings and inlay, one with Lannuier's label, came into the house and were later placed in the room.[33] The decorations of the Blue Room, with its Monroe furnishings, changed. Fabrics in a different shade of turquoise blue and wallpaper reproduced from a French document made by Jacquemart & Bénard, circa 1800, replaced the silk wall covering from 1962, and new, more elaborate draperies based on French pattern books were designed by Jones. Three additional gilded French chairs from Monroe's Oval Room were acquired, including the only survivor of two large enclosed armchairs—*bergères*—made for President and Mrs. Monroe.

A large and fine collection of New England Federal furniture, including two exceptional tambour desks, one with a pedimented top, a tall-case clock, and a sofa table and work table, all made by the father-son cabinetmakers, John and Thomas Seymour of Boston, were donated and/or purchased and placed in the Queens' Bedroom and other rooms in the private quarters in the 1970s. At President Nixon's request, a room on the ground floor, the Map Room, was turned into a sitting room, and eighteenth-century furnishings in the Chippendale style were placed there. Among them were several Philadelphia pieces such as a rare mahogany side chair bearing the label of James Gillingham (1736–81), a serpentine-shaped chest of drawers, a large side table with Chinese fret work, 1770–75, and a tall-case clock with works by Emanuel Rouse (working 1747–68) made about 1750. New York-made furniture included an armchair, circa 1755, attributed to Gilbert Ash (1717–85) and a triple-arched-back sofa with fret-carved legs and stretchers, circa 1760.

Acquisitions in the years 1969 to 1974 were substantial. Hundreds of pieces of furniture; lighting fixtures that included nineteen chandeliers and nine pair of rare eighteenth- and nineteenth-century Argand lamps; fireplace equipment; French, Chinese, and American porcelains (several examples of White House services from the Jackson, Polk, Pierce, Grant, and McKinley administrations); silver (a presentation cup made by Tiffany and Company in 1899 and given to the French ambassador to the United States for his assistance in the peace negotiations ending the Spanish-American War); and more than twenty handsome nineteenth-century carpets from France, England, Turkey, Iran, and China were placed throughout the house. The museum-like settings of the Nixon administration, with an emphasis on the high quality of furnishings, survive today in the Green Room and Red Room.

Succeeding administrations have continued to rely on the advice of the Committee for the Preservation of the White House, and works by American artisans and artists have

OPPOSITE:

SERVICE PLATE, DESSERT PLATE, AND CREAM SOUP CUP AND SAUCER
Castleton China, Inc., New Castle, Pennsylvania, 1968-72; designed by Tiffany & Co., New York

Lady Bird Johnson's interest in the natural world is reflected in the floral designs on the Johnson state service; wild flowers appear on the borders of the service plate, and the official flowers of each state and the District of Columbia were selected for the dessert plates.

WORK TABLE

Attributed to Duncan Phyfe
New York, c. 1810

*This extraordinary tapered-form table is
one of only four nearly identical tables
(two are in the White House). Made for
writing, sewing, or perhaps miniature
painting, its intricate design and extensive and beautiful fittings could only have
been executed by a highly skilled cabinetmaker such as Phyfe.*

entered the collection to continue Jacqueline Kennedy's vision. With the enormous growth
in the collections in the 1960s and early 1970s, there was less need for extensive acquisition
programs. Collecting concentrated on the refining of the collection, the addition of objects
associated with the White House and its former occupants, and materials such as historic
prints, photographs, and manuscripts that document the history of the house. President and
Mrs. Ford were in residence during the nation's bicentennial celebrations in 1976 and welcomed many heads of state that year. Patriotic Americans made several donations to the
White House. Among them was a Philadelphia easy chair, made before the Declaration of
Independence was issued, that joined other eighteenth-century furniture in the Map Room.
Attributed to Thomas Affleck (1740–95), it was made about 1760–70. Three pieces (a
plate and a pair of fruit coolers) from James and Dolley Madison's personal French dinner
service were acquired. A 1792 newspaper with the announcement and terms of a competition for a design for the President's House in the new city of Washington and a letter writ-

ten to Dolley Madison in 1809 recommending Baltimore cabinetmakers for the Madison Oval Room were added to the growing historical manuscript collection and archives of the Office of the Curator. Memorabilia such as a glass locket containing locks of Thomas Jefferson's hair and a carved ivory fan once owned by Edith Roosevelt were also acquired. Betty Ford took much pleasure in using examples of historic dinner services as service plates for small private dinners. The Hayes service with its unusual plant and animal motifs provided dinner conversation among the Fords' guests. She also emphasized American crafts, using works borrowed from museums as centerpieces at official dinners and as decorations during the Christmas holidays.

President and Mrs. Jimmy Carter had a deep appreciation for the historic house, took an interest in objects with historical associations, and had several pieces from White House storage brought into the private quarters, including a Victorian child's suite of furniture placed in their daughter Amy's room. Rosalynn Carter concentrated on expanding the paintings collection and added many important works. Especially noteworthy was a painting by George Caleb Bingham, *Lighter Relieving Steamboat Aground* (1847), depicting boatmen on the Missouri River. Recognizing that first ladies and curators should not have to raise funds continually for new acquisitions and the refurbishing of state rooms, Rosalynn Carter, an active honorary chair of the Committee for the Preservation of the White House, endorsed and supported the establishment of the private, nonprofit White House Preservation Fund in 1979 to provide an endowment for the benefit of the White House. Historic objects continued to be donated, and one of the most important was the only known surviving sofa from the Monroe French suite of 1817, a gift in 1979. When placed later in the Blue Room, its curving back fit perfectly into the oval shape of the room. For the Lincoln Bedroom, an English Victorian chandelier, once fitted for gas, was found. It closely resembled the chandelier that appeared in prints of the room in Lincoln's time. Mrs. Carter also accepted the gift of a wool coverlet in a nineteenth-century rose pattern specially handwoven by a generous citizen for the "Lincoln" bed, following Grace Coolidge's precedent in the 1920s. Ten additional Italian figures for the White House crèche were donated, and rare historic prints of the White House and maps of the District of Columbia were given. Of special importance was the earliest engraving of the President's House, printed in London in 1807, and the first printed plan of the city of Washington, dated 1792. Parts of the old nineteenth-century White House were returned—wallpaper swatches from McKinley's family rooms, a box made from the East Room oak floor removed in 1902, ceiling globes from the late-nineteenth-century East Room, and a bench from the pre-1902 elevator.

In 1981 Mrs. Ronald Reagan solicited contributions from private individuals for an extensive redecoration of the private quarters and the maintenance of the public spaces. More than 150 collection objects were conserved as were the marble walls, wood doors, and floors in the public rooms, and funds were also applied to improve collections storage. In 1988 the first comprehensive conservation survey of the furniture collection was conducted. Objects with White House and presidential associations continued to be added to the collection. Two of twenty-four chairs made for the East Room in 1818 were acquired as were eight pieces of Monroe's state dessert service and a rare American cut-glass decanter made for James Madison in 1816. A carpet in the Ispahan manner, made by Armenian girls in a Syrian orphanage of Near Eastern Relief in 1925, an eighteenth-century desk from Pennsylvania, and an English silver inkstand, all given to President and Mrs. Coolidge in the 1920s, were donated by their son. The Theodore Roosevelt Association presented Roosevelt's Nobel Peace Prize gold medal, awarded to him in 1906, and a brass and ivory presidential seal used by President Lincoln in the White House was a significant acquisition. Several objects on loan were converted to permanent acquisitions. Among them were important New York neoclassical furniture in the Red Room (a rosewood fire screen), the Green Room (a work table), and in the Library (a drum table).

Mrs. Reagan also commissioned a new porcelain state dinner and dessert service. The design was based on the first American-made service ordered by President and Mrs. Wilson in 1918 and incorporated her favorite red color prominently in the borders of the 220 place settings, each with nineteen pieces, which were made by Lenox.[34] The large and expensive service, donated with funds from a private foundation, was widely criticized at a time of federal budget cuts. Although such criticisms were not as extensive as those leveled at Martin Van Buren in 1840 or Mary Todd Lincoln in the 1860s, they were, nonetheless, another instance of White House acquisitions judged in a political context. Shortly before President and Mrs. Reagan left the White House, she received a delegation from the American Association of Museums, which had accredited the White House as a museum in 1988. The White House museum programs now met the highest standards of the museum community.[35]

President and Mrs. George Bush resided in the President's House during the celebrations in 1992 observing the 200th anniversary of the laying of the White House cornerstone, and they supported and participated in the activities planned by the White House Historical Association. Barbara Bush reactivated the Committee for the Preservation of the White House (it had not met during the Reagan years) with the appointment of curators and art historians from major museums and academic institutions. The committee approved an expanded and revised collections policy to govern acquisitions and loans, considered the state of the public rooms, and made recommendations for their improvement. The revised collections policy stated that the "overall objec-

OPPOSITE, ABOVE:
ARGAND LAMP
Probably Messinger & Son, Birmingham, England, c. 1830

English Argand lamps became popular in America after their invention in the 1780s because they produced brighter lighting with less smoke. The bronze and glass lamp was owned by Dolley Madison. The silver lamp has an unusual oval mirror to reflect light from the burner.

OPPOSITE, BELOW:
ARGAND LAMP
Matthew Boulton, Soho, England, c. 1786

BELOW:
ARMCHAIR
Possibly Thomas Affleck, Philadelphia, c. 1765-75

Armchairs with stuffed backs copied from a design by the English cabinetmaker Thomas Chippendale were seldom made in 18th-century America. The mahogany arm supports reflect the high quality of Affleck's carving.

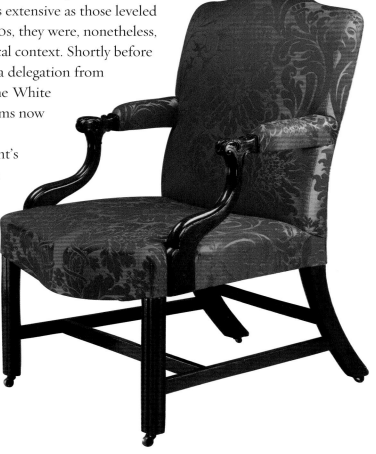

tive in the assemblage of the collection is to present a visual homogeneity of objects representative of those that once may have adorned this important structure, and through the exhibition of superior quality fine and decorative arts, to promote an awareness of the historic significance of the President's House through its ever changing occupancies."[36]

The committee established new procedures to review objects considered for the collection and recommended the acquisition of a mahogany card table with Charles-Honoré Lannuier's label. An example from the Lincoln state porcelain service (a custard cup) in a shape not represented in the White House China Room, was donated, as were a rare cut and engraved sherry glass, a finger bowl, and an ice cream plate from the Lincoln glassware service.

In the early 1990s, emphasis was placed on the conservation and storage of the objects that encompassed one of the most important collections of American decorative arts in the nation. Congress granted special appropriations for conservation, and many of the most historic objects in the house, such as the Monroe gilded bronze plateau, silver, and textiles, as well as furniture received treatment. In 1992 objects in off-site storage were moved to a new museum storage facility, managed by the National Park Service. For the first time, temperature-and-humidity controlled space and a conservation laboratory assured that White House objects would be preserved for future occupants. At the same time, a new computerized inventory and museum management system was developed to provide up-to-date documentation on the 30,000 objects in the White House.

Barbara Bush also supported the reorganization of the White House Preservation Fund, and it was revitalized as the White House Endowment Fund under the White House Historical Association, with the goal of raising a twenty-five million dollar endowment for acquisitions, the care and refurbishing of the public rooms, and conservation of the collection. Hillary Rodham Clinton actively continued to support the fund, and through her efforts, the goal was achieved in 1998.

President and Mrs. William Clinton, keen students of White House history, enjoyed learning about the history of the house, its rooms and objects, and were enthusiastic and supportive stewards of its museum role. Hillary Rodham Clinton, as honorary chairman, was an active participant in the Committee for the Preservation of the White House, and deeply involved in decisions on changes in the state rooms and acquisitions. President Clinton appointed additional members to the committee to broaden its expertise, and in 1995 Mrs. Clinton, with the advice of the committee, oversaw the refurbishment of the Blue Room (the first in twenty-five years) and the East Room. The Entrance Hall, Cross Hall, and Grand Staircase were refurbished in 1997 and the State Dining Room in 1998. For the Blue Room, early-nineteenth-century French wallpapers, made in the period of Monroe's presidency, were located and reproduced, new sapphire blue fabrics were custom

SERVICE PLATE, FISH/LUNCH PLATE, AND TEA CUP AND SAUCER
Lenox, Inc., Trenton, New Jersey, 1981-82

Nancy Reagan commissioned a new state service for 220. Its design was based on the first American service made for the White House in 1918, but Mrs. Reagan chose red, her favorite color, for the new service.

OPPOSITE:
The Map Room was converted into a sitting room in 1970, and major examples of 18th-century American furniture were acquired for it. The English cut-glass chandelier, c. 1771-73, has star pendants and a silvered bowl with its original wood liner.

DESSERT AND DINNER PLATES
SERVICE PLATE
Lenox, Inc., Pomona, New Jersey, 2000

First Lady Hillary Rodham Clinton, inspired by White House architectural details, commissioned this service to commemorate the two-hundredth anniversary of the White House. For the first time, images of the White House were used—the north view on the dinner plates (far right) and gilded service plates (below), and the south view on the yellow-bordered dessert plates (right).

made, and a new carpet, based on European designs of about 1815, was woven. The East Room was freshened with the removal of the faux marble paint from the red marble mantels and baseboards, and new carpets, incorporating details from the plaster ceiling, were made. The gilded furniture in the Entrance Hall and Cross Hall was covered in red fabric replicated from French design sources of the first quarter of the nineteenth century, and new carpets were designed. The walls of the State Dining Room were painted a stone color in keeping with the Georgian style paneling, and the room's architectural details were highlighted. New draperies in a Colonial Revival design and a new carpet using motifs of the 1902 ceiling were added, and several of the 1902 furnishings were conserved. The eagle pedestal console tables, painted and gilded in the early 1960s, were restored to their original mahogany, and the gilded chandelier and wall sconces were conserved to brighten their appearance.

In 1994 the Committee for the Preservation of the White House endorsed Mrs. Clinton's idea of a series of exhibitions of American sculpture by twentieth-century artists to be displayed in the Jacqueline Kennedy Garden. Working with museums throughout the country, the committee organized eight exhibitions. The committee also recommended updating the books in the White House Library to include definitive books on American thought published since the creation of the library in the early 1960s. Acquisitions for the permanent White House collection included a pair of eighteenth-century mahogany chairs with a history of having been purchased for George Washington's first presidential residence in New York in 1789, and two pairs of imitation bamboo side chairs that had been in the White House in the 1870s and used by President and Mrs. Rutherford B. Hayes and President and Mrs. James A. Garfield. A small square mahogany pier table, made 1805–10, with two of Lannuier's labels, that had been on long-term loan, was added, bringing to six the labeled pieces in the White House by this important New York cabinetmaker. A Boston card table with a spread-winged eagle pedestal, dating from 1815–20, a mate to a table in the Oval Office acquired in the 1970s, was added. A ruby-stained glass goblet and a tankard, both made in Bohemia between 1840 and 1860, with engraved images of the President's House copied from prints of the 1830s, attest to the growing popularity of depictions of the White House in the nineteenth century.

A rare drawing of the Blue Room in 1860 illustrating the Rococo revival suite of furniture chosen by Harriet Lane for James Buchanan was the only item acquired by the White House from the Jacqueline Kennedy Onassis estate sale in 1998. Drawings and fabrics from the New York office of Jansen, the firm that did so much work for Jacqueline Kennedy, were donated, as were the papers of Charles T. Haight, director of B. Altman & Company's design studio, who had overseen all of the interior design work during the Truman renovation in the 1950s. Tiffany Studio drawings for rugs commissioned especially for the Red Room and Green Room in the Coolidge administration were also added.

At the close of the twentieth century, attention focused on ways to commemorate the two-hundredth anniversary of the President's House. The White House Historical

SERVICE PLATE
BOULLION CUP AND SAUCER
Lenox, Inc., Kinston, North Carolina, 2008–09

This state service commissioned by First Lady Laura Bush looked to services used by former presidential families for inspiration. The basket weave border design on the service plates was inspired by early nineteenth-century French pieces associated with Dolley Madison in the White House collection. The gilded eagle in the center is based on a wooden inlay design in an early New England sideboard once owned by Daniel Webster.

Association observed this milestone through publications, exhibitions, films, lectures, and symposia. A new dinner and dessert service with design details from state rooms and images of the White House, suggested by Mrs. Clinton, was donated by the association, as was an elegant pair of French porcelain vases, circa 1820, with likenesses of George Washington and John Adams.

The delay in selecting a president in the election of 2000 left little time for President George W. Bush and Laura Bush to plan their move to the White House. Mrs. Bush called her mother-in-law, Barbara Bush, who told her there were already so many lovely and comfortable furnishings in the White House that they would need to bring very little.[37] They brought clothes, photos, and a single piece of furniture: a chest of drawers that had belonged to George Bush's grandmother.[38] Laura Bush's priority was to create a sense of serenity and comfort in the residence. She kept the sunny yellow walls of the Second Floor sitting rooms and corridor and added comfortable furniture covered in soft, muted greens. The first two rooms she devoted attention to were those of her twin daughters, Barbara and Jenna. She also oversaw the furnishing of the president's Second Floor office, the Treaty Room, where President Bush used Grant's 1869 cabinet table and sofa. Mrs. Bush commented that "There is a unique continuity in knowing your predecessors have walked these halls, have written on these tables, have sat in these chairs. And a particular comfort as well."[39]

In 2002 Laura Bush solicited the advice of the Committee for the Preservation of the White House regarding the Lincoln Bedroom, which had changed little since President Truman had moved objects associated with President Lincoln into the room in 1945. Relying on historic documents, prints, and photographs of the mid- and late-nineteenth-century President's House, replicas of the Lincoln-era mantel, wallpaper, window cornices and draperies, and a carpet were reproduced. The Lincoln Bed was draped in the purple silks favored by Mrs. Lincoln and received a copy of the carved and gilded cornice that hung above the bed for decades. A pair of Rococo

PHOTOGRAPH
Unknown photographer, 1865

This rare stereograph shows the North Portico of the White House draped in black mourning crape provided by Washington upholsterers after the death of President Lincoln in April of 1865.

RIGHT:
TALL CASE CLOCK
John and Thomas Seymour, Boston, c. 1805-1810; works possibly by James Doull, Charlestown, Massachusetts

A refined New England tall case clock, with sophisticated inlays characteristic of the Seymours' superb craftsmanship, is part of a large collection of New England Federal furniture in the White House.

OPPOSITE:
Each President of the United States has selected a special desk for use in the Oval Office. Presidents Kennedy, Carter, Reagan, Clinton, G.W. Bush, and President Obama chose the Resolute desk that was presented to President Hayes in 1880. It is shown here in 2011.

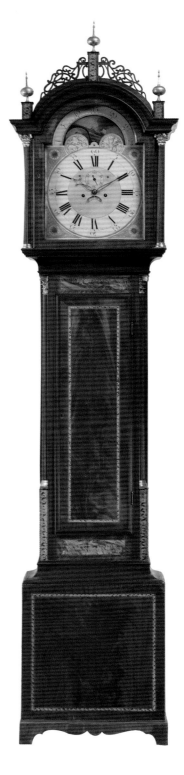

IMPORTANT ACQUISITIONS 1961–2014:
DUNCAN PHYFE
1768–1854

*One of the most highly skilled cabinetmakers
working in New York City in the early 19th
century, the Scottish-born Phyfe oversaw a large
workshop that produced sophisticated furniture
for wealthy patrons. Although none of his pieces was
in the early President's House, works of superb quality by or attributed to him are now in the
Green Room and Library.*

DESK AND BOOKCASE, C. 1815-20
*With its Gothic arched mullions and a cylinder front
with a fold-out writing surface, this bookcase bears*

DRESSING CHEST, C. 1805-1810
Chests of this innovative form were made in Rhode Island and Massachusetts, but the construction and details suggest a Seymour attribution.

TAMBOUR DESK, C.1793-1798
Ladies' writing desks with tambour shutters inlaid with a drapery design were a speciality of the Seymours. This is one of three rare desks with pedimented tops.

WORK TABLE, 1814
A receipt for a mahogany lady's work table accompanies this piece by Thomas Seymour, an early example of the influence of English Regency designs on Boston furniture.

SOFA TABLE, C. 1805-10
With its birch-veneered drawers and intricate stringing, this table is a refined example of a form uncommon in early 19th-century America.

IMPORTANT ACQUIS
1961–2014:
JOHN SEYM(
C.1738–1818
AND
THOMAS SEYM
1771–1848

An important group of furniture produ
John Seymour and/or his son Thomas was
by the White House in the 1970s. The Eng
Seymours worked in Boston where they
beautifully crafted Federal period furnit
featured fine and intricate inlays.

TAMBOUR DESK AND BOOKCASE, C.1798–1808
The Seymours are recognized for their desks with tambour doors modeled after English designs.
This desk has rich veneers and inlays, and urn-shaped ivory keyhole escutcheons.

CARD TABLE, C. 1810-15
Drawing on a variety of French and English sources,
Lannuier made several tables in this form. This one has brass
inlays of lyres, urns, and stars and gilded brass moldings.

LABEL, CENTER TABLE, C. 1810
Lannuier's work is well documented because many
pieces bear his stamp or bilingual label. This paper
label is underneath the center table top, at right.

PIER TABLE, C. 1805-10
Architectural in form, this table in the "antique"
taste resembles a similar but earlier French table
in the White House.

MIXING TABLE/ STAND, C. 1810-15
Inset with a green marble top, this small table with its
water-leaf carved balusters and legs represents the height
of New York neoclassical taste.

CENTER TABLE, C. 1810
*Lannuier's masterpiece, this unique table is modeled after French gueridons
(small circular tables). The beautiful inlays, handsome gilded bronze mounts,
and intricate Italian marble top distinguish this exquisitely crafted piece.*

SELECTED MAKER'S MARKS

Candelabrum, Paul Storr *(page 248)*

Plateau, John W. Forbes *(page 69)*

Mantel Clock, Denière & Matelin *(page 65)*

Presentation Cup, Tiffany & Co. *(page 179)*

Dinner Plate, Job & John Jackson *(page 95)*

Lighthouse Clock, Simon Willard & Son. *(page 235)*

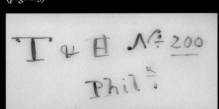

Dressing Table, Val-Kill Furniture Shop *(page 213)*

Pitcher, Tucker & Hulme *(page 241)*

Center Table, Herter Brothers *(page 150)*

Bookcase-Desk, John Shaw *(page 244)*

Waste Bowl, Robert Keyworth *(page 100)*

Mantel Clock, Thomire *(page 63)*

ENDNOTES

ABBREVIATIONS IN NOTES

GPO: Government Printing Office

LC: Library of Congress

MHS: Massachusetts Historical Society

NA/CREM: National Archives. Commission on the Renovation of the Executive Mansion. Record Group 220.

NA/HR: National Archives. House of Representatives. Record Group 233.

NA/JCC: National Archives. Joint Committees of Congress. Record Group 128.

NA/MTA: National Archives. Miscellaneous Treasury Accounts of the General Accounting Office, 1790–1894. Record Group 217.

NA/OPBG: National Archives. Office of Public Buildings and Grounds. Record Group 42. [Office of Public Buildings and Public Parks of the National Capital]

OCWH: Office of the Curator, The White House

CHAPTER I

1. George Washington to James Madison, March 30, 1789, *The Writings of George Washington*, ed. John C. Fitzpatrick (Washington, D.C.: GPO, 1931–44), 30:255.

2. Sarah Robinson to Kitty F. Wistar, April 30, 1789, Benjamin Pickman Papers, Peabody Essex Museum.

3. The list "Abstract of Accounts of sundry persons for Goods furnished and repairs done to the House occupied by the President of the United States . . ." is in the National Archives, Records of the Office of the Treasury, RG 53, vol. 138, 316–24. See also the Samuel Osgood Papers, New-York Historical Society, and Henry B. Hoffman, "President Washington's Cherry Street Residence," *The New-York Historical Society Quarterly Bulletin 23* (July 1939), 90–102.

4. Susan Detweiler and Charles Hummel, "Two Philadelphia Mahogany Side Chairs from President Washington's Official Residence in Philadelphia" (OCWH, 1993). A desk chair made by Thomas Burling is at Mount Vernon. The National Museum of American History, Smithsonian Institution, has a pair of chairs purchased from Thomas Burling that descended in the Washington family. See Helen Maggs Fede, *Washington Furniture at Mount Vernon* (Mount Vernon, Va.: Mount Vernon Ladies' Association, 1966), and Margaret B. Klapthor and Howard Morrison, *George Washington: A Figure Upon the Stage* (Washington, D.C.: Smithsonian Institution, 1982).

5. Gouverneur Morris to George Washington, January 24, 1790, Gouverneur Morris Papers, LC. Also quoted in Susan Detweiler, *George Washington's Chinaware* (New York: Harry N. Abrams, 1982).

6. James Thomas Flexner, *George Washington*, vol. 3, *George Washington and the New Nation, 1783-1793*. (Boston: Little, Brown, 1969), 209.

7. "Articles purchased from the Comte de Moustier," March 4, 1790, invoice in Mount Vernon Ladies' Association Archives, Mount Vernon, Va.

8. Washington to Tobias Lear, September 5, 1790, *Writings of George Washington*, 31:110. See also Harold Donaldson Eberlin, "190, High Street (Market Street Below Sixth) The Home of Washington and Adams, 1790–1800," *American Philosophical Society Transactions 43* (1953): 161–78.

9. Washington to Lear, November 7, 1790, *Writings of George Washington*, 31:146.

10. Washington to Lear, November 14, 1790, *Writings of George Washington*, 31:152–53.

11. Washington to Samuel Powel, September 20, 1791, *Writings of George Washington*, 31:372–73.

12. For further discussion of Washington's homes in New York and Philadelphia, see *White House History*, no. 6 (Fall 1999).

13. The inventory of the contents of the President's House in Philadelphia, "Household Furniture," is in the George Washington Papers, LC. It is not dated but appears to have been done in February, 1797.

14. Washington to Bartholomew Dandridge, April 3, 1797, *Writings of George Washington*, 35:428, and Washington to Mary White Morris, May 1, 1797, ibid. 441–42.

15. Lear to Washington, March 15, 1797, printed in "Household Furniture," Washington Papers, LC.

16. John Adams to Abigail Adams, February 9, 1797, quoted in Phyllis Lee Levin, *Abigail Adams* (New York: St. Martin's Press, 1987), 306.

17. Abigail Adams to John Adams, January 14, 1797, quoted in Edith B. Gelles, *First Thoughts: Life and Letters of Abigail Adams* (New York: Twayne Publishers, 1998), 123–24. While vice president, John Adams lived at Bush Hill, the home of William Hamilton outside of Philadelphia.

18. Act of Congress, March 2, 1797.

19. James Thomas Flexner, *George Washington*, vol. 4, *George Washington: Anguish and Farewell, 1793-1799* (Boston: Little, Brown, 1972), 337.

20. Abigail Adams to "My Dear Sister [Mary Cranch]," May 16, 1797, Abigail Adams, *New Letters of Abigail Adams, 1788–1801*, ed. Stewart Mitchell (Boston: Houghton Mifflin, 1947), 90.

21. John Adams to Heads of Departments, May 16, 1800, Letters from Presidents of the United States to Commissioners of Public Buildings, 1791–1869, Manuscript Division, LC.

22. Abigail Adams to Mrs. Catherine Johnson, August 20, 1800, Adams Papers, MHS.

23. John Adams to Abigail Adams, November 2, 1800, Adams Papers, MHS.

24. Thomas Claxton to John Adams, November 3, 1800, Adams Papers, MHS.

25. Abigail Adams to Johnson, October 10, 1800, Adams papers, MHS.

26. Abigail Adams to Mary Cranch, November 21, 1800, Adams, *New Letters*, 256–59.

27. Abigail Adams to Abigail Adams Smith, November 27, 1800, Abigail Adams, *Letters of Mrs. Adams, the Wife of John Adams*, ed. Charles Francis Adams (Boston: Wilkins, Carter, 1848), 384.

28. Abigail Adams to Smith, November 21, 1800, Adams, *Letters of Mrs. Adams*, 382–83.

29. U.S. Congress, *Report of the Joint Committee Appointed to Consider What further measures ought to be taken for the Accommodation of the President of the United States*, February 27, 1801, NA/JCC 128. The inventory was printed in *The Times and District of Columbia Daily Advertiser*, March 16, 1801. See also Margaret B. Klapthor, "A First Lady and a New Frontier, 1800," *Historic Preservation 15*, no. 3 (1963): 88–93.

30. *Report of the Joint Committee*.

31. Ibid.

32. Ibid.

33. John Adams Inventory, 1826, Adams Papers, MHS.

34. Abigail Adams to Cranch, February 7, 1801, Adams, *New Letters*, 266.

35. Thomas Claxton to Senator Wilson C. Nicholas, February 26, 1801, House Report, February 27, 1801. NA/HR 233. See also *Report of the Joint Committee*.

36. *Annals of Congress*, 6th Cong., 2d sess., 1069–70. See also *The National Intelligencer*, March 11, 1801.

37. Margaret Bayard Smith, *The First Forty Years of Washington Society* (New York: C. Scribner's Sons, 1906), 384–85.

38. *Annals of Congress*, 6th Cong., 2d sess., 1068–71, 1572.

39. "Message from the President of the United States, communicating a Report of the Surveyor of the public buildings at the city of Washington To the Senate and House of Representatives of the United States," *New York Herald*, December 22, 1804.

40. NA/MTA acct. 21304, voucher 6, February 3, 1809.

41. Marie G. Kimball, "The Original Furnishings of the White House," *Antiques* (June-July 1929).

42. Information about this chair can be found in the catalog for Sotheby's sale no. 6834, "The Estate of Jacqueline Kennedy Onassis," April 23, 1996, lot 40. See also Susan R. Stein, *The Worlds of Thomas Jefferson at Monticello* (New York: Harry N. Abrams, 1993).

43. Inventory of the President's House, February 19, 1809, Thomas Jefferson Papers, LC.

44. Smith, *Washington Society*, 29.

45. Ibid., 388.

46. Ibid., 392.

47. Catharine Mitchell to Margaretta A. Miller, January 2, 1811, quoted in Carolyn Hoover Sung, "Catharine Mitchell's Letters from Washington,

1806–1812," *The Quarterly Journal of the Library of Congress* 34, no. 3 (July 1977): 181.

48.   Conover Hunt-Jones, *Dolley and the "Great Little Madison"* (Washington, D.C.: American Institute of Architects Foundation, 1977), 31.

49.   Margaret Brown Klapthor, *Benjamin Latrobe and Dolley Madison Decorate the White House, 1809–1811,* Contributions from the Museum of History and Technology Paper 49 (Washington, D.C.: Smithsonian Institution, 1965). Also discussed in Hunt-Jones, *Dolley and "Great Little Madison."*

50.   NA/MTA acct. 24181, October 16, 1811.

51.   Elbridge Gerry, *The Diary of Elbridge Gerry, Jr.* (New York: Brentano's, 1927), 180. See also Ethel Lewis, *The White House: An Informal History of Its Architecture, Interiors and Gardens* (New York: Dodd, Mead, 1937), 69.

52.   Samuel Smith to Dolley Madison, March 10, 1809, OCWH.

53.   NA/MTA acct. 28634, voucher 2, September 16, 1809.

54.   Benjamin Latrobe to Dolley Madison, September 8, 1809, Private Collection. Copy, Archives of the OCWH. Drawings of the Latrobe furniture survive in the Maryland Historical Society. They were first published by Robert Raley, "Interior Designs by Benjamin Henry Latrobe for the President's House," *Antiques* (June 1959): 568–71. For a similar suite designed by Latrobe, see Jack L. Lindsey, "An Early Latrobe Furniture Commission," *Antiques* (January 1991): 208–19.

55.   Diary of Lord Francis Jeffrey, November 17, 1813, Private Collection. Copy in OCWH Archives.

56.   Gerry, *Diary,* 181. See also Jeffrey diary, November 19, 1813.

57.   Gerry *Diary,* 180.

58.   Jeffrey Diary, November 19, 1813.

59.   NA/MTA acct. 28634, voucher 14.

60.   For articles on the 1814 burning of the White House, see *White House History* (Fall 1998).

61.   Dolley Madison to Mary Latrobe, December 3, 1814, quoted in Allen Clark, *Life and Letters of Dolley Madison* (Washington, D.C.: The Press of W. F. Roberts Company, 1914), 166.

62.   NA/MTA acct. 28634, voucher 25, July 10, 1815, and NA/MTA acct. 28634, voucher 31, January 22, 1817.

63.   NA/MTA acct. 28634, voucher 38.

64.   Mrs. William (Anna Maria Brodeau) Thornton, "Diary of Mrs. William Thornton: Capture of Washington by the British," *Records of the Columbia Historical Society* 19 (1916): 174–76.

65.   The design was registered by Jacquemart et Bénard in 1798. Catherine Lynn Frangiamore to Clement E. Conger, November 8, 1973, OCWH.

66.   Montpelier inventories are in Hunt-Jones, *Dolley and "Great Little Madison,"* 120–23.

67.   Jane Shadel Spillman, *White House Glassware: Two Centuries of Entertaining* (Washington, D.C.: White House Historical Association, 1989), 24.

CHAPTER 2

1.   James Monroe to Samuel Lane, April 28, 1817, in NA/HR 233, House Report 79, 18th Cong., 2d sess., 1824–25, 213. The appraisal of Monroe's personal effects is in NA/MTA acct. 43754, voucher 86, April 28, 1817.

2.   For an account of the controversy that resulted from Monroe's sale of his personal articles to the government, see Lucius Wilmerding, Jr., "James Monroe and the Furniture Fund," *The New-York Historical Society Quarterly* 44, no. 2 (April 1960): 133–49.

3.   *Eastern Argus,* December 2, 1817.

4.   Monroe to Lane, May 30, 1818, James Monroe Papers, New York Public Library, quoted in Noble E. Cunningham, Jr., *The Presidency of James Monroe* (Lawrence, Ks.: University Press of Kansas, 1996), 145.

5.   NA/MTA acct. 43754, voucher 66, October 18, 1818.

6.   NA/MTA acct. 43754, voucher 70, December 17, 1818. See Anne C. Golovin, "Cabinetmakers and Chairmakers of Washington, D.C., 1791–1840," *Antiques* (May 1975): 898–922, and idem, "William King, Jr., Georgetown Furniture Maker," *Antiques* (May 1977): 1032–35. Also, Ronald L. Hurst and Jonathan Prown, *Southern Furniture 1680-1830: The Colonial Williamsburg Collection* (Williamsburg, Va.: Colonial Williamsburg Foundation, 1997), 155–60.

7.   NA/MTA acct. 43754, voucher 12, May 20, 1818.

8.   Spillman, *White House Glassware,* 25–29.

9.   NA/MTA acct. 837131, voucher 3, September 15, 1817, lists, in French, the articles shipped from France in 1817. A partial list appears in Hans Huth, "The White House Furniture at the Time of Monroe," *Gazette des Beaux Arts* (January 1946): 23–46; see also Clement E. Conger and Betty C. Monkman, "President Monroe's Acquisitions," *The Connoisseur* (May 1976): 56–63.

10.   For information on the French Empire style and craftsmen, see Madeline Deschamps, *Empire* (New York: Abbeville Press, 1994); Alvar Gonzalez-Palacios, *The French Empire Style* (London: Hamlyn, 1970); David Revere McFadden et al., *L'Art de Vivre: Decorative Arts and Design in France 1789–1989* (New York: Vendome Press for the Cooper-Hewitt Museum, Smithsonian Institution, 1989); and Serge Grandjean, *Empire Furniture, 1800–1825* (New York: Taplinger Publishing, 1966).

11.   Letter-book of Mary Stead Pinckney in Wilmerding, "Monroe and the Furniture Fund," 134. Examples of the Louis XVI style furniture are in the James Monroe Museum, Fredericksburg, Va. See Lee Langston-Harrison, *A Presidential Legacy—The Monroe Collection at the James Monroe Museum and Memorial Library* (Fredericksburg, Va.: James Monroe Museum, 1997), and Helen Comstock, "James Monroe's French Furniture," *Antiques* (September 1951): 184–85.

12.   James Draper, *The Arts Under Napoleon* (New York: Metropolitan Museum of Art, 1978).

13.   James Monroe, "Message From the President of the United States upon the Subject of the Furniture Necessary for the President's House," February 10, 1818. 15th Cong., 1st sess., 1.

14.   Joseph Russell to James Monroe, September 15, 1817, in NA/HR 233, House Report 79, 221.

15.   Russell to Monroe, April 10, 1824, ibid., 262.

16.   Russell to Monroe, September 15,1817, ibid., 221.

17.   James Monroe is depicted in a portrait by John Vanderlyn standing next to an oval-backed armchair from the Bellangé suite and another chair from the suite also appears in a portrait of Andrew Jackson by Ralph Earl. None of the oval backed chairs is known to exist.

18.   NA/MAT acct. 136728, January 17, 1860, lists White House items sold by James C. McGuire & Co., Washington, D.C.

19.   Russell to Monroe, May 25, 1818, in House Report 79, 262.

20.   Robert Donaldson, "Notes on a Journey Through the Most Interesting Parts of the United States and the Canadas," January 16, 1819, private collection.

21.   Senator John Taylor to John H. Bernard, January 5, 1823, Private Collection. Copy in OCWH Archives.

22.   *Samuel F. B. Morse: His Letter and Journals,* vol. 1 (New York: Kennedy Galleries, 1973), 227.

23.   John Pearce, "The 1817 Catalogue Drawing of the White House Plateau," *The Connoisseur* (August 1971): 284–86.

24.   Thomas Hill Hubbard to Phebe Hubbard, February 21, 1818. Copy in OCWH Archives.

25.   Samuel Breck, December 30, 1823, in "Broken Journal of a Session of Congress," 18th Cong., Historical Society of Pennsylvania, Philadelphia.

26.   Statement of William Lee, Esquire, March 9, 1818. 15th Cong., 1st sess., 5.

27.   Letter from Joseph Elgar, December 5, 1825, in House Records, 19th Cong., 1st sess.

28.   Golovin, "Cabinetmakers and chairmakers," 910.

29.   "Estimate of articles necessary to complete the furnishing of the President's House," January 25, 1825, 18th Cong., 2d sess., and John Adams, Jr., "Account with Furniture of the President's House," February 26, 1826, House Records, 19th Cong., 1st sess. See also NA/MTA acct. 51873 (1825) for vouchers for purchases during the John Quincy Adams administration.

30.   William S. Potts, "A Presbyterian Minister Calls on President John Quincy Adams, November 7–9, 1827," *The New England Quarterly,* 34 (September 1961): 379–82.

31.   Act of Congress, May 22, 1826.

32.   Quoted in Edwin A. Miles, "President Adams' Billiard Table," *The New England Quarterly* 45 (March 1972): 31–43.

33.   Miles, "President Adams' Billiard Table," 43.

CHAPTER 3

1.   Smith, *Washington Society,* 295–96.

2.   Robert V. Remini, *Andrew Jackson,* (New York: Harper & Brothers, 1949), 2:178.

3.   NA/MTA acct. 61369, vouchers 5, 24.

4. Captain Basil Hall, *Travels in North America in the Years 1827 and 1828* (Edinburgh: Cadell, 1829), 14.

5. *United States Telegraph*, December 1829.

6. Jonathan Elliot, *Historical Sketches of the Ten Miles Square Forming the District of Columbia* (Washington, D.C.: J. Elliot, Jr., 1830), 160.

7. Robert C. Smith, "Philadelphia Empire Furniture by Antoine Gabriel Quervelle," *Antiques* (September 1964): 304–9. See also *Three Centuries of American Art* (Philadelphia: Philadelphia Museum of Art, 1976), 276.

8. All seven tables were originally decorated with gilt stenciling, but nineteenth-century refinishing has erased all but fragmentary traces of it on the rosewood veneer crossbanding at the outer edge of the center tables. There is some evidence of oil gilding on the inner edge of the top and the base of the center column, and vert antique (green paint with gold powder as highlights) on the feet and the carved leafage just above the feet. See conservation treatment report by Robert Mussey Associates, 1997, OCWH.

9. Elliot, *Historical Sketches*, 161.

10. NA/MTA acct. 61369, voucher 39.

11. *Public Buildings and Statuary of the Government: The Public Buildings and Architectural Ornaments of the Capitol of the United States at the City of Washington* (Washington City: P. Haas, 1839), 37.

12. Diary of Captain Blair Bolling, March 19, 1836, Papers of the Ladies' Hermitage Association, Nashville, Tenn. Copy, OCWH.

13. Major Thomas H. Shelby, Sr., *A Journal and Other Papers Concerning the Travels of Major Thomas H. Shelby, Sr.* (New York: Privately Printed, 1962), 5.

14. Gustave de Beaumont to his mother, January 20, 1831, quoted in George Wilson Pierson, *Tocqueville in America* (Baltimore: Johns Hopkins University Press, 1996), 663.

15. Two portraits of Jackson were painted with the furniture. One is in the National Museum of American Art of the Smithsonian Institution, and one is in the Daughters of the American Revolution Museum.

16. Shelby, *Travels*, 5.

17. Frances Trollope, *Domestic Manners of the Americans* (New York: Alfred A. Knopf, 1949), 230.

18. *The People's Magazine* 1, no. 7 (June 15, 1833).

19. Samuel Lorenzo Knapp, *Sketches of Public Characters Drawn from the Living and the Dead. With Notices of Other Matters* (New York: E. Bliss Publishers, 1830), 112.

20. Spillman, *White House Glassware*, 32–39. Spillman believed that the examples of a panel-cut glassware service in the collection featuring the engraved coat-of-arms of the United States alongside grape leaves and vines, are from the 1829 Bakewell service. However, more recent scholarship suggests that this service was made later and thus may instead represent the service purchased by President Franklin Pierce in 1853.

21. NA/MTA acct. 70467, voucher 4.

22. NA/MTA acct. 70467, voucher 5.

23. Knapp, *Public Characters*, 111.

24. NA/MTA acct. 70467.

25. NA/MTA acct. 70469, voucher 1.

26. NA/MTA acct. 70467, vouchers 4, 6.

27. NA/MTA acct. 74067, voucher 30.

28. Elliot, *Historical Sketches*, 163.

29. Thomas F. Pendel, *Thirty-six Years in the White House* (Washington, D.C.: Neale Publishing, 1902), 172.

30. Philadelphia Museum of Art, *Three Centuries of American Art*, 293–94. See also Alice Cooney Frelinghuysen, *American Porcelain: 1770–1920* (New York: Metropolitan Museum of Art, 1989), 19, and idem, "Tucker Porcelain, Philadelphia, 1826–1838," *Antiques* (April 1989): 916–29.

31. James G. Barber, *Andrew Jackson: A Portrait Study* (Washington, D.C.: National Portrait Gallery, 1991), 56, 67.

32. Report of William Noland, Commissioner of Public Buildings, House Doc. 32, 26th Cong., 1st sess., December 30, 1839.

33. NA/MTA acct. 75138, voucher 1.

34. James Graham to William Graham, September 17, 1837, *The Papers of William Alexander Graham, 1825–1837*, ed. J. G. de Roulhac Hamilton (Raleigh, N.C.: State Department of Archives and History, 1957), 1:526.

35. Lucadia Niles to Richard Niles, October 4, 1838, Pease Papers, Austin Public Library, Austin Texas.

36. William Preston to Susan Marshall Preston, December 28, 1839, Preston Family Papers, The Filson Club, Louisville, Kentucky.

37. Ibid.

38. "Speech of Mr. [Charles] Ogle, of Pennsylvania, on the regal splendor of the President's Palace," Delivered in the House, April 14, 1840, and printed by Weeks, Jordan, and Company, Boston. See also "Furniture of the President's House," House Report 552, 27th Cong., 2d sess. (April 1842) for Jackson and Van Buren expenditures.

39. Speech of Mr. Levi Lincoln of Massachusetts, a Whig representative in Congress, in reply to Mr. Ogle's condemnation of the Van Buren appropriations for furnishings in the President's House, House, April 16, 1840, OCWH.

40. William Noland to Walter Coles, June 25, 1840. Letters Received, NA/OPBG.

41. Noland to R. H. Hammond, March 29, 1841. Letters Received, NA/OPBG.

42. Carol Kohan, *Historic Furnishings Report for "Lindenwald" Martin Van Buren National Historic Site* (Harpers Ferry, W.Va.: National Park Service, 1986), 187–90.

43. *The Jeffersonian*, March 27, 1841.

44. Catherina V. R. Bonney, *A Legacy of Historical Gleanings* (Albany, N.Y.: J. Munsell, 1875), 165.

45. NA/MTA acct. 87086 and NA/MTA acct. 93470, voucher 28.

46. Oliver Perry Chitwood, *John Tyler: Champion of the Old South* (New York: D. Appleton Century, 1939), 394.

47. NA/MTA acct. 87086, vouchers 1, 2, 5, 6, 11, 15, 16, 22, 24, 34 and NA/MTA acct. 87143, voucher 1.

48. Charles Dickens, *American Notes and Pictures from Italy* (London: Oxford University Press, 1957), 125.

49. *The Brooklyn Eagle*, March 6, 1845.

50. NA/MTA acct. 94370, vouchers 2, 3 and NA/MTA acct. 96137.

51. Diary of Elizabeth Dixon, December 1, 1845–February 19, 1847, Connecticut Historical Society Collection, Hartford.

52. NA/MTA acct. 93470, vouchers 4, 26.

53. NA/MTA acct. 96137, voucher 45.

54. John N. Pearce, Lorraine W. Pearce, and Robert C. Smith, "The Meeks Family of Cabinetmakers," *Antiques* (April 1964): 417.

55. Dixon Diary, December 19, 1845.

56. NA/MTA acct. 93470, voucher 21.

57. Dixon Diary, December 19, 1845.

58. "Inventory of Furniture in the President's House," January 1, 1849, Letters Received, NA/OPBG.

59. Joanna Lucinda Ruckner to Elizabeth C. Price, April 7, 1846, James K. Polk Papers, Tennessee State Archives, Nashville.

60. C. A. Goodrich, *The Family Tourist: A Visit to the Principal Cities of the Western Continent* (Hartford: Case, Tiffany and Company, 1848), 364.

CHAPTER 4

1. Holman Hamilton, *Zachary Taylor: Soldier in the White House* (New York: Bobbs-Merrill, 1951), 221.

2. NA/MTA acct. 101316, 102509, voucher 6.

3. NA/MTA acct. 105580, voucher 8, and NA/MTA acct. 107778, vouchers 1, 8.

4. NA/MTA acct. 105580, voucher 3, and NA/MTA acct. 107778, vouchers 6, 10.

5. Henry McCall Holmes Journal, 1850, Wilmot Stuart Holmes Papers, Southern Historical Collection, University of North Carolina Library, Chapel Hill.

6. Millard Fillmore to Solomon Haven, December 21, 1850, OCWH Archives.

7. William Easby to Janes, Beebe & Co., October 18, 1852, Letters Sent, NA/OPBG, v. 10.

8. Berry B. Tracy et al., *Nineteenth-Century America: Furniture and Other Decorative Arts* (New York: Metropolitan Museum of Art, exhib. cat., 1970). See also Ellen Marie Snyder, "Victory Over Nature: Victorian Cast-Iron Seating Furniture," *Winterthur Portfolio*, 20, no. 4 (Winter 1985): 221–42.

9. NA/MTA acct. 113810, voucher 8.

10. NA/MTA acct. 113810, voucher 4. See also Margaret Brown Klapthor, *Official White House China: 1789 to the Present* (New York: Harry N. Abrams, 1999), 76–81, and Spillman, *White House Glassware*, 59–62.

11. NA/MTA acct. 113810, voucher 3.

12. NA/MTA acct. 113810, voucher 10.

13. Mrs. Charles W. Upham to "My very dear Betty," January 14 and 21, 1855, OCWH Archives.

14. John B. Blake to Congressman J. Glancy Jones, December 17, 1856, House Doc. 62, 34th Cong., 2d sess.

15. NA/MTA acct. 130243 and NA/MTA acct. 139177.

16. NA/MTA acct. 136728.

17. NA/MTA acct. 136728, voucher 20.

18. Benjamin Brown French Journals, January 28, 1855, vol. 6, 73, LC.

19. William Ferguson, *America, By River and Rail* (London: J. Nisbet & Co., 1856), 155.

20. Ann Yonemura, Associate Curator of Japanese Art, Arthur M. Sackler Gallery, Smithsonian Institution, provided information on mid-nineteenth-century Japanese lacquer objects.

21. Helen Nicolay, *A Biography of John G. Nicolay* (New York: Longmans, Green and Co., 1949), 74–75.

22. William O. Stoddard, *Inside the White House in War Times* (New York: Charles L. Webster & Co., 1890), 13.

23. Elizabeth Todd Grimsley, "Six Months in the White House," *Illinois State Historical Society Journal*, 19 (October 1926–January 1927): 47.

24. Justin G. Turner and Linda Lovitt Turner, *Mary Todd Lincoln: Her Life and Letters* (New York: Alfred A. Knopf, 1972), 106.

25. Nicolay, *John G. Nicolay*, 96.

26. French Journals, December 16, 1861, vol. 8, 256.

27. Grimsley, "Six Months in the White House," 59.

28. NA/MTA acct. 141262 and NA/MTA acct. 141263.

29. NA/MTA acct. 145025.

30. Klapthor, *Official White House China*, 182–92. See also Spillman, *White House Glassware*, 66–83.

31. *Godey's Lady's Book and Magazine*, 57 (August 1858).

32. NA/MTA acct. 140775, voucher 10.

33. "The Lincolns Redecorate the White House," *Daily Alta California*, May 12, 1862.

34. Marvin D. Schwartz, et. al., *The Furniture of John Henry Belter and the Rococo Revival: An Inquiry into Nineteenth-Century Furniture Design Through a Study of the Gloria and Richard Manney Collection* (New York: E. P. Dutton, 1981).

35. OCWH Archives.

36. "Lincolns Redecorate," *Daily Alta California*, May 12, 1862.

37. Ibid.

38. Stoddard, *Inside the White House*, 173.

39. "Lincolns Redecorate," *Daily Alta California*, May 12, 1862.

40. Mary Clemmer Ames, *Ten Years in Washington or Inside Life and Scenes of Our National Capital as a Woman Sees Them*, (Hartford, Conn.: Hartford Publishing Company, 1882), 237.

41. Mary Todd Lincoln to James K. Kerr, January 9, 1865, to October 12, 1865, in Turner and Turner, *Mary Todd Lincoln*, 198–99, 262, 275–76.

42. French to Charles R. Train, Chairman, Committee on Public Buildings and Grounds, January 5, 1863, Letters Sent, NA/OPBG.

43. Mary Todd Lincoln to Alexander Williamson, January 17, 1866, in Turner and Turner, *Mary Todd Lincoln*, 327.

44. French Journals, July 14, 1865, vol. 9, 441.

45. Inventory of Furniture in President's House, May 26, 1865, Letters Received, NA/OPBG.

46. French Journals, January 11, 1866, vol. 10, 13.

47. Turner and Turner, *Mary Todd Lincoln*, 326.

48. A. A. E. Taylor, "An Afternoon at the White House," *Hours at Home* (December 1866).

49. NA/MTA acct. 157178.

50. French to Martha Patterson, July 15, 1865, Letters Sent, NA/OBPG.

51. NA/MTA acct. 157178.

52. French to E. V. Haughwout & Co., July 10, 1865, Letters Sent, NA/OPBG.

53. French Journals, May 6, 1866, vol. 10, 79.

54. French to Colonel Stephenson, April 20, 1866, Letters Sent, NA/OPBG.

55. French to Thaddeus Stevens, January 5, 1867, Letters Sent, NA/OPBG.

56. NA/MTA acct. 173118.

57. White House Inventory, February 1867, Letters Received, NA/OPBG.

58. John F. Ellis, *Guide to Washington City and Vicinity: a complete handbook, directing the stranger how to find public buildings, etc.* (Washington: John F. Ellis, 1868).

CHAPTER 5

1. Julia Dent Grant, *The Personal Memoirs of Julia Dent Grant*, ed. John Y. Simon (New York: G. P. Putnam's Sons, 1975), 174.

2. Ibid., 177.

3. Jesse R. Grant, *In the Days of My Father General Grant* (New York: Harper & Brothers, 1925), 57.

4. NA/MTA acct. 180754, voucher 6.

5. David A. Hanks, "Pottier & Stymus Mfg. Co.: Artistic Furniture & Decorations," *Art & Antiques* (September-October 1982): 84–90.

6. Moses King, ed., *King's Handbook of New York City*, 2d ed. (Boston: Moses King, 1893), 854.

7. NA/MTA acct. 180754, voucher 2.

8. It is now in the Rutherford B. Hayes Presidential Center in Fremont, Ohio.

9. Mary Clemmer Ames, *Ten Years in Washington* (Hartford: A. D. Worthington & Company, 1873), 257–59. See also Glenn Brown, *Memories 1860–1930* (Washington, D.C.: Press of W. F. Roberts Company, 1931), 110.

10. NA/MTA acct. 188179, voucher 9.

11. NA/MTA acct. 202494, voucher 36.

12. Katherine S. Howe, et al., *Herter Brothers: Furniture and Interiors for a Gilded Age* (New York: Harry N. Abrams, 1994).

13. Grant, *The Personal Memoirs of Julia Dent Grant*, 189.

14. Klapthor, *White House China*, 93–101.

15. *The Union Signal*, July 4, 1889.

16. "The Age of Innocence in the White House," *Literary Digest* 92 (February 5, 1927): 41.

17. Austine Snead ["Miss Grundy"], "How Presidents Live," *Boston Herald*, March 28, 1878.

18. Ibid.

19. Ibid.

20. Ibid.

21. H. Crook, *Through Five Administrations*, ed. Margarita S. Gerry, (New York: Harper & Brothers, 1907), 226–27.

22. NA/MTA acct. 224650.

23. Lucy Hayes to Theodore Davis, August 2, 1880, in Klapthor, *White House China*, 120.

24. A privately owned table acquired at a Washington sale in 1902 by Elliot Woods, architect of the U.S. Capitol, has the same eagle support legs and shields and was very likely made when the White House table was altered. The elaborate and heavily carved sideboard is in the Hayes Presidential Center. E. Jane Connell and Charles R. Muller, "Ohio Furniture 1788–1888," *Antiques* (February 1984): figure 7, 462–71.

25. A frame designed by Fry's associate, Benn Pitman, for the White House portrait of Lucy Hayes by Daniel Huntington, remained on the portrait until Chester Arthur replaced it with a simpler frame in 1884. It was commissiond by the Woman's Christian Temperance and the frame was carved by Pitman's students in the McMicken School of Design (now the Art Academy of Cincinnati). Most of Pitman's students were female. Jennifer L. Howe, ed., *Cincinnati Art Carved Furniture and Interiors* (Athens: Ohio University Press, 2003).

26. Rutherford B. Hayes to George Bancroft, November 23, 1880, quoted in *Hayes Historical Journal*, 1, no. 3 (Spring 1977): 221.

27. Rudolph Bauss interview, January 17, 1962, OCWH Archives.

28. Theodore Clark Smith, *Life and Letters of James Abram Garfield*, vol. 11 (New Haven: Yale University Press, 1925), 1174.

29. Charles A. Venable, *Silver in America, 1840–1940: A Century of Splendor* (New York: Harry N. Abrams, 1995), 318.

30. William H. Crook, *Memories of the White House*, ed. Henry Rood, (Boston: Little, Brown, 1911), 159–60, 163.

31. *Washington Evening Star*, April 13, 1882, and *Washington Post*, April 15, 1882.

32. Thomas C. Reeves, *Gentleman Boss: The Life of Chester Alan Arthur* (New York: Alfred A. Knopf, 1975), 270–71.

33. NA/MTA acct. 240684, voucher 41.

34. "The White House Refurnished," *Cincinnati Gazette*, December 1881, and Report of Col. A. F. Rockwell, U.S.A., Officer in Charge, for the Fiscal Year Ending June 30, 1882.

35. Wilson H. Faude, "Associated Artists and the American Renaissance in the Decorative Arts," *Winterthur Portfolio*, 10 (1975): 101–30. See also *In Pursuit of Beauty: Americans and the Aesthetic Movement* (New York: Metropolitan Museum of Art, 1986), and *The American Renaissance, 1876–1917* (New York: Brooklyn Museum, 1979).

36. Letters sent, vol. 4, and Letters received, vol. 6, NA/OPBG. See also Report of Col. Rockwell.

37. "The White House," *Artistic Houses*, vol. 2 (New York: Benjamin Blom, 1971), 97–99.

38. "The New Decorations at the White House," *Harper's Weekly*, January 6, 1883, and E. V. Smalley, "The White House," *The Century Magazine* (April 1884): 803–15.

39. NA/MTA acct. 236056, voucher 15, and NA/MTA acct. 240684, voucher 36.

40. Brown, *Memories 1860–1930*, 111.

41. *Washington Post*, January 22, 1903, and William Ryan and Desmond Guinness, *The White House: An Architectural History* (New York: McGraw-Hill, 1980), 161.

42. Col. J. M. Wilson to W. H. Houghton, 1886. Letters Sent, vol. 6, NA/OPBG.

43. NA/MTA acct. 267652, voucher 29.

44. *New York Times*, March 4, 1889, quoted in Lewis L. Gould, ed., *American First Ladies: Their Lives and Their Legacy* (New York: Garland Publishing, 1996), 254.

45. NA/MTA acct. 269704, voucher 27.

46. Klapthor, *White House China*.

47. Spillman, *White House Glassware*, 97–117.

48. E. S. Yergason Papers, OCWH.

49. Benjamin Harrison to Carrie Harrison, September 16, 1891, Marthena Harrison Williams Collection, Private Collection. Copy, OCWH Archives. For a further description of work in the house see Report of Col. Oswald H. Ernest, U.S.A. Officer in Charge, for the Fiscal Years Ending June 30, 1891, and June 30, 1892, and "Presidential Entertainments in the White House," *The Ladies Home Journal*, 7, no. 1 (December 1889). See also Frances Benjamin Johnston, "The White House," *Demorest's Family Magazine*, 26, no. 7 (May 1890).

50. NA/MTA acct. 282374, voucher 31, and NA/MTA acct. 287782, voucher 3.

51. "The President's Visitors," *Washington Evening Star*, June 8, 1889.

52. Johnston's photographs are in the Library of Congress. They were published in Frances Benjamin Johnston, *The White House* (Washington: Gibson Bros, 1893).

53. Ibid.

54. "Uncle Sam's Tenants," source unidentified, 1893. Copy, OCWH Archives.

55. Flora McDonald Thompson, "Art in the White House," *Harper's Weekly*, January 19, 1901, 143–48, and Gabrielle Marie Jacobs, "The Bric-a-Brac of the White House," *The Delineator* (August 1902): 244–50.

56. Abby Gunn Baker, "The China of the Presidents," *Munsey's Magazine*, 30, no. 3 (December 1903), and Abby Gunn Baker Papers, OCWH.

CHAPTER 6

1. Theodore Roosevelt, *Restoration of the White House: Message of the President of the United States Transmitting the Report of the Architects* (Washington, D.C.: GPO, 1903).

2. Brown, *Memories 1860–1930*, 110–11, and Glenn Brown, "The New White House," *Harper's Weekly*, July 14, 1906, 990.

3. A. Burnley Bibb, "The Restoration of the White House," *House and Garden*, March 1903, 135.

4. Brown, *Memories 1860–1930*, 114.

5. See Alan Axelrod, ed., *The Colonial Revival in America* (New York: W. W. Norton, 1985).

6. Charles F. McKim to Edith Roosevelt, undated. Copy in OCWH Archives.

7. James Stanford Bradshaw, "Grand Rapids Furniture in the White House," *Grand River Valley Review*, 8, no. 2 (1989): 14–23.

8. Invoices for the 1902 furnishings are in NA/MTA acct. 30215. A complete list of objects acquired from Davenport and other firms in 1902 appears in *Annual Report Upon Improvement and Care of Public Build-ings and Grounds: Annual Report of the Chief of Engineers for 1903* (Washington, D.C.: GPO, 1903), 2582–2665.

9. Anne Farnham, "A. H. Davenport and Company, Boston Furniture Makers," *Antiques* (May 1976): 1048–55. The firm merged with Irving and Casson in 1916 but went out of business in 1978. Photographs of fifteen drawings of the 1902 furniture and two original fabric samples from the State Dining Room were given by the firm to the White House in 1978. The location of the original drawings is unknown; however, a few working drawings of White House objects are in the firm's records at the Strong Museum, Rochester, New York.

10. Eleanor Wilson McAddo, "The Wilsons," *Saturday Evening Post*, January 2, 1937.

11. See *In Pursuit of Beauty* and *Nineteenth-Century America*.

12. Charles Moore, "The Restoration of the White House," *The Century Magazine*, 65, no. 6 (April 1903): 811.

13. *Washington Evening Star*, January 21, 1903, and *Washington Post*, January 22, 1903.

14. Jeni L. Sandberg, "Edward F. Caldwell and Company," *Antiques* (February 1998): 311–17.

15. Brown, *Memories 1860–1930*, 118–19.

16. Caldwell's design record books, including the White House fixtures, are in the New York Public Library; the archives of the firm, which closed in 1959, are held by the Cooper-Hewitt, National Design Museum, Smithsonian Institution, New York.

17. Klapthor, *White House China*, 145–51.

18. Spillman, *White House Glassware*, 108–13.

19. Thomas W. Symons to Abby Gunn Baker, February 25, 1904, NA/OPBG. See also Abby Gunn Baker Papers, OCWH.

20. Robin Hanson, *Silk Tabriz Carpet/The White House*, Conservation Report prepared for OCWH, 1999.

21. Moore, "Restoration of the White House," 829.

22. Montgomery Schuyler, "The New White House," *The Architectural Record*, 13 (April 1903): 383.

23. Helen Taft, *Recollections of Full Years* (New York: Dodd, Mead, 1914), 342.

24. Ibid., 337.

25. NA/MTA acct. 31336, voucher 44.

26. James A. Robinson, "Weaving in the Mountains of North Carolina," *The Art World*, August 1917, 484–85. See also Kathleen Curtis Wilson, "1913 Craft Show Inspires White House Redecoration," *Handwoven*, November/December 1997, 27–29, and Kathleen Wilson, *American Homespun for the President's House: Ellen Axson Wilson and the Decoration of the Blue Mountain Room* (Washington, D.C.: Woodrow Wilson House, 1997).

27. Edith Bolling Wilson, *My Memoirs* (New York: Bobbs-Merrill, 1938), 89.

28. Klapthor, *White House China*, 152–58.

29. NA/MTA acct. 66328, vouchers 18, 43, 112.

30. "How Laddie Boy Had Dinner with President Harding," *Boston Sunday Post*, December 25, 1921.

31. F. C. Sorenson to Mr. Hungate, memorandum, May 7, 1923. Copy in OCWH Archives. See also Carl Sferrazza Anthony, *Florence Harding: The First Lady, the Jazz Age, and the Death of America's Most Scandalous President* (New York: William Morrow, 1998).

32. Spillman, *White House Glassware*, 119–25.

33. Mrs. Calvin Coolidge, "When I Became the First Lady," *American Magazine*, September 1929, 106.

34. Mrs. Calvin Coolidge, "How I Spent My Days in the White House," *American Magazine*, October 1929, 16.

35. Grace C. Coolidge, *Grace Coolidge: The Autobiography*, ed. Lawrence E. Wikander and Robert H. Ferrell (Worland: High Plains Publishing, 1992), 63.

36. Mrs. Calvin Coolidge, "First Lady Makes a Coverlet," *Washington Evening Star*, February 12, 1928, and Mrs. Calvin Coolidge, "A Coverlet for the Ages," *New York Herald*, February 12, 1928.

37. Mrs. Calvin Coolidge, "Making Ourselves at Home in the White House," *American Magazine*, November 1929, 159.

38. Act of Congress, February 28, 1925.

39. Other members of the committee were Robert W. de Forest, president of the Metropolitan Museum of Art and president of the American Federation of Arts; New York architect William Adams Delano, who represented the Commission of Fine Arts; Francis C. Jones, National Academy of Fine Art; architect Charles E. Platt, representative of the American Institute of Architects; Luke Vincent Lockwood, an authority and writer on colonial furniture; Harriet B. Pratt, who became committee chairman; Mrs. Miles White, Jr., of Baltimore, a collector interested in colonial furnishings; and the officer in charge of public buildings and parks in Washington, the official charged with the care and maintenance of the White House.

40. "What Artists Think of the White House," *Literary Digest*, August 13, 1925, 25–26, 48–51.

41. "White House Furniture Correct," *The Connoisseur*, July 2, 1925.

42. "The Battle of the White House," *Literary Digest*, July 25, 1925, 27, and Carson G. Hathaway, "Censoring the White House Furniture," *The New York Times Magazine*, April 25, 1926.

43. "Early Americanizing the White House," *Antiques* (February 1930): 113–14.

44. Harriet I. Pratt to U. S. Grant III, December 22, 1928, Harriet I. Pratt Papers, OCWH.

45. Harriet B. Pratt Papers, OCWH.

46. Herbert Hoover, *The Memoirs of Herbert Hoover: The Cabinet and the Presidency 1920–1933* (New York: MacMillian, 1952), 320–28.

47. The original photographs and the manuscript "Study of White House Furnishings" by Dare Stark McMullin are in the Lou Henry Hoover Papers, Herbert Hoover Presidential Library, West Branch, Iowa. See also Dare Stark, "Heirlooms in the White House," *Woman's Home Companion*, March 1932.

48. "The Furnishings of President Hoover's Office," *Good Furniture and Decoration*, August 1930, 108–9, and James Stanford Bradshaw, "Grand Rapids Furniture in the White House," *Grand River Valley Review*, 8, no. 2 (1989).

49. Emily L. Wright, "Eleanor Roosevelt and The Val-Kill Industries 1927–1938" (master's thesis, State University of New York at Oneonta, 1982).

50. Bills of sale, June 12, 1933, and January 26, 1938, OCWH.

51. Lonore Kerr, "The Romance of White House Furniture," *Good Housekeeping*, November 1933, 106. See also Eleanor Roosevelt, *This I Remember* (New York: Harper & Brothers, 1949), 32–37, 80–81, and "Mrs. Roosevelt's Story of Val-Kill Furniture," *The Delineator*, November 1933, 22–23.

52. OCWH files and Andy Leon Harney, "WPA Handicrafts Rediscovered," *Historic Preservation*, 25, no. 3 (1973): 10–15.

53. Eleanor Roosevelt, *This I Remember*, 87.

54. Mrs. Harold I. Pratt to William Adams Delano, December 19, 1935, Pratt Papers, OCWH.

55. Procedure of the Sub-committee Upon Furnishings and Gifts for State Rooms of the White House, signed by Eleanor Roosevelt, March 17, 1941, Pratt Papers, OCWH.

56. Franklin D. Roosevelt to Gilmore Clarke, September 9, 1942, Pratt Papers, copy, OCWH.

57. Edouard Deladier, president of the Council of Ministries of France, to Franklin D. Roosevelt, September 21, 1933, OCWH Archives.

58. Klapthor, *White House China*, 159–65.

59. Spillman, *White House Glassware*, 121–32.

60. The piano is in the National Museum of American History, Smithsonian Institution.

61. The design of the eagle-shaped legs was inspired by the eagle console tables in the State Dining Room. Eric Gugler, "The White House Steinway," OCWH.

62. *Washington Sunday Star*, December 11, 1938.

63. Eleanor Roosevelt, "My Day" column, December 11, 1938, and Elise Kirk, *Music at the White House* (Urbana, Ill.: University of Illinois Press, 1986), 236–39.

64. J. B. West with Mary Lynn Kotz, *Upstairs at the White House: My Life with the First Ladies* (New York: Coward, McCann & Geohegan, 1973), 56–57.

65. See *White House History*, no. 5 (Spring 1999), for articles on the Truman renovation.

66. H. G. Crim to Mrs. Truman, September 30, 1950, NA/CREM.

67. David McCullough, *Truman* (New York: Simon and Schuster, 1992), 884.

68. NA/CREM and Charles T. Haight Papers, OCWH.

69. Klapthor, *White House China*, 166–69.

70. Commission on the Renovation of the Executive Mansion, *Report* (Washington, D.C.: GPO, 1952), 105–7. Many pieces ordered are illustrated in *The Beacon Hill Collection* (Cambridge, Mass.: Kaplan Furniture Company, [1956?]).

71. Glen E. Edgerton to Bunn Hill Martin, November 23, 1951, NA/CREM.

72. Harry S. Truman to Maury Maverick, January 7, 1950. Copy in OCWH Archives.

73. "White House Hunt Locates Antiques," *New York Times*, January 20, 1953.

74. *New York Sunday News*, May 8, 1952, 2.

75. Dwight D. Eisenhower, *Mandate for Change, 1953–1956* (New York: Doubleday, 1963), 259.

76. Klapthor, *White House China*, 7, 169–71.

77. "U. S. Will Accept Tableware Gift," *New York Times*, January 5, 1957. See also "White House Gets Famed Collection," *Washington Evening Star*, January 17, 1958, and Lonelle Aikman, "Inside the White House," *National Geographic* (January 1961): 36.

CHAPTER 7

1. Perry Wolff, *A Television Tour with Mrs. John F. Kennedy* (Garden City, N.J.: Doubleday, 1962), 231–32.

2. West, *Upstairs*, 197–98.

3. Mary Van Rensselaer Thayer, *Jacqueline Kennedy: The White House Years* (Boston: Little, Brown, 1967), 37.

4. Hugh Sidey, "The First Lady Brings History and Beauty to the White House," *Life*, September 1, 1961, 65.

5. West, *Upstairs*, 240.

6. John F. Kennedy Library, Papers of John F. Kennedy, White House Staff Files, Pierre Salinger Files, Press Releases, February 23, 1961, and April 18, 1961.

7. Du Pont's role in the White House is explored in Elaine Rice, "Furnishing Camelot: The Restoration of the White House Interiors 1961–1963 and the Role of H. F. du Pont" (master's thesis, Winterthur Program in Early American Culture, The University of Delaware at Newark, 1993).

8. Richard K. Howland and Margaret Brown Klapthor, "Remarks on a Philosophy of the Proposed Refurnishing of the White House," paper for OCWH, April 10, 1961, and H. F. du Pont to Fine Arts Committee for the White House, memorandum, May 3, 1961, with attachment by Lyman H. Butterfield and Julian P. Boyd, "The White House as a Symbol," April 24, 1961, OCWH Archives.

9. Lorraine Pearce, "Re-creating the White House," *Museum News* (December 1961): 14–19.

10. Jacqueline Kennedy to Lorraine Pearce, memorandum, April 25, 1962, OCWH Archives.

11. Nash Castro, "The Association's Twentieth Year," *White House History*, 1, no. 1 (1983): 23–27.

12. Public Law 87-286, 87th Cong., 1st sess., September 22, 1961. Congressional debate on the bill is in *Congressional Record: Daily Digest*, September 1, 1962.

13. White House objects not in use are now housed and conserved in the Executive Support Facility managed by the National Park Service.

14. John F. Kennedy Library, Papers of John F. Kennedy, White House Staff Files, Pierre Salinger Files, Press Releases, July 2, 1961.

15. Jacqueline Kennedy to Colonel and Mrs. [Edgar] Garbisch, July 27, 1961, OCWH Archives.

16. Sidey, "History and Beauty."

17. Bernice Shashy to Jacqueline Kennedy, February 15, 1962, OCWH Archives. See also Wolff, *Television Tour.*

18. Boudin's role is detailed in James A. Abbott and Elaine M. Rice, *Designing Camelot: The Kennedy White House Restoration* (New York: Van Nostrand Reinhold, 1998).

19. White House Historical Association, *The White House Library: A Short Title List* (Washington, D.C.: White House Historical Association, 1967).

20. Jacqueline Kennedy to J. H. Leroy Chambers, April 26, 1961, OCWH Archives.

21. Lorraine Waxman Pearce, "Lannuier in the President's House," *Antiques* (January 1961): 94–96, and Pearce, "American Empire Furniture in the White House," *Antiques* (May 1962): 515–18. Objects attributed to Lannuier in the early 1960s have been studied extensively and attributions have changed. See Peter Kinney, Frances F. Bretter, and Ulrich Leben, *Honoré Lannuier: Cabinetmaker from Paris* (New York: Metropolitan Museum of Art, 1998).

22. Martin Filler, "A Clash of Tastes at the White House," *New York Times Magazine*, November 2, 1980, 89.

23. Spillman, *White House Glassware*, 123–36.

24. Lady Bird Johnson, *A White House Diary* (New York: Holt, Rinehart and Winston, 1970), 53, 79.

25. Executive Order 11145, March 7, 1964.

26. Lyndon B. Johnson Library, White House Press Office Files, Press Release, March 7, 1964.

27. Johnson, *White House Diary*, 53.

28. Ibid., 511.

29. James R. Ketchum, "The White House Collection: Preliminary Catalogue Furniture, Furnishings, Fine Arts, Documents Acquired 1961–November 1964," prepared for the OCWH.

30. Klapthor, *White House China*, 172–82.

31. Edward Vason Jones, "Charles-Honoré Lannuier and Duncan Phyfe, Two Creative Geniuses of Federal New York," *The American Art Journal* (May 1977): 4–14.

32. Jones's career is documented in William R. Mitchell, Jr., *Edward Vason Jones: Architect, Connoisseur, and Collector* (Atlanta: St. Martin Publishing, 1995).

33. Clement E. Conger, "Decorative Arts at the White House," *Antiques* (July 1979): 112–33, and Clement E. Conger, "The White House," *The Connoisseur* (May 1976): 3–10. See also Berry B. Tracy, "Federal Period Furniture," *The Connoisseur* (May 1976): 11–15.

34. Klapthor, *White House China*, 184–87.

35. *The White House: The Ronald W. Reagan Administration 1981–1989* (Washington, D.C.: Office of the Chief Usher, Executive Residence, The White House, 1989), and Russell Lynes, "Architectural Digest Visits President and Mrs. Ronald Reagan at the White House," *Architectural Digest* (December 1981): 104–21.

36. *The White House: The George Bush Administration 1989–1993* (Washington, D.C.: Office of the Chief Usher, Executive Residence, The White House, 1997).

37. Betty C. Monkman, *The Living White House* (Washington, D.C.: White House Historical Association, 2007), 152.

38. Laura Bush, *Spoken from the Heart* (New York: Scribner, 2010), 167.

39. Ibid., 176-177.

40. Michelle Obama, interview with Donna Lawrence, Donna Lawrence Productions, March 19, 2013.

41. Ibid.

42. James Monroe, *Message from the President of the United States upon the Subject of the Furniture Necessary for the President's House*, February 10, 1818, 15th Cong., 1st sess. (1818), 1.

43. Wolff, *Television Tour*, 230–31.

CATALOG OF
ILLUSTRATED OBJECTS

WILLIAM G. ALLMAN

CHAPTER 1

TEA OR COFFEE URN (page 18)
Sheffield, England, circa 1785–88
Sheffield silverplate, ivory
Gift of Mr. and Mrs. Mark Bortman and Jane Bortman
Larus, 1964
1964.527.1
22 7/8 x 10 3/4 x 11 1/4 in. (58.1 x 27.3 x 28.6 cm.)
MARKS: None.
INSCRIPTIONS: Front engraved with cypher "JAA" for
John and Abigail Adams.
NOTES: Once owned by John and Abigail Adams, this
neoclassical vase-shaped urn, a type popular in England
circa 1770–1800, was possibly acquired when Adams was
American minister to England (1785–88). The "JAA"
cypher is an engraving form on some family silver docu-
mented in the inventory taken at Adams' death in 1826.
CONDITION: Heating iron and cylinder missing.
PROVENANCE: John and Abigail Adams; to their son
John Quincy Adams; to his son Charles Francis Adams;
to his son Henry Adams; to his sister Mary Adams
Quincy; to her daughter Dorothy Quincy Nourse; to her
daughter Dorothy Quincy Nourse Pope; sold to Israel
Sack, Inc., New York, circa 1946; sold to Mr. and Mrs.
Mark Bortman, 1953.
REFERENCES: John Adams inventory, 1826, John
Adams Papers, MHS. G. Bernard Hughes, *Antique
Sheffield Plate* (London: B. T. Batsford, 1970), 142. Joseph
D. Carr, "History in White House Silver," *White House
History*, no. 1 (1983): 37.

SIDE CHAIR (page 20)
Philadelphia, circa 1760–85
Mahogany / yellow pine, Atlantic white cedar
Gift of The Barra Foundation, 1994
1994.1736.2
38 1/16 x 23 1/4 x 21 1/2 in. (96.7 x 60.1 x 54.6 cm.)
MARKS: None.
NOTES: This chair, one of a pair at the White House,
was used by Presidents George Washington and John
Adams in the presidential residences in New York and
Philadelphia. Its "Gothic" splat was a classic Philadelphia
form synthesizing motifs found in Thomas Chippendale's 1762 *Director* (pls. X, XIII, XVI), but on this
chair in an extremely plain, flat, uncarved manifestation.
In the absence as well of carving on the crest rail, seat
rail, or knees of the front legs, these chairs could have
been from two sets—six and eight—of "plain mahogany"
chairs in a government purchase from Thomas Burling's
Ware Room in New York. The front seat rail of the
mate to this chair is incised with set number "III."

CONDITION: Battens added to interior of slip seats for
minimally invasive upholstery.
PROVENANCE: Possibly U.S. Government purchase
from Thomas Burling's Ware Room, New York; sold to
Peter Hinkle, Philadelphia, circa 1797–1800; to William
Gardner (nephew?); to a Dr. (?) Robinson; to Mrs.
Catherine Morrell; to Mrs. F. A. Hart; purchased by
Ferdinand Keller, Philadelphia dealer; sold to B. Frank
Clyde, circa 1903, to Vernon S. Prentice, to John S. Wal-
ton at Parke-Bernet, New York, 1952, and to Israel Sack,
Inc. (mate also sold circa 1903 and later to Israel Sack,
Inc.); both purchased by Lansdell K. Christie; sold by the
Christie estate, Sotheby Parke-Bernet 1972, to The
Barra Foundation (lent to White House 1972–94).
REFERENCES: "Abstract of Accounts of sundry persons
for Goods furnished and repairs done to the House
occupied by the President of the United States . . . ,"
316–24, vol. 38, NA/RG 53; Susan Gray Detweiler and
Charles Hummel, "Two Philadelphia Mahogany Side
Chairs from President Washington's Official Residence
in Philadelphia," 1993, OCWH. Thomas Chippendale,
The Gentleman & Cabinet-Maker's Director (1762; reprint,
New York: Dover, 1966). Morrison H. Heckscher,
*American Furniture in the Metropolitan Museum of Art, Late
Colonial Period: The Queen Anne and Chippendale Styles*
(New York: Random House, 1985), nos. 57–58.

SAUCE BOAT (page 21)
Royal Porcelain Manufactory of Sèvres, France,
circa 1778
Hard-paste porcelain
Gift of Mrs. Kate Upshur Moorhead, in memory of
Capt. John Upshur Moorhead, 1919
1919.2752.1
4 x 8 5/8 x 7 3/4 in. (10.2 x 21.9 x 19.7 cm.)
MARKS: Underside of foot—blue painted crowned
Sèvres factory cypher.
NOTES: One of four "saucers" (*sauciers*) at £4.10
(approximately $11) on the invoice of a 309-piece
French dinner service purchased personally by President
George Washington in New York in 1790 from the
agent of the former French minister, Comte de
Moustier. This service, much of which was purchased
from Sèvres in 1778, with supplements from other facto-
ries, was used as the state china during Washington's
terms in New York and Philadelphia. This piece is
the sole example of this service in the White House
collection; others are found at Mount Vernon and the
Smithsonian Institution.
PROVENANCE: Eléanor-Françoise Elie, Comte de
Moustier; George Washington; to Martha Washington;
to her granddaughter Martha Parke Custis Peter; to
her daughter America Peter Williams; to her daughter

Katherine Williams Upshur; to her daughter Kate
Upshur Moorhead.
REFERENCES: Invoice for "Articles purchased from the
Comte de Moustier," March 4, 1790, Archives of the
Mount Vernon Ladies Association. Margaret Brown
Klapthor, *Official White House China: 1789 to the Present* (New
York: Abrams, 1999), 23–26. Susan Gray Detweiler,
George Washington's China (New York: Abrams, 1982),
119–34.

ARMCHAIR (page 22)
Attributed to Adam Hains (1768–after 1820),
Philadelphia, circa 1793–97
Mahogany / ash, black walnut
Gift of Mr. and Mrs. Shepley Evans and the White
House Historical Association, 1975
1975.1182.1
34 1/8 x 23 x 23 in. (87.0 x 58.4 x 58.4 cm.)
MARKS: None.
NOTES: One of a pair, very similar to labeled Hains
armchairs at the Society for the Preservation of New
England Antiquities and the Museum of Fine Arts,
Boston. Unlabeled but closely related examples include a
suite upholstered for Massachusetts financier Andrew
Craigie by a French upholsterer in Philadelphia in 1793
(Longfellow National Historic Site, Cambridge, Mass.)
and a dispersed suite that may have belonged to
Alexander Hamilton (Smithsonian Institution, Museum
of the City of New York, and Federal Hall National
Memorial, New York). These various Philadelphia
chairs were probably derived from French chairs, such
as the similar Jefferson chair (page 34). Although the
labeled chairs have ball-tipped bellflower finials, this pair
has beehive-like finials composed of concentric disks.
CONDITION: Old, possibly original, arm pads preserved in modern non-invasive upholstery. Evidence of a
simple original tacking pattern around the base of the
seat rails.
PROVENANCE: Family tradition of acquisition from
George Washington when he left office in 1797; sold to
Alexander Fridge, Philadelphia; one given to a Mrs.
Alexander Murdoch, one to the mother of Fridge Murdoch (great nephew); descended to Mrs. Shepley Evans.
REFERENCES: Kathleen Catalano and Richard C.
Nylander, "New Attributions to Adams Hains, Philadel-
phia Furniture Maker," *Antiques* (May 1980): 1112.
Jonathan Fairbanks et al., *Collecting American Decorative Arts
and Sculpture 1771–1991* (Boston: Museum of Fine Arts), 40.

DINNER PLATE (page 23)
China, 1784–85
Porcelain
Gift of Miss Mary Custis Lee, 1915

1915.2747.1
9 1/2 in. (24.1 cm.)
MARKS: None.
NOTES: From the Society of the Cincinnati service purchased in New York in 1786 by Colonel Henry Lee for George Washington, first president of the society. Decorated with an underglaze blue "Fitzhugh" border and an overglaze figure of Fame holding the society's badge, this service was also used by Washington as president. Other examples are found at Mount Vernon, the Smithsonian Institution, the Department of State, and the Winterthur Museum.
PROVENANCE: George Washington; Martha Washington; to her grandson George Washington Parke Custis; to his daughter Mary Custis Lee (Mrs. Robert E.); removed from Arlington House by the federal government during the Civil War, but returned to their daughter Mary Custis Lee (donor in 1915) by order of President William McKinley.
REFERENCES: Klapthor, *White House China*, 20–21, 25. Detweiler, *George Washington's China*, 83–97.

SUGAR BOWL and TEAPOT COVER (page 23)
China, 1795
Porcelain
Gift of Miss Mary Custis Lee, 1917
1917.2751.1–2
Bowl—3 3/4 x 6 x 4 1/8 in. (9.5 x 15.2 x 10.5 cm.)
Cover—1 x 3 3/4 in. (2.5 x 9.5 cm.)
MARKS: None.
NOTES: Center sunburst with monogram "MW" for Martha Washington, to whom the Chinese Export service of which these pieces are a part was given in 1796 by a Dutch East India Company merchant. The outer border of a tail-grasping serpent represents eternity, while the inner border consists of a chain centering the names of the 15 states of the Union at the time. Other examples are found at Mount Vernon, the Smithsonian Institution, and other museums. This pattern was extensively reproduced in England, France, and the United States in the late 19th and early 20th centuries.
PROVENANCE: See dinner plate above.
REFERENCES: Detweiler, *George Washington's China*, 151–58.

ARMCHAIR (page 24)
France, circa 1780–85
Painted walnut
Gift of Mrs. Elsie Howland Quimby, 1962, in memory of Mrs. Duncan Cameron
1962.402.1
34 x 24 3/4 x 23 in. (86.4 x 62.9 x 58.4 cm.)
MARKS: None.
NOTES: In 1790, when George Washington occupied the New York residence of the former French minister, Comte de Moustier, he personally purchased furniture from de Moustier's agent. This chair (*fauteuil*) is believed to be from among those purchases.
CONDITION: Painted black when received, it was repainted gray based on the finish of a similar chair at Mount Vernon, also reportedly part of the de Moustier furnishings; in 1972, it was painted gray and white based

on traces of paint found on it or another French chair (see page 34). Crest rail finials are replacements.
PROVENANCE: Eléanor-Françoise Elie, Comte de Moustier; sold to President George Washington, 1790; sold 1797; by family tradition presented to Admiral Shubrick—presumably William B. Shubrick; presented to J. B. Cannon, Baltimore; to Mrs. Duncan Cameron; to her daughter, Mrs. Elsie Howland Quimby.
REFERENCES: Invoice for "Articles purchased from the Comte de Moustier," March 4, 1790, Archives of the Mount Vernon Ladies Association. William Howard Adams, ed., *The Eye of Thomas Jefferson*, National Gallery of Art, 1976, no. 373.

PRESENTATION SABER (page 25)
Klingenthal Armory, Klingenthal, Alsace, France, circa 1799–1800
Gilded brass, mother-of-pearl, steel
Gift of the French Republic, 1933
1933.1184.1
40 11/16 x 5 3/8 x 1 1/8 in. (103.4 x 9.2 x 2.9 cm.)
MARKS: None.
NOTES: Commissioned by the French volunteers in the American Revolution for George Washington, whose death prevented its presentation. Special features include an eagle-head pommel and an American eagle atop a wreathed "W" chased on one langet and gilt-etched on the blade. Similar but less elaborate French swords of this fashionable form decorated with a profile bust portrait of Washington on the langet were popular with American officers in the early 19th century.
CONDITION: Pearl grip cracked at langet on reverse.
PROVENANCE: Undocumented acquisition by the French government; sent by Edouard Deladier, president of the Council of Ministries of France, to President Franklin D. Roosevelt through General de Chambrun, a descendant of the Marquis de Lafayette, in 1933.
REFERENCES: Harold Peterson, *The American Sword, 1775–1945* (Philadelphia: Ray Riling Arms Books, 1965).

SOUP TUREEN AND STAND (page 31)
Royal Porcelain Manufactory of Sèvres, France, 1782
Porcelain
Gift of Mrs. Charles Francis Adams, 1932
1932.2980.1, 1932.2979.1
Tureen—13 x 7 3/8 x 6 1/2 in. (33.0 x 18.7 x 16.5 cm.)
Stand—17 3/4 x 14 1/8 in. (45.1 x 35.9 cm.)
MARKS: Tureen—underside—blue painted crowned factory cypher centering "ee" (1782, hard paste) and "IN / J" (unidentified painter "IN"); cover—none. Stand—underside—blue painted factory cypher (undated, soft-paste).
NOTES: From a family service of John and Abigail Adams. The donation also included two 1778 soft-paste plates. Examples are found also at the Adams National Historic Site, Quincy, Mass., and the Museum of Fine Arts, Boston.
CONDITION: The tureen may have had a liner, now absent, on which the cover would fit more fully than it does on the bowl alone.
PROVENANCE: John and Abigail Adams; to their son John Quincy Adams; to his son Charles Francis Adams; to his son Charles Francis Adams Jr.; to his widow Mary Hone Adams.

PRESERVES STAND (page 31)
Royal Porcelain Manufactory of Sèvres, France, 1782
Soft-paste porcelain
Gift of the White House Acquisition Trust, 1999
1999.1783.12
3 3/16 x 9 5/8 x 7 in. (8.1 x 24.4 x 17.8 cm.)
MARKS: Underside—blue painted "CC" / factory cypher / "Y" (unidentified painter).
NOTES: Factory model called a *plateau à deux pots à confiture* (tray with two pots for preserves). In the gold-trimmed white china purchased by President George Washington in 1790 from the agent of the former French minister to the United States, Comte de Moustier, there were four 1778 Sèvres stands of the same form in hard paste porcelain (three extant) which were called "Confection dishes."
CONDITION: The mate has one repaired cup lacking its cover.
PROVENANCE: Descended in the Adams family; John and Abigail Adams; to their son John Quincy Adams; to his son Charles Francis Adams; to his son John Quincy Adams II; to his daughter Abigail Adams Homans; descended through other family members; White House purchase at Northeast Auctions, Portsmouth, New Hampshire, March 21, 1999 (with 1782 mate; also five 1780 dinner plates, and six 1780 and 1782 soup plates).
REFERENCES: Detweiler, *George Washington's China*, 125–26.

ARMCHAIR (page 34)
France, circa 1784–89
Painted beechwood
Gift of an anonymous donor, 1972
1972.845.1
34 1/2 x 23 x 23 1/4 in. (87.6 x 58.4 x 59.0 cm.)
MARKS: None.
NOTES: Possibly from the household furniture, including 48 chairs, which Thomas Jefferson acquired in France in the 1780s and then had shipped from Paris to Philadelphia in 1790. On his resignation as secretary of state in 1793, the furniture was sent to Monticello. Related French armchairs (*fauteuils*) attributed to Jefferson ownership—one at the Baltimore Museum of Art (from a Washington family which once owned the two Bellangé side chairs returned to the White House in 1962) and two in a private collection (once owned by Jacqueline Kennedy).
CONDITION: In 1972, this chair was painted gray and white based on traces of paint found either on it or the George Washington chair (see page 24). Analysis by the Getty Conservation Center indicates that the original finish on the Jefferson chairs in a private collection was a warm tinted varnish to simulate mahogany, a more utilitarian finish than paint or gilding. No evidence of such a finish has survived on the White House chair.
PROVENANCE: Thomas Jefferson; Dolley Madison; gift to Doctor and Mrs. William Thornton (the architect of the U.S. Capitol); gift from Mrs. Thornton to Doctor and Mrs. Thomas Miller (physician to Presidents William Henry Harrison, James K. Polk, and Franklin Pierce), who lived with Mrs. Thornton in the 1830s and subsequently bought her Washington house from her; to

their daughters Mrs. Arthur Fendall and Miss Virginia Miller; to Mrs. Arthur Fendall's daughter; to her children Janet H. Harrison, Sara Scheetz, and Stirling M. Harrison; White House purchase with donated funds.
REFERENCES: Adams, *Eye of Thomas Jefferson*, no. 372. Sotheby's, New York, "Estate of Jacqueline Kennedy Onassis," 6834, April 23, 1996, Lot 40.

TABLESPOON (page 35)
Elizabeth Tookey (working circa 1767–74), London, 1768–69
Silver
White House Acquisition Fund, 1978
1978.1358.1
8 1/2 x 1 5/8 in. (21.6 x 4.1 cm.); 2 oz 3 dwt.
MARKS: Shaft reverse hallmarked "E.T," lion passant, crowned leopard head, Gothic "n."
INSCRIPTIONS: Handle face engraved "SBM" for Bathurst and Martha Skelton. Reverse of bowl engraved "This spoon belonged / to Thomas Jefferson 3d President of the United States and was in constant use at / Monticello. It came to him upon his marriage Jan. 1st 1772 / with Martha Wales dau. of John Wales and widow of / Bathurst Skelton. / It was made in London in 1768–9 and descended to Jefferson's / eldest dau Martha wife of Gov. Thos. Mann Randolph / to her son Col. Thos. Jeff. Randolph to his son Major / Thos Jeff Randolph, and finally to his son Mr. F. M. Randolph / of Keswick, Albemarle Co. Va. Jefferson's great / great grandson from whom it passed Dec. 1884 / to General Meredith Read whose great / grandfather George Read, of Delaware, the / Signer, was colleague of Mr. Jefferson in the / Continental Congress. The letters / B.M.S. stand for Bathurst / & Martha Skelton."
NOTES: In 1772 Thomas Jefferson made a list of English silver which his widowed bride, Martha Wayles Skelton, brought from her first marriage to Bathurst Skelton. This silver included a pair of salt cellars and four spoons; a ladle and one dozen teaspoons made by James Tookey; and one dozen tablespoons made by his wife Elizabeth Tookey. This tablespoon shares the provenance of and was sold at auction in 1978 with the ladle, salt cellars, and two salt spoons acquired by Monticello (the Thomas Jefferson Memorial Foundation). Two other tablespoons exist, both at Monticello (one on long-term loan from Yale University Art Gallery).
PROVENANCE: Bathurst and Martha Wayles Skelton; to Thomas and Martha Skelton Jefferson; to Thomas Jefferson; to his daughter Martha Jefferson Randolph; to her son Thomas Jefferson Randolph; to his son Thomas Jefferson Randolph; to his son Francis Meriwether Randolph; sold to General Meredith Reid 1884; by descent (?) to Mrs. John Bergen?; Sotheby Parke-Bernet, New York, 1978, Lot 576; S. J. Shrubsole, New York; White House purchase with donated funds.
REFERENCES: Susan R. Stein, *The Worlds of Thomas Jefferson at Monticello* (New York: Abrams, 1993), 314–16.

TEA SERVICE (Teapot, Cream Pitcher, Sugar Bowl) (page 41)
Sayre and Richards (working 1803–13), New York, circa 1803–13 (John Sayre, 1771–1852, and Thomas Richards, working 1802–30)

Silver, hardwood
Gift of Horace W. Harrison, 1986
1986.1593.1–3
Teapot—7 3/4 x 12 3/8 x 4 7/8 in. (19.7 x 31.4 x 12.4 cm.); 20 oz. 3 dwt.
Cream—5 3/4 x 5 3/4 x 2 7/8 in. (14.6 x 14.6 x 7.3 cm.); 8 oz.
Sugar—6 3/4 x 8 3/8 x 4 3/16 in. (17.2 x 20.6 x 10.6 cm.); 14 oz. 9 dwt.
MARKS: Underside—stamped "S&R" (oval), "F" (boxed).
INSCRIPTIONS: Body engraved with wreathed cypher "JM," reportedly for James Madison.
NOTES: Reportedly from the Madison family silver. Jacob Barker who helped cart away the Gilbert Stuart portrait of George Washington before the British burned the White House in 1814, was reportedly given these pieces because his loans to the government to finance the War of 1812 were not fully repaid. In 1803 the firm advertised that "They manufacture silver tea setts of the newest and most approved patterns," but few pieces of the partnership's work have survived.
PROVENANCE: James Madison; gift to Jacob Barker; to his daughter Sarah Barker Harrison; to her son Thomas B. Harrison; to his son Robert Harrison; to his son Horace W. Harrison.
REFERENCES: J. Madison Cutts, "Dolley Madison," *Records of the Columbia Historical Society*, vol. III (1900), 58–59. Ian M. G. Quimby, *American Silver at Winterthur* (Winterthur, Del.: Winterthur Museum, 1995), 284–85.

TEA BOX (page 42)
Chinese, circa 1811 / Jacquemart et Bénard, Paris, France, circa 1809–11
Painted wood / block-printed wallpaper
Gift of the White House Historical Association, 1971
1971.679.1
9 3/4 x 12 1/4 x 12 1/4 in. (24.8 x 31.1 x 31.1 cm.)
MARKS: Underside—stenciled "May 1811" (tea shipping date).
INSCRIPTIONS: Interior of box side to proper right of rear panel—inscribed in ink by Julia Latrobe "paper upon the Drawing room / of the President's house in / Mr Madison's time. / given to my mother by / Mrs Madison"; separate label in same hand "This pink paper was / given to my Mother by / her friend Mrs Madison. / It was that upon the walls / of the President's House / during Mr Madison's reign."
NOTES: Lined with a pink-ground French wallpaper (design registered by Jacquemart et Bénard in 1798) believed to have been installed in the White House prior to the 1814 fire.
Condition: Large loss in wallpaper at lower left of the inscribed panel.
PROVENANCE: Dolley Madison; given to Mary Elizabeth Hazelhurst Latrobe (wife of Benjamin Latrobe, the White House architect for Presidents Jefferson and Madison); descended in the Latrobe family.
REFERENCES: No. 1323, Li 14, Papiers de Tentures, Jacquemart, An VII, Bibiotheque Nationale, Paris. Catherine Lynn, *Wallpaper in America from the Seventeenth Century to World War I* (New York: Norton, 1980).

CRUET STAND (page 44)
Roch-Louis Dany (working circa 1779–1820), Paris, 1789
Silver
Bequest of James C. McGuire, 1931
1931.3684.1
12 7/8 x 10 11/16 x 6 3/8 in. (32.7 x 27.2 x 16.2 cm.); 36 oz.
MARKS: Underside of base—stamped maker's mark—crown / fleur-de-lis / "RLD"—and 1789 Paris warden and large silver duty charge marks; one saucer—maker, 1786 warden, 1782–89 duty charge and discharge marks for small silver; the other saucer—maker, 1787 warden, and 1782–89 charge for large silver (the saucers currently on the mate bear 1787–89 marks).
INSCRIPTION: Underside of base engraved "MADISON CASTOR RETURNED TO THE WHITE HOUSE BY BEQUEST OF JAMES CLARK McGUIRE 1931."
NOTES: Early in his first mission as minister to France (1794–97), James Monroe purchased household goods for his Paris residence. Silver from Dany included "2 columnar cruets" for 644 francs and "6 square candlesticks" for 1369 francs (228 francs each). These were sold in 1803 to his friend, James Madison, then secretary of state, to help defray personal expenses when Monroe returned to Paris to negotiate the Louisiana Purchase. Later used by the Madisons at their Virginia home, Montpelier.
CONDITION: Replacement cut-glass bottles made at the time of acquisition in 1931; the mate contains a simpler pair made in 1964.
PROVENANCE: James and Elizabeth Monroe; sold to James and Dolley Madison; to Dolley's son John Payne Todd; to James C. McGuire (Washington auctioneer and collector, creditor of Payne Todd); gift to his daughter-in-law Anna Madison Chapman McGuire, also a Madison great-grandniece; to her son James C. McGuire.
REFERENCES: Conover Hunt-Jones, *Dolley and the "Great Little Madison"* (Washington, D.C.: AIA Foundation, 1977), 24, figs. 25–26. Carr, "History in White House Silver," 37.

CANDLESTICKS (page 45)
Roch-Louis Dany (working circa 1779–1820), Paris, 1789
Silver
Bequest of James C. McGuire, 1931
1931.3783.1–2
11 x 4 x 4 in. (27.9 x 10.2 x 10.2 cm.); .1—20 oz. 8 dwt., .2—19 oz. 19 dwt.
MARKS: Underside of foot and interior of candle cup—stamped maker's mark—crowned "RLD"—and 1789 warden's and duty charge marks; interior of bobeche plug—maker's mark only.
INSCRIPTIONS: Foot underside engraved "MADISON CANDLESTICK RETURNED TO THE WHITE HOUSE BY BEQUEST OF JAMES CLARK McGUIRE 1931."
NOTES: See page 44. From a set of six; numbers "III" and "IIII" are marked on the interior of the foot.

DESSERT COOLER and SOUP TUREEN (*page 46*)
Nast manufactory (1783–1836), Paris, circa 1806
(Jean-Népomucène-Herman Nast, 1754–1817)
Porcelain
Gift of the White House Historical Association, 1976
1976.1250.2 and 1976.1246.1
Cooler—12 1/2 x 8 1/2 x 6 7/8 in. (31.8 x 21.6 x 17.5 cm.)
Tureen—6 3/4 x 13 1/2 x 7 7/8 in. (17.2 x 34.3 x 17.2 cm.)
MARKS: Underside—gold painted "nast."
NOTES: Fulwar Skipwith, the American commercial
agent in Paris, wrote to Secretary of State James Madison in 1806 that "Mr. Nast, the china manufacturer" had
at last executed Madison's order at "40% cheaper" than
Sèvres. This personal service—172 dinner pieces and 59
dessert pieces at $595.37—included "2 Soupieres ovales"
(180 francs, approximately $36) and "2 Glacieres vases"
(120 francs, $22). The service may have been used as the
state china when President and Mrs. Madison occupied
temporary quarters after the burning of the White
House in 1814. The White House has four additional
pieces—the matching cooler and three dinner plates
(diam. 9 1/4 in., all stencil-marked "NAST à Paris").
Two of the plates were received in 1905 from a donor
whose grandfather, Samuel Harrison Smith (publisher of
the *National Intelligencer*, 1800–1810, Washington newspaper of the Jefferson and Madison administrations),
reportedly was given them by Dolley Madison. The third
plate shares the tureen's provenance. Other pieces are at
the Smithsonian Institution.
CONDITION: The tureen cover is missing, perhaps as
early as an 1842 Madison inventory for "2 tureens—one
top"; one handle repaired. The liners are missing from
both repaired coolers (replaced by modern rings).
PROVENANCE: Coolers—James and Dolley Madison;
to her son Payne Todd; Robert Beale (probably 1851
sale); descended in his family to Florence B. Marshall;
lent to White House 1972–76; White House purchase
with donated funds. Tureen—James and Dolley Madison; possibly to her son Payne Todd; to her nephew
Richard D. Cutts (possibly at 1851 sale); to his daughter
Lucia Cutts; gift to Mrs. George B. Cutts (wife of
nephew); White House purchase with donated funds.
REFERENCES: Copy of original bill of April 18, 1806,
endorsed by Fulwer Skipwith on September 3, 1806,
James Madison Papers, New York Public Library.
"Inventory of Mrs. D. P. Madison's furniture in House
in Washington—Nov. 15, 1842," Dolley Madison Papers,
LC. Klapthor, *Official White House China*, 34–39. Hunt-
Jones, *Dolley*, 121, fig. 5.

DECANTER (*page 47*)
Bakewell, Page & Bakewell, Pittsburgh, 1816
Cut and engraved glass
Gift of the White House Preservation Fund with funds
from Mr. and Mrs. Lloyd Rappaport and funds in mem-
ory of Lila Acheson Wallace, 1986
1986.1590.1
8 11/16 x 4 1/2 in. (22.1 x 11.4 cm.)
MARKS: None.
INSCRIPTIONS: Shield engraved with initial "M" for
Madison.

NOTES: One of a pair given by the manufacturer, Benjamin Bakewell, to President James Madison in 1816.
The engraved eagle of the United States was personalized by the addition of the initial "M" on the breast
shield. During one of several fires, the stoppers to both
were lost and the mate was badly broken. The mate was
sold at auction in 1984 to a private collector by the son of
the consignor of this decanter.
CONDITION: Stopper missing.
PROVENANCE: President and Mrs. James Madison; to
Dolley's son Payne Todd; by the turn of the 20th century, both decanters were owned by the family of James
Monroe's nephew, Theodore Douglas Robinson, and
had come to be thought of as Monroe relics; to Miche-
line Robinson Geisen; C. G. Sloan & Co., Washington,
D.C., April 28, 1985, 769, Lot 1938; purchased by the
White House Preservation Fund—lent to White House
1985, donated 1986.
REFERENCES: Jane Shadel Spillman, *White House Glass-
ware: Two Centuries of Entertaining* (Washington, D.C.:
WHHA, 1989) 24, fig. 1. Hunt-Jones, *Dolley*, 43.

CHAPTER 2

BASKET (*page 52*)
Attributed to Denière et Matelin (circa 1797–1820),
Paris, circa 1817 (Jean-François Denière, 1774–1866;
François Matelin, ?–?)
Gilded bronze
U.S. Government purchase, 1817
1817.3676.1
15 3/4 x 9 3/8 in. (40.0 x 23.8 cm.)
MARKS: None.
NOTES: One of "2 other *corbeilles* mat gilt [with larger
"rich" basket of same description] of three figures on a
round foot with ivy leaves, having six lights decorated
with flowers" purchased for the "dining room" in 1817 to
accompany the plateau (with stands and urns at a total
cost of 6000 francs). Groupings of three such classical
female figures are generally assumed to depict the three
Graces, Greek goddesses of beauty and fertility. Those
on the larger companion basket (19 1/2 x 11 1/2) strongly
resemble, but are not identical to, those on the plateau.
Although the baskets and plinths are matched on all
three, the figures on the smaller pair are dressed, posed,
and coiffed differently. Based on the existence of the
marked White House plateau, an unsigned drawing of a
very similar plateau section (Musée des Arts Décoratifs,
Paris) has been attributed to Denière et Matelin. The
drawing also includes a basket, with figures similar to
those on the larger basket of this group, containing a
twelve-arm light structure.
CONDITION: Candle arms missing. Regilded as early as
1853.
REFERENCES: NA/MTA acct. 37131, voucher 3. Hans
Huth, "The White House Furniture at the Time of
Monroe," *Gazette des Beaux-Arts*, 6th ser., 29 (January
1946), 45. Clement E. Conger and Betty C. Monkman,
"President Monroe's Acquisitions," *The Connoisseur*
(May 1976): 58.

WINE COOLER (*page 55*)
Jean-Baptiste-Claude Odiot (1763–1850), Paris,
1798–1809
Silver
U.S. Government purchase, 1817
1817.3703.1
17 3/4 x 8 1/2 in. (45.1 x 21.6 cm.); 43 oz. 4 dwt.
MARKS: Underside—stamped maker's lozenge "JBCO"
and 1798–1809 Paris 1st standard silver and large excise
marks.
INSCRIPTIONS: Side engraved "President's House."
NOTES: From a set of four (all extant), thought to be
from among President Monroe's personal furnishings
purchased for use in the President's House in 1817,
although they are not clearly listed on the inventory of
his property. The "4 plated wine coolers, at $10," listed
after the enumeration of solid silver by weight, would
seem to be a serious undervaluing of these pieces.
Nonetheless, four coolers appear on the 1825 and all sub-
sequent White House inventories. If Monroe's, they
presumably would have been acquired during his diplomatic service in Europe, 1803–07.
CONDITION: Liners and collars missing.
REFERENCES: James Monroe to Samuel Lane, Commissioner of Public Buildings, April 28, 1817—NA/MTA
acct. 43754, voucher 86 [also in House Report 79, 18th
Cong., 2d session. (1824–25), 213–17]. Conger and
Monkman, "President Monroe's Acquisitions," 56, fig. 1.
Carr, "History in White House Silver," 33, fig. 1.

SALT SPOON (*page 56 left*)
Jacob Leonard (working circa 1810–27), Washington,
D.C., circa 1817–27
Gilded silver
U.S. Government purchase
1960.4008.1
4 1/8 in. (10.5 cm.); 5 dwt.
MARKS: Handle reverse—stamped "J. LEONARD"
(boxed).
INSCRIPTIONS: Handle face engraved "President's
House."
NOTES: One of a pair, the acquisition of which is
undocumented. Jacob Leonard took over the Washing-
ton customers of George Washington Riggs, when that
silversmith/merchant moved to Baltimore in 1810. He
provided four silver treaty skippet boxes to the State
Department in 1819, but was listed as a watchmaker at
another shop in an 1827 Washington city directory.
REFERENCES: Daughters of the American Revolution
Museum, *Magnificent Intentions: Decorative Arts of the District
of Columbia, 1791–1861* (Washington, D.C.: Daughters of
the American Revolution Museum, 1991), 20. Richard S.
Patterson and Richardson Dougall, *The Eagle and the Shield:
A History of the Great Seal of the United States* (Washington,
D.C.: GPO, 1976), 175. *The Washington Directory* (Wash-
ington, D.C.: S. A. Elliott, 1827), 49.

MUSTARD SPOON and SALT SPOON
(*page 56 right*)
Charles Alexander Burnett (1769–1848), Georgetown,
D.C., circa 1817–30
Gilded silver

U.S. Government purchase
1817.3718.1, 817.3719.1
Mustard—5 1/2 in. (14.0 cm.); 7 dwt.
MARKS: Handle reverse—stamped "C.A.B." (boxed).
Salt—4 in. (10.2 cm.); 5 dwt.
MARKS: Handle reverse—stamped "C.A.BURNETT" (boxed).
INSCRIPTIONS: Handle face engraved "President's House."
NOTES: The salt spoon is possibly from "6 salt spoons, $6.40" purchased from Burnett in 1817. The acquisition of the mustard spoon, one of a pair, is undocumented. Burnett, the District of Columbia's most prominent smith, supplied silver and fancy goods to the White House for several decades.
REFERENCES: NA/MTA acct. 43754, voucher 12. Cathrine B. Hollan, *In the Neatest, Most Fashionable Manner: Three Centuries of Alexandria Silver* (Alexandria, Va.: The Lyceum, 1994), 34–56.

ARMCHAIR *(page 57)*
William King, Jr. (1771–1854), Georgetown, D.C., 1818
Mahogany and mahogany veneer / oak, ash, tulip poplar; brass
Gift of Mr. and Mrs. John Ford Sollers, Sr., 1986
1986.1583.1
41 1/4 x 25 1/2 x 25 3/8 in. (104.8 x 64.8 x 64.4 cm.)
MARKS: None.
NOTES: From a suite of 24 armchairs and 4 sofas made for the East Room in 1818—$28 per chair, $184 per sofa—but not upholstered until 1829. Two additional examples have been returned to the White House—one in 1962, which had descended in the family of William J. MacPherson, who directed the 1873 redecoration of the East Room during which the suite was removed, and one in 1985, which was received without provenance data.
CONDITION: Refinished in 1989 to match the modern finish on the chair received in 1985; circular cup casters on the front legs duplicated for the front legs of the other two chairs and to fit on circular posts under the square rear legs of all three chairs.
PROVENANCE: White House; purchased by John T. Ford [a Ford provenance is shared by chairs at Ford's Theater, the Daughters of the American Revolution Museum (one of two), and at least three in private hands, as well as a sofa at the Smithsonian Institution]; to his daughter; to her son John Ford Sollers, Sr.
REFERENCES: NA/MTA acct. 43754, voucher 70. Anne Golovin, "William King, Jr., Georgetown Furniture Maker," *Antiques* (May 1977): 1033–34 (a family-owned chair, possibly a sample, is illustrated). William G. Allman, "Furnishing the Executive Mansion: Nineteenth Century Washington Sources," in *Our Changing White House*, ed. Wendell Garrett (Boston: Northeastern University Press, 1995), 139–42.

CANDLESTICK *(page 58)*
France, circa 1817
Gilded bronze
U.S. Government purchase
1817.1367.1
27 3/8 x 8 1/8 x 8 1/8 in. (69.5 x 20.6 x 20.6 cm.)

MARKS: Some plinth components—stamped "J·C" with sequential numbers [mate identically marked].
NOTES: One of an extant pair long attributed to the French purchases by James Monroe in 1817, possibly "1 Pr. engraved mat gilt bronze candlesticks" purchased for the Oval Room at 150 francs. By comparison with two pairs of figural candelabra (pages 62 and 64) at 1450 and 850 francs, however, they would seem to be too substantial to be that purchase. Inasmuch as other examples of this columnar form—some made by the Thomire and Denière firms—are fitted with candle arms, it is possible that they are in fact candelabra lacking their arm structures. In 1853 when small cut glass bowls were made for the figural holders on the Monroe plateau, two large matching bowls were made for these fixtures (they are shown filled with flowers and standing on the plateau in an 1870 engraving of a state dinner). In 1873 repairs were made to four candelabra and "2 large pilliars" which were presumably these fixtures.
REFERENCES: NA/MTA acct. 37131, voucher 3. Huth, "White House Furniture," 45–46. Conger and Monkman, "President Monroe's Acquisitions," 59.

STAND *(page 59)*
Possibly by Denière et Matelin (circa 1797–1820), Paris, circa 1817
Gilded bronze
U.S. Government purchase, 1817
1817.3677.1
15 1/8 x 11 7/8 in. (38.4 x 30.2 cm.)
MARKS: None.
NOTES: One of "2 rich mat gilt Trepieds copied after the antique"(both extant) purchased for the "dining room" in 1817 to accompany the Denière et Matelin plateau (with baskets and urns at a total cost of 6000 francs). A paw-footed leg similarly topped by a seated winged-sphinx figure, rather than a human or animal torso in a more fluid continuous line, appears as supports on a tripod table in the 1807 drawing book by English designer Thomas Hope, probably drawing on a French design or the same "antique" model which may have inspired this stand.
CONDITION: Regilded as early as 1853.
References: NA/MTA acct. 37131, voucher 3. Huth, "White House Furniture," 35–36, 46. Conger and Monkman, "President Monroe's Acquisitions," 62, fig. 6. Thomas Hope, *Household Furniture and Interior Decoration* (1807; reprint, New York: Dover, 1971), pl. XXV, no. 2.

SALON SUITE *(pages 60-61, 264)*
Pierre-Antoine Bellangé (1758–1827), Paris, circa 1817
Gilded beechwood
NOTES: A 53-piece "grand salon suite gilded wood with olive branch ornaments, covered in double-warp satin, fine crimson, two shades of gold, laurel-leaf design" for "the large oval room" (currently the Blue Room) in 1817. Two side chairs and one armchair are the only pieces at the White House to bear traces of the maker's stamp "P.BELLANGE". By 1825, of the 38 chairs (2 bergères, 18 armchairs, and 18 side chairs) 14 had been moved into the adjacent Green Room. By 1849, the chairs in the two rooms totaled only 28, the number—with the full complement of sofas, stools, footstools, and screens—which

was sold at auction by James C. McGuire in Washington D.C., January 17, 1860. A group of reproductions (seven arm, four side) was made in 1962 to supplement the three original chairs acquired in 1961-1962.
CONDITION: All pieces from the suite at the White House have been regilded.
REFERENCES: NA/MTA acct. 37131, voucher 3. Huth, "White House Furniture", 45. Conger and Monkman. "President Monroe's Acquisitions," 58.

ARMCHAIR *(page 60—see above)*
Gift of Catherine Bohlen, 1961
1961.14.1
38 5/8 x 25 3/4 x 25 3/4 in. (98.1 x 65.4 x 65.4 cm.)
MARKS: None.
NOTES: One of 18 *fauteuils* (four at the White House) purchased at 4893.02 francs. Three armchairs, all with Washington, D.C., provenances, are in other collections—Woodrow Wilson House, Daughters of the American Revolution Museum, and a private collection.
PROVENANCE: White House; descended to donor from her grandfather.

SOFA *(pages 60-61—see above)*
Gift of the Edison Institute, 1979
1979.1394.1
42 1/2 x 110 3/4 x 31 1/4 in. (108.0 x 281.3 x 79.4 cm.)
MARKS: None.
NOTES: One of two *sophas* (one extant at the White House) at 3368.74 francs.
PROVENANCE: White House; Henry Ford, 1930; the Edison Institute.

SIDE CHAIR *(page 61 upper—see above)*
Anonymous donation, 1962
1962.227.1
36 1/16 x 19 1/4 x 19 7/8 in. (91.6 x 48.9 x 50.5 cm.)
MARKS: Underside of front seat rail—trace of stamp "P. BELLANGE."
NOTES: One of eighteen *chaises* at 3454.38 francs. A second marked side chair descended in a different branch of the same family, also purchased by the White House with funds donated anonymously.
PROVENANCE: White House; Dr. John Moore McCalla (Washington, D.C., 1845–d.1897); to his daughter Isabel Hill McCalla Goldsborough; to her daughter Helen L. Goldsborough; White House purchase with donated funds.

ARMCHAIR *(page 61 lower—see above)*
Anonymous donation, 1972
1972.838.1
42 1/4 x 27 1/2 x 25 3/4 in. (107.3 x 69.8 x 65.4 cm.)
MARKS: None.
NOTES: One of two *bergères* (one extant at the White House) purchased at 798.28 francs. The bill also itemized the components of the upholstery of those two chairs (204.14 francs per chair), including "fine feathers" which would have been used for the seat cushion. It is unknown whether the two bergères were grouped among the 14 armchairs sold in 1860.
PROVENANCE: White House; possibly Estate of Violet Blair Janin (Mrs. Albert Janin), who lived near the White

House at 12 Lafayette Square; Union Trust Co., Washington, D.C.; Kemper Simpson, Washington, D.C. (1930s); Simpson estate sale at Adam A. Wechsler & Sons, Washington, D.C., 1971; United States Antiques, Washington, D.C.; White House purchase with donated funds.

CANDELABRUM (page 62)
Paris, circa 1817
Gilded bronze
U.S. Government purchase, 1817
1817.1424.1
42 x 13 1/2 x 12 1/4 in. (106.7 x 34.3 x 31.1 cm.)
MARKS: None.
NOTES: From among three pairs of figural candelabra (two pairs extant) purchased in 1817, these being the "oval room" set: "1 pair *Candélabres* female figure of antique bronze color holding overhead a cluster of 6 lights and ornaments, the figures mounted on square pedestals with military trophies, the branches and pedestals mat gilt," 1400 francs. Figures of this form, usually with wings as Victory or Fame, were made by several prominent Parisian bronzesmiths, probably after one of the earliest (1801) published designs by the noted French Empire designers Charles Percier (1764–1838) and Pierre-François-Léonard Fontaine (1762–1853). A matching trophy-mounted plinth appears on two pairs marked by Thomire & Co.; a nearly identical light structure and figure, but with wings, appears on a pair en suite with a clock marked "L. Ravrio."
CONDITION: Records do not reveal when the bronze-colored figures were gilded to match the arms and pedestals. Much of the gilding, however, has been lost and replaced with tinted lacquering. Interior scroll on one arm is a replacement.
REFERENCES: NA/MTA acct. 37131, voucher 3. Huth, "White House Furniture," 45. Conger and Monkman, "President Monroe's Acquisitions," 59. Charles Percier and Pierre-François-Léonard Fontaine, *Recueil de décorations intérieures* (1812; reprint, New York: Dover, 1991), pl. 18, no. 9.

PIER TABLE (page 63)
Pierre-Antoine Bellangé (1758–1827), Paris, circa 1817
Gilded beechwood, marble, mirror glass
U.S. Government purchase, 1817
1817.420.1
43 1/4 x 75 x 20 3/4 in. (109.9 x 190.5 x 52.7 cm.)
MARKS: None.
NOTES: See page 60-61. "1 Gilded wood console of 5 feet 10 inches long by 3 feet 4 inches high, double baluster legs, rear pilasters, a large mirror frame, carved and gilded" with the mirror glass and "1 white marble [top] of 5 feet 10 by 22 inches" totaling 715.40 francs. From a 53-piece suite purchased in 1817 for "the large oval room," this is the only piece to have remained continuously at the White House.
CONDITION: Regilded; replacement top and mirror glass.

MANTEL CLOCK (page 63)
Case by Thomire & Co. (Pierre-Philippe Thomire, 1751–1843); movement by Louis Moinet, Sr. (1768–1853), Paris, circa 1817

Gilded bronze / enameled iron; brass spring-driven movement
U.S. Government purchase, 1817
1817.1368.1
29 x 22 7/8 x 9 3/4 in. (73.7 x 58.1 x 24.8 cm.)
MARKS: Dial—inscribed "THOMIRE ET CIE / MOINET AINE HGER."
NOTES: "1 Pendule depicting Minerva leaning on a shield in which the movement is set, the whole mounted on a square bronze base, ornamented on three sides, bas-relief military trophy, with base molding, the whole of chased bronze gilded with mat gold, and Case," purchased at 2000 francs for the "large oval Room" (Blue Room) in 1817. Works by Moinet frequently were housed in cases by Thomire, including one with an identical figure of Minerva on a marble base ornamented with figures of the Muses (Christie's 1997), the arts being an attribute of Minerva in addition to her status as the Roman goddess of war.
CONDITION: Fully or partially regilded as early as 1853.
REFERENCES: NA/MTA acct. 37131, voucher 3. Huth, "White House Furniture," 35, 45, fig. 2. Conger and Monkman, "President Monroe's Acquisitions," 59, fig. 2.

CANDELABRUM (page 64)
Paris, circa 1817
Gilded bronze
U.S. Government purchase, 1817
1817.1503.1
33 3/4 x 13 1/8 x 12 1/4 in. (85.7 x 33.3 x 31.1 cm.)
MARKS: None.
NOTES: From among three pairs of figural candelabra (two pairs extant) purchased in 1817, this being the pair (both extant) for the "Sitting room or Parlor" (Red Room): "1 pair *Candélabres* with figures on square pedestals mat gilt with six lights," at 850 francs. On the mate the legs are crossed in reverse. A similar but ungilded figure is found on a pair signed by Claude-François Rabiat, circa 1805–15.
CONDITION: Fully or partially regilded as early as 1853. Much of the gilding, however, has been lost, replaced with tinted lacquering.
REFERENCES: NA/MTA acct. 37131, voucher 3. Huth, "White House Furniture," 45. Conger and Monkman, "President Monroe's Acquisitions," 59.

MANTEL CLOCK (page 65)
Case by Denière et Matelin (circa 1797–1820), Paris, circa 1817; movement by unidentified clocksmith.
Gilded bronze / enameled iron, brass spring-driven movement
U.S. Government purchase, 1817
1817.1362.1
23 x 18 1/2 x 6 3/4 in. (58.4 x 47.0 x 17.2 cm.)
MARKS: Dial—inscribed "Denière et Matelin / Fabts [fabricants] de Bronze à Paris"; right proper end of case—engraved "Denière et Matelin fabts de Bronze Dorés / a Paris."
NOTES: "One mat gilt Bronze *Pendule*, depicting Hannibal after the Battle of Cannae," purchased at 900 francs for "the Sitting room or Parlor" (Red Room) in 1817. The figure of the Carthaginian general, Hannibal (247–183/182 B.C.) stands beside the clock housing

marked "Cannae" for his greatest victory (216 B.C.) in Italy over the Romans during the Second Punic War. The Roman historian Livy wrote that Hannibal sent home to Carthage several corn measures of gold rings gathered from the bodies of Roman nobles slain at Cannae as evidence of the magnitude of his triumph. This story is represented by this figure of Hannibal fingering some of the rings in an urn. Earlier victories at the Trebia River (218 B.C.) and Lake Trasimenus (217 B.C.) are named on shields fronting crossed swords on the upper tier of the base, flanking a military mount centering "A" for the French "Annibal." Nearly identical clocks with unmarked cases bear works marked by clocksmiths LeRoy et Fils and Badier (private collections).
CONDITION: Fully or partially regilded as early as 1853. Small holes around the helmet-topped column indicate lost ornaments, probably an octagonal shield (on both nearly identical clocks) and possibly a prostrated Roman legionary standard (on one).
REFERENCES: NA/MTA acct. 37131, voucher 3. Huth, "White House Furniture," 35, 46. Conger and Monkman, "President Monroe's Acquisitions," 59, pl. A.

CENTER TABLE (page 66)
France, circa 1817
Mahogany and mahogany veneer / white oak, tulip poplar; marble, gilded bronze
U.S. Government purchase, 1817
1817.170.1
33 3/4 x 45 in. (85.7 x 114.3 cm.)
MARKS: None.
NOTES: "One round mahogany table, columnar supports, triangular base, white marble top of 3 1/2 feet diameter, the capitals and ornaments of chased mat gilt bronze," purchased at 500 francs for the "Sitting room or Parlor" (Red Room) in 1817. This characteristic French form was imitated in the United States, and two such tables, French or American, appear in two interior depictions—a Boston painting, *The Tea Party* by Henry Sargent, 1824 (Museum of Fine Arts, Boston), and a Baltimore drawing attributed to Robert Gilmour, Jr., circa 1817–18 (Maryland Historical Society).
CONDITION: Ball feet added 1962. Possibly original white marble top with some chipping of edges.
REFERENCES: NA/MTA acct. 37131, voucher 3. Huth, "White House Furniture," 45. Conger and Monkman. "President Monroe's Acquisitions," 59. D. Wendy Cooper, *Classical Taste in America 1800–1840* (New York: Abbeville, 1993) 39, pls. 15–16, 61.

VASES, pair (page 67 upper)
Paris, circa 1817
Porcelain
U.S. Government purchase, 1817
1817.1162.1–2
16 x 9 1/2 x 8 1/4 in. (40.6 x 24.1 x 21.0 cm.)
MARKS: None.
NOTES: "One Pair porcelain *Vases*, richly decorated, depicting views of Passy and the home of Franklin," purchased at 460 francs for the "Card Room" (now the Green Room) in 1817. Painted with scenes of Passy, the suburb of Paris where Benjamin Franklin lived when he was United States minister to France (1778–85). One

(.2) titled in a reserve on the foot, "Vue de la Maison de Franklin / a Passy," is a view of the Hotel Valentinois, in one wing of which Franklin resided. The other (.1) is of Passy from that house, entitled "Vue des environs de Passy prise de la maison de Franklin." The mansion was owned by Jacques-Donatien de Chaumont, a leading supplier of goods and munitions to the Americans during the Revolutionary War. A very similar pair of green-ground vases decorated with American naval scenes, also titled in French, was acquired by the Peabody Essex Museum, Salem, Mass., in 1998.

CONDITION: Both have been broken and conserved.

REFERENCES: NA/MTA acct. 37131, voucher 3. Huth, "White House Furniture," 46. Conger and Monkman, "President Monroe's Acquisitions," 61, pl. D.

VASES, pair (page 67 lower)
Paris, circa 1817
Porcelain
U.S. Government purchase, 1817
1817.1374.1–.1375.1
15 3/4 x 8 3/4 x 6 7/8 in. (40.0 x 22.2 x 17.5 cm.)
MARKS: None.

NOTES: "Two Porcelain *Vases*, richly decorated, depicting Homer & Belisarius," purchased at 500 francs for the "Sitting room or Parlor" (Red Room). One (.1374) shows a seaside scene of the Greek poet Homer, with a lyre slung over his back, addressing a boy. Its mate (.1375) shows a landscape scene of Byzantine general Belisarius (circa 505–565) carrying a boy, after a painting by Francis Gérard (1770–1837) (the Hermitage, St. Petersburg). Although he was briefly imprisoned by a suspicious Emperor Justinian, the legend of his being blinded and reduced to beggary, depicted here, is not true. Both scenes have appeared on other French vases.

REFERENCES: NA/MTA acct. 37131, voucher 3. Huth, "White House Furniture," 36, 45–46, fig. 6. Conger and Monkman, "President Monroe's Acquisitions," 59, fig. 3.

PLATEAU (page 68-69)
Denière et Matelin (circa 1797–1820), Paris, circa 1817
Gilded bronze, mirror glass
U.S. Government purchase, 1817
1817.3673.1
13 5/8 x 174 x 26 5/8 in. (34.6 x 442.0 x 65.1 cm.)
MARKS: Plinth foot face—script engraved "Deniere et Matelin."

NOTES: Purchased for the "dining room" in 1817—"1 chased bronze Surtout de table, mat gilt with garlands of fruit and vines with figure of Bacchus and Bacchantes and pedestals on which are 16 figures presenting wreathes for receiving lights [candles] and 16 cups for changing at will, composed of 7 pieces altogether 13 feet [sic 14] 6 inches long, over 2 feet wide, set with its mirrors." Accompanied by three baskets (now lacking original light arms) (see page 52), a pair of urns, and a pair of stands (see page 59), all extant, at a total cost of 6000 francs. In 1853 32 cut-glass dishes were acquired as an alternative to candles. Denière et Matelin was one of the largest French bronze workshops, with as many as 400 workmen. An unsigned drawing of a very similar plateau section and one similar basket (Musée des Arts Décoratifs, Paris) has been attributed to the firm based on the existence of the White

House plateau. Like the ball-mounted female figures in the contemporary candelabra (see page 62), the similar figures here are probably after an 1801 design by Percier et Fontaine. Another design attributed to Charles Percier, circa 1810, in the Odiot archives in Paris shows a very similar figure holding up two wreaths.

CONDITION: Regilded and mirrors resilvered as early as 1853. Original or early mercury gilding is largely intact on figures, but structural members and gallery were regilded at some time (possibly 1930s) in 24 karat gold electroplate. Fasteners tapped out and replaced with machine screws. Mirror plates resilvered or replaced.

REFERENCES: NA/MTA acct. 37131, voucher 3. Huth, "White House Furniture," 35–36, 46. Conger and Monkman, "President Monroe's Acquisitions," 61, figs. 4a–b. John Pearce, "The 1817 Catalogue Drawing of the White House Plateau," *The Connoisseur* (August 1971): 284–86. Madeleine Deschamps, *Empire* (New York: Abbeville, 1994), 96. Percier and Fontaine, *Recueil de décorations intérieures*, pls. 2 and 4.

PLATEAU (detail) (page 69)
John Wolfe Forbes (1781–1854), New York, circa 1820–25
Silver, mirror glass
Gift of Russell Hunter, 1962
1962.267.1
8 1/16 x 87 x 22 3/4 in. (20.5 x 221.0 x 57.8 cm.)
MARKS: Center section and one end section—stamped "I. W. FORBES." / (boxed) anchor, star, head?, "c."

NOTES: The plateau, a dining table centerpiece with a reflective mirrored floor, was popular in France in the Empire period, but very rare in America: only one other is known besides two made by John W. Forbes, the most distinguished of three silversmithing sons of a smith father. These were probably derived from the designs of Percier et Fontaine. One extremely similar French example, in gilded bronze rather than silver, differs mostly in having relief cherubs on eagle-less plinths. The second Forbes plateau, on exhibit at the Metropolitan Museum of Art in New York, was reportedly given by the citizens of New York to Governor DeWitt Clinton in 1825 on the opening of the Erie Canal. It is smaller, only 63-inches long, but nearly identical; the end plinths bear a relief trophy of an anchor, liberty cap, and caduceus, rather than the repeated classical figures of Flora and Pomona as on the White House example.

PROVENANCE: Probably John Hunter, New York; descended to Russell Hunter.

REFERENCES: Graham Hood, *American Silver: A History of Style, 1650–1900* (New York: Praeger, 1971), 202. Rachel B. Crawford, "The Forbes Family of Silversmiths," *Antiques* (April 1975): 730–34. Berry B. Tracy, et al., *19th Century America: Furniture and Other Decorative Arts* (New York: Metropolitan Museum of Art, 1970), no. 63.

SOUP TUREEN (page 70)
Jacques-Henri Fauconnier (1779–1839), Paris, circa 1817
Silver
U.S. Government purchase, 1817
1817.3685.1
14 5/8 x 18 1/4 x 11 5/8 in. (37.2 x 46.4 x 29.5 cm.); 193 oz.

MARKS: Underside of lid and stand—stamped "FAU-CONNIER / R. DUBAC / No. 58 A PARIS"; maker's lozenge—bird / "JF" / tower-and 1809–19 Paris 1st standard silver and large excise marks; tureen foot—maker and excise marks; liner underside—stamped "FAU-CONNIER" and makers lozenge; rim—excise mark.

NOTES: Of this pair (both extant) of "tureens with stands and liners" purchased in 1817, President James Monroe's agents, Russell & LaFarge, wrote: "The Plate has been manufactured by Fauconnier, an excellent artist and honest man; the tureens will, we hope, be found of the highest finish." With 188 pieces of flatware, the silver cost 615 francs. The finial was specially fashioned as an American eagle—shield-breasted, grasping arrows and olive branches. The lid, tureen, liner, and stand are engraved with a comparable American eagle aligned on one side of each. Unlike other White House silver, they are not engraved "President's House."

CONDITION: One hinged loop handle on .1 liner has been replaced by a fixed iron loop, the other handle repaired at a tear. Liner for .2 is missing.

REFERENCES: NA/MTA acct. 37131, voucher 3. House Report 79, 18th Congress, 2d sess., 1825. Huth, "White House Furniture," 36, 46. Conger and Monkman, "President Monroe's Acquisitions," 62, fig. 8. Carr, "History in White House Silver," 33, fig. 3.

FRUIT KNIVES (page 71)
J. B. Boitin (?–?), Paris, circa 1817
Gilded silver and mother-of-pearl
U.S. Government purchase, 1817
1817.3716.1–2
8 in. (20.3 cm.)
MARKS: Blade—stamped maker's lozenge—crowned "JB"—and 1809–19 Paris 1st standard silver and medium excise marks.

INSCRIPTIONS: Blade engraved "President's House."

NOTES: "36 Knives [*couverts*] vermeil blades, mother-of-pearl handles, gold coat-of-arms" (19 extant) were purchased for the "dining room" in 1817, among 188 pieces of flatware which, along with the Fauconnier tureens, cost 650 francs. The small shield mounted on the pearl handle is engraved with an American eagle emblem. One was apparently used by Mrs. Coolidge as a letter opener; it was returned to the White House by her son John in 1982 with an inkstand given to her by the Ladies of the Senate (see page 191). In 1866, New York retailer E. V. Haughwout was commissioned to produce china and silver to fill out existing services. The 29 knives then on hand were supplemented to a total of 48 by the acquisition of 19 copies (15 extant) made by Albert Coles & Co., New York, N.Y., $9 each.

REFERENCES: NA/MTA acct. 37131, voucher 3. Huth, "White House Furniture," 36, 46. Conger and Monkman, "President Monroe's Acquisitions," 62.

DESSERT PLATE (page 72-73)
Pierre-Louis Dagoty (1771–1840) and Edouard Honoré (?–1850) (partnership 1816–20), Paris, circa 1817
Porcelain
Gift of Mrs. R. C. Goetz and Mrs. Hugh Bullock, 1962
1962.292.1
8 5/16 in. (21.1 cm.)

MARKS: Reverse—red stenciled "M^ture de MADAME / d'Angoulême / P. L. Dagoty E. Honoré / á Paris."
NOTES: From among "7 dozen flat plates [assiettes plates]" in the 166-piece Monroe state dessert service, "A porcelain dessert service for thirty people, amaranth border with five vignettes representing Strength, Agriculture, Commerce, the Arts & the Sciences & the arms of the United States . . . ," purchased at 2182 francs. The eagle emblem may have been derived from the engraved letterhead stationery of the United States consulate in Paris, circa 1818–30s. The White House has one additional flat plate, while 32 flat plates are part of 64 pieces of the service in the collection of the Winterthur Museum.
PROVENANCE: White House; the donors' brother; Mrs. R. C. Goetz and Mrs. Hugh Bullock.
REFERENCES: NA/MTA acct. 37131, voucher 3. Klapthor, *Official White House China*, 40–46.

DESSERT COOLER AND BASKET (page 72–73)
Pierre-Louis Dagoty and Edouard Honoré (partnership 1816–20), Paris, circa 1817
Porcelain
Anonymous donation, 1986
1986.1591.1, 986.1591.4
Cooler—11 x 9 1/2 x 7 3/8 in. (27.9 x 24.1 x 18.7 cm.)
Basket—4 1/4 x 9 1/4 in. (10.8 x 23.5 cm.)
MARKS: None.
NOTES: From among four fruit coolers (*Glaciers*) and four baskets (*Corbeilles*) in the Monroe state dessert service. Four of the five transfer-printed reserves (no "commerce") appear on the cooler, with the eagle on both sides, but no eagle emblem or reserves appear on the basket. Other pieces from the same donation in the White House collection are 4 of 36 deep dessert plates, 2 of "24 diverse" compotes, and 1 of 4 footed bowls, all with the full five reserves. Another deep plate and 1 flat plate in the collection share a nearly identical provenance in the same family.
CONDITION: Cooler—crack down rear with two exterior staples; two reattached pieces at right rim, one including right handle.
PROVENANCE: White House; James C. McGuire, Washington, D.C., auctioneer; sold circa 1880 to Alexander McDonald Davis (pieces at Winterthur Museum sold to another family member); descended in family to donor.

SALT CELLAR (page 75)
Meissen, Saxony, early 19th century
Porcelain
Gift of Miss Mary Louisa Adams Clement, 1906
1906.2761.1
3 1/4 x 2 1/2 x 1 3/8 in. (8.3 x 5.4 x 3.5 cm.)
MARKS: Underside—hand painted factory mark of crossed lines.
NOTES: One of a pair from a John Quincy Adams family service in a blue and white onion pattern. Other pieces are in the Smithsonian Institution.
PROVENANCE: John Quincy and Louisa Catherine Adams; to their son John Adams II; to his daughter Mary Louisa Adams Johnson (born at the White House in 1828); to her daughter Louisa Catherine Adams Johnson Clement; to her daughter Mary Louisa Adams Clement.

CHAPTER 3

DINNER WINE GLASS, CELERY GLASS, WATER BOTTLE (page 80)
Bakewell, Page & Bakewell, Pittsburgh, Pennsylvania, 1829–30, and/or unidentified American glass houses, circa 1833–46
Cut and engraved glass
U.S. Government purchase, 1830–46
1830.3872. 1.1-4, .6.1-6, .4.1-12
Wine Glass—6 x 2 3/4 in. (15.2 x 7.0 cm.)
Celery Glass—10 1/4 x 5 in. (26.0 x 12.7 cm.)
Water Bottle—6 7/8 x 5 1/4 in. (17.5 x 13.3 cm.)
MARKS: None.
NOTES: These pieces are from the 425-piece "richest cut" Andrew Jackson state service—itemized on the "Invoice of Sundry Glass furnished the President of the United States by Bakewell Page & Bakewell Pittsburgh," January 27, 1830, $1,451.75—or reorders purchased in 1833, 1837, 1842, and 1846. The original order for colorless glassware included three entries for wine glasses—"6 doz cut clarets" at $20/dozen and five and seven dozen "wines to match." The celery glass, taller than matching celery or spoon glasses, may be from "3 pr. cut celeries" at $20/pair. The water bottle is probably from among four dozen at $36/dozen in the 1833 reorder.
REFERENCES: NA/MTA acct. 61369, voucher 54; acct. 70467, voucher 4. Spillman, *White House Glassware*, 32–58.

CENTER TABLE (page 84)
Anthony Gabriel Quervelle (1789–1856), Philadelphia, circa 1829
Mahogany, mahogany and rosewood veneers / mahogany, ash; marble; lead-filled die-stamped brass; brass
U.S. Government purchase, 1829
1829.239.1
29 1/2 x 40 1/2 in. (74.9 x 102.9 cm.)
MARKS: Underside of top brace—paper label "126 [street number on dressing glass image] / ANTHONY G. QUERVELLE'S / CABINET AND SOFA MANUFACTORY, / SOUTH SECOND STREET A FEW DOORS BELOW DOCK, / PHILADELPHIA."
NOTES: From "2 Round Tables Black & Gold Slabs," (both extant) at $100 each, purchased, along with one to match called "Large," at $135, for the East Room in 1829 from L. Veron & Co., Philadelphia. The larger table (29 1/2 x 49 1/2 in.) bears two of the paper labels.
CONDITION: Microscopic evidence of decorative finishes: gilding on molding around marble, leaves of shaft brackets, shaft gadrooning, and ring at base of shaft; gilt stenciling on rosewood outer crossbanding; ebonizing on inner crossbanding and edge of step atop plinth; vert antique on feet and leafage above feet. Modern finish (also on larger table) to complement old but non-original finish on mate. Foot scrolls used as model to cast carvable epoxy copies for mate. Reproduction casters on all three.
REFERENCES: NA/MTA acct. 61369, voucher 39. House Report 552, 27th Cong., 1st Sess., April 1, 1842, 61. Robert C. Smith, "Philadelphia Empire Furniture by Antoine Gabriel Quervelle" *Antiques* (September 1964): 304–9, fig. 10. Robert C. Smith, "The Furniture of

Anthony G. Quervelle, Part II: The Pedestal Tables," *Antiques* (July 1973): 90–99. Robert Mussey Associates, conservation report, 1997, OCWH.

PIER TABLE (page 85)
Anthony Gabriel Quervelle (1789–1856), Philadelphia, circa 1829
Mahogany and mahogany veneer / pine, tulip poplar, cherry; marble; mirror glass
U.S. Government purchase, 1829
1829.458.1
43 1/8 x 66 x 25 15/16 in. (109.5 x 167.6 x 65.9 cm.)
MARKS: Face of rear rail—paper label (see page 84).
NOTES: From "4 Pier Tables with Italian Slabs" at $175 each purchased for the East Room in 1829 from L. Veron & Co., Philadelphia. Removed from the East Room by early 1867, two cannot be traced further; one in very poor condition was destroyed in 1960.
CONDITION: Extensively restored: modern finish; replacement marble top; missing cherry molding under top replaced across front and proper right; non-original drawer removed from apron and missing flanking corner blocks replaced; missing mahogany plinth for proper right engaged column replaced; platform reveneered; new cherry rear feet based on table in collection of Chicago Historical Society; casters missing. Evidence of gilding on bird head and leaf on front supports and ring moldings on engaged columns.
REFERENCES: NA/MTA acct. 61369, voucher 39. House Report 552, 27th Cong., 1st Sess., April 1, 1842, 61. Smith, "Philadelphia Empire Furniture," 304–9, fig. 5. Robert C. Smith, "The Furniture of Anthony G. Quervelle, Part I: The Pier Tables," *Antiques* (May 1973): 984–94.

PART OF DINNER SERVICE (Sauce Boat, Mustard Stand, Cruet Stand, Vegetable Dish) (page 86)
Martin-Guillaume Biennais (1764–1843), Paris, 1809–19
Silver
U.S. Government purchase, 1833
1833.3700.2, 1833.3701.1, 1833.3694.2, 1833.3691.1
Sauce Boat—7 1/2 x 9 1/4 x 4 1/2 in. (19.1 x 23.5 x 11.4 cm.); 19 oz. 1 dwt.
Mustard Stand—3 5/8 x 4 x 2 3/4 in. (9.2 x 10.2 x 7.0 cm.); 5 oz. 16 dwt.
Cruet Stand—12 3/4 x 9 1/4 x 4 7/8 in.(32.4 x 23.5 x 12.4 cm.); 36 oz. 2 dwt.
Vegetable Dish—6 x 9 1/4 x 8 1/4 in. (15.2 x 23.5 x 21.0 cm.); 38 oz. 1 dwt.
MARKS: Body—stamped maker's lozenge—monkey / "B"—and 1809–19 Paris 1st standard silver and large excise marks.
INSCRIPTIONS: Side engraved "President's House."
NOTES: From a service of hollow and flatware purchased in 1833 from the estate of the "Baron de Tuyll" (Major General Baron Feodor Vasil'evich Teil'-fan-Serooskerken), former Russian Minister to the United States (1822–26), $4,308.62. All of the original quantities of each type shown here have survived except as noted: one of two "Sauce Boats" (mate missing by 1865, replaced

by an American copy in 1877), two "Mustard Stands," two "Setts Castors," and four "Vegetable Dishes".
CONDITION: None of the original glass cruets or caster liners has survived. The cruet bottles were made in 1964.
REFERENCES: NA/MTA acct. 70467, voucher 1. Carr, "History in White House Silver," 33–35, figs. 6–8.

SOUP TUREEN (page 88)
Martin-Guillaume Biennais (1764–1843), Paris, 1809–19
Silver
U.S. Government purchase, 1833
1833.3690.1
14 3/4 x 16 1/4 x 11 1/8 in. (37.5 x 41.3 x 28.3 cm.); 161 oz.
MARKS: Underside—stamped "BIENNAIS"; maker's lozenge—monkey / "B"—and 1809–19 Paris 1st standard silver and large excise marks.
INSCRIPTIONS: Side engraved "President's House."
NOTES: From "2 Soup Tureens" (both extant) from the de Tuyll service (see page 86). Originally 71 pieces of hollowware (63 extant), only the soup tureens, plates in two sizes, and platters in three sizes were stamped with the name "BIENNAIS" in addition to the maker's mark. Biennais, who operated a shop which employed up to 600 workers, was Napoleon's favorite silver producer, a master of the French Empire skill for contrasting smooth and sculpted surfaces in metal work. This tureen is more like the simpler work he executed for Napoleon's personal use, while a more elaborately ornamented tureen from a service commissioned by Napoleon's brother-in-law, the Prince Borghese, may be seen at the Metropolitan Museum of Art in New York. The name of his famous shop, the Purple Monkey, is reflected in his maker's mark.
REFERENCES: NA/MTA acct. 70467, voucher 1. Carr, "History in White House Silver," 33–34, fig. 5. Deschamps, Empire, 166–71.

COFFEE SERVICE (Coffeepots and Cream Jug) (page 89)
Martin-Guillaume Biennais (1764–1843), Paris, 1809–19
Silver, ivory
U.S. Government purchase, 1833
1833.3697.1, .3696.1, 3698.1
Coffeepot—10 1/2 x 7 x 4 3/4 in. (26.7 x 17.8 x 12.1 cm.); 25 oz. 17 dwt.
Coffeepot—13 3/8 x 8 3/4 x 5 1/4 in. (34.0 x 22.2 x 13.3 cm.); 51 oz. 18 dwt.
Cream Jug—10 1/4 x 6 5/8 x 4 1/4 in.(26.0 x 16.8 x 10.8 cm.); 33 oz. 3 dwt.
MARKS: Body—stamped maker's lozenge—monkey / "B"—and 1809–19 Paris 1st standard silver and large excise marks.
INSCRIPTIONS: Side engraved "President's House."
NOTES: "1 Large Coffee Pot," "1 Small Coffee Pot," and "1 Cream Jug," from the de Tuyll service (see page 86).
REFERENCES: NA/MTA acct. 70467, voucher 1. Carr, "History in White House Silver," 33–34.

TORCHÈRE (page 90)
France, circa 1830–37
Gilded bronze

Possible gift of Robert Patterson, circa 1829–37
1829.1320.1
64 1/2 x 22 1/2 in. (163.8 x 57.2 cm.)
MARKS: None.
NOTES: In the early 1880s, Thomas Pendel, White House doorkeeper, was told that this standing candelabrum, one of a pair (both extant), had been given by a General Patterson of Philadelphia to President Andrew Jackson. Early in the 20th century, Lucy Patterson claimed that this provenance applied to her grandfather, General Robert Patterson (1791–1881)—Philadelphia military officer, merchant, industrialist, and Jackson supporter—as told to her by her father. This gift is not mentioned, however, in the correspondence with Patterson in the Jackson Papers (Tennessee Historical Society). Lucy Patterson claimed that her grandfather had obtained them from the home of his friend Joseph Bonaparte (1768–1844), who resided in Bordentown, New Jersey circa 1815–32, 1837–39. These fixtures in the 18th-century rococo style, revived in France under King Louis Philippe (1830–48), could have been acquired for his fashionable country estate before or after Joseph Bonaparte's hiatus in England, 1832–37. The earliest image of them in the White House is an 1862 engraving of the Blue Room, showing the shafts topped by flowers with the candle arms removed. They appear in Blue Room photos from the late 1860s–early 1870s, both with and without arms.
PROVENANCE: (?) Joseph Bonaparte, Bordentown, New Jersey; to Robert Patterson (donor ?)

MANTEL CLOCK (page 91)
France, circa 1833
Marble/gilded brass; brass spring-driven movement
U.S. Government purchase, 1833
1833.3681.1
22 7/8 x 11 1/2 x 6 3/8 in. (58.1 x 30.2 x 21.6)
MARKS: None.
NOTES: Believed to be "1=4 Col. Black Marble Clock for the audience room 75.00" purchased from L. Veron & Co., Philadelphia, in 1833. This clock appears on the mantel in photographs of the President's Office (current Lincoln Bedroom), circa 1889–1902, and it was the clock in that same location in illustrations of that room from 1855 to 1866. Although no dust-shielding glass dome, often used over such portico clocks, was mentioned on the bill, one is shown in those pre-photo illustrations and mentioned in an 1849 inventory.
CONDITION: Numeral dial replaced or original Roman numerals missing with only scratched numerals remaining. Replacement movement.
REFERENCES: NA/MTA acct. 70467, voucher 4. "Inventory of Furniture &c in the President's House," January 21, 1849, Letters Received, Vol. 31, 3096, NA/OPBG.

VASES, near pair (page 92 and page 14)
William Ellis Tucker, Tucker & Hemphill, or Joseph Hemphill, Philadelphia, circa 1830–38
Porcelain
White House Acquisition Fund, 1988
1988.1629.1–2
.1—11 5/8 x 5 3/4 x 5 1/8 in. (29.5 x 14.6 x 13.0 cm.)

.2—11 3/8 x 5 5/8 x 5 1/4 in. (28.9 x 14.3 x 13.4 cm.)
MARKS: None.
NOTES: One (.1) is painted with an oval portrait of Andrew Jackson, with the black inscription—"Andrew Jackson / President of the United States"—in gilt wreath on the reverse. The mate (.2) is painted with an oval portrait of the Marquis de Lafayette, with an eagle holding an American flag on the reverse. In an attempt to manufacture American porcelain which could successfully compete with imports from Europe and the Far East, Tucker opened his Philadelphia factory in 1826. Trying to cope with financial burdens, he took in several partners, the last being Joseph Hemphill, who continued the firm's operations after Tucker's death in 1832.
PROVENANCE: Hirschl & Adler, New York; White House purchase.
REFERENCES: Philadelphia Museum of Art, Philadelphia: Three Centuries of American Art (Philadelphia: Philadelphia Museum of Art, 1976), 293–96. Alice Cooney Frelinghuysen, American Porcelain: 1770–1920 (New York: Metropolitan Museum of Art, 1989), 19, fig. 13. Alice Cooney Frelinghuysen, "Tucker Porcelain, Philadelphia, 1826–38," Antiques (April 1989): pl. XVII.

VASE (page 93)
France, circa 1825–30
Porcelain
White House Acquisition Fund, 1979
1979.1415.1
12 13/16 x 7 3/4 x 3 1/4 in. (32.5 x 19.7 x 8.3 cm.)
MARKS: None.
NOTES: Reserve portrait of Andrew Jackson entitled "Gen. Jackson," based on prints after a portrait by John Vanderlyn, circa 1819 (City Hall Collection, Charleston, South Carolina).
CONDITION: Repaired cracks in right handle; lower body staple-repaired and partially regilded.
Provenance: Herbert McKay; White House purchase with donated funds.
REFERENCES: James G. Barber, Andrew Jackson: A Portrait Study (Washington, D.C.: National Portrait Gallery, 1991), 67. Regine de Plinval de Guillebon, Porcelain of Paris, 1770–1850 (New York: Walker and Company, 1972).

PLATE (page 95)
Job & John Jackson, Burslem, England, 1831–43?
Transfer-printed earthenware
Gift of Mrs. Harry M. Ullman, 1961
1961.117.1
10 1/4 in. (26.0 cm.)
MARKS: Reverse—red printed "The / Presidents House / Washington." [script] above banner "JACKSONS WARRANTED."
NOTES: This image of the White House was taken from a popular engraving by Fenner, Sears & Co., after a drawing by H. Brown, as published by I. T. Hinton & Simpkin & Marshall, London, February 15, 1831. "An order of 'Job and John Jackson's Burslem Superior Ware' with 'very elegant American views'" was received by its New York agents by May 3, 1831. The firm produced at least forty American views in seven different colors. An example of this image printed in brown is also known, but it lacks the tall tree at lower left. The same image was used

by another Burslem manufacturer, Enoch Wood & Sons, for plates with a different border; the White House has a red soup plate, but examples in blue and black are known.
PROVENANCE: Rachel M. Ullman.
REFERENCES: Ellouise Baker Larsen, *American Historical Views on Staffordshire China*, 3d ed. (New York: Dover, 1975) nos. 400, 84.

WATER PITCHER (page 96)
G. C. Allen (working circa 1844–58), New York, 1858
Silver
Gift of Helen Singleton Green, 1913
1913.2856.1
12 1/2 x 8 1/2 x 4 1/2 in. (31.8 x 21.6 x 11.4 cm.); 39 oz. 2dwt.
MARKS: Underside—stamped thrice "G C ALLEN"
INSCRIPTIONS: Side engraved "Martin Van Buren / from / BFB December 3d 1811 / November 8th 1858."
NOTES: In his will, Benjamin Butler (attorney general 1833–38 in the Jackson and Van Buren administrations) directed that his executors "lay out at least three hundred dollars in the purchase of three pieces of plate, to be presented, in my name, to my early patron & friend Martin Van Buren ex-President of the United States, should he be living at the time of my death, and if not, then one piece to each of his three sons . . . Each of said pieces to be inscribed with the initials of my name, the date of my entering his office (December 3, 1811) and the date of my death." On December 13, 1858, Butler's son, Benjamin Jr. wrote that the pieces "are now being made, two pitchers and one ice bowl and will be very handsome." The other two pieces remain in the Van Buren family.
PROVENANCE: Estate of Benjamin F. Butler; bequest to President Martin Van Buren, 1858; to his son Abraham Van Buren; to his widow Angelica Singleton Van Buren; to her niece Helen Singleton Green.
REFERENCES: Carol E. Kohan, "Historic Furnishings Report for 'Lindenwald,'" National Park Service, 1986, nos. 11–12. Betty C. Monkman, "American Silver in the White House," *Washington Antiques Show Catalogue* (January 1980): 77, fig. 8.

CAMPAIGN TEXTILE (page 97)
Possibly American, circa 1840
Roller-printed cotton
Gift of John E. Walton, 1961
1961.163.1
20 x 25 1/2 in. (50.8 x 64.8 cm.)
MARKS: None.
NOTES: This brown-and-white cloth (detail shown) was produced to advertise William Henry Harrison's run for the presidency in 1840. His campaign against Martin Van Buren focused on his military successes against the Indians and his humble occupation as an Ohio farmer, a tactic seized on when his opponents derisively charged that the old warrior, actually born to the Virginia aristocracy, was better suited to retirement in a log cabin drinking hard cider. On this cloth these symbols—cabin and cider barrel—are joined by his portrait captioned "HARRISON AND REFORM."
CONDITION: Presumably cut from a larger piece of cloth.
PROVENANCE: John E. Walton.

REFERENCES: Florence Montgomery, *Printed Textiles: English and American Cottons and Linens, 1700–1850* (New York: Viking Press, 1970), fig. 402.

FRUIT BASKET (page 99)
France, circa 1820–30
Glazed and biscuit porcelain
Gift of Henrietta Bates McKee Brooke, Elliott McKee, Caroline Farnsworth, Frances Stone, and Fredrick H. Brooke, Jr., in memory of Mrs. Alfred E. Bates, 1957
1957.3754.1
16 3/8 x 16 1/4 x 8 1/2 in. (41.6 x 41.3 x 21.6 cm.)
MARKS: None.
NOTES: Believed to have been owned by President John Tyler. A circular basket with identical but gilded angel figures and a more elaborately molded basket and stand is marked by Marc Schoelcher, Paris, circa 1820.
CONDITION: Gilt wreath missing from one angel.
PROVENANCE: Sale of John Tyler effects; descended in purchaser's family to Mrs. Alfred E. Bates; gift of heirs.

PARTIAL TEA SERVICE (Waste Bowl, Cream Pitcher, Tongs) (page 100)
Robert Keyworth (1795–1856), Washington, D.C., circa 1835–51
Silver
U.S. Government purchase, circa 1837–51
1960.3724.1, 1960.3815.1, 1960.3816.1
Bowl—6 x 4 1/2 in. (15.2 x 11.4 cm.); 15 oz. 12 dwt.
Pitcher—7 1/2 x 6 1/2 x 4 in. (19.1 x 16.5 x 10.2 cm.); 10 oz. 1 dwt.
Tongs—6 1/2 in. (16.5 cm.); 3 oz. 2 dwt.
MARKS: Underside of foot of pitcher and bowl and interior of tongs handle—stamped R. KEYWORTH (boxed) twice on pitcher, four times in square around eagle on bowl.
INSCRIPTIONS: Side of pitcher and bowl and on handle arch of tongs "President's House."
NOTES: None of these pieces, singly or as a set, is mentioned on the extant vouchers for purchases from Keyworth, 1837–51. Since no sugar bowls, waste bowls, or compotes are listed in the 1849 inventory, it is likely that these pieces were acquired in the early 1850s. When the subject of White House furnishings, as a manifestation of the allegedly "regal" lifestyle of President Martin Van Buren, became a political issue in the 1840 election year, Keyworth, as "a respectable gold and silver smith of the City," was called in to certify that the dessert flatware at the White House was not solid gold, but silver gilt.
REFERENCES: Allman, "Furnishing the Executive Mansion," 153–54. Daughters of the American Revolution Museum, *Magnificent Intentions*, 38.

SIDE CHAIR (page 102)
J. & J. W. Meeks (circa 1836–55), New York, circa 1846 (John Meeks, 1801–75, and Joseph W. Meeks, 1806–78)
Walnut; walnut veneer / oak
U.S. Government purchase, 1846
1846.173.1
34 1/8 x 18 1/8 x 21 1/8 in. (86.7 x 46.0 x 53.7 cm.)
MARKS: None.

NOTES: The White House retains four from two sets of "12 B.W. [black walnut?] Gothic Chairs" purchased at $8 per chair from the Meeks firm, October 26, 1846. Purchased for the Cabinet Room (current Lincoln Bedroom), they appear in a 1856 illustration of the room and in images of the room during the Lincoln administration. Examples of this popular type of chair in other collections are made not only in walnut, but also in mahogany and oak, apparently by different cabinetmakers.
CONDITION: Replacement tacking rails; spring-filled seat; brackets or old reinforcing straps removed from inner face of rear legs; casters missing.
REFERENCES: NA/MTA acct. 96137, voucher 45. John N. Pearce, Lorraine W. Pearce, and Robert C. Smith, "The Meeks Family of Cabinetmakers," *Antiques* (April 1964): 414–20. John Pearce and Lorraine W. Pearce, "More on the Meeks Cabinetmakers," *Antiques* (July 1966): 69–73, figs. 7–8. "The President's House," *United States Magazine*, September 1856, 201. "President Lincoln and His Cabinet in Council at the White House," *Frank Leslie's Illustrated Newspaper*, March 30, 1861, 297, wood engraving. C. K. Stellwagen, Cabinet Room at the Presidents House (Cleveland: Western Reserve Historical Society, 1864), drawing. Francis B. Carpenter, *First Reading of the Emancipation Proclamation* (Washington, D.C.: U.S. Capitol, 1864), painting, and engravings after it by A. H. Ritchie, 1866.

SIDE CHAIR (page 103)
Charles A. Baudouine (1808–95), New York, circa 1845
Rosewood, ash; brass
U.S. Government purchase, 1845
1845.937.1
35 1/8 x 18 x 21 1/4 in. (89.5 x 45.7 x 54.0 cm.)
MARKS: None.
NOTES: The White House retains sixteen from among "42 Rosewood chairs in plush . . . $567" purchased on September 24, 1845, for the State Dining Room and described only three months later as "purple velvet chairs with carved rosewood frames . . . new and fresh." Chairs with matching legs appear in a photo of the Polk Cabinet taken in the State Dining Room. As early as 1849 these chairs were divided between the State and Family Dining Rooms. The rear of the plain rosewood lower back rail is enhanced with rosewood graining. The fan carving in the crux of the heart-shaped crest rail, a structurally under-supported ornament, appears in the earliest photos of the chairs (1870s) and is presumably an original element, although many were missing then.
CONDITION: The rosewood fans may be original, but mahogany ones, including the one seen here, are presumably replacements. Some were made circa 1961, when the chairs were brought together for use in the Treaty Room.
REFERENCES: NA/MTA acct. 93470, voucher 21. Diary of Elizabeth Dixon (Mrs. James E. Dixon), December 19, 1845, Papers of the Connecticut Historical Society.

POLK STATE CHINA SERVICE (page 104–105, 265)
Edouard Honoré (?–1855), Champroux, France, 1846
Porcelain
MARKS: Orange printed "ED HONORE / Bould Poissonniere No 6 / à PARIS / MANUFACTURE / à Champroux Allier / No / Prix".

NOTES: From "1 porcelain dinner and dessert service" purchased from Alexander T. Stewart & Co., New York, $979.40, March 23, 1846. The components were not itemized of the white dinner or green dessert services.
REFERENCES: NA/MTA acct. 93470 voucher 39. Klapthor, *Official White House China*, 68–72.

VEGETABLE DISH (page 104–105–see above)
Anonymous donation, 1987
1987.1624.1
3 3/8 x 11 x 9 1/4 in. (8.6 x 27.9 x 23.5 cm.)
MARKS: Underside—trace of printed mark; incuse "1901 / G."
CONDITION: Lid missing.
PROVENANCE: White House; Adam Weschler & Sons, Washington, D.C., December 4, 1987; White House purchase with donated funds.

SOUP PLATE (page 104–105–see above)
Gift of Mrs. Daniel Digges and Miss Mary Forsyth, 1909
1909.2883.1
9 3/4 in . (24.8 cm.)
MARKS: Reverse—trace of printed mark; incuse "1901 G."
PROVENANCE: White House; the donors' grandparents reportedly acquired this soup plate, a Polk dessert plate, and other White House pieces at 19th-century sales of White House property; Mrs. Daniel Carroll Digges and Miss Mary Forsyth.

FRUIT BASKET (page 104–105–see above)
Gift of Mrs. Jeanne Delattre-Seguy, 1964
1964.533.1
10 x 10 7/8 in. (25.4 x 27.6 cm.)
MARKS: Underside—trace of printed mark.
CONDITION: Missing section of the shaft was created using a Polk compote in the collection of the Smithsonian Institution as a model.
PROVENANCE: White House; Mrs. Jeanne Delattre-Seguy.

DESSERT PLATE (page 104–105–see above)
Gift of Mrs. Daniel Digges and Miss Mary Forsyth, 1909
909.2881.1
9 1/8 in. (23.2 cm.)
MARKS: Reverse—printed mark.
PROVENANCE: See soup plate.

CHAPTER 4

CENTER TABLE (page 110)
Attributed to John Henry Belter (1804–63), New York, circa 1861
Rosewood; marble; brass
U.S. Government purchase, 1861
1861.74.1
30 1/8 x 40 5/8 in. (76.8 x 103.2 cm.)
MARKS: None.
NOTES: Probably "1 Rich Rosewood Center Table 350.00" purchased from Philadelphia retailer Wm. Carryl in 1861. It was placed along with a ten-piece rosewood bedroom suite (see pages 130–131) in the principal

guest bedroom in the Lincoln White House. The carving of the apron is virtually identical (excepting leaves rather than flowers within the scrolls above the grape cluster) to that on a labeled Belter table at the Museum of the City of New York.
REFERENCES: NA/MTA acct. 140775, voucher 10. Marvin D. Schwartz et al., *The Furniture of John Henry Belter and the Rococo Revival* (New York: Dutton, 1981). Berry B. Tracy et al., *19th Century America: Furniture and Other Decorative Arts* (New York: Metropolitan Museum of Art, 1970), no. 119.

GOBLET (page 112)
Bohemia, circa 1840–60
Engraved and cut ruby-stained glass
Gift of the White House Historical Association, 1993
1993.1721.1
4 15/16 x 2 15/16 in. (12.5 x 7.5 cm.)
MARKS: None.
NOTES: The southwest view of "THE PRESIDENT'S HOUSE. / WASHINGTON" engraved on this goblet was derived from popular prints engraved from a drawing by H. Brown, circa 1831. Once thought to be of American manufacture, such non-lead glassware is now considered to have been made in Bohemia for the American market. A contemporary tankard engraved with the same scene also was donated to the White House in 1993.
CONDITION: Small scratches and two blemishes in the scene. Small chips with loss of stain along foot edges.
PROVENANCE: Wolfe's Auction, Cleveland, November 16, 1990, no. 354B. William Schwind Jr., Antiques, Yarmouth, Maine; purchased by the White House with donated funds.
REFERENCES: Jane Shadel Spillman, "Glasses with American Views," *Journal of Glass Studies* 19 (1977): 134–46, figs. 16–17 (front and rear of nearly identical goblet) and "Glasses Engraved with American Views," *Antiques* (July 1994): 78–85.

SIDE CHAIR (page 113)
American, circa 1850–60
Mahogany / ash; brass
Gift of Mr. and Mrs. Morton D. May, Jr., 1961
1961.140.2
36 1/4 x 18 1/2 x 18 1/2 in. (92.1 x 47.0 x 47.0 cm.)
MARKS: None.
NOTES: The crest rail of this Rococo Revival style chair is carved with a labeled bust of Zachary Taylor ("Z [backwards] TAYLOR") in general's uniform. Its mate bears a bust of Martin Van Buren ('M V BUREN"). They may be from a larger set, but no documentation of such exists.
CONDITION: "L" missing from "TAYLOR."
PROVENANCE: Reportedly descended in the family of John C. Breckenridge, Vice President under James Buchanan; David Stockwell, Inc.; White House purchase with donated funds.

GARDEN SETTEE (page 114)
Attributed to Janes, Beebe & Co., New York, circa 1852
Painted cast iron
U.S. Government purchase, 1852
1852.3833.1
37 1/2 x 64 x 19 1/2 in. (95.3 x 162.6 x 49.1 cm.)

MARKS: None.
NOTES: In August 1852, Janes, Beebe & Co. of New York replied to an inquiry from the chairman of the House Committee on Public Buildings and Grounds with a sketch and price quote for "60 of their strongest iron settees." As a result, Congress appropriated $840 for the acquisition of a "suitable number of iron settees to be placed in the public grounds at the Capitol and President's House," and the commissioner of public buildings ordered from that firm 60 settees to match the sketch, at the quoted price of $14 per settee delivered, each to be "5.2 in front and 4.4 in on the back of the seat . . . painted bronze green." The dimensions mentioned closely approximate the ten extant White House examples of the larger size of these "Gothic" style settees. Smaller matching settees appear in an 1856 photograph of the White House from the South Lawn by Titian Ramsey Peale (Division of Photographic History, National Museum of American History). Two such settees, painted a dark color, also stood on the South Portico between the Blue Room windows, as seen in an April 1861 photo and an 1862 Mathew Brady photo. Six of these (35 1/2 x 46 5/8 x 47 1/8 x 16 1/2 in.) remain at the White House. Many other American companies also produced this type of settee, patented in England 1846 and in the United States by 1848, some of which cast their names in the pieces, including James W. Carr of Richmond, Virginia, the Kramer Bros. of Dayton, Ohio, and the Chase Bros. of Boston. In its 1857 Descriptive Catalogue, the New York firm Hutchinson and Wickersham illustrated this form of "Gothic Settee" at $17 and $20.
REFERENCES: Letters Received, vol. 33, 3266, and Letters Sent 1851–53, 377. NA/OPBG. Tracy, *19th Century America*, no. 124. Ellen Marie Snyder, "Victory Over Nature: Victorian Cast-Iron Seating Furniture," *Winterthur Portfolio* 20, no. 4 (Winter 1985): 232. David A. Hanks, *Innovative Furniture in America from 1800 to the Present* (New York: Horizon Press, 1981), no. 57.

HOT WATER URN and SUGAR BOWL
(page 116)
Wood & Hughes, New York, circa 1858
Silver
Gift of the WHHA, 1973 and 1992
1973.982.1 and 1992.1719.1
Urn—17 x 10 3/4 x 10 3/4 in. (43.2 x 27.3 x 27.3 cm.); 83 oz. 10 dwt.
Sugar Bowl—9 3/4 x 8 1/4 x 5 1/2 in. (24.8 x 21.0 x 14.0 cm.); 24 oz. 17 dwt.
MARKS: Urn: None. Sugar: Underside of body—stamped "WOOD & HUGHES."
INSCRIPTIONS: Urn—rear center panel engraved "Millard Filmore [sic] / No2." Front panel on sugar engraved "Mrs. Millard Fillmore / (no7) / 1853."
NOTES: According to an 1858 article, when her husband became president in 1850, Abigail Fillmore was presented with a carriage and horses by a group of New York State friends. Since the gift was a perishable commodity and too grand for the Fillmores' style of private life after leaving the White House in 1853, it was sold to buy a set of silver as "a more imperishable record." Abigail Fillmore died only three weeks after leaving the

White House in 1853, so the silver reportedly "manufactured to order in New York and numbered from one to twelve," was probably not acquired by former President Millard Fillmore until his second marriage in 1858. The only other piece known is a kettle-on-stand acquired by the White House in 2013.

PROVENANCE: Millard Fillmore; to his widow Caroline Fillmore or his son Millard P. Fillmore; possibly sold to other family members. Urn—Graham Gallery, New York, N.Y.; White House purchase with donated funds, 1973. Sugar Bowl—descended in a collateral line of the Fillmore family; White House purchase with donated funds, 1992.

REFERENCES: *Harper's Weekly*, June 19, 1858. Herbert Collins, *Presidents on Wheels* (Washington, D.C.: Acropolis Books, 1971), 69–71. Monkman, "American Silver," 77, fig. 9.

COMPOTE *(page 117)*
Haughwout & Dailey, New York, 1853,
with French blank
Porcelain
Anonymous donation, 1986
1986.1591.11
5 1/2 x 11 1/8 in. (14.0 x 28.3 cm.)
MARKS: None.
NOTES: From the 269-piece Franklin Pierce state dinner service purchased from Haughwout & Dailey for $536.24 (no itemized costs for the types of pieces)—probably one of "2 low comports." For the New York Crystal Palace exposition opened by President Franklin Pierce in 1853, the firm prepared two special china designs to attract his patronage. An eagle-decorated design was not selected (although it was chosen in 1861 by Mary Todd Lincoln), but Pierce selected the other, with the removal from the escutcheon of the personalizing initial "P". "The designs are chiefly copies from works executed abroad. . . ." was the comment in a published description of the firm's exhibited goods.
PROVENANCE: White House; reportedly Mr. and Mrs. William Forsyth purchased china and glassware at White House sales in the second half of the 19th century; to their granddaughters Mary A. Forsyth and Mrs. Daniel Carroll Digges (who donated 12 pieces, including a plate and cup and saucer from this service, to the White House in 1909); sold circa 1919 to Anton Heitmuller; to his daughter Mrs. Ernest T. Love; sold to the donor.
REFERENCES: NA/MTA acct. 113810, voucher 4. Klapthor, *Official White House China*, 76–81.

WATER BOTTLE *(page 117)*
possibly Haughwout & Dailey, New York, 1853 or later reorder
Cut and engraved glass
U.S. Government purchase, 1853
1960.3874.1.8.1–7
6 7/8 x 5 1/4 in. (17.5 x 13.3 cm.)
MARKS: None.
NOTES: Believed to be from "4[Doz] Water Bottles" in a 778-piece glass service ordered for President Franklin Pierce from Haughwout & Dailey, New York, in 1853 at $801.87. Seven bottles, which sold for $38/dozen, are the

only pieces of the service to have remained continuously at the White House.
REFERENCES: NA/MTA acct. 113810, voucher 4. Spillman, *White House Glassware*, 59–63, fig. 23.

WINE GLASS *(page 117—see above)*
Possibly Haughwout & Dailey, New York, 1853, or later reorder
Cut and engraved glass
Gift of Mrs. Daniel Digges and Miss Mary Forsyth, 1909
1909.2969.1
4 5/8 x 2 1/8 in. (11.8 x 5.4 cm.)
NOTES: Believed to be from the 1853 Pierce glassware service.
PROVENANCE: White House; reportedly Mr. and Mrs. William Forsyth purchased china and glassware at White House sales in the second half of the 19th century; to their granddaughters Mary A. Forsyth and Mrs. Daniel Carroll Digges (who donated this and 11 other pieces, including three pieces of Pierce china, to the White House in 1909).

OVERMANTEL MIRROR *(page 118)*
L. R. Menger, New York, 1853
Gilded gesso on wood, mirror glass
U.S. Government purchase, 1853
1853.1047.2
102 x 72 x 6 3/4 in. (259.1 x 182.9 x 17.2 cm.)
MARKS: None.
NOTES: In 1853, L. R. Menger supplied a large quantity of gilded furnishings—18 mirror frames, 2 pier tables, and 14 window cornices. Illustrated in an 1856 engraving of the Green Room are this mirror and its mate ($110 each) and an extant pier table ($83), all of which remained there until 1902. For the Blue Room Menger supplied two elaborate mirrors ($330) also drawing on symbols of the United States and classical Rome—a pedimental U.S. shield on each, with legionary standards on the stiles of one, fasces with axes on the other.
REFERENCES: NA/MTA acct. 113810, voucher 8. "The President's House," *United States Magazine*, 200.

CENTERPIECE *(page 119)*
Haughwout & Dailey, New York, 1853,
with French blank
Porcelain and Parian ware
U.S. Government purchase, 1853
1853.2770.1
25 1/2 x 14 1/2 in. (64.8 x 36.8 cm.)
MARKS: None.
NOTES: "1 Centre Piece" from the 269-piece Franklin Pierce state dinner service purchased from Haughwout & Dailey for $536.24 (no itemized costs for the types of pieces) (see page 103). This is the only piece from the service that has remained continuously in the White House since its purchase. A similar piece was shown by the Minton factory at the London Crystal Palace exhibition of 1851. The Moorish "Alhambra" pattern that was not selected by President Pierce in 1853, but was chosen by Mrs. Lincoln in 1861, does appear on two matching pieces, one lacking its bowl, the latter having descended in

the family of Jacob Thompson, Secretary of the Interior for President James Buchanan.
CONDITION: Cover or surmounting ring or crown missing.
REFERENCES: NA/MTA acct. 113810, voucher 4. Klapthor, *Official White House China*, 76–81.

CENTER DIVAN, OTTOMAN, and ARMCHAIR *(page 120)*
Gottlieb Vollmer (1816–83), Philadelphia, 1859
Gilded ash / (divan only) white pine
U.S. Government purchase, 1860
1860.413.1, 1860.581.1, 1860.571.1
Divan—43 x 60 1/4 in. (109.2 x 153.0 cm.)
Ottoman—17 1/8 x 22 1/4 x 19 3/8 in. (43.5 x 56.5 x 49.2 cm.)
Chair—45 1/2 x 25 3/8 x 30 1/8 in. (115.6 x 64.4 x 76.5 cm.)
MARKS: None.
NOTES: One center divan ($285), one of "2 Ottomans" ($80), and one of "4 Arm chairs" ($360) from suite of gilded furniture—including two pairs of sofas ($185 and $165), four "Chairs without arms" ($260), and four reception chairs ($140), all in blue brocatelle with additional blue chintz covers ($89)—ordered in 1859, delivered in early 1860 for the Blue Room where the suite was used until 1902. All of the pieces are extant at the White House except one pair of sofas. Also on the 1860 bill was "1 Rich gilt ornament for Centre Divan 65.00," which shows in many Blue Room photos, but has been missing since 1902. A copy divan was given to President and Mrs. Eisenhower in 1955 by Mrs. Eisenhower's mother and sister as a house warming gift for their farm in Gettysburg, Pennsylvania (now the Eisenhower National Historic Site).
CONDITION: Regilded as early as 1873. Casters missing from divan.
REFERENCES: NA/MTA acct. 136728, voucher 20. Philadelphia Museum of Art, *Philadelphia*, 377–78.

CHIGAI-DANA *(page 122)*
Japan, circa 1854
Lacquered and gilded wood, white metal
Gift of the emperor of Japan
1860.338.1
25 7/8 x 26 3/4 x 14 7/8 in. (65.7 x 68.0 x 37.8 cm.)
MARKS: None.
NOTES: Believed to be from among the gifts brought back from Japan in 1855 by Commodore Matthew C. Perry.
CONDITION: Extensively conserved.
REFERENCES: Benjamin Brown French Journals, January 28, 1855, vol. 6, 73, LC. William Ferguson, *America by River and Rail* (London: James Nisbet and Co., 1856), 159. "White House Treasures," *New-York Tri-Weekly Tribune*, December 23, 1901. Gabrielle Marie Jacobs, "The Bric-a-Brac of the White House," *The Delineator* (August 1902). Dallas Finn, "Guests of the Nation: The Japanese Delegation to the Buchanan White House," *White House History* 12 (2003).

DESSERT WINE GLASS and COMPOTE *(page 124)*
Christian Dorflinger's Greenpoint Glass Works, Brooklyn, N.Y., 1861, or New England Glass Co., Cambridge,

Mass., 1865, or E. V. Haughwout, New York, 1866, or Hoare & Dailey/Corning Glass Works, Corning, N.Y., 1873, or T. G. Hawkes, Corning, N.Y., 1885
Cut and engraved glass
U.S. Government purchase, 1861–85
1861.3876.1.3.1–53 & .14.1–6
Wine Glass—4 5/8 x 2 1/4 in. (11.8 x 5.7 cm.)
Compote—8 1/4 x 9 1/4 in. (21.0 x 23.5 cm.)
MARKS: None.
NOTES: The compote is from "one sett of Glass Ware rich cut & eng'd with U.S. Coat of Arms: $1500" purchased in 1861 from A. P. Zimaudy, an unidentified retailer or glass company agent, or from the 1866 reorder from E. V. Haughwout, New York. The red-bowl wine glass may be from either of these or several reorders.
REFERENCES: NA/MTA acct. 141158, no voucher. Spillman, *White House Glassware*, 67–82, fig. 31.

DINNER PLATE (page 124)
E. V. Haughwout, New York, 1861, with blank by Haviland & Co., Limoges, France.
Porcelain
U.S. Government purchase, 1861
1861.3837.1.1.1–47
9 1/4 in. (23.5 cm.)
MARKS: None.
NOTES: From among "Ninety-Six Dinner Plates 9 inch" from "One fine Porcelain Dining Service of One Hundred, and ninety pieces . . . 190 . . . decorated Royal purple, and double gilt, with the Arms of the United States on each piece" purchased from E. V. Haughwout & Co., New York, in 1861. This design was not selected when shown by the predecessor firm, Haughwout & Dailey, to President Franklin Pierce in 1853. It was chosen by Mrs. Lincoln, however, with the original blue color replaced by the newly fashionable "solferino" or "royal purple."
REFERENCES: NA/MTA acct. 14151, voucher 14. Klapthor, *Official White House China*, 82–92.

BED (page 128)
American, circa 1861
Rosewood, rosewood veneer, and rosewood-grained black walnut / pine
U.S. Government purchase, 1861
1861.60.1
112 1/4 x 73 1/4 x 102 3/4 in. (285.1 x 186.1 x 261.0 cm.)
MARKS: Headboard, head posts, footboard, and side rails—stamped "29."
NOTES: An invoice dated May 29, 1861, from Wm H. Carryl and Bro., a Philadelphia retailer, includes "1 Rosewood Bedstead" as part of a 10-piece suite of furniture costing $800—see chest (page 131), chairs (page 130). Also on this invoice was "1 Rich Rosewood Centre Table," (see page 110). An 1862 newspaper article quite fully describes this bed in its guest room setting: "The guests' room, now known as the Prince of Wales' room since that youth occupied it [Albert Edward, Prince of Wales, later King Edward VII, was received at the White House on October 4, 1860], has been thoroughly ornamented and refurnished . . . The principal feature of the room is the bed. It is eight feet wide and nine feet long, of solid rosewood. The sides are cushioned and covered with purple figured satin. The head board is a piece of rich carved work, rising

eight feet above the bed, and having an oval top. Twenty feet above the floor, overspreading the whole, is a magnificent canopy, from the upper carved work of which the drapery hangs in elegant folds, being in the form of a crown, the front ornament upon which is the American shield with the Stars and Stripes carved thereon." (Daily Alta California, San Francisco, May 12, 1862). Although the crown with its patriotic shield ornamentation was certainly a special commission, it is unlikely that the bedstead itself was. Many examples of very similar beds are known to exist, some bearing makers' marks. This bed has no marks indicating its manufacturer. It was used by President and Mrs. Theodore Roosevelt and by President Woodrow Wilson. Grace Coolidge used it and crocheted a special coverlet for it (see page 205). In 1921 it was placed in the northwest bedroom, called the "Lincoln Bedroom," which had been the Prince of Wales bedroom in 1861. In 1945, President Truman had it moved to the southeast bedroom which had been Lincoln's office and which remains the "Lincoln Bedroom" today.
CONDITION: Flat rosewood surfaces refinished. Possibly original pine slats.
REFERENCES: NA/MTA acct. 140775, voucher 10.

ARMCHAIR and SIDE CHAIR (page 130)
American, circa 1861
Rosewood / brass and hardwood
U.S. Government purchase, 1861
1861.98.1, 1861.293.1
Armchair—42 1/2 x 23 7/8 x 28 1/2 in. (108.0 x 60.6 x 73.4 cm.)
Side Chair—35 1/2 x 18 1/2 x 17 in. (90.2 x 47.0 x 43.2 cm.)
MARKS: None.
NOTES: Probably part of "2 Arm Chairs" and "4 Wall Chairs" purchased from Philadelphia retailer Wm. Carryl & Bro. in 1861 for the principal guest bedroom in the Lincoln White House as part of an $800 suite (see pages 128 and 131). Although the second armchair is missing, possibly since 1903, the other side chairs have survived. These chairs are of the quality of the work of John Henry Belter (1804–63, active in New York 1844–63), whose name has become synonymous with elaborately carved Rococo Revival furniture. Although there are no known Belter design books or catalogs in which pattern names might have been recorded, chairs matching these have been referred to as the "Lincoln pattern," perhaps in response to the White House examples.
CONDITION: Original or old cake and springs retained in minimally invasive reupholstery. Original hardwood-wheel casters on the armchair only.
REFERENCES: NA/MTA acct. 140775, voucher 10. Schwartz, *Furniture of John Henry Belter*. Hanks, *Innovative Furniture*, nos. 36–37. David B. Warren et al., *American Decorative Arts and Paintings in the Bayou Bend Collection* (Houston: Museum of Fine Arts, 1998), F232-33.

CHEST OF DRAWERS (page 131 left)
American, circa 1861
Rosewood, rosewood veneer / mahogany, rosewood; marble; mirror glass; brass
U.S. Government purchase, 1861
1861.61.1

94 1/8 x 49 7/8 x 21 7/8 in. (239.1 x 126.7 x 55.6 cm.)
MARKS: None.
NOTES: Probably "1 bureau" purchased from Philadelphia retailer Wm. Carryl & Bro. in 1861 (see pages 128 and 130). A second rosewood bedroom suite was purchased from Washington upholster/paperhanger, John Alexander, in 1864; "1 Rosewood bureau & Glass" at $265 in this later suite might be this chest.
REFERENCES: NA/MTA acct. 140775, voucher 10, 1861. NA/MTA acct. 157178, voucher 7, 1864. Eileen and Richard Dubrow, *American Furniture of the 19th Century* (Atglen, Pa.: Schiffer Publishing Co., 1983), 148-154.

DRESSING CHEST OF DRAWERS (page 131 right)
American, circa 1865–70
Rosewood, rosewood veneer / oak, pine, tulip poplar; mirror glass; brass
U.S. Government purchase
1869.72.1
98 3/8 x 69 1/2 x 23 1/8 in. (249.9 x 176.5 x 58.7 cm.)
MARKS: None.
NOTES: This chest bears carved Renaissance Revival ornamentation that is more subdued than its ebonized or marquetry counterparts on French Second Empire furniture or some of its New York imitations. As with contemporary mirrored parlor consoles, the tall mirror was reflective of both the person dressing and the other furnishings in the room. Although its acquisition is undocumented, it was attributed presumably for stylistic reasons to the Grant administration in Mrs. Herbert Hoover's 1931 study of White House furnishings. It first appears in a room photograph in 1902.
CONDITION: Old, possibly original finish. Replacement veneer atop both tiers of drawers.
REFERENCES: Donald C. Peirce, *Art & Enterprise: American Decorative Art, 1825–1917* (Atlanta: High Museum of Art, 1999), no. 64.

DECANTER (page 134)
Christian Dorflinger's Greenpoint Glass Works, Brooklyn, New York, 1861, or E. V. Haughwout, New York, with blanks from Brooklyn Flint Glass Works, 1866
Cut and engraved glass
U.S. Government purchase, 1861–66
1861.3876.1.17.1
10 1/2 x 4 in. (26.7 x 10.2 cm.)
MARKS: None.
NOTES: (See page 124) E. V. Haughwout of New York was commissioned in 1865 to provide replacements for lost or broken White House silver and china of the first Lincoln pattern. "A set of glass such as Mrs. Patterson [Andrew Johnson's daughter] may select" proved to be a reorder of the Lincoln glassware (534 pieces at $2,596), the 17 itemized forms including 12 each of pint and quart decanters. The one example of each size which has survived at the White House may be from that reorder or from the non-itemized original order purchased in 1861.
REFERENCES: NA/MTA acct. 141158, no voucher; acct. 157178, voucher 18. Spillman, *White House Glassware*, 67–82, fig. 25.

FRUIT BASKET *(page 134)*
E. V. Haughwout, New York, with blanks from Haviland & Co., Limoges, France, 1861 or 1866
Porcelain
U.S. Government purchase, 1861 or 1866
1861.3837.1.19.1-4
7 7/8 x 9 1/2 in. (20.1 x 24.1 cm.)
MARKS: None.
NOTES: (See page 126.) On January 17, 1866, an order was placed with E. V. Haughwout, New York, for "rich China Ware with the Arms and Crests of the U.S. to replace broken and lost of the Solferine set," the first Lincoln state china service. The 331 pieces ordered included "2 round baskets," the original set having had eight. Two types of circular baskets have survived, each of a number, however, that prevents an attribution of either type specifically to one order.
REFERENCES: NA/MTA acct. 14151, voucher 14; acct. 15178, voucher 18. Klapthor, *Official White House China*, 82–92.

SIDE TABLE *(page 137)*
Probably A. & H. Jenkins (1837–57), Baltimore, circa 1853 (Anthony Hearn Jenkins, circa 1805–84, and Henry Worthington Jenkins, 1814–78)
Walnut / walnut, pine
U.S. Government purchase
1960.455.1
35 3/8 x 58 3/8 x 24 in. (89.8 x 148.3 x 61.0 cm.)
MARKS: None.
NOTES: From a set of four, one of which appears in the earliest photos of the State Dining Room (1870s). In Mrs. Herbert Hoover's 1931 study of surviving White House furnishings, they were attributed to acquisition in the late 1860s during the Andrew Johnson administration. For the 1853 redecoration of the public rooms, however, the Jenkins brothers had provided a dining table, two walnut sideboards, and "4 walnut side tables @ $60" each, presumably for the State Dining Room since they also repaired and reupholstered 30 chairs used in that room. Contemporary with mirrors bearing the shield of the United States placed in the Green Room and Blue Room, those 1853 side tables may be the extant set of four which also bear the U.S. shield. These tables remained in the State Dining Room until 1902. The Jenkins family made furniture in Baltimore for more than one hundred years.
CONDITION: Modern plywood added under top.
REFERENCES: NA/MTA acct. 113810, voucher 10. Gregory R. Weidman, *Furniture in Maryland, 1700–1840* (Baltimore: Maryland Historical Society, 1984), nos. 72, 293.

CHAPTER 5

DINNER PLATTER *(page 142)*
Haviland & Co., Limoges, France, 1880, from a design by Theodore Russell Davis (1840–94)
Porcelain
U.S. Government purchase, 1880
1880.3840.1.1-2
20 x 12 7/8 in. (50.8 x 32.7 cm.)

MARKS: Reverse—orange printed "FABRIQUE PAR / HAVILAND & Co. / d'apres les dessins / DE"; black signature "Theo: R. Davis"; brown "LIMOGES / HAVILAND & Co." over brown "1879" through entwined red, white, and blue pennant; green double-understruck "H&C°."
NOTES: In 1879 Haviland & Co. was commissioned to execute a state service for President and Mrs. Rutherford B. Hayes by a contract of February 20. After a chance meeting with Mrs. Hayes in the White House conservatory, Theodore R. Davis, an artist for *Harper's Weekly*, who advocated a service designed with American flora and fauna, was asked to assume direction of the designing. From his drawings, etchings were produced for transfer of the outlines to the ware; the White House has a turkey platter etching by Félix Bracquemond (1833–1914). Basic coloring was applied by chromolithographic and decalcomania processes and then shaded by decorators. In response to his unusual designs for new dish shapes and their decoration, the contract was renegotiated and the service was delivered in two parts on June 30 and December 29, 1880. In the second shipment were the four types and sizes of platters, two of each type, all with rolled corners. The dinner platters (both extant) were described as painted with "a magnificent wild turkey, who struts through the light snow, upon which are seen delicate reflections from his rich-colored plumage . . . [on] this most perfectly American dish."
REFERENCES: NA/MTA acct. 225211, voucher 56. Klapthor, *Official White House China*, 102–21, appendices I–II, 201–89, including a full reprinting of a Haviland booklet of the designs.

CENTER TABLE *(page 144)*
American, circa 1875–85
Black walnut, marquetry
U.S. Government purchase
1881.297.1
28 1/2 x 47 x 28 1/2 in. (72.4 x 119.4 x 72.4 cm.)
MARKS: None.
NOTES: This table first appears in room photographs of the Green Room after 1891, but it may have been acquired during the redecoration of the room begun by Lucretia Garfield and completed for President Chester Arthur, circa 1881–82. Many elaborate marquetry panels, such as the center of the top of this table, seem to have been imported from Paris.
REFERENCES: Katherine S. Howe, et al., *Herter Brothers: Furniture and Interiors for a Gilded Age* (New York: Abrams, 1994), 137–38, 142–43.

SOFA and ARMCHAIR *(page 146)*
Pottier & Stymus Manufacturing Co., New York, 1869
Black walnut / ash; brass
U.S. Government purchase, 1869
1869.212.1, 1869.197.1
Sofa—45 3/8 x 78 x 32 in. (115.2 x 198.1 x 81.3 cm.)
Chair—38 x 28 1/2 x 25 1/2 in. (96.5 x 72.4 x 64.8 cm.)
MARKS: Sofa—top of one arm—stamped "1838 US." Armchair—none.
NOTES: The "Sofa in Tapestry" ($235) and one of a pair of armchairs (the mate not extant) at $180 from a suite of "Walnut French" furniture purchased for the Cabinet

Room (then on the second floor of the White House) in 1869 for President Ulysses S. Grant. Also extant at the White House are the conference table (page 147), two tub chairs, and the revolving desk chair, with the secretary desk at the Rutherford B. Hayes Presidential Center, Fremont, Ohio.
CONDITION: Two non-original casters on the sofa, model for replacements on sofa and chair.
REFERENCES: NA/MTA acct. 180754, voucher 2.

CONFERENCE TABLE *(page 147)*
Pottier & Stymus Manufacturing Co., New York, 1869
Walnut / mahogany, tulip poplar; leather
U.S. Government purchase, 1869
1869.209.1
28 3/4 x 96 1/2 x 48 in. (73.0 x 245.1 x 121.9 cm.)
MARKS: None.
NOTES: One "table for 8 persons" from a suite of furniture (see page 146) purchased for the Cabinet Room in 1869. Eight locking drawers were available to the President and the seven Cabinet officers as of 1869 (State, War, Treasury, Navy, Interior, Attorney General, and Postmaster General). The table continued to be used by the Cabinet until 1902 when a new Cabinet Room was provided in the newly constructed Executive Office Building (West Wing). In 1961, Mrs. Kennedy reassembled the surviving pieces from the suite—this table, the sofa, and four chairs in that same second floor room, renamed the Treaty Room, which had served as the Cabinet Room from 1865 to 1902. The historic documents which have been signed on this table include: 1. The Peace Protocol ending hostilities of the Spanish-American War, August 12, 1898, witnessed by President William McKinley in the Cabinet Room. 2. The Pact of Paris (Kellogg-Briand Peace Pact), 1929, signed by President Calvin Coolidge in the East Room. 3. Arms and nuclear testing treaties with the Soviet Union signed in the East Room by Presidents Nixon (1972), Ford (1976), Reagan (1987), and Bush (1990). 4. Treaties with former Soviet republics (Russia, Ukraine, Kazakhstan), 1992, signed by President George Bush in the East Room. 5. Middle East peace documents including: Egyptian-Israeli Peace Treaty, 1979, on the North Lawn, witnessed by President Jimmy Carter; and The Israel-Palestinian Declaration of Principles, 1993, on the South Lawn, hosted by President Bill Clinton.
CONDITION: Remains of call button system at one end.
REFERENCES: NA/MTA acct. 180754, voucher 2.

MANTEL CLOCK *(page 148)*
France, circa 1869
Marble; malachite/enameled iron, brass spring-driven movement; barometer, thermometer, perpetual calendar mechanism
U.S. Government purchase, 1869
1869.3742.1
23 1/2 x 26 1/4 x 10 1/2 in. (59.7 x 61.6 x 26.7 cm.)
MARKS: Dial—inscribed "BROWNE & SPAULDING / NEW-YORK"; movement plates—stamped "3186."
NOTES: "1 Marble and Malachite French Clock, Day, week, month change of moon, etc. $500" was purchased from New York retailers Browne & Spaulding, November 9, 1869. It was accompanied by "1 pair of bronze

vases Naids" ($45) and "1 pair of side pieces for clock" ($75). The clock and kylix-form cups which may have been the "side pieces" were used on the mantel in the Cabinet Room until 1902. Neither the side pieces nor the vases are extant at the White House. Other French mantel clocks purchased in 1869 from Browne & Spaulding have movements marked by the two noted Montbeliard firms—Vincenti and S. Marti.
REFERENCES: NA/MTA acct. 176595, voucher 59.

CENTER TABLE (page 150)
Herter Brothers, New York, circa 1875
Rosewood / black walnut; satinwood, holly, and boxwood; brass
U.S. Government purchase, 1875
1875.78.1
30 1/2 x 53 x 32 3/4 in. (77.5 x 134.6 x 83.2 cm.)
MARKS: Underside of top—remains of printed paper label (engraving of the company building) / HERTER BROTHERS, / Furniture & Decorations / _____ FURNITURE, / _____ BROADWAY, / _____ STREETS / _____ [N]EW YORK."
NOTES: "1 Rich rosewood inlaid & gilt centre table"— grouped with two pairs of gilded chairs at a cost of $450 in a December 23, 1875, acquisition from Herter Brothers of thirteen pieces of furniture for the Red Room. A gaping-mouth version of the lion motif appeared on one pair of the gilded chairs (one extant—page 151) and on four pieces, a pair of sofas and a pair of armchairs from an eight-piece rosewood suite, probably sold in 1903.
CONDITION: Replacement urn on stretcher crossing.
REFERENCES: NA/MTA acct. 202494, voucher 36. Katherine S. Howe, Herter Brothers, figs. 96 and 110.

ARMCHAIR (page 151)
Herter Brothers, New York, circa 1875
Gilded ash / cherry; brass
U.S. Government purchase, 1875
1875.2656.1
30 1/2 x 26 1/8 x 23 1/4 in. (77.5 x 66.4 x 59.1 cm.)
MARKS: Left seat rail—stamped "3209" (Herter serial number).
NOTES: One of "2 all gilt Lady's chairs, one covered in blue lampas, and one with red and gold Japanese brocade" purchased in 1875, obviously made to complement the labeled center table (page 150) and a rosewood suite of two settees and six chairs, all placed in the Red Room. A matching suite with "3000" numbers was purchased for the Goodwin mansion in Hartford in 1874, now at the Wadsworth Atheneum.
CONDITION: Partially regilded. Mate destroyed 1926.
REFERENCES: NA/MTA acct. 202494, voucher 36. Howe, Herter Brothers, 51.

FIRE SCREEN (page 152)
Edward A. Richter, Vienna, Austria, circa 1876
Gilded wood, glass; embroidery (silk, wool, and cotton) and beadwork (glass and metal) on perforated cardboard
Gift of Edward A. Richter, 1877
1877.433.1
56 1/2 x 31 1/4 x 23 5/16 in. (143.5 x 79.4 x 59.2 cm.)

MARKS: Rear of crest rail—brass plaque engraved "Edward A. Richter / VIENNA / Centennial Exhibition, 1876"; cardboard—trace of seal " . . . ers / London."
NOTES: The Austrian minister to the United States, Count Ladislas Hoyoz, wrote to Secretary of State Hamilton Fish on February 1, 1877: "Mr. Richter of Vienna, manufacturer of embroideries, who has taken part in the Exhibition of Philadelphia applied some time ago to this Legation with the view to be authorized to present His excellency the President of the Unites States with an embroidered screen and a portfolio on a stand, both destined for the White house [sic] . . . it is understood that General Grant accepts Mr. Richter's presents only under the condition that they have to belong to the furniture of the Executive Mansion."
REFERENCES: General Records Department of State, Notes, Austria, vol. 7, January 1, 1875–May 31, 1880, NA/RG 59. Robert C. Post, ed., 1876: A Centennial Exhibition (Washington, D.C.: Smithsonian Institution, 1976).

TOBACCO BOX (page 152)
George B. Sharp (working circa 1844–74), Philadelphia, circa 1869
Silver
Gift of the White House Historical Association, 1973
1973.1034.1
9/16 x 2 3/4 x 13/16 in. (1.4 x 7.0 x 2.1 cm.); 1 oz. 10 dwt.
MARKS: Interior bottom of longer compartment— stamped "S" flanked by opposed lions passant.
INSCRIPTIONS: Hinged lids engraved "President / U.S. Grant. / from / A.E. Borie."
NOTES: Small top compartment contains lighter wheel with external knob; light gold wash on interior of larger tobacco compartment.
PROVENANCE: Gift from Adolph E. Borie (1809–80), Philadelphia financier and first secretary of the navy in the Grant Cabinet (1869), to President Ulysses S. Grant; Sotheby Parke-Bernet, 3571, November 15–17, 1973, no. 658; White House purchase with donated funds.
REFERENCES: Monkman, "American Silver," 78, fig. 10. Quimby, American Silver, 445–46.

CENTERPIECE (page 153)
Gorham Mfg. Co., Providence, R.I., 1871
Silver, mirror glass
Possibly a gift of Gorham Mfg. Co., 1876
1876.1409.1
34 x 44 1/2 x 19 in. (86.4 x 113.0 x 48.3 cm.); boat—128 oz. 7 dwt.
MARKS: Stern of boat—stamped lion passant (octagon), anchor (boxed), "G" (octagon) / "STERLING / D."
NOTES: Called "Hiawatha's Boat" for its depiction of the title character of Henry Wadsworth Longfellow's poem, The Song of Hiawatha, sailing on the water of a mirrored plateau. It was selected by Mrs. Grant at the Centennial Exposition in Philadelphia in 1876; there is no record of its purchase by the government, so it may have been donated by the manufacturer. The boat is separate from the plateau; some of the plateau ornaments are removable as well—the two lily pads and thirteen numbered shoreline ornaments, including two salamanders and one copper turtle. In relief on the opposite lengths of the frame are two lines of the poem: "SWIFT OR SLOW AT

WILL HE GLIDED VEERED TO RIGHT OR LEFT AT PLEASURE" (chap. VII, "Hiawatha's Sailing") and "ALL ALONE WENT HIAWATHA THROUGH THE CLEAR TRANSPARENT WATER" (chap. VIII, "Hiawatha's Fishing").
CONDITION: Replacement shield and head feathers.
REFERENCES: Julia Dent Grant, The Personal Memoirs of Julia Dent Grant, John Y. Simon, ed. (New York: Putnam's, 1975), 189. Henry Wadsworth Longfellow, The Complete Poetical Works of Longfellow (Boston, Houghton Mifflin, 1963), 129–30. "The White House Porcelain Service for State Dinners," The Ladies' Home Journal (July 1889), 4. Monkman, "American Silver," 78, fig. 1. Charles H. Carpenter, Jr., Gorham Silver (New York: Dodd, Mead & Co., 1982), 58–62. Post, 1876: A Centennial Exhibition, 121.

COMPOTE, CAKE STAND, and DINNER PLATE (page 154)
Haviland & Co., Limoges, France, 1869–70 and 1874
Porcelain
U.S. Government purchase, 1870 and 1874
1870.3839.8.1-5, 6.1-3, and 1.1-15
Compote—5 3/4 x 8 7/8 in. (14.6 x 22.5 cm.)
Cake Stand—3 x 9 in. (7.6 x 22.9 cm.)
Plate—9 3/8 in. (23.8 cm.)
MARKS: Compote and stand foot underside—red printed "FABRIQUE PAR HAVILAND & CO. / POUR / J.W. BOTELER & BRO. / WASHINGTON." Plate—None.
NOTES: In 1869, "one State Dinner service 587 pieces with flowers and Coats-of-Arms," at $3,000, was ordered by President and Mrs. Ulysses S. Grant from Washington retailer J. W. Boteler & Bro. Although the components of the set, received in February 1870, were not specified, this unmarked plate may be from that original order. In preparation for the wedding of their daughter Nellie in May 1874, Mrs. Grant ordered supplemental pieces from Boteler in 1873: 160 plates in three sizes, 115 sets of cups and saucers in three sizes, and 6 each of four types of serving stands. This compote and stand are presumably from 2 types of "compotes" at $51.30 and $58.80 for 6 of each. All of the extant standing pieces bear the printed Haviland/Boteler mark, which also appeared on an accompanying reorder of pieces in the Lincoln "royal purple" pattern.
REFERENCES: NA/MTA acct. 176596, voucher 15; acct. 192686, voucher 29. Klapthor, Official White House China, 93–99.

SIDE CHAIR (page 155)
Probably New York, circa 1873–77
Maple / ash; brass
Gift of the White House Historical Association, 1995
1995.1746.4
33 1/16 x 19 1/2 x 20 1/4 in. (84.0 x 49.5 x 51.4 cm.)
MARKS: Caster plate—stamped "PAT. MAY 20 73."
NOTES: After its display at the Philadelphia Centennial Exposition in 1876, Japanese bamboo furniture grew in popularity in the United States as did its American imitations. An early example of such faux bamboo furniture is a suite (chairs, bed, bedside stand, wash stand, dressing chest, tall chest, wardrobe, center table, and window cornices) used in the bedroom occupied by President and

Mrs. Rutherford B. Hayes and by President and Mrs. James A. Garfield. Of undocumented acquisition, the suite may have come to the White House during the Grant administration. This chair, from one of two very similar pairs believed to be from that suite and retrieved for the White House in 1995, were reportedly given to A. E. Kennedy (White House decorative work circa 1893–1904) by President Grover Cleveland. Other parts of the suite were probably sold at auction in 1903.
CONDITION: Some replacement finials/drops.
PROVENANCE: White House, gift to A. E. Kennedy; descended to granddaughter Margaret W. Queen; sold at Tim Gordon Auctions, Frederick, Md., June 17, 1995; White House purchase with donated funds.
REFERENCES: Austine Snead ("Miss Grundy"), "How Presidents Live," *Boston Herald*, March 28, 1878. Tracy, *19th Century America*, no. 228. Peirce, *Art & Enterprise*, no. 120.

CANDELABRUM *(page 156)*
Probably European, circa 1880
Gilded brass
U.S. Government purchase, 1880
1880.3806.3
30 15/16 x 16 in. (78.6 x 40.6 cm.)
MARKS: Plates inside base—stamped "G T(?)."
NOTES: From one of two pairs purchased as "4 Gilt Candelabra at $125 / For State Dining Table of Executive Mansion 500.00" from Tiffany & Co., New York, October 8, 1880. These were ordered on June 30 from photographs and drawings submitted.
REFERENCES: Letters Sent, vol. 2, 316, NA/OPBG; NA/MTA acct. 224650, voucher 1. "White House Porcelain, " *Ladies' Home Journal*, 4.

DINNER SERVICE *(page 157)*
Haviland & Co., Limoges, France, 1880, from designs by Theodore Russell Davis (1840–94)
Porcelain
U.S. Government purchase, 1880
1880.3840.2.1-46, .3.1-2, .4.1-27, .13.1-32, .10.1-49, .9.1-42, .11.1-40, .6.1-34, .7.1-21, .8.1-69, .16.1-8, .17.1-15, .14.1-8, .15.1-28
Dinner Plate—10 1/8 in. (25.7 cm.); "Big Horn"
Game Platter—18 x 11 1/2 in. (45.7 x 29.2 cm.); "On Chesapeake Bay"
Game Plate—9 in. (22.9 cm.); "Ruffed Grouse"
Ice Cream Plate—6 3/4 x 7 1/2 in. (17.2 x 19.0 cm.)
Cheese Plate—8 3/4 in. (22.2 cm.)
Oyster Plate—8 3/4 in. (22.2 cm.)
Salad Plate—7 1/4 in. (18.4 cm.)
Fish Plate—8 3/8 in. (21.2 cm.); "Sheep's Head"
Soup Plate—9 in. (22.9 cm.); "Mountain Laurel"
Dessert/Fruit Plate—9 1/2 x 8 1/4 in. (24.1 x 20.9 cm.); "Ohio Golden Rod"
Demitasse Cup—2 1/2 x 3 x 1 7/8 in. (6.4 x 7.6 x 4.8 cm.)
Demitasse Saucer—4 3/4 in. (12.1 cm.)
Tea Cup—2 1/8 x 4 1/2 x 2 3/4 in. (5.4 x 11.4 x 7.0 cm.)
Tea Saucer—5 1/2 in. (14.0 cm.)
MARKS: See catalog entry for dinner platter, page 292.
NOTES: See catalog entry for dinner platter, page 292. The complexity of the dish shapes and decoration designed by Theodore Davis for the Rutherford B. Hayes state service led to the renegotiation of the origi-

nal 1879 contract with Haviland & Co. so that the service was delivered in two parts on June 30 and December 29, 1880. The White House received examples of all twelve designs for four plate types (dinner, game, fish, dessert/fruit), but only nine of twelve soup plate designs. Pieces of the Hayes designs and forms were made for public sale as well, but on these the dated pennant mark unique to the White House service was replaced by a blue 1880 patent mark. Two small reorders in 1884 (3 plates) and 1886 (22 plates) would have been some of the patent examples, some of which have survived in the White House collection.
REFERENCES: NA/MTA acct. 225211, voucher 56. Klapthor, *Official White House China*, 102–21, appendices I–II, 201–89.

PARTNER'S DESK *(page 159)*
William Evenden, Royal Naval Dockyard at Chatham, England, probably from a design by Morant, Boyd & Blanford, London, 1880; kneehole panel by Rudolph Bauss, Washington, D.C., 1945
White oak, mahogany / white oak, teak
Gift of Queen Victoria, 1880
1880.177.1
29 x 72 x 48 in. (73.7 x 182.9 x 121.9 cm.)
MARKS: Underside on the of all exterior drawer fronts—stamped "MORANT BOYD & BLANFORD / 91 NEW BOND STREET"; lock plates—stamped company armorial mark "BY ROYAL / LETTERS PATENT / FOUR LEVERS / SAFETY LOCK / COMYN CHINC & Co."
INSCRIPTIONS: "H.M.S. 'Resolute', forming part of the expedition sent in search of Sir John Franklin in 1852, was abandoned in Latitude 74°41' N. Longitude 101°22' W. on 15th May 1854. She was discovered and extricated in September 1855, in Latitude 67° N. by Captain Buddington of the United States Whaler 'George Henry'. The ship was purchased, fitted out and sent to England, as a gift to Her Majesty Queen Victoria by the President and People of the United States, as a token of goodwill & friendship. This table was made from her timbers when she was broken up, and is presented by the Queen of Great Britain & Ireland, to the President of the United States, as a memorial of the courtesy and loving kindness which dictated the offer of the gift of the 'Resolute.'"
NOTES: Called the "Resolute desk," this double-pedestal desk was made from the oak timbers of the British ship HMS *Resolute* as a gift to President Rutherford B. Hayes from Queen Victoria in 1880. The desk was used in the President's Office on the second floor of the Residence, 1880–1902, and in the President's Study, 1902–48. President Franklin D. Roosevelt requested that one side of the kneehole be fitted with a panel carved with the presidential coat-of-arms, which was installed in 1945 before the eagle was redirected toward the olive branch in President Harry S. Truman's 1945 redefinition of the Presidential Seal. Used in the Broadcast Room on the Ground Floor 1952–61, it was first used in the Oval Office by President John F. Kennedy, 1961–63. On off-site exhibit 1964–77, it has been used again in the Oval Office 1977–89 (Carter, Reagan) and 1993–present (Clinton). A proposal for the desk, not as

actually executed, was depicted in *Frank Leslie's Illustrated Newspaper* in 1880 while a description from the *Chatham* (England) *News* reported that it was made by William Evenden, "a skilled wood carver and joiner, employed in Chatham Dockyard." Another desk was made from the timbers for the wife of American merchant Henry Grinnell, who financed two expeditions to search for John Franklin (Whaling Museum, New Bedford, Mass.).
CONDITION: A plinth, installed in 1961 to elevate the kneehole, was replaced in 1986.
REFERENCES: *Chatham* (England) *News*, September 13, 1879, cited in the *Chatham, Rochester, and Gillingham News*, January 28, 1911. *Frank Leslie's Illustrated Newspaper*, December 11, 1880. Rutherford B. Hayes to George Bancroft, November 23, 1880, in *Hayes Historical Journal*, 1, no. 3 (Spring 1977): 221. Rosamund Allwood, "Luxury Furniture Makers of the Victorian Period," *Antique Collecting* (June 1988): 5.

TEAPOT *(page 160)*
Dominick & Haff, New York, 1881
Silver, ebony
U.S. Government purchase, 1881
1881.3888.1
4 5/8 x 11 3/8 x 5 1/4 in. (11.8 x 28.9 x 13.3 cm.); 20 oz. 8 dwt.
MARKS: Underside—stamped "115 / STERLING"; box-circle-diamond with "925" in box and "1881" arranged in points; "M.W. GALT BRO. & CO."
INSCRIPTIONS: Side engraved "President's House / 1881."
NOTES: On March 22, 1881, Washington retailer M. W. Galt Bro. & Co. sent to Lucretia Garfield a small silver teapot and a drawing of a larger matching one. The larger one was ordered that day at $100.
REFERENCES: Letters Received, 96, March 23, 1881, NA/OPBG. Allman, "Furnishing the Executive Mansion," 153–54. Charles L. Venable, *Silver in America, 1840–1940: A Century of Splendor* (New York: Abrams, 1995), 318.

SOFA *(page 164)*
American, circa 1881
Painted wood / oak; brass
Gift of Lenox R. Lohr, 1962
1962.228.1
40 x 70 x 28 in. (101.6 x 177.8 x 71.1 cm.)
MARKS: None.
NOTES: Colonel A. F. Rockwell, officer in charge of Public Buildings & Grounds, reported that the East Room had received new furniture and window hangings in 1881. Pre-1887 photos of the room show two suites of seat furniture, each probably consisting of two sofas, two corner chairs, four arm chairs, and six side chairs, which were supplied by W. B. Moses, Washington, D.C. An armchair from the other suite was also received in the same 1962 donation.
CONDITION: Later black paint.
PROVENANCE: White House; sold 1903 to a Washington furniture dealer; purchased circa 1930 by Lenox Lohr.
REFERENCES: "The White House Refurnished," *Cincinnati Gazette*, December 1881. Report of Col. A. F.

Rockwell, U.S.A., Officer in Charge, for the Fiscal Year Ending June 30, 1882.

VASE (page 169 upper)
Chinese, circa 1883
Porcelain
U.S. Government purchase, 1883
1883.1511.1
36 1/2 x 13 5/8 in. (92.7 x 34.6 cm.)
MARKS: None.
NOTES: When Associated Artists redecorated parts of the White House for President Chester Arthur, 1882–84, among the furnishings provided by Louis C. Tiffany & Co. for the Red Room in July 1883 was "1 Pr. Large Satsuma vases" at $210 with "2 Pedestals for vases" at $50. These Chinese Medallion style vases, inexplicably called by the name of Japanese ware which had become increasingly fashionable after its exhibition at the 1876 Philadelphia Exposition, were used in the Red Room only briefly before being moved to the Green Room, circa 1884–85.
CONDITION: The mate to this vase has been repaired.
REFERENCES: NA/MTA acct. 240684, voucher 19.

VASE (page 169 lower)
American, circa 1884
Earthenware
U.S. Government purchase, 1884
1884.1510.1
40 3/4 x 11 3/4 in. (103.5 x 29.9 cm.)
MARKS: None.
NOTES: In July 1884, Louis C. Tiffany & Co. provided "2 Vases" at $150, which may have been the pair for which replacements were shipped but a few months later in December. This vase "Captive Love" (*L'Amour Captif*—painted on underside) or an identical example shows in a photograph of the Tiffany store at Union Square in New York. With its mate, "The Invigorating Fountain" (*La Fontaine Enivrante*), they first appear in an 1885 photograph of the Red Room replacing a pair of large oriental vases supplied by Tiffany in 1883. The decoration of these vases, of a form inspired by "rouleau" vases made at Sévres in the early 19th century, was probably copied from French examples by an American craftsman. Curiously, turn-of-the-century articles correctly attribute their acquisition to President Chester Arthur, but at a tenfold inflated price of $1,500.
REFERENCES: NA/MTA acct. 24332, voucher 5. Letters Received, Vol. 452, December 13, 1884, NA/OPBG. Thompson, "Art in the White House," 144. Waldon Fawcett, "Rare Bric-a-Brac at the White House," *The Ledger Monthly* (March 1902).

PEPPER SHAKER (page 170)
Adams & Shaw Co., New York, for Tiffany & Co., circa 1882
Silver electroplate
U.S. Government purchase, 1882
1882.3893.1
3 13/16 x 1 1/2 in. (9.7 x 3.8 cm.)
MARKS: Underside of foot—stamped "4073 / TIFFANY & Co / MAKERS / AS [flanking brackets overlaid "CO"] / SILVER-SOLDERED 13 / F."

NOTES: From "6 Pepper Boxes," $6 each (3 extant), part of a large assortment of silver tableware purchased from Tiffany & Co., May 16, 1882. Tiffany bought plated ware from Adams & Shaw Co., from 1874 until it absorbed that firm, circa 1885.
REFERENCES: For all on page 170: NA/MTA acct. 223637, voucher 45. Charles H. Carpenter, Jr., with Mary Grace Carpenter, *Tiffany Silver* (New York: Dodd, Mead & Co., 1978)

COMPOTE (page 170—see above)
Tiffany & Co., New York, circa 1882
Gilded silver electroplate
U.S. Government purchase, 1882
1882.3895.1
6 x 9 7/8 in. (15.2 x 25.1 cm.)
MARKS: Underside—stamped "3056 / TIFFANY & Co / MAKERS / SILVER-SOLDERED / 87 / C."
Inscriptions: Side of bowl engraved "President's House."
NOTES: One of "6 Comports," $35 each (all extant). There is no evidence that these were originally gilded. Six gilded copies were made in 1950 by S. Kirk & Sons, Baltimore.

OLIVE DISH (page 170—see above)
Tiffany & Co., New York, circa 1882
Silver electroplate
U.S. Government purchase, 1882
1882.3894.1
2 3/4 x 7 3/8 x 5 in. (7.0 x 18.7 x 12.7 cm.)
MARKS: Underside—stamped "3056 / TIFFANY & Co / MAKERS / SILVER-SOLDERED / 85 / 6."
INSCRIPTIONS: Side engraved "President's House."
NOTES: One of "2 Olive Dishes," $30 each (extant).

OYSTER FORK (page 170—see above)
Tiffany & Co., New York, circa 1882
Silver
U.S. Government purchase, 1882
1882.3889.1
5 3/4 in. (14.6 cm.); 10 dwt.
MARKS: Handle reverse—stamped "M TIFFANY & Co STERLING"
INSCRIPTIONS: Handle face engraved "President's House."
NOTES: One of "5 dozen Oyster forks," $20 per dozen. (53 extant). Supplemental forks were made by Gorham, one dozen each in 1895 and 1898.

SALT SPOON (page 170—see above)
Tiffany & Co., New York, circa 1882
Silver
U.S. Government purchase, 1882
1882.3892.1
3 1/2 in. (8.9 cm.); 7 dwt.
MARKS: Handle reverse—stamped "TIFFANY & Co."
INSCRIPTIONS: Handle face engraved "President's House."
NOTES: From "1 Dozen Salt spoons," $9 per dozen (2 extant). "Whittier" pattern.

PLATE (page 170)
Worcester Royal Porcelain Co., England, 1881, painted by Charles H.C. Baldwyn (1859–1943)

Porcelain
U.S. Government purchase, 1882
1882.2990.1
9 1/4 in. (23.5 cm.)
MARKS: Reverse—red printed "MANUFACTURED. BY.THE.WORCESTER.ROYAL.PORCELAIN.Co" in oval ring around "FOR / TIFFANY & Co / NEW YORK"; incuse crowned factory mark / "WORCESTER" and "S10"; red-painted mark "W / 487."
NOTES: On May 16, 1882, Tiffany & Co. provided President Chester Arthur's White House with silver tableware (see page 170), jardinieres, and a selection of 23 "Plates." The latter, not identified by type, size, or decoration, was recorded as 13 entries differing by price—from $2.75 to $10.50 each. In addition to 7 singles, two groups of 3 and two groups of 4 may also have been unique plates grouped not by design but only by price. The numbers and costs suggest ornamental plates such as the six unique ones which have been exhibited in the china collection since 1904 as having been acquired during the Arthur administration, including this one bearing the only Tiffany-specific mark.
REFERENCES: NA/MTA acct. 223637, voucher 45. Klapthor, *Official White House China*, 122–25.

PLATE (page 170—see above)
Probably England, circa 1881
Porcelain
1882.2877.1
U.S. Government purchase, 1882
9 1/8 in. (23.2 cm.)
MARKS: Reverse—incuse circled cypher "JG."
NOTES: See above.

SCONCE (page 173)
American?, circa 1891
Brass, cut glass / electric light fixture
U.S. Government purchase, 1891
891.1127.4
27 1/4 x 9 3/4 x 8 3/4 in. (70.5 x 24.8 x 22.2 cm.)
MARKS: None.
NOTES: From set of "4—A.P.B. [antique polished brass?] 1-light electric Brackets with cut glass globes at $65" (all extant) purchased for the Family Dining Room from the Edison General Electric Company of New York as part of "Introducing Electric lamps into Executive Mansion," March 16, 1891. They were removed to the West Sitting Hall on the second floor in 1902, remaining there until they were retired in 1948. A matching 7-light chandelier which cost $175 was probably sold in the 1903 sale.
REFERENCES: NA/MTA acct. 282374, voucher 31.

BREAKFAST PLATE and DINNER PLATE (page 173)
Tressemannes & Vogt, Limoges, France, 1891
Porcelain
U.S. Government purchase, 1892
1892.3841.3.1-51 and .1.1-74
Breakfast Plate—8 1/2 in. (21.6 cm.)
Dinner Plate—9 1/2 in. (24.1 cm.)
MARKS: Reverse—gilt printed "T.V. (on bell) / FRANCE / DÉCORÉ POUR / M.W. BEVERIDGE. /

WASHINGTON, D.C." / gilt "HARRISON 1892" / green "T&V (boxed) / FRANCE."
NOTES: Washington retailer M. W. Beveridge solicited samples of plates made from a design suggested by Caroline Harrison and executed by Paul Putzki, a Washington teacher of china painting. Two samples submitted by Tressemannes and Vogt were selected. Six dozen each of dinner ($189) and soup ($186) plates of Sample A (blue-bordered) and breakfast ($186) and tea ($171) plates of Sample B (white-edged) were received on December 30, 1891, and paid for in January 1892. Five dozen after-dinner cups and saucers were then ordered, but Mrs. Harrison died (October 24, 1892) before their arrival on January 3, 1893. The pattern was reordered in 1898, 1899, 1900, and 1908, but later breakfast plates were apparently of the Sample A design.
REFERENCES: NA/MTA acct. 288960, voucher 18; acct. 294899, voucher 14. Klapthor, *Official White House China*, 127–31, 140, 143–44, 150–51, appendix III, 290.

WATER GOBLET *(page 173)*
C. Dorflinger & Sons, White Mills, Pennsylvania, 1891
Cut and engraved glass
U.S. Government purchase, 1891
1891.3877.1.1-41
6 1/8 x 3 3/8 in. (15.6 x 8.6 cm.)
MARKS: None.
NOTES: From "5 dozen goblets at $46.50 per dozen" in the Benjamin Harrison state glass service purchased through Washington retailer, M. W. Beveridge. The service included five dozen each of Apollinaris tumblers, finger bowls, ice cream plates, and four other stemware forms, with eight water bottles and eight decanters, at a total cost of $1,973.50. Reorders of the service in succeeding administrations, 1896–1918, were made by Dorflinger and by T. G. Hawkes & Co., Corning, N.Y.
REFERENCES: NA/MTA acct. 287852, voucher 74. Spillman, *White House Glassware*, 96–116, figs. 42–43.

DINNER FORK and BREAKFAST FORK
(page 175)
William B. Durgin, Concord, N.H., 1894
Gilded silver
U.S. Government purchase, 1894
1894.3902.1–87, 894.3904.1–80
Dinner Fork—7 7/8 in. (20.0 cm.); 2 oz. 1 dwt.
Breakfast Fork—7 1/8 in. (18.1 cm.); 1 oz. 10 dwt.
MARKS: Shaft—stamped "D (script) STERLING" and "HARRIS & SHAFER".
INSCRIPTIONS: Handle face engraved with the Great Seal of the United States; handle reverse engraved "President's House;" rear of bowl engraved "1895."
NOTES: "16 doz. Silver Forks, metal furnished by U.S."—eight dozen each of dinner and breakfast sizes—were purchased from Harris & Shafer, Washington, D.C., October 23, 1894. These were made with silver provided by melting down old White House flatware ("84 silver forks and 57 gilt forks") at a cost of $204.81 plus $144 for engraving them with the "U.S. coat of arms." Those forks were further engraved, probably with "President's House" and the incorrect date "1895," when an additional seven dozen dinner forks were purchased in 1896. In 1950, S. Kirk & Sons in Baltimore was commissioned to make 120 each of

fish, salad, and oyster forks to complement the dinner and breakfast forks of the 1890s. In 1994, to bring quantities up to 150, Kirk Stieff Co., Baltimore, provided supplements to the breakfast forks and the three 1950 types. Dessert spoons were made to be used with the breakfast forks for the dessert course at formal dining.
REFERENCES: NA/MTA acct. rec. November 1894, voucher 28; acct. rec. June 1896, vouchers 23, 27; acct. 14493, voucher 23, 1898. "New Spoons of Old Silver," *The Jewelers' Weekly*, April 7, 1897, 14.

CANDELABRUM *(page 177)*
Gorham Mfg. Co., Providence, Rhode Island, circa 1898
Silver electroplate
U.S. Government purchase, 1898
1898.3921.1
20 x 16 in. (50.8 x 40.6 cm.)
MARKS: Underside of foot—stamped anchor "GORHAM CO. / 0315."
INSCRIPTIONS: Top of foot engraved "President's House"; underside of foot rim engraved "1898."
NOTES: One of "6 plated candelabra" (5 extant) purchased from Galt & Bro., Washington, D.C., December 29, 1898, $35 each. These were supplemented in 1899 and 1900 by purchases from Galt & Bro. of six matching Baroque-style candelabra. Silverplate was an appropriate medium for such candelabra because of the limited wear involved in their usage. Some of these candelabra appear on the banquet table in the Cross Hall for President William McKinley's dinner in 1899 for Admiral George Dewey, hero of the Spanish-American War.
Condition: Only 8 of the 12 arm structures have survived.
REFERENCES: NA/MTA acct. 14493, voucher 23, 1898, and voucher 34, 1899; acct. 17693, voucher 32, 1900. Charles Carpenter, *Gorham Silver*.

VASE *(page 178)*
National Porcelain Manufactory of Sèvres, France, 1898
Porcelain, gilded metal
Gift of the French Republic
1898.1291.1
34 x 17 1/2 x 15 5/8 in. (86.4 x 44.4 x 39.7 cm.)
MARKS: None.
INSCRIPTIONS: Metal plinth—engraved brass plaque "FELIX FAURE / PRESIDENT OF THE FRENCH REPUBLIC / TO WILLIAM MCKINLEY / PRESIDENT OF THE UNITED STATES / IN COMMEMORATION OF THE INAUGURATION / OF THE NEW FRANCO-AMERICAN CABLE / AUGUST 17, 1898."
NOTES: On August 17, 1898, the inaugural day of a new trans-Atlantic cable, messages were exchanged between French President Félix Fauré at Le Havre and President William McKinley in the "war room of the White House" (current Lincoln Sitting Room). To commemorate that event Fauré sent McKinley a pair of large vases, one of a number of variants of a shape modeled about 1840, listed in the Sèvres archives under the factory name, "Vase de la Vendage" (Vase of the Grape Harvest), possibly in reference to their deep blue color. They are recorded in a sales book in July 1898, prior to the event, at 3500 francs each, with delivery to "M. MacKinley" in January 1899. Although there is no correspondence documenting the

gift, an article, circa 1900, mentioned that the vases "did not reach the White House until after the death of M. Faure" (February 16, 1899).
REFERENCES: Tamara Prèaud, Archivist at Sèvres, letter of August 3, 1999, OCWH. Jacobs, "Bric-a-Brac." Thompson, "Art in the White House," 144.

PRESENTATION CUP *(page 179)*
Tiffany & Co., New York, 1899
Silver with partial gold wash
White House Acquisition Fund, 1972
1972.834.1
13 3/4 x 12 1/8 in. (34.9 x 30.7 cm.); 103 oz. 11 dwt.
MARKS: Underside of base—stamped "TIFFANY & CO / 14073 MAKERS 6606 / STERLING SILVER / 925-1000 / T"; neck and foot—stamped oval mark of standing swan.
INSCRIPTIONS: Neck in relief "Presented by the President of the United States [William McKinley] to his Excellency M. Jules Cambon, Ambassador of France, in token of his friendly services in the negotiation of the Protocol of Peace between the United States and Spain, August 12, 1898."
NOTES: Three olive-branch handles rise from the seals of the United States, Spain, and France on the body, positioned above three eagles clustered as the pedestal. Gold-washed bowl interior. Tiffany's holloware ledger (Tiffany archives) lists this as "14073 / Love Cup / Cambon" (order 6606 of June 29, 1899), made of 103.8 oz. of silver at $994.30. The Peace Protocol was signed in the White House Cabinet Room (now the Treaty Room).
PROVENANCE: Jules Cambon; Adam A. Weschler & Sons, Washington, D.C., February 1972; White House purchase with donated funds.
REFERENCES: Illustrated on a Tiffany & Co. advertising page in the "Official Souvenir Program" of the 1901 inauguration of President McKinley, OCWH. Carpenter with Carpenter, *Tiffany Silver*, 148, no. 209. David B. Warren et al., *Marks of Achievement: Four Centuries of American Presentation Silver* (New York: Abrams, 1987), 137. Monkman, "American Silver," 78–79, fig. 11.

CHAPTER 6

CHANDELIER *(page 184)*
William Parker, London, circa 1774
Cut glass, gilded metal
Anonymous donation, 1946
1946.1432.1
72 x 42 in. (182.9 x 106.9 cm.)
MARKS: None.
NOTES: One of a pair of chandeliers received in 1946 for the Cross Hall, where they remain today. Parker was the preeminent London maker of cut-glass chandeliers and other lighting fixtures in the late 18th century, his clients including the Prince of Wales for Carlton House and the Duke of Devonshire at Chatsworth.
CONDITION: One replacement nozzle on this chandelier; three nozzles and one arm on its mate.
PROVENANCE: Purchased in 1790 in London for the townhouse of the Count of Porto Covo in Lisbon, Portugal; sold to Hyde and Knudsen, New York, in 1940

when the house was sold to the British government; sold to anonymous donor for the White House in 1946.
REFERENCES: Chandelier Cleaning & Restoration, "Historical Report," 8, OCWH. Temple Newsam, *Country House Lighting, 1660–1890* (Leeds, England: Leeds City Art Galleries 1982), 43–44.

SIDE CHAIR (page 187 left)
A. H. Davenport, Boston, 1902, from a design by McKim, Mead & White
Mahogany
U.S. Government purchase, 1903
1903.466.1
43 1/4 x 21 1/2 x 25 1/2 in. (109.9 x 54.5 x 64.8 cm.)
MARKS: None.
NOTES: From a set of fifty Queen Anne–style side chairs purchased for the State Dining Room as part of a non-itemized contract of October 1, 1902 (paid January 24, 1903), "For furniture, carpets, curtains, &c . . . / Placed in State Dining room, Family Dining room, and four new bedrooms over East room, Executive Mansion," $12,698. The side chairs were listed in the 1903 inventory as 50 "Chairs, high back, no arms, tapestry covered, mahogany," at $40 each. In December 1953, ten additional side chairs were purchased. Although Irving & Casson–A. H. Davenport was invited to bid on making these supplements, the original Davenport chairs were copied instead by the Gunlocke Co., Waylande, N.Y., at $110 each. In May 1957, four armchairs were acquired from the same source.
REFERENCES: NA/MTA acct. 30215, voucher 35. Thomas W. Symons and Theodore A. Bingham, Corps of Engineers, U.S. Army, *Annual Report upon the Improvement and Care of Public Buildings and Grounds. . . .* (Washington, D.C.: GPO, 1903), 2656. Brooklyn Museum, *The American Renaissance, 1876–1917* (New York: Pantheon Books, 1979), no. 115 (drawing no. 110). Anne Farnam, "A. H. Davenport & Company, Boston Furniture Makers," *Antiques* (May 1976): fig. 3.

ARMCHAIR (page 187 right)
A. H. Davenport, Boston, 1902, from a design by McKim, Mead & White
White oak, cane
U.S. Government purchase, 1903
1903.517.1
56 7/8 x 27 x 27 3/4 in. (144.5 x 68.6 x 70.5 cm.)
MARKS: None.
NOTES: From six William & Mary–style armchairs purchased for the State Dining Room as part of the same non-itemized contract of October 1, 1902, as were the side chairs. Listed in the 1903 inventory as 6 "Chairs, oak, carved, armchairs, velvet cushions" at $100 each. The Irving & Casson–A. H. Davenport papers at the Strong Museum, Rochester, New York includes a drawing of a nearly matching chair, with less surface carving, entitled "F.E. PEABODY / SIMILAR CHAIR MADE FOR / WHITE HOUSE."
REFERENCES: NA/MTA acct. 30215, voucher 35. Brooklyn Museum, *American Renaissance*, no. 114. Farnam, "A. H. Davenport," fig. 3.

CONSOLE TABLE (page 189)
A. H. Davenport, Boston, 1902, from a design by McKim, Mead & White
Mahogany / ash; marble, brass
U.S. Government purchase, 1902
1902.655.1
44 1/8 x 120 1/8 x 31 in. (112.1 x 355.1 x 78.7 cm.)
MARKS: Top of center brace—stenciled "MADE BY / A. H. DAVENPORT / BOSTON, MASS."
NOTES: From a set of eagle-pedestal tables—one double and two single—purchased for the State Dining Room as part of a non-itemized contract of October 1, 1902 (see page 187). The larger table was listed in the 1903 inventory as one "Long sideboard, mahogany, carved eagle legs, marble top, brass trimmings" at $600. The pair of smaller tables was listed as "Serving tables, 'Console' tables, mahogany, carved eagle supports" at $310 each. These tables were derived from a double-pedestal table in the dining room of the home of Stanford White, partner in the architectural firm of McKim, Mead & White. Sketches on a piece of the firm's stationery were entitled "Mr. White's / all gilt Sideboard / Suggestions for White House / Dining R." That table (private collection) shows in an illustration of White's dining room in the catalog of the 1907 sale of furnishings after his 1906 death.
CONDITION: The green marble top was replaced at an early date in 1909. The wings on both eagles have been broken and repaired. In 1961 the eagles were gilded atop dark brown plinths, while the table frame was painted white with gilt trim. In 1998, this table and its similarly treated mates were restored to a mahogany finish.
REFERENCES: NA/MTA acct. 30215, voucher 35; acct. 11220, voucher 51 (1909). Symons and Bingham, *Annual Report*, 1903, 2656. Brooklyn Museum, *American Renaissance*, no. 111 (design). Farnam, "A. H. Davenport." Channing Blake, "Architects as Furniture Designers," *Antiques* (May 1976).

BENCH (page 190)
L. Marcotte & Co., New York, 1903
Gilded cherry
U.S. Government purchase, 1903
1903.555.1
20 x 54 x 18 1/2 in. (50.8 x 137.2 x 47.0 cm.)
MARKS: None.
NOTES: From a suite of thirteen purchased for the East Room in 1902. Part of an unitemized contract of December 5, 1902, for "Furniture for East and Blue rooms . . . ," $11,175.26, they were listed in the June 1903 inventory of the East Room as "Banquettes, 11, 4 feet 6 inches by 1 foot 6 inches; 2, 2 feet 9 inches by 1 foot 6 inches; richly carved, gildedde genes, finished with gimp, loose covers of yellow figured linen," $2,651.96. Underside of stretcher stamped with set number "4."
CONDITION: Fully or partially regilded as early as 1906. Five of the 54-inch benches have been altered; two were enlarged to 72 inches in 1951, and four were cut down to 34 inches in 1961 to match the original two smaller benches.
REFERENCES: NA/MTA acct. 30125, voucher 18. Symons and Bingham, *Annual Report*, 1903, 2652.

ANDIRON (page 190)
France, 1903
Brass / iron
U.S. Government purchase, 1903
1903.1365.1–2
14 7/8 x 14 x 6 1/2 in. (37.8 x 35.6 x 16.5 cm.)
MARKS: None.
NOTES: From one of two pairs in an Egyptian-revival style purchased for the Blue and Red Rooms in 1903. By a bill of March 7, L. Marcotte & Co. provided "1 pair of gilt andirons" at $135 for the Red Room, but by a bill of May 23, an additional set was provided for the Blue Room at only $100.
CONDITION: Iron log rest, with spherical stop, missing from both pairs.
REFERENCES: NA/MTA acct. 32386, voucher 16. Brooklyn Museum, *The American Renaissance*, no. 160.

ARMCHAIR (page 191)
L. Marcotte & Co., New York, 1902
Painted and gilded cherry
U.S. Government purchase, 1903
1903.614.1
42 1/8 x 29 1/4 x 28 in. (107.0 x 74.3 x 71.1 cm.)
MARKS: None.
NOTES: From a set of four armchairs, with four matching side ("single") chairs, one sofa, and four footstools purchased for the Blue Room. Twelve shield-back ("small") side chairs were also acquired for the Blue Room and the Red Room. Both were part of a non-itemized contract of December 5, 1902, for "Furniture for East and Blue rooms . . . ," $11,175.26. In the June 1903 inventory, they were listed as part of a suite "Richly carved, white and gold, covered with brocade, trimmed with gimp" at a collective cost of $3,697.91. The armchair was probably based on a suite made by François-Honoré-Georges Jacob-Desmalter (1770–1814) in 1809 for the Salon des Fleurs at the Château de Compiègne in France.
REFERENCES: NA/MTA acct. 30125, voucher 18. Symons and Bingham, *Annual Report*, 1903, 2654. Louise Ade Boger, *Furniture Past & Present* (Garden City, New York: Doubleday & Co., 1966), 209. Jean-Marie Moulin, *Le Chateau de Compiegne* (Paris: Editions de la Réunion des musées nationaux, 1987), 94. Brooklyn Museum, *American Renaissance*, nos. 120–21.

SIDE CHAIR (page 191)
L. Marcotte & Co., New York, 1902
Painted birch
U.S. Government purchase, 1903
1903.620.1
37 5/8 x 23 x 23 in. (95.6 x 58.4 x 58.4 cm.)
MARKS: None.
NOTES: (See Armchair above.)

CHANDELIER (page 193)
Christoph Palme & Co., Parchen, Bohemia, 1902, for Edward F. Caldwell & Co., New York
Cut glass, gilded brass / electric light fixtures
U.S. Government purchase, 1902
1902.3057.1
129 x 68 in. (327.7 x 172.7 cm.)
MARKS: None.

NOTES: From a set of three (all extant) purchased for the East Room from Edward F. Caldwell & Co., New York, under a comprehensive White House lighting contract of September 25, 1902—"For furnishing and placing in position between Sept. 25th, 1902, and date [December 31] certain electric light and gas fixtures," $19,061.50. Design sketches dated July 2, 1902, include these chandeliers as "C.11837" and "White House / East Room / glass fixture." Only a short time later, during fiscal year 1903–04, the chandeliers were taken down and "the diameter of the lower portion reduced in size" by Caldwell at no charge.

CONDITION: Shortened and modified during the Truman renovation. The crown of gilded metal leaves was replaced by cut-glass plumes. At the center of the neck, the projecting metal scrolls and swags of glass pendants were removed. Glass pendants were added to the glass bobeches and around the bottom drop. The three tiers of interior arms paralleling the main ring were replaced by one tier of lights, with additional lights in the bowl and in the crown.

REFERENCES: NA/MTA acct. 30215, vouchers 15, 72. Edward F. Caldwell & Co. Records, Design Records, vol. 2, New York Public Library. Jeni L. Sandberg, "Edward F. Caldwell and Company," *Antiques* (February 1998): 311–17. Chandelier Cleaning & Restoration Services Limited, "The White House, Washington, D.C., United States of America. Historical Report," 1997, 11, OCWH. Thomas W. Symons and Charles S. Bromwell, Corps of Engineers, U.S. Army, *Annual Report upon the Improvement and Care of Public Buildings and Grounds. . . .* (Washington, D.C.: GPO, 1904), 3901.

LIGHT STANDARD (page 194)
Edward F. Caldwell & Co., New York, 1902
Gilded metal, cut glass, marble / electric light fixtures
U.S. Government purchase, 1902
1902.1297.1
123 3/8 x 29 3/4 in. (312.5 x 75.6 cm.)
MARKS: None.
NOTES: From a set of four (all extant) purchased from Caldwell under a comprehensive White House lighting contract of September 25, 1902—"For furnishing and placing in position between Sept. 25th, 1902, and date [December 31] certain electric light and gas fixtures," $19,061.50. They were listed in the June 1903 inventory of the East Room as "Electric standards, 12 light, dark fire gilt, marble bases, candelabra lamps" at $900 each. The column is based closely on a French Empire candelabrum. Design sketches dated July 2, 1902, include these standards as "C.11834".
CONDITION: Some of the simplification of glasswork during the early 1960s has been corrected. Tubing, installed in 1902 to reinforce the candle arms in transport, was left in place with glass pendants suspended from it. The original red marble bases were replaced during the Truman renovation to match new red marble baseboards, mantels, and hearths.
REFERENCES: NA/MTA acct. 30215, vouchers 15, 72. Symons and Bingham, *Annual Report*, 1903, 2652. Alexander Speltz, *Styles of Ornament* (1904 ; reprint, London: Bracken Books, 1996), 597–98, pl. 381, fig. 1. Caldwell,

"Design Records." Sandberg, "Edward F. Caldwell," 311–17.

TEA CUP AND SAUCER and OYSTER PLATE (page 195)
Josiah Wedgwood & Sons, Ltd., Etruria, England, 1903
Porcelain
U.S. Government purchase, 1903
1903.3858.7.1, .8.1-82, .2.1-38
Cup—1 15/16 x 4 1/4 x 3 1/2 in. (4.9 x 10.8 x 8.9 cm.)
Saucer—5 1/2 in. (14.0 cm.)
Plate—10 1/8 x 9 in. (25.7 x 22.9 cm.)
MARKS: Underside—printed company mark—vase / 3 stars / "WEDGWOOD" / star / "ENGLAND" and "FROM / THE VAN HEUSEN CHARLES Co / ALBANY, N.Y. / Rd No 399026 [British patent office registry number] / PATENT APPLIED FOR."
NOTES: The Theodore Roosevelt state service, purchased from the Van Heusen Charles Co., Albany, New York, in 1903, was an eight-piece service for 120 accompanied by 12 each of two sizes of platters, totaling 1,296 pieces at $8,094. The ten dozen oyster plates cost $99.75 per dozen, and the ten dozen tea cups and saucers $119.25 per dozen. The design is Wedgwood's "Ulunda" pattern (number X5333), probably designed by Armand Leger, with the addition of a polychrome Great Seal of the United States. In 1910, the Tafts reordered four types, but also added three new types to the service—dessert plates and breakfast coffee cups and saucers.
REFERENCES: NA/MTA acct. 32386, voucher 85; acct. 16827, voucher 28. Klapthor, *Official White House* China, 145–51.

CABINET (page 196)
Gustav Stickley (1858–1942), Eastwood, New York, circa 1904
White oak, glass, copper
U.S. Government purchase, 1904
1904.412.1
69 1/8 x 36 1/8 x 14 in. (175.6 x 91.8 x 35.6 cm.)
MARKS: Top center of backboard—boxed red stamped joiners compass centering "als ik kan" [Flemish version of William Morris's motto—"all I can"] / "Stickley" signature stamp.
NOTES: From a pair (one extant), described as "Cabinet, fumed" (oak given a weathered finish by exposure to ammonia fumes"). Purchased from W. B. Moses & Sons, Washington, D.C., February 1904, at $55 each, with an additional $14 charge for "adding 3" [inches] to legs of 2 Cabinets & furnishing 8 new feet, with ball bearing castors," they were acquired for display of White House china at the east end of the Ground Floor Corridor. Col. Thomas W. Symons, the commissioner of public buildings and grounds, wrote that President Theodore Roosevelt "for the first time saw the cabinets and china" on February 22, 1904, and "was very much delighted at the idea and himself proposed that we should try to get some representative china of each administration. . . ." On the matter of ordering additional cabinets, he advised a quick decision "for it takes quite a bit of time to get them." In May 1904, the Washington decorating firm of A. E. Kennedy was paid $86 for "Furnishing & making 4 Oak China Closets" for the Ground Floor Corridor. These

replaced the two Stickley cabinets which, according to the 1905 inventory, were moved to the second floor.
CONDITION: Replacement lower proper right glass pane. Drapery mounts remain on the door interior.
REFERENCES: NA/MTA acct. 34380, voucher 63. Col. Thomas W. Symons to Abby Gunn Baker, February 25, 1904, Abby Gunn Baker Papers, OCWH. NA/MTA acct. 34600, voucher 27. Leslie Greene Bowman, *American Arts & Crafts: Virtue in Design* (Los Angeles County Museum of Art, 1995), 70–72.

PRAYER RUG (page 197)
Tabriz, Persia, circa 1850
Silk; emerald, tourmaline, aquamarine, pearl
Gift of Hayozoun Hohannes Topakyan, 1909
1909.471.1
69 x 44 1/4 in. (175.3 x 112.5 cm.)
MARKS: None.
INSCRIPTIONS: Brass plaque on original display case engraved "PRESENTED TO THE UNITED STATES OF AMERICA BY H. H. TOPAKYAN / 1907 [sic, 1909]."
NOTES: This extremely rare example of a jeweled Persian prayer rug, made after the 19th century revival of Persian weaving, is of a form displayed on ceremonial occasions at the Ottoman court in the 16th and 17th centuries. Possibly unique in America, it is set with 34 emeralds, 14 tourmalines, and one aquamarine, all stitched to the weave foundation in prepared pile-less places; 26 adhered turquoises; over 15,000 small pearls and 150 larger pearls; and seed pearl fringe. It is woven with lines of 13th century Farsi poetry by Sa'di, pseudonym of Sheikh Muslih-al-Din. Top band: "It is a green leaf, a gift of a dervish. What can the poor person do? That is all that he possesses." Bottom band: "To bring the leg of a locust to a king is improper; however, it is quite an achievement if an ant brings it." This may be "the rug the President [Theodore Roosevelt] has so much admired" in the collection of H. H. Topakyan, the Persian consul general in New York. On February 17, 1909, just two weeks before leaving office, President Roosevelt wrote Topakyan to accept for the government "the beautiful jeweled rug which you delivered to The White House today."
CONDITION: Some fading, especially at the top. Restitching of some gems. One emerald, seven tourmalines, the single aquamarine, and some larger pearls are replacements; two turquoises and numerous small pearls are missing. Pearl fringe has been restrung on brass wire at a reduced density.
REFERENCES: H. H. Topakyan to William Loeb, Secretary to the President, October 12, 1908, Theodore Roosevelt Papers, LC. Theodore Roosevelt to H. H. Topakyan, February 17, 1909, Theodore Roosevelt Papers, Letters Sent, Vol. 91, 232, LC. Robin Hanson, "Silk Tabriz Pile Carpet, The White House," February 1999, OCWH.

TEA AND COFFEE SET (*Coffeepot, Sugar Bowl, Teapot*) (page 199)
Lenox, Inc., Trenton, New Jersey, 1911
Silver-overlaid china
Gift of Charles P. Taft, 1966
1966.592.2-3-1

Coffee—6 5/8 x 5 5/8 x 2 3/4 in. (16.8 x 14.3 x 7.0 cm.)
Sugar—2 3/4 x 4 3/4 x 3 in. (7.0 x 12.1 x 7.6 cm.)
Tea—4 5/8 x 7 x 4 in. (11.8 x 17.8 x 10.2 cm.)
MARKS: Underside of teapot and sugar bowl—painted company mark—wreathed script "L" / LENOX.
INSCRIPTIONS: Shield on front of each engraved "T / 1886–1911."
NOTES: President and Mrs. William Howard Taft celebrated their twenty-fifth wedding anniversary at a gala garden party at the White House on June 19, 1911. Mrs. Taft wrote: "silver was showered upon us until we were almost buried in silver," including gifts from the Congress and foreign heads of state. In 1966, their son donated to the White House two of the gifts they received (original donors not identified), this silver-overlaid cobalt blue china service and a silver cream pitcher and sugar bowl with cobalt glass liners.
REFERENCES: Helen Taft, *Recollections of Full Years* (New York: Dodd, Mead, 1914), 391–92. William Seale, *The President's House: A History*, 2 vols. (Washington, D.C.: WHHA, 1986), 760–63.

GARDEN SETTEE (page 201)
Northern Europe, circa 1900
Painted limestone
U.S. Government purchase
1960.3830.1
30 3/4 x 54 1/2 x 18 in. (78.1 x 138.4 x 45.7 cm.)
MARKS: None.
NOTES: In 1913 Ellen Wilson invited the noted landscape designer, Beatrix Jones Farrand (1872–1959) to redesign the east garden. Completed before Mrs. Wilson's death in the White House on August 6, 1914, the garden contained a ten-piece suite of stone furniture—two settees (both still in the garden) at the east ends of the east-west walk-ways, four chairs (three extant) in one corner, and four stools (two extant) at the corners of a central pool. The acquisition of the furniture is undocumented, although it was long-assumed to have been acquired by Farrand. This settee, however, shows in a grounds photo taken before Theodore Roosevelt left office in 1909, so some or all of the suite was at the White House before Farrand executed a sketch (Woodrow Wilson House in Washington) showing two settees recessed into the east end of the garden.
CONDITION: Repainted and repaired. The three extant chairs are missing parts of their backs.
REFERENCES: Jane Brown, *Beatrix: The Gardening Life of Beatrix Jones Farrand, 1872–1959* (New York: Viking, 1995), 106, 108. William M. Harts, Corps of Engineers, *Report upon the Improvement and Care of Public Buildings and Grounds . . .* (Washington, D.C.: GPO, 1914), 3342.

SERVICE PLATE, ENTREE/FISH PLATE, and RAMEKIN AND PLATE (page 202)
Lenox, Inc., Trenton, New Jersey, 1918
China
U.S. Government purchase, 1918
1918.3859.1.1-91, .5.1-202, .17.1-9, .18.1
Service Plate—11 1/8 in. (28.3 cm.)
Entree/Fish Plate—8 7/8 in. (22.5 cm.)
Ramekin—1 5/8 x 3 3/8 in. (3.1 x 8.6 cm.)

Ramekin Plate—5 1/16 in. (12.9 cm.)
MARKS: Underside of plates—gilt printed factory mark—wreathed script "L" and "LENOX / DULIN & MARTIN CO. / WASHINGTON, D.C. / THE WHITE HOUSE / 1918"; underside of cup—incuse) "1221."
NOTES: The Woodrow Wilson state service (1,522 pieces), purchased from Washington retailer Dulin & Martin in 1918 for $11,251.60, was the first state service made in the United States. Ordered on March 28, 1918, it was received in five shipments during that year. Eight pieces were ordered for 120, with the entree and fish plates actually being the same at $42.75 per dozen. Only eight dozen were ordered of four types, including the service plates at $198.50 per dozen. Four types more likely used for breakfasts or luncheons were ordered in smaller quantities, including two dozen each of ramekins and plates at $45.50 per dozen. Frank Graham Holmes, the chief designer at Lenox, described his design for this service as simple but rich, "supremely patriotic—the stars and stripes and the Seal of the United States." President Wilson however, personally suggested the replacement of the Great Seal with the Presidential arms. The "stars and stripes" motif was used as the rim band on all pieces except the service plates, where it was the shoulder band on the only pieces to have the cobalt blue border and heavy gold rim. Lenox designates its ware "china" or "fine china" rather than porcelain. The service remained in use and was reordered during several administrations. In 1925, four dozen ramekins were ordered, but in a cheaper form without the Presidential arms. During the Clinton administration, Lenox produced 139 supplemental service plates bearing the 1918 and modern company marks.
REFERENCES: NA/MTA acct. 58310, voucher 106; acct. 64016, voucher 84. Abby Gunn Baker, news release, October 13, 1918, Baker Papers, OCWH; and "First American Made China for the White House," *Washington Evening Star*, October 20, 1918. Klapthor, *Official White House China*, 152–58.

WATER GOBLET (page 203 upper)
Central Glass Works, Wheeling, West Virginia, 1921
Gold-overlaid glass
Gift of the Harding Memorial Association, 1968
1968.616.6
7 5/8 x 3 5/8 in. (19.4 x 9.2 cm.)
MARKS: None.
NOTES: In May 1921, new First Lady Florence Harding received from the Central Glass Works a gift of a 336-piece glass service in its "Dragon" pattern with the initial "H." A trade journal of May 26 reported: "It goes with the historic White House gold service [flatware] and will be used only on state occasions. It is Mrs. Harding's own property and will be taken away with her when she leaves the White House." The service included not only stemware and tumblers, but plates, cruets, and accessories. The gift to the White House in 1968 consisted of nine pieces—finger bowl and plate, tumbler, and stemware for water, wine, champagne, liqueur, sherbet, and juice.
PROVENANCE: Florence Kling Harding; the Harding Memorial Association.

REFERENCES: Spillman, *White House Glassware*, 119–20, 124–25.

DESSERT PLATE (page 203 lower)
Lenox, Inc., Trenton, New Jersey, circa 1920
China
Gift of the Harding Memorial Association, 1959
1959.3569.1
8 3/16 in. (20.8 cm.)
MARKS: Underside printed with green company mark—wreathed "L" / "LENOX"; handwritten gold "7 / M3."
NOTES: From a personal service owned by President and Mrs. Warren G. Harding, this plate was donated with a matching demitasse cup and saucer.
PROVENANCE: President and Mrs. Warren G. Harding; Harding Memorial Association.
REFERENCES: Susan G. Detweiler, *American Presidential China* (Washington, D.C.: Smithsonian Traveling Exhibition Service, 1975), 77.

RUG DESIGN (page 204)
Bollentin and Thompson for Tiffany Studios, New York, 1926
Watercolor on paper
Gift of the White House Historical Association, 1995
1995.1755.1
18 1/2 x 14 1/4 in. (47.0 x 36.2 cm.)
MARKS: Lower drawing margin—stamped "BOLLENTIN AND THOMPSON" and inscribed "ORDER #157" and "#1784." Lower left inscribed in pencil with manufacturing instructions. New and original mats—inscribed "Aubusson Rug / made 1927 for the / Green Room in the / WHITE HOUSE / Washington, D.C. / by / TIFFANY STUDIOS."
NOTES: In June 1926, the White House ordered from Tiffany Studios "Aubusson Rugs for the Red Room and Green Room . . . per sketches and yarns submitted and approved," $5,680. This drawing shows the lower right quadrant of the Green Room rug with the polychrome presidential arms as an oval center medallion. Although the extant rug (927.1574.1) was actually executed with the arms as a circular medallion, this drawing is undoubtedly from among the submitted "sketches" mentioned on the voucher because there are manufacturing instructions written in pencil on the lower left margin to weave the scrolls as drawn, not as discussed, with a note "that there are 13 stars & 13 little circles over the stars." Also acquired in 1995 is a design for the companion Red Room rug that shows the full rug with a circular medallion of the Great Seal of the United States rather than the executed Presidential arms.
PROVENANCE: Tiffany Studios; Rockland County (New York) Antique Show; Post Road Gallery, Larchmont, N.Y.; Hirschl & Adler, New York; C. G. Sloan & Co., Rockville, Md., September 17, 1995; White House purchase with donated funds.
REFERENCES: Order 3449-H, June 10, 1926, and voucher 501, March 23, 1927, OCWH.

COVERLET (page 205)
Grace Goodhue Coolidge (1879–1957), Washington, D.C., 1925–27
Crocheted shoe thread

Gift of Grace Coolidge, 1927
1927.1691.1
108 x 76 3/4 in. (274.3 x 195.0 cm.)
MARKS: At head—crocheted "GRACE COOLIDGE";
left proper edge—"THE PRESIDENT'S HOUSE";
right proper side—"AUGUST 3, 1923–MARCH 4,
1929"; near center—"E PLURIBUS UNUM."
NOTES: First Lady Grace Coolidge made a coverlet for
the "Lincoln bed" (see page 128) which, as she wrote, was
intended to be a "token which shall go down through the
ages to serve as a definite and visible link connecting the
present and the past." It was made of pieces—three large
panels and the motto strip as the top, two side inserts,
and three sections of border. She wrote: "The making of
the coverlet was accomplished in two years, the greater
part being done in the White House and the final
stitches being taken on board the U.S.S. Mayflower [the
presidential yacht] during the President's review of the
fleet at Hampton Roads [Virginia] in June, 1927." On
October 31, 1928, Washington decorator James B. Henderson sold to the White House a "Blue Taffeta Spread
[not extant] to be used on Lincoln bed under Mrs.
Coolidge's knitted coverlet," $43.
REFERENCES: Mrs. Calvin Coolidge, "First Lady Makes
a Coverlet," *Washington Evening Star* (February 12, 1928),
33; and "A Coverlet for the Ages," *New York Herald* (February 12, 1928), 16–17. Henderson bill, OCWH.

SOUP SPOON, DINNER KNIFE, DINNER
FORK (page 207)
International Silver Co., Wallingford, Conn.,
circa 1926–60
Silver / stainless steel (knife blades)
Gift of International Silver Co., 1926, or U.S. Govern-
ment purchase, 1929–60
1926.3973.1.1-96, .11.1-67, .23.1-93
Soup Spoon—7 in. (17.8 cm.); 1 oz. 14 dwt.
Dinner Knife—9 5/8 in. (24.4 cm.); 2 oz. 3 dwt.
Dinner Fork—7 7/8 in. (20.0 cm.); 1 oz. 19 dwt.
MARKS: Reverse of all pieces except knives—stamped
"INTERNATIONAL STERLING PATD"; knife han-
dles—stamped "STERLING HANDLE"; blades—
etched "INTERNATIONAL / STAINLESS."
INSCRIPTIONS: Handle face engraved "President's
House."
NOTES: A flatware service in International Silver's
"Minuet" pattern was selected by Grace Coolidge in
1926 and donated by the manufacturer. The pattern,
both flatware and hollowware, was described in advertising as part of "a great new decorative movement" that
began in 1924 with the opening of the American Wing of
the Metropolitan Museum of Art in New York. "Minuet! Dance of lovely Colonial society! Design with the
grace of America's most graceful period! Expressing that
everlasting good taste which comes to us from early
America." It was apparently unclear whether the service
was a gift to Mrs. Coolidge personally since it was not
recorded in the White House inventories until after her
departure. "Found and added" in the 1929 and 1931
inventories were 20 each of most of sixteen types of
knives, forks, and spoons with 12 types of serving uten-
sils. From the administrations of Herbert Hoover

through Richard Nixon, 1929 to 1973, supplements of
most of these types were purchased as the service was
increased in size—to 70 of most types in 1950, to 100 in
1960. Several types not original to the 1926 set also were
ordered, including fish knives and forks first ordered in
1929 and steak knives in 1957. The Minuet service was
used at luncheons and dinners until 1974 and continues
to be used by White House families.
REFERENCES: Letter from E. P. Hogan, historian,
International Silver Co., June 11, 1980, OCWH. "Minuet: A Service in International Sterling" promotional
brochure, 1932, OCWH. Vouchers 208 and 339, from
Berry & Company, Washington, D.C., 1929, OCWH.

INKSTAND (page 208)
John Wakelin & Robert Garrard I (partnership
1792–1802), London, 1800–1801
Silver, glass
Gift of Mr. and Mrs. John Coolidge, 1982
1982.1506.1
1 1/8 x 9 1/4 x 6 3/8 in. (2.9 x 23.5 x 16.2 cm.); 18 oz.
MARKS: Underside and one bottle lid—hallmarked "IW
/ RG," lion passant, crowned leopard's head, "E."
INSCRIPTIONS: Underside engraved "Presented / to /
Mrs Coolidge / by / The Ladies of the Senate / March 4,
1929."
NOTES: At her departure from the White House in
1929, Grace Coolidge received from the Ladies of the
Senate this English silver inkstand to be used on a walnut
Pennsylvania slant-front desk, circa 1790, with a New
England maple and rush side chair, circa 1820. All three
pieces were donated to the White House by her son in
1982. The inkstand was accompanied by one of the
Monroe pearl-handled fruit knives which Mrs. Coolidge
apparently used as a letter opener (see page 71).
CONDITION: Scroll and floral engraving added in the
later 19th century.
PROVENANCE: A. Schmidt & Sons, Washington, D.C.;
sold to the Ladies of the Senate for presentation to
Grace Coolidge, 1929; to her son John Coolidge.

DESK (page 211)
Morris W. Dove (1878–1968), Washington, D.C., 1932
Mahogany / mahogany plywood; marble; brass; leather
U.S. Government purchase, 1932
1932.391.1
57 5/8 x 38 x 34 (open) in. (148.9 x 96.5 x 86.4 cm.)
MARKS: None.
NOTES: Early in his first mission as minister to France
(1794–97), James Monroe purchased furnishings for his
Paris residence, including a fall-front desk (*secrétaire à
abattant*) now on exhibit at the James Monroe Museum
and Memorial Library, Fredericksburg, Virginia. On the
desk, which was among the personal furnishings brought
by the Monroes to the White House, President Monroe
reportedly signed his 1823 Annual Message to Congress,
the section of which concerning European non-interfer-
ence in the Americas is now called the "Monroe Doctrine." This desk is among seven pieces in the Monroe
Museum collection that were copied for Lou Hoover in
1932 and placed in what she called the "Monroe Room"
(now the Treaty Room) at the White House. Much of
the $1,480 bill was spent on the desk ($450) and copies

of contemporary but similarly unmarked French pieces—
commode ($380) and tea table ($180). Dove, an immigrant from Russia in 1912, had a long association with
the White House. From 1913 to his retirement in 1952,
he made replacement chairs for the Cabinet Room as
they were needed to fulfill the tradition of Cabinet officers receiving their individual chairs by purchase or gift
from staff or friends.
REFERENCES: Account 91020, voucher 64, OCWH.
Lee Langston-Harrison, A *Presidential Legacy: The Monroe
Collection* (Fredericksburg, Va.: James Monroe Museum
and Memorial Library, 1997), 83–85. Dare Stark
McMullin, "Hoover Furniture Study," 1932, Herbert
Hoover Library.

DRESSING TABLE (page 213)
Otto Berge, The Val-Kill Furniture Shop, Hyde Park,
New York, circa 1933
Maple / white pine
U.S. Government purchase, 1933
1933.911.1
29 1/8 x 38 x 19 3/4 in. (74.0 x 96.5 x 50.2 cm.)
MARKS: Top of drawer front—branded "Val Kill" (dou-
ble-boxed); under top at right—branded "Otto" and
"10M" [the 14th example of type no. 10].
NOTES: To provide jobs or greater economic security
for rural men and women, Eleanor Roosevelt helped
established a small furniture factory on the family estate
at Hyde Park, New York. At The Val-Kill Furniture
Shop, Italian and Norwegian craftsmen recruited from
New York City began work in 1927 to "copy early American furniture, doing it as nearly as possible in the same
ways as the early Americans did it." From the start the
furniture had been expensive; so when the Depression
came, there was a serious decline in orders. By her own
admission, Mrs. Roosevelt remained the shop's best customer. In May 1933, only two months after moving into
the White House, Mrs. Roosevelt directed that eleven
pieces of Val-Kill furniture be purchased for the White
House from the New York furniture store W. & J.
Sloane. All five pieces of a maple bedroom suite placed in
a small guest bedroom on the Second Floor were
branded with a craftsman's first name: this dressing table
($62) and a night table ($42) by "Otto" Berge, a stool
($28) by "Arn" Berge, a bed ($62) by "Karl" Johannsen,
and a small mirror ($28) by "Frank" Landolfa. The other
six pieces were small tables, three of walnut and three of
mahogany; none of the three extant tables is marked with
a maker name. In January 1938, a supplemental maple
chest of drawers was purchased from Sloane.
REFERENCES: Voucher 460, OCWH. Emily L.
Wright, "Eleanor Roosevelt and the Val-Kill Industries
1927–38" (master's thesis, State University of New
York at Oneonta, 1982).

SALAD PLATE (page 215 right)
Lenox, Inc., Trenton, New Jersey, 1934
China
U.S. Government purchase, 1934
1934.3860.7.1–78
7 1/4 in. (18.4 cm.)
MARKS: Underside of plates—gilt printed "THE
WHITE HOUSE / 1934" / wreathed script "L" /MADE

IN THE U.S.A./"LENOX / WM. H. PLUMMER & CO., LTD. / NEW YORK CITY."
NOTES: The Franklin D. Roosevelt state service was purchased from New York retailer Wm. H. Plummer & Co. in 1934 for $9,301.20. Ordered on October 13, 1934, the 1722-piece service was received in January 1935. Eight pieces were ordered for 120, with the salad plates at $66 per dozen. Only eight dozen were ordered of several types and fewer of some others. In the design, patriotic rim stars and a polychrome rendering of the Presidential arms was personalized by a band of gilt roses separated by sets of three feathers, derived from the Roosevelt family arms. During the Clinton administration (1994), Lenox produced 2,289 supplements of thirteen pieces, including 155 salad plates bearing the 1934 and modern company marks.
REFERENCES: National Capital Parks, acct. 978388, voucher 463, OCWH. Klapthor, *Official White House China*, 159–63.

WATER GOBLET and FINGER BOWL
(page 215 left)
T. G. Hawkes & Company, Corning, N.Y., 1938, with blanks by Tiffin Glass Co., Tiffin, Ohio
Cut and engraved glass
U.S. Government purchase, 1938
1938.3878.1.1-127 & .7.1-143
Water Goblet—6 x 3 3/8 in. (15.2 x 8.6 cm.)
Finger Bowl—2 1/2 x 5 1/4 in. (6.4 x 13.3 cm.)
MARKS: Underside—etched "HAWKES."
NOTES: The Franklin D. Roosevelt state glassware service was first ordered in late 1937 from Washington retailer Martin's. The Hawkes "Venetian" pattern was selected, which the firm renamed "White House," with the addition of an engraved eagle emblem. The invoice survives for ten dozen each of goblets and finger bowls at $95 per dozen; the acquisition of the matching dinner wine glasses is uncertain, but ten dozen each of dessert wine and sherry glasses were first acquired in 1941 from Martin's. In 1946 champagnes without the emblem were purchased. After that the various types were reordered.
REFERENCES: National Capital Parks, acct. 1119052, voucher 427, OCWH. Spillman, *White House Glassware*, 120–23, 130–32.

PIANO and BENCH (page 216–17)
Steinway and Sons, Long Island City, New York, 1938; design by Eric Gugler (1889–1974); legs by Albert Stewart (1900–); decoration by Dunbar Beck (1902–86)
Mahogany, gilded wood, gold-plated brass / piano works
Gift of Steinway & Sons, 1938
1938.1287.1–.1288.1
Piano—38 3/8 x 115 x 59 3/4 in. (97.5 x 292.1 x 151.8 cm.)
Bench—19 1/2 x 41 1/4 x 16 1/4 in. (49.5 x 104.8 x 41.3 cm.)
MARKS: Iron frame—relief "300,000 / 1938" "STEIN-WAY & SONS / NEW YORK," "STEINWAY FOUNDRY CASTING," "STEINWAY & SONS / (lyre) / NEW YORK / REGISTERED / U.S. PAT. OFF"; "11 / 1.B / 1253 / (rosette)."
INSCRIPTIONS: Ivory plaque above keyboard engraved "Presented to / THE UNITED STATES OF AMER-ICA / By / STEINWAY & SONS."

NOTES: At a ceremony on December 10, 1938, this grand piano was presented to President Franklin D. Roosevelt for the White House by Mr. Theodore Steinway, on behalf of the Steinway family. The 300,000th Steinway piano, it was built to replace another Steinway at the White House—no. 100,000, a gilded and painted grand piano that had been given in 1903 (now at the Smithsonian Institution). Seeking to create a unique and distinguished "State Piano," Eric Gugler—a New York architect, friend of the Roosevelts, and White House consultant in the 1930s—chose a square form with simpler lines than the routine double-curve form. At Mr. Steinway's suggestion, Dunbar Beck, a muralist, executed the gold leaf decoration, with painted details, representing "five music forms indigenous of America"—a New England barn dance; a cowboy playing his guitar; the Virginia reel; two black field hands, one clapping and one dancing; and an Indian ceremonial dance. Albert Stewart, a sculptor, executed the three gilded mahogany legs carved as American eagles.
CONDITION: The instrument was rebuilt by Steinway within its original case, 1979. Replacement gold-plated handles.
REFERENCES: "The White House Steinway," booklet prepared by the manufacturer, 1938–39, OCWH. Eric Gugler Papers, OCWH. Elise K. Kirk, *Music at the White House: A History of the American Spirit* (Urbana, Ill.: University of Illinois Press, 1986), 236–39.

SERVICE PLATE, SOUP PLATE, and BOUILLON CUP AND SAUCER (page 220)
Lenox, Inc., Trenton, New Jersey, 1951
China
U.S. Government purchase, 1951
1951.3862 .1.1-114, .5.1-119, .11.1-106, .12.1-114
Service Plate—11 3/8 in. (28.9 cm.)
Soup Plate—9 1/8 in. (23.2 cm.)
Cup—2 1/4 x 5 1/4 x 3 1/2 in. (5.7 x 13.3 x 8.9 cm.); Saucer—6 in. (15.2 cm.)
MARKS: Underside of plates—gilt printed wreathed script "L" / WHITE HOUSE SERVICE / BY LENOX / X-308 / MADE IN U.S.A. / B. ALTMAN & CO." (X-308 on all but X-307 on service plates.)
NOTES: The Truman state service was purchased in 1951 from New York retailer B. Altman & Co., the firm which handled the refurbishing of the White House during the Truman renovation. It was designed by Charles T. Haight, head of Altman's design department. The 2,572-piece service, 13-piece place settings for 120, cost $26,944.10. The service plates cost $270.11 per dozen, the soup plates $177.50, and the sets of bouillon cups and saucers $266.57. Received on October 30, 1951, it was first used on April 3, 1952, at a luncheon for Queen Juliana of the Netherlands, only a week after the Trumans had moved back into the building. The green banding complemented the walls of the State Dining Room, painted a celadon green in the renovation.
REFERENCES: National Capital Parks, acct. 138797, voucher 463, OCWH. Klapthor, *Official White House China*, 165–68.

CHIFFONIER (page 221)
Kaplan Furniture Co., Cambridge, Mass., circa 1951

Mahogany; mahogany and satinwood veneers / mahogany, red pine; mirror glass, leather
U.S. Government purchase, 1952
1952.3227.1
53 1/4 x 37 3/4 x 20 1/8 in. (135.3 x 95.9 x 51.1 cm.)
MARKS: Interior of upper drawer—paper label—19th century Boston street scene / "BEACON HILL COLLECTION / (REG. U.S. PAT. OFFICE) / Piece Number" [handwritten] "828."
NOTES: Purchased as part of B. Altman's contract for furnishings for the Truman renovation—"1 No. 828 Chiffonier" for $368, February 2, 1952. Founded early in the 20th century, the Kaplan Furniture Co. specialized in reproducing or adapting fine antique furniture. Its "Beacon Hill Collection" was shown in New York at B. Altman & Co., which ordered many pieces from that line for use in the White House. This piece was described in the Beacon Hill catalogues as "No. 828 MARLOWE—Sheraton High Chest, recreated from American design of the period 1790. Mahogany, inlaid with satinwood; ivory escutcheons . . ." and as "Chiffonier . . . Ideal chest for the head of the house." It was acquired for use in President Truman's bedroom.
REFERENCES: Kaplan Furniture Co., *The Beacon Hill Collection* (Boston: Kaplan Furniture Co., circa 1950–56), 159. Kaplan Furniture Co., *Selections from the Beacon Hill Collection* (Boston: Kaplan Furniture Co., circa 1950), 17.

OVERMANTEL GLASS WITH PAINTING
(page 222)
England, circa 1695
Gilded red pine, mirror glass, brass / oil on canvas
Gift of King George VI, 1951
1951.3327.1
80 x 55 x 4 in. (203.2 x 139.7 x 10.2 cm.)
MARKS: None.
NOTES: Presented by Princess Elizabeth of Great Britain (now Queen Elizabeth II) on behalf of her father, King George VI, on November 3, 1951, at a ceremony in the Rose Garden of the White House. Given toward the conclusion of the Truman Renovation (the Trumans would move back in on March 24, 1952), the princess cited world interest in the project and said: " . . . we are glad to join with you in celebrating its restoration; and my father, who has many happy memories of his own stay in the house [in 1939], has wished to mark the event with a personal gift. It gave the King great pleasure when he found the overmantel which is before you now. The work of Eighteenth Century artists, and embodying the finest British craftsmanship, it seems perfectly suited for the place which it will occupy. . . . It is his hope, and mine, that it will be a welcome ornament to one of your proudest national possessions and that it will remain here, as a mark of our friendship, so long as the White House shall stand." President Truman hung it in the State Dining Room. Reportedly made for the residence of Sir Fisher Tench, circa 1695, this overmantel mirror of an early-18th-century style, called "a chimney looking glass" or "mantel-tree looking glass" in its period, is framed together with a still life painting by an unidentified artist.

CONDITION: The gilding has been conserved. Small brass sconce arms missing.
PROVENANCE: Purchased from a British dealer for donation by King George VI.
REFERENCES: *Washington Post*, November 3, 1951. Herbert F. Schiffer, *The Mirror Book* (Exton, Penn.: Schiffer Publishing, 1983), fig. 126. Joseph Downs, *American Furniture: Queen Anne and Chippendale Periods* (New York: Viking, 1967 reprint of 1952), no. 251.

MANTEL CLOCK (page 223)
Case possibly by Pierre-Joseph Gouthière (1732/40–?) / movement by Michel-François Piolaine (working 1787–circa 1810), Paris, circa 1780–90
Gilt bronze, marble / enameled metal, spring-driven clock and organ movements
Gift of President Vincent Auriol of France, 1952
1952.3502.1
25 1/2 x 18 x 8 in. (64.8 x 45.7 x 20.2 cm.)
MARKS: Dial—inscribed "Piolaine / A PARIS."
NOTES: Shortly after they moved back into the renovated White House, President and Mrs. Harry Truman received gifts especially selected by President Vincent Auriol of France. This musical *pendule* and a pair of gilded bronze candelabra were presented on April 18, 1952, by Henri Bonnet, French ambassador to the United States, "in token of the gratitude and friendship of the French people for the people of the United States." A nearly identical case, with works by Edme-Philibert Guydamour, is known; it has a floral swag suspended beneath the drapery pole that is also found on many other very similar non-musical clocks, with the clock works and cherub-goat support structure on a low marble base, one with works by Piolaine. Those smaller clocks all have a reclining Bacchante, rather than Athena, atop the clock dial.
CONDITION: Possibly missing a floral swag from the drapery pole.
PROVENANCE: Acquired by President Vincent Auriol of France for presentation to the White House.
REFERENCES: *Washington Evening Star*, April 18, 1952. Bernard Pin, "Retrouvailles," *Nouvelle Revue de L'Association des Amis Des Instruments et de la Musique Mechanique* (Paris: 4th Trimester, 1984), 870–71.

WINE COOLER (page 224)
Paul Storr (1771–1844), London, 1809–10, for Rundell, Bridge & Rundell
Gilded silver
Bequest of Margaret Thompson Biddle, 1957
1957.4147.1
13 7/8 x 13 1/4 in. (35.2 x 33.7 cm.); 202 oz.
MARKS: Base edge of urn and underside of stand—hallmarked "P.S", lion passant, crowned leopard head, "O," king head; body liner side—all but leopard; rim liner side—all but leopard and king; base flange of urn—stamped "RUNDELL BRIDGE ET RUNDELL AURIFICES REGIS ET PRINCIPIS WALLIAE LONDINI FECERUNT"; underside of stand—stamped "RUNDELL BRIDGE ET RUNDELL LONDINI"; fillet below horses—chased "AD 1809".
INSCRIPTIONS: All components engraved with an unidentified British armorial including an earl's coronet.

NOTES: From a set of four received in January 1958 as part of a collection of gilded silver bequeathed by Margaret Thompson Biddle, heiress to a Montana mining fortune. Her collection of gilded silver was shared among homes in New York and Paris and on the French Riviera. This cooler is after a design by John Flaxman (1755–1826) or William Theed (1764–1817) found in a book of drawings for London retailers Rundell, Bridge & Rundell—"Design for Plate by John Flaxman, etc." (Victoria & Albert Museum). The form is derived from the famous Medici Krater as engraved by Piranesi in 1778. The decoration of a bacchanalian procession is after a second century A.D. Roman sarcophagus as published in a book on the Vatican Museum, 1782–1802. The first examples may be a set of eight by Benjamin Smith, 1808, in the British Royal Collection. In this set of four made by Storr in the following year, three are stamped "44," but each bears a set number from "1" to "4." A matching pair, engraved with an elaborate baronial arms, was also received in the bequest.
CONDITION: Electroplated prior to donation.
PROVENANCE: Margaret Thompson Biddle.
REFERENCES: N. M. Penzer, *Paul Storr, 1771–1844, Silversmith and Goldsmith* (London: Spring Books, 1971) pl. XXIX. Henry Hawley, *Neo-Classicism, Style and Motif* (Cleveland, Ohio: Cleveland Museum of Art, 1964), fig. 182. Charles Oman, "A Problem of Artistic Responsibility," *Apollo* (March 1966) (attribution to William Theed, head designer and partner in Rundell, Bridge & Rundell).

ASSORTED TABLEWARE (page 225)
Gilded silver
Bequest of Margaret Thompson Biddle, 1957

WATER AND WINE EWERS (page 225—see above)
Richard Sibley (working circa 1793–1836), London, 11817–18
957.4142.2 & .1
Water—16 13/16 x 8 3/8 x 7 in. (42.7 x 21.3 x 17.8 cm.); 143 oz. 13 dwt.
Wine—16 5/8 x 8 3/4 x 7 in. (42.6 x 22.2 x 17.8 cm.); 145 oz. 17 dwt.
MARKS: Spout—hallmarked "RS" [script, boxed], lion passant, crowned leopard head, "b," king head.
NOTES: These ewers—a seated triton with a sea serpent head and waterleaves on one for water, a satyr with a ram's head and grapevine on the mate for wine—were based on a popular form made by the Wedgwood pottery in black basalt ware. In 1775 Wedgwood & Bentley paid model-caster John Flaxman, Sr., for "A pair of vases one with a Satyr & the other with Triton Handle" that were probably castings, or possibly designs, from an antique or Renaissance metal prototype. A remarkably similar "Design for Vases' was drawn by French designer, Jean Le Paurte, circa 1661.
REFERENCES: Christie's, sale 7822, January 22, 1994, no. 386. Sotheby's, sale 5761, October 28–29, 1988, no. 65, citing Reilly and Savage, *The Dictionary of Wedgwood* and Harry Barnard, *Wedgwood Chats*, 224.

PUNCH BOWL (page 225—see above)
George Wickes (1698–1761), London, 1739–40
1957.4182.1

7 7/8 x 11 1/2 x 10 3/4 in. (20.0 x 29.2 x 27.3 cm.); 63 oz. 5 dwt.
MARKS: Base edge—hallmarked with fleur de lis / "GW" [Gothic in trefoil box], lion passant, crowned leopard head, "d."
INSCRIPTIONS: Unidentified engraved armorial—dragon passant over cypher-like scrolls centering inescutcheon hand.
NOTES: Wickes, goldsmith to Frederick, Prince of Wales (son of King George II), founded, circa 1735, a London firm that evolved into the current firm of R. Garrard, royal goldsmith since 1830. This is the second oldest English piece in the Biddle collection.

ENTREE PLATE (page 225—see above)
Gorham Mfg. Co., Providence, Rhode Island, 1916
1957.4234.1-12
9 in. (22.9 cm.); 11 oz. 6 dwt.
MARKS: Reverse—stamped lion passant, anchor, "G [gothic] / STERLING / K Y D / E.A. BROWN CO.," hatchet datemark.
INSCRIPTIONS: Center engraved with cypher "MAT" for Margaret Thompson [Biddle].
NOTES: From a service for twelve in five sizes of plates, with matching serving platters, pierced in a neoclassical design of cornucopia and fruit baskets.
REFERENCES: Charles Carpenter, *Gorham Silver*.

GOBLET (page 225—see above)
Tiffany & Co., New York, 1937–47.
1957.4279.1-12
6 x 3 3/16 in. (15.2 x 8.1 cm.); 8 oz.
MARKS: Foot underside—stamped "TIFFANY & Cº / MAKERS / 22397 / STERLING SILVER / 925-1000 / m [gothic]."
INSCRIPTIONS: Side engraved with cypher "MTB" for Margaret Thompson Biddle.
NOTES: From a set of twelve of a simple form first registered by Tiffany in 1937–38. Accompanied by twelve each of two sizes of more conical Tiffany goblets without monograms.
REFERENCES: Carpenter with Carpenter, *Tiffany Silver*.

GOBLET (page 225—see above)
Joseph Jackson (working 1775–1807), Dublin, circa 1775–87
1957.4277.1-2
6 3/4 x 3 3/4 in. (17.2 x 9.5 cm.); 7 oz. 1 dwt.
MARKS: Base—hallmarked "I.I" [boxed], crowned harp [in conforming frame used until 1787], Hibernia.
NOTES: One of a pair, the only Irish pieces in the Biddle collection.
REFERENCES: Smithsonian Institution Traveling Exhibition Service, *Irish Silver From the Seventeenth to the Nineteenth Century*, 1982, 42, 47–48.

JAM POT (page 225—see above)
Philippe-Jean-Baptiste Huguet (working circa 1800–1816), Paris, 1809–16
1957.4208.1
8 x 7 1/2 x 5 3/4 in. (20.3 x 19.1 x 14.6 cm.); 23 oz. 3 dwt.
MARKS: Lid—stamped maker's lozenge "PJBH" and 1809–19 Paris 1st standard silver and medium excise marks.

NOTES: The neoclassical decoration of this glass-lined pot includes a medallion of a female face with grapes in her hair, perhaps suggestive of its fruity contents.

SWEETS SERVERS (page 225—see above)
Robert Gainsford (working 1808–?), Sheffield, England, 1812–13
1957.4178.1-3
4 1/2 x 9 in. (11.4 x 22.9 cm.); 12 oz. 8 dwt.
MARKS: Underside—hallmarked "R.G" (boxed), lion passant (king head?), crowned "D."
INSCRIPTIONS: Underside engraved "Was the Property / of H. Royl Highn^ss the / Duke of York. / Bought with the / Prize Monies of / Vittoria [sic Vitoria, Spain] June 21st / 1813 and / Waterloo June 10th / 1815."
NOTES: From a set of three. Gainsford was registered with the assay office in Sheffield in 1808, by which time the city, which was granted an assay office only in 1773, was more famous for its production of less expensive silverplated ware than for its silver.
PROVENANCE: Frederick, Duke of York (1767–1827), second son of King George III, from a set of three purchased with prize monies from the Napoleonic wars.

SUGAR POT (page 225—see above)
Benjamin and James Smith (partnership 1809–16), London, 1810–11; (Benjamin, working 1791–1822)
1957.4207.1-4
7 7/8 x 5 1/2 x 4 5/8 in. (20.0 x 14.0 x 11.8 cm.); 31 oz. 4 dwt.
MARKS: Body underside—hallmarked "B S / I.S" (boxed), lion passant, crowned leopard head, "P," king head; lid—maker, lion, date letter; finial—maker and lion.
NOTES: From a set of four. Benjamin Smith was one of the foremost English Regency silversmiths. In a series of partnerships, including one with his brother James, he frequently supplied ware to the crown jewelers and goldsmiths, Rundell, Bridge and Rundell, a firm known for its classical-revival ware, sometimes modeled by notable sculptors such as John Flaxman, Jr. (1755–1826). This form was reportedly derived from an antique vase from the collection of the Marquess of Lansdowne, and a drawing of a similar vase, circa 1805, is among the Flaxman materials at the Victoria & Albert Museum, London. Some were made in 1805 by Smith in partnership with Digby Scott. In the British Royal Collection are seven by Benjamin and James Smith, 1809. From 1813, the form was also made by Smith's great rival, Paul Storr.
REFERENCES: Sotheby's, sale 6071, October 12, 1990. Penzer, *Paul Storr*, pl.LII.

SALT CELLAR (page 225—see above)
Paul Storr (1771–1844), London, 1809–10
1957.4216.1-12
2 5/8 x 4 1/8 in. (6.7 x 10.5 cm.); 12 oz. 2 dwt.
MARKS: Underside—hallmarked lion passant, crowned leopard head, "P.S," "O," king head.
INSCRIPTIONS: Unidentified engraved armorial device—earl's coronet over griffin head.
NOTES: From a set of twelve. Matching Storr salts made in 1811 are known, as are simpler 1810 examples without the rim shells or side swags. The leading English Regency silversmith, Storr often provided silver to the firm of

Rundell, Bridge, and Rundell jewelers and goldsmiths to the Crown, before joining that partnership, 1811–19.
REFERENCES: Morrie A. Moss, *The Lillian and Morrie Moss Collection of Paul Storr Silver* (Miami: Roskin Book Productions, 1972), pl. 37 (matching 1808 pair). Sothebys, Los Angeles, sale 331, March 1–3, 1982.

TALL CASE CLOCK (page 226)
Effingham Embree, New York, circa 1790–1800; unidentified cabinetmaker
Mahogany / maple; light and dark wood inlays, brass / brass, painted iron, brass weight-driven movement
Gift of the National Society of Colonial Dames in America, 1973
1973.976.1
95 3/4 x 18 1/4 x 10 in. (243.2 x 46.4 x 25.4 cm.)
MARKS: Dial—inscribed "Effingham Embree / New York."
NOTES: This pagoda-top case, with its eagle-inlay, seems to have been Embree's favorite form; at least nine nearly identical or very similar cases with marked faces are known, five of which are in museum collections—Brooklyn Museum of Art, Henry Ford Museum, Museum of Early Southern Decorative Arts, Boscobel (Garrison, N.Y.), and Florence Griswold Museum (Old Lyme, Conn.). This is the only works with musical chimes among them; the six tunes played are identified on the dial as: "March" (2), "Minuet" (2), "Dance," and "Air." Cases of the same general form were also used by some clocksmiths from the greater New York region—examples from Poughkeepsie, New York, and New Brunswick and Elizabethtown, New Jersey, are known. Two Elizabethtown clocks have musical chimes. The White House collection also contains a tall case clock and a bracket clock made when Embree worked in an earlier partnership with Joseph or Thomas Pearsall, circa 1785–90.
CONDITION: Extensively inpainted dial.
PROVENANCE: Israel Sack, Inc., New York; Berry B. Tracy, New York; purchased by the White House with donated funds.
REFERENCES: Brooks Palmer, *Treasury of American Clocks* (New York: Macmillan, 1967), no. 28. Kate Van Winkle Keller, "Musical Clocks in Early America and their Music," *Bulletin of the National Association of Watch & Clock Collectors* (June 1982): 253.

CHAPTER 7

MANTEL CLOCK (page 232)
Dubuc (possibly Jean-Baptiste b. 1743), Paris, France, circa 1815; unidentified bronzier
Gilded bronze / enameled metal, brass spring-driven movement
Gift of Dudley P. K. Wood, 1961
1961.116.1
18 x 14 x 5 1/2 in. (45.7 x 35.6 x 14.0 cm.)
Marks: Dial—inscribed "Dubuc / Rue Michel-le-Comte No. 33 / A PARIS." Main spring— "Fournier 1815 jeuillet" (July 1815).
NOTES: Dubuc, listed from 1806 to 1817 on the street recorded on the dial, frequently supplied this form for

the American market. Beneath the dial is a drapery mount bearing the famous words spoken by General Henry ("Light-Horse Harry") Lee in his "Funeral Oration upon George Washington" before both houses of Congress in Philadelphia, December 26, 1799: "WASHINGTON. / First in WAR. / First in PEACE. / First in the HEARTS of his COUNTRYMEN." The figure of Washington seems to have been derived from a 1796 engraving by Thomas Chessman after John Trumbull's painting, Washington Before the Battle of Trenton, with a spyglass in his right hand replaced by a rolled document. The relief image on the plinth represents Washington's resignation of his commission in 1783, both he and the other men in the scene wearing a toga-like drapery over their period clothing, perhaps an allusion to a similar return to civilian life by the Roman hero Cincinnatus. Although this case is most often found with a dial marked by Dubuc (matching examples at the Metropolitan Museum of Art, New York, and the Saint Louis Art Museum), others are known with dials marked by Charles Oudin of Paris (Butterfields' 1992) and Thomas Demilt of New York (Christie's 1992). The latter bears, as do some Dubuc clocks, a different eagle.
PROVENANCE: Dudley P. K. Wood.
REFERENCES: Hugh Honour, *The European Vision of America* (Cleveland: Cleveland Museum of Art, 1976), no. 225. Donald P. Fennimore, *Metalwork in Early America: Copper and Its Alloys from the Winterthur Collection* (Winterthur Museum, 1996), 303. Marshall B. Davidson and Elizabeth Stillinger, *The American Wing at the Metropolitan Museum of Art* (New York: Alfred A. Knopf, 1985), fig. 86.

LINEN PRESS (page 234)
Annapolis, Maryland, circa 1790–1800
Mahogany and mahogany veneer / pine and tulip poplar; maple banding; lightwood and stained inlays
Anonymous donation, 1971
1971.701.1
38 x 39 x 20 in. (96.5 x 99.1 x 50.8 cm.)
MARKS: Backboard—large indistinct chalk mark.
NOTES: Also called a clothespress or wardrobe, the linen press—a form most often produced in the Federal period in the southern states and in New York—is usually a cabinet of sliding drawers for the storage of clothing set atop a chest of drawers, one exception being a Baltimore chest-on-cabinet (Maryland Historical Society), unusual for its inverted arrangement of cases. The White House freestanding press, with its handsomely inlaid top, was clearly meant to serve without any surmounting cabinetry. Its doors, faced with a veneer oval set in a mitered panel, resemble those on the Baltimore cabinet and several other sophisticated pieces of Baltimore case furniture.
CONDITION: Four sliding trays replaced temporarily by modern plywood shelves; small splines spaced into back of both doors to correct warpage.
PROVENANCE: Reportedly originated in the Paca family of Maryland; David Stockwell, Inc., Wilmington, Delaware; purchased by the White House with donated funds.
REFERENCES: William G. Allman, "Federal Flora: Inlaid Furniture in the White House," *Washington Antiques*

Show Catalogue (January 1988), 149–53. Weidman, *Furniture in Maryland*, no. 75.

LIGHTHOUSE CLOCK (page 235)

Simon Willard (1753–1848) & Son, Roxbury, Mass., circa 1825; unidentified cabinetmaker
Mahogany and mahogany veneer / pine; brass, gilded metal, glass; glass sulphide / enameled metal, brass weight-driven movement
Gift of Mr. and Mrs. A. H. Meyer, 1961
1961.167.6
29 1/2 x 9 1/4 in. (74.9 x 23.5 cm.)
MARKS: Dial—inscribed "SIMON WILLARD & SON'S / PATENT."
NOTES: In an 1822 advertisement, Simon Willard announced: "the President of the United States [James Monroe] has granted him a PATENT RIGHT for his newly invented ALARUM TIMEPIECE." The ad was illustrated with an engraving of a lighthouse clock much like this one, some of the early examples of which were alarm clocks. Designed to resemble the famous Eddystone Lighthouse off Plymouth, England, many of the Willard lighthouse clocks have brass leaf-capped ball feet, a form used on this clock as the chime finial. The juncture between the circular shaft and octagonal plinth (sometimes circular or square) is filled here with simple mahogany moldings rather than gilt metal collars. At the invitation of President James Monroe and the Congress, the Marquis de Lafayette made a year-long "Triumphal Tour" throughout the twenty-four states of the United States, 1824–25. He was received by his friend Monroe at the White House on several occasions in the fall and winter and stayed at the White House with President John Quincy Adams in the summer of 1825. During his visit, the park north of the White House was named "Lafayette Square." Shortly after his return to Paris, he sent Monroe a small bronze bust (James Monroe Museum and Memorial Library), copied from an original bust that is believed to be the source for the portrait executed as a sulphide medallion set into this clock, presumably around the time of Lafayette's visit. A plaster copy of the bronze bust was given to the White House in 1930.
CONDITION: Door on rear of plinth missing. Replacement glass dome.
PROVENANCE: Israel Sack & Co.; purchased by Mr. and Mrs. A. H. Meyer, for donation to the White House.
REFERENCES: William H. Distin and Robert Bishop, *The American Clock* (New York: Dutton, 1976), 102–3. John Ware Willard, *Simon Willard and His Clocks* (1911; reprint, Mamaroneck, N.Y.: Paul P. Appel, 1962). Tracy, *19th Century America*, no. 62. Clement E. Conger et al., *Treasures of State* (New York: Abrams, 1991), fig. 153.

SIDE CHAIR (page 236)

Salem, Mass., circa 1800, carving possibly by the shop of Samuel McIntire (1757–1811)
Mahogany / pine
Gift of the White House Historical Association, 1961
1961.68.3
36 7/8 x 21 1/2 x 20 1/2 in. (93.7 x 54.6 x 52.1 cm.)
MARKS: None.

NOTES: The back with its interlaced arched splats and drapery-carved tablet is derived from George Hepplewhite's 1794 *The Cabinet-Maker and Upholsterer's Guide*. The star-punched ground of the tablet is a feature often associated with the fine decorative carving executed for both furniture and architectural elements in the Salem shop of the notable architect and carver Samuel McIntire. The White House has eight of this type of chair. This one, with a wider tablet (7 7/8 in.) was received with two with a similarly carved but smaller tablet (5 7/8 in.) that renders their crest rail arches more flat and elongated.
CONDITION: Double-lined brass ornamental nailing, part of a minimally invasive upholstery, is based on original pattern evidence.
PROVENANCE: John S. Walton, New York, N.Y.; purchased by the White House with donated funds.
REFERENCES: George Hepplewhite, *The Cabinet-Maker and Upholsterer's Guide* (1794; reprint, New York: Dover, 1969), pl. 9. Patricia E. Kane, *300 Years of American Seating Furniture* (Boston: New York Graphic Society, 1976), no. 215.

SIDE CHAIR (page 237)

James Gillingham (1736–81), Philadelphia, circa 1768–73
Mahogany / yellow pine
Gift of Mr. and Mrs. Mitchel Taradash, 1970
1970.669.1
38 3/4 x 23 1/2 x 18 1/2 in. (98.5 x 59.7 x 47.0 cm.)
Marks: Rear seat rail interior—paper label "James Gillingham / Cabinet and Chair Maker, / [in] Second Stree[t] / Between / Walnut & Chestnut Streets, / PHILADELPHIA."
NOTES: The existence of this and two matching chairs, all very rare labeled pieces by James Gillingham, has led many such trefoil-pierced-splat chairs to be attributed to Gillingham or at least called the Gillingham type. It was, however, a form popular among Philadelphia cabinet-makers, being derived from Thomas Chippendale's *Director* (1754 and 1762 editions). Many other chairs of this type, including some attributed to Thomas Tufft, are more heavily carved on their knees, seat front, and crest rail. The front seat rail and slip seat bear the set mark "IIII."
CONDITION: Broken tenons at the rear of each side seat rail have been repaired.
PROVENANCE: Mr. and Mrs. Mitchel Taradash.
REFERENCES: Chippendale, *Director*, pls. X, XXIV. Luke Vincent Lockwood, *Colonial Furniture in America* (New York: Charles Scribner's Sons, 1901, Rev. ed. 1926), figs. 558–559. Hecksher, *American Furniture in the Metropolitan*, no. 54.

SETTEE (page 238)

Philadelphia, circa 1800–10
Mahogany and mahogany veneer / ash; stained lightwood inlay
Gift of Mr. and Mrs. A.H. Meyer, 1961
1961.167.1
36 1/2 x 75 x 23 1/2 in. (92.7 x 190.5 x 59.7 cm.)
MARKS: None.
NOTES: Settees of chairback types were illustrated in the drawing books of both George Hepplewhite (1788)

and Thomas Sheraton (1794/1802). This example is from a suite with four armchairs at the White House and four side chairs in the Kaufman Collection, which Michael Flanigan has called, "as fine a set of chairs as Federal Philadelphia produced." Very similar armchairs, but with a padded oval in the back (Winterthur Museum), were called by Charles Montgomery, "among the richest expressions of the American cabinet- and chairmaker of the Federal period." The chairs, are not strictly a set with the settee, differing in the placement of some of the carving—splat plumes carved on, rather than below, the crest rail, and ribbon ends carved on, not atop, the oval splat. In fact, in those details the settee more closely resembles the armchairs at Winterthur. Similar side chairs with a carved oval at the center of the oval splat are also known.
CONDITION:. The feet, seemingly intact on the settee, have been worn down or cut down on the chairs. Evidence of an ornamental tacking pattern of two straight parallel lines was uncovered during the application of minimally intrusive upholstery.
PROVENANCE: William and Mary Sloan Frick (by tradition an 1816 wedding gift); descended to great-granddaughter Mary Frick Montgomery; Israel Sack, Inc., New York; Mr. and Mrs. A. H. Meyer.
REFERENCES: J. Michael Flanigan, *American Furniture from the Kaufman Collection* (Washington, D.C.: National Gallery of Art, 1986), no. 45. Charles F. Montgomery, *American Furniture, The Federal Period, in the Henry Francis du Pont Winterthur Museum* (New York: Viking Press, 1966), no. 93. Philadelphia Museum of Art, Philadelphia, no. 174.

BOOKCASE (page 239)

Philadelphia, circa 1800–10
Mahogany and mahogany veneer / mahogany and pine; holly; glass
Gift of Yale University in honor of Francis P. Garvan, 1962
1962.352.1
107 1/8 x 73 1/2 x 21 1/2 in. (222.1 x 186.7 x 54.6 cm.)
MARKS: None.
NOTES: This is one of a very rare pair of bookcases once owned by a son of prominent Philadelphia banker Thomas Willing, who was a member of the Second Continental Congress and later president of the first Bank of the United States. The mate, with a fall-front butler's desk in place of a center drawer, is at the Yale University Art Gallery. The mullion pattern in the glazed upper case doors appears to be derived from "No. 1 " among six "Doors for Bookcases" in Thomas Sheraton's *The Cabinet-Maker and Upholsterer's Drawing-Book*, 1793. The delicate urn and scroll inlay at the center of the pediment flanked by urn-decorated panels on the final plinths are an unusual contrast with the otherwise strong, linear Federal ornamentation below.
CONDITION: Some repairs to mock-fluting; replacement locks; deep discoloration on center draw front. The upper case interior was first lined and illuminated in 1962.
PROVENANCE: Richard Willing; to Edward Shippen Willing, 1858; to J. Rhea Barton Willing; Louis Guerineau Myers; Myers sale at American Art Gallery, February 24, 1921, no. 642; the pair was purchased by Francis

P. Garvan and given to Yale University in the 1930s as part of the Mabel Brady Garvan Collection.
REFERENCES: Philadelphia Museum of Art, *Philadelphia*, no. 165. Thomas Sheraton, *The Cabinet-Maker and Upholsterer's Drawing-Book* (1793; reprint, New York: Dover, 1973), pl. 29. William MacPherson Horner, Jr., *Blue Book: Philadelphia Furniture, William Penn to George Washington* (Philadelphia: n.p., 1935), pl. 400.

WALLPAPER *(page 240–41)*
Jean Zuber et Cie, Rixheim, France, circa 1834–36
Block-printed wallpaper
Gift of the National Society of Interior Designers, 1961
1961.98.1
86 1/8 x 94 in. (218.8 x 238.8 cm.)
MARKS: None.
NOTES: In the first half of the 19th century, many handsome French wallpapers were imported into the United States, but such papers were not used just in the city or country homes of the most wealthy. In an 1830s stone house in the small town of Thurmont, Maryland, was hung a set of the panoramic paper entitled *Vues de l'Amerique du Nord* ("Views of North America") that was removed and installed in the White House in 1961. It was designed by Jean-Julien Deltil (1791–1863), probably after engravings of American scenes executed by French artists in the 1820s, but wallpaper historian Catherine Lynn has noted about this "General View of Boston" that, "Although the State House at the top of the hill clearly marks the scene as Boston, the foreground bears a close resemblance to waterside views of European ports pictured on other scenic papers." Block-printed in thirty-two panels using 1,674 wood blocks, this paper has been reprinted repeatedly in the 19th and 20th centuries. In addition to this scene of Boston, the paper consists of "General View of New York" (from Weehawken, New Jersey), "Review at the Military Academy at West Point," "Indian Calumet Dance by the Rock Bridge in the Allegheny Mountains" (Winnebago Indians at the Natural Bridge of Virginia), and "Niagara Falls." For installation in the Diplomatic Reception Room, supplemental panels of New York, Winnebago Indians, and West Point were acquired. In 1852, Zuber and Co. issued another paper, *Vues de la Guerre d'Indépendance Americaine* ("Views of the American War of Independence"), using the backgrounds from the "North America" paper onto which were hand-painted military figures of the American Revolution, creating four fanciful scenes. A set of this paper was also acquired for the White House in 1961.
PROVENANCE: Installed in the center hall of a house in Thurmont, Maryland; the house was purchased in 1891 by D.R. Rouzer; to his daughter, Mary Gertrude Rouzer Stoner, who sold the building about 1961; wallpaper to Peter Hill, Washington, D.C. (he purchased the rights to remove it just before demolition of the building began); purchased by the White House with donated funds.
REFERENCES: Henri Clouzet and Charles Folot, *Histoire du Papier Peint en France* (Paris: Editions d'Art Charles Moreau, 1935), 185. Lynn, *Wallpaper in America*, 192–93, 201.

PITCHER *(page 241)*
William Ellis Tucker and John Hulme (partnership 1828), Philadelphia, 1828
Porcelain
Gift of Mr. and Mrs. Raymond G. Grover, 1962
1962.264.1
7 1/2 x 4 1/2 x 3 3/4 in. (19.1 x 11.4 x 9.5 cm.)
MARKS: Underside—red handwritten "T & H N°200 / Philᵃ."
NOTES: In an attempt to manufacture American porcelain that could successfully compete with imports from Europe and the Far East, William Ellis Tucker opened a relatively short-lived Philadelphia factory in 1826. Trying to cope with financial burdens, he took in a series of partners, including John Hulme for but a few months in 1828. In the Tucker pattern book (Philadelphia Museum of Art), this is listed as the "Walker" shape, named for Andrew Craig Walker, who molded the finer pitchers for the Tucker works. Made in four sizes, this is one of two larger than the one-pint size, the only one for which a volume was recorded; both larger sizes sold for $1 each. At least eight of this form are known to carry a full "Tucker and Hulme" mark, some dated "1828."
CONDITION: Lower end of handle cracked; crack in bottom; chip on spout.
REFERENCES: "Tucker rarity to the White House," *Antiques* (July 1962): 79. Philadelphia Museum of Art, *Philadelphia*, 293–96. Frelinghuysen, *American Porcelain*, 14–20, fig. 11; and Frelinghuysen, "Tucker Porcelain," pl. XIV.

ARGAND LAMP *(page 242)*
Matthew Boulton, Soho, England, 1784
Sheffield silverplate, glass / electric light fixtures
Gift of the American Institute of Interior Designers, 1962
1962.328.1
19 3/8 x 12 7/8 x 5 7/8 in. (49.2 x 32.7 x 14.9 cm.)
MARKS: None.
NOTES: One of pair of lamps believed to have been presented to Major General Henry Knox (1750–1806), commander of artillery in the American revolution, by his friend and comrade in arms, the Marquis de Lafayette, during his first return visit to the United States in 1784. Knox would become the first secretary of war (1789–94) and was known for entertaining in New York and Philadelphia "in the style of a prince," a life style for which these lamps would have been most appropriate. After their sale in 1958, these double-burner peg lamps, designed to be fit into candlesticks or sconces, were mounted on their current vasiform shafts. In 1784, Swiss-born scientist François-Pierre-Ami Argand (1750–1803) received a British patent for his 1780 invention of a tubular oil burner with chimney—"a lamp that is so constructed to produce neither smoak [sic] nor smell, and to give considerably more light than any lamp hitherto known." He joined forces with William Parker & Son, the foremost London manufacturer of glass lighting fixtures, and Matthew Boulton, the Birmingham manufacturer of silverplate and brass, to form Argand's Patent Lamp Co. In August 1785, he gave to King Louis XVI a pair of lamps in this pattern, called "Louis" (no.

10565 in a Matthew Boulton sales catalog), atop a tall candlestick. Another "Louis" pattern lamp, supported on a glass pedestal, once belonged to George Washington (Smithsonian Institution). At the same time, other types of the very popular Argand lamps were purchased by Thomas Jefferson for Monticello and for his friend James Madison.
CONDITION: Electrified. Repaired chimney rings and replacement chimneys. Repaired urn stem on mate.
PROVENANCE: By tradition, the Marquis de Lafayette to Major General Henry Knox; Parke-Bernet, New York, November 16, 1956, no. 368; Frank Ganci Antiques; Melanie Kahane as part of the A.I.D. donation of furnishings for the Library of the White House.
REFERENCES: John J. Wolfe, *Brandy, Balloons, & Lamps: Ami Argand, 1750–1803* (Carbondale, Ill.: Southern Illinois University Press, 1999), pls. 5–6, figs. 2.20–2.22.

LOOKING GLASS *(page 243)*
New York or Boston, circa 1800–10
Gilded wood, reverse-painted glass, mirror glass
Gift of Vernon C. Stoneman, 1970
1970.662.1
63 x 35 1/2 x 6 in. (160.0 x 90.2 x 15.2 cm.)
MARKS: None.
NOTES: Federal looking glasses often were ornamented with *églomisé* panels, on a small group of which appears various depictions of an American eagle derived from the Great Seal of the United States. These patriotic eagles—holding the arrows, olive branch, and "E Pluribus Unum" motto banner, always beneath floral swags—were usually executed in a upright pose, as on the Seal, exposing an American shield on their breasts. On this unusually large mirror with its elaborate double-column stiles, the eagle, however, is crouched, its breast not exposed, which makes it somewhat less a static icon.
CONDITION: Extensive regilding. Resilvered glass.
PROVENANCE: Vernon C. Stoneman.
REFERENCES: Schiffer, *The Mirror Book*, fig. 159.

DESK AND BOOKCASE *(page 244)*
John Shaw (1745–1829), Annapolis, Maryland, 1797
Mahogany and mahogany veneer / tulip poplar, yellow pine, white oak; light, dark, and stained inlays; glass, baize, brass
Gift of the Hendler Foundation, in memory of Lionel Manuel Hendler, 1963
1963.471.1
98 5/8 x 45 3/4 x 36 1/4 in. (250.6 x 115.2 x 92.1 cm.)
MARKS: Center of bookcase interior back—printed paper label "JOHN SHAW, / CABINET-MAKER, / ANNAPOLIS" with handwritten "W 1797 T."
NOTES: Scottish-born John Shaw immigrated to Annapolis in the 1760s, during the height of its colonial affluence, and became the city's foremost cabinetmaker of the late 18th century. In 1797, the same year this desk was made, he crafted furniture—24 arm chairs and 11 desks—for the Senate chamber in the Maryland State House in Annapolis. An identical label has survived on one of those desks; the initials "WT" stand for a apprentice or journeyman in Shaw's shop, possibly William Tuck, whose brother Washington was apprenticed to Shaw in 1798. One of Shaw's most impressive and ele-

gant creations, this desk is stylistically transitional, a substantial basically Chippendale form lightened with Federal neoclassical inlays, including a large conch shell on the face of the fall board, and the delicately pierced pediment. The Museum of Early Southern Decorative Arts, Winston-Salem, North Carolina, has an extremely similar but unlabeled desk with diamond rather than oval mullions and an American eagle inlay instead of the acorn inlay on the prospect door. Another desk attributed to Shaw has a lower case of a true Federal form with cabinet doors and tall French feet.
CONDITION: Finial missing. Replacement proper right rear foot. Repaired pediment, feet, and base blocking. Modern green baize on writing board.
PROVENANCE: By family tradition, made for John Randall, Annapolis merchant; to his daughter Henrietta Randall Magruder; to John Randall Magruder; to Peter Hagner Magruder; purchased at Magruder estate auction, Galton-Osborn Co., Baltimore, Maryland, 1948, by Lionel Manuel Hendler; Hendler Foundation.
REFERENCES: William Voss Elder III and Lu Bartlett, *John Shaw, Cabinetmaker of Annapolis* (Baltimore: Baltimore Museum of Art, 1983), nos. 40, 49, 51. "New in the Mesda Collection," *The Luminary* (Fall 1998): 6.

SOFA (page 245)
New York, circa 1810–25
Mahogany and gilded and painted pine / pine
Gift of Eugene W. Bolling and the Honorable and Mrs. C. Douglas Dillon, 1961
1961.119.1
34 x 84 1/2 x 24 in. (86.4 x 214.6 x 61.0 cm.)
MARKS: None.
NOTES: This sofa is the least broad (by 8–20 inches) of several similar New York sofas, most in museum collections, which are among the high points of American cabinetmaking in the Empire style. Scrolled-arm "Grecian" sofas, which appear in the 1802 edition of the *London Chair-Makers' and Carvers' Book of Price for Workmanship*, became a popular early-19th-century American form, but this group shares an especially bold design with a scrolling arm and leg fashioned as one integral entity. The sinuous dolphin form, a neoclassical motif often seen as supports on Renaissance fountains, was also adapted for consoles on pier tables made in the 1820s. One of the most beautiful examples of this sofa form, at the Metropolitan Museum of Art, New York, has a scroll-ended concave crest rail and a Greek-key-inlaid seat rail. A similar but carved crest rail appears on one at the U.S. Navy Museum, Washington, D.C., the only one to have a nautical provenance—reportedly used on the USS *Constitution*—in character with its ornamentation.
CONDITION: Gilding and vert antique restored; small replaced sections of belly fins. Plate casters are missing, replaced by non-original wooden plinths.
PROVENANCE: Received by Eugene W. Bolling, circa 1910, from his father-in-law who acquired it circa 1880; partial donation.
REFERENCES: Tracy, *19th Century America*, no. 45. Oscar Fitzgerald, *Three Hundred Years of American Furniture* (Englewood Cliffs, N.J.: Prentice-Hall, 1983), VI-13.

CARD TABLE (page 246 left)
Probably New York, circa 1825
Mahogany, quarter-sawn oak and burl ash veneers, parcel-gilt mahogany, gilded and painted wood / pine, tulip poplar; cut glass
Gift of the Honorable and Mrs. C. Douglas Dillon, 1961
1961.21.1
29 1/2 x 36 x 18 in. (74.9 x 91.4 x 45.7 cm.)
MARKS: None.
NOTES: After about 1815, the lyre, as an emblem of antique classicism, became a structural element in American furniture, often used as the splat on chairs, benches, and settees and as the supports for card, work, and sofa tables. Its use may have originated with a lyre-back side chair sketched by Duncan Phyfe in New York, circa 1815, but it quickly became fashionable in other cities as well. A lyre support is unusual on such a stretcher-form card table, but very similar swan-head examples are also found on New York card tables of a platform type, circa 1815–25, including a mahogany pair donated to the White House in 1972. The glass mounts are also unusual; similar shapes of a different decorative pattern are found on a pair of pier tables sharing the use of oak veneers, one with a foot is marked "J. Young," possibly piece work provided to a larger shop by James or Joseph Young, who worked in New York circa 1819–26.
CONDITION: Conserved veneer and gilding.
PROVENANCE: Israel Sack, Inc., New York; purchased by the White House with donated funds.
REFERENCES: Peter M. Kenny et al., *Honoré Lannuier, Cabinetmaker from Paris* (New York: Metropolitan Museum of Art, 1998), pl. 45. Lorraine W. Pearce, "Lannuier in the President's House," *Antiques* (January 1962):3, 95. J. Michael Flanigan, letter of May 24, 1990, OCWH.

SOFA TABLE (page 246 right)
New York, in the manner of Charles-Honoré Lannuier, circa 1815–20
Mahogany and mahogany veneer, gilded and painted wood / tulip poplar, pine, mahogany
Gift of the Honorable and Mrs. C. Douglas Dillon, 1961
1961.12.1
28 1/2 x 55 3/4 (open) x 28 in. (72.4 x 141.6 x 71.1 cm.)
MARKS: None.
NOTES: One of the rarer forms in American cabinetmaking, the sofa table, a long rectangular drop-leaf table intended for placement before a sofa, was most often crafted with pedestal ends composed of square or turned posts, lyres, or, in the case of this bold example, pairs of turned and carved posts. This table and a nearly identical table at Bayou Bend (the Museum of Fine Arts, Houston) were further ornamented with winged caryatids, in the manner of the great New York cabinetmaker, Charles-Honoré Lannuier, filling each side atop the stretchers. It was acquired with an Lannuier attribution that was reassessed by Peter Kenny for the Lannuier exhibition at the Metropolitan Museum of Art, 1998.
CONDITION: Non-original finishes, the vert antique painting of the feet based on microscopic evidence.
PROVENANCE: Ginsburg & Levy, New York; purchased by the White House with donated funds.

REFERENCES: Kenny, *Honoré Lannuier*, xii. Lorraine Pearce, "Lannuier in the President's House," 95. Philip D. Zimmerman, "The American sofa table," *Antiques* (May 1999): 744–53, pl. I.

CANDELABRUM (page 248)
Paul Storr (1771–1844), London, 1810–11
Silver
Gift of Mrs. Dorothea S. Wiman, 1964
963.413.113
27 1/4 x 18 in. (69.2 x 45.7 cm.); 192 oz. 11 dwt.
MARKS: Base and arm cluster—hallmarked "P.S.," lion passant, crowned leopard head, "P," king head; cup liners—all but leopard; cups—all but leopard and date; bobeches—only maker and lion; edge of base—stamped "RUNDELL BRIDGE ET RUNDELL AURIFICES REGIS ET PRINCIPIS WALLIAE LONDINI" (Latin ascription, "Rundell, Bridge, and Rundell, Goldsmiths to the Crown and to the Prince of Wales, London," frequently added to works commissioned by the firm from independent smiths, including Paul Storr, who became a partner in the firm in 1811.)
INSCRIPTIONS: Base and arm cluster engraved with armorial device, ducal crown over tree rising from coronet, and overlaid with boxed "THROUGH" (Duke of Hamilton motto).
NOTES: This candelabrum is from a set of six (four at the White House) which once belonged to the Dukes of Hamilton. Made in 1810–11 by Paul Storr, they were presumably acquired by Alexander, Marquis of Douglas and Clydesdale (10th duke of Hamilton in 1819) (1767–1854), probably to supplement an official ambassadorial service of Storr silver that he received from the crown when appointed British ambassador to Russia in 1806. These candelabra, which bear no royal arms, were sold in 1919 with 250 pieces of the Hamilton ambassadorial service, made by Paul Storr, 1806–7 (104 dinner plates, 5 covered meat platters, and 2 covered chop plates were received by the White House from same donor). With a scaly-paneled shaft derived from mid-18th-century candlesticks, they have a removable arm structure for four lights (with finial) or five lights. The candlesticks are numbered 2, 3, 4, and 6, but other components of the original set of six were interchanged, numbered variously 1–6.
CONDITION: Two finials are missing.
PROVENANCE: Alexander, 10th Duke of Hamilton; sale of Hamilton estate silver at Christie, Manson & Woods, London, November 4, 1919, no. 33, six candelabra; Mrs. Dorothea S. Wiman (1964 addition to her 1963 donation).
REFERENCES: Christie, Manson & Woods, (London) Duke of Hamilton sale, November 4, 1919, no. 33. Moss, *Moss Collection*. pl. 37 (matching 1808 pair). Penzer, *Paul Storr*, pl. XXIV (nearly identical candlestick with two-arm branch).

RUG (page 249)
France, circa 1815
Wool
Anonymous donation, 1961
1961.154.1
230 x 174 in. (584.2 x 426.7 cm.)
MARKS: None.

NOTES: This rug may have been made at the Savonnerie factory, a 17th-century Paris producer of knotted-pile carpets which was revived as the Imperial Manufactory of Savonnerie under the patronage of Emperor Napoleon after 1805. It produced highly valued rugs in the Empire style, some after designs by Charles Percier (1764–1838). Huge carpets were made for the Tuileries palace, for the chateaux at Saint-Cloud and Compiègne and for other Napoleonic residences. Its bold neoclassical design includes a wide band of roses and daisies in the center medallion that is very similar to that on the rug in Napoleon's bedroom at the Grand Trianon; the ball-tipped arcade motif and block border are more general elements shared by both of those rugs. This rug was acquired in 1961 as a floor covering for the Red Room with its newly acquired Empire-style furniture. Retired in 1965 due to its condition, it has been reproduced three times—in 1965, 1971, and most recently in 1997—so that this particular Empire design has remained almost continuously in the Red Room.
CONDITION: Extensive wear and some reweaving.
PROVENANCE: Coury Rugs, Inc., New York; purchased by the White House with donated funds.
REFERENCES: Deschamps, *Empire*, 114, 149–52. Stéphane Faniel et al., *Le Dix-neuvième siècle Français* (Paris: Hachette, 1957), 172.

DESSERT COOLER (page 251 left)
France, circa 1815–25
Porcelain
Gift of Grafton Minot, 1962
1962.311.1
15 3/4 x 11 1/2 x 8 1/4 in. (40.0 x 29.2 x 21.0 cm.)
MARKS: None.
INSCRIPTIONS: Body front marked with cypher "WCE" for William and Caroline Eustis.
NOTES: One of a pair reportedly given to William and Caroline Eustis by the Marquis de Lafayette during his 1824–25 visit to the United States. As governor of Massachusetts, Eustis, a surgeon in the Continental Army, received his "old friend" (as Lafayette called himself in an 1816 letter) in August 1824 for a state banquet in Boston and a night's stay at his home in Roxbury. It is also possible, however, that Eustis received these from Lafayette during his service as minister to the Netherlands (circa 1815–18), possibly in 1816 when he gave a pair of prints to Lafayette. A shipping manifest of Eustis property, circa 1816, listed "5 covered vases," which may include these coolers. Ice cream or fruit ices held in the liner were set down into ice filling the rest of the body. The tall spool-like cover is comparable to the necks on some French porcelain vases and coffeepots.
CONDITION: Left proper handle on each cooler repaired; chip in edge of covers; body of mate also repaired.
PROVENANCE: By tradition, William and Caroline Eustis as a gift from the Marquis de Lafayette; gift to John Minot, aide to Eustis; descended in family to Grafton Minot.
REFERENCES: John Bradford Hermanson, "The Shirley-Eustis House, Roxbury, Massachusetts," *Antiques* (August 1991): 206–18. Michel Bloit, *Trois Siècles de Porcelaine de Paris* (Paris: Editions Hervas, 1988), 73. Plinval de Guillebon, *Porcelain of Paris*, pl. 66.

URN (page 251 right)
Barr Flight & Barr, Worcester, England, circa 1807
Porcelain
Gift of A. P. Rochelle Thomas, 1961
1961.17.1
16 3/8 x 9 1/4 x 7 1/2 in. (41.6 x 23.5 x 19.1 cm.)
MARKS: Underside of foot—red printed crown / "Barr Flight & Barr / Worcester / Flight & Barr / Coventry Street / London / Manufacturers to their / Majesties and / Royal Family."
INSCRIPTIONS: Side—"To Commemorate / A VICTORY obtain'd by H.M.S. BLANCHE / 38 Guns, over the French Frigate Le [sic La] GUERRIERE / of 50 Guns, after a close engagement of 45 Minutes. / This GALLANT EXPLOIT was achiev'd / without the loss of a SINGLE MAN on the / part of the BLANCHE thro' the persevering / Activity and superior Seamanship of / CAPTAIN, now SIR THOˢ LAVIE, / to whom this VASE is dedicated / by his most sincere Friend and / affectionate Brother in Law / THOˢ: St. JOHN."
NOTES: Made to commemorate the capture of the French frigate *La Guerrière* by Royal Navy Captain Thomas Lavie in command of HMS *Blanche*, July 18, 1806. For this victory off the Faroe Islands without the loss of a single British life, Lavie received a knighthood of the Order of the Bath. An inscription panel about this "gallant exploit" appears on one side; on the opposite side is a scene of a female figure, probably representing England, pointing toward a naval battle. The other decoration is nautical or the oak and laurel symbolic of victory. The same shell and dolphin handles were used on a Worcester vase, circa 1808, painted with shells. After its capture, the *Guerrière* was incorporated into the Royal Navy. On August 19, 1812, during the War of 1812, she in turn was captured and sunk by the USS *Constitution* under the command of Captain Isaac Hull, the battle in which the latter ship received its nickname, "Old Ironsides." Having seen President John F. Kennedy seated before a painting of this battle, Mr. Thomas was prompted to donate the urn to the White House, and President Kennedy selected it for display in the Oval Office.
PROVENANCE: Sir Thomas Lavie; purchased from Lavie's descendants by A. P. Rochelle Thomas.
REFERENCES: John Sanden, "Shell-Decorated Worcester Porcelain," *Antiques* (June 1992): pl. XV.

SERVICE, PLATE, DESSERT PLATE, and CREAM SOUP CUP AND SAUCER (page 253)
Castleton China, Inc., New Castle, Pennsylvania, 1968–72; designed by Tiffany & Co., New York
Porcelain
Anonymous donation, 1968
1968.620.2.1.1-216, .5.1-204, .6.1-216, .7.1-216
Service Plate—11 5/8 in. (29.5 cm.)
Dessert Plate—9 in. (22.9 cm.)
Cream Soup Cup—2 x 6 1/2 x 5 in. (5.1 x 16.5 x 12.7 cm.)
Cream Soup Saucer—7 1/8 in. (18.1 cm.)
MARKS: (printed in gold on underside) "THE WHITE HOUSE / 1968" and "DESIGNED BY TIFFANY AND COMPANY / MADE BY CASTLETON CHINA CO. / U.S.A."; (on the dessert plate between the other two marks) "TEXAS / BLUEBONNET / Lupinus subcarnosus."

NOTES: Since prior services—Truman, Roosevelt, Wilson—had comprised only 120 place settings each, the need to accommodate larger numbers for state dinners led to the ordering of the Johnson state service in 1967. The 2,208-piece service, 216 10-piece place settings, with 24 each of two sizes of serving or flower bowls, was received in 1968, the dessert plates (only 204) not until 1972. The service was designed by Tiffany: the general design, including the "gold-dot vaulting," by Van Day Truex, the paintings of the American eagle emblem and flowers by André Piette. Lady Bird Johnson suggested that the service plate be decorated with a center eagle, derived from the Monroe state service of 1817, and wildflowers on the rim, while the dinner plate had the eagle and different flowers on its rim. The dessert plates were handpainted with the official flowers of the fifty states and the District of Columbia (four of each), the drawings of which may be found at the Smithsonian Institution. Extra place settings were especially provided for the china collections of the White House and Smithsonian Institution, the Johnson Library, and the firms involved in the manufacture.
REFERENCES: Anthony Holberton-Wood, Tiffany & Co., to Bess Abell, December 4, 1967; Abell to Holberton-Wood, February 8, 1968, Lyndon Baines Johnson Library. Klapthor, *Official White House China*, 172–82. André Piette Papers, Archives Center, National Museum of American History.

WORK TABLE (pages 254 and 255)
Attributed to Duncan Phyfe (1768–1854), New York, circa 1810
Mahogany and mahogany veneer / mahogany and tulip poplar; mirror glass; gilded brass
Gift of the Richard King Mellon Foundation, 1971
1971.716.1
28 1/4 x 23 x 16 in. (71.8 x 58.4 x 40.6 cm.)
MARKS: None.
NOTES: This intricately outfitted work table is one of four very similar examples known, all attributed to Duncan Phyfe's shop because of their quality and inventiveness. The tapered cabinet section, an English Regency form in *le style antique* called "sarcophagus" in the 1805 *Supplement to the Cabinet-Makers London Book of Prices*, is related to a Phyfe-labeled work table, circa 1815, with a partial tapered body on a four-column pedestal. The White House table and a nearly identical table at the Metropolitan Museum of Art, New York, have front panels bearing very similar, possibly contemporaneous veneering. The sinuous brackets, the authenticity of which has been questioned for concealing ornamental details of the cabinet, may have been added at an early date to increase the strength of the form. Another example, placed on loan at the White House in 1971 and acquired in 1981, differs structurally in having two slides in the box, one with a pivoting mirror, the other a frame perhaps for needlework.
CONDITION: In a 1935 photograph, the table now at the Metropolitan Museum bore no corner brackets; and when exhibited together in the 1960s, neither it nor the White House table had them. With evidence of mortises in the corners of the top section and plinth, however, the former was fitted by 1971 with brackets found in a conservation shop. The White House table was acquired in

1971 with reproduction brackets in place. One leg has been repaired. Regilded hardware.
PROVENANCE: Israel Sack, Inc., New York, circa 1963; Harry Arons Antiques, Inc., Bridgeport, Connecticut; purchased by the White House with contributed funds.
REFERENCES: Tracy, *19th Century America*, no. 24. "Brochure no. 11, May 1963," *American Antiques from Israel Sack Collection*, 1 (Washington, D.C.: Highland House, 1969), no. 645. Tracy, "Federal Period Furniture," pls. A–B. Nancy McClelland, *Duncan Phyfe and the English Regency* (New York: William R. Scott, 1939), pl. 187

ARGAND LAMP (page 256 lower)
Matthew Boulton, Soho, England, circa 1786
Sheffield silverplate, mirror glass, glass / electric light fixture
Gift of the Richard King Mellon Foundation, 1971
1971.737.1
20 1/2 x 5 x 5 in. (52.1 x 12.7 x 12.7 cm.)
MARKS: None.
NOTES: One of a pair, this lamp features an unusual mirrored oil font as a reflector for its Argand burner, popular for its brighter and more smoke-free and odor-free light. Invented by François-Pierre-Ami Argand (1750–1803) in 1780 and patented in Great Britain in 1784, many of the lamps produced for Argand's Patent Lamp Co. were produced by Matthew Boulton at his metals factory outside Birmingham. The graceful swag and scroll cresting topped by a classical kylix urn is another unusual feature.
CONDITION: Electrified. Replacement chimneys.
PROVENANCE: Hyde & Shepard, New York; purchased by the White House with donated funds.
REFERENCES: Wolfe, *Brandy, Balloons, & Lamps*, fig. 10.13.

ARGAND LAMP (page 256 upper)
Possibly Messinger & Son, Birmingham, England, circa 1830
Parcel gilt bronze, cut glass, glass / electric light fixtures
Gift of Mrs. Edward W. C. Russell, 1976
1976.1244.1
19 3/4 x 16 1/2 x 7 7/8 in. (50.2 x 41.9 x 20.0 cm.)
MARKS: Burner front—relief plaque "B.GARDINER / N.YORK."
NOTES: One of a pair (the other apparently destroyed) reportedly given by Dolley Madison to one of her freed slaves, with a tradition of having been given to her by Joseph Bonaparte, a brother of Napoleon who lived in New Jersey, circa 1815–32, 1837–39. Baldwin Gardiner, a New York silversmith and importer, 1827–48, imported comparable Argand lamps from Birmingham manufacturer Thomas Messinger; a set of three similarly marked by Gardiner, but also by the maker, is at the Baltimore Museum of Art. The contrast of patinated bronze and gilded ornament is less obvious on this lamp with its abundance of glass components.
CONDITION: Electrified.
PROVENANCE: By tradition, given by Dolley Madison to freed slave Mammy Jones; to her son Charles Jerome Jones; to his daughter Jenny Jones; one to her niece Irene Jones Milliner (mate to a cousin, broken by his children); gift to Barbara Russell.
REFERENCES: Cooper, *Classical Taste*, 158–59, pl. 116.

ARMCHAIR (page 257)
Possibly Thomas Affleck (1740–95), Philadelphia, circa 1765–75
Mahogany / red oak and yellow pine; brass
Gift of Mr. and Mrs. Bertram Lippincott, 1976
1976.1280.1
43 x 27 x 31 1/2 in. (109.2 x 68.6 x 80.0 cm.)
MARKS: None.
NOTES: One of a pair of chairs that were separated in the mid-19th century when they passed to great-grandsons of the original owner. A rectangular brass plaque—"OWNED BY / JOSEPH WHARTON OF WALNUT GROVE / BORN AUGUST 4th 1707 / DIED JULY 27th 1779"—was on this chair. The mate, sold at Sotheby's in 1996, bears an oval brass plate attributing its ownership to Joseph Wharton as well. Stuffed-back armchairs were rare in America, the largest and most elegant examples of which were made in Philadelphia. These were derived from two designs for "French Chairs" in Thomas Chippendale's 1762 *Director*. Thomas Affleck, who came to Philadelphia in 1763, is known to have owned a copy, and a large heavily carved set of chairs of this type, associated with Governor John Penn, are attributed to his workmanship.
PROVENANCE: Descended in the family of Philadelphia merchant Joseph Wharton, who reportedly used it at his country home, "Walnut Grove"; to his son Charles Wharton; to his son William Wharton; to his son Joseph Wharton, Philadelphia industrialist and philanthropist (the mate to his brother Charles William Wharton); to his daughter Joanna Wharton Lippincott; to her son Bertram Lippincott.
REFERENCES: Chippendale, *Director*, pl. XIX. Horner, Blue Book, pl. 268. Sotheby's sale 6801, January 20, 1996, no. 202. Philadelphia Museum of Art, *Philadelphia*, no. 79.

SERVICE PLATE, FISH/LUNCH PLATE, and TEA CUP AND SAUCER (page 259)
Lenox, Inc., Trenton, New Jersey, 1981–82
China
Gift of the Knapp Foundation, 1982
1982.1500.2.1.1-220, .3.1-221, .16.1-279, .17.1-221
Service Plate—11 5/8 in. (29.5 cm.)
Fish/Lunch Plate—9 1/8 in. (23.2 cm.)
Tea Cup—2 x 4 3/4 x 4 in. (5.1 x 12.1 x 10.2 cm.)
Tea/Bouillon Saucer—6 in. (15.2 cm.)
MARKS: Underside—gold printed wreathed script "L" / [copyright mark] "LENOX / MADE IN U.S.A. / THE WHITE HOUSE / 1981."
NOTES: To accommodate the increasing size and diversity of state dinners and other functions, the Reagan state service was purchased from Lenox, Inc., in 1982. The 4,370-piece service, 19-piece place settings for 220 with platters and serving plates, cost $210,399. Reflecting Mrs. Reagan's interest, the service plates and dessert plates have a full red rim overlaid with gilt cross-hatching, the other pieces narrow red rim bands. Six extra place settings were especially produced for the china collections of the White House and Smithsonian Institution, the Reagan Library, President and Mrs. Reagan, the manufacturer, and the donor. Twenty additional buffet plates, marked to match the original service, were produced by Lenox in 1988.

REFERENCES: Lenox invoices, 1982, OCWH.
Klapthor, *Official White House China*, 184–87.

DESSERT PLATE AND DINNER PLATE, SERVICE PLATE (page 260)
Lenox, Inc., Pomona, New Jersey, 2000
China
Gift of the White House Acquisition Trust
2000.1796. 5.1-311, .2.1-312, . 1.1-301
Service plate—12 in. (30.5 cm.)
Dinner plate—10 5/8 in. (27 cm.)
Dessert plate—9 1/4 in. (23.5 cm.)
MARKS: Underside—"THE WHITE HOUSE / 200th ANNIVERSARY / 1800–2000" / gold-printed wreathed script "L" / [copyright mark] "LENOX / MADE IN U.S.A."
NOTES: This service, with 12-piece place settings for 300, was commissioned to commemorate the 200th anniversary of the first occupancy of White House in 1800. The designs were inspired by architectural motifs in the State Dining Room, East Room, and Diplomatic Reception Room, and included the first use of images of the White House—the north front at the center of the gold-rimmed service plate and on the yellow rim of the dinner plate, the south front on the yellow rim of the dessert plate.

SERVICE PLATE, BOUILLON CUP AND SAUCER (page 261)
Lenox, Inc., Kinston, North Carolina, 2008–2009
China
Gift of the White House Acquisition Trust, 2008
2008.1875.1.1-320, .9.1-320, .10.1-320
Service plate—11 3/4 in. (30 cm.)
Bouillon cup—2 3/16 x 5 1/2 x 3 3/4 in. (5.6 x 14 x 9.5 cm.)
Bouillon saucer—5 3/4 in. (14.6 cm.)
MARKS: Underside—"THE WHITE HOUSE / 2008" / gold-printed wreathed script "L" / [copyright mark] "LENOX / MADE IN U.S.A."
NOTES: The design for the George W. Bush State China Service—fourteen-piece place settings for 320—was derived from contemporary objects in the White House collection—a green net or basket-weave border based on a French dinner service, c.1799–1805, believed to have been owned by James and Dolley Madison (pieces donated to the White House china collection in 1934) and an eagle emblem based on an inlay on a Massachusetts sideboard, c.1795–1805, believed to have been owned by Daniel Webster (donated in 1962).

TALL CASE CLOCK (page 262 left)
John Seymour (circa 1738–1818) and Thomas Seymour (1771–1848), Boston, circa 1805–1810; movement possibly by James Doull, Charlestown, Mass.
Mahogany and mahogany veneer / pine; crotch birch, satinwood; gilded brass, glass / painted iron, brass weight-driven movement
Gift of the White House Historical Association, 1972
1972.919.1
106 x 23 3/4 x 10 3/8 in. (269.2 x 60.3 x 26.4 cm.)
MARKS: Front seat board—pencil inscribed "JS."
NOTES: This clock case is an important example of the superb craftsmanship of father and son cabinetmakers John and Thomas Seymour, who immigrated from England to

Falmouth (now Portland, Maine) in 1785 and moved to Boston in 1794. Conservator Robert Mussey, who is currently studying the Seymours, wrote: "This is one of the great masterpieces of Boston clock casework of the Federal period, showing innovation in inlay, great care in choice and layout of veneers, and impressive height." The initials "JS" were discovered by Mussey, who noted that of the six clock cases of this type, this is the only one so marked. Although the lunette inlay, so often associated with the Seymours, can be found on other Massachusetts furniture, the double lunette inlay of opposing and alternating lunettes remains a sophisticated Seymour ornament. Although it appears on a small group of very similar Seymour clock cases with dials signed by James Doull of Charlestown (one example at the Metropolitan Museum of Art), on this clock with an unmarked dial, it was fashioned in its most refined and innovative form with small wood-burned triangles between the curves.

CONDITION: Per Robert Mussey, it is in "superb condition." Some inpainting on the dial. Silk missing from bonnet side-lights with replacement glass. Replacement finials; regilded brasses.

PROVENANCE: Vernon Stoneman sold this clock, along with many other pieces from his large collection of furniture attributed to the Seymour workshops, to the White House in 1972, purchased with donated funds.

REFERENCES: Vernon Stoneman, *A Supplement to John and Thomas Seymour: Cabinetmakers in Boston, 1794–1816* (Boston: Special Publications, 1965), no. 72. Robert Mussey, Survey of Seymour Furniture in the White House collection, 1997. Tracy, "Federal Period Furniture," fig. 6.

FIRE SCREEN (page 264)
Pierre-Antoine Bellangé (1758–1827), Paris, circa 1817
Gilded beechwood
Gift of the George B. Hartzog Jr. White House Acquisition Trust
2012.1883.1
MARKS: none
NOTES: See pages 60–61 and 238 for other pieces from the suite. One of two *écrans* (one at the White House) purchased at 511.42 francs as part of a 53-piece "grand salon suite gilded wood with olive branch ornaments, covered in double-warp satin, fine crimson, two shades of gold, laurel-leaf design" for "the large oval room" (currently the Blue Room) in 1817. The two screens plus 28 of 38 chairs and the full complement of sofas, stools, and footstools were sold at auction by James C. McGuire in Washington, D.C., January 17, 1860.
CONDITION: Remnants of original gesso and gilding under later layers. Remnants of post-1837 blue show fabric and pre-1837 (possibly 1817) red threads. Linen foundation possibly original.
REFERENCES: NA/MTA 37131, v-3. Hans Huth, "The White House Furniture at the Time of Monroe," *Gazette des Beaux-Arts*, series 6, vol. 29, (January 1946), 45. Clement E. Conger and Betty C. Monkman. "President Monroe's Acquisitions," *The Connoisseur* (May 1976), 58.
PROVENANCE: White House; Lawrence G. C. Maguire; Maguire estate sold at Grogan & Co., Dedham, Massachusetts, May 20, 2012.

CONFECTIONARY STAND (page 265)
Edouard Honoré (?–1855), Champroux, France, 1846
Porcelain
Gift of the George B. Hartzog, Jr. White House Acquisition Trust.
2013.1891.1
17 ½ x 9 ¼ in. (19.1 x 23.5 cm.)
MARKS: Underside—orange printed "ED HONORE/Bould Poissonniere No 6/ à PARIS/ MANUFACTURE/ à Champroux Allier/ No/ Prix"
NOTES: See pages 103–105 and 288 for other pieces of the service. From the James K. Polk state service— "1 porcelain dinner and dessert service" purchased from Alexander T. Stewart & Co., New York, $979.40, March 23, 1846. The components of the white dinner and green dessert services were not itemized on the bill, but this three-tiered stand is possibly from "2 Stands for confectionary" listed in the inventory of January 21, 1849, taken at the end of the Polk administration. A second example, with a Polk service soup plate substituted for the bottom tier, presumably due to damage, is part of the Robert L. McNeil collection of presidential china at the Philadelphia Museum of Art.
REFERENCES: NA/MTA v-39. Margaret Brown Klapthor, *Official White House China*, 68–72.
PROVENANCE: White House; West Coast family; Christie's New York, September 25, 2013.

SOFA (page 266 upper left)
Duncan Phyfe (1768–1854), New York, circa 1810
Mahogany and mahogany veneer / poplar; cane
Gift of the American Institute of Interior Designers, 1961
961.169.2
35 1/2 x 72 x 22 1/2 in. (90.2 x 182.9 x 57.2 cm.)
MARKS: None.
NOTES: One of pair en suite with two armchairs and six side chairs which by family tradition were purchased from Duncan Phyfe for the Allamuchy, New Jersey, home of the son of prominent politician John Rutherfurd. In writing about a very similar sofa attributed to Phyfe at the Winterthur Museum, Charles Montgomery cited the description of "A Scroll Back Cane Sofa" from *The New-York Revised Prices for Manufacturing Cabinet and Chair Work* for 1810—"The center legs [back] running up and forming three panels, elliptic front, bored for caning." Calling that sofa "much rarer [than a similar upholstered example] because of the caning," he acknowledged that a price book listing meant that cabinetmakers besides Phyfe were capable of making such a piece. The Winterthur sofa has a "Bell seat" and conforming arms more in character with the chairs in the White House suite and other Phyfe chairs at Winterthur than the flat arms and seat sides of this sofa, its mate, and an example at the Yale University Art Gallery. The reeding and carving of the arm supports is not repeated on the armchairs.
CONDITION: Recaned. On both sofas the two center rear legs have been replaced, after the originals had been removed in the past and replaced with a single center leg. Casters missing.
PROVENANCE: Duncan Phyfe to Robert W. Rutherfurd; descended to his grandson Winthrop Rutherfurd; to his children—Winthrop, John, Hugo, and Guy Rutherfurd,

Barbara Rutherford Knowles, and Arturo Peralta (widower of Alice Rutherfurd); part of the A.I.D. donation of furnishings for the Library of the White House, 1961–62.
REFERENCES: Charles Montgomery, *American Furniture*, figs. 65–67, 278. Kane, *American Seating Furniture*, no. 229.

PIER TABLE (page 266 upper right)
Attributed to Duncan Phyfe (1768–1854), New York, circa 1815
Mahogany and mahogany veneer / white pine; marble; gilded brass
Gift of Soloman Grossman, 1971
1971.778.1
34 5/8 x 35 1/4 x 18 in. (88.0 x 89.5 x 45.7 cm.)
MARKS: None.
NOTES: Two identical tables, possibly mates though acquired by the White House from different sources, share a strong reed-cluster pedestal not seen on other pier tables or similar card tables. Two other examples of such a tripod pier table attributed to the Phyfe shop are somewhat more elaborately ornamented with a carved center tablet and blocks on a satinwood-veneered apron and a leaf-carved urn pedestal. The basic form, described as "Solid Eliptic Pillar and Claw" in the 1810 *New-York Prices for Manufacturing Cabinet and Chair Work*, was also utilized for many New York card tables, including one stamped by Michael Allison, another noted New York cabinetmaker in the Federal period.
CONDITION: Regilded casters.
PROVENANCE: Soloman Grossman—lent to the White House before donation. [the second example was purchased from Joe Kindig, Jr. & Son, York, Pennsylvania in 1971—gift of the Richard King Mellon Foundation].
REFERENCES: McClelland, *Duncan Phyfe*, pl. 187. Christie's, sale 8208, June 21, 1995, no. 272; Sotheby's, sale 6444, June 24, 1993, no. 541.

SIDE CHAIR (page 266 lower left)
Attributed to Duncan Phyfe (1768–1854), New York, circa 1810–20
Mahogany / oak; white pine, gilded composition, gilded brass
White House Acquisition Fund, 1962
1962.194.2
33 x 20 x 20 in. (83.8 x 50.8 x 50.8 cm.)
MARKS: None.
NOTES: Derived from the folding chair of an ancient Roman magistrate, the "curule" form was shown as stools in many of the early 19th century design books but appeared as part of "Chairs with Grecian Cross Fronts" in the 1808 Supplement to the *London Chair-Makers' and Carvers' Book of Prices*. Probably in 1815, Duncan Phyfe sketched a side chair of this form, with a reeded curule leg structure at the front echoed by a back splat of the same shape, and apparently submitted it as a proposal to a prospective Philadelphia client who bought furniture from him in January 1816 (the drawings and bill survive in the manuscript collection at the Winterthur Museum). It was offered with two forms of seat—"Cane bottoms" at $19 with "Cushions—Extra" at $3 or "Stuffed bottom" at $21. The sketch does not include the reeding of the back frame nor the castered paw feet on this chair, from a near set of

three. Other chairs have the curule legs on both sides, including twelve that by tradition were purchased from Phyfe by Thomas Pearsall of New York, circa 1810 (Metropolitan Museum of Art, New York). The form was extremely popular in New York and not exclusively the province of the Phyfe shop.

CONDITION: The composition lion's masks on the crossing of the curule legs are reproduced from a gilded brass mask on an identical chair in the Museum of the City of New York. One pine medial seat brace is a replacement. Regilded castered paw feet.

PROVENANCE: The Searchers—Antiques, Washington, D.C.; purchased by the White House with donated funds.

REFERENCES: Charles Montgomery, *American Furniture*, nos. 72–72A. Tracy, "Federal Period Furniture," fig. 4. Tracy, *19th Century America*, fig. 15.

PIER TABLE *(page 266 lower center)*

Duncan Phyfe (1768–1854), New York, circa 1834
Mahogany / white pine and tulip poplar; marble; mirror glass
White House Acquisition Fund, 1961
1961.45.1
35 1/2 x 42 3/4 x 18 1/8 in. (90.2 x 108.6 x 46.0 cm.)
MARKS: None.

NOTES: This table was one of a "Pair Piere Tables" purchased from Duncan Phyfe in 1834 for $260, part of an acquisition of thirty pieces of bedroom, dining room, and parlor furniture at $1,154.50. Prior to the sale of this table to the White House in 1961, its mate had been sold by another family member who also had sold the dining table and ten of twelve chairs. The latter sale was accompanied by the now unlocated original bill of August 16, 1834, signed "D. Phyfe" (photocopy OCWH). Thomas Gordon Smith, a historian of neoclassical style, has called this "the earliest documented piece of plain-style Grecian furniture by Duncan Phyfe." Phyfe made a nearly identical labeled table for his daughter, Eliza Vail (Museum of the City of New York). Two sideboard tables of the same form and a complementary cellarette were part of furnishings that Phyfe provided in 1841 for Millford Plantation in South Carolina. A dressing table of the same form with the addition of a surmounting mirror box on a wooden top is attributed to Phyfe. These tables may be based on the form of a similar attributed pier table, but one with canted consoles (Metropolitan Museum of Art, New York), that may have been derived from a French design plate by La Mésengère, 1825–27.

PROVENANCE: Purchased by Benjamin Clark, for his home "Fanewood" near Newburgh, New York, 1834; descended to his great-granddaughter Mary Zeigler (the mate to her brother); purchased by the White House in 1961 with donated funds.

REFERENCES: Loraine W. Pearce, "American Empire Furniture in the White House," *Antiques* (September 1962): fig. 6. McClelland, *Duncan Phyfe*, pl. III. Thomas Gordon Smith, "Millford Plantation South Carolina," *Antiques* (May 1997): 738–41. Davidson and Stillinger, *American Wing*, fig. 98. Tracy, *19th Century America*, no. 80.

ARMCHAIR *(page 266 lower right)*

Duncan Phyfe (1768–1854), New York, circa 1810
Mahogany and mahogany veneer / tulip poplar; cane

Gift of the American Institute of Interior Designers, 1961, 961.169.4
35 1/2 x 72 x 22 1/2 in. (90.2 x 182.9 x 57.2 cm.)
MARKS: None.

NOTES: From a suite of two nearly identical sets of chairs—one arm and three sides each—and two complementary sofas. A design for a scroll-back chair with double crossed bannisters appeared in *The London Chair-Makers' and Carvers' Book of Prices*, 1802 and 1807. The chairs of this suite, with a family history of acquisition from Phyfe, are closely related to two sets of chairs purchased from Phyfe by wealthy New Yorker William Bayard in 1807. The back is similar to that on one Bayard set (Winterthur Museum) except for the splat crossing ornamentation; those twelve have quatrefoil rosettes, while these two sets have either a diamond or no carved lozenge at all. The arms, seat, and front legs are similar to those on the second Bayard set with only a single cross splat. The design, however, was not exclusive to Phyfe, and an armchair long-attributed to him (Metropolitan Museum of Art) has been discovered to bear a fragment of the label of his talented New York contemporary, Charles-Honoré Lannuier. Although bell seats were an option for sofas as well, those from this suite do not have such.

CONDITION: Replacement upper cross in splat. Patch on rear of each rear leg after removal of a rabbeted extension at the foot.

PROVENANCE: See sofa above.

REFERENCES: Charles Montgomery, *American Furniture*, figs. 65–67. V. Isabella Miller, *Furniture by New York Cabinetmakers, 1650 to 1860* (New York: Museum of the City of New York, Exh. cat. 1956), nos. 100–101. Peter M. Kenny, "R.T.H. Halsey: American Wing founder and champion of Duncan Phyfe", *Antiques* (January 2000): 190, pls. VII–VIIA

DESK AND BOOKCASE *(page 267)*

Attributed to Duncan Phyfe (1768–1854), New York, circa 1815–20
Mahogany; mahogany, satinwood, and rosewood veneers / mahogany, tulip poplar, pine; glass; brass
Gift of the Richard King Mellon Foundation, 1974
1974.1102.1
96 1/4 x 41 1/2 x 21 1/2 in. (244.5 x 105.4 x 54.6 cm.)
MARKS: None.

NOTES: Related desks with a fold-out writing board in place of the cylinder desk include one twice-labeled by Phyfe (private collection) and one purchased from Phyfe in 1816 (Telfair Museum of Art, Savannah, Georgia). The latter has tiered Gothic-arched mullions very similar to those on the White House example. Two very similar cylinder desks, which share a somewhat differently configured interior and legs topped by a spiral turning, differ principally in the bookcase section—one with pilasters and sinuous mullions (Metropolitan Museum of Art, New York), the other with diamond and curving mullions and a heavy triangular pediment.

CONDITION: Replacement baize on the writing board; replacement brasses.

PROVENANCE: Edward Vason Jones; to his daughter Jeanette Jones Balling; purchased by the White House with donated funds.

REFERENCES: McClelland, *Duncan Phyfe*, pl. 251. Page Talbott, *Classical Savannah: Fine and Decorative Arts, 1800–1840* (Savannah: Telfair Museum of Art, 1995) 227. Tracy, *19th Century America*, no. 20. Bernard and S. Dean Levy, *In Search of Excellence* (June 1995 dealer catalog), 67.

DRESSING CHEST *(page 268 upper left)*

Attributed to Thomas Seymour (1771–1848), possibly with John Seymour (c. 1738–1818), Boston, 1805–10
Mahogany, mahogany veneer / mahogany, white pine, walnut; satinwood; mirror glass; brass, ivory
Gift of Mrs. Bradley Randall, 1962
1962.231.1
70 3/4 x 37 3/4 x 21 1/4 in. (179.7 x 95.9 x 54.0 cm.)
MARKS: Underside of upper drawers—chalk "N N2" (right), "No 1" (left).

NOTES: The dressing chest may be an American innovation, the marriage of an English dressing glass, which in the first half of the 19th century became unfashionable because "they scarcely show more than your head, and are easily upset," with a New England case form. Two similar chests, nearly identical to each other, have the same crossbanding with patch-like sapwood sections, but differ in other ornamental and structural features from the White House chest. Since all three have Rhode Island histories and one bears a manuscript label stating it was made for an 1813 wedding dowry by Joseph Rawson & Son, Providence, they all at one time had been attributed to Rawson. Although the use of the lunette inlay was once considered to be an exclusive hallmark of the Seymour shop in Boston, structural characteristics do suggest that the White House chest and a similar chest sold at auction in 1999 are very likely from the Seymour shop.

CONDITION: Three-inch birch repair of lost lunette inlay on proper left side; other veneer repairs.

PROVENANCE: William Jones, Governor of Rhode Island 1811–1817; to his daughter Mrs. Thomas Coles Hoppin; to her son Augustus Hoppin; to his niece Louise Hoppin; to her niece Eleanor Vinton Randall.

REFERENCES: Christopher P. Monkhouse and Thomas S. Michie, *American Furniture in Pendleton House* (Providence: Rhode Island School of Design, 1986), Fig. 14, citing Eliza Leslie, *House Book or, A Manual of Domestic Economy* (Philadelphia, 1840). Eleanore Bradford Monahon, "The Rawson family of cabinetmakers in Providence, Rhode Island," *Antiques* (July 1980), Fig. 12. Robert Christie's, sale 9054, January 16, 1999, #722.

TAMBOUR DESK *(page 268 upper right)*

John Seymour (circa 1738–1818) and Thomas Seymour (1771–1848), Boston, 1793–98.
Mahogany and mahogany veneer / oak and pine; curly maple and lightwoods; enamel, brass, ivory
Gift of Vernon Stoneman, 1973
1973.1018.1
59 7/8 x 38 x 19 5/8 in. (152.1 x 96.5 x 49.9 cm.)
MARKS: "No." and "EB" inscribed in pencil on the upper surface of the drawer bottom and the upper-left letter drawer of the desk interior.

NOTES: The finest examples of the tambour desk, or lady's writing table with tambour shutters, are attributed to John and Thomas Seymour. This desk shares such specific details as the swag-inlaid doors and enamel pulls of the four seasons on the two-drawer Seymour-labeled desk at the Winterthur Museum. Matching single-capped inlaid pilasters on the lower case and curly maple pilasters on the upper case are found on a two-drawer unlabeled desk with slatted tambour doors in the Kaufman Collection. Only three examples, however, have pedimental compartments. Two of them are three-drawered, with correspondingly taller pediments atop mahogany case tops, one of which (also Kaufman Collection) descended in the family of a Thomas Seymour business partner. The White House desk, which descended in the family of Seymour contemporaries in both Falmouth (now Portland, Maine) and Boston, has a pine case top suggesting that its pediment, shallower than the other two in proportion to its two-drawer case, was not an option nor something that might be easily removed and discarded.

CONDITION: Conservator Robert Mussey, who studied the works of the Seymours, claims that of the dozens he has examined "this is probably in the most original condition, though it has some minor repairs, and has been refinished." The original finial is missing.

PROVENANCE: William and Hannah Cranch Bond; to their son William Cranch Bond; descended to his great-granddaughters; Vernon Stoneman (lent to White House 1970–73).

REFERENCES: Stoneman, *John and Thomas Seymour*, no. 34. Mussey, *The Furniture Masterworks of John & Thomas Seymour*. Tracy, "Federal Period Furniture," fig. 2. Charles Montgomery, *American Furniture*, no. 186. Warren, *Bayou Bend Collection*, F178. Flanigan, *American Furniture*, no. 84.

WORK TABLE (*page 268 lower left*)
Attributed to Thomas Seymour (1771–1848), Boston, 1814
Mahogany and mahogany veneer / white pine, Spanish cedar; ebony; brass
Gift of the White House Historical Association, 1972
1972.916.1
30 1/2 x 21 3/4 x 16 3/4 in. (77.5 x 55.2 x 42.6 cm.)
MARKS: Underside of top drawer—partly printed paper receipt "M [printed] Ralph Haskins / Feby 17 1814[hand] Bought at Boston Cabinet Manufactory, / CONGRESS STREET. [printed] / 1 Mahogany Ladys work Table $36. / Rec^d payment / Ths Seymour Agent [hand]."
NOTES: Thomas Seymour, English-born cabinetmaker who worked for many years with his father, John, as part of a very talented shop, ran the Boston Furniture Warehouse, 1805–8, and then opened his Boston Cabinet Manufactory in 1812, advertising that he would sell "Useful, and Ornamental Cabinet Furniture all made by or under the direction of Thomas Seymour." According to Robert Mussey, who studied the works of the Seymours, this table, with a writing board in the top drawer and a sewing bag slide, is perhaps the earliest documented example in Boston of the more restrained English Regency style, decorated with subtle ebony stringing instead of lightwood veneers and inlay.
CONDITION: Replacement baize on the writing board; original sewing bag missing.
PROVENANCE: Vernon Stoneman sold this table, along with many other pieces from his large collection of furni-

ture attributed to the Seymour workshops, to the White House in 1972, purchased with donated funds.
REFERENCES: Vernon Stoneman, *John and Thomas Seymour: Cabinetmakers in Boston, 1794–1816* (Boston: Special Publications, 1959), 151. Mussey, *The Furniture Masterworks of John & Thomas Seymour*.

SOFA TABLE (*page 268 lower right*)
John Seymour (circa 1738–1818) and/or Thomas Seymour (1771–1848), Boston, circa 1805–10
Mahogany, mahogany and birch veneers / white pine, birch; light wood and dark wood inlays; brass
Gift of the White House Historical Association, 1975
1975.1181.1
27 1/2 x 53 3/4 (open) x 33 in. (69.8 x 136.5 x 83.8 cm.)
MARKS: None.
NOTES: The sofa table is one of the rarer forms in American cabinetmaking, probably introduced very early in the 19th century from England. Thomas Sheraton in his 1803 *Cabinet Dictionary* explained that "the ladies chiefly occupy them [before sofas] to draw, write, or read." A small group of tables similar to this one, also showing construction and decorative techniques associated with the very talented English-born Seymours, father and son, in Boston, may be among the earliest examples of the sofa table in America. This table shows extensive work by a stringing craftsman, not only in the lines but in the striped diamonds on the corner blocks. It has one real and one sham drawer on each side.
CONDITION: All four legs apparently were bolted to the pedestals, the bolt heads covered by plugged mortises on the inside faces, possibly accompanied by the replacement of the metal brackets under the legs. One fractured leg repaired with splines in the underside.
PROVENANCE: Israel Sack, Inc., New York; purchased by the White House with donated funds.
REFERENCES: Philip D. Zimmerman, "The American Sofa Table," *Antiques* (May 1999): 744–53, pl. V. Mussey, *The Furniture Masterworks of John & Thomas Seymour*. Survey of Seymour Furniture, supplement.

TAMBOUR DESK AND BOOKCASE (*page 269*)
Attributed to Thomas Seymour (1771–1848) probably with John Seymour (circa 1738–1818), Boston, circa 1778–1808
Mahogany, mahogany and curly maple veneers / pine; glass; reverse-painted glass, ivory, brass
Gift of an anonymous donor and the WHHA, 1974
1974.1073.1
81 1/2 x 36 9/16 x 28 3/8 (open) in. (207.0 x 92.9 x 72.1 cm.)
MARKS: Middle case bottom board and rear of lower case backboard—pencil inscribed "No 2" [in distinctive Seymour hand].
NOTES: That the top of the middle case is made of finished mahogany suggests that the bookcase is not original to the piece, but conservator Robert Mussey, who studied the works of the Seymours, claims it was "added in the Seymour shop not long after original manufacture." A very similar desk, with a different and now removed bookcase, is in the collection of the Winterthur Museum.
CONDITION: Old but probably not original finials. Some inpainting of églomisé decoration and nail evidence of numerous interior curtains on bookcase doors. The tambour doors have been repaired and relined (including part

of an 1890 newspaper) and at least two mahogany slats replaced. Non-original blue paper drawer lining over early, probably original blue paper.
PROVENANCE: Israel Sack, Inc., New York; sold to George Lorrimer in the early 1930s; Israel Sack, Inc.; purchased by the White House with donated funds.
REFERENCES: Stoneman, *John and Thomas Seymour*, no. 50. Mussey, *The Furniture Masterworks of John & Thomas Seymour*. Christie's, New York, 8842, January 16, 1998, no. 269. Charles Montgomery, *American Furniture*, no. 186. Tracy, *19th Century America*, no. 63.

CARD TABLE (*page 270 upper left*)
Charles-Honoré Lannuier (1779–1819), New York, circa 1810–15
Mahogany, mahogany veneer / mahogany, tulip poplar; ebony, gilded brass, die-stamped brass; iron
Gift of the White House Preservation Fund, 1992
1992.1704.1
29 1/2 x 36 1/8 x 18 1/8 in. (74.9 x 91.7 x 46.0 cm.)
MARKS: Maker's bilingual printed paper label on underside of top—"HONORÉ LANNUIER / CABINET MAKER, / (FROM PARIS) / Keeps his Ware-house and Manufactory / AND CABINET WARE OF THE / NEWEST FASHION, / AT No. 60 BROAD-STREET. / HONORÉ LANNUIER / EBENISTE / (DE PARIS) / LIENT SON MAGASIN / DE MEUBLES, LES PLUS / A-LA-MODE, / BROAD-STREET No. 60 / NEW-YORK."
NOTES: One of a pair; the mate is in a private collection. A pair of extremely similar but unlabeled tables, which may have belonged to Napoleon's brother, Joseph Bonaparte, during his residence in America, circa 1815–39, consists of one acquired by the White House in 1974, the other an anonymous loan to the Metropolitan Museum of Art in 1998. Peter Kenny cites the diversity of sources influencing the design of this table—its precise upper section, in *le goût antique* on Tuscan columns of French origin, as part of a basically English "pillar-and-claw" form with classic New York leaf carving on the legs (with reeding as well on the attributed tables). The delicate French-inspired classical inlays include a lyre, urns, loop rosettes, and six- and eight-pointed stars. The attributed pair has simple circles in place of the eight-pointed stars on the face of the shaft plinth.
CONDITION: Large veneer patch on apron center. Proper right front foot repaired.
PROVENANCE: By tradition, Isaac Bell, New York, in 1810; descended in the family, but at some point laterally to Dr. Edward Bell Krumbhaar (the mate continued by direct descent); Robert T. Trump, Flourtown, Pa.; Edward Vason Jones (lent to the White House 1973–80); to his daughter Mrs. Jeanette Jones Balling (lent 1980–92); purchased by the White House with donated funds.
REFERENCES: Kenny, *Honoré Lannuier*, 76, nos. 57–58, pl. 22; nos. 59–60, pl. 58 (both plates depict non–White House mates). Edward V. Jones, "Charles-Honoré Lannuier and Duncan Phyfe, Two Creative Geniuses of Federal New York," *The American Art Journal* (May 1977), fig. 18.

MIXING TABLE/STAND (*page 270 lower right*)
Charles-Honoré Lannuier (1779–1819), New York, circa 1810–15
Mahogany / pine, maple, tulip poplar; marble, brass

Gift of the White House Historical Association, 1973
1973.965.1
28 1/4 x 23 3/4 x 16 1/4 in. (71.7 x 60.3 x 41.2 cm.)
MARKS: Maker's bilingual printed paper label on underside of top (virtually illegible).
NOTES: This stand is an unusual form, its inlaid green marble top perhaps designed to accommodate alcoholic or hot beverages which might otherwise damage a wooden top. Although Lannuier is known for his creative integration of French and American design elements, this is a choice example of him working more purely in the New York classical style. The typical New York waterleaf carving on the balusters and legs is robustly and deeply cut, but, per Lannuier scholar Peter Kenny, not so distinctively as to be a clear indicator of Lannuier's work.
CONDITION: Evidence of vert antique or dark paint on paw feet; replacement casters. Brass molding at base of apron on one canted corner is a replacement.
PROVENANCE: By tradition Rufus King, Jamaica, N.Y. (statesman, diplomat, last Federalist Presidential candidate in 1816); to his son James Gore King, possibly on his 1813 marriage; to Edward King; to his daughter Elizabeth Gracie King; to her daughter Gracie King Keyes, who sold it (and a stamped Lannuier bureau now in the Warner Collection, Gulf States Paper Corporation, Tuscaloosa, Alabama) to Berry B. Tracy, New York; purchased by the White House with donated funds.
REFERENCES: Kenny, *Honoré Lannuier*, no. 118, pl. 68, 182. Berry B. Tracy, "For 'One of the Most Genteel Residences in the City,'" *The Metropolitan Museum of Art Bulletin* (April 1967), fig. 3.

PIER TABLE (page 270 lower left)
Charles-Honoré Lannuier (1779–1819), New York, circa 1805–10
Mahogany veneer / mahogany, white pine, tulip poplar; gilded brass, mirror glass, marble
Gift of Robert Knox, 1961
1961.168.1
35 x 41 1/2 x 19 in. (88.9 x 105.4 x 48.2 cm.)
MARKS: Maker's bilingual printed paper label on rear rail face.
NOTES: In the years just before Lannuier came from France to America in 1803, the Directoire style, known as *le goût moderne*, was being replaced by *le goût antique* of the Consulat period (1799–1804), with its "more massive, architec-

tural, and archeologically correct forms." Peter Kenny states that this table, the second piece of labeled Lannuier furniture acquired by the White House in 1961, is "one of the rare early pier tables in the 'antique taste'." A similar but smaller labeled table stands on gilded ball feet (private collection). A similar French table with its columns on rounded plinth projections was also received by the White House in 1961.
Provenance: By tradition, Thomas Cornell Pearsall, New York merchant, patron of Phyfe and Lannuier; to his daughter Phoebe Pearsall; to her niece Frances Pearsall Bradhurst Field; to her daughter Mary Field Payne; to her nieces Frances Field Walker and Mary Field Hoving; purchased at Parke-Bernet, November 9, 1946, no. 137 by Robert Knox.
REFERENCES: Lorraine Pearce, "American Empire Furniture in the White House," 516, figs.4–5. Kenny, *Honoré Lannuier*, no. 94, pl. 28, xi.

CENTER TABLE (page 271)
Charles-Honoré Lannuier (1779–1819), New York, circa 1810
Mahogany, and rosewood, satinwood, and possibly sycamore veneers / tulip poplar, white pine, and mahogany; parcel-gilded brass; vert antique; marbles
Gift of the Honorable and Mrs. C. Douglas Dillon, 1961
961.33.2
29 3/4 x 26 in. (75.9 x 68.6 cm.)
MARKS: Maker's bilingual printed paper label on underside of top.
NOTES: In his 1998 study of Lannuier, Peter Kenny wrote about this unique small Lannuier *guéridon*, derived from a French circular center table form: "The great masterpiece of Lannuier's amalgamated style is a superbly balanced and proportioned gueridon . . . that miraculously incorporates within its compact form the warmth and color of figured mahogany, satinwood, patinated metalwork, and soft-toned Italian marbles . . . In this small gem, one of the first examples of its kind made in America, Lannuier seamlessly melds typical New York serpentine legs of a type sometimes seen on seating forms such as chairs and window benches . . . into his design, transforming them into term supports with gilded and bronzed cast-metal classical busts . . . ." The mounts were probably made in France, the specimen top of colored Italian marbles. This was the first piece of labeled Lannuier furniture acquired for the White House.

CONDITION: Repairs to veneers and leg joinery. Old, possibly original, fire-gilding on tiaras and necklaces of brass busts atop the legs. Old, possibly original, vert antique on feet with microscopic evidence of applied gold flakes. Casters missing.
PROVENANCE: Possibly John Robert Livingston or his son Robert Montgomery Livingston; to his son Charles Octavius Livingston; to his son Charles Victor Livingston; to his widow Nellie Hasbrouck Livingston, whose estate sold it to Kingston, New York dealer Eugene Brossard, 1961; purchased by White House with donated funds.
REFERENCES: Kenny, *Honoré Lannuier*, 76–77, no. 116, pls. 10, 33, and p. 2. Lorraine Pearce, "Lannuier in the President's House," 3, 96, and frontispiece. Robert Mussey, conservation report, 1992, OCWH. Tracy, "Federal Period Furniture," fig. D.

QUILT (detail) (endpapers)
A. E. Kennedy, Washington, D.C., circa 1897–1901
Silk, velvet
Gift of the White House Historical Association, 1995
995.1747.1
92 1/2 x 65 3/4 in. (235.0 x 167.0 cm.)
MARKS: None.
NOTES: The patterned patchwork face is made of fragments from work done for the White House by A. E. Kennedy, a Washington decorating/upholstery firm that contracted with the White House circa 1893–1904. Three satin-weave fabrics in appropriate colors have been identified as those on seat furniture in the East Room, Green Room, and Red Room prior to 1902. The gold East Room fabric had been used on the two suites of seat furniture in the room, including the sofa (page 164). A random patchwork pillow sham from the same acquisition is backed by a red-and-cream-striped fabric used on a Red Room armchair in which Ida McKinley was photographed in the White House greenhouse, circa 1900. These textiles were acquired with other White House objects (see page 155).
CONDITION: Tears in one cream-colored fragment.
PROVENANCE: A. E. Kennedy; descended to granddaughter Margaret W. Queen; sold at Tim Gordon Auctions, Frederick, Md., June 17, 1995.
REFERENCES: Robin M. Hanson, "Technical Study: Crazy Quilt and Sham in the Collection of the White House," 1995, OCWH.

PICTURE CREDITS

All photographs in this book are copyright © White House Historical Association, unless otherwise noted below. All paintings, drawings, prints, and historical photographs are in the White House collection and are copyright © White House Historical Association, unless noted below:
Abbie Rowe, National Park Service (The White House): 108 bottom left, 218, 231 all three; Art Commission of the City of New York: 54; Collection of Mrs. John M. Scott: 51 top; Daughters of the American Revolution Museum: 83; Dwight D. Eisenhower Library: 226 right;

Erik Kvalsik, The White House: 79 bottom, 149, 263; Herbert Hoover Library: 210; Historical Society of Pennsylvania: 21 bottom, 77 inset, 107 inset, 139 inset; John Fitzgerald Kennedy Library: 108 bottom right, 141 bottom; Library of Congress: 19, 33, middle, 78 bottom, 129 right, 136, 140 top right and bottom, 141 top right, 159 bottom, 163 top left and right, 167, 168, 171, 174, 182 top right, 183, 230 bottom; Martin Luther King Memorial Library, Washington, D.C.: 161; Maryland Historical Society: 39 all three, 48-49; Massachussetts Historical Society: 27; National Archives: 87, 125, 160

bottom, 196 top right, 213 bottom, 230 top; National Gallery of Art: 26; New York Public Library (Edward F. Caldwell Lighting Company Records, Astor, Lenox and Tilden Foundation): 192, 194 left; Rutherford B. Hayes Presidential Center, Fremont, Ohio: 108 top left, 155 bottom; St. John's Church: 51 bottom; Smithsonian Institution: 94 both; book jacket, back flap, bottom: Steven White. 242–43. The two objects on the third and fourth shelves to the right of the window are included with the permission of the National Museum of the American Indian, Smithsonian Institution.

SELECTED BIBLIOGRAPHY

Adams, Abigail. *Letters of Mrs. Adams, the Wife of John Adams.* Edited by Charles Francis Adams. Boston: Wilkins, Carter and Co., 1848.

———. *New Letters of Abigail Adams, 1788–1801.* Edited by Stewart Mitchell. Boston: Houghton Mifflin Co., 1947.

Allman, William G. "Furnishing the Executive Mansion: Nineteenth-Century Washington Sources," in *Our Changing White House.* Edited by Wendell Garrett. Boston: Northeastern University Press, 1995.

Allman, William G. and Melissa Naulin. *Something of Splendor: Decorative Arts from the White House.* Washington, D.C.: White House Historical Association, 2011.

Ames, Mary Clemmer. *Ten Years in Washington.* Hartford, Conn.: A. D. Worthington & Co., 1874.

Axelrod, Alan, ed. *The Colonial Revival in America.* New York: W. W. Norton & Co., 1985.

Baker, Jean H. *Mary Todd Lincoln: A Biography.* New York: W. W. Norton & Co., 1987.

Brooklyn Museum of Art. *The American Renaissance: 1876–1917.* New York: Pantheon Books, 1979.

Bush, Barbara. *A Memoir: Barbara Bush.* New York: Charles Scribner's Sons, 1994.

Bush, Laura. *Spoken from the Heart.* New York: Scribner, 2010.

Caemmerer, H. Paul. *The Commission of Fine Arts, 1910–63: A Brief History.* Washington, D.C.: Government Printing Office, 1964.

Carpenter, Charles H., Jr. *Gorham Silver.* New York: Dodd, Mead & Co., 1982.

Carpenter, Charles H., Jr., and Mary Grace Carpenter. *Tiffany Silver.* New York: Dodd, Mead & Co., 1978.

Carpenter, Francis B. *Six Months in the White House with Abraham Lincoln.* New York: Hurd & Houghton, 1866.

Carr, Joseph D. "History in White House Silver." *White House History* 1, no. 1 (1983): 29–37.

Carter, Rosalynn. *First Lady from Plains.* Boston: Houghton Mifflin, 1984.

Chitwood, Oliver Perry. *John Tyler: Champion of the Old South.* New York: D. Appleton Century Co., 1939.

Clinton, Hillary Rodman. *Living History.* New York: Scribner, 2004.

Comstock, Helen. *American Furniture: Seventeenth, Eighteenth, and Nineteenth Century Styles.* New York: Viking Press, 1962.

Committee for the Preservation of the White House. *Report of the Committee for the Preservation of the White House 1964–1969.* Washington, D.C.: The Committee, 1969.

Conger, Clement E. "Decorative Arts at the White House." *Antiques* (July 1979): 112–34.

Conger, Clement E., and Betty C. Monkman. "President Monroe's Acquisitions." *The Connoisseur* (May 1976): 56–63.

Conger, Clement E., et al. *Treasures of State.* New York: Harry N. Abrams, 1991.

Coolidge, Grace G. "When I Became the First Lady." *American Magazine* 108 (September 1929): 11–13, 104, 106, 108.

———. "How I Spent My Days at the White House." *American Magazine* 108 (October 1929): 16–17, 138, 140, 142.

———. "Making Ourselves at Home in the White House." *American Magazine* 108 (November 1929): 20–21, 159–60, 163–4.

———. *Grace Coolidge: The Autobiography.* Edited by Lawrence E. Wikander and Robert H. Ferrell. Worland, Wyo.: High Plains Publishing Co., 1992.

Cooper, Wendy A. *In Praise of America: American Decorative Arts, 1650–1830.* New York: Alfred A. Knopf, 1980.

———. *Classical Taste in America 1800–1840.* New York: Abbeville Press, 1983.

Crook, William H. *Memories of the White House.* Boston: Little, Brown, and Co., 1911.

Daughters of the American Revolution Museum. *Magnificent Intentions: Decorative Arts of the District of Columbia, 1791–1861.* Washington, D.C.: Daughters of the American Revolution Museum, 1991.

Detweiler, Susan. *George Washington's Chinaware.* New York: Harry N. Abrams, 1982.

Draper, James David. *The Arts under Napoleon.* New York: Metropolitan Museum of Art, 1978.

Eisenhower, Julie Nixon. *Pat Nixon: The Untold Story.* New York: Simon and Schuster, 1986.

Eisenhower, Susan. *Mrs. Ike: Memories and Reflections on the Life of Mamie Eisenhower.* New York: Farrar, Straus and Giroux, 1996.

Elder, William Voss, III. "The White House and Its Furnishings." *Historic Preservation* 16 no. 2 (1964): 70–78.

———. *Baltimore Painted Furniture 1800–1840.* Baltimore: Baltimore Museum of Art, 1972.

Fairbanks, Jonathan, and Elizabeth Bidwell Bates. *American Furniture, 1620 to the Present.* New York: Richard Marek Publishers, 1981.

Fede, Helen Maggs. *Washington Furniture at Mount Vernon.* Mount Vernon, Va.: Mount Vernon Ladies' Association and the Union, 1966.

Fennimore, Donald L. *Metalwork in Early America: Copper and Its Alloys from the Winterthur Collection.* Winterthur, Del.: Henry Francis du Pont Winterthur Museum, 1996.

Fitzpatrick, John C., ed. *The Writings of George Washington.* 39 vols. Washington, D.C.: Government Printing Office, 1931–44.

Flanigan, J. Michael, et al. *American Furniture from the Kaufman Collection.* Washington, D.C.: National Gallery of Art, 1986.

Flexner, James Thomas. *George Washington.* 4 vols. Boston: Little, Brown and Co., 1965–72.

Ford, Betty, with Chris Chase. *The Times of My Life.* New York: Harper & Row, 1978.

Freidel, Frank, and William Pencak, eds. *The White House: The First Two Hundred Years.* Boston: Northeastern University Press, 1994.

Frelinghuysen, Alice Cooney. *American Porcelain: 1770–1920.* New York: Metropolitan Museum of Art, 1989.

French, Benjamin Brown. *Witness to the Young Republic: A Yankee's Journal, 1828–70.* Edited by Donald B. Cole and John J. McDonough. Hanover, N.H.: University Press of New England, 1989.

Garrett, Wendell, ed. *Our Changing White House.* Boston: Northeastern University Press, 1995.

Geer, Emily Apt. *First Lady: The Life of Lucy Webb Hayes.* Kent, Ohio: Kent State University Press, 1984.

Gelles, Edith B. *First Thoughts: Life and Letters of Abigail Adams.* New York: Twayne Publishers, 1998.

Gerry, Elbridge, Jr. *The Diary of Elbridge Gerry, Jr.* Edited by Claude B. Bowers. New York: Brentano's, 1927.

Golovin, Anne Castrodale. "Cabinetmakers and Chairmakers of Washington, D.C., 1791–1840." *Antiques* (May 1975): 896–916.

Gould, Lewis L., ed. *American First Ladies: Their Lives and Their Legacy.* New York: Garland Publishing, 1996.

Grant, Julia Dent. *The Personal Memoirs of Julia Dent Grant.* Edited by John Y. Simon. New York: G. P. Putnam's Sons, 1975.

Guidas, John. *The White House: Resources for Research at the Library of Congress.* Washington, D.C.: Government Printing Office, 1992.

Guillebon, Regine de Plinval de. *Porcelain of Paris, 1770–1850.* New York: Walker and Co., 1972.

Hoover, Irwin H. *Forty-Two Years in the White House.* Boston: Houghton Mifflin Co., 1934.

Howe, Katherine S., et al. *Herter Brothers: Furniture and Interiors for a Gilded Age.* New York: Harry N. Abrams, 1994.

Hunt-Jones, Conover. *Dolley and the "Great Little Madison."* Washington, D.C.: American Institute of Architects Foundation, 1977.

Huth, Hans. "The White House Furniture at the Time of Monroe." *Gazette des Beaux-Arts*, series 6, v. 29 (January 1946): 23–46.

Jacobs, Gabrielle Marie. "The Bric-a-Brac of the White House." *The Delineator* (August 1902): 244–50.

Jaffray, Elizabeth. *Secrets of the White House.* New York: Cosmopolitan Book Corp., 1927.

Johnson, Lady Bird. *A White House Diary.* New York: Holt, Rinehart and Winston, 1970.

Jones, Edward Vason. "Charles-Honoré Lannuier and Duncan Phyfe, Creative Geniuses of Federal New York." *The American Art Journal* (May 1977): 4–14.

Kane, Patricia E. *300 Years of American Seating Furniture.* Boston: New York Graphic Society, 1976.

Kenny, Peter M., et al. *Honoré Lannuier, Cabinetmaker from Paris.* New York: Metropolitan Museum of Art, 1998.

———. *Duncan Phyfe: Master Cabinetmaker in New York.* New York: Metropolitan Museum of Art, 2011.

Ketchum, William C., with the Museum of American Folk Art. *American Cabinetmakers: Marked American Furniture, 1640–1940.* New York: Crown Publishers, 1995.

Kimball, Marie G. "The Original Furnishings of the White House." *Antiques* (June 1929): 481–86; (July 1929): 33–37.

Klapthor, Margaret Brown. "Benjamin Latrobe and Dolley Madison Decorate the White House, 1809–1811." *Contributions from the Museum of History and Technology,* Paper 49. Washington, D.C.: Smithsonian Institution, 1965.

———. *Official White House China: 1789 to the Present.* 2d ed. New York: Harry N. Abrams, 1999.

Kloss, William, et al. *Art in the White House: A Nation's Pride.* Washington, D.C.: White House Historical Association, 2007.

Leech, Margaret. *Reveille in Washington, 1860–1865.* New York: Harper & Brothers, 1941.

Levin, Phyllis Lee. *Abigail Adams.* New York: St. Martin's Press, 1987.

Lewis, Ethel. *The White House: An Informal History of Its Architecture, Interiors and Gardens.* New York: Dodd, Mead & Co., 1937.

Logan, Mrs. John A. *Thirty Years in Washington.* Hartford, Conn.: A. D. Worthington & Co., 1901.

Lynn, Catherine. *Wallpaper in America: From the Seventeenth Century to World War I.* New York: W. W. Norton, 1980.

Malone, Dumas. *Jefferson and His Time.* 6 vols. Boston: Little, Brown, and Co., 1948–81.

McClelland, Nancy. *Duncan Phyfe and the English Regency: 1795–1830.* New York: William R. Scott, 1939.

Metropolitan Museum of Art. *In Pursuit of Beauty: Americans and the Aesthetic Movement.* New York: Metropolitan Museum of Art, 1986.

Monkman, Betty C. "The White House: 1873–1902." *Nineteenth Century* 3 (Spring 1978): 76–81.

———. "American Silver in the White House." *Washington Antiques Show Catalogue* (January 1980): 74–79.

———. *The White House 1792–1992: Image in Architecture.* Washington, D.C.: American Architectural Foundation, 1992.

———. "Furniture and Interiors: Change and Continuity," in *Our Changing White House.* Edited by Wendell Garrett. Boston: Northeastern University Press, 1995.

———. *Treasures of the White House.* New York: Abbeville Press, 2001.

———. *The Living White House.* Washington, D.C.: White House Historical Association, 12th ed., 2007.

———. *The Living White House.* Washington, D.C.: White House Historical Association, 13th ed., 2013.

Montgomery, Charles F. *American Furniture, The Federal Period, in the Henry Francis du Pont Winterthur Museum.* New York: Viking Press, 1966.

Morris, Sylvia Jukes. *Edith Kermit Roosevelt: Portrait of a First Lady.* New York: Coward, McCann & Geoghegan, 1980.

Mussey, Robert. *The Furniture Masterworks of John & Thomas Seymour.* Salem, Massachusetts: Peabody Essex, 2003.

Nesbitt, Henrietta. *White House Diary.* New York: Doubleday & Co., 1948.

Niven, John. *Martin Van Buren: The Romantic Age of American Politics.* New York: Oxford University Press, 1983.

Palmer, Arlene. *Artistry and Innovation in Pittsburgh Glass, 1808-1882: From Bakewell & Ensell to Bakewell, Pears & Co.* Pittsburgh: Frick Art & Historical Center, 2004.

Pearce, Lorraine Waxman. "Lannuier in the President's House." *Antiques* (January 1962): 94–96.

———. "American Empire Furniture in the White House." *Antiques* (May 1962): 515–19.

———. "Fine Federal Furniture at the White House." *Antiques* (September 1962): 273–77.

Peirce, Donald C. *Art & Enterprise: American Decorative Art, 1825–1917, The Virginia Carroll Crawford Collection.* Atlanta: High Museum of Art, 1999.

Pendel, Thomas F. *Thirty-Six Years in the White House.* Washington, D.C.: Neale Publishing Co., 1902.

Penzer, N. M. *Paul Storr.* London: Spring Books, 1971.

Philadelphia Museum of Art. *Philadelphia: Three Centuries of American Art.* Philadelphia: Philadelphia Museum of Art, 1976.

Raley, R. L. "Interior Designs by Benjamin Henry Latrobe for the President's House." *Antiques* (June 1959): 568–71.

Reagan, Nancy, with William Novak. *My Turn: The Memoirs of Nancy Reagan.* New York: Random House, 1989.

Remini, Robert V. *Andrew Jackson.* 3 vols. New York: Harper & Row, 1977–84.

Restoration of the White House, Washington, D.C.: Government Printing Office, 1903.

Roosevelt, Eleanor. *This I Remember.* New York: Harper & Brothers, 1949.

Ross, Ishbel. *Grace Coolidge and Her Era: The Story of a President's Wife.* New York: Dodd, Mead & Co., 1962.

Saunders, Frances W. *Ellen Axson Wilson: First Lady Between Two Worlds.* Chapel Hill: University of North Carolina Press, 1985.

Schwartz, Marvin D., Edward J. Stanek, and Douglas K. True. *The Furniture of John Henry Belter and the Rococo Revival: An Inquiry into Nineteenth-Century Furniture Design Through a Study of the Gloria and Richard Manney Collection.* New York: E. P. Dutton, 1981.

Seale, William. *The President's House: A History.* 2 vols. Washington, D.C.: White House Historical Association, 2008.

———. *The White House: The History of an American Idea.* Washington, D.C.: American Institute of Architects Press, 2001.

———, ed. *The White House: Actors and Observers.* Boston: Northeastern University Press, 2002.

Singleton, Esther. *The Story of the White House.* 2 vols. New York: McClure Co., 1907.

Smith, Margaret Bayard. *The First Forty Years of Washington Society.* New York: C. Scribner's Sons, 1906.

Spillman, Jane Shadel. *White House Glassware: Two Centuries of Entertaining.* Washington, D.C.: White House Historical Association, 1989.

Stoddard, William O. *Inside the White House in War Times.* New York: Charles L. Webster & Co., 1890.

Stoneman, Vernon. *John and Thomas Seymour: Cabinetmakers in Boston, 1794–1816.* Boston: Special Publications, 1959.

Taft, Helen. *Recollections of Full Years.* New York: Dodd, Mead & Co., 1914.

Thayer, Mary Van Rensselaer. *Jacqueline Kennedy: The White House Years.* Boston: Little, Brown and Co., 1967.

Thompson, Flora McDonald. "Art in the White House." *Harper's Bazar* (January 19, 1901): 143–48.

Tracy, Berry B. "[White House] Federal Period Furniture." *The Connoisseur* (May 1976): 11–15.

Tracy, Berry B., and William H. Gerdts. *Classical America, 1815–1845.* Newark: Newark Museum Association, 1963.

Tracy, Berry B., et al. *19th Century America: Furniture and other Decorative Arts.* New York: Metropolitan Museum of Art, 1970.

Turner, Justin G., and Linda Lovitt Turner. *Mary Todd Lincoln: Her Life and Letters.* New York: Alfred A. Knopf, 1972.

United States. *Report of the Commission on the Renovation of the Executive Mansion.* Washington, D.C.: Government Printing Office, 1952.

United States. The White House. Office of the Chief Usher. *The White House: The Ronald W. Reagan Administration 1981–1989.* Washington, D.C.: White House Historical Association, 1989.

United States. The White House. Office of the Chief Usher. *The White House: The George Bush Administration 1989–1993.* Washington, D.C.: White House Historical Association, 1997.

United States. The White House. Office of the Chief Usher. *The White House: The William J. Clinton Administration 1993-2001.* Washington, D.C.: White House Historical Association, 2004.

United States. The White House. Office of the Curator. *The White House Collection. Preliminary Catalogue.* N.p.: 1964.

Venable, Charles L. *Silver in America, 1840–1940: A Century of Splendor.* New York: Harry N. Abrams, 1995.

Warren, David B., et al. *American Decorative Arts and Paintings in the Bayou Bend Collection.* Houston: Museum of Fine Arts, Houston, 1998.

Weidman, Gregory R. *Furniture in Maryland, 1700–1840.* Baltimore: Maryland Historical Society, 1984.

West, J. B., and Mary Lynn Kotz. *Upstairs at the White House: My Life with the First Ladies.* New York: Coward, McCann & Geoghegan, 1973.

The White House: An Historic Guide. Washington, D.C.: White House Historical Association, editions 1–23. 1962–2011.

White House History. Washington, D.C.: White House Historical Association, no.1, 1983; no. 2–33, 1997–2013.

Wilson, Edith Bolling. *My Memoir.* Indianapolis: Bobbs-Merrill Co., 1938.

Wolff, Perry. *A Tour of the White House with Mrs. John F. Kennedy.* Garden City, N.Y.: Doubleday & Co., 1962.

INDEX